Glencoe Spanish 3

¡Buen viaje!

Conrad J. Schmitt
Protase E. Woodford

Teacher's Manual

Glencoe
McGraw-Hill

New York, New York   Columbus, Ohio   Woodland Hills, California   Peoria, Illinois

Glencoe/McGraw-Hill

A Division of The **McGraw·Hill** *Companies*

Send all inquiries to:
Glencoe/McGraw-Hill
21600 Oxnard Street
Suite 500
Woodland Hills, CA 91367

ISBN 0-02-641814-2 (Teacher's Wraparound Edition)

2 3 4 5 6 7 8 9 071 08 07 06 05 04 03 02 01 00 99

Contents

About the Authors

Conrad J. Schmitt

Conrad J. Schmitt received his B.A. degree magna cum laude from Montclair State College, Upper Montclair, NJ. He received his M.A. from Middlebury College, Middlebury, VT. He did additional graduate work at Seton Hall University and New York University.

Mr. Schmitt has taught Spanish and French at the elementary, junior, and senior high school levels. He was Coordinator of Foreign Languages for Hackensack, New Jersey, Public Schools. He also taught Spanish at Upsala College, East Orange, NJ; Spanish at Montclair State College; and Methods of Teaching a Foreign Language at the Graduate School of Education, Rutgers University, New Brunswick, NJ. He was editor-in-chief of Foreign Languages and Bilingual Education for McGraw-Hill Book Company and Director of English language Materials for McGraw-Hill International Book Company.

Mr. Schmitt has authored or co-authored more than eighty books, all published by Glencoe/McGraw-Hill, or other divisions of the McGraw-Hill Companies. He has addressed teacher groups and given workshops in all states of the U.S. and has lectured and presented seminars throughout the Far East, Europe, Latin America, and Canada. In addition, Mr. Schmitt has travelled extensively throughout Spain, Central and South America, and the Caribbean.

Protase E. Woodford

Protase "Woody" Woodford has taught Spanish at all levels from elementary through graduate school. At the Educational Testing Service in Princeton, NJ, he was Director of Test Development, Director of Language Programs, Director of International Testing Programs, and Director of the Puerto Rico Office. He was appointed "Distinguished Linguist" at the U.S. Naval Academy in 1988. He is the author of over two dozen Spanish and English language textbooks for schools and colleges. He has served as a consultant to the American Council on the Teaching of Foreign Languages (ACTFL), the National Assessment of Educational Progress, the College Board, the United Nations Secretariat, UNESCO, the Organization of American States, the U.S. Office of Education, the United States Agency for International Development (AID), the World Bank, the Japanese Ministry of International Trade and Industry, and many ministries of education in Asia, Latin America, and the Middle East. In 1994 he was invited to chair the National Advisory Council on Standards in Foreign Language Education. Mr. Woodford served on the Board of Directors of the Northeast Conference during the period 1982-85. He received the 1993 NYSFLT National Distinguished Leadership Award, and the 1994 Central States Paul Simon Award for Support of Language and International Studies. From 1996-2000 he served as Chairman of the Board of Trustees, Center for Applied Linguistics.

Introduction

Welcome to **_Glencoe Spanish_**, the junior high and high school Spanish series from Glencoe/McGraw-Hill, a division of the McGraw-Hill Companies. Every element in this series has been designed to help you create an atmosphere of challenge, variety, cooperation, and enjoyment for your students. From the moment you begin to use **_Glencoe Spanish_**, you will notice that not only is it packed with exciting, practical materials and features designed to stimulate young people to work together towards language proficiency, but that it goes beyond by urging students to use their new skills in other areas of the curriculum.

Glencoe Spanish uses an integrated approach to language learning. From the introduction of new material, through reinforcement, evaluation, and review, its presentations, exercises, and activities are designed to span all four language skills. Another characteristic of this series is that students use and reinforce these new skills while developing a realistic, up-to-date awareness of Spanish culture.

The Teacher's Wraparound Edition you are reading has been developed based on the advice of experienced foreign language educators throughout the United States in order to meet your needs as a teacher both in and out of the foreign language classroom. Here are some of the features and benefits which make **_Glencoe Spanish_**, a powerful set of teaching tools:

- random access format
- student-centered instruction
- balance among all four language skills
- contextualized vocabulary
- thorough, contextual presentation of grammar
- an integrated approach to culture.

Features and Benefits

RANDOM ACCESS FORMAT While we have taken every opportunity to use the latest in pedagogical developments in order to create a learning atmosphere of variety, vitality, communication, and challenge, we have also made every effort to make the *Glencoe Spanish* series "teacher-friendly." And this is where the flexibility, which is especially important to Level 3 teachers, comes in. For example, some third-year students need a great deal of grammar review. Other groups are ready to read unabridged literature. *Glencoe Spanish 3 (¡Buen viaje!)* meets the needs of all third-year classes by providing a variety of materials in each chapter that can be taught independently of each other.

The Student Textbook and the Teacher's Wraparound Edition provide an instructional method that, if covered in its entirety, will provide a solid foundation of advanced Spanish study for high school students. Each chapter of the Student Textbook includes seven sections: *Cultura, Conversación, Lenguaje, Repaso de estructura, Periodismo, Estructura,* and *Literatura.* (The content of each section is described in detail on pages T13 and T14.) You may decide to cover all the sections in a chapter or to omit an entire section or sections. For example, *Repaso de estructura* typically recycles two or three grammar points from *Glencoe Spanish 1* and *2.* However, if your class has an excellent background in this grammar, you may decide to skip this section in one or more chapters, or to cover only those points you feel students need to review. You may also decide to cover material in a different order from that in which it appears in a chapter. For example, you may wish to present communicative strategies from *Lenguaje* at the beginning of a chapter, as a means of motivating students by allowing them to quickly participate in some of the chapter's real-life situations. Because the material in *¡Buen viaje! Level 3* does not become progressively more difficult, and there are easy and difficult sections in each chapter, plenty of room has been built in for you to be flexible. You can draw on your own education, experience, and personality in order to tailor a language program that is suitable and rewarding for the individual "chemistry" of each class.

In the Student Textbook, there is a marked difference between learning exercises (*Práctica*) and communication-based activities (*Actividades comunicativas*), both of which are provided in each chapter. The former serve, as their name implies, as exercises for the acquisition and practice of new vocabulary and structures, while the latter are designed to get students communicating in open-ended contexts using the Spanish they have learned. You can select the exercises and activities that best suit the needs of your students.

We have been looking only at the Student Textbook. The abundance of suggestions for techniques, strategies, additional practice, chapter projects, independent (homework) assignments, informal assessments, and more, which are provided in this Teacher's Wraparound Edition—as well as the veritable banquet of resources available in the wide array of ancillary materials provided in the series—are what make *Glencoe Spanish* truly flexible and "teacher-friendly." They guarantee you a great pool of ideas and teaching tools from which to pick and choose in order to create an outstanding course.

STUDENT-CENTERED INSTRUCTION Teaching a foreign language requires coping with different learning styles and special student needs. It requires the ability to capitalize on the great cultural and economic diversity present in many classrooms and to turn this diversity into an engine for learning by putting students together in goal-oriented groups. And it often requires effective techniques for managing large classes.

Glencoe Spanish anticipates these requirements by offering ideas for setting up a cooperative learning environment for students. Useful suggestions to this end accompany each chapter, under the heading Cooperative Learning, in the bottom margin of the Teacher's Wraparound Edition. Additional paired and group-work activities are found in the Student Textbook (*Actividades comunicativas*), and under other headings such as Additional Practice and Paired Activities in the Teacher's Wraparound Edition.

Besides cooperative learning strategies, *Glencoe Spanish* contains many other student-centered elements that allow students to expand their learning experiences. Here are a few examples: Suggestions are offered in the Teacher's Wraparound Edition for out-of-class projects on topics related to the chapter theme. The Audio Program allows students to work at their own pace. They may stop the tape whenever necessary to make directed changes in the language or to refer to their activity sheets in the Student Tape Manual.

These and other features discussed elsewhere in this Teacher's Manual have been designed with the student in mind. They assure that each individual, regardless of learning style, previous preparation, background, or age, will have the necessary resources for becoming proficient in Spanish.

Balance Among All Four Language Skills

Glencoe Spanish provides a balanced focus on the listening, speaking, reading, and writing skills throughout all phases of instruction. And since it is "teacher-friendly," it gives you leeway if you wish to adjust the integration of these skills to the needs of a particular individual, group, or class. Several features of the series lend themselves to this: the overall flexibility of format, the abundance of suggested optional and additional activities, and the design of the individual activities themselves. Flexibility was discussed above. Let's look at some sections of a typical chapter as examples of the other two characteristics mentioned.

Four of the seven chapter sections (*Cultura, Conversación, Periodismo,* and *Literatura*) begin with a

brief introduction and an illustrated vocabulary presentation. If the suggested Teaching Vocabulary section is followed, students are introduced to new words and phrases in the *Vocabulario* sections by the teacher and/or by the audio presentation. The focus is on listening and speaking through modeling and repetition. The *Práctica* that accompany each *Vocabulario* section can be performed with books either closed (accentuating listening and speaking) or open (accentuating reading, listening, and speaking). However, these *Práctica* can just as well be assigned or reassigned as written work if the teacher wishes to have the whole class or individuals begin to concentrate on reading and writing. Throughout the *Vocabulario* sections, optional and additional reinforcement activities are suggested in the Teacher's Wraparound Edition.

Reading and writing activities, while present from the earliest stages in the *Glencoe Spanish* series, naturally become more sophisticated and receive greater emphasis in *Glencoe Spanish 3*. In each chapter there is an original cultural reading, two or three authentic pieces from contemporary Spanish magazines and newspapers, and one to three unabridged selections from Hispanic literature. Writing activities range from grammar exercises to literary analysis. These textbook activities are further reinforced in the Writing Activities Workbook.

Let's take a closer look at how each of the four skills is woven into the Student Textbook, the Teacher's Wraparound Edition, and the ancillary materials.

LISTENING You are the primary source for listening as you model new vocabulary, dialogues, sample language, structure, and pronunciation. Share your knowledge of Spanish culture, history, geography, and literature with the students and talk to them about their lives and your own, or engage in culturally oriented activities and projects. And as always, it is your ability to use Spanish as much as possible with your students, both in and outside of the classroom, which determines how relevant and dynamic their learning experience will be.

Glencoe Spanish offers numerous ways in which to develop the listening skill. There are teacher-focused activities, which provide the consistent modeling that students need. Teachers who use the Audio Program will find that these recordings help students become accustomed to a variety of voices, as well as rates of speech. And activities in which students interact with each other develop listening spontaneity and acuity.

In the Student Textbook, new vocabulary will be modeled by the teacher. Following each *Vocabulario* presentation (found in the *Cultura, Conversación, Periodismo,* and *Literatura* sections) are several exercises for practicing the new vocabulary. These can be done with books closed for listening comprehension practice. The readings in the *Cultura* and *Periodismo* sections and the new language in the *Lenguaje* section can be modeled by the teacher, while the *Escenas de la vida* dialogues from the *Conversación,* and the *Literatura* selections are featured on the Audio Program. At the end of each of these sections there are comprehension exercises (*Comprensión*) and *Actividades comunicativas,* in which students may work in pairs or groups and must listen to each other in order to find information, take notes, or report to others on what was said in their group. In the *Estructuras* sections, students listen as the teacher models grammatical material and then are given a chance to practice each structure in several exercises. Once again, closing the book will provide increased focus on the listening skill.

In addition to the Student Textbook, the Teacher's Wraparound Edition offers several other listening-based activities correlated to the chapters, including those suggested under the headings Cooperative Learning, Paired Activities, and Additional Practice, all of which are found in the bottom margins of each Teacher's Wraparound Edition chapter.

The Audio Program has two main listening components. The first is practice-oriented, wherein students further reinforce vocabulary and grammar, following directions and making changes in utterances. They can self-check their work by listening to the correctly modeled utterances, which are supplied after a pause.

The second part of the program places more emphasis on receptive listening skills. Students listen to language in the form of dialogues, announcements, or advertisements—language delivered at a faster pace

and in greater volume—and then are asked to demonstrate their understanding of the main ideas and important details in what they have heard. The Student Tape Manual contains activity sheets for doing this work, and the Teacher's Edition contains the complete transcript of all audio materials to assist you in laying out listening tasks for your class.

SPEAKING The twin centerpieces of each chapter, in terms of spoken Spanish, are the *Conversación* and *Lenguaje* sections. Each presents the language as it is currently spoken in everyday functional contexts so that, from the start, your students will be accustomed to speaking in a way that is reflective of contemporary Spanish. The *Escenas de la vida* dialogues from the *Conversación* may be repeated by the students after they are modeled by the teacher or the audio cassettes, or may be read aloud by students taking the roles of the various characters. The functional language in *Lenguaje* may also be modeled by the teacher. Each section is followed by *Actividades comunicativas* that allow students to use new language in role-plays and real-life situations. Here, students are engaged in meaningful, interesting sessions of sharing information, all designed to make them want to speak and experiment with the language.

In addition, most of the areas of the Student Textbook and the Teacher's Wraparound Edition described above, under **Listening,** also simultaneously develop the speaking skill. After hearing a model in the *Vocabulario* or *Estructura* sections, students may repeat it, either as a whole class, in small groups, or as individuals. From these modeled cues, they will progress to visual ones—the photos and art in the textbook. The real aim of the *Práctica* accompanying these two sections is to get students to produce this new material actively.

The speaking skill is stressed in the first part of each recorded chapter of the Audio Program, where pauses are provided for the student to produce directed, spoken changes in the language. This is an excellent opportunity for those students who are self-conscious about speaking out in class to feel more comfortable speaking Spanish. The Audio Program gives these students a chance to work in isolation. And the format of making a change in the language, uttering the change, and then listening for the correct model may improve the speaking skill. Sensitively administered, the Audio Program can serve as a confidence-builder for such students, allowing them to work their way gradually into more spontaneous speech with their classmates.

The packet of Situation Cards provides students with yet another opportunity to produce spoken Spanish. They put the student into a contextualized, real-world situation. Students must ask and/or answer questions in order to perform successfully.

READING Each chapter of the Student Textbook opens with a *Cultura* reading that establishes the theme of the chapter. The *Periodismo* section contains two or three authentic readings taken from contemporary Spanish language magazines and newspapers. All selections are preceded by an introduction with background information for the English-speaking student and a *Vocabulario* that presents key vocabulary students will encounter. The readings are followed by comprehension exercises and activities. The final section of each chapter, *Literatura*, contains the most challenging readings. It features from one to three unabridged selections of Hispanic literature from a variety of periods, each accompanied by a pre-reading activity, a vocabulary presentation with exercises, an historical introduction, comprehension exercises, and communicative activities.

The Writing Activities Workbook offers additional readings under the heading *Un poco más*. These selections, and the accompanying exercises, focus on reading strategies such as cognate recognition, building vocabulary through related word forms, and the use of context clues.

In addition to the reading development discussed above, students are constantly presented with authentic Spanish texts such as announcements from periodicals, telephone listings, transportation schedules, labeled diagrams, floor plans, travel brochures, school progress reports, etc., as sources of information. Sometimes these documents serve as the bases for language activities, and other times they appear in order to round out a cultural presentation.

But, in varying degrees, they all require students to apply their reading skills.

WRITING Written work is interwoven throughout the language learning process in **Glencoe Spanish**. The exercises, which occur throughout the *Vocabulario* and *Estructura* sections of each chapter in the Student Textbook, are designed in such a way that they can be completed in written form as well as orally. Frequently, you may wish to reassign exercises that you have gone over orally in class as written homework. The Teacher's Wraparound Edition makes special note of this under the topic Independent Practice. At the end of each *Cultura, Periodismo*, and *Literatura* section, direct focus is placed on writing in the *Actividades comunicativas*. Here students are given the opportunity to do more extensive writing tasks. These may be descriptive, narrative, argumentative, or analytical. They may also appear in the form of dialogues or interviews. Often a context is set up and then students are asked to develop an appropriate written response.

The Writing Activities Workbook is the component in which writing skills receive the most concentrated attention. All of the exercises in it are writing-based, and they vary in length from one-word answers to short compositions. They are designed to focus on the same vocabulary and grammar presented in the corresponding chapter of the Student Textbook, but they are all new and all contextualized around fresh visual material or situational vignettes. Since they often have students making lists, adding to charts and labeling, they provide an excellent means for them to organize the chapter material in their minds and make associations that will help them retain it. As the students' knowledge of Spanish increases, longer written pieces are required of them.

Besides these major sources of writing, students are asked to make implicit use of writing almost everywhere in the series. They are constantly taking notes, listing, categorizing, labeling, summarizing, comparing or contrasting on paper. Even the Audio Program involves students in writing through the use of activity sheets. By choosing among these options, you can be sure that your students will receive the practice they need to successfully develop their writing skills.

Contextualized Vocabulary

From the moment students see new words at the beginning of each chapter in **Glencoe Spanish**, they see them within an identifiable context. This contextualization remains consistent throughout the practice, testing, and recycling phases of learning.

In the *Vocabulario* segments of the *Cultura*, *Periodismo*, and *Literatura* sections, a context for new and relevant vocabulary is established through a brief *Introducción*. The vocabulary is then presented together with interesting, colorful visuals. And so, from the start, students learn to group words by association, thereby enhancing their ability to assimilate and store vocabulary for long-term retention. The result is that students see at a glance the new language set into a real-life situation that provides "something to talk about"—a reason for using it. The accompanying exercises enrich this context. Each *Práctica* item labeled *Historieta* is related to the others within the set, so that when taken together they form a meaningful vignette or story. Throughout the chapter, these words and phrases are reintroduced frequently.

Moreover, future chapters build on vocabulary and grammar from previous ones. Chapter themes introduced in Levels 1 and 2 are reintroduced in Level 3 along with additional related vocabulary. Special attention has been given to vocabulary in the reading sections of the series as well. For example, in *Periodismo* and *Literatura*, students are encouraged to stretch their vocabularies in order to get as much meaning as possible from these authentic and unsimplified selections.

Thorough, Contextual Presentation of Grammar

A quick look through the chapters of *¡Buen viaje! Level 3* will show the role grammar plays in the overall approach of the **Glencoe Spanish** series. Although grammar is by no means the driving force behind the series, it is indeed an important aspect. In **Glencoe Spanish 3**, grammar is presented in two of the seven sections in each chapter. *Repaso de estructura* recycles two or three grammar points from Levels 1 and 2, while *Estructura* reviews points from the second half of Level 2, beginning with the present subjunctive, and goes on to introduce advanced grammar topics. Depending on the ability of the class, these sections may be used to review Spanish 1 and 2 material or to present grammar points for the first time. What makes this series particularly effective is that, as well as being thorough, the presentation of grammar runs concurrent with, and is embedded in, the chapter-long situational themes. Students are presented with Spanish structures both directly, as grammar, and as a set of useful functions that will aid them in communication, in expanding and improving their Spanish across the four skills, and in learning about Spanish culture as well as other areas of the school curriculum. Another important characteristic is that each *Estructura* section has been divided into short, coherent "doses" of related grammar points, which prevents grammar from becoming overwhelming to the student.

Throughout this series you will see that as you teach the various grammar topics, student interest remains high because each exercise relates to a communicative topic and the format always varies. As is the case with many of the vocabulary exercises, the individual practice items in the grammar exercises are often related to each other contextually, in order to heighten student interest. All such exercises are labeled *Historieta*.

You will find that it is easy to alternate the teaching of grammar with that of other sections of a chapter or other components as you see fit. This is true for several reasons: the grammar segments are short and intelligently divided, each one providing a good sense of closure; language elements—including grammar—taught in one section have been included as much as possible in the others; and again, there is a coherent contextual theme.

Aside from the Student Textbook and Teacher's Wraparound Edition, with their focus on grammar in the *Estructura* sections of each chapter, **Glencoe Spanish** offers students opportunities to practice grammar in other series components as well. Chapter by chapter, the Writing Activities Workbook provides ample tasks in which students must put into writing the new grammar points on which they have been working in class. The Audio Program includes recorded sections in every chapter of the Student Tape Manual that correspond directly to grammar topics in the Student Textbook. Grammatical structures are also practiced in the Situation Cards.

An Integrated Approach to Culture

True competence in a foreign language cannot be attained without simultaneous development of the awareness of the culture in which the language is spoken. That is why **Glencoe Spanish** places such great emphasis on culture. Accurate, up-to-date information on Hispanic culture is present from the very beginning of each chapter. The *Cultura* section sets the stage on which the other chapter materials will be played out, presenting a variety of materials about a specific cultural theme that will be recycled and expanded either implicitly or explicitly throughout every phase of language learning and in every component of the series. Many culturally oriented questions raised by students may be answered in this introductory *Cultura* section. Through vocabulary presentations, readings, captioned visuals, and guided activities, these sections provide fundamental knowledge about such topics as Spanish travel and tourism, the media, and leisure and pastimes, among many others. This information is presented with the idea that culture is a product of people—their attitudes, desires, preferences, differences, similarities, strengths, and weaknesses—and that it is ever changing. Students are always encouraged to compare or contrast what they learn

about Spanish culture with their own, thereby learning to think critically and progress towards a more mature vision of the world.

The presentation of all language in each chapter of the Student Textbook is embedded in running contextual themes, and these themes richly reflect the cultures of the Spanish-speaking countries. Even in chapter sections that focus primarily on vocabulary or grammar, the presence of culture comes through in the language used as examples or items in exercises, as well as in the content of the accompanying illustrations, photographs, charts, diagrams, maps, or other reproductions of authentic documents in Spanish. This constant, implicit inclusion of cultural information creates a format that not only aids in the learning of new words and structures, but also piques student interest, invites questions, and stimulates discussion of the people behind the language.

Culture is also important in the two other reading sections of each chapter, *Periodismo* and *Literatura*. The readings here serve as valuable sources of information on current events in Spanish-speaking countries and on the rich tradition of Spanish literature.

All of the cultural material described in the Student Textbook can be augmented by following a variety of suggestions in the Teacher's Wraparound Edition. There are guidelines for culturally rich instruction and activities, as well as useful, interesting facts for the teacher, under headings such as Chapter Projects, About the Spanish Language, Geography Connection, History Connection, Critical Thinking, Literature Connection, Art Connection, Did You Know? and others.

Series Components

In order to take full advantage of the student-centered, "teacher-friendly" curriculum offered by *Glencoe Spanish*, you may want to refer to this section to familiarize yourself with the various resources the series has to offer. Level 3 of *Glencoe Spanish* contains the following components:

◆ Student Edition
◆ Teacher's Wraparound Edition
◆ Writing Activities Workbook, Student Edition
◆ Writing Activities Workbook, Teacher's Annotated Edition
◆ Student Tape Manual, Student Edition
◆ Student Tape Manual, Teacher's Edition (Student edition and tapescript)
◆ Audio Program (cassette or compact disc)
◆ Video Program (videocassette or videodisc)
◆ Video Activities Booklet
◆ Bell Ringer Review Transparencies
◆ Transparency Binder
◆ Computer Testmaker Software (Windows/Macintosh)
◆ Situation Cards
◆ Chapter Quizzes with Answer Key
◆ Testing Program with Answer Key, Test Cassettes
◆ Block Scheduling Lesson Plans
◆ Lesson Plans
◆ Expansion Activities
◆ Online Internet Activities
◆ Electronic Teacher's Classroom Resources

Organization of the Student Textbook

Each of the eight chapters of *¡Buen viaje! Level 3* is divided into the following sections:

◆ *Cultura*

◆ *Conversación*

◆ *Lenguaje*

◆ *Repaso de estructura*

◆ *Periodismo*

◆ *Estructura*

◆ *Literatura*

CULTURA This section contains original readings on one aspect of contemporary Hispanic life. High interest level has been a prerequisite in the choice of topics, which range from vacation preferences of the Spanish-speaking people, to breakthroughs in scientific research. Each reading is preceded by a brief introduction to the chapter theme. New vocabulary is then presented through a combination of illustrations and definitions in Spanish. Vocabulary is then practiced through various contextualized *Práctica*. The reading is followed by two tiers of activities: *Comprensión*, which enables students to demonstrate their understanding of the material at the word, sentence, paragraph, and main idea levels; and *Actividades comunicativas*, which ask students to analyze and personalize what they have read in oral and written tasks.

CONVERSACIÓN This section presents advanced vocabulary in the situational contexts of real-life conversations related to the chapter theme. Each *Conversación* section begins with a vocabulary presentation with exercises similar to those in *Cultura*. The focal point of the section, *Escenas de la vida*, presents a series of authentic, culturally rich dialogues that can be used for class or individual repetitions, for

reading aloud by students, or for role-playing or adaptation through substitution. The dialogue is accompanied by comprehension exercises. Then students are invited once again to recombine and use all the new language in a variety of oral group and paired activities, many of them role-plays, via the *Actividades comunicativas*.

LENGUAJE Each presentation offers students communicative strategies that will allow them to negotiate such real-life situations as extending invitations, expressing opinions, and making small-talk. The language presented is always that spoken by contemporary Spanish people, never the "complete sentence" textbook Spanish that leaves students who travel to a Spanish-speaking country for the first time wondering what language they have been studying all these years! Each *Lenguaje* presentation is followed by one or more *Actividades comunicativas*, which ask students to imagine themselves in various situations and react accordingly, using the new language.

REPASO DE ESTRUCTURA This is the first of two grammar sections in each chapter. It recycles two or three grammar points from *Glencoe Spanish 1* and *2*. Depending on the ability and background of each class, the teacher will decide to use this section as a review or as a new grammar presentation. Each of the segments provides a step-by-step description in English of how the new grammatical structure is used in Spanish, accompanied by examples, tables, and other visuals. This description, while concise, does not assume previous knowledge on the part of students. Each segment's presentation is followed by a series of flexible and contextualized *Práctica*; examples as well as items in the exercises are never separate and unrelated but always fit together in vignettes to enhance meaning.

These vignettes are always directly related to the overall chapter theme.

PERIODISMO   This section introduces students to the type of material people in Spain and Latin America read every day—newspaper and magazine articles, headlines, weather reports, advertisements—with a good deal of linguistic and cultural support to make it meaningful to them. Each section opens with an *Introducción* containing cultural and historical background information and a description of the texts they will read. Then, there follows an illustrated vocabulary presentation with exercises, which introduces key words and expressions they will encounter in the selections. Each *Periodismo* section contains two or three authentic readings, and each selection is followed by comprehension items and *Actividades comunicativas* that ask students to go beyond the readings in oral and written open-ended tasks including letter-writing and oral presentations.

ESTRUCTURA   This second grammar section of the chapter follows the format established by *Repaso de estructura*, but here students are presented with advanced grammar topics not usually taught in the first two years of Spanish study (*El pluscuamperfecto, El presente perfecto del subjuntivo*), as well as recycled structures from the second half of *Glencoe Spanish 2* (*Formación del subjuntivo, Cláusulas con si*). As with *Repaso de estructura*, clear explanations of formation and usage are given in English, and the practice exercises offer communicative contexts for using the new structures.

LITERATURA   This section introduces students to a sample of the great literature produced throughout the Spanish-speaking world. Great care has been taken to select pieces that students can read in their original, unsimplified forms that nevertheless do not overwhelm with their level of difficulty. Included are poems, songs, and excerpts from novels and plays. Emphasis has been placed on contemporary literature, but classics have also been included. To begin each *Literatura* section, *Antes de leer* encourages the students to recall relevant thematic or linguistic information they may already have. A vocabulary presentation with exercises follows. To support students in their first attempts at reading unadapted Spanish literature, the *Introducción* places the selection and its author in historical and literary context. The selection itself contains marginal glosses for those words whose meanings students cannot be expected to guess from their contexts. A series of *Comprensión* exercises after the reading establishes students' grasp of the content and asks them to draw some basic inferences about it. Several *Actividades comunicativas*, ranging from creative-writing topics based on the theme of the reading to elementary literary analysis, end the section.

VISTAS   After every two chapters of the Student Textbook, *Glencoe Spanish* provides a unique section called *Vistas*. This presentation was prepared by the National Geographic Society. Each *Vista* focuses on one Spanish-speaking country via a dazzling display of photos representative of both that country's past as well as its present. Students have the opportunity to read the photo captions accompanying these *Vista* pages.

Suggestions for Teaching the Student Textbook

On the first day of class, teachers may wish to reiterate the importance of the Spanish language and reasons for continuing the learning process in the third year. Some suggested activities are:

◆ Show students a map (the maps located on pages 408–410 of *¡Buen viaje! Level 3* can be used) to remind them of the extent of the Spanish-speaking world.

◆ Have students discuss the areas within North America in which there is a high percentage of Spanish speakers. Ask them to name local Spanish-speaking sources, including any individuals or groups they may know in their community.

◆ Make a list of place names such as San Francisco, El Paso, San Antonio, or names in your locality that are of Spanish origin.

◆ Explain to students the possibility of using Spanish in numerous careers such as: foreign service, teaching, business, (banking, import/export), tourism, translating.

◆ Do a brief survey of the textbook, showing students that this year they will have the opportunity to read authentic Spanish language newspaper and magazine articles and unabridged literary texts.

◆ On the first day you may wish to find out whether your students used Spanish names in last year's Spanish class. If they didn't, this is a good time to give students a Spanish first name, or to let them take a new Spanish name, if they wish.

Teaching Various Sections of the Chapter

One of the major objectives of the *Glencoe Spanish* series is to enable teachers to adapt the material to their own philosophy and teaching style and to their students' needs. As a result, a variety of suggestions are offered here for teaching each section of the chapter.

Vocabulario

New vocabulary is introduced in four of the seven chapter sections: *Cultura, Conversación, Periodismo,* and *Literatura.* All vocabulary presentations follow the same format and may be taught in similar ways. The *Vocabulario* section always contains some words that are accompanied by an illustration that depicts the meaning of the new word. Other new words and expressions are defined in Spanish with brief explanations or synonyms. All *Vocabulario* sections are available as overhead transparencies.

GENERAL TECHNIQUES All the *Vocabulario* sections in each chapter are recorded on the Audio Program. Have students listen to the new vocabulary and then ask them to repeat these words after you.

SPECIFIC TECHNIQUES: OPTION 1 This option for the presentation of vocabulary best meets the needs of those teachers who consider the development of oral skills a prime objective.

◆ While students have their books closed, read each new term or play the audio cassette/compact disc, or project the appropriate overhead transparency. Have students repeat the word after you several times. Enhance this presentation by giving explanations of the new terms using known vocabulary, cognates, gestures, and mime. After you have presented several words in this manner, ask questions such as:
En un embotellamiento, ¿hay muchos coches?
¿Cómo está la autopista cuando hay un embotellamiento?

¿Qué tiempo hace durante una tempestad?
(*¡Buen viaje! Level 3*, Chapter 1, *Conversación*)

◆ To teach the new vocabulary terms that are defined with explanations or synonyms, read the words or play the audio cassette or compact disc, having students repeat each new item. For each term, read the definition given in the textbook, expanding it if necessary to make sure students understand. Then ask questions about the item. For example, the following items appear in *¡Buen viaje! Level 3*, Chapter 2, *Cultura*: **sembrar: plantar granos, vegetales, etc.** The teacher should illustrate the meaning of **sembrar** by pretending to sow imaginary seeds. Then, to check comprehension, the teacher could ask:

¿En qué estación del año siembras los vegetales?
¿Qué vegetales (flores) prefieres sembrar?
Additional questions to provide practice with new vocabulary are provided for you in the presentation section of each *Vocabulario* in the Teacher's Wraparound Edition.

◆ After this basic presentation of each *Vocabulario* section, have students open their books and read the new vocabulary for additional reinforcement.

◆ Go over the exercises that follow each *Vocabulario* orally.

◆ Assign the exercises for homework. Also assign the corresponding vocabulary exercises in the Writing Activities Workbook.

◆ The following day, go over the exercises that were assigned for homework.

OPTION 2 This option will meet the needs of those teachers who wish to teach the oral skills but consider reading and writing equally important.

◆ Have students repeat each word once or twice after you. Enhance this presentation by giving explanations of the new term using the definitions in the textbook, explanations with known vocabulary, cognates, gestures, and mime.

◆ Ask students to open their books. Have them read the *Vocabulario* section. Correct pronunciation errors as they are made.

◆ Go over the exercises that follow the *Vocabulario*.

◆ Assign the exercises for homework. Also assign the vocabulary exercises in the Writing Activities Workbook.

◆ The following day, go over the exercises that were assigned for homework.

OPTION 3 This option will meet the needs of those teachers who consider the reading and writing skills of utmost importance.

◆ Have students open their books and read the *Vocabulario* items as they look at the illustrations and read the definitions.

◆ Give students several minutes to look at the vocabulary exercises. Then go over the exercises.

◆ Assign the exercises as well as the corresponding vocabulary exercises in the Writing Activities Workbook for homework, and then go over them the following day.

Additional Activities

Teachers may use any one of the following activities from time to time. These can be done in conjunction with any of the options previously outlined.

◆ After the vocabulary has been presented, have students open their books and make up as many original sentences as they can, using the new words. This can be done orally or in writing.

◆ Have students work in pairs or small groups. As they look at the illustrations in the textbook, have them make up as many questions as they can. They can direct their questions to their peers. Individuals or teams can compete to make up the most questions in three minutes. This activity provides the students with an excellent opportunity to use interrogative words.

◆ Call on one student to read to the class one of the vocabulary exercises that tells a story. Then call on a more able student to retell the story in his/her own words.

◆ With slower groups, you can have one student go to the front of the room. Have him or her think of one of the new words. Let classmates give the student the new words from the *Vocabulario* until they guess the word that the student in the front of the room has in mind. This is a very easy way to have the students recall the words they have just learned.

Cultura and *Periodismo*

After the preliminary vocabulary presentations in both of these sections, there are one or more readings accompanied by comprehension exercises and communicative activities. The readings in each of these sections can be taught in similar ways.

OPTION 1 In some units, depending on time and interest, the teacher may want the students to go over the reading selection thoroughly. In this case, all or any combination of the following techniques can be used.

◆ Read the *Introducción* that precedes the section to give students a brief synopsis of the section theme.

◆ Ask brief comprehension questions about the *Introducción*.

◆ Have students open their books. Call on individuals to read.

◆ Ask questions about what was just read.

◆ Have students read the selection at home and complete the accompanying comprehension exercises.

◆ Go over the exercises in class the next day.

◆ Call on a student to give a summary of the selection in his/her own words. If necessary, guide students in the development of their summaries. Ask several questions, the answers to which review the main points of the reading. After the oral review, students can take several minutes to write a summary of the section.

OPTION 2 Teachers may wish to be less thorough in the presentation of some of the reading selections. In this case, the following techniques should be helpful:

◆ Call on an individual to read a paragraph.

◆ Ask questions about the paragraph.

◆ Assign the entire reading to be read at home. Have students do the *Comprensión* exercises that accompany the reading selection.

◆ Go over the exercises the following day.

OPTION 3 Sometimes, teachers may wish merely to assign the readings and exercises for homework and then go over them the following day. The *Actividades comunicativas* that follow each *Cultura* or *Periodismo* selection assist students in working independently with the language. In some cases, teachers may want the whole class to do all the activities. In other cases, teachers can decide which activities the whole class will do. Another possibility is to break the class into groups and have each group work on a different activity.

Conversación

SPECIFIC TECHNIQUES After the initial vocabulary presentation with exercises, this section provides a series of related dialogues in thematic context. These *Escenas de la vida* dialogues appear on the Audio Program, which can be used in their presentation. Teachers may wish to vary the presentation of the *Conversación* from one chapter to another. In some chapters, the dialogues can be presented thoroughly and in other chapters they may be presented quickly as a reading exercise. Some possible options are:

◆ Have the class repeat each dialogue after you. Then have students work in pairs to prepare and present one of the *Escenas de la vida* dialogues to the class. The dialogue does not have to be memorized. If students change it a bit, all the better.

◆ Have students read the dialogues several times on their own. Then have them work in pairs and read one of the dialogues as a skit. Encourage them to be animated and to use proper intonation and gestures, when appropriate.

◆ Instead of reading the dialogue together, students can work in pairs on a related activity. One makes up as many questions as possible related to the dialogue and the other answers his/her questions.

- Once students can complete the *Comprensión* exercise(s) that accompany the dialogue(s) with relative ease, they know the dialogue sufficiently well without having to memorize it.
- Students can tell or write a synopsis of the dialogue.
- You may wish to assign a class period for the preparation and presentation of the role-plays in *Actividades comunicativas,* or ask students to prepare one or more of the activities outside of class and present them during the following class period. You may want to have the whole class do all the activities, to select some activities the whole class will do, or to break the class into groups and have each group work on a different activity.

Lenguaje

SPECIFIC TECHNIQUES The techniques suggested for teaching *Conversación* may also be used to present the functional language in *Lenguaje.* Teachers should make the context clear by reading the brief introductions that precede each language box and by using the appropriate gestures and intonation. Students should repeat each utterance after the teacher. Exercises can be done in class or assigned for homework, and the *Actividades comunicativas* that end each *Lenguaje* section can be prepared at home or in class and then presented in class.

Repaso de estructura and *Estructura*

The *Estructura* sections of the chapter open with a grammatical explanation in English. Each grammatical explanation is accompanied by many examples. Related grammar points are grouped together within an *Estructura* section; for example, *Repaso de estructura* in Chapter 1 presents *El pretérito, Pretérito de los verbos de cambio radical,* and *Pretérito de los verbos irregulares.* Whenever the contrast between

English and Spanish poses problems for students in the learning process (for example, with the subjunctive), a contrastive analysis between the two languages is made.

Learning Exercises

The exercises that follow the grammatical explanation are constructed to build from simple to more complex. The first few exercises that follow the grammatical explanation are considered **learning exercises** because they assist the students in grasping and internalizing the new grammar concept. These learning exercises are immediately followed by test exercises—exercises that make students use all aspects of the grammatical point they have just learned. This format greatly assists teachers in meeting the needs of the various ability levels of students in their classes. Every effort has been made to make the grammatical explanations as succinct and complete as possible. We have purposely avoided extremely technical grammatical or linguistic terminology that most students would not understand. Nevertheless, it is necessary to use certain basic grammatical terms.

Since the structures in each *Estructura* section are recycled from the second half of **Glencoe Spanish 2**, teachers who feel students need more practice with certain grammar points can use exercises from **¡Buen viaje! Level 2** to supplement those in the Level 3 Student Textbook.

The exercises in the Writing Activities Workbook also parallel the order of presentation in the Student Textbook. The Teaching Resource boxes and the Independent Practice topics in the Teacher's Wraparound Edition indicate when certain exercises from the Writing Activities Workbook can be assigned.

Specific Techniques for Presenting Grammar

OPTION 1 Some teachers prefer the deductive approach to the teaching of grammar. When this is the preferred method, teachers can begin each *Estructura* section by presenting the grammatical rule to students or by having them read the rule in their textbooks. After they have gone over the rule, have them read the examples in their textbooks or write the examples on the chalkboard. Then proceed with the exercises that follow the grammatical explanation.

OPTION 2 Other teachers prefer the inductive approach to the teaching of grammar. If this is the case, begin the *Estructura* section by writing the examples that accompany the rule on the chalkboard or by having students read them in their textbooks. Let us take, for example, the placement of direct and indirect object pronouns with the infinitive and the gerund. The examples the students have in their textbooks (*¡Buen viaje! Level 3,* Chapter 4, page 187) are:

INFINITIVE

Ella me lo quiere decir.	**Ella quiere decírmelo.**
Ella me lo va a decir.	**Ella va a decírmelo.**
Ella me acaba de decir el nombre.	**Ella acaba de decirme el nombre.**

GERUND

Ella me lo estaba diciendo.	**Ella estaba diciéndomelo.**
Ahora ella se lo está diciendo a ellos.	**Ahora ella está diciéndoselo a ellos.**
Ella les sigue hablando.	**Ella sigue hablándoles.**

In order to teach this concept inductively, teachers can ask students to do or answer the following:

◆ Using the examples with infinitives, have students find the object pronouns in the first sentence of each pair. Say them or underline the pronouns if they are written on the board.

◆ Have students find the pronouns in the second sentence of each pair. Say them or underline them on the board. Now ask students to explain the differences they see.

◆ Ask students what else happens when the object pronouns are attached to the verb. Ask students why they think the written accent is necessary.

◆ Ask students to compare the pairs of sentences and say whether or not the meaning changes depending on the placement of the pronoun(s).

◆ Now go through the same procedure using the examples containing gerunds.

By answering these questions, students have induced, on their own, the rule from the examples. To further reinforce the rule, have students read the grammatical explanation and then continue with the grammar exercises that follow. Further suggestions for the inductive presentation of the grammatical points are given in the Teacher's Wraparound Edition.

Specific Techniques for Teaching Grammar Exercises

In the development of the **Glencoe Spanish** series, we have purposely provided a wide variety of exercises in the *Estructura* section so that students can proceed from one exercise to another without becoming bored. The types of exercises they will encounter are: short conversations, answering questions, conducting or taking part in an interview, making up questions, describing an illustration, filling in the blanks, multiple-choice, completing a conversation, completing a narrative, etc. In going over the exercises with students, teachers may want to conduct the exercises themselves or they may want students to work in pairs. The *Estructura* exercises can be gone over in class before they are assigned for homework or they may be assigned first. Many teachers may want to vary their approach.

All the *Práctica* in the Student Textbook can be done with books open. Many of the exercises such as question-answer, interview, and transformation can also be done with books closed.

Literatura

The literary selections in this section can be taught implementing many of the same techniques used for the readings in *Cultura* and *Periodismo*. However, because these readings contain more sophisticated concepts and language, they may present special problems. For example, very often in a literary selection there will be a long descriptive or detailed paragraph that students will find difficult to understand. Encourage students to read this sort of passage for the main idea or the most important information it contains. Facilitate this type of reading by asking them to find the answers to only a few questions about the passage. You may want to give them the questions before they read. Example: *La tía Julia y el escribidor* (*¡Buen viaje! Level 3,* Chapter 7, page 347).

◆ **¿A quién le habla el doctor Quinteros mientras le preparan el desayuno?**

◆ **¿Cómo sabemos que hoy es sábado?**

◆ **¿Adónde va el doctor Quinteros después del desayuno?**

If students can answer these questions correctly, it indicates that they have understood the main idea of the passage.

Students may find the poetry selections especially daunting, since many of them will not have learned to read poetry in English. One technique that is especially effective in presenting poetry is the paraphrase. The teacher may read several lines of poetry aloud, then paraphrase them before going on to the next few lines. After giving the paraphrase, you may wish to ask a few quick comprehension questions about it, then have the students read the lines silently or aloud. Then call on a student to paraphrase what he/she just read in his/her own words. Continue with the rest of the poem.

Organization of the Teacher's Wraparound Edition

One important component that distinguishes *Glencoe Spanish* and adds to the series' flexible, "teacher-friendly" nature is the Teacher's Wraparound Edition (TWE), of which this Teacher's Manual is a part. Each two-page spread of the TWE "wraps around" a slightly reduced reproduction of the corresponding pages of the Student Textbook and offers in the expanded margins a variety of specific, helpful suggestions for every phase in the learning process. A complete method for the presentation of all the material in the Student Textbook is provided—basically, a complete set of lesson plans—as well as techniques for background-building, additional reinforcement of new language skills, creative and communicative recycling of material from previous chapters, and a host of other alternatives from which to choose. This banquet of ideas has been developed and conveniently laid out in order to save valuable teacher preparation time and to aid you in designing the richest, most varied language experience possible for you and your students. A closer look at the kinds of support in the TWE, and their locations, will help you decide which ones are right for your pace and style of teaching and the differing "chemistries" of your classes.

The notes in the Teacher's Wraparound Edition can be divided into two basic categories:

1. Major topics, which appear in the left- and right-hand margins, are those that most directly correspond to the material in the accompanying two-page spread of the Student Textbook.
2. Additional topics, which appear in the bottom margin, are meant to be complementary to the material in the Student Textbook. They offer a wide range of options aimed at getting students to practice and use the Spanish they are learning in diverse ways, individually and with their classmates, in the classroom and for homework.

The enrichment notes also include tips to the teacher on clarifying and interconnecting elements in Spanish language, culture, geography, and history—ideas that have proved useful to other teachers and that are offered for your consideration.

Description of Major Topics in the Teacher's Wraparound Edition

OVERVIEW At the beginning of each chapter there is a brief description of the language functions that students will be able to perform by chapter's end.

Organization of the Teacher's Edition

NATIONAL STANDARDS Due to the importance of standards in second language learning, we have highlighted student pages where the National Standards apply most obviously. The Communication standard is consistently identified early in each chapter, since communication in Spanish is the overall objective throughout the *Glencoe Spanish* series. Examples of the other four National Standards—Cultures, Connections, Comparisons, and Communities—are cited as they occur on specific pages in the Student Textbook.

TEACHING VOCABULARY (CONVERSATION, STRUCTURE, READING) Step-by-step suggestions for the presentation of the material in the major sections in each chapter: *Conversación, Repaso de Estructura, Periodismo, Estructura,* and *Literatura* are presented in the left- and right-hand margins. They offer the teacher suggestions on what to say, whether to have books open or closed, whether to perform tasks individually, in pairs or in small groups, expand the material, reteach, and assign homework. These are indeed suggestions. You may wish to follow them as written or choose a more eclectic approach to suit time constraints, personal teaching style, and class "chemistry".

BELL RINGER REVIEWS These short activities recycle vocabulary and grammar from previous chapters and sections. They serve as effective warm-ups, urging students to begin thinking in Spanish, and helping them make the transition from their previous class to Spanish. In *¡Buen viaje! Level 3,* the Bell Ringer Review topics are directly related to the lesson about to begin. Minimal direction is required to get the Bell Ringer Review activity started, so students can begin meaningful, independent work in Spanish as soon as the class hour begins, rather than wait for the teacher to finish administrative tasks, such as attendance, etc. Bell Ringer Reviews occur consistently throughout each chapter of Level 3.

ABOUT THE SPANISH LANGUAGE Since Spanish is such a growing, living language, spoken in so many different places of the world by people of different cultures and classes, the usage and connotation of words can vary greatly. In this section, information is offered on the differences. The most important feature of this section is the presentation of regionalisms. In the student text itself, we present those words that are most universally understood. The many regional variants are given in this About the Spanish Language section.

GEOGRAPHY CONNECTION These suggestions encourage students to use the maps provided in the Student Textbook or those available from outside sources in order to familiarize them with the geography of the Spanish-speaking world. These optional activities are another way in which *Glencoe Spanish* crosses boundaries into other areas of the curriculum. Their use will instill in students the awareness that Spanish class is not just a study of language, but an investigation into a powerful culture that has directly or indirectly affected the lives of millions of people all over the globe. Besides studying the geography of the Spanish-speaking world, students will be urged to trace the presence of Spanish culture throughout Europe, Africa, the Americas, Asia, and the Pacific. The notes include interesting geographical and historical background information that you may decide to share with your students.

VOCABULARY EXPANSION These notes provide the teacher handy access to vocabulary items that are thematically related to those presented within the Student Textbook. They are offered to enrich classroom conversations, allowing students more varied and meaningful responses when talking about themselves, their classmates, or the topic in question. Note that none of these items, nor any other information in the TWE, is included in the Chapter Tests accompanying *Glencoe Spanish*.

HISTORY CONNECTION This information provides teachers with a very effective springboard from the Spanish classroom into the history and social studies areas of the curriculum. Students are invited to discuss the cultural, economic, and political forces that have shaped the Spanish-speaking world. The notes will assist you in providing this type of information yourself or in creating projects in which students do their own research, perhaps with the aid of a history teacher. By making the history connection, students are encouraged to either import or export learning between the Spanish classroom and the History or Social Studies realms.

Description of Additional Topics in the Teacher's Wraparound Edition

CHAPTER PROJECTS Specific suggestions are given at the start of each chapter for launching individual students or groups into a research project in keeping with the chapter theme. Students are encouraged to gather information by using resources in school and public libraries, visiting local Spanish institutions, or by interviewing Spanish-speaking people or other persons knowledgeable in the area of Spanish culture whom they may know. These types of projects may serve as another excellent means for students to make connections between their learning in the Spanish classroom and other areas of the curriculum.

LEARNING FROM ILLUSTRATIONS, PHOTOS, AND REALIA Each chapter of *Glencoe Spanish* contains many colorful photographs and reproductions of authentic Spanish documents filled with valuable cultural information. In order to help you take advantage of this rich source of learning, notes containing additional, interesting information have been provided to assist you in highlighting the special features of this up-to-date realia. Questions designed to enhance learners' reading and critical thinking skills are supplied so that you may challenge your students to examine the photos and realia thoughtfully and incisively.

COOPERATIVE LEARNING There are cooperative learning activities included in each chapter. These activities include guidelines both on the size of groups and on the tasks the groups will perform. They reflect two basic principles of cooperative learning: (a) that students work together, being responsible for their own learning, and (b) that they do so in an atmosphere of mutual respect and support, where the contributions of each peer are valued. For more information on this topic, please see the section in this Teacher's Manual entitled COOPERATIVE LEARNING.

ADVANCED GAMES Advanced games appear in the *Vocabulario* and *Estructura* sections throughout the textbook and can often be adapted for use in chapters other than the one in which they first appear. All games are essentially cooperative learning activities.

PAIRED ACTIVITIES In every chapter there are paired activities that complement the activities in the Student Textbook.

ADDITIONAL PRACTICE There are a variety of Additional Practice activities that complement the

presentation of material in the Student Textbook. The additional practice focuses on personalization of the new material and employs more than one language skill. It provides you with ample additional material for extra practice beyond the Student Textbook.

INDEPENDENT PRACTICE Many of the exercises in each chapter lend themselves well to assignment or reassignment as homework. In addition to providing extra practice, reassigning exercises that were performed orally in class as homework makes use of additional language skills and aids in informal assessment. Suggestions for independent practice from the Student Textbook and from the Writing Activities Workbook are included.

CRITICAL THINKING ACTIVITY To broaden the scope of the foreign language classroom, suggestions are given that will encourage students to make inferences and organize their learning into a coherent "big picture" of today's world. These and other topics offered in the enrichment notes provide dynamic content areas to which students can apply their Spanish language skills and their growing knowledge of Spanish culture. The guided discussions suggested here are based on the chapter themes and encourage students to make connections between what they learn in the Spanish program and other areas of the curriculum.

DID YOU KNOW? This is a teacher-resource topic containing information on a large variety of subjects related to the chapter theme. This topic might help you expand your own knowledge and give you some interesting information to share with your students to spur their interest in research projects, enliven class discussions, and round out their awareness of Spanish culture, history, and geography.

LITERATURE CONNECTION This topic gives background material on the *Literatura* readings and authors and on the various literary periods and movements related to them. When appropriate, these notes also appear in other sections of the chapters.

LITERARY ANALYSIS These analytical questions may be used by teachers whose classes are ready to go beyond the activities in the *Literatura* section of the student text. They ask students to analyze specific parts of the reading in more depth than the student book activities.

ART CONNECTION AND MUSIC CONNECTION These topics give background material as needed on Spanish-speaking artists, composers, and musicians and their works.

Additional Ancillary Components

All ancillary components are supplementary to the Student Textbook. Any or all parts of the following ancillaries can be used at the discretion of the teacher.

The Writing Activities Workbook

The consumable workbook offers additional writing practice to reinforce the vocabulary and grammatical structures in each chapter of the Student Textbook. The workbook exercises are presented in the same order as the presentation of material in the Student Textbook. The exercises are contextualized, often centered around line-art illustrations. Workbook activities employ a variety of elicitation techniques. There are short answers, matching columns, personalized questions, and compositions. The workbook provides further reading skills development in the *Un poco más* section, in which students are introduced to a number of reading strategies such as scanning for information, distinguishing fact from opinion, drawing inferences, and reaching conclusions, for the purpose of improving their reading comprehension and expanding their vocabulary. The *Un poco más* section also expands the cultural themes presented in the corresponding Student Textbook chapter. The Writing Activities Workbook, Teacher's Annotated Edition, provides the teacher with all the material from the student edition of the Writing Activities Workbook plus the answers—wherever possible—to the activities.

The Student Tape Manual

The Student Tape Manual contains the activity sheets that students will use when listening to the audio cassette recordings. The Teacher's Edition of the Student Tape Manual contains, in addition, the answers to the recorded activities, plus the complete script of all recorded material.

The Audio Program (Cassette or Compact Disc)

The recorded material for each chapter of **Glencoe Spanish 3** is divided into two parts—*Primera parte* and *Segunda parte*. The *Primera parte* consists of additional listening and speaking practice for the *Vocabulario* presentations (from the *Cultura*, *Conversación*, *Periodismo*, and *Literatura* sections) and the two *Estructura* sections of each chapter. There is also a dramatization of the *Escenas de la vida* dialogues from the *Conversación* section of the Student Textbook, and a reading of the *Literatura* selection. (In the case of longer selections, only excerpts are read.)

The *Segunda parte* contains a series of activities designed to further stretch students' receptive listening skills in more open-ended, real-life situations. Students indicate their understanding of brief conversations, advertisements, announcements, etc., by making the appropriate response on their activity sheets located in the Student Tape Manual. The *Segunda parte* concludes with student interviews on the basic themes presented in a given chapter of the textbook.

The Video Program (Videocassette or Videodisc)

The **Glencoe Spanish 3** video consists of one hour-long video and an accompanying Video Activities Booklet. Together, these two components reinforce the chapter themes found in the **Glencoe Spanish 3** Student Textbook. The video contains authentic commercial footage from a variety of Spanish-speaking countries including Spain, Mexico, Argentina, Ecuador, and Bolivia. Each video segment is related to a corresponding reading in the Student Textbook. The Video Program encourages students to be active listeners and viewers by asking them to respond to each video segment through a variety of pre-viewing, viewing, and post-viewing activities. Students are asked to view the same video segment multiple times as they are led, via the activities in the Video Activities Booklet, to look and listen for more detailed information.

VIDEO ACTIVITIES BOOKLET The Video Activities Booklet is the vital companion piece to the hour-long video. It consists of a series of pre-viewing, viewing, and post-viewing activities on blackline masters. These activities include specific instructions to students on what to watch and listen for as they view a given segment of the video. It also helps students to draw upon and expand their knowledge of the Spanish language and culture gained through the various readings in the Student Textbook. In addition to the student print activities, the Video Activities Booklet contains an Answer Key, a Teacher's Manual, Culture Notes, and a complete transcript of the video soundtrack.

Transparency Binder

There are four categories of transparencies, all of which are packaged in a binder: Bell Ringer Reviews, Vocabulary, Maps, and Fine Art.

Additional Ancillary Components

COMPUTER TESTMAKER SOFTWARE Available for Windows PC and Macintosh, this software program allows the teacher to print out ready-made chapter tests, or customize a ready-made test, by adding or deleting test items. The computer software comes with a User's Guide as well as a printed transcript of all test items. The testmaker program includes a randomizer, so that each time the teacher prints out a test, the items are presented in a different order.

EXPANSION ACTIVITIES For each chapter of the Student Textbook, there are several activities on blackline masters that provide further opportunities for

students to practice their communication skills in motivating, gamelike formats. Some activities are designed for paired work, while others are whole-class activities, and still others, such as crossword puzzles, can be done individually. Any or all of these activities can be used in block scheduling configurations or as independent practice.

Situation Cards

This is another component of *Glencoe Spanish* aimed at developing listening and speaking skills through guided conversation. For each chapter of the Student Textbook, there is a corresponding set of guided conversational situations printed on hand-held cards. Working in pairs, students use appropriate vocabulary and grammar from the chapter to converse on the suggested topics. Although they are designed primarily as paired activities, the Situation Cards may also be used in preparation for the speaking portion of the Testing Program or for informal assessment. Additional uses for the Situation Cards are described in the Situation Cards package, along with specific instructions and tips for their duplication and incorporation into your teaching plans. The cards are in blackline master form for easy duplication.

Lesson Plans

Flexible lesson plans have been developed to meet a variety of class schedules. The various support materials are incorporated into these lesson plans at their most logical point of use, depending on the nature of the presentation material on a given day. For example, the Vocabulary Transparencies and the Audio Program can be used most effectively when presenting the chapter vocabulary. On the other hand, the Chapter Quizzes are recommended for use one or two days after the initial presentation of vocabulary, or following the presentation of a specific grammar topic. Because student needs and teacher preferences vary, space has been provided on each lesson plan page for the teacher to write additional notes and comments in order to adjust the day's activities as required.

Block Scheduling Lesson Plans

The Block Scheduling Lesson Plans have been developed to show how the material may be distributed over the *¡Buen viaje! Level 3* course in a logical and progressive manner. The plans may be used as presented or they are flexible enough to allow for the teacher's own creative adaptation. There are no specific time limits placed on any teaching activity. Space has been provided on each day's lesson plan for the teacher to write additional and/or alternate teaching activities to those suggested. The plans include use of the numerous support materials comprising the Level 3 teaching package.

Internet Activities

The online Internet Activities serve as a dynamic, real-world connection between cultural themes introduced in *Glencoe Spanish 3* and related topics available via the Internet. In addition to serving as an innovative avenue for cultural reinforcement, the activities encourage both students and teachers to view the Internet as an engaging and valuable tool for learning the Spanish language. Through this medium, students are able to further their knowledge of the Spanish language, as well as increase their opportunities for participating in Spanish-speaking communities around the world. The Internet activities encourage students to establish an ongoing key pal (pen pal) relationship with Spanish-speaking teenagers abroad.

The Internet Activities include directions for the activities, student response sheets that can be downloaded and printed, and accompanying background teacher information, all on a chapter-by-chapter basis. Students will find the information required to complete each Internet activity by going to one or more of the Web sites whose addresses are provided.

Chapter Quizzes with Answer Key

There is a brief quiz for every vocabulary section and every individual structure point in each chapter. These quizzes are provided on blackline masters, and all answers appear at the end of the Chapter Quizzes booklet.

Tests with Answer Key

Because one of the goals of *Glencoe Spanish 3* is to give teachers the flexibility to select the material from each chapter that is most appropriate for their classes, each chapter section has its own test, which will take approximately one-half a class period to administer. The following chapter sections are represented in the testing program:

- *Cultura* These tests evaluate new vocabulary acquisition through fill-in-the-blanks, matching, multiple-choice items, and comprehension questions on the cultural information in the readings.

- *Conversación/Lenguaje* These two chapter sections have a combined test that evaluates new vocabulary acquisition and the students' ability to react to different thematic and functional situations using the new expressions presented in the *Lenguaje* section.

- *Repaso de estructura* and *Estructura* Separate tests for both sections ensure that students have learned the grammar points presented in each of these sections, through such discrete-point techniques as fill-in-the-blanks, short answers, true/false, and multiple choice.

- *Periodismo* and *Literatura* Each selection in these two sections has its own test, unless there are two or more very short readings in a section. Each test evaluates the acquisition of active vocabulary (those words and expressions introduced in the *Vocabulario* presentations). The tests go on to ask students to demonstrate comprehension of the reading selection and to analyze it in more open-ended, essay-type answers.

◆ *Global Listening Comprensión Test* Every chapter has one listening comprehension test which covers the entire chapter but emphasizes the *Conversación*, *Lenguaje*, and *Estructura* sections. This test is designed to be useful to all teachers using **¡Buen viaje! Level 3**, whether or not they complete all sections of a chapter. For this reason, factual recall of cultural or literary material is not tested here. The test relies heavily on the new active vocabulary and grammar presented in the chapter.

In addition to the section tests described above, there are comprehensive chapter tests provided for **¡Buen viaje! Level 3.** All tests are provided on blackline masters, and all answers appear in an Answer Key at the end of the Testing Program.

National Standards Glencoe Correlation
¡Buen viaje! Spanish 3

NATIONAL STANDARDS FOR FOREIGN LANGUAGE LEARNING

OBJECTIVES	PAGE REFERENCES

COMMUNICATION
Communicate in Languages Other Than English

Standard 1.1: Students engage in conversations, provide and obtain information, express feelings and emotions, and exchange opinions.

Student Edition: xii, 58, 150, 294

Standard 1.2: Students understand and interpret written and spoken language on a variety of topics.

Student Edition: 200, 244

Standard 1.3: Students present information, concepts, and ideas to an audience of listeners or readers on a variety of topics.

Student Edition: 352

CULTURES
Gain Knowledge and Understanding of Other Cultures

Standard 2.1: Students demonstrate an understanding of the relationship between the practices and perspectives of the culture studied.

Student Edition: 69, 96, 107, 154, 175, 264, 269, 393

Standard 2.2: Students demonstrate an understanding of the relationship between the products and perspectives of the culture studied.

Student Edition: 6, 24, 46, 49, 53, 62, 94, 99, 145, 192, 194, 198, 240, 241, 284, 290, 340, 346, 396, 401, 406

CONNECTIONS
Connect with Other Disciplines and Acquire Information

Standard 3.1: Students reinforce and further their knowledge of other disciplines through the foreign language.

Student Edition: 27, 83, 248, 324, 325, 352, 357, 373, 384

Standard 3.2: Students acquire information and recognize the distinctive viewpoints that are only available through the foreign language and its cultures.

Student Edition: 205, 236

NATIONAL STANDARDS FOR FOREIGN LANGUAGE LEARNING

OBJECTIVES

PAGE REFERENCES

COMPARISONS
**Develop Insight into the Nature
of Language and Culture**

Standard 4.1: Students demonstrate understanding of
the nature of language through comparisons of the
language studied and their own.

Student Edition: 9, 35, 75, 218

Standard 4.2: Students demonstrate understanding of
the concept of culture through comparisons of the
cultures studied and their own.

Student Edition: 68, 394

COMMUNITIES
**Participate in Multilingual Communities at Home
and Around the World**

Standard 5.1: Students use the language both within
and beyond the school setting.

Student Edition: 195, 292

Standard 5.2: Students show evidence of becoming
life-long learners by using the language for personal
enjoyment and enrichment.

Student Edition: 99, 143, 243, 349

ACTFL Proficiency Guidelines

The *Glencoe Spanish* series, *¡Buen viaje! Levels 1, 2,* and *3,* follow a logical progression through the ACTFL Proficiency Levels from Novice through Advanced. The initial chapters of *¡Buen viaje! Level 1,* for example, present and practice the formulaic language typical of the Novice level: greetings, expressions of courtesy, numbers, days, and dates. Later chapters of *¡Buen viaje! Level 1* have students describing in some detail, expressing likes and dislikes, narrating in present and past, which are language behaviors representative of the Intermediate-Mid and High levels.

It should be noted that it would be extremely rare for a student to perform at the same ACTFL level across all four language skills. What is usually to be expected is that the student will demonstrate a higher level of performance in receptive skills than in production skills. An Intermediate level speaker may be a fairly competent Advanced level listener. An Advanced level reader might be an intermediate level writer.

It is also the case that in the *Glencoe Spanish* materials, as in real life, the language level varies within any given situation. Superior level writers may leave notes written at an Advanced or even at an Intermediate level. Advanced level speakers may respond to a question with a single word, a response usually associated with the Novice level. Nevertheless, the steady, overall progression of complexity from Novice to Advanced holds true throughout the series.

Glencoe Spanish 3

¡Buen viaje!

Glencoe Spanish 3

¡Buen viaje!

ABOUT THE FRONT COVER
Plaza de Mayo, Buenos Aires, Argentina, showing the old Cabildo (Town Hall) in the foreground. The Cabildo was the town hall during the colonial period. Today it is a national historical museum. Also located in the Plaza de Mayo is the Casa Rosada, the official residence of the President of Argentina. The Plaza de Mayo is located in the center of Buenos Aires. It has been the scene of many of the most important events in the history of Argentina.

ABOUT THE BACK COVER
(top) El altiplano, Perú; *(middle)* La Mezquita, Córdoba, España;
(bottom) Plaza Mayor, Madrid, España

NATIONAL GEOGRAPHIC SOCIETY

The colorful and inviting **Vistas** featured in this textbook were designed and developed by the National Geographic Society's Educational Division. Their purpose is to give greater insight into the people and places found in the Spanish-speaking countries listed below.

VISTAS DE BOLIVIA
pages 102A–102B

VISTAS DE LA ARGENTINA
pages 200A–200B

VISTAS DE COLOMBIA
pages 294A–294B

VISTAS DE VENEZUELA
pages 408A–408B

Glencoe Spanish 3

¡Buen viaje!

CONRAD J. SCHMITT

PROTASE E. WOODFORD

Glencoe McGraw-Hill

New York, New York   Columbus, Ohio   Woodland Hills, California   Peoria, Illinois

The National Geographic Society

The **National Geographic Society**, founded in 1888 for the increase and diffusion of geographic knowledge, is the world's largest nonprofit scientific and educational organization. Since its earliest days, the Society has used sophisticated communication technologies and rich historical and archival resources to convey knowledge to a worldwide membership. The Education Division supports the Society's mission by developing innovative educational programs—ranging from traditional print materials to multimedia programs including CD-ROMs, videodiscs, and software.

Meet our Authors

Conrad J. Schmitt

Conrad J. Schmitt received his B.A. degree *magna cum laude* from Montclair State College, Upper Montclair, NJ. He received his M.A. from Middlebury College, Middlebury, VT. He did additional graduate work at Seton Hall University and New York University. Mr. Schmitt has taught Spanish and French at the elementary, junior, and senior high school levels. In addition, he has travelled extensively throughout Spain, Central and South America, and the Caribbean.

Protase E Woodford

Protase "Woody" Woodford has taught Spanish at all levels from elementary through graduate school. At Educational Testing Service in Princeton, NJ, he was Director of Test Development, Director of Language Programs, Director of International Testing Programs, and Director of the Puerto Rico Office. He has served as a consultant to the United Nations Secretariat, UNESCO, the Organization of American States, the U.S. Office of Education, and many ministries of education in Asia, Latin America, and the Middle East.

Glencoe/McGraw-Hill

A Division of The McGraw·Hill Companies

Send all inquiries to:
Glencoe/McGraw-Hill
21600 Oxnard Street, Suite 500
Woodland Hills, CA 91367

ISBN: 0-02-641813-4   (Student Edition)
ISBN: 0-02-641814-2   (Teacher's Wraparound Edition)

Printed in the United States of America.

2 3 4 5 6 7 8 9 10   003   08 07 06 05 04 03 02 01 00 99

Contenido

CAPÍTULO 4
Pasajes

CAPÍTULO 5
Sucesos y acontecimientos

viii

CAPÍTULO 8
Raíces

Apéndices

Chapter 1 Overview ◆◆◆◆◆◆◆◆◆◆◆◆◆◆◆◆◆◆◆◆◆

SCOPE AND SEQUENCE pages xiiA–xiiB

TOPICS	FUNCTIONS	STRUCTURE	CULTURE
◆ Vacations ◆ Travel ◆ Weather	◆ How to discuss travel habits of people in Spanish-speaking areas of the world ◆ How to make and cancel plane or train reservations ◆ How to ask for information in different travel situations ◆ How to describe complete actions in the past ◆ How to read and discuss newspaper articles about Mexico City, trains in Spain, and the weather ◆ How to talk about actions that may or may not take place ◆ How to express opinions, wishes, preferences, and commands ◆ How to describe specific things ◆ How to read and discuss literary works by Gertrudis Gómez de Avellaneda, Juan Ramón Jiménez, and Emilia Pardo Bazán	◆ **El pretérito** ◆ **Pretérito de los verbos de cambio radical** ◆ **Pretérito de los verbos irregulares** ◆ **Formación del subjuntivo** ◆ **Subjuntivo con expresiones impersonales** ◆ **Subjuntivo en cláusulas nominales** ◆ **Sustantivos masculinos que terminan en *a*** ◆ **Sustantivos femeninos en *a*, *ha* inicial**	◆ Chichén Itzá ◆ Tourist locations in Peru and Argentina ◆ The National Cathedral of San Ángel, México, D.F. ◆ The AVE train in Spain ◆ A weather report for the Caribbean **Literatura** ◆ «**¡Al partir!**», Gertrudis Gómez de Avellaneda ◆ «**El viaje definitivo**», Juan Ramón Jiménez ◆ «**Temprano y con Sol**», Emilia Pardo Bazán

CHAPTER 1 RESOURCES

PRINT	MULTIMEDIA

Planning Resources

Lesson Plans Block Scheduling Lesson Plans	Interactive Lesson Planner

Reinforcement Resources

Writing Activities Workbook Student Tape Manual Video Activities Booklet Glencoe Foreign Language Web Site User's Guide	Transparencies Binder Audiocassette/Compact Disc Program Videocassette/Videodisc Program Online Internet Activities Electronic Teacher's Classroom Resources

Assessment Resources

Situation Cards Chapter Quizzes Testing Program	Testmaker Computer Software (Macintosh/Windows) Listening Comprehension Audiocassette/Compact Disc

Motivational Resources

Expansion Activities	Café Glencoe: **www.cafe.glencoe.com**

Chapter 1 Planning Guide

SECTION	PAGES	SECTION RESOURCES
Cultura Lugares de interés turístico *El turismo*	2–7	🔦 Transparency 1 🎧 Audiocassette 1A/Compact Disc 1 📁 Writing Activities Workbook, pages 1–3 📁 Student Tape Manual, pages 1–3 📁 Chapter Quizzes, page 1 💾 Testing Program, pages 5–7
Conversación Un vuelo anulado	8–13	🔦 Transparency 2 🎧 Audiocassette 1A/Compact Disc 1 📁 Writing Activities Workbook, pages 4–5 📁 Student Tape Manual, pages 3–5 📁 Chapter Quizzes, page 2 💾 Testing Program, pages 8–9
Lenguaje De viaje	14–15	🔦 Transparency 3 🎧 Audiocassette 1B/Compact Disc 1 📁 Writing Activities Workbook, page 5 📁 Student Tape Manual, page 5 💾 Testing Program, pages 8–9
Repaso de estructura El pretérito Pretérito de los verbos de cambio radical Pretérito de los verbos irregulares	16–20	🎧 Audiocassette 1B/Compact Disc 1 📁 Writing Activities Workbook, pages 6–9 📁 Student Tape Manual, page 6 📁 Chapter Quizzes, pages 3–5 💾 Testing Program, pages 10–11
Periodismo San Ángel: «San Ángel, un oasis capitalino» El AVE «AVE: De Madrid a Sevilla en menos de tres horas» El tiempo	21–34	🔦 Transparencies 4A–4B, 5, 6–7 🎧 Audiocassette 1B/Compact Disc 1 📁 Writing Activities Workbook, pages 10–12 📁 Student Tape Manual, pages 7–8 📁 Chapter Quizzes, pages 6–8 💾 Testing Program, pages 12–19
Estructura Formación del subjuntivo Subjuntivo con expresiones imperso- nales Subjuntivo en cláusulas nominales Sustantivos masculinos que terminan en *a* Sustantivos femeninos en *a*, *ha* inicial	35–43	🎧 Audiocassette 2A/Compact Disc 1 📁 Writing Activities Workbook, pages 13–15 📁 Student Tape Manual, pages 11–12 📁 Chapter Quizzes, pages 9–13 💾 Testing Program, pages 20–22
Literatura «¡Al partir!», Gertrudis Gómez de Avellaneda «El viaje definitivo», Juan Ramón Jiménez «Temprano y con Sol», Emilia Pardo Bazán	44–57	🔦 Transparencies 8–10 🎧 Audiocassette 2A–2B/ Compact Discs 1–2 📁 Writing Activities Workbook, pages 16–21 📁 Student Tape Manual, pages 13–14 📁 Chapter Quizzes, pages 14–16 💾 Testing Program, pages 23–29

OVERVIEW

In this chapter students will learn about the vacation habits of Spanish-speaking people. While they are learning this new material, a great deal of information from *¡Buen viaje! Level 1* and *Level 2* will be reincorporated. In the *Conversación* section additional vocabulary needed to resolve travel problems, such as canceled flights or missed trains, will be presented.

National Standards

✿ *Communication* Students will engage in conversation, provide and obtain information, and express and exchange opinions on the topic of travel. They will listen to and read authentic language on the same topic.

Learning From Photos

La foto es de Tossa de Mar. Tossa está en la Costa Brava en la provincia de Gerona. Tossa es uno de los lugares turísticos más importantes de la zona.

CAPÍTULO 1

Los viajes

Objetivos

In this chapter you will do the following:

- read about the travel habits of people in the Hispanic world
- make and cancel plane or train reservations
- review how to get the information you need in different travel situations
- review how to describe completed past actions
- read and discuss newspaper articles about Mexico City, trains in Spain, and the weather
- review how to talk about actions that may or may not take place; and how to express opinions, wishes, preferences, and demands of others
- review how to talk about specific things
- read and discuss the following literary works: «¡Al partir!» by Gertrudis Gómez de Avellaneda, «El viaje definitivo» by Juan Ramón Jiménez, and «Temprano y con Sol» by Emilia Pardo Bazán

inter NET CONNECTION

The Glencoe Foreign Language Web site (http://www.glencoe.com/sec/fl) offers these options that enable you and your students to experience the Spanish-speaking world via the Internet:

- At **Café Glencoe**, the interactive "after-school" section of the site, you and your students can access a variety of additional online resources, including online newspapers, interactive games, and a send-a-postcard feature.
- The online **Proyectos** are correlated to the chapters and utilize Hispanic Web sites around the world.

DIFFICULTY PLATEAUS

Each chapter of *¡Buen viaje! Level 3* is divided into the following sections: *Cultura, Conversación, Lenguaje, Repaso de estructura, Periodismo, Estructura,* and *Literatura. Estructura* presents advanced grammar, which includes new topics as well as the grammar taught in the last six chapters of *¡Buen viaje! Level 2.*

The following is a rating of the difficulty level of the various sections of each chapter of the book:

Easy: Conversación, Lenguaje, Repaso de estructura

Intermediate: Cultura

Intermediate/Difficult: Periodismo

Difficult: Literatura, Estructura

Each structure topic, conversation, and reading selection is rated as follows:

◆   **Easy**

◆◆   **Intermediate**

◆◆◆ **Difficult**

Please note that the material in *¡Buen viaje! Level 3* does not become increasingly difficult as the students progress. Within each chapter there are easy and difficult sections.

The overall rating of this chapter is: ◆ **Easy.**

RANDOM ACCESS

Because of the above type of rating, it is not necessary to follow the sequencing of the book exactly. You should feel free to omit any selection that does not interest you or that does not meet the needs of your students.

EVALUATION

Quizzes There is a quiz for every vocabulary section and every structure point.

Tests To accompany *¡Buen viaje! Level 3* there are global tests for both *Estructuras,* a combined *Conversación/Lenguaje* test, and one test for each reading in the *Cultura, Periodismo,* and *Literatura* sections. There is also a comprehensive chapter test.

uno ❧ **1**

Chapter Projects

1. Divida Ud. la clase en cuatro grupos. Cada grupo debe hacer una investigación sobre cómo los miembros de cada grupo pasan sus vacaciones de verano. Compare Ud. los resultados de cada grupo con los hábitos de los hispanos.

2. Pídales a los alumnos que escojan una región o una ciudad en España, en México, en el Caribe o en Sudamérica y que hagan un folleto turístico para convencer a los turistas que visiten esta región.

3. Pídales a los alumnos que escojan una región de los Estados Unidos y que preparen un folleto turístico para promover el turismo en este lugar.

4. Cada persona en el grupo va a ser autora. Debe escribir un cuento sobre un viaje. Su viaje puede ser verdadero o imaginario.

1

Bell Ringer Review

Use the BRR Transparency 1-1, or write the following on the board:
**Hagan Uds. algunas oraciones con las palabras siguientes:
a orillas del mar
la playa
broncearse
nadar
esquiar en el agua
correr las olas
dar un paseo, pasear**

TEACHING TIPS

A. If you wish to present this *Introducción* thoroughly, you can call on individual students to read it aloud. You may ask some questions such as those in the ADDITIONAL PRACTICE on page 3.

B. You may, however, wish to have students read the *Introducción* silently. Then, you may call on one or two individuals to explain it in a few sentences.

HISTORY CONNECTION

Se dice que Chichén Itzá tiene las ruinas más impresionantes de los maya-toltecas. Si las ruinas de Chichén Itzá son las más impresionantes, las de Uxmal son las más bonitas. Las ruinas de Uxmal son de los mayas. Los arqueólogos creen que las ruinas de Uxmal datan de los siglos 7 a 9.

CULTURA
Lugares de interés turístico

Pirámide, Uxmal, México

Figura maya

Introducción

A mucha gente le gusta viajar durante sus vacaciones. El destino que escoge cada viajero o turista depende de sus gustos e intereses personales. Si a algunos les gusta nadar, su destino es una playa o balneario. Si a otros les gusta esquiar, van para las montañas. A otros les gustan el camping, el alpinismo o las caminatas. Hay quienes viajan por motivos culturales a un sitio arqueológico, por ejemplo. Y a los naturalistas les encanta ir a un lugar donde puedan observar la flora y la fauna en su hábitat natural. Desde el punto de vista turístico, el mundo hispano ofrece una variedad enorme de lugares donde uno puede disfrutar de una estadía placentera. Hay algo para todos los gustos e intereses.

Learning From Photos

En la segunda foto vemos la famosa escultura de piedra de Chac Mool recostado. Esta escultura está en Chichén Itzá. Chac Mool es el dios de la lluvia.

Vocabulario

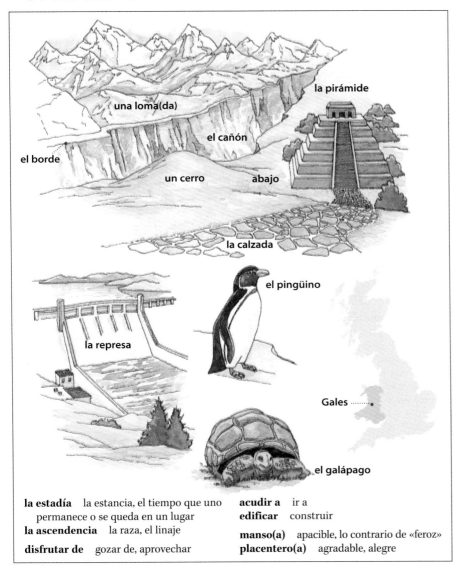

una loma(da)

la pirámide

el cañón

el borde

un cerro

abajo

la calzada

el pingüino

la represa

Gales

el galápago

la estadía   la estancia, el tiempo que uno
permanece o se queda en un lugar
la ascendencia   la raza, el linaje
disfrutar de   gozar de, aprovechar

acudir a   ir a
edificar   construir

manso(a)   apacible, lo contrario de «feroz»
placentero(a)   agradable, alegre

RESOURCES

- Vocabulary Transparencies
- Audio Cassette 1A/Compact Disc 1
- Student Tape Manual
- Workbook
- Chapter Quizzes

TEACHING VOCABULARY

A. Show the Vocabulary Transparency. Point to each item as students repeat the word after you or Cassette 1A/Compact Disc 1.

B. Definitions: Give students several minutes to peruse the definitions silently. Then call on individuals to read the definitions aloud.

ABOUT THE SPANISH LANGUAGE

- Note that **Gales** is the noun and **galés** is the adjective.

Additional Practice

You may wish to ask the following questions about the *Introducción*.

1. ¿Cuándo le gusta viajar a mucha gente?
2. ¿De qué depende el destino que escogen?
3. ¿Cuáles son algunos motivos por los cuales la gente viaja?
4. ¿Qué es un naturalista? ¿Qué le interesaría?

❧Práctica❧

A. Have one student read the questions. Another one responds.

B. Call on a student to read the statement. The same student determines if the statement is true or false.

C. You may wish to allow students to prepare *Práctica C* before going over it in class.

ANSWERS

Práctica

A **1. ancha**
  2. sí
  3. sí
  4. sí
B **1. no**
  2. no
  3. sí
  4. sí
  5. sí
  6. no
  7. sí
C **1. al borde**
  2. un cerro
  3. disfrutar de
  4. acude a
  5. Han edificado
  6. placenteros
  7. ascendencia

GEOGRAPHY CONNECTION

Benalmádena es un pueblo de menos de 2.000 habitantes en un lugar muy pintoresco y bello. El turismo es su única industria.

❧Práctica❧

A **La geografía**   Contesten según el dibujo.

  1. ¿Es estrecha o ancha la loma(da)?
  2. ¿Está entre dos cerros la loma(da)?
  3. ¿Está la fortaleza al borde de un cañón?
  4. ¿El río corre bajo la loma?

B **¿Verdad o no?**   ¿Sí o no?

  1. Los lados de una pirámide son rectangulares.
  2. Gales es una provincia de Francia.
  3. Una calzada es un tipo de camino o carretera.
  4. Los pingüinos tienen alas y son excelentes nadadores.
  5. El galápago es una tortuga de mar.
  6. Los tigres son animales mansos.
  7. La represa es un lugar donde se detiene o se contiene el agua.

C **Las definiciones**   Expresen de otra manera.

  1. Está *a la orilla* del precipicio.
  2. Está en *una colina alta*.
  3. Ellos van a *gozar de* sus vacaciones en la playa.
  4. Mucha gente *va a* la orilla del mar en el verano.
  5. *Han construido* muchos hoteles a todo lo largo de la Costa del Sol en el sur de España.
  6. Van a pasar unos días *agradables* en Marbella, en la Costa del Sol.
  7. Él es de *raza* india.

HOTEL ALAY
BENALMADENA
COSTA DEL SOL

29630 BENALMADENA - COSTA
COSTA DEL SOL
MÁLAGA - ESPAÑA
TELEF: (952) 44 14 40
TELEX: 77034 ALAY-E
FAX: (952) 44 63 80
-20%

Independent Practice

Assign any of the following:
  1. Exercises, page 4
  2. Workbook, *Cultura*

El turismo

El verano es la estación en que muchos individuos toman sus vacaciones. A muchos veraneantes les gusta pasar un par de días o semanas en una playa a orillas del mar para volver a casa bronceados y descansados. ¿Qué dices? ¿Te gustaría pasar tus vacaciones en un balneario fantástico? Pues, hay muchas posibilidades en el mundo hispano.

A todo lo largo de las costas de España y de México hay playas fantásticas a las cuales acuden miles de turistas cada año.

Rincón, en el Canal de la Mona en la costa occidental de Puerto Rico, es un paraíso para los «surfers». Y si piensas en Punta del Este, Mar del Plata o Viña del Mar, no olvides de planear tus vacaciones para diciembre, enero o febrero, cuando estos lugares disfrutan del verano.

¿Te interesa la arqueología? Entonces, ¿por qué no vas a Machu Picchu en el Perú, a Tikal en Guatemala o a Copán en Honduras? En Machu Picchu están las famosas ruinas de una ciudad incaica descubiertas por el senador estadounidense Hiram Bingham en 1911. Machu Picchu se

Playa de Acapulco

Did You Know?

Como dice la lectura, Punta Tombo tiene el criadero de pingüinos magallánicos más grande del mundo. Punta Tombo está cerca de la ciudad de Puerto Madryn. Esta ciudad fue fundada por los galeses en 1865. Aún hoy se conserva la lengua galesa como lengua oficial.

GEOGRAPHY CONNECTION

Acapulco está en la costa del Pacífico a unas 260 millas al sur de la Ciudad de México. La Bahía de Acapulco tiene uno de los mejores puertos naturales del mundo. A los turistas les encantan las playas y el clima de Acapulco. El sol brilla casi siempre.

Durante la época colonial, Acapulco fue un puerto importante para los españoles. De este puerto salieron los barcos para los países del Lejano Oriente. Hoy Acapulco es una de las ciudades más grandes de México con una población de más de dos millones de habitantes.

TEACHING TIPS

In this section students will learn about Spanish-speaking countries as tourist destinations and the travel habits and vacation preferences of Spanish-speaking peoples.

A. Tell students to look for the following important information as they read: **¿Dónde hay playas fantásticas a las cuales acuden miles de turistas cada año? ¿Dónde están las famosas ruinas de una ciudad incaica? ¿Dónde están situadas las ruinas de Tikal? ¿Qué construyeron en Tikal?**

B. You may wish to call on individuals to read sections of the reading selection aloud, or you may wish to read the selection (or parts of it) to the class as the students follow along in their books.

C. You may have students read the selection silently and then proceed to the exercises.

D. Go over the comprehension exercises.

Machu Picchu, Perú

patios, baños, mercados, plazas, calzadas (carreteras) y represas—todo en medio de una jungla de densa vegetación.

Si eres naturalista, es posible que te interese visitar la península Valdés, cerca de Puerto Madryn, en la Argentina. Pero cuidado con los elefantes marinos que se crían aquí. Estas criaturas inmensas son bastante tranquilas mientras no se les bloquee el acceso al mar. No muy lejos de la península Valdés está Punta Tombo, el criadero más grande del mundo de pingüinos magallánicos. ¿Sabes cómo recibieron su nombre estas aves adorables? Pues, «pingüino» viene del galés «pengwyn». La palabra significa «cabeza blanca». Es el nombre que se les dio en el siglo XVI, cuando un miembro de una expedición inglesa vio un pingüino por primera vez en Puerto Deseado, cerca de Punta Tombo. En toda esta región de la Patagonia argentina siguen viviendo muchos galeses.

halla a unos 2.300 metros sobre el nivel del mar. Las maravillosas y misteriosas ruinas están situadas en una lomada estrecha entre dos cerros, al borde del cañón de Urubamba por cuyo fondo, 400 metros más abajo, serpentea el río del mismo nombre. No sabemos quiénes edificaron y habitaron esta ciudad aunque sin duda era gente de raza incaica. Sin embargo, hay varias teorías: pudo haber sido una fortaleza militar, un santuario religioso o una escuela para la nobleza.

Las ruinas de Tikal están situadas en medio de una vasta jungla tropical del Petén, en Guatemala. Estas famosas ruinas mayas son muy misteriosas porque nadie sabe de dónde ni cuándo vinieron los mayas, y tampoco se sabe cómo ni por qué desaparecieron. Pero en Tikal construyeron pirámides de hasta 20 pisos de altura. Construyeron también magníficos palacios,

Punta Tombo, Península Valdés, Patagonia, Argentina

Comprensión

A **¿Qué dices?** Contesten personalmente.

1. ¿Te gustaría pasar unos días en una playa o balneario?
2. O, ¿preferirías ir a las montañas?
3. ¿Prefieres las vacaciones de verano o de invierno?
4. ¿Te interesaría visitar un sitio arqueológico?

B **Machu Picchu** Contesten.

1. ¿En qué país está Machu Picchu?
2. ¿Qué hay en Machu Picchu?
3. ¿Quién las descubrió?
4. ¿Cuándo las descubrió?
5. ¿Dónde está situada Machu Picchu?
6. ¿A qué altura está?
7. ¿Para qué servía la ciudad?
8. ¿Qué pudo haber sido?

C **Tikal** Corrijan las oraciones falsas.

1. Las ruinas de Tikal están en el Perú.
2. Las ruinas de Tikal están en las montañas.
3. Las ruinas de Tikal son de los incas.
4. En la jungla tropical hay muchas piedras y rocas.

D **La Patagonia** ¿Sí o no?

1. La península Valdés está en la Patagonia argentina.
2. Los elefantes marinos son pequeños.
3. Los elefantes marinos son siempre feroces.
4. Los elefantes marinos se quedan siempre en el mar.
5. Los elefantes marinos siempre quieren tener acceso al mar.
6. Los pingüinos tienen cabezas blancas.
7. Los pingüinos son pequeños pero feroces.
8. Muchos galeses viven en la Patagonia.
9. Gales es una parte de Gran Bretaña.

Costa Brava, España

Actividades comunicativas

A **Las vacaciones** Imagínese que Ud. está pasando sus vacaciones en la Costa Brava de España. Ud. acaba de comprar una tarjeta postal. Escríbasela a un(a) buen(a) amigo(a) diciéndole todo lo que Ud. está haciendo.

B **Las ruinas mayas** Copán, Honduras y Mérida, en la península de Yucatán de México, son lugares que también tienen ruinas magníficas de los misteriosos mayas. Busque información en una enciclopedia o en el Internet sobre estos sitios arqueológicos de fama mundial. Prepare un informe escrito sobre uno de estos lugares.

ANSWERS

Comprensión

A Answers will vary.

B 1. El Perú.
2. Hay famosas ruinas de una ciudad incaica.
3. Las descubrió Hiram Bingham, senador estadounidense.
4. Las descubrió en 1911.
5. Está situada en una lomada estrecha entre dos cerros.
6. Está a 2.300 metros sobre el nivel del mar.
7. No sabemos por cierto.
8. Pudo haber sido una fortaleza militar, un santuario religioso o una escuela para la nobleza.

C 1. Las ruinas de Tikal están en Guatemala.
2. Las ruinas de Tikal están en medio de una vasta jungla tropical.
3. Las ruinas de Tikal son de los mayas.
4. En la jungla tropical hay densa vegetación.

D 1. sí   6. sí
2. no   7. no
3. no   8. sí
4. no   9. sí
5. sí

Actividades comunicativas

ANSWERS

A and **B** Answers will vary.

Cooperative Learning

Actividades comunicativas A and B: Have students divide into small groups and choose a leader. The leader makes final corrections on the postcard and report, then shares corrections with the group to come to a consensus.

Learning From Photos

La Costa Brava está al nordeste de Barcelona en Cataluña. Comienza en Blanes y continúa hasta Port-Bou en la frontera con Francia. Aquí el paisaje es de una belleza extraordinaria. Las montañas bajan al agua azul del Mediterráneo. Por todo lo largo de la costa hay centenares de bahías o calas adonde acuden los veraneantes en busca del sol.

ABOUT THE SPANISH LANGUAGE

«Brava», cuando se refiere al mar, quiere decir «enfurecida» o «violenta».

7

Conversación

Un vuelo anulado

TEACHING VOCABULARY

A. Have students open their books to page 8. Have them repeat each word, expression, or sentence after you or Cassette 1A/Compact Disc 1.

B. Call on one student to read the words and another student to read the definition.

C. You can intersperse the questions from *Práctica A* as you are presenting the vocabulary.

D. With more able groups, you may call on individuals to use the new words in original sentences.

ABOUT THE SPANISH LANGUAGE

◆ In some countries the term **el colectivo** is used to refer to a taxi that picks up people along a set route. **El taxi** is a taxi that does not stop for other people. In Argentina, however, **el colectivo** is a municipal bus.

◆ **La autopista** is the most commonly used term for a freeway, but you will also see and hear **la autovía**.

Vocabulario

la autopista · una tormenta · una tempestad · el embotellamiento

la terminal · TAXI · el taxímetro · la parada de taxis

ESTACIÓN DE ATOCHA · TAXI

El viajero tiene prisa.
Se da prisa.
Va a perder el tren.

pronosticar   predecir el futuro
deducir   restar algo
reembolsar   devolver el dinero pagado

el monto   la suma, el total
el retraso   acción de llegar tarde, la tardanza
la demora   el retraso

Critical Thinking Activity

Thinking skills: identifying consequences

¿Qué influencia ejerce el mal tiempo en los transportes? ¿Cuáles son las consecuencias? ¿Cuáles son las causas frecuentes de los embotellamientos en muchas carreteras y autopistas de los países industrializados?

✥Práctica✥

A HISTORIETA ¿Qué pasa?

Contesten según el dibujo.

1. ¿Tiene prisa este señor?
2. ¿Adónde fue?
3. ¿Cómo fue?
4. ¿Ya salió el tren?
5. ¿Perdió el tren?
6. ¿Había un embotellamiento en la autopista?
7. ¿Había una tormenta o hacía buen tiempo?

B Otra palabra ¿Cúal es la palabra?

1. una fila larga de coches
2. un lugar donde se puede encontrar un taxi
3. la suma
4. una tempestad con viento y lluvia
5. sustraer (restar algo) de una suma
6. hacer un pronóstico
7. un aparato en un taxi que indica el precio del trayecto (recorrido)
8. una llegada con demora
9. devolver dinero

CONVERSACIÓN

nueve ∽ **9**

✥Práctica✥

EXPANSION Students can describe the illustration in their own words. In more able groups you may have the students use the words in *Práctica B* in original sentences.

ANSWERS
Práctica

A 1. Sí, el señor tiene prisa.
2. Fue a la estación.
3. Fue en taxi.
4. Sí, ya salió el tren.
5. Sí, perdió el tren.
6. Sí, había un embotellamiento en la autopista.
7. Había una tormenta.

B 1. un embotellamiento
2. la parada de taxis
3. el monto
4. una tormenta
5. deducir
6. pronosticar
7. el taxímetro
8. un retraso
9. reembolsar

National Standards

Comparisons
Students will learn formulas of politeness appropriate in Hispanic culture for requesting information.

Independent Practice

Assign any of the following:
1. Exercises, page 9
2. Workbook, *Conversación*

TEACHING THE CONVERSATION

A. You may wish to divide the conversation into three parts or present the entire conversation at once.

B. Have students listen to the *Conversación* on Cassette 1A/ Compact Disc 1 with their books closed.

C. Call on students to read the *Conversación* aloud. Each one takes a different part.

D. You may wish to do the corresponding *Comprensión* exercise each time you complete a section of the *Conversación*.

Escenas de la vida

En el aeropuerto

SEÑOR: He perdido mi vuelo a Sevilla. Pasé media hora en un embotellamiento en la autopista.

AGENTE: Pero Ud. no ha perdido su vuelo.

SEÑOR: ¡Qué suerte! ¿No ha salido todavía? ¿Hay un retraso?

AGENTE: No, se ha anulado el vuelo a causa de un problema mecánico.

SEÑOR: ¿Cuándo sale el próximo vuelo?

AGENTE: Hay otro vuelo que debe salir a las trece y veinte, pero están proyectando una demora de dos horas.

SEÑOR: ¿Debido a qué? ¿Otro problema técnico?

AGENTE: No, pero está haciendo muy mal tiempo en Sevilla y habrá demoras a causa del control del tráfico aéreo.

SEÑOR: Creo que voy a tomar el tren. ¿Puede Ud. devolverme lo que pagué por el billete?

AGENTE: Sí, ¡cómo no! ¿Ud. lo puso en una tarjeta de crédito?

SEÑOR: Sí.

AGENTE: Entonces le daré una ficha de reembolso y el monto será deducido de su cuenta.

SEÑOR: Gracias, pero tengo mucha prisa. Mi agente de viajes lo hará.

AGENTE: De acuerdo.

SEÑOR: ¿Dónde puedo encontrar un taxi?

AGENTE: Al salir de la terminal, Ud. verá a mano izquierda una parada de taxis.

10 ∽ *diez*

Learning From Photos

Ask students the following: **¿Qué está pasando en el mostrador de la línea aérea? Imagine otra conversación entre el pasajero y la agente.**

"Business" in the sign refers to business class on the plane. Many airlines now offer three classes of service on their intercontinental routes: First, Business, and Economy.

En el taxi

SEÑOR: La estación de Atocha, por favor.
TAXISTA: Sí, señor.
SEÑOR: Quisiera estar en la estación en veinte minutos. ¿Le parece posible?
TAXISTA: A esta hora no anda mal el tráfico. ¡Ya veremos! Con un poco de suerte llegaremos.
SEÑOR: ¿Cuánto es para ir a Atocha?
TAXISTA: Lo que indique el taxímetro.

En la estación de ferrocarril

SEÑOR: ¿A qué hora sale el próximo tren para Sevilla?
EMPLEADO: Hay un rápido que sale a las trece y cuarenta y cinco.
SEÑOR: ¿A qué hora sale el AVE?
EMPLEADO: A las catorce horas. Hay que pagar un suplemento, pero en menos de tres horas estará Ud. en Sevilla.
SEÑOR: ¡Increíble! Una plaza en clase preferente, ida y vuelta, por favor. Aquí tiene mi tarjeta de crédito.
EMPLEADO: Muchas gracias. Y aquí tiene su billete. Andén 3, vía A.

CONVERSACIÓN
once ◦ **11**

Cross-Cultural Comparison

The Spanish State Railroad is called **RENFE—Red Nacional de Ferrocarriles Españoles.** Recent new construction and upgrading of services have greatly improved train service in Spain.

The fastest train in Spain is **El ave** (see article, page 27). Another deluxe train is the **Talgo.** The **ELT** or **electrotrén** is, as the name implies, electric. Local trains are the **Corail** and **InterCity. Rápidos** and **expresos** are actually the slower trains.

Puente aéreo, as seen on the sign at the airport, refers to the shuttle service between Madrid and Barcelona. There are flights every hour.

Another important shuttle service operates between Buenos Aires and Montevideo. Flights leave every hour from the downtown **aeroparque** in Buenos Aires, not from Ezeiza, the international airport, which is much farther from the city center. The shuttles arrive at the international airport in Montevideo, which is not far from the center of the capital.

VOCABULARY EXPANSION

You may wish to teach the following expressions:
Largo recorrido (*long distance*)
aventa anticipada (*advance sales*)

Critical Thinking Activity

Thinking skills: supporting statements with reasons, problem solving

1. **Da tu opinión. ¿Hizo bien el señor cuando decidió ir a la estación de ferrocarril? ¿Por qué?**
2. **¿Cómo y por qué resuelven algunos problemas ecológicos los transportes públicos?**

ABOUT THE SPANISH LANGUAGE

◆ In most areas a domestic flight is **un vuelo nacional.** In Argentina and Uruguay, however, they are called **vuelos de cabotaje.**
◆ **El puente aéreo** is the expression used for the shuttle.

11

TEACHING TIPS

A, B, and C After you go over each exercise, call on a student to retell the corresponding part of the conversation in his/her own words.

EXPANSION Have students make up and answer their own questions about the conversation.

ANSWERS

A 1. **El viajero iba a Sevilla.**
  2. **Él no perdió nada.**
  3. **Llegó tarde porque hubo un embotellamiento.**
  4. **No, el vuelo no había salido.**
  5. **El vuelo fue anulado a causa de un problema técnico.**
  6. **El vuelo saldrá con demora porque hace mal tiempo.**
  7. **El señor va a tomar el tren.**
  8. **Sí, el agente le puede reembolsar el dinero.**
  9. **El agente le dará una ficha de reembolso.**
  10. **El señor irá a su agencia de viajes porque no tiene tiempo.**
  11. **Quiere ir a la estación de ferrocarril en taxi.**
  12. **El señor puede encontrar un taxi al salir de la terminal.**

B 1. **El pasajero va a la estación de Atocha.**
  2. **Él quiere llegar dentro de veinte minutos.**
  3. **Sí, es posible que llegue en veinte minutos.**
  4. **El tráfico no anda mal.**
  5. **La tarifa será lo que indique el taxímetro.**

C 1. **... trece y cuarenta y cinco.**
  2. **... rápido.**
  3. **... catorce horas.**
  4. **... en menos de tres horas.**
  5. **... una plaza en clase preferente de ida y vuelta.**
  6. **... andén 3, vía A.**

Comprensión

A **HISTORIETA** El viajero
Contesten.
  1. ¿Adónde iba el viajero?
  2. ¿Qué perdió?
  3. ¿Por qué llegó tarde al aeropuerto?
  4. ¿Ya había salido su vuelo?
  5. ¿Por qué fue anulado el vuelo?
  6. ¿Por qué saldrá con una demora el próximo vuelo?
  7. ¿Qué va a tomar el señor?
  8. ¿Le puede reembolsar el agente el dinero que pagó por su billete?
  9. ¿Qué le dará el agente?
  10. ¿Por qué irá el señor a su agencia de viajes?
  11. ¿Cómo quiere ir a la estación de ferrocarril?
  12. ¿Dónde puede encontrar un taxi?

El aeropuerto de Barajas, Madrid, España

B **HISTORIETA** A la estación de ferrocarril
Contesten.
  1. ¿A qué estación va el pasajero?
  2. ¿Cuándo quiere llegar a la estación?
  3. ¿Es posible?
  4. ¿Por qué?
  5. ¿Cuál es la tarifa desde el aeropuerto de Barajas hasta la estación de Atocha?

El AVE

C **El tren** Completen.
  1. El próximo tren para Sevilla sale a las ___.
  2. Es un ___.
  3. El AVE sale a las ___.
  4. Llega a Sevilla ___.
  5. El pasajero toma ___.
  6. El tren sale del ___.
  7. Hay que pagar ___.
  8. El señor paga con ___.

LITERATURE CONNECTION

1. Los poetas famosos Gustavo Adolfo Bécquer, Antonio Machado y Vicente Aleixandre nacieron en Sevilla.
2. Cervantes fue encarcelado (prisionero) en Sevilla y fue en esta ciudad donde empezó a escribir *El Quijote*. Es aquí donde «nació» don Quijote.

Did You Know?

El aeropuerto internacional de Barajas no está muy lejos del centro de la ciudad. Hay un servicio de autocar del aeropuerto al centro mismo de la ciudad. Los autocares salen cada 25 minutos. Hacen el trayecto de Barajas a la Plaza Colón en el Paseo de la Castellana en unos 25 minutos.

Actividades comunicativas

A **De viaje a Madrid** Ud. va de Nueva York a Madrid. Está en el mostrador de la línea aérea. Trabaje con un(a) compañero(a) de clase. Uno(a) de Uds. tomará (hará) el papel del/de la pasajero(a), y el/la otro(a) tomará el papel del/de la agente de la compañía aérea. Preparen una conversación. Si por casualidad Uds. han olvidado algunas palabras, aquí tienen las palabras que ya han aprendido y que necesitarán para su conversación.

> el boleto, la tarjeta de embarque, el talón, la sección de no fumar, el equipaje de mano, el número del asiento, el pasaporte, el destino, la puerta de salida, el equipaje, facturar, la aduana, el reclamo de equipaje

B **A Sevilla** Ud. va de Madrid a Sevilla. Está en la estación de ferrocarril en Madrid. Trabaje con un(a) compañero(a) de clase. Preparen una conversación en la estación de ferrocarril. Aquí tienen algunas de las palabras que necesitarán.

> la ventanilla, la sala de espera, el maletero, el billete sencillo, el billete de ida y vuelta, el andén, el vagón, la litera, el coche-cama, el coche-comedor, transbordar

C **El hotel** Ud. ha llegado a su hotel en Sevilla. Trabaje con un(a) compañero(a) de clase. Uno(a) de Uds. será el/la cliente. El/La otro(a) será el/la recepcionista. Preparen una conversación. Aquí tienen una lista de las palabras que ya han aprendido y que posiblemente necesitarán.

> la ficha, el ascensor, el botones, la llave, un cuarto sencillo (doble), la caja, la cuenta, el monto, la ducha, los gastos, la cama, el balcón, el baño, el aire acondicionado, el televisor

El patio de un hotel, Sevilla, España

trece 13

TEACHING TIPS

A. You may wish to have students select the activity they prefer to do. It is not necessary that all students do all activities.

B. You can do these activities as paired activities or they can be done in a group. Students assist one another in polishing the final version of their conversations.

Actividades comunicativas

ANSWERS

A, B, and C Answers will vary.

HISTORY CONNECTION

1. Los árabes o los moros invadieron a España en el año 711 y no fueron expulsados hasta 1492. Por eso se ve mucha influencia musulmana en España, sobre todo en Andalucía.
2. Los reyes Fernando y Pedro el Cruel están enterrados en la catedral de Sevilla.
3. El rey Carlos V se casó en Sevilla.
4. Don Juan, el hijo de Fernando e Isabel, los reyes católicos, nació en Sevilla.
5. Cristóbal Colón está enterrado en la catedral de Sevilla.
6. Américo Vespucio y Fernando de Magallanes salieron de Sevilla para explorar el Nuevo Mundo.

Cooperative Learning

Have students work in groups of four. Each group member discusses the advantages and disadvantages of travel by train, airplane, and car. The group decides on a preferable mode of transportation and reports to the class.

Independent Practice

Assign any of the following:
1. Exercises and activities, pages 12–13
2. Workbook, *Conversación*

Bell Ringer Review

Use the BRR Transparency 1-4, or write the following on the board:
Escriba cinco lugares que le gustaría visitar en España. ¿Por qué?

OVERVIEW

The language section gives students the opportunity to use real-life expressions they would need in all types of travel situations.

REGISTER

You may wish to give students some information concerning register as they learn to ask questions.

Formal
   Perdón, ¿podría Ud. decirme...?
   ¿Pudiera decirme...?
Less formal
   Perdón, ¿me puede decir...?
Informal
   ¿El Hotel Alejandro, por favor?
   ¿La hora, por favor?

TEACHING TIPS

A. It is suggested that you read the explanatory information to the class.

B. Have the class repeat the expressions. This can be done in unison. Have the students use as much expression as possible. Pay particular attention to intonation.

Lenguaje
De viaje

Cuando alguien sale de viaje, Ud. le puede decir:

> **¡Buen viaje!**

Cuando Ud. está de vacaciones o cuando viaja, es necesario informarse (enterarse) de muchas cosas. Hay que saber dónde, cuándo y a qué hora algo tendrá lugar. Si quiere pedirle información a alguien, para ser cortés, puede comenzar su pregunta diciendo:

> **Perdón.**
> **Perdóneme, pero...**
> **Perdón. ¿Podría decirme...**
> **Perdón. ¿Puede Ud. decirme...**
>   **dónde está el correo?**
>   **cuándo será el concierto?**
>   **a qué hora sale el tren para Sevilla?**

Si Ud. quiere saber cómo debe hacer algo, puede preguntar:

> **¿Qué hago para llamar a los Estados Unidos?**
> **¿Qué debo hacer para llamar a los Estados Unidos?**

Antes de comprar algo, es necesario saber el precio. Si Ud. compra mercancías, puede preguntar:

> **¿Cuál es el precio de esta camisa?**
> **¿Cuánto cuesta?**
> **¿Cuánto es esta canasta?**

Si Ud. quiere comprar comida (alimentos), puede preguntar:

> **¿A cuánto están las manzanas?**
> **¿A cómo es la salchicha?**

Si alguien le hace una pregunta y Ud. no la sabe contestar, puede decir:

> **Lo siento mucho pero...**
>   **no soy de aquí.**
>   **no sé.**
>   **no tengo idea.**
>   **no le puedo ayudar.**

Actividad comunicativa

A **Pidiendo información** Imagínese que Ud. está de viaje en España y se encuentra en las siguientes situaciones. Trabaje con un(a) compañero(a) de clase.

1. Ud. va a tomar un vuelo de Madrid a Tenerife en las Canarias. Vaya a una agencia de viajes y pídale al/a la agente toda la información que necesita.
2. Ud. va a tomar el tren de Madrid a Sevilla. Vaya a la estación de ferrocarril, pida la información que necesita y compre un billete.
3. Ud. quiere tomar un taxi de Barajas, el aeropuerto de Madrid, al centro de la ciudad. Hable con el/la agente de información y con el taxista.
4. Ud. llega a un hotel en Tenerife. Pida la información necesaria para conseguir una buena habitación.
5. Su cantante favorita está en Madrid. Ud. quiere ir al concierto. Hágale al/a la recepcionista del hotel todas las preguntas necesarias para poder ir al concierto.

La Giralda, Sevilla

6. Ud. está en Badajoz y quiere saber cómo se hace para usar el teléfono público. Pregúnteselo a alguien.
7. Ud. está en una tienda de departamentos. Hay algunas cosas que quisiera comprar. Entérese de los precios.

NOTE The major objective of this activity is to have students formulate questions correctly.

RECYCLING

 This activity recycles vocabulary dealing with the following communicative topics: **la estación de ferrocarril, el aeropuerto, en el taxi, al hotel, algunas actividades culturales, de compras, una llamada telefónica.**

TEACHING TIPS

A. Have students select the situation they wish to do.
B. You may wish to assign partners or have students select partners.
C. Call on pairs to present their conversation to the class.

ANSWERS
Answers will vary.

HISTORY CONNECTION

La famosa Giralda es el símbolo de la ciudad de Sevilla. La Giralda fue construida entre 1184 y 1196 por los moros. Fue la torre de la gran Mezquita. Cuando los cristianos derrumbaron la Mezquita para construir una catedral, se dieron cuenta de la belleza de esta torre y no la pudieron destruir. La incorporaron en su catedral.

Did You Know?

Las islas Canarias reciben su nombre del latín *canis* que significa *perro,* y no del pájaro canario. Se dice que los primeros exploradores encontraron muchos perros allí.

GEOGRAPHY CONNECTION

Lanzarote es una de las islas del archipiélago canario. Es la más próxima a España.

Las islas Canarias pertenecen a España y están situadas en el Atlántico a poca distancia de la costa del Marruecos meridional (del sur).

Repaso de estructura

Completed past actions
El pretérito

1. The preterite is used to state actions that began and ended sometime in the past. To form the root for the preterite, drop the infinitive ending of the verb. Add the corresponding endings to these roots.

hablar	habl-ar	habl-
comer	com-er	com-
vivir	viv-ir	viv-

2. Review the following forms.

INFINITIVE	hablar	comer	vivir
yo	hablé	comí	viví
tú	hablaste	comiste	viviste
él, ella, Ud.	habló	comió	vivió
nosotros(as)	hablamos	comimos	vivimos
vosotros(as)	*hablasteis*	*comisteis*	*vivisteis*
ellos, ellas, Uds.	hablaron	comieron	vivieron

3. Some frequently used time expressions that accompany past actions in the preterite are:

ayer	el año (mes) pasado
anoche	la semana pasada
ayer por la tarde	hace una semana (un año)
ayer por la mañana	

4. Note the similarity in the preterite of the verbs **dar** and **ver** and the special spelling of the **yo** form of the preterite of verbs that end in **-car, -gar, -zar.**

INFINITIVE	buscar	jugar	empezar		dar	ver
yo	busqué	jugué	empecé		di	vi
tú	buscaste	jugaste	empezaste		diste	viste
él, ella, Ud.	buscó	jugó	empezó		dio	vio
nosotros(as)	buscamos	jugamos	empezamos		dimos	vimos
vosotros(as)	*buscasteis*	*jugasteis*	*empezasteis*		*disteis*	*visteis*
ellos, ellas, Uds.	buscaron	jugaron	empezaron		dieron	vieron

 Bell Ringer Review

Use the BRR Transparency 1-5, or write the following on the board:
Ponga las oraciones siguientes en el presente:
1. **Pasé todo el día en la playa.**
2. **Vi a mis amigos.**
3. **Nadamos.**
4. **Nos bronceamos.**
5. **Natalia alquiló un barco pequeño.**
6. **Roberto no terminó su trabajo.**
7. **No esperamos a Roberto en la playa.**

TEACHING STRUCTURE

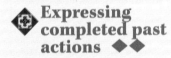 **Expressing completed past actions** ◆◆

A. Many groups should be able to skip the review of this topic.

B. Have students repeat the forms. Write them on the board and underline the endings.

C. Have students open their books and read the paradigms aloud.

D. Call on students to read the expressions in step 3.

ABOUT THE SPANISH LANGUAGE

◆ In many areas **a** is not used with the verb **jugar. Jugar fútbol** and **jugar al fútbol** are both correct.

16

Cooperative Learning

After completing the Práctica on page 17, have students do the following activity. Have students work in groups of four. Give them the following verbs and phrases: **viajar, trabajar, esperar el tren.** Students 1–3 will prepare a mini-conversation for each verb or phrase and Student 4 will report to the class.

For example:
E1: ¿Con quién viajaste?
E2: Viajé con mi amigo.
E3: ¿Cuándo viajaron Uds.?
E2: Viajamos el verano pasado.
E4 *(a la clase)*: **E2 y su amigo viajaron el verano pasado.**

⊹Práctica⊱

A **El verano** Contesten.

1. ¿Pasaste el fin de semana en la playa?
2. ¿Nadaste?
3. ¿Esquiaste en el agua?
4. ¿Usaste crema protectora?
5. ¿Comiste en un restaurante a orillas del mar?
6. ¿Comiste solo(a) o con algunos amigos?
7. ¿Comieron mariscos?
8. ¿Qué comieron?
9. ¿Quién pagó la cuenta?
10. ¿Dejaron Uds. una propina para el mesero?
11. ¿A qué hora salieron del restaurante?
12. ¿A qué hora volviste a casa?
13. ¿Te acostaste en seguida?
14. ¿Te dormiste en seguida?

B **HISTORIETA Un concierto**

Completen con el pretérito.

—Anita, ¿tú ___ (salir) anoche?
—Sí ___ (oír) cantar a Ricky Martin.
—¿Él ___ (dar) un concierto?
—Sí, en el estadio municipal.
—¿Qué tal te ___ (gustar)?
—Mucho. Como siempre, él ___ (cantar) muy bien.
—¿Quién más ___ (asistir)? ¿Maripaz?
—Maripaz, no. Pilar me ___ (acompañar).
—¿A qué hora ___ (empezar) el concierto?
—___ (Empezar) a las ocho y media y nosotras no ___ (salir) del concierto hasta las once menos cuarto.
—¿A qué hora ___ (volver) Uds. a casa?
—___ (Volver) a eso de las once y cuarto.
—Dime, ¿cuánto les ___ (costar) las entradas?
—Mil pesos cada una.
—Yo quería ir al concierto. ¿Por qué no me ___ (invitar)?
—Yo te ___ (llamar) la semana pasada antes de comprar las entradas pero no ___ (contestar) nadie.
—Entiendo. Si me ___ (llamar) el viernes por la noche, (yo) no ___ (contestar) porque todos nosotros ___ (salir) para el fin de semana.

Ricky Martin, un cantante puertorriqueño

C **Vimos a Ricky Martin.** Escriba de nuevo la conversación de la Práctica B en forma narrativa.

D **¿Quién jugó? Yo jugué.** Escriban el siguiente párrafo cambiando **nosotros** en **yo**.

Anoche nosotros llegamos al parque. Buscamos a unos amigos y empezamos a jugar al fútbol. Jugamos bien. Lanzamos el balón y marcamos tres tantos en quince minutos.

REPASO DE ESTRUCTURA

Independent Practice

Assign any of the following:
1. Exercises, page 17
2. Workbook, *Repaso de estructura*

Did You Know?

Ricky Martin is a well-known Puerto Rican singer and actor. As a boy, he was a member of the singing group *Menudo*.

TEACHING TIPS

A. This exercise can be done with books closed, open, or once each way.

B. This exercise can be done in pairs with books open.

EXPANSION Have students give the information from this exercise in their own words.

ANSWERS
Práctica

A Answers can be negative.
1. **Sí, pasé el fin de semana en la playa.**
2. **Sí, nadé.**
3. **Sí, esquié en el agua.**
4. **Sí, usé crema protectora.**
5. **Sí, comí en un restaurante a orillas del mar.**
6. **Comí solo(a) (con algunos amigos).**
7. **Sí, comimos mariscos.**
8. **Comimos...**
9. **(Mi amigo[a]) pagó la cuenta.**
10. **Sí, dejamos una propina para el mesero.**
11. **Salimos del restaurante a las...**
12. **Volví a casa a las...**
13. **Sí, me acosté en seguida.**
14. **Sí, me dormí en seguida.**

B
saliste	volvieron
oí	Volvimos
dio	costaron
gustó	invitaste
cantó	llamé
asistió	contestó
acompañó	llamaste
empezó	contesté
Empezó	salimos
salimos	

C All verbs will be in the third person.

D
llegué	Jugué
Busqué	Lancé
empecé	marqué

17

Repaso de estructura

TEACHING STRUCTURE

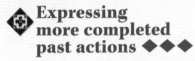 Expressing more completed past actions ◆◆◆

A. Have students repeat the verbs in steps 1 and 2 of the structure explanation after you.

B. Write the forms of the verbs on the board.

¡OJO! To avoid doing large segments of grammar at one time, you may wish to intersperse the grammar points as you are doing other sections of the lesson. If your students need to do the review grammar, you may wish to go over these points as you are doing the *Cultura, Conversación,* and *Lenguaje* sections of the chapter. If you prefer, however, you can spend two or three class periods in succession doing the review grammar.

TEACHING TIPS

A. This exercise can be done with books open, closed, or once each way.

EXPANSION Have students give the information from this exercise in their own words.

ANSWERS

A 1. Pedí
2. Pidieron
3. Prefirieron
4. Sirvieron
5. pedimos
6. Pedí
7. Me gustó
8. me medí
9. guardé

More completed past actions
Pretérito de los verbos de cambio radical

1. The verbs **sentir, preferir,** and **sugerir** have a stem change in the preterite. In the third person singular forms (**él, ella**) and plural forms (**ellos, ellas**), the **e** changes to **i.** The **o** of the verbs **dormir** and **morir** changes to **u** in the third person singular and plural forms. Review the following.

preferir	dormir
preferí	dormí
preferiste	dormiste
prefirió	durmió
preferimos	dormimos
preferisteis	*dormisteis*
prefirieron	durmieron

2. The stem of the verbs **pedir, servir, freír, medir, repetir, seguir,** and **sonreír** also changes from **e** to **i** in the third person singular and plural forms.

pedir	servir
pedí	serví
pediste	serviste
pidió	sirvió
pedimos	servimos
pedisteis	*servisteis*
pidieron	sirvieron

Restaurante **EL MERO**

ESPECIALIDADES: Pescaíto Frito
Dorada a la Sal
Variada de Marisco
Cazuela de arroz Marinera
Carnes

-10%

☎ 44 07 52

 Práctica

A HISTORIETA ¿Qué pediste en el restaurante?

Contesten según se indica.

1. ¿Qué pediste anoche cuando fuiste al restaurante? (mariscos en salsa verde)
2. ¿Y qué pidieron tus amigos? (una combinación de biftec y langosta)
3. ¿Qué prefirieron, el biftec o la langosta? (la langosta)
4. ¿Con qué sirvieron el biftec y la langosta? (tostones, arroz y frijoles)
5. Después, ¿pidieron Uds. un postre? (sí)
6. Y tú, ¿qué pediste? (flan)
7. ¿Te gustó? (mucho)
8. ¿Te mediste la cintura *(waist)* después de comer todo eso? (no)
9. No guardaste tu régimen, ¿verdad? (es verdad)

Learning From Realia

1. **El restaurante se llama El Mero. El mero es un pescado delicioso** *(grouper).*
2. You may wish to have students describe the specialties.

B Historieta Un problema en el restaurante

Completen.

—¡Oiga, camarero!

—Sí, señor.

—Perdón, pero yo ___ (pedir) una langosta y Ud. me ___ (servir) camarones.

—Lo siento, señor. Pero la verdad es que yo le ___ (sugerir) la langosta y Ud. ___ (pedir) los camarones.

—De ninguna manera. Yo sé lo que ___ (pedir).

—Y yo también sé lo que Ud. ___ (pedir).

—Y además yo le ___ (pedir) un puré de papas y Ud. me ___ (servir) arroz.

—Es imposible, señor. No tenemos puré de papas. Yo sé exactamente lo que Ud. ___ (pedir), señor. Además yo le ___ (repetir) la orden y Ud. no ___ (decir) nada.

—Lo siento, pero lo que Ud. ___ (repetir) no es lo que me ___ (servir).

—Señor, al fin y al cabo, no hay problema. Si Ud. quiere una langosta, se la puedo servir con mucho gusto. Pero el puré de papas no se lo puedo servir, porque no lo tenemos. Lo siento mucho.

More completed past actions
Pretérito de los verbos irregulares

A number of frequently used verbs are irregular in the preterite. Many of these verbs can be grouped together because they have irregularities in common. Review the following forms.

andar	tener	estar
anduve	tuve	estuve
anduviste	tuviste	estuviste
anduvo	tuvo	estuvo
anduvimos	tuvimos	estuvimos
anduvisteis	*tuvisteis*	*estuvisteis*
anduvieron	tuvieron	estuvieron

decir	traer	conducir
dije	traje	conduje
dijiste	trajiste	condujiste
dijo	trajo	condujo
dijimos	trajimos	condujimos
dijisteis	*trajisteis*	*condujisteis*
dijeron	trajeron	condujeron

poner	poder	saber	querer	venir
puse	pude	supe	quise	vine
pusiste	pudiste	supiste	quisiste	viniste
puso	pudo	supo	quiso	vino
pusimos	pudimos	supimos	quisimos	vinimos
pusisteis	*pudisteis*	*supisteis*	*quisisteis*	*vinisteis*
pusieron	pudieron	supieron	quisieron	vinieron

ir, ser
fui
fuiste
fue
fuimos
fuisteis
fueron

B This exercise can be done in pairs with books open.

EXPANSION You may wish to call on students to summarize the problem in the restaurant in narrative form.

ANSWERS

B	
pedí	pedí
sirvió	sirvió
sugerí	pidió
pidió	repetí
pedí	dijo
pidió	repitió
	sirvió

Bell Ringer Review

Use the BRR Transparency 1-6, or write the following on the board:

Complete en el presente.

1. Yo lo ___ y tú lo ___. (preferir)
2. Él ___ y nosotros ___. (dormir)
3. La profesora ___ y los alumnos ___. (repetir)
4. Ella ___ y nosotros ___. (sonreír)
5. Yo lo ___ pero Ud. no lo ___. (pedir)
6. Yo ___ pero ellos no ___. (servir)

TEACHING STRUCTURE

◈ Describing more completed past actions ◆◆◆

A. Have students open their books and read the paradigms aloud in unison.

B. Pay particular attention to stress as well as spelling changes.

C. Have students pay particular attention to the spelling of **dijeron, trajeron, condujeron,** and **fueron.**

Additional Practice

1. **Dígale a un(a) compañero(a) todo lo que Ud. hizo anoche cuando volvió a casa. Luego, pregúntele al (a la) compañero(a) lo que él (ella) hizo. Después determinen si hicieron las mismas cosas.**

2. **Con un(a) compañero(a), escriba un párrafo sobre un problema que tuvo lugar en un restaurante.**

Independent Practice

Assign any of the following:
1. Exercises, pages 18–19
2. Workbook, *Repaso de estructura*

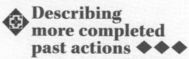

Repaso de estructura

TEACHING TIPS

EXPANSION Have students retell the information from these exercises in their own words.

C and D Have students prepare these exercises before going over them in class.

ANSWERS

Práctica

A Answers can be negative.

1. Sí, hice un viaje el año pasado.
2. Fui a…
3. Sí, puse las maletas en la maletera del carro.
4. Hice el viaje con…
5. (Mi amigo[a]) condujo el carro.
6. Sí, trajimos mucho equipaje.

B 1. fue
   2. vio
   3. vinieron
   4. fueron
   5. Anduvieron
   6. hizo
   7. puso
   8. llevaron
   9. Pusieron

C hiciste
   vino
   fuimos
   Fueron
   quiso
   tuvimos

D 1. Carmen fue a El Corte Inglés.
   2. Manolo vino a su casa.
   3. Los dos fueron de compras.
   4. Fueron en el metro.
   5. No pudieron ir en coche porque el padre de Carmen no quiso darle el coche.

Práctica

A HISTORIETA **El viaje que hice**

Contesten.

1. ¿Hiciste un viaje el año pasado?
2. ¿Adónde fuiste?
3. ¿Pusiste las maletas en la maletera del carro?
4. ¿Con quién(es) hiciste el viaje?
5. ¿Quién condujo el carro?
6. ¿Trajeron mucho equipaje?

B HISTORIETA **Él fue al mercado.**

Cambien en el pretérito.

1. Felipe va al mercado en Toluca.
2. En el mercado ve a algunos amigos.
3. Ellos vienen en carro.
4. En el mercado van de un puesto a otro.
5. Andan por todo el mercado.
6. Felipe hace muchas compras.
7. Él pone sus compras en una canasta grande.
8. Sus amigos lo llevan a casa.
9. Ponen sus compras en la maletera del carro.

Un mercado en México

C HISTORIETA **¿Qué hiciste anoche?**

Completen.

—Carmen, ¿qué ___ (hacer) tú anoche?
—Pues, Manolo ___ (venir) a mi casa y después nosotros ___ (ir) a El Corte Inglés.
—¿ ___ (Ir) Uds. en coche?
—No, mi padre no ___ (querer) darme el coche. Así nosotros ___ (tener) que tomar el metro.

D **A la tienda de departamentos** Contesten según la conversación.

1. ¿Qué hizo Carmen anoche?
2. ¿Quién vino a su casa?
3. ¿Adónde fueron los dos?
4. ¿Cómo fueron?
5. ¿Por qué no pudieron ir en coche?

Independent Practice

Assign any of the following:

1. Exercises, page 20
2. Workbook, *Repaso de estructura*

Learning From Photos

El Corte Inglés is a well-established and respected department store chain in Spain. There are stores located throughout the country.

Periodismo

San Ángel

Una tienda en San Ángel | La Catedral Nacional, México D.F., México

Introducción

Aun las grandes ciudades tienen sus lugares tranquilos donde los habitantes o los turistas pueden escaparse del movimiento y de la actividad de la gran metrópoli. Hasta la Ciudad de México, la ciudad más grande del mundo con más de 22 millones de habitantes, tiene lugares apacibles y agradables. La Ciudad de México es una ciudad muy cosmopolita. Tiene un barrio comercial, Insurgentes; una zona colonial, el Zócalo; un gran bulevar como los de París o Buenos Aires, la Reforma; y un parque fabuloso, el Bosque de Chapultepec. Muy cerca de la Ciudad de México, o como dicen los mexicanos del «Distrito Federal», en Teotihuacán, se encuentran las famosas pirámides del Sol y de la Luna.

Desde el centro de la ciudad se pueden ver los dos volcanes Ixtaccíhuatl y Popocatépetl que están a unos 60 kilómetros de la ciudad. Pero, desgraciadamente no se ven todos los días debido a que la bellísima Ciudad de México sufre de una grave contaminación del aire. Es una de las ciudades más contaminadas del mundo y no es raro ver a la gente llevando máscaras por las calles.

San Ángel es una colonia (un barrio) del Distrito Federal. Es un oasis de tranquilidad en esta gran metrópoli. En San Ángel hay un mercado especial que se llama el Bazar Sábado. Vamos a ver por qué se llama así en el artículo que vamos a leer.

Este artículo apareció en *Places*, una revista que se distribuye gratuitamente a los turistas que visitan a México. México es el país latinoamericano que recibe a más turistas anualmente.

PERIODISMO

veintiuno ∾ **21**

TEACHING TIPS

You can have students read this *Introducción* aloud or silently.

HISTORY CONNECTION

La Catedral Nacional en México es la catedral más antigua y más grande de la América Latina. Su construcción comenzó en 1573 y continuó unos tres siglos. Al lado de la catedral está la pequeña iglesia, el Sagrario, construida en el siglo XVIII.

Hace unos 50 años, zonas como San Ángel y Coyoacán fueron incorporadas en México D.F. Antes habían sido municipios separados.

Did You Know?

Because parts of Mexico City are constructed on a series of canals, much of the land is quite spongy. For this reason the cathedral has sunk considerably. A project has been underway for some time to stabilize it.

TEACHING VOCABULARY

A. Have students look at the illustrations on page 22 as you present the vocabulary.

B. Definitions: Call on one student to read the new word. Another reads the definition.

C. Proceed with the accompanying exercise.

ABOUT THE SPANISH LANGUAGE

- In Spain **sacar fotografías** means to take pictures. In Latin America **tomar fotografías** is used.
- In most areas, **una caminata** is a hike, **un paseo** is a walk. In Mexico, however, **una caminata** is also used for a walk.
- **Descender del minibús** (to get off the bus) in Spain is often **bajar** or **bajarse del bus.** The reflexive pronoun is used in more constructions in Latin America than in Spain.

INFORMAL ASSESSMENT

Now that all types of verbs have been reviewed in the preterite tense, have students respond to the following:

1. **¿Qué hiciste anoche?**
2. **¿Qué hicieron tú y tus compañeros ayer?**
3. **¿Qué hiciste durante las vacaciones?**
4. **¿Qué hiciste en la escuela?**
   Have students give as many answers as possible to each question.

22

Vocabulario

tomar fotografías

descender del minibús

una calle angosta

dar una caminata

un dibujo

El dibujante está dibujando.
Es una caricatura.

unas miniaturas de aves la vendedora el vendedor

una blusa bordada

unas golosinas

unos juguetes de madera

unos dulces

un prendedor

una pulsera un arete

el bazar

el lugar el sitio
los comensales los que comen en la misma mesa
el trayecto la distancia entre dos lugares

ubicado(a) situado(a)
disfrutar (de) pasarlo bien, divertirse
confeccionar hacer, fabricar

Cooperative Learning

Have students do the following paired activity: **Trabaje con un(a) compañero(a). Hable de todo lo que hizo el verano pasado. Diga a la clase si Uds. hicieron la misma cosa o algunas cosas diferentes.**

Práctica

A **Los turistas** Contesten.

1. ¿Descienden los turistas del minibús en la esquina?
2. ¿Dan una caminata por la plaza?
3. ¿Toman fotografías de la plaza?
4. ¿Salen muchas calles angostas de la plaza?
5. ¿Hay un bazar en la plaza?
6. ¿Es un bazar de antigüedades?
7. ¿Hay muchos vendedores en el bazar?
8. ¿Qué venden?

B **¿Qué compra el turista?** Contesten según el dibujo.

 1.

 2.

 3.

 4.

 5.

 6.

C **¿Qué hacen?** Expresen de otra manera.

1. Están *haciendo* blusas bordadas.
2. El bazar está *situado* en el jardín.
3. Vamos a *pasarlo bien durante* nuestras vacaciones.
4. *Los que están comiendo juntos* están probando varios platillos combinados de comida mexicana.
5. Es un *sitio* muy atractivo y acogedor.
6. Es un *recorrido* corto en el metro.
7. *(Se) bajan* del autobús.

D **¿Qué es?** Identifiquen.

joya   juguete   comida   ropa   artesanía   obra de arte

1. unos aretes
2. un balón
3. unas golosinas
4. un dibujo
5. unos dulces
6. una blusa bordada
7. un prendedor
8. una pulsera
9. una miniatura
10. una acuarela

TEACHING TIPS

This exercise can be done with books open, closed, or once each way.
EXPANSION You may have the students give the information from this exercise in their own words.
B, C, and D These exercises can be done with books open.

ANSWERS
Práctica
A 1. sí
2. sí
3. sí
4. sí
5. no
6. no
7. sí
8. juguetes de madera, dulces, golosinas, pulseras, blusas bordadas, miniaturas de aves, aretes, prendedores
B 1. unos aretes
2. un juguete
3. una pulsera
4. una blusa bordada
5. un dibujo (una caricatura)
6. unos dulces
C 1. confeccionando
2. ubicado
3. disfrutar de
4. Los comensales
5. lugar
6. trayecto
7. Descienden
D 1. joya
2. juguete
3. comida
4. obra de arte
5. comida
6. ropa
7. joya
8. joya
9. artesanía
10. obra de arte

Independent Practice

Assign any of the following:
1. Exercises, page 23
2. Workbook, *Periodismo*

23

SAN ÁNGEL: UN OASIS CAPITALINO ◆

Bell Ringer Review

Use the BRR Transparency 1-8, or write the following on the board: **En cinco o seis oraciones, describa la región donde Ud. vive.**

TEACHING THE READING

A. You may wish to have the students read this selection in detail. You may intersperse their reading with questions from *Práctica A* as they read aloud.

B. La idea principal: En tu opinión, ¿cuál es la idea principal de este artículo?

C. Go over the *Comprensión* exercises on page 25.

GEOGRAPHY CONNECTION

When reading paragraph 5 you may wish to point out the following to the students: **La República o la Confederación de México se compone de 28 estados, 3 territorios y un distrito federal. Oaxaca, Chiapas y Jalisco son estados mexicanos.**

DISTRITO FEDERAL

SAN ÁNGEL
un oasis capitalino

Para el Distrito Federal–con más de 22 millones de habitantes en la capital y el área metropolitana–siempre resulta reconfortable saber que quedan algunos lugares donde se puede disfrutar de apacibles[1] horas en un ambiente que invita a realizar una saludable[2] caminata, tomar fotografías, visitar algún bazar de antigüedades o simplemente observar las angostas calles cubiertas de empedrados[3] y las añejas[4] casas de estilo colonial.

Este lugar se llama San Ángel, al sur de la Ciudad de México.

En San Ángel se puede afirmar que habita la tranquilidad de domingo a viernes desde hace muchos años. Los sábados, hay un cambio repentino[5] desde las primeras horas de la mañana, cuando decenas de vendedores de artesanías y pintores se congregan en lo que es el jardín principal.

En este lugar existe uno de los más completos centros artesanales con productos traídos desde diversos lugares del país; se llama Bazar Sábado, ubicado en el número 11 de la plaza de San Jacinto.

Curiosamente, sólo abre sus puertas una vez a la semana: el día sábado. En ese día cientos de capitalinos y turistas llegan para comprar faldas y blusas bordadas tejidas en Oaxaca o Chiapas; objetos de piedra de ónix, cerámica de Jalisco; lámparas, aretes, pulseras y prendedores

hechos por artesanos que allí mismo los confeccionan; juguetes de madera así como dulces y golosinas.

En el patio central existe un restaurante que ofrece variados platillos de la cocina mexicana mientras los comensales pueden escuchar diversos grupos musicales folklóricos.

Pero en San Ángel hay más por visitar: en el jardín principal también ese día se reúnen decenas de pintores y escultores que ofrecen sus obras producidas a lo largo de la semana. Lo mismo puede encontrar paisajes de Taxco, Guerrero, como de San Miguel de Allende, Guanajuato, que pinturas con paisajes del volcán Popocatépetl o la montaña Ixtaccíhuatl, cuadros de estampas[6] típicas, etc.

También, otros artistas venden óleos y acuarelas con rostros de indígenas así como miniaturas de aves, flores y diversidad de ornamentos.

Hay dibujantes que en unos minutos le pueden hacer un boceto[7] a lápiz o su caricatura.

Para trasladarse a San Ángel basta tomar un minibús o autobús en la avenida Insurgentes a la altura de la Estación Metro Insurgentes, en dirección sur, que anuncia San Ángel, o simplemente C.U. (Ciudad Universitaria) y en un trayecto de 30 a 35 minutos–dependiendo del tráfico por esa artería–estará frente al Monumento a Obregón. Allí descienda y camine una cuadra hacia la avenida Revolución. De inmediato, usted notará el contraste de esta gigantesca urbe[8] con las empedradas calles del lugar.

ANDRÉS GARCÍA

---

[1] **apacibles** *peaceful*	[4] **añejas** antiguas	[7] **boceto** *sketch*
[2] **saludable** *healthy*	[5] **repentino** *sudden*	[8] **urbe** ciudad
[3] **empedrados** *paved with stones*	[6] **estampas** *engravings*	

National Standards

Communication
Students learn about the products of regions of Mexico and about some ways that residents of the capital enjoy their leisure time.

Critical Thinking Activity

Thinking skills: supporting statements with reasons **¿Por qué es bueno tener algunos lugares tranquilos y apacibles en el centro de las grandes ciudades?**

ABOUT THE SPANISH LANGUAGE

◆ **México** is spelled with an **x** throughout Latin America but with a **j** —**Méjico** and **mejicano**— in Spain.

Comprensión

A **En el bazar**   Contesten.

1. ¿Qué es el Distrito Federal?
2. ¿Dónde está San Ángel?
3. ¿Por qué hay un cambio repentino en el ambiente de San Ángel los sábados?
4. ¿Dónde tiene lugar el Bazar Sábado?
5. ¿Qué compran los turistas y los capitalinos en el Bazar Sábado?
6. ¿Qué venden los pintores y escultores?

B **En México**   Den los informes siguientes.

1. el número de habitantes que tiene la Ciudad de México
2. los nombres de algunos estados mexicanos
3. el estado donde se encuentra Taxco
4. el estado donde se encuentra San Miguel de Allende
5. los nombres de dos volcanes

C **En San Ángel**   Describan lo siguiente.

1. las calles de San Ángel
2. el Bazar Sábado

San Ángel

Actividades comunicativas

A **En la Ciudad de México**   Ud. está en la Ciudad de México y alguien le pregunta cómo ir del centro de la ciudad a San Ángel. Indíquele cómo.

B **Es un lugar tranquilo.**   Escoja una ciudad cerca de donde Ud. vive. Descríbala. Indique si dentro de la ciudad hay un lugar tranquilo parecido a San Ángel. Descríbalo. Prepare una lista de lugares que serían de interés para los turistas en esta ciudad.

C **Me gustaría vivir en Sevilla.**   Ud. ha aprendido mucho sobre las ciudades de España y de Latinoamérica. Escoja una ciudad española o latinoamericana que le gustaría visitar. En un párrafo, explique por qué.

D **Vamos a Taxco.**   Taxco y San Miguel de Allende son dos pueblos fabulosos en México. Vaya Ud. a una agencia de viajes. En un folleto publicitario sobre México, busque información sobre estos dos pueblos. Luego, prepare su propio folleto publicitario sobre estas dos ciudades.

Independent Practice

Assign any of the following:

1. *Comprensión* exercises, page 25
2. **Workbook,** *Periodismo*

ANSWERS

Comprensión

A 1. **Es la capital de México.**
2. **Está al sur de la ciudad.**
3. **Decenas de vendedores se congregan en el jardín principal.**
4. **En el número 11 de la plaza de San Jacinto.**
5. **Compran ropa, artesanías y joyas.**
6. **Venden sus obras de arte.**

B 1. **La Ciudad de México tiene más de 22 millones de habitantes.**
2. **Oaxaca, Chiapas, Jalisco, Guanajuato y Guerrero son estados mexicanos.**
3. **Taxco se encuentra en Guerrero.**
4. **San Miguel de Allende se encuentra en Guanajuato.**
5. **Dos volcanes son Ixtaccíhuatl y Popocatépetl.**

C Answers will vary.

TEACHING TIPS

A. You may wish to have the students select the activity they prefer to do. It is not necessary that all students do all activities.

B. **Actividades A and B:** You can do these activities as paired activities or they could be done in a group. Students assist one another in polishing the final version of their presentations.

C. **Actividad C:** This paragraph might be put on a bulletin board after being presented to the class orally.

D. **Actividad D:** This may be done as a group activity. Students assist one another in the preparation of the brochures.

ANSWERS

A–D Answers will vary.

25

TEACHING TIPS

You can have students read the *Introducción* aloud or silently.

RESOURCES

- Vocabulary Transparencies
- Audio Cassette 1B/Compact Disc 1
- Student Tape Manual
- Workbook
- Chapter Quizzes
- Testing Program

TEACHING VOCABULARY

Have students repeat the words, sentences, and definitions after you or Cassette 1B/Compact Disc 1.

TEACHING TIPS

Call on individuals to read the completed sentences aloud.

EXPANSION Have students make up questions about each statement.

ANSWERS
Práctica
A 1. recorre
   2. tramos
   3. apetece
   4. aseos
   5. inodoro
   6. lavamanos

El AVE

Introducción

¿Qué es un ave? Un ave es un pájaro. Y un pájaro vuela. El vuelo indica velocidad, rápidez. En España el A V E son las siglas para el tren de ALTA VELOCIDAD ESPAÑOLA. Es un tren que anda a 250 kilómetros por hora y hasta a 300 en algunos tramos.

He aquí algunos trozos de un artículo sobre el AVE que apareció en la revista española *Tiempo*.

Vocabulario

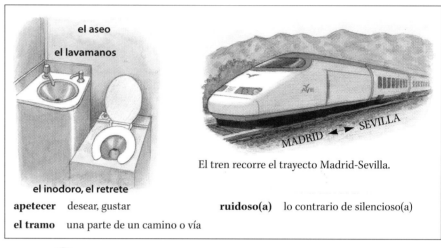

el aseo
el lavamanos
el inodoro, el retrete

El tren recorre el trayecto Madrid-Sevilla.

apetecer   desear, gustar

el tramo   una parte de un camino o vía

ruidoso(a)   lo contrario de silencioso(a)

Práctica

A **HISTORIETA** **En el tren**

Completen.

El tren ___ el trayecto Madrid-Sevilla a 250 kilómetros por hora. Pero en algunos ___ del trayecto puede alcanzar una velocidad hasta de 300 kilómetros por hora. ¿Le ___ tomar algo? No hay problema. Puede pasar al coche-cafetería. El tren es tan cómodo que aun los ___ tienen aire acondicionado. En el aseo hay un ___ y también un ___ para lavarse las manos.

Critical Thinking Activity

Thinking skills: supporting statements with reasons **¿Por qué tiene tanta importancia la velocidad en la vida moderna?**

AVE: De Madrid a Sevilla en menos de tres horas

CON la inauguración de la Expo el AVE realizó su primer viaje. A 250 kilómetros por hora, el tren de alta velocidad recorre el trayecto Madrid-Sevilla en dos horas y cincuenta minutos.

Los viajeros del AVE pueden realizar el trayecto Madrid-Sevilla en dos horas y cincuenta minutos y elegir, entre otros servicios, cuál de los tres canales de video prefieren o qué tipo de música ambiental les apetece oír durante el viaje.

Cada tren lleva ocho coches y un total de 330 plazas, 39 de la clase club, 78 de la preferente y 213 de turista.

El AVE es muy similar a la segunda generación del TGV francés, el primer tren de alta velocidad del mundo, inaugurado en 1981, y que realizaba el trayecto París-Lyon a 260 kilómetros por hora. El modelo español, sin embargo, ha adoptado un diseño más aerodinámico y utiliza equipos informáticos más parecidos a los de los aviones que a los de los trenes modernos.

El tren de alta velocidad es rápido y poco ruidoso. RENFE cambió su nombre de TAV (Tren de Alta Velocidad) a AVE después de pensarlo mucho, precisamente para que se asociara el tren con la idea de «silencio y poesía».

Los colores del AVE son blanco, gris y azul. El coche-cafetería está diseñado para que los viajeros puedan contemplar el paisaje mientras toman una copa sin agacharse¹ ni un milímetro. Dispone de teléfonos, aseos especialmente acondicionados para niños y de zonas familiares con mesa de juegos…

De cumplirse las previsiones de la Comunidad Europea, en el año 2015 la Red Europa de Alta Velocidad tendrá 30.000 kilómetros y se podrá viajar de Madrid a París, por ejemplo, en menos de ocho horas y a Londres, en diez.

¹**agacharse** bend

TEACHING THE READING

A. You may wish to have students read this selection in detail. If so, you may intersperse their reading of it with questions from *Comprensión A* on page 28 as they read aloud.

B. Go over *Comprensión B* on page 28 in class as students look for the information.

ABOUT THE SPANISH LANGUAGE

1. Trying to find the proper word for a public bathroom is not always an easy matter. **El cuarto de baño** is used only for the bathroom in a home or hotel room since it must have a bathtub. For a public facility one can ask **¿Dónde está el servicio? ¿Dónde está el aseo? or ¿Dónde están los aseos? ¿Dónde está el doble v, c (W.C.)? ¿Dónde está el sanitario?** Other less frequently heard terms are **¿Dónde está el excusado? ¿Dónde está el tocador? ¿Dónde está la toilette** (often pronounced **tualé**). One often heard **el retrete,** but lately it has come to be somewhat vulgar, often referring to the toilet itself, almost synonymous with **el inodoro,** which is the toilet bowl.

2. **El lavamanos** is also called **el lavabo.**

3. The verb **apetecer** is often used when asking someone if he/she would like to have some food or drink:
   ¿Te (Le) apetece…?
   ¿Qué tal te apetece…?

National Standards

Connections
Students connect with mathematics seeing real-life use of the metric system for speeds and distances and should be encouraged to calculate the stated speeds and distances using the U.S. system.

ANSWERS
Comprensión

A 1. Tarda dos horas, cincuenta minutos.

2. Es un tren de alta velocidad.

3. Es similar al TGV francés.

4. El tren español tiene un diseño más aerodinámico y utiliza equipos informáticos más parecidos a los de los aviones.

5. Se asocia con el silencio y la poesía.

6. Pueden contemplar el paisaje.

7. Están acondicionados para los niños.

B 1. Hay tres canales de video.

2. Hay ocho coches en cada tren.

3. Hay un total de 330 plazas.

4. Hay tres clases.

5. Las clases son club, preferente y turista.

6. La sigla para la compañía nacional española de ferrocarriles es RENFE.

7. Los colores del tren son blanco, gris y azul.

Actividad comunicativa

ANSWERS

Answers will vary.

Comprensión

A **El AVE** Contesten.

1. ¿Cuánto tiempo tarda el trayecto Madrid-Sevilla?
2. ¿Qué es el AVE?
3. ¿A qué tren es similar el AVE?
4. ¿Cuáles son algunas diferencias entre el TGV francés y el AVE español?
5. ¿Con qué idea se asocia el nombre del tren?
6. ¿Qué pueden contemplar los pasajeros desde el coche-cafetería?
7. ¿Para quiénes están acondicionados los aseos?

B **¿Dónde dice?** Busquen la información siguiente.

1. el número de canales de video que hay
2. el número de coches que tiene cada tren
3. el total de plazas
4. el número de clases
5. el nombre de cada clase
6. la sigla para la compañía nacional española de ferrocarriles
7. los colores del tren

HORARIOS A PARTIR DEL 26•9 HASTA 29•1

TRENES LARGA DISTANCIA

El estilo de viajar

Menos tiempo de viaje

AVE

Actividad comunicativa

A **El tren es muy popular** El tren es un medio de transporte importante y popular en España pero no lo es en la mayoría de los países latinoamericanos a causa del terreno. Es difícil construir ferrocarriles por los Andes o las selvas tropicales. Sin embargo, hay algunos trayectos que son sumamente interesantes para los turistas. Búsquelos en un mapa.

PERÚ	Cuzco-Machu Picchu
	Lima-Huancayo-Huancavelica
ECUADOR	Quito-Riobamba
ARGENTINA	Buenos Aires-San Carlos de Bariloche
	Buenos Aires-Mendoza
PANAMÁ	Panamá-Colón
COSTA RICA	San José-Puntarenas
	San José-Limón

Learning From Realia

You may wish to ask students the following questions about the realia on page 28: **¿Qué es este documento? (un horario de trenes) ¿Para qué trenes es? ¿Para qué período de tiempo son válidos los horarios?**

Independent Practice

Assign any of the following:
1. *Comprensión* exercises, page 28
2. Workbook, *Periodismo*

El tiempo

Introducción

El tiempo le interesa mucho al viajero porque un día en la playa con cielo claro y sol brillante es una maravilla. En cambio, un día en la playa es un horror cuando el cielo está nublado y hay chubascos. Cuando hace buen tiempo, los aviones salen a tiempo. Cuando hay una tempestad o una nevada, los vuelos salen con demora o se anulan. Por consiguiente, los turistas o viajeros quieren saber el tiempo que hará. Escuchan el pronóstico meteorológico en la radio o en la televisión o lo leen en el periódico.

He aquí, del periódico más importante de Cataluña, *La Vanguardia* de Barcelona, el resumen meteorológico para la región. Y para saber el tiempo en el Caribe tenemos otro pronóstico, del periódico *El Nuevo Día* de San Juan, Puerto Rico.

Un huracán

 Bell Ringer Review

Use the BRR Transparency 1-10, or write the following on the board: **Conteste. ¿Qué tiempo está haciendo hoy? Donde Ud. vive, ¿qué tiempo hace en el invierno? ¿Y en el verano?**

INTRODUCIÓN

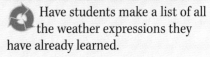 **RECYCLING**

Have students make a list of all the weather expressions they have already learned.

TEACHING TIPS

Before reading the *Introducción*, ask students to make a list of adjectives under each type of weather they came up with for the Recycling activity above. Now ask volunteers to describe how the weather affects them emotionally.

Learning From Photos

After completing the section on *El tiempo*, have students describe the photo with as much detail as possible.

29

RESOURCES

- Vocabulary Transparencies
- Audio Cassette 1B/Compact Disc 1
- Student Tape Manual
- Workbook
- Chapter Quizzes
- Testing Program

TEACHING VOCABULARY

A. Have students look at the overhead transparency and repeat each word or sentence after you or Cassette 1B/Compact Disc 1.

B. Have students open their books to page 30 and read the words and sentences aloud.

C. Upon completion of the vocabulary presentation, have students list storms according to severity.

Vocabulario

Formas de precipitación

un chubasco

La lluvia cae en chubascos.

un aguacero

Cuando la lluvia cae con mucha fuerza y en grandes cantidades es un aguacero.

un temporal

Los temporales ocurren cuando la lluvia cae en grandes cantidades acompañada de vientos fuertes.
Un temporal puede durar varios días.

el granizo

La lluvia helada puede tomar la forma de granizo.

un huracán

una tormenta, una tempestad

Los temporales muy fuertes son huracanes.

Cooperative Learning

Have students write in groups and discuss the following topics:

1. **Las tempestades (no) me asustan.**
2. **Donde nosotros vivimos (no) tenemos que preocuparnos por las tempestades.**

una nevada

Cuando la lluvia helada cae del cielo en copos blancos y ligeros hay una nevada.

despejado y soleado

Durante un día despejado y soleado el sol brilla y hace muy buen tiempo.

soplar

Los vientos soplan del este a más de cinco millas por hora.
Los vientos son leves, no son fuertes.

Práctica

A **El tiempo** Completen.

1. El ___ que cayó anoche era del tamaño de bolas de golf.
2. El cielo está ___. No hay ni una nube.
3. Lloverá muy poco mañana. Sólo habrá algunos ___ por la tarde.
4. Los ___ ahora llevan nombres de hombres y mujeres. Algunos han causado millones de dólares en daños y destrucción.
5. Los vientos de treinta a treinta y cinco millas por hora no son ___.
6. No salgas ahora. Espera que termine el ___. La calle está como un lago.

TEACHING TIPS

This exercise can be done orally with books open as soon as the vocabulary presentation is completed.

ANSWERS
Práctica
A 1. **granizo**
   2. **despejado**
   3. **chubascos**
   4. **huracanes**
   5. **leves**
   6. **aguacero**

INFORMAL ASSESSMENT

Have students give a complete description of today's weather.

31

EL TIEMPO ◆

TEACHING THE READING

A. Ask students to scan the article and try to determine what season of the year this would be in the U. S.

B. Ask the students to compare the weather in the United States with that described in Puerto Rico.

C. It is suggested that you have students read this selection silently as if they were leisurely reading the newspaper.

LA VANGUARDIA *Barcelona, España*

El Tiempo

Cataluña: Durante la jornada[1] de ayer el tiempo en general fue bastante bueno, con predominio de los cielos despejados o casi despejados. Las temperaturas fueron muy agradables y únicamente se registraron algunas ligeras precipitaciones en puntos de los Pirineos. Los vientos aún soplaron algo fuertes en puntos de la zona del litoral[2] catalán.

Y EL TIEMPO EN EL CARIBE

Pronóstico del tiempo para hoy

HOY EN LA ISLA Un clima relativamente seco prevalece sobre el área de Puerto Rico y las Islas Vírgenes. No se anticipa cambio alguno en el presente patrón[3] del tiempo hasta pasado el viernes entrante. El sol sale a las 5:48 a.m. y se ocultará a las 7:03 p.m. Hay luna nueva.

MARÍTIMO Alta presión atmosférica al nordeste de la región. Vientos del este de 10 a 15 millas, más leves en la noche. El oleaje[4] es de cerca de dos pies con marejadas[5] del este de tres a cinco pies.

SAN JUAN Soleado en la mañana y semisoleado en la tarde con un 20 por ciento de probabilidad de lluvia. Temperatura cerca de 89 grados con vientos del este de 10 a 15 millas por hora.

PONCE Y MAYAGÜEZ En Ponce, mayormente soleado con un 20 por ciento de probabilidad de lluvia en la tarde y de temperatura cerca de 88 grados. En Mayagüez, soleado en la mañana. Parcialmente nublado por la tarde con 40 por ciento de probabilidad de aguaceros o tronadas[6].

TEMPERATURAS
AYER: Máxima 90° Mínima 76°
HOY: Máxima 90° Mínima 76°

ATLANTA	65° MIN. 85° MAX.
BOSTON	57° MIN. 77° MAX.
CHICAGO	56° MIN. 76° MAX.
DALLAS	70° MIN. 91° MAX.
DETROIT	53° MIN. 76° MAX.
HARTFORD	53° MIN. 76° MAX.

¿Va de pesca?

Marea[7] alta: 9:30 a.m. 11:08 p.m.
Marea baja: 5:33 a.m. 3:26 p.m.

[1] **jornada** día
[2] **litoral** costa
[3] **patrón** pattern
[4] **oleaje** surf
[5] **marejadas** swells
[6] **tronadas** thunderstorms
[7] **marea** tide

Did You Know?

El Niño El Niño es una corriente marina muy cálida que se origina ocasionalmente frente a la costa del Ecuador y el Perú. La llegada de esta corriente generalmente coincide con la Navidad y por esta razón se llama «El Niño» *(the Christ child)*. La llegada de El Niño produce una enorme cantidad de lluvia y otros cambios atmosféricos que afectan aun la costa oeste de los EE.UU.

La garúa La garúa es un tipo de neblina que cubre la ciudad de Lima en el invierno o sea de julio a octubre. Durante estos meses es raro que salga el sol en Lima.

La tramontana Es un viento fuerte (en España) que sopla del norte hacia el sur, hacia el Mediterráneo. Puede venir del otro lado de los Pirineos.

Las estaciones En muchas partes de Latinoamérica el verano y el invierno tienen más que ver con la precipitación que con la temperatura. El invierno es la temporada lluviosa y el verano es la estación seca.

❧ Comprensión ❧

A **¿Cómo estuvo el tiempo?** ¿Sí o no?

1. Hizo mal tiempo ayer en Cataluña.
2. Por lo general casi no hubo nubosidad.
3. En algunas partes de las costas de la región, hubo vientos fuertes.
4. No llovió en las montañas.

B **El pronóstico para el Caribe** Escojan.

1. El tiempo no cambiará antes ___
   a. de esta noche
   b. de mañana
   c. del viernes que viene

2. A las 7:03 de la tarde el sol ___.
   a. saldrá
   b. está de mediodía
   c. se pondrá

3. Comparadas con las de ayer, las temperaturas de hoy son ___.
   a. más bajas
   b. exactamente iguales
   c. un poco más altas

4. Quince millas por hora representa ___.
   a. la fuerza de los vientos
   b. el tamaño de las olas
   c. la temperatura máxima en el mar

5. La ciudad de ___ tendrá la temperatura más alta mañana.
   a. San Juan
   b. Ponce
   c. Mayagüez

6. Es más probable que llueva en ___.
   a. San Juan
   b. Ponce
   c. Mayagüez

7. Hay ___ mareas en un día.
   a. dos
   b. tres
   c. cuatro

8. La ciudad con la temperatura más alta fue ___.
   a. Atlanta
   b. Detroit
   c. Dallas

ANSWERS
Comprensión

A **1.** no
   2. sí
   3. sí
   4. no

B **1.** c
   2. c
   3. b
   4. a
   5. a
   6. c
   7. c
   8. c

Learning From Photos

Have students describe the scene in each of the photos. You may wish to ask: **¿En cuál de las fotos se ve una tormenta? ¿Cuál de las fotos es del invierno?**

33

C 1. Los vientos vienen del este.

   2. Los vientos soplan de 10 a 15 millas por hora.

   3. Las marejadas vienen del este.

   4. El tiempo en San Juan estará soleado por la mañana.

   5. Por la tarde estará semi-soleado.

   6. El tiempo en Ponce estará soleado.

   7. La probabilidad de precipitación es del 20%.

   8. El cielo estará parcialmente nublado por la tarde en Mayagüez.

   9. La marea alta está a las 9:30 de la mañana y a las 11:08 de la noche.

  10. Ayer la temperatura máxima en San Juan fue 90º y la mínima fue 76º.

ANSWERS

A–E Answers will vary.

National Standards

✦ Comparisons

Students learn how contrary-to-fact statements are expressed in Spanish. Although the subjunctive is less used in English, students recognize that the concept is expressed in English as well, but using an infinitive construction.

C **El tiempo y la temperatura** Contesten.

   1. ¿De dónde vienen los vientos?

   2. ¿A cuántas millas por hora soplan?

   3. ¿De dónde vienen las marejadas?

   4. ¿Cómo estará el tiempo en San Juan por la mañana?

   5. ¿Y por la tarde?

   6. ¿Cómo estará el tiempo en Ponce?

   7. ¿Cuál es la probabilidad de precipitación?

   8. ¿En qué ciudad estará el cielo parcialmente nublado por la tarde?

   9. ¿A qué hora está la marea alta?

  10. Ayer, ¿cuál fue la temperatura máxima en San Juan? ¿Y la mínima?

Actividades comunicativas

A **Un mapa meteorológico** Estudie el mapa meteorológico un momento. ¿En qué parte de la península preferiría estar Ud. y por qué?

B **Y el tiempo para hoy…** Ud. es el/la meteorólogo(a) de su emisora local de televisión. Prepare Ud. el pronóstico para el día 8 de febrero. Empiece con: «Y ahora, estimado público, el pronóstico del tiempo para mañana, 8 de febrero…»

C *El Alcázar* He aquí los titulares del periódico *El Alcázar*. ¿Cómo estará el tiempo? ¿Qué les pasó a dos montañeros? ¿Dónde?

D **El pronóstico meteorológico** Lea el pronóstico meteorológico en su periódico local. Imagínese que Ud. tiene que indicarle el tiempo que hará a un(a) amigo(a) que sólo habla español. Dele el pronóstico en español.

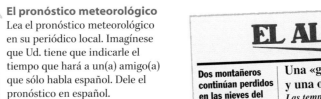

EL ALCÁZAR

Dos montañeros continúan perdidos en las nieves del Pirineo navarro

Una «gota fría» provoca nevadas y una ola de intenso frío
Las temperaturas subirán a partir de hoy

E **En el verano hace calor.** Describa el tiempo que hace donde Ud. vive durante cada estación del año: el verano, el otoño, el invierno y la primavera.

Independent Practice

Assign any of the following:

  1. *Comprensión* exercise, page 34

  2. Workbook, *Periodismo*

Estructura

Discussing what may or may not take place
Formación del subjuntivo

1. The subjunctive mood is used frequently in Spanish to express an action that is desired or hoped for but that is not necessarily real. The indicative mood is used to indicate or express actions that definitely are taking place, did take place, or will take place. Analyze the following sentences.

> **Carlos paga sus gastos personales.**
> **Los padres de Carlos quieren que él pague sus gastos personales.**

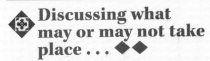

The first sentence is an independent statement of fact—*Charles pays his personal expenses.* The second sentence contains a dependent clause—*that Charles pay his personal expenses.* The action expressed in this dependent clause is an action desired but not necessarily real. It is dependent upon, and subordinate to, the verb of the main clause "want." What Charles' parents want may or may not occur. Since it may or may not occur, the verb in the dependent clause must be in the subjunctive mood.

2. To form the present subjunctive drop the **o** ending of the first person singular of the present indicative.

hablo	**vendo**	**recibo**	**pongo**	**salgo**	**conozco**
habl-	**vend-**	**recib-**	**pong-**	**salg-**	**conozc-**

Then add to this root the endings for the present subjunctive. The vowel of the subjunctive endings is the opposite of the vowel used for the present indicative. Verbs ending in **-ar** take the vowel **e**, and verbs ending in **-er** and **-ir** take the vowel **a.**

INFINITIVE	hablar	vender	recibir	poner	salir	conocer
yo	hable	venda	reciba	ponga	salga	conozca
tú	hables	vendas	recibas	pongas	salgas	conozcas
él, ella, Ud.	hable	venda	reciba	ponga	salga	conozca
nosotros(as)	hablemos	vendamos	recibamos	pongamos	salgamos	conozcamos
vosotros(as)	*habléis*	*vendáis*	*recibáis*	*pongáis*	*salgáis*	*conozcáis*
ellos, ellas, Uds.	hablen	vendan	reciban	pongan	salgan	conozcan

---

RESOURCES

- Workbook
- Student Tape Manual
- Audio Cassette 2A/Compact Disc 1
- Computer Software: *Estructura*
- Chapter Quizzes
- Testing Program

TEACHING STRUCTURE

Discussing what may or may not take place . . . ◆◆

RECYCLING If students have already completed most of *¡Buen viaje! Level 2*, this section will be a review.

¡OJO! You may wish to intersperse the grammar as you present other parts of the chapter. For example:

1. You may wish to present the present subjunctive as you are doing the *Conversación* or one of the *Periodismo* selections.
2. Or, you may wish to present *Formación del subjuntivo* in one class period, then do a selection from another section of the chapter followed by *Subjuntivo con expresiones impersonales* and *Subjuntivo en cláusulas nominales.*

TEACHING TIPS

A. Go over steps 1–6.
B. Have students repeat the forms after you for practice.
C. On the board, write the **yo** form of each verb from the chart. Cross out the endings and have students repeat the subjunctive forms.

35

¡OJO! The most important concept for the students to grasp is that the indicative is used when reporting an objective, real fact. The subjunctive is used when reporting something that is not necessarily real, or that depends upon something else. It, therefore, may or may not happen. When students understand this concept, they no longer have to memorize the long list of expressions that are followed by the subjunctive. It is a question of logic.

3. Any verb that has an irregular **yo** form in the present tense of the indicative will maintain that irregularity in all forms of the present subjunctive.

INFINITIVE	present indicative (yo)	present subjunctive
poner	pongo	ponga
traer	traigo	traiga
hacer	hago	haga
tener	tengo	tenga
salir	salgo	salga
venir	vengo	venga
oír	oigo	oiga
decir	digo	diga
conocer	conozco	conozca
conducir	conduzco	conduzca
construir	construyo	construya

4. Some -**ar** and -**er** stem-changing verbs have the same stem change in the subjunctive as in the present indicative.

INFINITIVE	pensar	contar	perder	volver
yo	piense	cuente	pierda	vuelva
tú	pienses	cuentes	pierdas	vuelvas
él, ella, Ud.	piense	cuente	pierda	vuelva
nosotros(as)	pensemos	contemos	perdamos	volvamos
vosotros(as)	penséis	contéis	perdáis	volváis
ellos, ellas, Uds.	piensen	cuenten	pierdan	vuelvan

5. The -**ir** stem-changing verbs such as **preferir** and **dormir** have an additional change in the present subjunctive. Note that the **nosotros** and **vosotros** forms of **preferir** have an **i,** and the **nosotros** and **vosotros** forms of **dormir** have a **u.**

preferir	dormir
prefiera	duerma
prefieras	duermas
prefiera	duerma
prefiramos	durmamos
prefiráis	durmáis
prefieran	duerman

Costa del Sol

Puerto Marina

Learning From Photos

You may wish to ask students to describe the postcard on page 36. Ask questions such as: **¿Dónde está la Costa del Sol? ¿Qué tipo de edificios vemos en esta foto? ¿Quiénes ocupan estos apartamentos? ¿Creen Uds. que estos apartamentos son muy exclusivos?**

6. The **e** of **-ir** stem-changing verbs, such as **pedir** and **servir,** changes to **i** in all forms of the present subjunctive. **Dar, estar, ir, saber,** and **ser** are the only verbs that do not follow the normal pattern for the formation of the present subjunctive.

pedir	servir
pida	sirva
pidas	sirvas
pida	sirva
pidamos	sirvamos
pidáis	*sirváis*
pidan	sirvan

dar	estar	ir	saber	ser
dé	esté	vaya	sepa	sea
des	estés	vayas	sepas	seas
dé	esté	vaya	sepa	sea
demos	estemos	vayamos	sepamos	seamos
deis	*estéis*	*vayáis*	*sepáis*	*seáis*
den	estén	vayan	sepan	sean

Práctica

A **Los padres de Graciela** Los padres de Graciela quieren que ella haga muchas cosas. Es probable que ella las haga, pero es también posible que ella no las haga. Por consiguiente, es necesario usar el subjuntivo. Sigan el modelo.

> **estudiar**
> **Los padres de Graciela quieren que ella estudie.**

1. estudiar mucho
2. tomar cinco cursos
3. trabajar duro
4. aprender mucho
5. leer mucho
6. comer bien
7. vivir con ellos
8. recibir buenas notas
9. asistir a la universidad
10. tener éxito
11. salir bien en los exámenes
12. decir siempre la verdad
13. tener buenos modales
14. ser cortés
15. conducir el coche con cuidado
16. hacerse rica

B **HISTORIETA** ¿Qué quieren sus amigos?

Sigan el modelo.

> **hacer el viaje**
> **Los amigos de Carlos quieren que él haga el viaje.**

1. llamar al hotel
2. reservar un cuarto
3. hacer el viaje
4. salir con ellos
5. no conducir
6. tomar el tren
7. ir con ellos

TEACHING TIPS

The purpose of these exercises is to have students use the verbs in the subjunctive form.

EXPANSION Have students redo the exercises with **Mis padres quieren que nosotros…**

ANSWERS
Práctica

A **Los padres de Graciela quieren que ella …**
1. **estudie mucho.**
2. **tome cinco cursos.**
3. **trabaje duro.**
4. **aprenda mucho.**
5. **lea mucho.**
6. **coma bien.**
7. **viva con ellos.**
8. **reciba buenas notas.**
9. **asista a la universidad.**
10. **tenga éxito.**
11. **salga bien en los exámenes.**
12. **diga siempre la verdad.**
13. **tenga buenos modales.**
14. **sea cortés.**
15. **conduzca el coche con cuidado.**
16. **se haga rica.**

B **Los amigos de Carlos quieren que él…**
1. **llame al hotel.**
2. **reserve un cuarto.**
3. **haga el viaje.**
4. **salga con ellos.**
5. **no conduzca.**
6. **tome el tren.**
7. **vaya con ellos.**

Independent Practice

Assign any of the following:
1. Exercises, page 37
2. Workbook, *Estructura*

Paired Activity

Have students do the following paired activity: **Trabaje con un(a) compañero(a). Dígale algunas cosas que sus padres quieren que Ud. haga. Su compañero(a) le dirá si sus padres quieren que él/ella haga las mismas cosas. Después, decidirán lo que sus padres tienen en común.**

37

TEACHING STRUCTURE

◆ Expressing necessity or possibility ◆◆

Read the explanation with the students. Have them repeat the model sentences.

ANSWERS
Práctica

A Some answers can be negative.
1. Sí, es posible que pasen...
2. Sí, es probable que viajen...
3. Sí, es posible que viajen...
4. Sí, es necesario que siempre tengan...
5. Sí, es importante que lleven...

B Es probable que él...
1. haga el viaje...
2. pase unos días...
3. vaya a...
4. vaya al...
5. compre algunas...
6. compre algunos...
7. dé los regalos...

Necessity or possibility
Subjuntivo con expresiones impersonales

1. The subjunctive is used after the following impersonal expressions.

Es posible	Es bueno
Es imposible	Es mejor
Es probable	Es fácil
Es improbable	Es difícil
Es importante	Es necesario

Es posible que ellos vengan mañana.
Es imposible que lleguen a tiempo.
Es probable que haya mucho tráfico en la carretera.
De todos modos, es necesario que ellos estén aquí a las seis.

2. Note that all of the above expressions take the subjunctive, since the action of the verb in the dependent clause may or may not take place.

A HISTORIETA Posibilidades

Contesten.
1. ¿Es posible que ellos pasen sus vacaciones en Europa?
2. ¿Es probable que ellos viajen en avión de un país a otro?
3. ¿Es posible que viajen por el Mediterráneo en un crucero?
4. ¿Es necesario que siempre tengan su pasaporte?
5. ¿Es importante que lleven cheques de viajero?

B HISTORIETA ¿Es probable?

Sigan el modelo.

ir a México
Es probable que él vaya a México.

1. hacer el viaje en avión
2. pasar unos días en la capital
3. ir a San Ángel
4. ir al Bazar Sábado
5. comprar algunas antigüedades
6. comprar algunos regalos
7. dar los regalos a sus amigos y parientes

Learning From Photos

Point out to students the use of **os** in the realia: **Puede haceros ganar...** In Latin America it would be **Puede hacerles ganar.**

Did You Know?

Trasmediterránea This is a ferry company that operates vessels between Spain, North Africa, and several of the Mediterranean islands.

C **¿Es necesario?** Sigan el modelo.

> **tener sus documentos**
> **Es necesario que los turistas tengan sus documentos.**

1. hacer una reservación
2. llamar al hotel de antemano
3. tener cheques de viajero
4. cambiar su dinero en el banco
5. viajar en grupo

D HISTORIETA **Es probable que nos llamen.**

Completen.

1. Es posible que ellos ___ (llegar) mañana.
2. Es posible que ellos ___ (venir) en autobús.
3. ¿Tú lo crees? Es probable que ellos ___ (tener) el carro, ¿no?
4. Pues, yo no sé. Pero es necesario que yo ___ (saber) a qué hora van a llegar.
5. ¿Por qué es tan importante que tú lo ___ (saber)?
6. Pues, es mejor que yo ___ (estar) en casa, ¿no?
7. Pero es difícil que tú ___ (volver) a casa antes de las cuatro de la tarde, ¿no?
8. Sí, es bastante difícil que yo ___ (salir) de la escuela antes de las tres y media.
9. ¿Quieres que yo los ___ (esperar)?

E HISTORIETA **El hotel**

Contesten.

1. ¿Es posible que el hotel esté completo?
2. ¿Es mejor que yo haga una reservación?
3. Al llegar al hotel, ¿es necesario que nosotros vayamos a la recepción?
4. ¿Es posible que el botones nos ayude con el equipaje?
5. ¿Es raro que los hoteles no acepten tarjetas de crédito?

La Paz, Bolivia

EXPANSION Have students work in small groups. Assign different questions from *Práctica E* to each group and have them work together to come up with as many answers as possible. When the time is up, allow students to circulate in the room to add answers to the other groups' lists or have each group present its list orally to the class.

ANSWERS
Práctica

C **Es necesario que los turistas…**
1. **hagan una reservación.**
2. **llamen al hotel de antemano.**
3. **tengan cheques de viajero.**
4. **cambien su dinero en el banco.**
5. **viajen en grupo.**

D 1. **lleguen**
2. **vengan**
3. **tengan**
4. **sepa**
5. **sepas**
6. **esté**
7. **vuelvas**
8. **salga**
9. **espere**

E 1. **Sí, es posible que el hotel esté completo.**
2. **Sí, es mejor que tú hagas una reservación.**
3. **Sí, es necesario que nosotros vayamos (Uds. vayan) a la recepción.**
4. **Sí, es posible que el botones nos ayude con el equipaje.**
5. **Sí, es raro que los hoteles no acepten tarjetas de crédito.**

Paired Activity

Have students do the following paired activity: **Trabaje con un(a) compañero(a). Dígale todo lo que es necesario que Ud. haga antes de hacer un viaje en avión. Él/Ella le dirá todo lo que es necesario que él/ella haga. Hagan Uds. una lista de todas las cosas que Uds. dos tienen que hacer.**

Independent Practice

Assign any of the following:
1. Exercises, pages 38–39
2. Workbook, *Estructura*

TEACHING STRUCTURE

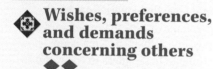

◆ **Wishes, preferences, and demands concerning others**
◆◆

Reinforce the idea that the information that follows **que** may or may not take place and that is why the subjunctive is used. Understanding this concept is more important than memorizing the expressions that take the subjunctive. Have the students read the model sentences aloud.

**A B O U T   T H E
S P A N I S H   L A N G U A G E**

◆ The realia states **El mundo en una bolsa.** The word **bolsa** is used in many countries for a bag—**bolsa de papel, bolsa de plástico, bolsa de papas fritas,** etc. In some areas you will also hear **el saco. La bolsa** can also mean pocketbook (purse) but the gender will vary. You will hear both **la bolsa** and **el bolso. La Bolsa** with a capital B is the Stock Market.

◆ In the Dominican Republic, **la bolsa** is a vulgar term and the word used for a bag is **la funda. La funda** in other areas is a pillow case. **La funda** is also a wrapper.

ANSWERS

Práctica

A Yo quiero que...
1. Uds. me esperen.
2. Uds. salgan...
3. nosotros vayamos...
4. Uds. me ayuden...
5. Uds. no le digan...

B Mamá insiste en que...
1. nos levantemos...
2. tomemos...
3. salgamos...
4. no lleguemos...
5. estudiemos y aprendamos.
6. seamos...

40

Wishes, preferences, and demands concerning others
Subjuntivo en cláusulas nominales

The subjunctive is also used after the following verbs.

desear	to desire
esperar	*to hope*
preferir	*to prefer*
mandar	*to order*
insistir en	*to insist*

Note that the use of the subjunctive is extremely logical in Spanish. Whether one desires, hopes, prefers, demands, or insists that another person do something, one can never be sure that the person will in fact do it. Therefore, the action of the verb in the dependent clause is not necessarily real and the subjunctive must be used.

> **Los padres de Carlos quieren que él sea serio.**
> **Desean que su hijo tenga éxito.**
> **Esperan que él esté estudiando mucho en la escuela.**
> **Insisten en que él estudie bastante.**
> **De todos modos, ellos prefieren que él pague sus gastos personales.**

◆Práctica◆

A HISTORIETA *¿Qué quieres?*

Yo quiero que...
1. Uds. me esperan.
2. Uds. salen conmigo.
3. Todos nosotros vamos juntos a la tienda.
4. Uds. me ayudan a buscar un regalo para Cristina.
5. Uds. no le dicen nada a Cristina.

B HISTORIETA *¿En qué insiste mamá?*

Mamá insiste en que...
1. Nos levantamos temprano.
2. Tomamos un buen desayuno.
3. Salimos a tiempo.
4. No llegamos tarde a la escuela.
5. Estudiamos y aprendemos.
6. Somos diligentes.

Madrid, España

Paired Activity

Práctica A–D, pp. 40–41: Have students work in pairs. One student reads the question and the other answers. They then reverse roles. After everyone has had time to do all the exercises orally, call on selected pairs to give the answers.

Hint: As students work, you may wish to circulate to listen to the students and help them with individual questions and problems.

C HISTORIETA ¿Qué prefiere él?

Él prefiere que...

1. Yo lo espero delante de la escuela.
2. Yo conduzco.
3. Vamos juntos al partido.
4. Nos sentamos en la primera fila.
5. Yo no hablo durante el partido de fútbol.

D HISTORIETA ¿Qué espera Julia?

Sigan el modelo.

Su amigo llega a tiempo.
Julia espera que su amigo llegue a tiempo.

1. Su padre le permite usar el carro.
2. Su padre le da permiso para usarlo.
3. El tanque está lleno.
4. Su amigo viene a la casa a tiempo.
5. Ellos tienen las entradas para el partido.
6. Sus amigos llegan temprano al estadio.

La Copa mundial

E HISTORIETA ¿Al teatro o al cine?

Contesten.

1. ¿Prefieres que vayamos al Teatro Colón o que vayamos al Cine Goya?
2. ¿Quieres que yo compre las entradas?
3. ¿Esperas que queden localidades?
4. ¿Deseas que yo invite a Carmen?
5. ¿Insistirá ella en que nos sentemos en la primera fila?
6. Yo prefiero que comamos después de la función. ¿Qué prefieres tú?
7. ¿Prefieres que lleguemos temprano a casa?
8. ¿Quieres que Carmen vaya al restaurante con nosotros?
9. ¿Prefieres que ella venga a nuestra casa o que yo la vaya a buscar?

F HISTORIETA En el banco

Completen.

—Buenos días, señora. ¿En qué puedo servirle?
—Buenos días. Quiero que Uds. me ____ (dar) dólares por pesos.
—¿Cuántos pesos quiere Ud. cambiar?
—Depende. Espero que el valor del dólar no ____ (estar) muy alto hoy.
—Está a doscientos veinte.
—Espero que no ____ (bajar) mañana.
—Ay, señora, nadie sabe a cómo estará el dólar mañana.

ESTRUCTURA

cuarenta y uno 41

ANSWERS
Práctica
C Él prefiere que...
1. yo lo espere delante de la escuela.
2. yo conduzca.
3. vayamos juntos al partido.
4. nos sentemos en la primera fila.
5. yo no hable durante el partido de fútbol.
D Julia espera que...
1. su padre le permita usar el carro.
2. su padre le dé permiso para usarlo.
3. el tanque esté lleno.
4. su amigo venga a la casa a tiempo.
5. ellos tengan las entradas para el partido.
6. sus amigos lleguen temprano al estadio.
E Answers can be negative.
1. Prefiero que vayamos al...
2. Sí, quiero que tú compres las entradas.
3. Sí, espero que queden localidades.
4. Sí, deseo que tú invites a Carmen.
5. Sí, ella insistirá en que nos sentemos en la primera fila.
6. Prefiero que comamos después de la función.
7. Sí, prefiero que lleguemos temprano a casa.
8. Sí, quiero que Carmen vaya al restaurante con nosotros.
9. Prefiero que ella venga a nuestra casa (que tú la vayas a buscar).
F 1. den
2. esté
3. baje

Cooperative Learning

Have students do the following activity:
Trabajen en pequeños grupos. Decidan lo que quieren que sus profesores no hagan. Indiquen lo que prefieren que hagan. Preparen una lista.

Independent Practice

Assign any of the following:
1. Exercises, pages 40–41
2. Workbook, *Estructura*

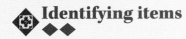

TEACHING STRUCTURE

◆ Identifying items
◆◆

Have the students read the explanation and ask them to repeat the words aloud.

 It is recommended that you go over this point quickly. Students will, however, need much reinforcement of the correct agreement.

TEACHING TIPS

Práctica A and **B** can be done with books open.

ANSWERS
Práctica
A 1. un, el
  2. El, del, el, del
  3. el, el, los, el, los
  4. El
B 1. la, la
  2. el/la
  3. la, la

LITERATURE CONNECTION

Lope de Vega fue un gran dramaturgo español del siglo XVII. El siglo XVII se llama el Siglo de Oro por su gran producción literaria clásica. Los cuatro dramaturgos más famosos de la España del siglo XVII son Lope de Vega, Tirso de Molina, Calderón de la Barca y Juan Ruiz de Alarcón.

Identifying items
Sustantivos masculinos que terminan en **a**

There are several nouns in Spanish that end in **a** but are masculine. These nouns are derived from Greek roots. They take the definite article **el** and the indefinite article **un.**

el clima	el poema
el día	el programa
el drama	el sistema
el mapa	el telegrama
el planeta	el tema

Note that the noun **la mano** is irregular. Even though **la mano** ends in **o,** it is feminine— **la mano. La foto** is also used as a shortened version of **la fotografía.** The noun **radio** can be either **la radio** or **el radio.** The gender varies according to the country.

❖Práctica❖

A Palabras de origen griego Completen.
1. Es ___ día estupendo y ___ clima de esta región es estupendo.
2. ___ tema ___ poema es ___ clima de ___ planeta desconocido.
3. En la clase de español los estudiantes estudian ___ mapa de España, ___ mapa de la América del Sur, ___ poemas de Rubén Darío, ___ poeta nicaragüense y ___ dramas de Lope de Vega, el dramaturgo español.
4. ___ tema de este capítulo es el turismo.

B ¡No la toques! Completen.
1. ¡Nene! No pongas ___ mano en ___ foto.
2. Lo escuchamos en ___ radio.
3. Levanta ___ mano si sabes lo que aparece en ___ foto.

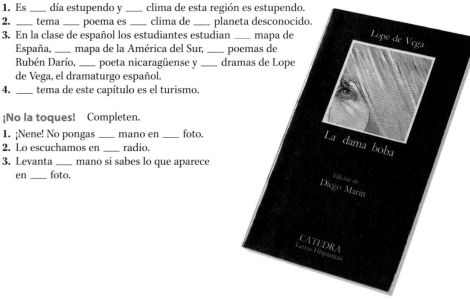

Additional Practice

1. Prepare Ud. una lista de cosas que sus padres siempre quieren que Ud. haga. Luego compare su lista con la de otro(a) compañero(a) de clase.
2. Prepare Ud. una lista de cosas que su profesor(a) de español exige que Ud. haga.
3. Prepare Ud. una lista de las cosas que son fáciles que Ud. haga. Luego prepare una lista de las cosas que son difíciles que Ud. haga.
4. Prepare Ud. una lista de cosas que es posible o probable que le ocurran. De esta lista, escoja las cosas que Ud. quiere que le ocurran y las cosas que Ud. prefiere que no ocurran.

Identifying more items
Sustantivos femeninos en **a, ha** inicial

Feminine nouns that begin with a stressed **a** or the silent **h** followed by a stressed **a** take the masculine definite article **el** or the indefinite article **un**. The reason such nouns take the articles **el** and **un** is that it would be difficult to pronounce the two vowels—**la a, una a**—together. Since the nouns are feminine, the plural articles **las** and **unas** are used and any adjective modifying the noun is in the feminine form.

el agua	las aguas	*water*
el (un) águila	las águilas	*eagle*
el (un) área	las áreas	*area*
el (un) arma	las armas	*firearm*
el (un) hacha	las hachas	*ax*
el (un) ala	las alas	*wing*
el hambre		*hunger*

 **Práctica**

A **Los sustantivos** Completen.

1. ___ agua del río es dulce pero ___ agua del mar es salada.
2. ___ área que van a visitar ___ turistas no es peligrosa.
3. ___ águilas beben ___ agua dulce del río pero no beben ___ agua salada del mar.
4. ___ alas grandes de ___ águilas son increíbles. Pero, ¡mira! ¡Qué pena! ___ águila pequeña tiene ___ ala rota.
5. ___ arma que llevan los policías es una pistola.
6. ___ área alrededor de una ciudad se llama un suburbio. ___ áreas suburbanas suelen ser bastante hermosas.

Edificios de apartamentos en un área suburbana de Madrid, España

TEACHING STRUCTURE

◆ **Identifying more items** ◆◆

Guide the students through the explanation and have them repeat after you the singular and plural forms.

TEACHING TIPS

This exercise can be done with books open.

ANSWERS
Práctica
A 1. El, el
2. El, los
3. Las, el, el
4. Las, las, El, un
5. El
6. El, Las

Learning From Photos

These buildings are typical of the large apartment complexes built on the outskirts of Madrid.

Independent Practice

Assign any of the following:
1. Exercises, pages 42–43
2. Workbook, *Estructura*

43

TEACHING TIPS

Have students do the pre-reading activity. They will encounter many of these words in the reading after the vocabulary presentation.

RESOURCES

- 📖 Vocabulary Transparencies
- 🎧 Audio Cassette 2A/Compact Disc 1
- 📁 Student Tape Manual
- 📁 Workbook
- 📁 Chapter Quizzes
- 💾 Testing Program

TEACHING VOCABULARY

A. Have students repeat the new words after you or Cassette 2A/Compact Disc 1.

B. To vary the procedure, you may wish to read definitions to the students. To help the students better understand the words being defined, you may wish to use them in sentences: **Las estrellas brillan en el cielo de noche. Las olas del mar bañan las orillas. Navegar el buque es el trabajo del capitán.**

LITERATURE CONNECTION

You may wish to give students a brief definition of a sonnet and a verse.

Un soneto es una composición poética de catorce versos, ordenados en dos cuartetos (de cuatro versos) y dos tercetos (de tres versos).

El verso es la frase o parte de una frase en la que las sílabas tienen un orden rítmico determinado.

44

Literatura
¡Al partir!

de Gertrudis Gómez de Avellaneda

Antes de leer

Hay muchos motivos para viajar. Algunos son muy agradables—como, por ejemplo, pasar una semana de vacaciones en un lugar exótico, un paraíso o edén. Otros motivos son más serios, como los de un viaje de negocios. Y otros pueden ser tristes, como el exilio. Al leer este soneto, Ud. decidirá cuáles son las emociones de la autora.

Vocabulario

la estrella · la vela · el cielo · el velo · el suelo · el buque · el ancla · las olas

acudir   venir, llegar
alzar   levantar
partir   salir

el dolor   la tristeza
el oído   la oreja   **el hado**   el destino (*fate*)   **ardiente**   muy caliente

---

Additional Practice

You may wish to ask students the following questions: **¿Quién es un poeta inglés o americano que ha escrito sonetos? ¿Cuál es un soneto que Ud. ha leído que le gustó mucho?**

❖Práctica❖

A **El mar** *Completen.*

1. El mar tiene ___ y el ___ tiene nubes.
2. Este barco, o buque, tiene ___. No tiene motor.
3. Hay que alzar o levantar el ___ antes de que salga el buque del puerto.
4. Mucha gente ___ al puerto para ver la salida del barco.
5. Las ___ brillan en el ___ de noche.
6. La arena cubre el ___ a lo largo de la costa.

B **Al partir** *Escojan.*

1. alzar el ancla	a. salir
2. izar las velas	b. la oreja
3. partir	c. levantar las velas
4. el hado	d. acudir
5. el oído	e. el barco
6. ir a	f. levantar ancla
7. el buque	g. el destino
8. el dolor	h. la tristeza

Una vista de la costa de San Juan, Puerto Rico, desde el fuerte de San Jerónimo

TEACHING TIPS

A and B It is recommended that you have the students prepare these exercises before going over them in class.

ANSWERS
Práctica

A 1. **olas, cielo**
   2. **vela**
   3. **ancla**
   4. **acude**
   5. **estrellas, cielo**
   6. **suelo**

B 1. **f**
   2. **c**
   3. **a**
   4. **g**
   5. **b**
   6. **d**
   7. **e**
   8. **h**

Learning From Photos

Un «morro» es un monte o peñasco escarpado que sirve de marca a los navegantes en la costa. El fuerte de San Jerónimo es conocido como «El Morro.»

Independent Practice

Assign any of the following:
1. Exercises, page 45
2. Workbook, *Literatura*

45

TEACHING TIPS

A. Ask students if they have ever heard of Gertrudis Gómez de Avellaneda.

B. You may have students read the *Introducción* aloud or silently. Tell them: **Van a leer una biografía de la autora Gertrudis Gómez de Avellaneda.**

C. After going over the *Introducción*, have students give three or four salient points about Avellaneda's life.

LECTURA ◆ ◆ ◆

TEACHING THE READING

A. Before doing the reading, ask students the following question: **Imagina que tienes que salir de tu país y nunca volverás. ¿Cuáles son tus sentimientos?**

B. Tell students: **Vamos a leer un poema de una autora cubana.**

C. Give the students some time to read the selection silently either at home or in class. Ask them to think about the mood of the poem.

D. After an individual student has read a stanza, you may wish to ask some questions.

E. With more able groups, you may wish to ask the analytical questions in LITERARY ANALYSIS at the bottom of page 46.

Introducción

Gertrudis Gómez de Avellaneda

Gertrudis Gómez de Avellaneda nació en Camagüey, Cuba, en 1814. Empezó a escribir poesía cuando era muy joven. Su padre siempre quiso llevar a la familia a España, su país natal. Pero murió bastante joven y su esposa se casó en segundas nupcias con un coronel español que no quería quedarse a vivir en las colonias. El día 9 de abril de 1836, Gertrudis se embarcó con su madre y su padrastro en el puerto de Santiago de Cuba con destino a Burdeos, Francia, en una fragata francesa. Aquel día Gertrudis Gómez de Avellaneda compuso el soneto que sigue.

Lectura

¡Al partir!

¡Perla del mar! ¡Estrella de Occidente!
¡Hermosa Cuba! Tu brillante cielo
la noche cubre con su opaco velo
como cubre el dolor mi triste frente.

¡Voy a partir!... La chusma° diligente,
para arrancarme° del nativo suelo
las velas iza°, y pronta a su desvelo°
la brisa acude de tu zona ardiente.

¡Adiós, patria feliz, edén querido!
¡Doquier° que el hado en su furor me impela,
tu dulce nombre halagará° mi oído!

¡Adiós!... ¡Ya cruje° la turgente° vela...
el ancla se alza... el buque, estremecido°,
las olas corta y silencioso vuela!

la chusma *crew*
arrancarme *to uproot me*
iza *hoists*
desvelo *sleeplessness*

doquier *wherever*
halagará *will delight*

cruje *creak*
turgente *swollen*
estremecido *shaken*

El Morro, La Habana, Cuba

Literary Analysis

1. **Indique los cuartetos y los tercetos de este soneto.**
2. **Un soneto consta de catorce versos y trata de un solo pensamiento. ¿Cuál es el pensamiento de este soneto?**
3. **¿Cuál es el giro al pensamiento en el primer terceto de este soneto? ¿Cuál es la palabra que enfatiza el sentimiento al comienzo del primer terceto?**

National Standards

Cultures
Students experience, discuss and analyze an expressive product of the culture: the poem «¡Al partir!» by Gertrudis Gómez de Avellaneda.

Después de leer

Comprensión

A El poema   Contesten.

1. ¿De dónde sale la autora?
2. ¿Cómo se siente?
3. ¿Quién levanta (iza) las velas?
4. ¿A quién le dice «adiós» la autora?
5. ¿Sale de noche o por la mañana?

B La autora dice que...   ¿Sí o no?

1. La autora dice que Cuba es hermosa.
2. Gertrudis Gómez de Avellaneda está muy contenta con hacer el viaje en buque.
3. El cielo es brillante.
4. Ella sale por la mañana.
5. La tripulación del buque no trabaja bien.
6. La brisa viene de una región muy fría.
7. La autora dice que sabe precisamente adónde va.
8. El buque hace mucho ruido.

C Otra palabra   ¿Cómo lo dice la autora?

1. Tu *claro* cielo
2. ¡Voy a *salir*!
3. La *tripulación* diligente *levanta* las velas para *llevarme* del nativo suelo.
4. La brisa acude de tu zona *cálida*.
5. ¡Adiós, patria feliz, *paraíso*!
6. *Dondequiera* que *el destino* en su *ira (rabia)* me *lleve (empuje)*
7. tu dulce nombre *agradará* mi oído
8. ... *el barco*, estremecido, *anda rápido* y *sin ruido navega*

El Palacio del Valle, Cienfuegos, Cuba

Actividades comunicativas

A El soneto   En el soneto la autora menciona a Cuba seis veces. ¿Qué términos utiliza para referirse a Cuba?

B Una carta   Imagínese que Ud. es Gertrudis Gómez de Avellaneda. Escríbale una carta a su mejor amigo(a) describiéndole su salida de Cuba y sus emociones.

ANSWERS
Comprensión

A 1. Sale de Cuba.
   2. Se siente triste.
   3. La chusma levanta (iza) las velas.
   4. Le dice «adiós» a Cuba, su país natal.
   5. Sale de noche.

B 1. sí   5. no
   2. no   6. no
   3. no   7. no
   4. no   8. no

C 1. brillante
   2. partir
   3. chusma, iza, arrancarme
   4. ardiente
   5. edén
   6. Doquier, el hado, furor, impela
   7. halagará
   8. el buque, las olas cortas, silencioso vuela

Actividades comunicativas

ANSWERS

A 1. Perla del Mar
   2. Estrella de Occidente
   3. Hermosa Cuba
   4. nativo suelo
   5. patria feliz
   6. edén querido

B Answers will vary.

Critical Thinking Activity

Thinking skills: supporting statements with reasons   ¿Por qué puede causar muchos problemas emocionales y aun psicológicos el destierro o el exilio?

Independent Practice

Assign any of the following:
1. Exercises, page 47
2. Workbook, *Literatura*

GEOGRAPHY CONNECTION

Cienfuegos, a seaport on Cuba's southern coast, is the third largest city in Cuba and one of its most important commercial centers. The Palacio del Valle was the summer house of a very wealthy family. Its style is reminiscent of the Moorish palaces of Spain. Today, the palace is a cultural center.

RESOURCES

- Vocabulary Transparencies
- Audio Cassette 2A/Compact Disc 1
- Student Tape Manual
- Workbook
- Chapter Quizzes
- Testing Program

TEACHING VOCABULARY

A. Have students repeat the new words and expressions after you or Cassette 2A/Compact Disc 1.

B. Call on a student to make up an original sentence using the words for which definitions are given.

ABOUT THE SPANISH LANGUAGE

- Point out to students that **el rincón** is often the corner of a room and **la esquina,** the street corner or the corner of a building (exterior). **El rincón** can also mean a small space.

- **El huerto, la huerta,** and **el jardín** are all heard with equal frequency. A **jardín** is usually for flowers only.

El viaje definitivo

de Juan Ramón Jiménez

Antes de leer

La muerte es un tema que a menudo aparece en las letras hispanas. Para muchos, la muerte es un viaje, sea el viaje final o como la llama el poeta Juan Ramón Jiménez, el viaje definitivo.

Vocabulario

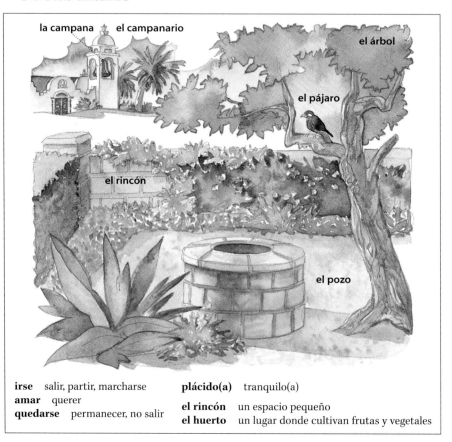

irse salir, partir, marcharse
amar querer
quedarse permanecer, no salir

plácido(a) tranquilo(a)
el rincón un espacio pequeño
el huerto un lugar donde cultivan frutas y vegetales

Learning From Illustrations

Have students describe the illustration in their own words.

Práctica

A **En el huerto** Contesten según se indica.

1. ¿Dónde cantan los pájaros? (en el huerto)
2. ¿Qué hay en el huerto? (un árbol)
3. ¿Qué más hay? (un pozo)
4. ¿Qué sacan del pozo? (agua)

5. ¿Dónde está el árbol? (en el rincón)
6. ¿Qué tocan? (las campanas)
7. ¿Dónde tocan las campanas? (en el campanario)

B **Se dice así.** Expresen de otra manera.

1. Los pájaros están en *el jardín* y *no salen.*
2. *Permanecen.*

3. El señor *quiere mucho a* los pájaros.
4. En *el jardín* hay un ambiente *muy tranquilo.*

Introducción

Juan Ramón Jiménez nació en Moguer, en la provincia de Huelva, Andalucía, en 1881. Estudió el bachillerato en un colegio jesuita en el Puerto de Santa María, cerca de Cádiz. Más tarde, estudió derecho en la Universidad de Sevilla.

De joven Jiménez no gozó de muy buena salud. Era un niño enfermizo y delicado. Sufrió trastornos nerviosos por lo que estuvo en un sanatorio. Cuando tenía sólo 18 años, fue a Madrid donde escribía en una habitación acorchada[1] porque no quería oír los ruidos de la calle. Vivió también en Nueva York, donde se casó con Zenobia Camprubí, una americana, hija de un español y una puertorriqueña. Durante la Guerra Civil española, Juan Ramón Jiménez se desterró y pasó los últimos 22 años de su vida en los Estados Unidos y Puerto Rico, donde murió en 1958. Dos años antes de su muerte le otorgaron el Premio Nóbel de Literatura por su extraordinaria obra lírica.

[1] **acorchada** *lined with cork*

Juan Ramón Jiménez

La Plaza Colón, San Juan, Puerto Rico

La poesía lírica de Juan Ramón Jiménez es como lo fue su vida—solitaria, nostálgica y melancólica. Vivía en constante temor de una muerte repentina. «El viaje definitivo» es una imagen de la muerte que algún día vendrá. Al leer el poema, piense en las siguientes preguntas.

Cuando muera el poeta, ¿cambiará el mundo o no? ¿Seguirá igual? ¿Quiénes morirán? ¿Quiénes nacerán?

TEACHING TIP

A and B Have students prepare these exercises before going over them in class.

ANSWERS
Práctica

A 1. **Los pájaros cantan en el huerto.**
2. **En el huerto hay un árbol.**
3. **Hay también un pozo.**
4. **Sacan agua del pozo.**
5. **El árbol está en el rincón.**
6. **Las campanas tocan.**
7. **Las campanas tocan en el campanario.**

B 1. **Los pájaros están en el huerto y no se marchan (parten).**
2. **Se quedan.**
3. **El señor ama mucho a los pájaros.**
4. **En el huerto hay un ambiente muy plácido.**

TEACHING TIP

Have students read the *Introducción* aloud or silently.

National Standards

Cultures
Students experience, discuss, and analyze an expressive product of the culture: the poem «El viaje definitivo» by Juan Ramón Jiménez.

Additional Practice

You may wish to ask the following questions about the *Introducción:*

1. **¿Dónde nació Juan Ramón Jiménez?**
2. **¿Dónde está Moguer?**
3. **¿Qué estudió y dónde?**
4. **¿Cómo era de niño?**
5. **¿Cuándo fue a Madrid?**
6. **¿Dónde escribía y por qué?**
7. **¿Dónde se casó?**
8. **¿Con quién se casó?**
9. **¿Cuándo se desterró Juan Ramón Jiménez?**
10. **¿Dónde vivió?**
11. **¿Dónde murió?**
12. **¿Qué premio recibió y cuándo?**

TEACHING TIPS

A. Because the language of this selection is quite simple, you may wish to have students read the entire selection silently. Then call on individual students to read parts of the poem aloud. Encourage them to use as much expression as possible.

B. Ask students if there was any part they did not understand. Call on other students to explain.

C. Assign the selection to be read for homework and have students write the answers to the *Comprensión* exercises on page 51.

D. With more able groups you may wish to ask the analytical questions in LITERARY ANALYSIS at the bottom of page 50.

LITERATURE CONNECTION

La obra lírica de Juan Ramón Jiménez se identifica con su propia vida. La esencia de la poesía está en su propia alma. Su poesía es bella, pura, sencilla y sin adorno. Sus descripciones son estados de ánimo, frecuentemente melancólicos. Prefiere las imágenes de la naturaleza como el otoño, los jardines, las hojas, etc. Definición. Una metáfora es una figura retórica por la cual se transporta el sentido de una palabra a otra, mediante una comparación mental.

Lectura

El viaje definitivo

Y yo me iré. Y se quedarán los pájaros cantando;
y se quedará mi huerto, con su árbol verde,
y con su pozo blanco.
Todas las tardes el cielo será azul y plácido;
y tocarán, como esta tarde están tocando,
las campanas del campanario.
Se morirán los que me amaron
y el pueblo se hará nuevo cada año;
y lejos del bullicio° distinto, sordo°, raro
del domingo cerrado,
del coche de las cinco, de las siestas del baño
en el rincón secreto de mi huerto florido° y encalado°,
mi espíritu errará°, nostálgico.
Y yo me iré y seré otro, sin hogar, sin árbol
verde, sin pozo blanco,
sin cielo azul y plácido...
Y se quedarán los pájaros cantando.

bullicio ruido
sordo *muffled*

florido con flores
encalado pintado de blanco
errará andará como un vagabundo

Literary Analysis

1. ¿Qué es el viaje definitivo?
2. ¿Qué seguirá igual?
3. ¿Qué no seguirá igual?
4. ¿Qué nostalgia sentirá el poeta?
5. En sus poesías, Juan Ramón Jiménez se refiere mucho a la naturaleza. Dé ejemplos de tales referencias en esta poesía.
6. Busque las frases, expresiones o palabras que le dan a la poesía un tono melancólico.

ABOUT THE SPANISH LANGUAGE

◆ In the original versions of Jiménez's poems, the words with *g* such as **nostálgico** were spelled with *j*—**nostáljico.** This was an idiosyncrasy of the author.

Después de leer

Comprensión

A **¿Qué pasará?** Contesten.

1. ¿Quién se irá?
2. ¿Quiénes se quedarán?
3. ¿Qué más se quedará?
4. ¿Qué tiene su huerto?
5. ¿Cómo será el cielo?
6. ¿Cuándo?
7. ¿Qué tocarán?
8. ¿Dónde?
9. ¿Están tocando ahora?
10. ¿Quiénes se morirán?
11. ¿Dónde errará el espíritu del poeta?
12. ¿Adónde irá él?

B **Símbolos** Expliquen.

1. ¿Por qué se hará nuevo el pueblo?
2. ¿Qué sentimientos evoca este poema lírico?
3. ¿Qué es el viaje definitivo?

C **Los colores** Contesten.

El poeta usa varios colores en este poema. ¿Cuáles son los colores? ¿Qué describe al usar estos colores?

D **El poeta** ¿Cómo lo dice el poeta?

1. Yo *saldré*.
2. *Permanecerán* los pájaros cantando.
3. Y se quedará mi *jardín*.
4. Y *cada tarde* el cielo será azul y *tranquilo*.
5. Se morirán los que me *querían*.
6. Mi espíritu *vagará*.
7. Y seré otro, sin *casa*, sin árbol.

Actividades comunicativas

A **El título** Explique el significado del título del poema.

B **Los críticos** Muchos críticos literarios dicen que en la obra de Juan Ramón Jiménez hay una nota musical unida a un sentimiento melancólico y a elementos visuales de color impresionista. Escriba uno o dos párrafos sobre el arte impresionista. Mire un cuadro de un artista impresionista y luego trate de dibujar lo que Ud. ve al leer el poema «El viaje definitivo».

C **La muerte** Para Ud., ¿es la muerte un viaje definitivo? ¿Por qué? Trate de explicar su filosofía sobre la muerte.

LITERATURA

cincuenta y uno **51**

ANSWERS

Comprensión

A 1. El poeta se irá.
2. Los pájaros se quedarán.
3. El huerto se quedará.
4. Tiene un árbol verde y un pozo blanco.
5. El cielo será azul y plácido.
6. Será azul y plácido todas las tardes.
7. Las campanas tocarán.
8. Tocarán en el campanario.
9. Sí, están tocando ahora.
10. Los que amaron al poeta se morirán.
11. Su espíritu errará en el rincón secreto de su huerto.
12. Él irá a ser otro.

B Answers will vary.

C Árbol verde, pozo blanco, cielo azul.

D 1. me iré
2. Se quedarán
3. huerto
4. todas las tardes, plácido
5. amaron
6. errará
7. hogar

Actividades comunicativas

ANSWERS

A–C Answers will vary.

Independent Practice

Assign any of the following:
1. *Comprensión*, page 51
2. Workbook, *Literatura*

TEACHING TIPS

You may wish to read this paragraph aloud to the class.

RESOURCES

- Vocabulary Transparencies
- Audio Cassette 2B/Compact Disc 2
- Student Tape Manual
- Workbook
- Chapter Quizzes
- Testing Program

TEACHING VOCABULARY

A. Have students repeat the words and sentences after you or Cassette 2B/Compact Disc 2.

B. Ask questions using the new words as you present the vocabulary. Examples are:
¿Llega el tren a la frontera?
¿Cruza el tren la frontera o tienen que transbordar en la frontera los pasajeros?
¿Tienen las familias ricas o pobres una criada?
¿Qué limpia la criada?
¿Paga la familia a la criada?

C. After presenting all the vocabulary orally, call on students to read the definitions aloud for additional reinforcement.

Temprano y con Sol

Adaptado de Emilia Pardo Bazán

Antes de leer

Hay muchos motivos para viajar. En la mayoría de los casos es simplemente para pasar unos ocho o quince días de vacaciones. A veces es para satisfacer el espíritu aventurero—para ir a un país lejano y desconocido.

En el cuento *Temprano y con Sol* de Emilia Pardo Bazán los dos niños que son los protagonistas del cuento tienen otro motivo. ¡A ver lo que es! Al empezar el cuento los vemos comprando dos billetes en la estación de ferrocarril.

Vocabulario

Es la frontera.
El tren llega a la frontera.
Es un tren directo. Va a cruzar la frontera.
Los pasajeros no tienen que transbordar o cambiar de tren.

La niña siempre soñaba con viajes largos.
Soñaba con viajes a países desconocidos—que no conocía.

la manía   deseo fuerte, una obsesión de la imaginación
la criada   la muchacha o señora que hace los quehaceres domésticos por un salario
la frontera   línea que separa un país de otro

tonto(a)   loco(a), estúpido(a)
lejano   que está muy lejos, lo contrario de cercano

volver a   hacer una vez más, repetir una cosa
internar   encerrar, retener a una persona en un lugar
avisar   dar noticia de una cosa, advertir
echar a correr escalera abajo   ir a bajar la escalera rápidamente

---

Additional Practice

¿Cuál es la palabra?
1. un lugar donde crecen muchos árboles y otros arbustos
2. muy conocido, renombrado
3. no del pasado, de hoy
4. exigirle a alguien que pague
5. el que dicta cursos en la universidad
6. conceder

Práctica

A **En el tren** Contesten según se indica.
1. ¿Hay muchos o pocos pasajeros en el tren? (muchos)
2. ¿Adónde llega el tren? (a la frontera)
3. ¿Es un tren directo? (no)
4. ¿Cruza la frontera el tren? (no)
5. ¿Qué tienen que hacer los pasajeros que quieren cruzar la frontera? (transbordar, es decir tomar otro tren)
6. ¿Quién les avisa que no es un tren directo? (el agente en la estación de ferrocarril)

B **¿Cómo se dice?** Expresen de otra manera.
1. Es un país *que no conocemos*.
2. Es un país *que está lejos de aquí*.
3. La niña siempre *tenía sueños*.
4. Tienen que *cambiar de tren*.
5. Yo sé que lo van *a retener* allí.
6. ¿Quién le va a *dar noticia de la situación*?
7. Él *volvió a decir* la misma cosa.

C **¿Cuál es la palabra?** Completen.
1. Los Pirineos forman una ___ natural entre España y Francia.
2. La niña siempre ___ ___ viajes largos y exóticos.
3. Ella está un poco loca. Tiene muchas ___.
4. Pero no es una condición grave. No la van a ___ en el hospital.
5. La ___ limpia la casa, lava los platos, etc., y la familia le paga un salario.
6. Ellos no subieron la escalera. Corrieron ___ ___.

Los Pirineos

TEACHING TIPS

A. *Práctica A* can be done orally with books closed.
B. After reviewing *Práctica A*, call on a student to retell all the information in his or her own words.
C. Have students prepare *Práctica B* and C before going over them in class.

ANSWERS
Práctica

A 1. Hay muchos pasajeros en el tren.
2. El tren llega a la frontera.
3. No es un tren directo.
4. El tren no cruza la frontera.
5. Los pasajeros que quieren cruzar la frontera tienen que transbordar.
6. El agente en la estación de ferrocarril les avisa que no es un tren directo.

B 1. Es un país desconocido.
2. Es un país lejano.
3. La nina siempre soñaba.
4. Tienen que transbordar.
5. Yo sé que lo van a internar allí.
6. ¿Quién le va a avisar?
7. Él repitió la misma cosa.

C 1. frontera
2. soñaba con
3. manías
4. internar
5. criada
6. escalera abajo

National Standards

 Cultures
Students experience, discuss, and analyze an expressive product of the culture: the excerpt from the short story «Temprano y con Sol» by Emilia Pardo Bazán.

Independent Practice

Assign any of the following:
1. Exercises, page 53
2. Workbook, *Literatura*

53

TEACHING TIPS

A. Have the students read the *Introducción* silently or aloud.

B. You may wish to ask the following questions about the *Introducción*.

¿Es la autora de una familia aristócrata?

¿Cómo se llama ella?

¿Dónde nació?

¿Cómo fue la mujer?

¿Qué tipo de novelas escribió ella?

¿Qué describe en sus novelas más importantes?

¿Cuál es otro género literario que cultivó Pardo Bazán?

TEACHING THE READING

A. Because the language of this selection is fairly simple, you may wish to have students read the entire selection aloud quickly, having individuals read parts. Have pairs of students read the dialog sections aloud. Encourage them to use as much expression as possible.

B. Ask students if there was any part they did not understand. Call on other students to explain.

C. After two or three paragraphs have been read, ask comprehension questions about the paragraphs.

D. Assign the selection to be read for homework and have students write the answers to the *Comprensión* exercises on pages 56–57.

Introducción

Emilia Pardo Bazán (1852–1921), la condesa de Pardo Bazán, es considerada una de las novelistas más importantes de la literatura española. Nació en La Coruña, Galicia, de una familia aristócrata. Fue una mujer culta de gran curiosidad intelectual y talento vigoroso.

Su obra incluye varias novelas psicológicas y regionales. En sus dos novelas regionales, *Los Pazos de Ulloa* y

La madre naturaleza, la autora estudia y describe la decadencia de la aristocracia gallega. Pardo Bazán cultivó el cuento también. Su obra incluye varias colecciones de cuentos y se le considera una maestra de este género literario.

La condesa de Pardo Bazán alcanzó el honor de ser la primera mujer a quien se le dio una cátedra en la Universidad Central.

Lectura

Temprano y con sol

El empleado que vendía billetes en la oficina de la estación quedó sorprendido al oír una voz infantil que decía:

—¡Dos billetes, de primera clase, para París!...

Miró a una niña de once o doce años, de ojos y pelos negros, con un rico vestido de color y un bonito sombrerillo.° De la mano traía a un niño casi de la misma edad que ella, el cual iba muy bien vestido también. El chico parecía confuso; la niña muy alegre. El empleado sonrió y murmuró paternalmente:

—¿Directo, o a la frontera? A la frontera son ciento cincuenta pesetas, y...

—Aquí está el dinero —contestó la niña, abriendo su bolsa. El empleado volvió a sonreír y dijo:

—No es bastante.

—¡Hay quince duros° y tres pesetas! —exclamó la niña.

—Pero no es suficiente. Si no lo creen, pregunten ustedes a sus papás.

El niño se puso rojo, y la niña, dando una patada° en el suelo, gritó:

—¡Bien... , pues... , dos billetes más baratos!

—¿A una estación más próxima? ¿Escorial; Ávila?...

—¡Ávila, sí... , Ávila!... —respondió la niña.

Vaciló el empleado un momento; luego entregó los dos billetes. Subieron los dos chicos al tren y, al verse dentro del coche, comenzaron a bailar de alegría.

sombrerillo *little hat*

duros *five peseta coins*

dando una patada *stamping*

¿Cómo empezó aquel amor apasionado? Pues comenzó del modo más simple e inocente. Comenzó por la manía de los dos chicos de formar colecciones de sellos.

El papá de Finita y la mamá de Currín, ya enviudados° los dos, apenas se conocían, aunque vivían en el mismo edificio. Currín y Finita, en cambio, se encontraban siempre en la escalera, cuando iban a la escuela.

Una mañana, al bajar la escalera, Currín notó que Finita llevaba un objeto, un libro rojo, ¡el álbum de sellos! Quería verlo. La colección estaba muy completa y contenía muchos sellos de varios países. Al ver un sello muy raro de la república de Liberia, exclamó Currín:

—¿Me lo das?

—Toma —respondió Finita.

—Gracias, hermosa —contestó Currín.

Finita se puso roja y muy alegre.

—¿Sabes que te he de decir una cosa? —murmuró el chico.

—Anda, dímela.

—Hoy no.

Ya era tarde y la criada que acompañaba a Finita la llevó a la escuela. Currín se quedó admirando su sello y pensando en Finita. Currín era un chico de carácter dulce, aficionado a los dramas tristes, a las novelas de aventuras y a la poesía. Soñaba con viajes largos a países desconocidos. Verdad es que, aquella noche, soñó que Finita y él habían hecho una excursión a una tierra lejana.

Al día siguiente, nuevo encuentro en la escalera. Currín tenía unos sellos que iba a dar a Finita. Finita sonrió y se acercó a Currín, con misterio, diciendo:

—Dime lo que me ibas a decir ayer...

—No era nada... .

—¡Cómo nada! —exclamó Finita furiosa. —¡Qué idiota! ¿Nada, eh?

Currín se acercó al oído de la niña y murmuró:

—Sí, era algo... . Quería decirte que eres... ¡muy guapita!

Al decir esto, echó a correr escalera abajo.

Currín escribía versos a Finita y no pensaba en otra cosa más que en ella. Al fin de la semana eran novios.

Cierta tarde creyó el portero del edificio que soñaba. ¿No era aquélla la señorita Finita? ¿Y no era aquél el señorito Currín? ¿Y no subían los dos a un coche que pasaba? ¿A dónde van? ¿Deberé avisar a los padres?

—Oye —decía Finita a Currín, cuando el tren se puso en marcha; —Ávila, ¿cómo es? ¿Muy grande? ¿Bonita, lo mismo que París?

—No —respondió Currín. —Debe de ser un pueblo de pesca.°

—Yo quiero ver París; y también quiero ver las Pirámides de Egipto.

enviudados *widowed*

Paris, a principios del siglo XX

de pesca *fishing*

TEACHING THE READING

A. Context: Explain to students that one of the tactics that they will use to guess the meaning of unknown words is guessing from context. Tell them not to worry if they encounter a word that they do not know. They can often guess the meaning from the entire sentence. Point out to them that they do not understand everything when they read in their own language, but, unconsciously, they guess from the context. Such guessing can be based on: plain common sense, knowledge of the world around us, use of synonyms or antonyms in the text surrounding the unknown word or expression.

B. Glosses: These also help students read, of course. However, you may ask your students to hide them at first and see if they can guess the meaning of the words glossed.

C. Word derivation: It may be difficult at first, but students should be asked whenever possible what familiar word they can recognize in a derived word or expression.

D. Cooperative learning: It may be useful to have students work in small groups and share their problem-solving strategies so that they become aware of the various techniques available.

∼Después de leer∼

TEACHING TIPS

A. Go over all of the *Después de leer* activities after completing the reading.

B. The *Después de leer* activities can be written as a homework assignment.

ANSWERS
Comprensión

A 1. **dos billetes de primera clase, en la estación de ferrocarril**
 2. **París**
 3. **bastante dinero**
 4. **Ávila**
 5. **Se pusieron muy alegres.**
 6. **sellos**
 7. **en el mismo edificio**
 8. **no**
 9. **sí**

—Sí... —murmuró Currín, —pero... ¿y el dinero?

—¿El dinero? –contestó Finita. —Eres tonto. ¡Se puede pedir prestado°!

—¿Y a quién?

—¡A cualquier persona!

—¿Y si no nos lo quieren dar?

—Yo tengo mi reloj que empeñar°. Tú también. Y puedo empeñar mi abrigo nuevo. Si escribo a papá, nos enviará dinero.

—Tu papá estará furioso... . ¡No sé qué haremos!

—Pues voy a empeñar mi reloj y tú puedes empeñar el tuyo. ¡Qué bien vamos a divertirnos en Ávila! Me llevarás al café... y al teatro... y al paseo...

Cuando llegaron a Ávila, salieron del tren. La gente salía y los novios no sabían a dónde dirigirse.

—¿Por dónde se va a Ávila? —preguntó Currín a un mozo que no les hizo caso. Por instinto se encaminaron a una puerta, entregaron sus billetes y, cogidos por un solícito agente de hotel, se metieron en el coche, que los llevó al Hotel Inglés.

Entretanto el gobernador de Ávila recibió un telegrama mandando la captura de los dos enamorados. Los fugitivos fueron llevados a Madrid, sin pérdida de tiempo. Finita fue internada en un convento y Currín quedó en una escuela, de donde no fueron permitidos salir en todo el año, ni aun los domingos.

Como consecuencia de aquella tragedia, el papá de Finita y la mamá de Currín tuvieron de conocerse muy bien, y creció su mutua admiración de día en día. Aunque no tenemos noticias exactas, creemos que Finita y Currín llegaron a ser... hermanastros.

pedir prestado *borrow*

empeñar *pawn*

Ávila, a principios del siglo XX

Madrid, a principios del siglo XX

∼Después de leer∼

◆ Comprensión ◆

A **El cuento**   Contesten.

1. ¿Qué compraba la niña? ¿Dónde?
2. ¿Adónde quería ir?
3. ¿Qué no tenía la niña?
4. ¿Para dónde compró el billete?
5. ¿Cómo se pusieron los dos niños cuando subieron al tren?
6. ¿Qué coleccionaban los niños?
7. ¿Dónde vivían ellos?
8. ¿Se conocían sus padres?
9. ¿Habían enviudado sus padres?

Learning From Photos

Ávila
¿Es una fotografía nueva de Ávila?
¿Hay murallas alrededor de Ávila?
¿Es Ávila una ciudad grande?

Madrid
¿Es una foto del Madrid de hoy?
¿De cuándo data la foto?
¿Había mucho tráfico en Madrid a principios del siglo?
¿Había muchos coches?
¿Había autobuses o tranvías?

10. ¿Dónde se veían los niños cuando iban a la escuela?
11. Un día, ¿por qué le habló Currín a Finita?
12. ¿Con qué soñaba Currín? Y una noche, ¿con qué soñó?
13. ¿Por qué se puso tan sorprendido el portero de su edificio?
14. ¿Qué hicieron los dos niños cuando llegaron a Ávila?
15. ¿Qué recibió el gobernador de Ávila?
16. ¿Dónde fue internada Finita? ¿Y Currín?

B **Descripciones**
   1. Describa Ud. a Finita.
   2. Describa Ud. a Currín.

C **¿Cómo puede ser?**   Expliquen.
Al final del cuento dice: «Aunque no tenemos noticias exactas, creemos que Finita y Currín llegaron a ser... hermanastros.» Expliquen cómo es posible esto.

D **Estudio de palabras**   Pareen.

   1. dio una sonrisa   **a.** murmuró
   2. dijo en voz muy baja   **b.** estúpido
   3. como un padre   **c.** paternalmente
   4. de un niño   **d.** sonrió
   5. suficiente   **e.** bastante
   6. tonto   **f.** infantil

⟨Actividades comunicativas⟩

A **Un drama o una comedia**
Trabajando en grupos de dos preparen un drama entre el padre de Finita y la mamá de Currín. En su «obra» incluyan el diálogo que tuvo lugar en las siguientes circunstancias:
► cuando se conocieron
► cuando se dieron cuenta de lo que habían hecho sus hijos
► cuando decidieron hacer
► cuando creció su mutua admiración

ANSWERS
Comprensión
   10. en la escalera
   11. Quería ver el albúm de sellos que llevaba.
   12. Soñaba con viajes largos a países desconocidos. Soñó que Finita y él habián hecho una excursión a una tierra lejana.
   13. Porque los dos salieron juntos.
   14. Salieron del tren, se encaminaron hacia una puerta, hablaron con un agente de un hotel y se metireon en un coche para ir al hotel.
   15. un telegrama
   16. en un covento; en una escuela
B 1. Finita: Tenía once o doce anos. Tenía ojos y pelos negros.
   2. Currín: Tenía unos once o doce anos. Estaba bien vestido.
C Posiblemente el padre de Finita y la madre de Currín se casaron.
D 1. d
   2. a
   3. c
   4. f
   5. e
   6. b

⟨Actividad comunicativa⟩

ANSWERS
Answers will vary.

Independent Practice

Assign any of the following:
   1. Exercise, page 57
   2. Workbook, *Literatura*

Chapter 2 Overview ◆◆◆◆◆◆◆◆◆◆◆◆◆◆◆◆◆◆◆◆◆◆◆

SCOPE AND SEQUENCE pages 58A–58B

TOPICS	FUNCTIONS	STRUCTURE	CULTURE
◆ Lifestyles in rural and urban areas ◆ Routine invitations	◆ How to discuss daily routines of Hispanic youths ◆ How to extend invitations as well as accept or refuse them ◆ How to talk about habitual past actions ◆ How to distinguish between recurring and completed actions in the past ◆ How to read and discuss magazine articles about Hispanic youths ◆ How to express doubt or uncertainty ◆ How to give advice and make suggestions ◆ How to express emotional reactions to the actions of others ◆ How to read and discuss literary works by Nicanor Parra and Laura Esquivel	◆ **El imperfecto** ◆ **El imperfecto y el pretérito** ◆ **Dos acciones en la misma oración** ◆ **Subjuntivo con expresiones de duda** ◆ **Subjuntivo con verbos especiales** ◆ **Subjuntivo con expresiones de emoción**	◆ Daily life for a Puerto Rican student versus a young Indian boy in Bolivia ◆ An American exchange student in Spain ◆ Nonverbal gestures for refusing food or drink ◆ Lowering the voting age ◆ First day of classes at a school in Sevilla **Literatura** ◆ «**Sueños**», Nicanor Parra ◆ *Como agua para chocolate,* Laura Esquivel

CHAPTER 2 RESOURCES

PRINT	MULTIMEDIA

Planning Resources

Lesson Plans Block Scheduling Lesson Plans	Interactive Lesson Planner

Reinforcement Resources

Writing Activities Workbook Student Tape Manual Video Activities Booklet Glencoe Foreign Language Web Site User's Guide	Transparencies Binder Audiocassette/Compact Disc Program Videocassette/Videodisc Program Online Internet Activities Electronic Teacher's Classroom Resources

Assessment Resources

Situation Cards Chapter Quizzes Testing Program	Testmaker Computer Software (Macintosh/Windows) Listening Comprehension Audiocassette/Compact Disc

Motivational Resources

Expansion Activities	Café Glencoe: **www.cafe.glencoe.com**

SECTION	PAGES	SECTION RESOURCES
Cultura **La vida diaria** *Dos jóvenes: Débora e Hipólito*	60–65	Transparencies 11A–11B Audiocassette 3A/Compact Disc 2 Writing Activities Workbook, pages 29–31 Student Tape Manual, pages 18–21 Chapter Quizzes, page 17 Testing Program, pages 33–35
Conversación **La estudiante extranjera**	66–71	Transparency 12 Audiocassette 3A/Compact Disc 2 Writing Activities Workbook, page 32 Student Tape Manual, page 22 Chapter Quizzes, page 18 Testing Program, pages 36–38
Lenguaje **Ofreciendo comida** **Para invitar**	72–74	Transparency 13 Audiocassette 3B/Compact Disc 2 Writing Activities Workbook, page 33 Student Tape Manual, page 23 Testing Program, pages 36–38
Repaso de estructura **El imperfecto** **El imperfecto y el pretérito** **Dos acciones en la misma oración**	75–79	Audiocassette 3B/Compact Disc 2 Writing Activities Workbook, pages 34–36 Student Tape Manual, page 24 Chapter Quizzes, pages 19–21 Testing Program, pages 39–40
Periodismo **El voto para los jóvenes** **«¿Rebajar la edad para votar?»** **El primer día de clases** **«Carteras»**	80–87	Transparencies 14A–14B, 15 Audiocassette 3B/Compact Disc 2 Writing Activities Workbook, pages 37–39 Student Tape Manual, pages 25–26 Chapter Quizzes, pages 22–23 Testing Program, pages 41–45
Estructura **Subjuntivo con expresiones de duda** **Subjuntivo con verbos especiales** **Subjuntivo con expresiones de emoción**	88–91	Audiocassette 4A/Compact Disc 3 Writing Activities Workbook, pages 40–42 Student Tape Manual, page 29 Chapter Quizzes, pages 24–26 Testing Program, pages 46–47
Literatura **«Sueños», Nicanor Parra** *Como agua para chocolate,* **Laura Esquivel**	92–101	Transparencies 16, 17 Audiocassette 4A–4B/Compact Disc 3 Writing Activities Workbook, pages 43–46 Student Tape Manual, page 30 Chapter Quizzes, pages 27–28 Testing Program, pages 48–52

OVERVIEW

In this chapter students will learn more about Spanish-speaking people and their daily lives. Rural life will be explored, as well as city life in different parts of the Hispanic world. Students will also learn how to extend, accept, and decline invitations politely.

National Standards

Communication Students will engage in conversations, provide and obtain information, express feelings, and exchange opinions on the topics of daily routines, including schools and education and the rights and privileges of youth.

Learning From Photos

La vista es de la famosísima Avenida 9 de Julio en Buenos Aires, la capital argentina. Según los argentinos es la avenida más ancha del mundo. El 9 de Julio conmemora la independencia de la Argentina el 9 de julio de 1816.

CAPÍTULO 2

Rutinas

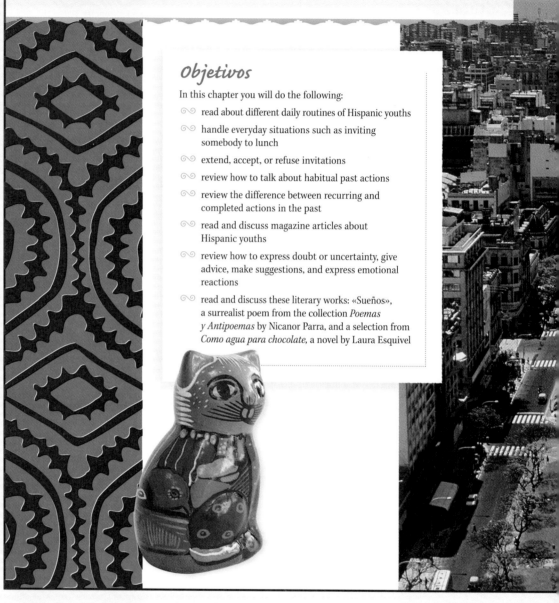

Objetivos

In this chapter you will do the following:

- read about different daily routines of Hispanic youths
- handle everyday situations such as inviting somebody to lunch
- extend, accept, or refuse invitations
- review how to talk about habitual past actions
- review the difference between recurring and completed actions in the past
- read and discuss magazine articles about Hispanic youths
- review how to express doubt or uncertainty, give advice, make suggestions, and express emotional reactions
- read and discuss these literary works: «Sueños», a surrealist poem from the collection *Poemas y Antipoemas* by Nicanor Parra, and a selection from *Como agua para chocolate*, a novel by Laura Esquivel

 *inter*NET
CONNECTION

The Glencoe Foreign Language Web site (http://www.glencoe.com/sec/fl) offers these options that enable you and your students to experience the Spanish-speaking world via the Internet:

- At **Café Glencoe**, the interactive "after-school" section of the site, you and your students can access a variety of additional online resources, including online newspapers, interactive games, and a send-a-postcard feature.
- The online **Proyectos** are correlated to the chapters and utilize Hispanic Web sites around the world.

DIFFICULTY PLATEAUS

In all chapters, each reading selection in *Cultura, Periodismo,* and *Literatura* as well as the *Conversación* and each structure topic will be rated as follows:

◆ **Easy**
◆◆ **Intermediate**
◆◆◆ **Difficult**

Please note that the material in *¡Buen viaje! Level 3* does not get progressively more difficult. Within each chapter there are easy and difficult sections.

The overall rating of this chapter is ◆◆ **Intermediate.**

RANDOM ACCESS

You may follow the exact order of the chapter or you may omit certain sections that you feel are not necessary for your students. Similarly, you may wish to present a literary selection without interruption or you may intersperse some material from the *Estructura.*

EVALUATION

Quizzes There is a quiz for every vocabulary section and every structure point.

Tests There are global tests for both *Estructuras,* a combined *Conversación/Lenguaje* test, and one test for each reading in the *Cultura, Periodismo,* and *Literatura* sections. There is also a comprehensive chapter test.

cincuenta y nueve ◌ **59**

Chapter Projects

Las rutinas urbanas y rurales: Haga que los estudiantes, trabajando en pequeños grupos, preparen un informe que contraste las rutinas típicas de los jóvenes que viven en áreas rurales y en los centros urbanos.

CAPÍTULO 2
Cultura

TEACHING TIPS

Have students read the *Introducción* aloud or silently.

RESOURCES

- ✍ Vocabulary Transparencies
- 🎧 Audio Cassette 3A/Compact Disc 2
- 📁 Student Tape Manual
- 📁 Workbook
- 📁 Chapter Quizzes

VOCABULARY EXPANSION

You may wish to provide students with **divertirse** as a synonym for **entretenerse**. **Días de fiesta** is an expression synonymous with **días festivos** and may be more familiar to some students. **Indígenas** literally means "indigenous" or "indigenous peoples," people native to a particular place. In Latin America **indígena** always refers to Amerindians.

TEACHING VOCABULARY

A. Using the Vocabulary Transparencies, have students repeat the new words in unison after you or Cassette 3A/Compact Disc 2.

B. To vary the procedure, give students several minutes to read the definitions silently to themselves.

C. Then have the class repeat each new word or phrase once or twice in unison.

CULTURA
La vida diaria

Introducción

Los bebés comen, lloran, duermen. Los adolescentes se levantan, van a la escuela, juegan, comen, estudian, duermen. Los adultos se levantan, van y vuelven del trabajo, comen, se entretienen un poco, duermen. Es la rutina diaria. De cuando en cuando hay un cambio. Hay días festivos, vacaciones o eventos especiales: un nacimiento, una boda, una muerte.

Estas rutinas son más o menos las mismas en casi todas partes del mundo. Pero hay algunas diferencias en cuanto a los detalles. El indígena del altiplano boliviano se levanta, va y vuelve del trabajo, se entretiene un poco y duerme, al igual que su compatriota, el banquero de La Paz. Pero las formas en que trabajan, comen y se divierten son muy distintas.

Vocabulario

el entrenador

las ovejas

las llamas

Did You Know?

Llamas, vicuñas, alpacas, and **guanacos** are all similar, varying primarily in size, color, and texture of wool. They are ruminants (cud chewers) and are related to the camel. Originally they came from Andean South America.

los tejidos

la comida chatarra

sembrar plantar granos, vegetales, etc.
cosechar recoger los productos agrícolas
regar darle agua a, echarle agua a, irrigar
acudir a presentarse, visitar, llegar

el altiplano un área llana de los Andes, la mayor parte está en Bolivia
los aymarás un grupo indígena de Bolivia y el Perú

el ama de casa la señora de la casa o familia
las faenas labores, tareas, trabajos o actividades
los vecinos los que habitan un mismo pueblo, barrio o vecindad

Una calle de San Juan, Puerto, Rico

Práctica

A **Pareen.** Escojan.

1. las disputas
2. las sesiones
3. resolver
4. deshidratado
5. humilde
6. obviamente

a. dehydrated
b. obviously
c. disputes
d. sessions
e. to resolve
f. humble

B **El trabajo diario** Expresen de otra manera.

1. El joven ayuda con *las tareas* del campo.
2. *La señora* lleva a sus hijos a la escuela.
3. Los agricultores tienen que *irrigar* las plantas de frijol.
4. Primero los agricultores *plantan* sus granos y vegetales.
5. Generalmente los agricultores son personas muy *modestas*.

C **¿Estás de acuerdo?** ¿Sí o no?

1. La comida chatarra se sirve en restaurantes caros y lujosos.
2. El entrenador les da instrucciones a los jugadores.
3. Son vecinos porque viven en pueblos diferentes.
4. Muchas casas en los EE.UU. reciben programas de televisión por cable.
5. La alpaca es un tipo de lana que se obtiene de la llama.
6. Primero se cosechan y luego se siembran el choclo (maíz) y la papa.

El altiplano

CULTURA

sesenta y uno 61

Dos jóvenes: Débora e Hipólito

Débora Rodríguez vive en Ponce, Puerto Rico. Ella tiene catorce años. Débora se levanta a las seis de la mañana. Se desayuna con su familia: sus padres, su hermana y sus dos hermanos. Su padre es ingeniero y su madre es ama de casa. Débora suele desayunar con jugo de naranja natural, o jugo de china como ellos lo llaman, y un cereal frío, como copos de maíz[1] con leche. Su mamá lleva a los muchachos en carro al Colegio Ponceño, un colegio privado, y allí los deja hasta las tres de la tarde cuando los va a recoger. Los muchachos comen en el colegio. Les dan una hora al mediodía para comer. Ellos pueden llevar la comida de casa o pueden comprarla en la cafetería. En este colegio la mayoría de los cursos se dan en inglés. Los de religión y, obviamente, español, se dan en español. Débora juega al softball por la tarde con su equipo. Su padre es el entrenador del equipo. La familia cena a las 7:00 y Débora estudia después por un par de horas antes de acostarse a las 10:00. Algunas noches cuando no tiene mucha tarea, Débora mira la televisión con la familia. Como tienen cable, ella puede ver programas tanto en inglés como en español. De vez en cuando, toda la familia va al centro a comer «comida chatarra»: pollo frito, hamburguesas, papas fritas y Coca-Cola. Después van a la heladería. Hay helados de todos los sabores, vainilla y chocolate, por supuesto, pero también guanábana, tamarindo, coco y guayaba[2] ¡Qué rico!

Hipólito Moricio es boliviano y tiene trece años. Hipólito es aymará, miembro de un grupo indígena que representa un 30% de la población boliviana. Vive en un pueblecito del altiplano. Hipólito tiene mucha suerte, él va a la escuela. De los niños de su edad en las zonas rurales, solamente el 16% asiste a la escuela. Hipólito ha aprendido bastante español en la escuela, pero su lengua materna es el aymará.

[1] **los copos de maíz** *cornflakes*
[2] **la guanábana, el tamarindo, el coco, la guayaba** *frutas tropicales*

Un colegio en San Juan, Puerto Rico

Plaza y Catedral de la Guadalupe, Ponce

TEACHING THE READING

◆ Dos jóvenes: Débora e Hipólito ◆

A. This section contains some very useful vocabulary. Call on several students to read this section aloud.

B. Assign the *Comprensión* exercises on page 64 and the Workbook.

ABOUT THE SPANISH LANGUAGE

Although the traditional three meals are called **el desayuno, el almuerzo,** and **la cena,** there are variations. In many places the main meal of the day is still eaten in the afternoon and is called **la comida,** not **el almuerzo.** In some parts of Mexico and the U.S. Southwest, breakfast is **el almuerzo.**

HISTORY CONNECTION

Los estudiantes puertorriqueños aprenden la historia de Puerto Rico. Pero además, aprenden la historia de España y de los EE.UU. ¿Por qué? ¿De qué es el mapa en la pared?

Cooperative Learning

Have students work in teams. Each team is responsible for designing a magazine. They need to choose material that is appropriate for a teenage audience. Each team then reports their ideas to the class.

National Standards

Cultures

Students are introduced to the daily routines of peers in two Hispanic cultures, Puerto Rico and Bolivia. They are shown the relationship between the products and perspectives of Bolivian culture.

Una escuela en Bolivia y un niño aymará

Hipólito se levanta muy temprano para ayudar a su padre con sus faenas. Los Moricio son agricultores. En su pequeña parcela de tierra cultivan papas y un poco de maíz, o choclo. Ellos también tienen unas cuantas ovejas y llamas. Hipólito ayuda a su papá y a los vecinos a esquilar[3] las ovejas y llamas. La madre de Hipólito y otras señoras hacen de la lana preciosos tejidos para mantas y chompas[4] que venden luego en la ciudad. La lana de la llama es muy fina. Se conoce como alpaca.

El padre de Hipólito, Lucas Moricio, es una persona importante en el pueblo. En los tiempos antiguos hubiera sido «el amauta», o sabio del pueblo. Los vecinos acuden al señor Lucas para resolver disputas.

Antes de salir para la escuela, Hipólito toma un té de coca. Los hombres mascan[5] hojas de coca mientras trabajan. Les ayuda a resistir el frío y las alturas de más de 3.000 metros. A Hipólito le gustan los platos típicos que se preparan con papa deshidratada por el frío. Este alimento se llama «chuño» y los antiguos incas y aymarás lo comían hace más de mil años. En la escuela Hipólito aprende matemáticas básicas y, lo que es muy importante para él, a hablar y leer el español. El padre de Hipólito comprende muy poco español. Clemencia, la madre de Hipólito, habla bastante español, ya que tiene que usar el idioma cuando vende sus tejidos en la ciudad. Hipólito vuelve de la escuela al mediodía. Por razones económicas, hay dos sesiones en su escuela, una por la mañana y otra por la tarde. Los vecinos ayudaron a construir la escuela. El gobierno contribuyó con los materiales y los vecinos con la mano de obra. La escuela no tiene luz eléctrica ni agua corriente, pero todos están muy contentos con ella sin que importe lo humilde que sea. Por la tarde, Hipólito trabaja con su padre. Según la época, puede ayudarle a sembrar, regar o cosechar las papas y el choclo. Les da de comer a los animales y ayuda con el rodeo y esquileo del ganado. Antes de caer el sol, Hipólito les lee a sus padres de su cuaderno de ejercicios. A los padres les encanta escucharle. Lo más probable es que un día Hipólito también llegue a ser «amauta» como su padre. Y quizás sea amauta en el mundo más allá del pueblo, en La Paz, por ejemplo. Quizás llegue a ser hasta presidente de la República.

[3] **esquilar** *to shear an animal*
[4] **las chompas** *los suéteres*
[5] **mascan** *chew*

Paraphrasing Have students paraphrase the following:
1. "**Hipólito ayuda a su papá y a los vecinos a quitar la lana de las ovejas y llamas.**" They may say: "**Hipólito ayuda a su padre y a los residentes del pueblo a esquilar las ovejas y llamas.**"
2. "**… para ayudar a su papá con sus tareas.**" They may say: "**… para ayudar a su padre con sus faenas (con su trabajo).**"

ABOUT THE SPANISH LANGUAGE

A sweater has a number of different names in Spanish: **jersey, suéter, pulóver,** and, of course, **chompa.**

GEOGRAPHY CONNECTION

La enfermedad que afecta a las personas en las alturas extremas de los Andes se llama «el soroche». Algunos síntomas del soroche son dolores de cabeza, falta de aliento (dificultad en respirar) y fatiga. En el aeropuerto de El Alto en La Paz, hay enfermeros con tanques de oxígeno para los pasajeros afectados por la altura.

Cooperative Learning

Have pairs of students interview each other. One student will play the role of Débora Rodríguez and the other will be Hipólito Moricio. They should ask each other about their daily routines, school, food, work, and play.

Learning From Photos

Los muchachos en la foto están en el patio de la escuela durante el descanso o el recreo. Ellos están jugando con el tobogán. Probablemente hay un columpio *(swing)* en el patio también. Describa lo que se ve en la foto. ¿En qué parte del país estará la escuela? ¿Qué dice el letrero en la pared? ¿Qué edad tendrán los niños?

CULTURAL CONNECTION

Indians of the Andean region for centuries have chewed the leaves of the coca plant. Today, even in the international hotels of La Paz, Cuzco, etc., a tea is brewed from coca (**té de coca**) and available all day to guests. It is supposed to alleviate the effects of the extremely high altitude.

ANSWERS

Comprensión

A 1. Hipólito
  2. Hipólito
  3. Débora
  4. Débora
  5. Débora
  6. Débora
  7. Hipólito
  8. Débora
  9. Hipólito
 10. Débora

B 1. Débora
  2. jugo de naranja, cereal frío con leche
  3. Los muchachos pueden llevar la comida de casa o pueden comprarla en la cafetería.
  4. Es el inglés.
  5. el padre de Débora
  6. las hamburguesas, las papas fritas y la Coca-Cola

C 1. boliviano
  2. en el altiplano
  3. es agricultor
  4. aymará
  5. Su padre esquila las llamas y su madre hace chompas y mantas.

D 1. Los vecinos de Hipólito mascan coca porque les ayuda a resistir el frío y las alturas.
  2. Las señoras hacen chompas y mantas para venderlas.
  3. Débora habla inglés y español mientras Hipólito habla español y aymará.
  4. Hipólito trabaja. El padre de Hipólito necesita la ayuda de su hijo para sembrar, regar y cosechar.

Comprensión

El altiplano

A **¿Quién es?** ¿Es Débora o Hipólito?

1. Vive en una zona de gran altura.
2. Va a la escuela a pie.
3. Come helado de coco y guanábana.
4. Su padre le enseña a jugar al softball.
5. Donde vive, nunca hace frío.
6. Toma y le gusta la Coca-Cola.
7. Su padre ayudó en la construcción de la escuela.
8. La madre lleva a los hijos a la escuela en carro.
9. La madre vende sus productos en la ciudad.
10. Habla inglés y español.

B **En Puerto Rico** Contesten.

1. ¿Quién es puertorriqueña?
2. ¿Cuál es el desayuno de la muchacha?
3. ¿Qué alternativas tienen para el almuerzo los muchachos en el Colegio Ponceño?
4. ¿Cuál es el idioma que más se usa en el Colegio Ponceño?
5. ¿Quién es el entrenador del equipo de softball?
6. ¿Cuáles son algunos ejemplos de «comida chatarra»?

C **En el altiplano** Corrijan las oraciones falsas.

1. Hipólito es puertorriqueño.
2. Él vive en la costa.
3. Su padre es ingeniero.
4. En casa, Hipólito habla inglés.
5. Su madre esquila las llamas y su padre hace chompas y mantas.

D **Comentarios** Expliquen y comenten.

1. ¿Por qué mascan coca los vecinos de Hipólito?
2. ¿Qué hacen las señoras para contribuir a la economía de la familia?
3. Contrasten el bilingüismo de Débora con el bilingüismo de Hipólito.
4. ¿Cuál de los jóvenes trabaja? ¿Cómo trabaja y por qué?

Una vista de Ponce, Puerto Rico

Critical Thinking Activity

Thinking skills: making inferences **La tierra que se ve en la foto en la página 65, ¿será fácil o difícil de cultivar? ¿Por qué?**

Learning From Photos

Have the students say all they can about the photo. Have the students locate Ponce on a map of Puerto Rico.

Indígenas bolivianos

Actividades comunicativas

A **Mis rutinas** Imagínese que Ud. es Hipólito Moricio quien está aprendiendo español. Su maestro le pide que escriba en su cuaderno de ejercicios lo que hace todos los días. Escriba unos párrafos describiendo su rutina diaria.

B **Un poco de historia** Ponce es la segunda ciudad de Puerto Rico. Lleva el nombre de don Juan Ponce de León, el primer gobernador de la isla. En 1898, durante la guerra con España, el general norteamericano Nelson Miles desembarcó en un lugar de Puerto Rico cerca de Ponce. Busque información sobre la historia de Puerto Rico en un libro de historia o una enciclopedia, y prepare un breve informe.

C **Una investigación demográfica** Hipólito es aymará. El mayor grupo indígena de Bolivia son los quechuas. Hay también otro grupo importante, los guaraníes. ¿Quiénes son? ¿Dónde viven? Prepare un pequeño cuadro demográfico de Bolivia que indique los grupos importantes de indígenas, el tamaño de cada grupo y los lugares en donde viven.

D **Necesitamos un entrenador**. El padre de Débora es un excelente entrenador de softball. Escríbale una carta invitándole a venir a entrenar el equipo de la escuela de Ud.

Disfruta lo que billones de años han creado para ti...

PARQUE DE LAS CAVERNAS DEL RIO CAMUY

Un maravilloso mundo de escenarios naturales que jamás olvidarás.

CULTURA

sesenta y cinco 65

TEACHING TIPS

B and **C** Have the students divide into two teams. One team does *Actividad B* while the other works on *Actividad C*. The reports can be presented when convenient.

> **Actividades comunicativas**

ANSWERS
A–D Answers will vary.

GEOGRAPHY CONNECTION

1. La ciudad de Ponce, Puerto Rico, lleva el nombre del primer gobernador de Puerto Rico, don Juan Ponce de León (1460–1521) quien desembarcó en Borinquén (Puerto Rico) en 1508, fundando la ciudad de San Juan. Ponce de León descubrió la Florida en 1512.

2. Las Cavernas de Camuy están en Puerto Rico. Son enormes cavernas subterráneas. ¿Saben cómo es que se forman cavernas de ese tipo? Se forman con la erosión de la tierra por los ríos subterráneos. ¿Hay cavernas subterráneas en los EE.UU.? ¿Dónde? ¿Cómo se llaman?

Independent Practice

Assign any of the following:
1. Exercises, pages 64–65
2. Workbook *Cultura*

Learning From Photos

You may wish to have students say all they can about the photo, or you may wish to ask them: **¿Dónde están estos señores? ¿Qué hacen ellos? ¿Parece muy fértil la tierra? ¿Hace mucho calor allí? ¿Por qué sí o por qué no?**

Bell Ringer Review

Use the Bell Ringer Transparency 2-3, or write the following on the board:

1. **Escriba una lista de todas las formas de transporte que conoce.**
2. **Describa la casa o el apartamento donde Ud. vive.**

RESOURCES

- Vocabulary Transparencies
- Audio Cassettes 3A/Compact Disc 2
- Student Tape Manual
- Workbook
- Chapter Quizzes

TEACHING VOCABULARY

A. Present the new vocabulary and have the students repeat after you or Cassette 3A/Compact Disc 2.
B. Call on individuals to read each new word or phrase and its definition.

VOCABULARY EXPANSION

The literal meaning of **cacharro** is a clay pot, especially a broken one. It also can mean any broken-down piece of equipment.

Conversación

La estudiante extranjera

Vocabulario

el barrio

una tienda de videos

un cacharro

la boca del metro

el piso el apartamento
el horario el tiempo indicado para diferentes actividades
el capricho deseo para algo innecesario

particular privado(a)
encantador(a) muy agradable, simpatiquísimo(a)
propio(a) que es propiedad de una persona
raro(a) infrecuente, muy diferente
valenciano(a) de la región de Valencia

acostumbrarse familiarizarse con algo
sorprenderse recibir una sorpresa, descubrir algo raro
ponerse llegar a ser
tener razón estar correcto(a)
estar a gusto estar satisfecho(a), estar contento(a)

66 ❧ *sesenta y seis*

Did You Know?

El primer sistema de trenes subterráneos fue el de Londres en 1868. El *Métropolitain* de París fue inaugurado en 1900 y el *Metro* de Madrid en 1919. Hoy el Metro de Madrid consiste de unas 10 líneas. En los últimos años se han inaugurado varias extensiones del sistema que llegan a los suburbios.

En Latinoamérica hay sistemas de metro modernos en México D.F., Caracas y Santiago de Chile. El metro más antiguo de Latinoamérica es el de Buenos Aires.

❦Práctica❦

A **¿De qué hablamos?** Contesten según las fotos.

1. ¿Es una tienda o es un metro?
2. ¿Qué tipo de tienda es?
3. ¿Qué es la señorita?
4. ¿Es un coche privado o un taxi?
5. ¿Es un coche elegante o es un cacharro?

B **Pareen.** Escojan la palabra que se define.

> **la secundaria** **el metro** **cenar**
> **el elefante** **el mediodía**

1. Las doce del día.
2. El tren subterráneo de una ciudad.
3. En los Estados Unidos la escuela para los grados del noveno hasta el duodécimo.
4. Un animal enorme, herbívoro, que vive en África y Asia.
5. Tomar la comida de la noche.

C **Definiciones** Completen.

1. Me ___ mucho lo que dices. Es difícil de creer.
2. Sí, ella compró un coche de color de rosa, es un ___ de ella.
3. Ella es simpatiquísima, es ___, pero su gusto es muy raro.
4. Pero el coche es de ella, es su ___ coche y ella puede hacer lo que quiera con él.
5. Pues yo nunca podría ___ a un coche color de rosa.

CONVERSACIÓN

sesenta y siete ∽ **67**

TEACHING TIPS

It is recommended that you go over the *Práctica* in class after the students have prepared them at home.

__ANSWERS__
Práctica
A 1. **Es una tienda.**
   2. **Es una tienda de videos.**
   3. **La senorita es una empleada.**
   4. **Es un coche privado.**
   5. **Es un cacharro.**
B 1. **el mediodía**
   2. **el metro**
   3. **la secundaria**
   4. **el elefante**
   5. **cenar**
C 1. **Sorprendo**
   2. **capricho**
   3. **encantadora**
   4. **propio**
   5. **estar a gusto**

Learning From Photos

The old jalopy in the photo is typical of the cars to be found in Havana. Most cars in Cuba prior to the Revolution (1958) were American. An embargo imposed by the U.S. in the 1960s stopped the importation of American cars. Cubans have somehow kept these pre-embargo museum pieces running.

Did You Know?

European videos use a different system than in the U.S. Videos bought in Europe cannot be played on standard American videocassette decks.

Independent Practice

Assign any of the following:
1. Exercises, page 67
2. Workbook, *Conversación*

Escenas de la vida

Bell Ringer Review

Use the BRR Transparency 2-4, or write the following on the board: **Escriba todo lo que Ud. hizo esta mañana antes de salir para la escuela.**

TEACHING THE CONVERSATION

◆ Escenas de la vida ◆◆

A. Call on individual students with good pronunciation to read the conversation aloud to the class with as much expression as possible. Have the others follow along in their books as they listen.

B. If you wish, you can intersperse the questions from *Comprensión A* and *C* on page 70.

RECYCLING

 Have students recall vocabulary to describe their homes: **apartamento/cuarto/habitación/ dormitorio/cocina/sala/cuarto de baño/comedor/casa particular (privada)/piso/ascensor/garaje**

National Standards

Comparisons
Students are helped to acquire an understanding of the concept of culture by contrasting aspects of American culture and the culture of Spain through the perspective of their peers.

Escenas de la vida

La estudiante extranjera

PACO: ¿De qué parte de Estados Unidos eres, Linda?

LINDA: Soy de California, cerca de Los Ángeles.

PACO: ¿Dónde vives aquí en Madrid?

LINDA: En un piso en el barrio de Argüelles, cerca de la boca del metro, con los Serra, una familia valenciana. En California vivía en una casa particular.

PACO: Y, ¿qué tal? ¿Estás a gusto allí?

LINDA: Pues, sí, hombre. Estoy contentísima. La familia es encantadora, y puedo practicar mi español con ellos todos los días.

PACO: Es muy diferente la vida aquí a la de los Estados Unidos, ¿no?

LINDA: Sí, tuve que acostumbrarme a mucho, especialmente el horario. Cenar a las diez de la noche me era un poco raro. Y volver a casa a comer al mediodía era nuevo para mí. Nosotros almorzábamos en la cafetería de la escuela, en sólo media hora. Ahora como en casa con la familia. Y, ¡qué comida! Me voy a poner como un elefante.

PACO: ¿Qué más te sorprendió de la vida aquí?

LINDA: Pues, tuve que aprender a tomar el bus y el metro para ir a cualquier parte. En California siempre vamos en coche. Yo tenía mi propio coche, un cacharro, pero andaba muy bien.

PACO: En América muchos estudiantes de secundaria trabajan, ¿verdad?

LINDA: Yo trabajaba los sábados y todos los veranos. Era dependienta en una tienda de videos. Gastaba el dinero que ganaba en caprichos. Compraba discos compactos, ropa, iba al cine. No tenía que pedirles dinero a mis padres.

PACO: Aquí es muy raro que un estudiante trabaje. Si necesito algo se lo pido a mis padres. Hmm… Creo que vosotros tenéis más libertad que nosotros.

LINDA: Sí, creo que tienes razón. Pero también es muy bonito poder depender de tus papás para todo.

CONVERSACIÓN

sesenta y nueve 〜 **69**

ABOUT THE SPANISH LANGUAGE

Puede indicarles a los estudiantes el uso muy natural de *vosotros* cuando Paco dice: «*Creo que vosotros tenéis más libertad que nosotros.*» Puede recordarles que *vosotros* es el plural de *tú* y que es la forma normalmente usada en la mayor parte de España aunque no se emplea en Latinoamérica.

National Standards

Cultures

Have the students discuss the apparent differences in parental attitudes toward teenagers in Spain and the United States with regard to independence. Ask them to indicate the advantages and disadvantages of being a teenager in each of the two cultures.

PARAPHRASING You may wish to ask students to provide as many variants as they can think of for: **En California vivía en una casa particular.** They may say: **En California vivía en una casa privada.** Or **Mi casa en California era una casa privada,** etc.

Paired Activity

Have pairs of students prepare a work resumé of all the jobs they ever had, including "jobs" at home such as housecleaning, garbage hauling, etc. They should describe their job responsibilities in as much detail as possible.

A 1. Es de California.
2. No, es de cerca de Los Ángeles.
3. Vive en Argüelles.
4. No, vive con una familia española.
5. Sí, le gusta mucho.
6. Es encantadora.
7. No, es valenciana.
8. Practica su español.
9. Está cerca de la boca del metro.
10. No, cree que es muy diferente.

B 1. horario
2. escuela
3. cenar
4. a comer
5. media hora
6. trabajan
7. casa particular

C 1. En España Linda come mucho.
2. En California ella va a todas partes en coche.
3. Su coche era un cacharro.
4. Ella trabajaba los sábados y los veranos.
5. Ella trabajaba en una tienda de videos.
6. Ella compraba caprichos con el dinero que ganaba.
7. Paco dice que es muy raro que un estudiante español trabaje.
8. Paco cree que los estudiantes españoles tienen menos libertad que los norteamericanos.

Comprensión

A **Preguntas** Contesten.

1. ¿De dónde es Linda?
2. ¿Ella es de la ciudad de Los Ángeles?
3. ¿En qué parte de Madrid vive Linda ahora?
4. ¿Vive ella ahora con su familia de California?
5. ¿A Linda le gusta donde está?
6. ¿Cómo es la familia con la que ella vive en Madrid?
7. ¿Es madrileña la familia de Argüelles?
8. ¿Qué hace Linda con la familia todos los días?
9. ¿Cerca de qué está el apartamento en Argüelles?
10. ¿Cree Linda que la vida en Madrid es igual a la vida en California?

B **La vida de Linda** Completen.

1. Linda tuvo que acostumbrarse al ___.
2. En California ella almorzaba en la ___.
3. Ella creía que era raro ___ a las diez de la noche.
4. En Madrid ella vuelve a casa ___ al mediodía.
5. En California ella tenía sólo ___ para almorzar.
6. Paco le pregunta si en los EE.UU. muchos estudiantes de secundaria ___.
7. En los Estados Unidos, Linda vivía en una ___.

C **¿Sí o no?** Corrijan las oraciones falsas.

1. En España Linda come muy poco.
2. En Madrid ella va a todas partes en coche.
3. Su coche era nuevo y elegante.
4. Ella trabajaba los domingos y los inviernos.
5. Ella trabajaba en un supermercado.
6. Ella compraba libros de texto con el dinero que ganaba.
7. Paco dice que muchos estudiantes españoles trabajan también.
8. Paco cree que los estudiantes españoles tienen más libertad que los norteamericanos.

Los Ángeles, California

Argüelles, Madrid

TEACHING TIPS

A. For *Actividad D,* have students tell what **caprichos** they would spend their money on.

B. For *Actividad E,* ask students if they have noticed any differences between one part of the United States and another.

Actividades comunicativas

ANSWERS

A-E Answers will vary.

Did You Know?

El nombre completo que los españoles dieron a Los Ángeles fue: El Pueblo de Nuestra Señora Reina de los Ángeles, probablemente porque llegaron al lugar el 1º de agosto de 1769, cuando los misioneros franciscanos celebraban la fiesta de Nuestra Señora de los Ángeles.

Actividades comunicativas

A **Posible empleo**   Una tienda de videos en Madrid necesita un dependiente. Ud. quiere el trabajo. Hable con el dueño/la dueña (tu compañero/a). Ud. quiere saber los días y horas de trabajo, el pago, etc.

B **No puede comer más.**   Ud. vive con la familia Serra. Es la hora de comer y la Sra. Serra quiere que Ud. coma más. Ud. se está poniendo muy gordo(a). Explique, cortésmente, el problema. ¡Buena suerte!

C **¿Trabaja Ud.?**   Su amigo español (su compañero/a) quiere saber si Ud. trabaja y qué tipo de trabajo hace. Contéstele y dígale en qué trabaja. Después cambien de rol.

D **Paco necesita dinero.**   Ud. es Paco. Necesita dinero para varios «caprichos». Pídale el dinero a uno de sus padres (su compañero/a) y explíquele para qué quiere el dinero.

E **Diferencias**   En la conversación Paco y Linda hablan de algunas diferencias entre la vida en Madrid y la vida en Los Ángeles o cualquier parte de los Estados Unidos. Trabaje con un(a) compañero(a) de clase. Den sus opiniones sobre las diferencias que discuten Pablo y Linda.

CONVERSACIÓN

setenta y uno **71**

Learning From Photos

The apartments shown are near **Argüelles.** They are on the **Paseo de Rosales** across from the **Parque del Oeste.** This is a very desirable residential neighborhood. The famous author Ramón Gómez de la Serna called the **Paseo de Rosales,** *"El mirador del mundo"*.

Independent Practice

Assign any of the following:
1. Exercises, pages 70–71
2. Workbook, *Conversación*

Lenguaje

TEACHING TIPS

A. Read the explanatory material to the class. Have the class repeat the expressions in unison.

B. Call on individuals to complete the incomplete statements. For example: **¿Te doy más...? ¿Te doy más ensalada?**

CULTURAL NOTE

Gestures The usual gesture to indicate refusal of food or drink is one or both hands up, palms out, in an "I surrender" gesture but with the hand(s) about chest high.

If food or drink is being refused in a public setting, such as saying "no" to a waiter who wants to pour more coffee or tea, a back and forth or wagging motion with the index finger facing outward is normal.

¿Te doy más pastel?

Gracias, pero no puedo más.

Ofreciendo comida

Cuando quiere ofrecerle algo a alguien, le puede preguntar:

> **¿Te doy más ___?**
> **¿Te sirvo ___?**
> **¿Te apetece ___?**
> **¿Te pongo ___?**
> **¿Quieres un poco de ___?**

Si le ofrecen algo, Ud. puede decir:

> **Por favor. Sí, me gusta el ___.**
> **Sí, me encanta la ___.**

Si Ud. quiere lo que le ofrecen, nunca diga «gracias», porque «gracias» quiere decir «no, gracias». Si no quiere lo que le ofrecen, diga:

> **Gracias, pero no puedo más.**
> **No, muchas gracias.**
> **¡Todo estuvo rico / bueno / excelente, pero ya no puedo, gracias!**

Paired Activity

After introducing the expressions, have pairs of students offer and accept **una limonada, una taza de té, un helado, un bocadillo.**

Then have pairs of students offer and decline **más sopa, otra chuleta, otro sándwich, más limonada, otro plato de fruta.**

Para invitar

Si Ud. va a invitar a alguien, diga:

> **¿Quieres ir a... conmigo/con nosotros?**

Si quiere indicar que Ud. va a pagar, diga:

> **Te invito a... esta noche. ¿Puedes acompañarme?**

Si Ud. es la persona invitada y quiere aceptar, diga:

> **Sí, con mucho gusto.**
> **Pues, sí, encantado(a).**

Si Ud. quisiera aceptar, pero no puede, diga:

> **Ay, no puedo esta noche, pero me gustaría acompañarte en otra ocasión.**
> **Esta noche no puedo, pero otra noche, sí.**

ABOUT THE SPANISH LANGUAGE

The verb **invitar** is a synonym of **convidar.** It carries a connotation of gift or offering. There is an old saying: **"El que invita, paga."** One would never **"invitar"** and expect the invitee to pay.

¿Quieres ir al café conmigo?

Sí, con mucho gusto.

Additional Practice

Have pairs of students extend and accept invitations **al cine, a un partido de fútbol, a un concierto, a cenar, a tomar un refresco, a una fiesta.**

Then have pairs of students extend and decline invitations **al teatro, a la zarzuela, a una exposición de arte, a la playa, a un café.**

Si Ud. no tiene interés en aceptar nunca, diga:

> **Lo siento, pero no puedo.**
> **Gracias, pero no puedo.**
> **Lo siento. Tengo otro compromiso.**

Si Ud. no está seguro(a) y quiere saber más, diga:

> **Me gustaría, pero de momento no sé si puedo. Te llamaré.**
> **Voy a mirar mi calendario, pero entretanto, dime más.**
> **Me interesa. ¡Cuéntame más!**

Actividades comunicativas

A **Pero abuela...** Preparen Uds. una conversación entre una abuela, que quiere que el/la nieto(a) coma un postre rico, y el/la nieto(a). La abuela le ofrece el postre. El/la nieto(a) acepta. La abuela insiste en que el/la nieto(a) coma aún más. El/la nieto(a) resiste.

B **Sí, claro que sí.** Ud. quiere salir con una persona muy interesante. Invítele a alguna actividad. Su compañero(a) es la persona, y acepta. Ahora cambien de papel. El/La compañero(a) le invita a Ud. a salir. Ud. quiere ir, pero no puede. Dígaselo. Finalmente, Ud. invita a su compañero(a) a salir. Él o ella no quiere salir nunca con Ud. Cambien de papel y repitan la conversación.

C **Una invitación** Lea estas reglas para escribir una invitación. El texto debe ser claro, sencillo y completo. Incluya lo siguiente: nombres, lugar, día y hora. Ahora, invite por escrito a un(a) amigo(a) a una fiesta en casa. Indique la ocasión que se celebra. Déle la invitación a un(a) compañero(a) de clase. Él o ella aceptará, o no, la invitación por escrito.

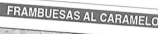

FRAMBUESAS AL CARAMELO

74

Repaso de estructura

Talking about habitual, recurring past actions
El imperfecto

1. The imperfect tense is, after the preterite, the most frequently used tense to express past actions. Review the forms of the imperfect. Note that the same endings are used for both **-er** and **-ir** verbs.

INFINITIVE	hablar	leer	escribir
yo	hablaba	leía	escribía
tú	hablabas	leías	escribías
él, ella, Ud.	hablaba	leía	escribía
nosotros(as)	hablábamos	leíamos	escribíamos
vosotros(as)	hablabais	leíais	escribíais
ellos, ellas, Uds.	hablaban	leían	escribían

2. Note that verbs that have a stem change in either the present or the preterite do not have a stem change in the imperfect.

INFINITIVE	querer	sentir	pedir
yo	quería	sentía	pedía
tú	querías	sentías	pedías
él, ella, Ud.	quería	sentía	pedía
nosotros(as)	queríamos	sentíamos	pedíamos
vosotros(as)	queríais	sentíais	pedíais
ellos, ellas, Uds.	querían	sentían	pedían

3. The following verbs are the only irregular verbs in the imperfect tense.

INFINITIVE	ir	ser	ver
yo	iba	era	veía
tú	ibas	eras	veías
él, ella, Ud.	iba	era	veía
nosotros(as)	íbamos	éramos	veíamos
vosotros(as)	ibais	erais	veíais
ellos, ellas, Uds.	iban	eran	veían

RESOURCES

- 📁 Workbook
- 📁 Student Tape Manual
- 🎧 Audio Cassette 3B/Compact Disc 2
- 💾 Computer Software: *Estructura*
- 📁 Chapter Quizzes
- 💾 Testing Program

Bell Ringer Review

Use the BRR Transparency 2-5, or write the following on the board:
Complete en el presente:
1. Yo ___ (querer) ir al cine.
2. Nosotros ___ (querer) ir al teatro.
3. Nosotros ___ (ir) a la escuela.
4. Yo ___ (ser) una persona bien educada.
5. Yo lo ___ (sentir) mucho.
6. Yo no ___ (conocer) a mucha gente aquí.

TEACHING STRUCTURE

◆ Talking about habitual, recurring past actions◆◆◆

A. *Steps 1, 2, and 3:* Have the students repeat the verb forms aloud. Permit them to read the explanatory material silently or omit it. Most students learn the forms by hearing, seeing, and using them.

B. It is recommended that you not give students English equivalents for the imperfect. "Used to" implies that it is not anymore.

C. *Steps 4 and 6:* Have the students read the explanation and the model sentences aloud. In step 6, you may wish to have the students read all the sentences together to form a descriptive narrative.

D. *Step 5:* Explain to the students that the important thing to keep in mind is continuity. The beginning and end times of the action are not important. Have students read the time expressions and the model sentences aloud.

ANSWERS

Práctica

A Some answers may vary.

1. Yo me levantaba a las... todos los días.
2. Sí, jugaba con mis amiguitos.
3. Nosotros jugábamos...
4. Nosotros tomábamos las vacaciones en el verano (en el invierno).
5. Nosotros íbamos a...
6. Durante las vacaciones comíamos...
7. Cuando era pequeño(a), prefería...
8. No sabía...
9. Sí, mis padres me leían.
10. Me acostaba a las...

---

4. The imperfect tense form of the impersonal expression **hay** is **había**.

> Había mucha gente en la fiesta.
> Había por lo menos doscientas personas.

5. The imperfect tense is used to express habitual or repeated actions in the past. When the event began or ended is not important. Several time expressions that typically accompany the imperfect are:

todos los domingos	siempre
los domingos	muchas veces
cada día	con frecuencia
todos los días	a menudo

> La profesora siempre hablaba español en clase.
> Los viernes, ella nos daba un examen.
> De vez en cuando, nosotros escribíamos en la pizarra.
> Y a menudo leíamos artículos en periódicos hispanos.

6. The imperfect is also used to describe persons, places, and things in the past.

> El general era alto, fuerte y muy valiente.
> Él luchaba (entraba en batalla) por la nación.
> Él tenía sólo cuarenta y seis años.
> Pero estaba muy cansado y triste.
> Quería volver a su casa y a su familia.
> Pero no podía porque la patria lo necesitaba.
> Era invierno. Hacía frío y nevaba.
> Era Nochevieja. Era la medianoche.
> Pronto iba a comenzar la batalla.

Una estatua de José de San Martín

Práctica

A HISTORIETA **(Cuando era pequeño(a)**

Contesten.

1. ¿A qué hora te levantabas todos los días?
2. ¿Jugabas con tus amiguitos?
3. ¿A qué jugaban Uds.?
4. Tú y tu familia, ¿cuándo tomaban Uds. sus vacaciones, en el verano o en el invierno?
5. ¿Adónde iban durante las vacaciones?
6. ¿Dónde comían durante las vacaciones?
7. ¿Qué preferías hacer cuando eras pequeño(a)?
8. ¿Qué no sabías hacer?
9. ¿Te leían tus padres?
10. ¿A qué hora te acostabas?

Niños españoles

Additional Practice

For more practice with the imperfect, bring in pictures of important historical figures such as San Martín, Bolívar, José Martí, Eva Perón, Cristóbal Colón, el Cid, Isabel la Católica. Ask students to describe them in detail using the imperfect tense.

Learning From Photos

You may wish to have students describe the scene in the lower photo.

B HISTORIETA La campesina

Completen con el imperfecto.

Rosaura Jiménez ___ (vivir) en un pueblo pequeño de Bolivia. Ella y sus padres ___
(trabajar) en los campos. Ellos ___ y ___ (sembrar, cosechar) maíz y papas. Cuando
Rosaura no ___ (tener) que trabajar, ___ (asistir) a la escuela. Aunque ella sólo ___
(poder) asistir de vez en cuando, ___ (recibir) buenas notas. Su maestra ___ (saber) que
Rosaura ___ (ser) inteligente y trabajadora. La maestra ___ (hacer) todo lo posible para
ayudar a la niña. ___ (Parecer) imposible pero Rosaura pudo ir a la universidad. Hoy es
maestra también. Ella recuerda siempre cómo ___ (ser) su vida cuando ___ (ir) a la
escuela. Rosaura es una maestra excelente. Ella dice: —Nosotros ___ (trabajar)
mucho pero ___ (saber) que un día todo ___ (ir) a ser
mejor. Y así es.

C HISTORIETA El soldado

Escriban el siguiente párrafo en el imperfecto, cambiando
yo en **mi abuelo.**

Yo me llamo Aníbal Valladares. Soy soldado. Lucho por la
independencia de la nación. Tengo veinte años y estoy cansado
de luchar. Quiero ver el final de la guerra. Siempre me siento
triste cuando veo tanta destrucción. Hace mucho tiempo que
no estoy contento. Las batallas son constantes. Nunca puedo
descansar. Creo que voy a morir en una batalla.

Soldados en Guadalajara, México

Talking about past events
El imperfecto y el pretérito

1. The choice of the preterite or imperfect depends upon whether the speaker is describing
an action completed in the past or a continuous, recurring action in the past. Use the
preterite to express actions or events that began and ended at a definite time in
the past.

> **Salí de casa a las seis y media el sábado pasado.**
> **Fui al cine, donde vi una película extranjera.**
> **Cuando la película terminó, fui a un restaurante y comí con unos amigos.**

2. Use the imperfect to express a continuous, repeated, or habitual action in the past. The
moment when the action began or ended is not important.

> **Yo salía de casa a las seis y media todos los sábados.**
> **Iba al cine, donde veía películas extranjeras.**
> **Cuando la película terminaba, iba a un restaurante y comía con unos amigos.**

REPASO DE ESTRUCTURA

Cooperative Learning

Trabajen en grupos pequeños. Un(a) estudiante será el/la secretario(a) del grupo. Díctenle un cuento de horror que Uds. crearán juntos. Un(a) alumno(a) empezará con algunas oraciones. Por ejemplo: *Era de noche. No había estrellas en el cielo. No se podía ver nada.*

Cada alumno(a) dará una oración hasta que tengan un cuento completo. Den algunas descripciones completas y misteriosas. Después, lean su cuento a la clase.

TEACHING TIPS

Have students write *Práctica C*. Call
on an individual to read the paragraph as the students correct their
own papers.

ANSWERS
Práctica
B **1. vivía**
  2. trabajaban
  3. sembraban
  4. cosechaban
  5. tenía
  6. asistía
  7. podía
  8. recibía
  9. sabía
  10. era
  11. hacía
  12. Parecía
  13. era
  14. iba
  15. trabajábamos
  16. sabíamos
  17. iba
C **Mi abuelo se llamaba Aníbal
  Valladares. Era soldado.
  Luchaba por la independencia
  de la nación. Tenía veinte años y
  estaba cansado de luchar.
  Quería ver el final de la guerra
  (batalla). Siempre se sentía
  triste cuando veía tanta
  destrucción. Hacía mucho
  tiempo que no estaba contento.
  Las batallas eran constantes.
  Nunca podía descansar. Creía
  que iba a morir en una batalla.**

TEACHING STRUCTURE

 **Talking about past
events**◆◆◆

Steps 1, 2, and 3: Have students read
the explanations and the model sentences aloud.

TEACHING TIPS

EXPANSION Have individual students tell the story in *Práctica A* or *B* in their own words.

ANSWERS
Práctica

A 1. fue   6. sabía
    2. quería   7. recordó
    3. llegó   8. era
    4. estaba   9. volvió
    5. había

B 1. Don Paco era minero.
    2. Trabajaba en las minas.
    3. Iba al trabajo seis días a la semana.
    4. Operaba máquinas.
    5. Leía y miraba la tele.
    6. Tuvo un accidente.
    7. Él se retiró.
    8. Le dieron una fiesta.
    9. Se sentían tristes.
   10. Les dijo adiós.

TEACHING STRUCTURE

 Expressing two past events in the same sentence◆◆◆

Have students read the explanatory material and sentences in steps 1, 2, and 3 aloud.

 GEOGRAPHY CONNECTION

You may wish to remind students: **Grandes áreas de Chile y la Argentina se encuentran al extremo sur, en regiones muy frías. Los glaciares y los *icebergs* son bastante comunes en esas regiones. ¿Entre qué latitudes se encuentran las regiones del sur de Chile y la Argentina?**

---

3. Use the imperfect with verbs such as **querer, saber, pensar, preferir, desear, sentir, poder,** and **creer** that describe a state of mind or a feeling.

    Él no podía ir.   **Lo sentía mucho.**   **Queríamos salir.**

⟡ Práctica ⟡

A  **El correo**

Completen.

Ayer mi hermana ___ (ir) al correo. Ella ___ (querer) comprar unos sellos. Cuando ella ___ (llegar) al correo, el correo ___ (estar) cerrado. No ___ (haber) nadie allí. Ella no ___ (saber) qué hacer. Por fin, ella ___ (recordar) que ___ (ser) día de fiesta y ___ (volver) a casa.

B **HISTORIETA El trabajo**

Contesten según se indica.

1. ¿Qué era don Paco? (minero)
2. ¿Dónde trabajaba don Paco? (en las minas)
3. ¿Cuántos días a la semana iba al trabajo? (seis)
4. ¿Qué hacía en el trabajo? (operar máquinas)
5. ¿Qué hacía después del trabajo? (leer y mirar la tele)
6. ¿Qué le pasó el año pasado? (tener un accidente)
7. ¿Qué hizo él entonces? (retirarse)
8. ¿Qué hicieron sus compañeros? (darle una fiesta)
9. ¿Cómo se sentían los compañeros? (tristes)
10. ¿Qué hizo don Paco después de la fiesta? (decirles adiós)

Expressing two past events in the same sentence
Dos acciones en la misma oración

1. Often a sentence in the past will have two verbs. Both may be in the same tense, or each one in a different tense. In the sentence below, both verbs are in the preterite because they express two simple actions or events that began and ended in the past.

    Rosa llegó y Martín salió.

2. In the sentence below, the two verbs are in the imperfect because both express continuous, repeated actions in the past.

    Todos los inviernos yo patinaba y mi hermana esquiaba.

Independent Practice

Assign any of the following:
1. Exercises, pages 76–79
2. Workbook, *Repaso de estructura*

3. In the following sentence, one verb is in the imperfect and the other is in the preterite. The verb in the imperfect, **hablaba,** describes what was going on. The verb in the preterite, **llamó,** expresses an action or event that intervened and interrupted what was going on.

> **Yo hablaba por teléfono cuando alguien llamó a la puerta.**

Práctica

A HISTORIETA Anoche

Completen.

1. Anoche yo ___ (trabajar) cuando ___ (sonar) el teléfono.
2. Yo ___ (levantarse) y ___ (ir) a contestar el teléfono.
3. Yo ___ (hablar) por teléfono cuando ___ (llegar) mi amigo Carlos.
4. Carlos ___ (sentarse) en la sala. Mientras yo ___ (hablar) por teléfono él ___ (leer) el periódico.
5. Cuando yo ___ (terminar) de hablar por teléfono, mi amigo y yo ___ (salir). ___ (ir) a un café.
6. En el café nosotros ___ (pedir) un refresco. Mientras nosotros ___ (hablar) y ___ (tomar) el refresco, ___ (entrar) otros amigos nuestros en el café.
7. Ellos ___ (sentarse) con nosotros y todos nosotros ___ (empezar) a hablar.

B HISTORIETA En la oficina

Combinen las dos oraciones y cambien el tiempo de los verbos al pasado.

1. La directora habla por teléfono. El secretario entra.
2. El secretario espera. La directora sigue hablando.
3. La directora termina. El secretario le habla.
4. El secretario le explica un problema. El teléfono suena otra vez.
5. La directora le dice al secretario que no puede atenderlo. El secretario se va.

C HISTORIETA ¿Qué pasaba cuando...?

Contesten.

1. ¿Miraba Juan la televisión cuando sonó el teléfono? ¿Contestó el teléfono?
2. ¿Leía su madre el periódico cuando Juan la llamó al teléfono? ¿Fue su madre al teléfono?
3. ¿Hablaba su madre por teléfono cuando Juan salió? ¿Fue Juan a un restaurante?
4. ¿Caminaba Juan al restaurante cuando vio a su amiga Lola? ¿Fueron juntos al restaurante?
5. En el restaurante, ¿hablaban Juan y Lola cuando llegaron dos amigos más?
6. ¿Hablaban los amigos cuando el mesero vino a la mesa?

CAPÍTULO 2
Repaso de estructura

TEACHING TIPS

Práctica A, B, and *C* You may assign these exercises as homework before going over them in class the next day.

ANSWERS
Práctica

A 1. trabajaba, sonó
2. me levanté, fui
3. hablaba, llegó
4. se sentó, hablaba, leía
5. terminé, salimos, Fuimos
6. pedimos, hablábamos, tomábamos, entraron
7. se sentaron, empezamos

B 1. hablaba, entró
2. esperaba, seguía
3. terminó, habló
4. explicaba, sonó
5. dijo, podía, se fue

C Answers will vary.
1. Sí, Juan miraba la televisión cuando sonó el teléfono. Sí, contestó el teléfono.
2. Sí, su madre leía el periódico cuando Juan la llamó al teléfono. Sí, ella fue al teléfono.
3. Sí, su madre hablaba por teléfono cuando Juan salió. Sí, Juan fue a un restaurante.
4. Sí, Juan caminaba al restaurante cuando vio a su amiga Lola. Sí, fueron juntos al restaurante.
5. Sí, Juan y Lola hablaban en el restaurante cuando llegaron dos amigos más.
6. Sí, los amigos hablaban cuando vino el mesero a la mesa.

Learning From Photos

You may wish to ask the students questions about the photo on page 79: **¿Dónde están estas personas? ¿Qué están haciendo? ¿Qué tiempo hace?**

Learning From Realia

In regard to the ad on page 79, you may wish to ask the following: **¿Para qué es el anuncio? ¿En qué ciudad está Florida Park? ¿Cerca de qué parque está? ¿Qué se puede hacer en Florida Park? ¿Cuántas líneas de teléfono tienen? ¿Por qué dan los números de teléfono?**

80

Bell Ringer Review

Use the BRR Transparency 2-6, or write the following on the board:

Paree la palabra con su definición.

1. las elecciones
2. el servicio militar
3. el adolescente
4. la cárcel
5. la demografía

a. el estudio de las poblaciones
b. la penitenciaría, donde ponen a los criminales
c. la condición de ser soldado
d. la oportunidad de votar por los candidatos
e. la persona de edad entre 13 y 17 años

TEACHING TIPS

Have students read the *Introducción* silently.

TEACHING VOCABULARY

A. To vary the procedure, you may wish to have students go over the vocabulary on their own without oral presentation in class. It is quite easy to get the meaning of these words. Have students study them and prepare the *Práctica* on page 81.

ABOUT THE SPANISH LANGUAGE

◆ Although **viejo** and **anciano** are often used interchangeably, there is a subtle difference between the two words. The Vulgar Latin **vetulus,** from which **viejo** is derived, actually meant "not very old." Today, **anciano** is usually reserved to describe the very old.

Introducción

Una de las rutinas más importantes en los países democráticos es la de votar en las elecciones. Los ciudadanos votan en elecciones municipales, estatales o provinciales y nacionales. En el pasado, tanto en España como en los Estados Unidos, la edad mínima para votar era de 21 años. Después la edad se rebajó a los 18 en los dos países. ¿Cuál debe ser la edad mínima para votar? Un joven de 17 años puede hacer el servicio militar. A los

dieciséis años, un criminal adolescente puede ir a una cárcel para adultos. En los EE.UU. hay 40.000 jóvenes menores de 16 años con licencia para manejar un automóvil, y en algunos estados jóvenes de 14, 13 y hasta 12 años de edad pueden contraer matrimonio, pero no pueden votar. El siguiente artículo de Bonifacio de la Cuadra apareció en el periódico español, *El País*.

Vocabulario

el bebé

el adulto

el joven, el niño

la persona mayor, el anciano

rebajar	bajar, reducir	**el discernimiento**	inteligencia, capacidad de distinguir
asegurar	afirmar, dar garantía	**el/la pensionista**	persona que recibe una pensión
suministrar	proveer, dar	**el envejecimiento**	proceso de ponerse viejo

las viejas

los viejos

los jubilados, la tercera edad

Práctica

A **Los viejos** Completen.

1. Ellos son viejos, todos son de la ___ edad.

2. La señora es ___, recibe una pensión del gobierno.

3. Don Andrés ya no trabaja. Él es ___. Se retiró hace muchos años.

4. Él se está poniendo viejo. Se le nota los efectos del ___.

B **¿Cómo se dice?** Expresen de otra manera.

1. Los medios de comunicación *proveen* mucha información.

2. Y nadie propone *reducir* la cantidad de información.

3. Dicen que con más información la gente mejora su *capacidad de distinguir*.

4. Pero nadie puede *afirmar* que es verdad.

C **Palabras afines** Pareen.

1. ejercer   **a.** audacious, bold

2. apto   **b.** decrepitude, senility

3. justificar   **c.** electorate, voters

4. la longevidad   **d.** to justify

5. el electorado   **e.** apt, capable

6. la decrepitud   **f.** to exercise, to use

7. audaz   **g.** longevity, long life

PERIODISMO

ochenta y uno

B. The next day, call on several students to read the new words and definitions aloud before going over the vocabulary exercises.

ANSWERS
Práctica

A 1. tercera

   2. pensionista

   3. jubilado

   4. envejecimiento

B 1. suministran

   2. rebajar

   3. discernimiento

   4. asegurar

C 1. f

   2. e

   3. d

   4. g

   5. c

   6. b

   7. a

ABOUT THE SPANISH LANGUAGE

◆ **Jubilado** refers to the person who, because of advanced age, retires from employment, usually with a pension. The verb is **jubilarse,** which also means "to rejoice", "to be jubilant." In Latin America "retirado" and "retirarse" are more commonly used to express "retired" and "to retire."

◆ **La tercera edad** is the Spanish equivalent of "senior citizens."

Independent Practice

Assign any of the following:

  1. Exercises, page 81

  2. Workbook, *Periodismo*

TEACHING THE READING

A. Have students read the article at home.

B. You may wish to divide the class into two groups, one in favor of and the other opposed to lowering the voting age, and have students from each group give their ideas on the issue.

C. Go over the *Comprensión* exercises on page 83.

¿Rebajar la edad para votar?

Bonifacio de la Cuadra

«Se me ocurre proponer que los niños voten» palabras de Blanca Vásquez, psicóloga.

¿Cuándo deben comenzar los ciudadanos a ejercer el derecho al voto? ¿Deben seguir votando a partir de los 18 años? ¿Y por qué no desde los 13, o los 15, o al menos desde los 16, edad legalmente apta aun—no se olvide—para ingresar en una cárcel de adultos?

¿Es hoy la frontera de los 18 años un límite sólido que justifique dejar fuera de la participación política esencial en una democracia a todos los menores de esa edad?

¿Existe algún estudio que nos asegure que el niño de 13, 14, 15 ó 16 años, habitante de la aldea[1] global y receptor diario de la abundancia de información suministrada[2] cada segundo, no tiene la capacidad para expresar su voto en igualdad de condiciones que un adulto?

Además de otras muchas razones en favor de rebajar la edad para votar hay razones demográficas. El aumento de la longevidad ha producido hoy el envejecimiento del electorado. En España existen dos millones de jubilados y pensionistas con derecho al voto, un legítimo lobby en defensa de sus intereses y que, sin duda, influye[3] en las políticas sociales de los gobiernos y de los partidos políticos.

Una inyección de votos juveniles, además de contribuir a equilibrar el peso político legítimo de la tercera edad, probablemente haría volver la cabeza de los políticos hacia problemas educativos, de desempleo juvenil y formación profesional que ahora se ven solamente desde la perspectiva de unos representantes elegidos por votantes mayores de 18 años.

Y no se diga que un ciudadano de 14, 15 ó 16 años no tiene capacidad hoy para elegir políticamente lo que más le interesa. Cuestionarse si algunos adolescentes tienen capacidad de discernimiento nos obligaría a reconsiderar el derecho al voto de algunos ancianos nonagenarios y nos acercaría a una no deseable «guerra generacional». Parece mucho más democrático aumentar por el lado juvenil el volumen de votantes.

No se asuste nadie tampoco porque se proponga extender a los adolescentes el derecho al voto. Mucho más audaces parecían las primeras mujeres que intentaron demandarlo.

[1] **aldea** *village*
[2] **suministrada** *supplied*
[3] **influye** *influences*

Critical Thinking Activity

Thinking skills: evaluating information
The text refers to the **aldea global.** You may wish to ask students to give their interpretation of the term "global village."

Additional Practice

After having gone over the reading you may wish to ask students the following additional questions:

¿Cuál es la edad mínima en España para ingresar en la cárcel?

¿Qué haría que los políticos se interesaran más en los problemas de los jóvenes?

Comprensión

A Los votantes Contesten.

1. ¿Qué es lo que se le ocurrió a la psicóloga Blanca Vásquez?
2. ¿Cuál es la pregunta a la que se dirige este artículo?
3. ¿A qué edad pueden votar hoy en España y en los EE.UU.?
4. ¿Qué factor ha producido el envejecimiento del electorado?
5. ¿Cuántos pensionistas y jubilados en España pueden votar?
6. ¿A quiénes pueden influir con su voto los pensionistas y jubilados?

B Detalles Indiquen donde dice:

1. que los votos de los jóvenes podrían proveer un balance a los votos de los viejos
2. cuáles son algunos de los problemas importantes para los jóvenes
3. cuál es el punto de vista de los representantes actuales
4. lo que hay que reconsiderar al cuestionar la capacidad de discernimiento de los jóvenes
5. el tipo de «guerra» que podría acercarse

C ¿Qué quiere decir? Expliquen.

1. ¿Es hoy la frontera de los 18 años un límite sólido que justifique dejar fuera de la participación política en una democracia a todos los menores de esa edad?
2. Parece mucho más democrático aumentar por el lado juvenil el volumen de votantes.
3. Mucho más audaces parecían las primeras mujeres que intentaron demandarlo.
4. la aldea global

Actividades comunicativas

A Un debate actual Con su grupo preparen un debate sobre el tema «rebajar la edad de votar, ¿sí o no?» Dividan el grupo en dos. Un grupo debe tomar la posición a favor de rebajar la edad del voto, el otro grupo la posición en contra. Preparen sus argumentos y presenten el debate ante la clase.

B Un poco de historia Fue en 1920 cuando las mujeres de los Estados Unidos por fin ganaron el derecho al voto. Algunas figuras importantes en esta lucha fueron: Elizabeth Cady Stanton, Susan B. Anthony, Lucretia Mott y Lucy Stone. En Francia las mujeres no podían votar hasta 1945, y todavía hay países donde las mujeres no pueden votar. Seleccione uno de los siguientes temas, busque la información y prepare un informe para dar a la clase:

▶ una líder en la lucha por el voto en los EE.UU.
▶ el derecho al voto hoy día para las mujeres en varios países del mundo

---

TEACHING TIPS

A. You may wish to have students prepare the answers to this exercise and then go over them orally in class.

B. Students can look up the information as they are reading silently.

ANSWERS
Comprensión

A 1. Proponer que los niños voten.
   2. ¿Rebajar la edad para votar?
   3. A los 18 años.
   4. El aumento de la longevidad.
   5. Dos millones.
   6. A los políticos.
B and **C** Answers will vary.

Actividades comunicativas

ANSWERS

A and **B** Answers will vary.

National Standards

Connections Students will reinforce and further their knowledge of history and civics by doing a research paper on women's suffrage.

Learning From Photos

The voters in the photo are receiving their ballots to be filled out. Students may be more familiar with voting booths and machines used in our elections. The United States is the only country that uses voting machines extensively. In Spain and Latin America voters use a paper ballot called a **papeleta.**

Independent Practice

Assign any of the following:
1. Exercises, page 83
2. Workbook, *Periodismo*

TEACHING TIPS

Have the students read the *Introducción* silently.

RESOURCES

- 🖌 Vocabulary Transparencies
- 🎧 Audio Cassette 3B/Compact Disc 2
- 📁 Student Tape Manual
- 📁 Workbook
- 📁 Chapter Quizzes
- 📁 Testing Program

TEACHING VOCABULARY

Present the new words and have students repeat them after you or Cassette 3B/Compact Disc 2, two or three times in unison.

El primer día de clases

Introducción

En Europa y en Norteamérica ocurre a fines de agosto o principios de septiembre. Al sur del ecuador, ocurre a principios de marzo. Es el comienzo del otoño, es el comienzo del año escolar. Es una rutina que se repite año tras año. Para algunos, tristemente, se repite durante muy pocos años. Para otros, puede repetirse hasta 15 ó 20 veces.

El siguiente artículo por Antonio de la Torre apareció en el periódico *ABC* de Sevilla, un jueves, 16 de septiembre, el día después del comienzo de curso. Se publicó durante una época de mucha discusión sobre leyes y proyectos en el campo de la educación española.

Vocabulario

el pozo

la cartera

el/la aprendiz(a) la persona que está aprendiendo un oficio, un(a) alumno(a)
el dineral una gran cantidad de dinero
la etapa una época o un avance en el desarrollo de una acción
hojear pasar las páginas de un libro

precisar necesitar

agridulce agrio y dulce al mismo tiempo
soñoliento(a) con sueño
ilusionado(a) con ilusiones

Did You Know?

En las escuelas españolas, tanto públicas como privadas, los alumnos tienen que comprar sus propios libros. El Ministerio de Educación aprueba los libros que se pueden usar y las escuelas escogen entre los libros aprobados. Se venden libros de texto en las librerías, obviamente, pero también en los supermercados y los quioscos de periódicos.

⊰Práctica⊱

A **¿Cuál es la palabra?** Contesten.

1. ¿En qué llevan los alumnos los libros y documentos?
2. Todavía no es carpintero, pero está aprendiendo. ¿Qué es?
3. Pasa las páginas del libro sin leerlo. ¿Qué hace?
4. Tiene un sabor *(taste)* que es una combinación de agrio y dulce. ¿Qué tipo de sabor tiene?
5. Cuesta millones. ¿Qué habrá que pagar para comprarlo?

B **La palabra** Completen.

1. Es un pueblo que parece dormir; allí no pasa nada nunca. Es un pueblecito ___.
2. Este proceso es bastante complicado. Tiene una variedad de ___ en su desarrollo.
3. Para hacerlo bien se ___ excelentes instrumentos y condiciones.
4. No debes estar muy ___ por los primeros resultados.
5. Guarda los papeles en tu ___ para que nadie los vea.

Un colegio en España

TEACHING TIPS

Práctica A can be done with books open or closed. *Práctica B* can be done with books open as a reading exercise.

ANSWERS
Práctica

A 1. **en una cartera**
   2. **aprendiz**
   3. **hojea**
   4. **agridulce**
   5. **un dineral**
B 1. **soñoliento**
   2. **etapas**
   3. **precisan**
   4. **ilusionado(a)**
   5. **cartera**

RECYCLING

Have pairs of students make up lists of everything they might carry in their **mochila.** The partners must guess what's in the **mochila.**

Learning From Photos

Have students describe the scene in the photo in as much detail as possible. You may wish to ask questions such as: **¿Dónde están los jóvenes? ¿Qué son ellos? ¿Qué ropa llevan? ¿Es una escuela mixta o no? ¿Qué edad, más o menos, tienen ellos?**

Independent Practice

Assign any of the following:
1. Exercises on page 85
2. Workbook, *Periodismo*

85

◈ **Al día: Carteras**
◆◆◆

🖌 Bell Ringer Review

Use the BRR Transparency 2-9, or write the following on the board:
Complete con la forma correcta del imperfecto o del pretérito.
1. Las carteras ___ (brillar) con sus vivos colores.
2. El artículo ___ (aparecer) en el periódico *ABC* un jueves en Sevilla.
3. Ella ___ (hojear) las páginas de la revista mientras que ___ (esperar) a su amigo.
4. Yo no ___ (poder) ir.
5. Anoche yo ___ (estudiar) cuando ___ (sonar) el teléfono.

TEACHING THE READING

You may have the students read this selection silently, aloud, or once each way, depending on the interests of the particular group. This passage is somewhat difficult because of the use of metaphors.

ABOUT THE SPANISH LANGUAGE

Metaphors and similes are frequent in journalistic prose. You may wish to provide the following definitions: **La metáfora es una figura retórica que consiste en cambiar el sentido exacto de una palabra a otro figurado en lugar de una comparación.**

El símil es una comparación expresa de una cosa con otra. Por ejemplo: "El amor es como una flor".

ABC DE SEVILLA

Jueves, 16 de septiembre

N.º 334

Al día
CARTERAS

Las carteras y las mochilas que ayer por la mañana se veían por las calles de Sevilla constituyen uno de los ingredientes más característicos de ese guiso[1] agridulce del primer día de clases que, ceremoniosamente, se repite cada año convirtiéndose en una rutinaria noticia. Pegados a ellas, soñolientos, apesadumbrados[2] e ilusionados al mismo tiempo, van esos aprendices de la vida de los que solemos decir que tienen el futuro en sus manos.

Ahora mismo, ellos no entienden de leyes ni de reformas ni de plazas[3] ni de profesorado. Su devenir[4] a lo largo de los próximos nueve meses va a girar en torno a esa cartera que ayer llevaban sobre sus espaldas y de esos libros nuevos que han costado un dineral y que un interés —más que un interés todavía ausente—les ha hecho hojear por encima durante estos últimos días de vacaciones veraniegas.

Compañeras inseparables de aventuras y desventuras, las carteras que ayer brillaban con sus vivos colores en el asfalto sevillano son algo más que un instrumento de transporte de libros y material escolar. En realidad constituyen el símbolo de una etapa de la vida del hombre que probablemente marcará y determinará el desarrollo de las posteriores. En esas carteras se irán guardando éxitos y fracasos, aciertos[5] y errores, inquietudes y letargos[6], desvelos[7] y añoranzas[8]. En esas carteras se está almacenando[9] un modelo de infancia que influirá decisivamente en lo que será la sociedad del mañana.

Ellos serán, en efecto, los protagonistas[10] del futuro. Pero que su destino sea feliz o aciago[11] depende tanto de sus propios esfuerzos como de los que hagamos quienes estamos protagonizando el presente. Tenemos que ayudarles a llenar las carteras de todas esas cosas que precisan para que, cuando llegue el momento, el bagaje[12] que están atesorando[13] en esta etapa crucial e irrepetible no se diluya[14] en el pozo de la frustración.

[1] **guiso** comida, plato
[2] **apesadumbrados** deprimidos
[3] **plazas** puestos, empleos, cargos
[4] **devenir** futuro
[5] **aciertos** éxitos, logros
[6] **letargos** faltas de energía
[7] **desvelos** preocupaciones, insomnio
[8] **añoranzas** nostalgia
[9] **almacenando** guardando, acumulando
[10] **protagonistas** actores principales
[11] **aciago** desgraciado, infeliz
[12] **bagaje** equipaje, impedimenta
[13] **atesorando** guardando
[14] **diluya** desvanezca, pierda

Additional Practice

Have students indicate the main idea and prepare a simple **précis** of the article.

Learning From Photos

Have the students describe the young people in the photo. You may wish to ask: **¿Qué serán estos jóvenes? ¿Se visten iguales, los varones y la muchacha? ¿Por qué? ¿Qué son ellos y dónde están? ¿Cree Ud. que están en una región tropical o no? ¿Por qué?**

❧ Comprensión ❧

A **Las preguntas** Contesten.
1. ¿Qué día comenzaron las clases?
2. ¿De qué ciudad trata el artículo?
3. ¿Quiénes son los «aprendices de la vida»?
4. ¿Qué precio han tenido los textos?
5. ¿Qué han hojeado los chicos durante los últimos días de vacaciones?
6. ¿Cuál es la duración del año escolar en España? ¿Dónde lo dice el autor?

B **Las frases** ¿Qué querrá decir... ?
1. «esos aprendices de la vida de los que solemos decir que tienen el futuro en sus manos»
2. «vacaciones veraniegas»
3. «En esas carteras se irán guardando éxitos y fracasos, aciertos y errores, inquietudes y letargos, desvelos y añoranzas».

C **Los comentarios** Comenten.
1. El autor habla de los «protagonistas del futuro» y de los que «estamos protagonizando el presente». ¿De quiénes habla y qué dice de los dos grupos?
2. El autor alude a las discusiones políticas sobre la educación. ¿Dónde hace esta alusión?
3. Según el autor, ¿de qué depende el futuro de los jóvenes?
4. Al final del artículo, el autor escribe de la cartera en forma simbólica. Explique lo que el autor quiere decir en la última frase del artículo.

❧ Actividades comunicativas ❧

A **¿Sabes por qué... ?** Explique por qué las clases en Chile o en la Argentina comienzan en marzo y no en septiembre.

B **Temas y debates** Trabajando en grupo, preparen un debate sobre el siguiente tema: «¿Deben los políticos influir en la educación o no, y por qué?» Un grupo debe presentar argumentos a favor y el otro, en contra.

VOCABULARY EXPANSION

The article talks about **las vacaciones veraniegas.** You may wish to provide students with the other adjectives for the seasons: **primaveral, invernal, otoñal.** You might ask students: **¿En qué meses podríamos tener vacaciones primaverales, vacaciones invernales y vacaciones otoñales?**

TEACHING TIPS

Have students complete the *Comprensión* exercises as they are reading the selection. It is recommended that you allow them to look up the answers as they read rather than use the exercises for factual recall.

ANSWERS
Comprensión

A 1. **el quince de septiembre**
2. **Sevilla**
3. **Los estudiantes**
4. **Los textos cuestan un dineral.**
5. **Han hojeado sus libros nuevos.**
6. **Dura de septiembre a junio. El autor habla de las vacaciones veraniegas.**

B and **C** Answers will vary.

INFORMAL ASSESSMENT

After going over the exercises once, you may want to do them again very quickly just to see how much of the factual information the students recall.

TEACHING TIPS

B You may wish to have volunteer groups perform the actual debate in class with the remainder of the class acting as judges.

Actividades comunicativas

ANSWERS
A and **B** Answers will vary.

87

Paired Activity

Have pairs of students create original conversations between the young people in the **librería.** Some questions might be: **¿Qué estás leyendo? ¿Estás buscando libros de texto? ¿Venden los libros a buen precio aquí?** You may also have students tell what books they would buy in a bookstore and why.

Independent Practice

Assign any of the following:
1. Exercises, page 87
2. Workbook, *Periodismo*

Estructura

🔔 Bell Ringer Review

Use the BRR Transparency 2-10, or write the following on the board:
Escriba todo lo que Ud. quiere hacer esta semana.

TEACHING STRUCTURE

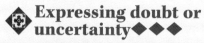

◆ Expressing doubt or uncertainty ◆◆◆

Steps 1, 2, and 3: Have the students read the explanation and the model sentences aloud.

  Step 4: Have the students repeat the expressions for the subjunctive and indicative after you.

Expressing doubt or uncertainty
Subjuntivo con expresiones de duda

1. The subjunctive is used after any expression that implies doubt or uncertainty, since it is not known if the action in the dependent clause will take place.

> **Yo dudo que ellos lleguen a tiempo.**
> **No creo que ellos vengan en avión.**

2. If the statement implies certainty rather than doubt, the indicative is used in the dependent clause, not the subjunctive. The future tense is often used in a clause that follows an expression of certainty. Although it might seem logical to use the subjunctive, the emphasis is on the certainty of the event taking place. For this reason the indicative is used.

> **Yo creo que ellos vendrán mañana.**
> **Estoy seguro de que ellos vendrán en avión.**

3. In a question containing an expression of doubt, the speaker chooses between the use of the subjunctive or the indicative, depending upon the meaning he or she wishes to convey. Observe and analyze the following questions.

> **¿Crees que ellos vengan mañana?**

In this question, the speaker uses the subjunctive, not the indicative, to ask if you think they will come tomorrow. The speaker's choice of the subjunctive indicates that he or she does not think they will come tomorrow. The speaker indicates his / her own doubt or uncertainty by using the subjunctive.

> **¿Crees que ellos vendrán mañana?**

The speaker repeats the question. This time, however, he or she uses the indicative, not the subjunctive. The use of the indicative indicates the speaker's certainty that they will come tomorrow.

4. Here is a list of typical expressions of doubt and certainty.

SUBJUNCTIVE	INDICATIVE
dudar	no dudar
es dudoso	no es dudoso (no hay duda)
no estar seguro	estar seguro
no creer	creer
no es cierto	es cierto

Advanced Game

1. Before class, prepare a list of situations that end with a verb or phrase requiring the subjunctive. For example: **La clase comenzó hace diez minutos. El profesor no está. Es necesario que...**, or **Siempre llegas tarde. Yo quiero que...**

2. Divide the class into two or three teams with the leader from each team at the front of the class.

3. Read the situations to the class. Students must write down an appropriate ending to the sentence within a certain time limit.

4. Each student on the team then reads his/her answer to the class, ending with the leader. The team gets a point for each answer that is identical or similar to the leader's answer.

Hint: The team can switch leaders at any time to give all students the chance to be up front.

⊹Práctica⊹

A **¿Lo crees o lo dudas?** Sigan el modelo.

Elena cree que ellos vienen pronto.
Pero yo dudo que vengan pronto.

1. Elena cree que ellos vienen pronto.
2. Ella cree que llegarán hoy.
3. Ella cree que conocen el camino.
4. Ella cree que traerán buenas noticias.
5. Ella cree que todos estaremos contentos.

B **¿Cree que sí, o lo duda?** Escojan.

1. Pedro: «¿Crees que ellos irán a Chile?»
   a. Pedro cree que ellos van a ir a Chile.
   b. Pedro duda que ellos vayan a Chile.
2. Carolina: «¿Crees que ellos tengan bastante dinero para el viaje?»
   a. Carolina cree que ellos tienen el dinero.
   b. Carolina duda que ellos tengan el dinero.
3. Pedro: «¿Crees que sus padres les den el dinero?»
   a. Pedro cree que sus padres les darán el dinero.
   b. Pedro duda que sus padres les den el dinero.
4. Carolina: «¿Crees que ellos puedan trabajar en Chile?»
   a. Carolina cree que ellos podrán trabajar.
   b. Carolina duda que ellos consigan trabajo.

Giving advice and making suggestions
Subjuntivo con verbos especiales

1. A number of verbs state or imply a command, an order, advice, or a suggestion. These verbs are followed by the subjunctive because, even though we ask, tell, advise, or suggest that someone do something, it is not certain that the person will actually do it.

Some frequently used verbs that state or imply a command, an order, advice, or a suggestion are:

decir	*to tell*	**rogar**	*to beg, plead*	**aconsejar**	*to advise*
escribir	*to write*	**mandar**	*to order*	**recomendar**	*to recommend*
pedir	*to ask, request*	**exigir**	*to demand, require*	**sugerir**	*to suggest*

TEACHING TIPS

It is suggested that you go over these exercises orally in class. They can then also be assigned for homework.

ANSWERS
Práctica
A Pero yo dudo que...
1. ellos **vengan** pronto.
2. **lleguen** hoy.
3. **conozcan** el camino.
4. **traigan** buenas noticias.
5. todos **estemos** contentos.

B 1. a
    2. b
    3. b
    4. b

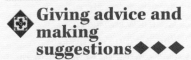

ABOUT THE SPANISH LANGUAGE

Have students look at the photo and provide as many names for luggage as they can. This list might be helpful: **el equipaje, la maleta, el baúl, el maletín, la valija, el veliz, el bolso.**

TEACHING STRUCTURE

◆ **Giving advice and making suggestions**◆◆◆

A. Have the students read the explanation in step 1 aloud and repeat the list of verbs in unison after you.

Advanced Game

1. Before class, prepare two sets of cards, one with verbs and expressions from Chapters 1 and 2 that take the subjunctive and the other with verbs featured in the grammar presentation on page 88. For example:

EXPRESIONES/VERBOS   OTROS VERBOS
es posible que   **creer**
es dudoso que   **estar seguro**
es necesario que   **es cierto**

2. Give the students several cards from each pile. Have them work together in teams to make as many sentences as possible illustrating either the use of the subjunctive or the indicative. They can write on butcher paper and have other teams check their work or they can turn the work in for a grade.
Hint: Use a timer to keep students focused on their work.

B. Have the students repeat the model sentences in step 2 aloud. You may want to have them explain why the subjunctive is used.

C. Have the students read the explanatory material in step 3 silently. You may then wish to write the model sentences on the board and ask volunteers to explain the differences. Perhaps the more able students might make up original sentences to illustrate this point.

TEACHING TIPS

You may wish to assign *Práctica A, B,* and *C* for homework and go over them the next day to ensure that the students have a proper understanding of this concept.

ANSWERS
Práctica
A Mi hermano me exige que...
1. **no salga de noche.**
2. **traiga mis libros a casa.**
3. **no mire mucha televisión.**
4. **duerma bastante.**
5. **me levante temprano.**
B Él nos pide que...
1. **no salgamos sin él.**
2. **vayamos en metro.**
3. **compremos los boletos.**
4. **nos sentemos en la primera fila.**
C Le escribe que...
1. **trate bien a su hermanita.**
2. **coma bastante.**
3. **se acueste temprano.**
4. **tenga buenos modales.**
5. **la vaya a visitar.**

90

---

2. Observe and analyze the following sentences.

> *Le* digo que venga.
> *Les* ruego que lleguen temprano.
> *Les* aconsejo que salgan antes de las ocho a causa del tráfico.
> Anita *me* pide que (yo) la ayude.
> *Te* ruego que la ayudes también.
> La directora exige que *le* demos ayuda.

These verbs often take an indirect object pronoun in the main clause.

3. Note that the subjunctive follows the verbs **decir** and **escribir** only when they imply a command. If someone simply is giving information, the subjunctive is not used. Observe the following sentences.

Ella me dice que viene mañana.	*She tells me that she's coming tomorrow.*
Ella me dice que venga mañana.	*She tells me to come tomorrow.*

Práctica

A **Lo que mi hermano mayor (me) exige**
Sigan el modelo.

> **¿Qué te exige tu hermano? (estudiar más)**
> **Mi hermano me exige que estudie más.**

1. no salir de noche
2. traer mis libros a casa
3. no mirar mucha televisión
4. dormir bastante
5. levantarme temprano

B **¿Qué pide?**   Sigan el modelo

> **¿Qué les pide Pedro? (esperar)**
> **Él nos pide que esperemos.**

1. no salir sin él
2. ir en metro
3. comprar los boletos
4. sentarnos en la primera fila

C **Le escribe su abuela**.   Sigan el modelo.

> **¿Qué le escribe su abuela? (ser bueno)**
> **Le escribe que sea bueno.**

1. tratar bien a su hermanita
2. comer bastante
3. acostarse temprano
4. tener buenos modales
5. ir a visitarla

Critical Thinking Activity

Thinking skills: supporting arguments with reasons **En muchos países los jóvenes caminan o toman el transporte público para ir a la escuela. En los EE.UU. es común que haya buses escolares o que los alumnos vayan a la escuela en auto privado. ¿Cuáles son las ventajas y desventajas de ir a la escuela en el bus escolar?**

Independent Practice

Assign any of the following:
1. Exercises, pages 89–90
2. Workbook, *Estructura*

Expressing emotions
Subjuntivo con expresiones de emoción

1. The subjunctive is also used in a clause that modifies a verb or expression conveying any kind of emotion. Some verbs or expressions of emotion are:

alegrarse de	*to be happy about*	gustar	*to like*
estar contento(a)	*to be glad*	es una lástima	*it's a pity*
estar triste	*to be sad*	temer	*to fear*
sorprender	*to surprise*	tener miedo de	*to be afraid*

2. Unlike the other expressions that take the subjunctive, the information in a clause following a verb or expression of emotion can be factual. If the information in the clause is real, why is the subjunctive used? Observe and analyze the following sentences.

> **Me alegro de que Teresa esté con nosotros.**
> **¿Estás contento de que Teresa esté aquí?**
> **Creo que es una lástima que esté con nosotros.**

3. In the sentences above, Teresa's presence is a fact, but the subjunctive is used because the clause is introduced by an expression of feeling. As illustrated by the examples, feelings can be positive or negative and vary from person to person.

Práctica

A HISTORIETA ¿Cómo te sientes?

Sigan el modelo.

> **Ganamos el partido. (Me alegro)**
> **Me alegro de que ganemos el partido.**

1. Paco viene con nosotros. (Me sorprende)
2. Nadie quiere estar con él. (Siento)
3. Paco se porta mejor ahora. (Me alegro de)
4. Marta lo invita a la fiesta. (Estoy contento[a])
5. Paco se va el jueves. (Es una lástima)
6. Pero Roberto vuelve hoy. (Me gusta)

B ¿Qué emoción sientes? Contesten con frases completas.

1. La economía está mucho mejor.
2. Muchas personas no tienen hogar.
3. Los atletas profesionales ganan millones de dólares.
4. Algunos niños pasan mucha hambre.
5. Quieren reducir las vacaciones.
6. Piensan dar más exámenes.
7. Te dan 20.000 dólares.

ESTRUCTURA

Paired Activity

Have pairs of students create at least three original sentences that might be spoken by the young man in the photos on this page.

Independent Practice

Assign any of the following:
1. Exercises, page 91
2. Workbook, *Estructura*

TEACHING STRUCTURE

◆ Expressing emotions ◆ ◆

A. Guide students through the explanations in Steps 1 and 2.

B. Have students repeat after you the verbs and expressions in Step 1.

C. You may wish to give additional model sentences patterned after those in Step 2, as this concept may be more difficult for the average student to assimilate.

TEACHING TIPS

You may wish to give students time in class to work on *Práctica B* before going over it in class.

ANSWERS
Práctica

A 1. **Me sorprende que Paco venga con nosotros.**
2. **Siento que nadie quiera estar con él.**
3. **Me alegro de que Paco se porte mejor ahora.**
4. **Estoy contento(a) que Marta lo invite a la fiesta.**
5. **Es una lástima que Paco se vaya el jueves.**
6. **Me gusta que Roberto vuelva hoy.**

B 1. **me alegro de que, estoy contento(a)/esté**
2. **estoy triste, es una lástima/tengan**
3. **estoy contento(a), me alegro de que, me sorprende/ganen**
4. **es una lástima, estoy triste/pasen**
5. **temo, tengo miedo de que, estoy triste, es una lástima/quieran**
6. **temo, tengo miedo de que, estoy triste, es una lástima/piensen**
7. **estoy contento(a), me alegro de que, me sorprende/den**

91

TEACHING TIPS

Have students do the pre-reading activity.

RESOURCES

- Vocabulary Transparencies
- Audio Cassette 4A/Compact Disc 3
- Student Tape Manual
- Workbook
- Chapter Quizzes
- Testing Program

TEACHING VOCABULARY

As you show the Vocabulary Transparency, have students repeat the new words and expressions after you or Cassette 4A/Compact Disc 3.

ABOUT THE SPANISH LANGUAGE

You may wish to remind students that **-illo(a)** is another diminutive ending like **-ito(a).** You might want to mention the more regional diminutive endings such as **-iño(a)** (Galicia) and **-ico(a)** (Aragón and Navarra).

The **hoja de afeitar** goes in the **navaja** or "safety razor." **Navaja** is also a straight razor or a folding knife.

Another word for coffin, less elegant though more descriptive, is **caja de muertos.**

Bigote singular and **bigotes** plural are both used.

Bencina is the word for gasoline in Chile. In most other areas the word is **gasolina.**

Literatura
Sueños
de Nicanor Parra

Antes de leer

Cuando pensamos en la poesía, muchos pensamos en algo sublime, florido y grandilocuente. Los temas son heroicos, románticos, trágicos. Pero no tiene que ser así. También hay poemas que tratan de lo cotidiano, de lo sencillo. Sin embargo, las cosas no son siempre lo que parecen.

Vocabulario

los pajarillos voladores

el aviso luminoso

la bomba de bencina

la cruz

los anteojos

los bigotes

la hoja de afeitar

el ataúd

darle cuerda a una victrola

el cadáver   el cuerpo de un muerto
el lujo   la opulencia, la riqueza
el pejerrey   un tipo de pescado muy sabroso

atravesar   cruzar, ir de un lado al otro
arrastrar   tirar, halar (jalar), llevar por el suelo

Additional Practice

Darle cuerda is "to wind up." You may wish to say to the students: **Se le da cuerda a la antigua victrola. También se le da cuerda al reloj si no es electrónico. ¿A qué otras cosas se le da cuerda?**

Literary Analysis

Have students explain in their own words the meaning of the following words in the *Antes de leer* section: **sublime, florido, grandilocuente, heroico, romántico, trágico.**

⊱Práctica⊰

A. Sinónimos Escojan.

1. la bencina
2. los anteojos
3. el ataúd

a. la caja de muertos
b. las gafas/los lentes
c. la gasolina

B. ¿Cúal es la palabra? Completen.

1. Hay un excelente restaurante al otro lado; hay que ___ el puente para llegar allí.
2. Desde aquí puedes ver el ___ luminoso.
3. ¡Camina, hombre! No debes ___ los pies. ¡Corre!

C. ¿Qué es? Identifiquen.

1. el cuerpo de un muerto
2. el pelo sobre el labio superior
3. la riqueza, la opulencia
4. lo que se pone para ver mejor
5. el nombre de un pescado

TEACHING TIPS

A. Have students prepare the *Práctica* at home and then go over them in class.

B. Call on individual students to read their responses. To save time, each student should do two or three items before the next student is called on.

ANSWERS
Práctica

A 1. c
   2. b
   3. a

B 1. atravesar
   2. aviso
   3. arrastrar

C 1. el cadáver
   2. el bigote (los bigotes)
   3. el lujo
   4. los anteojos
   5. el pejerrey

Learning From Photos

"La Flor y Nata" is a play on words in the neon sign. **Nata** is the word for "cream." But the expression **"flor y nata"** means "the very best of its kind." You may wish to ask the students what kind of shop it is, and why they chose a name that means **"lo más selecto de su especie."**

Independent Practice

Assign any of the following:
1. Exercises, page 93
2. Workbook, *Literatura*

93

TEACHING TIPS

Read the *Introducción* to the class or paraphrase it.

TEACHING THE READING

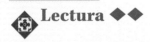 **Lectura** ◆◆

A. Have students read the *Comprensión* exercises on page 95 so they can look for the information as they read the poem.
B. Read the poem once aloud to the class or have the students listen to Cassette 4A/Compact Disc 3.
C. Call on a student to read aloud.
D. With more able groups, you may wish to ask the analytical questions in LITERARY ANALYSIS at the bottom of this page.

 LITERATURE CONNECTION

El mismo Nicanor Parra ha dicho que un antipoema «a la postre, no es otra cosa que el poema tradicional enriquecido con la savia surrealista—surrealismo criollo o como queráis llamarlo». El surrealismo se define como «movimiento literario y artístico que intenta sobrepasar lo real impulsando con automatismo psíquico lo imaginario o irracional».

Dos importantes poetas que colaboraron en el movimiento son el español Federico García Lorca y el chileno Pablo Neruda. En la pintura, los españoles Pablo Picasso y Salvador Dalí fueron grandes exponentes del surrealismo.

Introducción

Nicanor Parra, chileno, nació en Chillán, una ciudad en la región de Bío Bío en el valle central de su país, en 1914. Su primer libro de poemas fue publicado en 1937. Nicanor Parra era ingeniero. Estudió en la Universidad de Brown en los EE.UU. y llegó a ser director de la Escuela de Ingeniería de la Universidad de Chile. En 1966 fue profesor en la Universidad de Louisiana en los EE.UU.

Nicanor Parra

Lectura

Sueños

Sueño con una mesa y una silla
Sueño que me doy vuelta en automóvil
Sueño que estoy filmando una película
Sueño con una bomba de bencina
Sueño que soy un turista de lujo
Sueño que estoy colgando de una cruz
Sueño que estoy comiendo pejerreyes
Sueño que voy atravesando un puente
Sueño con un aviso luminoso
Sueño con una dama de bigotes
Sueño que voy bajando una escalera
Sueño que le doy cuerda a una victrola
Sueño que se me rompen los anteojos
Sueño que estoy haciendo un ataúd
Sueño con el sistema planetario
Sueño que estoy luchando con un perro
Sueño que estoy matando una serpiente.

Sueño con pajarillos voladores
Sueño que voy arrastrando un cadáver
Sueño que me condenan a la horca°
Sueño con el diluvio° universal
Sueño que soy una mata de cardo°.

Sueño también que se me cae el pelo.

la horca *the gallows*
el diluvio *una gran lluvia como en la Biblia*
una mata de cardo *a thistle bush*

Literary Analysis

En otra versión del poema la última frase dice: «Sueño también que se me caen los dientes».

¿Qué tienen en común las dos frases? ¿Por qué será que el poeta decidió terminar el poema con esas frases?

National Standards

Cultures
Students experience, discuss, and analyze an expressive product of the culture: the poem «Sueños» by the Chilean poet Nicanor Parra.

Después de leer

Comprensión

A **Sueño que...** Contesten.

1. Cada vez que el poeta dice «sueño que», se refiere a algo que él hace o algo que le está pasando. Dé Ud. los ejemplos que pueda del poema.
2. Cuando el poeta dice «sueño con», se refiere a otras cosas o criaturas que no son él. Dé Ud. algunos ejemplos.

B **Las clasificaciones** Clasifiquen.

1. ¿Cuáles de los sueños tratan de cosas rutinarias?
2. ¿Cuáles son fantásticos?
3. ¿Cuáles se refieren a la muerte?

C **Antipoemas** Piensen.

Este poema aparece en un libro con el título *Poemas y Antipoemas*. ¿Por qué llevará el libro ese título? ¿Qué querrá decir el autor? Comenten.

Actividades comunicativas

A **Tres poetas** De Chile han venido tres importantes poetas del siglo XX: Nicanor Parra, Pablo Neruda y Gabriela Mistral. Preparen biografías breves de estos tres poetas.

B **Un antipoeta** Nicanor Parra describe un «antipoeta» de esta manera:

¿Qué es un antipoeta?
¿Un comerciante en urnas y ataúdes?
¿Un general que duda de sí mismo?
¿Un sacerdote que no cree en nada?
¿Un bailarín al borde del abismo?
¿Un poeta que duerme en una silla?

Comenten. ¿Cuál de las descripciones es la más válida? ¿Cómo describen Uds. a un «antipoeta»?

C **Todos soñamos.** Los sueños pueden ser realistas o absurdos. Escriba Ud. un poema basado en sus propios sueños. No se preocupe de la rima. Puede usar *Sueños* como modelo.

Pablo Neruda

Gabriela Mistral

Independent Practice

Assign any of the following:
1. Exercises, page 95
2. Workbook, *Literatura*

Did You Know?

Chile, a pesar de ser un país de escasa población (menos de 15 millones), ha producido muchas importantes figuras literarias, entre ellas los poetas Pablo Neruda y Gabriela Mistral, y los novelistas contemporáneos José Donoso e Isabel Allende.

ANSWERS
Comprensión

A 1. Answers will vary.
me doy una vuelta en automóvil
soy un turista de lujo
le doy cuerda a una victrola
voy bajando una escalera
se me rompen los anteojos

2. una mesa y una silla
una bomba de bencina
pajarillos voladores
el diluvio universal

B 1. una mesa y una silla
bomba de bencina
vuelta en automóvil
comer pejerreyes
atravesar un puente
aviso luminoso
bajar una escalera
dar cuerda a una victrola
rompérsele los anteojos
caérsele el pelo
pajarillos voladores

2. filmar una película
ser turista de lujo
colgar de una cruz
una dama de bigotes
el sistema planetario
luchar con un perro
matar una serpiente
condenarse a la horca
el diluvio universal
ser una mata de cardo

3. hacer un ataúd
colgar de una cruz
arrastar un cadáver
condenarse a la horca

C Answers will vary.

Actividades comunicativas

ANSWERS
A–C Answers will vary.

95

RESOURCES

- 🔊 Vocabulary Transparencies
- 🎧 Audio Cassette 4B/Compact Disc 3
- 📁 Student Tape Manual
- 📁 Workbook
- 📁 Chapter Quizzes
- 💾 Testing Program

TEACHING THE READING

A. You may wish to have students read the *Antes de leer* section aloud.

B. Ask the following questions: **¿Cuál es la primera costumbre que se menciona? ¿En qué clase de familias era costumbre? ¿Cuál es la segunda costumbre? ¿Cuál era, muchas veces, el resultado de estas costumbres? ¿A qué se refería la expresión «quedarse para vestir santos»?**

TEACHING VOCABULARY

A. Have students repeat the new words several times after you or the cassette.

B. Have students study the new words and prepare the *Práctica* on page 97.

C. The next day call on several students to read the new words and definitions aloud before going over the vocabulary exercises.

VOCABULARY EXPANSION

Caldo is a broth or stock made from chicken or beef, etc. **Sopa** originally had to include bread. Until recently, field workers in Andalucía ate a **sopa** or **gazpacho** consisting simply of olive oil, vinegar, water, and bread.

96

Como agua para chocolate
de Laura Esquivel

Antes de leer

Una costumbre de las familias mexicanas de clase alta era la de obligar a la hija menor a nunca casarse, a permanecer soltera y a cuidar de la madre hasta la muerte de ésta. También era costumbre en muchos lugares no permitir casarse una hija menor antes de que se casara la mayor. El dolor y la angustia que resultaban de estas costumbres son materia de leyenda en muchas familias. Todo el mundo le tenía pena a la hija que «se quedaba para vestir santos», cruel expresión que nos da una imagen de la vieja solterona que pasa sus días decorando las estatuas de los santos en la iglesia.

Vocabulario

colar

rociar

un caldo
una gota

vaciar

la miel
una cucharada

azucarar   cristalizarse   **empanizar**   tomar forma
destrozar   arruinar

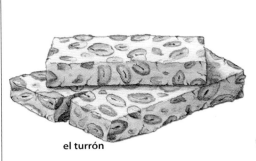

el turrón

batir

ajeno   de otra persona
de golpe   de repente, sin anuncio o preparación
flojo   no muy sólido, no firme

el carmín   ingrediente para dar color rojo a la comida
clara   parte blanca del huevo, contrario de yema

A | **La receta**   Completen.

1. El pastel no está muy firme, al contrario, está muy ___.
2. Y es de color ___ un rojo muy brillante.
3. No usamos azúcar. Le echamos ___ para hacerlo dulce.
4. Y vamos a echar poquísimo jugo de limón, sólo dos o tres ___.
5. Es necesario ___ el caldo para que no quede mucha grasa.
6. Para hacer merengue el cocinero tiene que ___ los huevos y para hacer nata es necesario ___ la crema.
7. Esta receta lleva sólo ___ de los huevos, no las yemas.
8. No debemos arruinar o ___ la propiedad ___; es decir la propiedad de otros.

B | **En la cocina**   Pareen.

1. la espátula   **a.** texture
2. la textura   **b.** to reveal
3. alterar   **c.** spatula
4. revelar   **d.** to dissolve
5. disolver   **e.** to alter

TEACHING TIPS

These exercises are not difficult and can be done orally in class.

ANSWERS
Práctica
A 1. flojo
  2. carmín
  3. miel
  4. gotas
  5. colar
  6. batir, batir
  7. las claras
  8. destrozar, ajena
B 1. c
  2. a
  3. e
  4. b
  5. d

VOCABULARY EXPANSION

Turrón usually refers to the almond nougat candy «bricks» that are a typical Christmas treat in Spain and Latin America. In this story, however, the **turrón** is the frosting or the icing on the wedding cake being prepared by Nacha.

National Standards

Culture   The custom of having the youngest daughter of a well-to-do Mexican family dedicate her life to caring for her mother is a foreign concept to most American students. This is a good opportunity to discuss ways in which elderly relatives are cared for in the United States and in other cultures with which the students may be familiar.

Independent Practice

Assign any of the following:
1. Exercises, page 97
2. Workbook, *Literatura*

TEACHING THE READING

A. You may wish to have students read the *Introducción* aloud.
B. Ask the following questions:
¿Cuántas novelas escribió la autora antes de *Como agua para chocolate*? ¿Cuándo se publicó la novela? ¿A cuántos idiomas fue traducida? ¿Quién es Tita? ¿Dónde se encontraba el rancho? ¿En qué época histórica ocurre gran parte de la accion? ¿Quién es Nacha? ¿Con qué comienza cada capítulo?

 HISTORY CONNECTION

Much of the action of this novel occurs during the period of the Mexican Revolution, which began with the fall of the Porfirio Díaz regime in 1911. Mexico suffered an extended period of upheaval from 1911 until the 1920s. Legendary figures of the Revolution include Francisco (Pancho) Villa and Emiliano Zapata. In 1916 some of Villa's troops crossed the border and attacked Columbus, New Mexico. President Wilson ordered General Pershing to pursue Villa and capture him. The Americans chased Villa throughout Chihuahua for 11 months but never found him. The expedition failed.

Como agua para chocolate (fragmento)

de Laura Esquivel

Introducción

Como agua para chocolate es la primera novela de la autora mexicana, Laura Esquivel. La novela se publicó en 1989 y enseguida llegó a ser número uno en ventas en México. Poco después se tradujo al inglés, lengua en la que fue también «best seller», y a docenas de otros idiomas. En 1992 se hizo de la novela una película popularísima.

La protagonista de la novela es Tita, la hija menor de Mamá Elena, matriarca de la familia de la Garza, cuyo rancho se encuentra en Piedras Negras, no muy lejos de la frontera con los Estados Unidos. Gran parte de la novela ocurre durante la época de la Revolución mexicana. Una de las hermanas de Tita, Gertrudis, llega a ser «Generala» de un ejército revolucionario.

Tita se enamora de un joven, Pedro Muzquiz, que quiere casarse con ella, pero Mamá Elena se opone y le obliga a Tita a seguir la vieja tradición de la hija menor. Mamá Elena le propone al padre de Pedro que su hijo se case con Rosaura, la hermana mayor de Tita.

En el fragmento que sigue, Tita está en la cocina con Nacha, de 85 años, vieja sirvienta de los de la Garza. Mamá Elena le ha ordenado a Tita ayudarle a Nacha a preparar el pastel para la boda de Pedro y Rosaura. La vieja Nacha también se ha quedado «para vestir santos».

Cada capítulo de la novela comienza con una receta. De hecho, el subtítulo de la obra es *«Novela de entregas mensuales con recetas, amores y remedios caseros»*. Este fragmento también comienza con una receta, la receta para el fondant, la pasta de azúcar que cubrirá el pastel.

Laura Esquivel

Additional Practice

You may wish to show the film version of *Como agua para chocolate*. It was quite popular in the United States and should be readily available.

Lectura

Para el fondant:

800 gramos de azúcar granulado
60 gotas de jugo de limón más bastante agua para disolver

Se ponen en una cacerola, el azúcar y el agua al fuego sin dejar de moverla hasta que empieza a hervir. Se cuela en otra cacerola y se vuelve a poner al fuego agregándole el limón hasta que tome punto de bola floja, limpiando de vez en cuando los bordes de la cacerola con un lienzo° húmedo para que la miel no se azucare; cuando ha tomado el punto anteriormente indicado se vacía en otra cacerola húmeda, se rocía por encima y se deja enfriar un poco.

Después, con una espátula de madera, se bate hasta que se empaniza.

Para aplicarlo, se le pone una cucharada de leche y se vuelve a poner al fuego para que se deslíe, se pone después una gota de carmín y se cubre con él únicamente la parte superior del pastel.

Nacha se dio cuenta de que Tita estaba mal, cuando ésta le preguntó si no le iba a poner el carmín.

—Mi niña, se lo acabo de poner, ¿no ves el color rosado que tiene?

—No...

—Vete a dormir, niña, yo termino el turrón. Sólo las ollas saben los hervores° de su caldo, pero yo adivino los tuyos, y ya deja de llorar, que me estás mojando° el fondant y no va a servir, anda, ya vete.

Nachita cubrió de besos a Tita y la empujó fuera de la cocina. No se explicaba de dónde había sacado nuevas lágrimas°, pero las había sacado y alterado con ellas la textura del turrón. Ahora le costaría doble esfuerzo dejarlo en su punto. Ya sola se dio a la tarea de terminar con el turrón lo más pronto posible, para irse a dormir. El turrón se hace con 10 claras de huevo y 500 gramos de azúcar batidos a punto de hebra° fuerte.

Cuando terminó se le ocurrió darle un dedazo° al fondant, para ver si las lágrimas de Tita no habían alterado el sabor, pero, sin saber por qué, a Nacha le entró de golpe una gran nostalgia. Recordó uno a uno todos los banquetes de boda que había preparado para la familia de la Garza con la ilusión de que el próximo fuera el suyo. A sus 85 años no valía la pena llorar, ni lamentarse de que nunca hubieran llegado ni el esperado banquete ni la esperada boda, a pesar de que el novio sí llegó, ¡vaya que había llegado! Sólo que la mamá de Mamá Elena se había encargado de ahuyentarlo°. Desde entonces se había conformado con gozar de las bodas ajenas y así lo hizo por muchos años sin repelar. No sabía por qué lo hacía ahora. Sentía que era una reverenda tontería, pero no podía dejar de hacerlo.

un lienzo *cloth*

los hervores *boiling; figuratively, heartaches*

mojando *wetting*

lágrimas *tears*

hebra *thread*
darle un dedazo *stick a finger in*

ahuyentarlo *driving him away*

National Standards

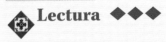

Cultures Students experience, discuss, and analyze an expressive product of the culture: the excerpt from the novel *Como agua para chocolate* by Laura Esquivel.

TEACHING THE READING

Lectura ◆◆◆

A. You may wish to have students read the selection silently.
B. Call on individuals to read aloud, or you may wish to have the silent reading suffice and not do the reading selection intensively.
C. You may wish to ask students to figure out the meaning from the context of some difficult words and phrases such as:
doble esfuerzo
entró de golpe
no valía la pena llorar
¡Vaya que había llegado!
repelar
una reverenda tontería
no tuvo ánimos
no los complacería

National Standards

Communities Students are encouraged to use the language outside the classroom for personal enjoyment and enrichment by seeing the film or reading the entire novel, *Como agua para chocolate*.

Additional Practice

You may wish to ask additional comprehension questions such as:
¿Cuáles son los ingredientes del turrón?
¿Qué edad tiene Nacha?
¿Cuál fue la ilusión de Nacha al preparar cada uno de los banquetes de boda?

ABOUT THE SPANISH LANGUAGE

◆ The recipe that opens the reading is an excellent example of the passive voice **se** construction. You may wish to ask students to identify each use of this construction in the recipe.

Did You Know?

Pedro and Tita's sister Rosaura will be married in church. However, they will have to have a civil ceremony as well in order to be legally wed. Mexico and some other Latin American countries require a civil ceremony. Families are, of course, free to have a religious ceremony in addition to the civil one.

Cubrió con el turrón° lo mejor que pudo el pastel y se fue a su cuarto, con un fuerte dolor de pecho. Lloró toda la noche y a la mañana siguiente no tuvo ánimos para asistir a la boda.

Tita hubiera dado cualquier cosa por estar en el lugar de Nacha, pues ella no sólo tenía que estar presente en la iglesia, se sintiera como se sintiera, sino que tenía que estar muy pendiente° de que su rostro no revelara la menor emoción. Creía poder lograrlo siempre y cuando su mirada no se cruzara con la de Pedro. Ese incidente podría destrozar toda la paz y tranquilidad que aparentaba°.

Sabía que ella, más que su hermana Rosaura, era el centro de atención. Los invitados, más que cumplir con un acto social, querían regodearse° con la idea de su sufrimiento, pero no los complacería, no. Podía sentir claramente cómo penetraban por sus espaldas los cuchicheos° de los presentes a su paso.

—¿Ya viste a Tita? ¡Pobrecita, su hermana se va a casar con su novio! Yo los vi un día en la plaza del pueblo, tomados de la mano. ¡Tan felices que se veían!

el turrón *icing (in this context)*

pendiente *aware*

aparentaba *feigned*

regodearse *take delight in*

los cuchicheos *whisperings*

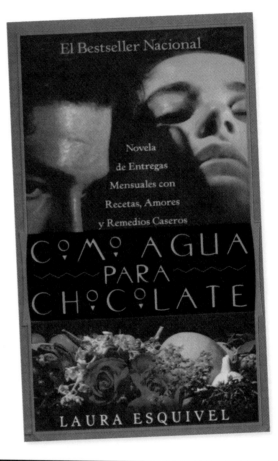

Critical Thinking Activity

Thinking skills: evaluating information

Students may have heard that Hispanic culture is **machista** or male-dominated. Yet there are examples of very strong women in this novel, evident in this short selection. You may wish to ask students to select one of the women and give their impressions of her character and personality.

~Después de leer~

Comprensión

A **El fondant de Nacha** Contesten.

1. ¿Qué es lo que le dio el color rosado al fondant?
2. ¿Qué le indicó a Nacha que Tita no estaba bien?
3. Algo alteró la textura del turrón. ¿Qué?
4. ¿Qué le metió Nacha al fondant para probar el sabor?
5. ¿Cuál es la «reverenda tontería» a la que se refiere Nacha?

B **Nachita** Completen.

1. La receta con que comienza este fragmento es para ___.
2. Nachita le dio muchos ___ a Tita y la echó de la cocina.
3. Nacha quería terminar pronto con el turrón, porque tenía ganas de ___.

C **En otras palabras** ¿Qué quiere decir... ?

1. Sólo las ollas saben los hervores de su caldo, pero yo adivino los tuyos,...
2. ... la mamá de Mamá Elena se había encargado de ahuyentarlo
3. Tita hubiera dado cualquier cosa por estar en el lugar de Nacha...
4. Los invitados... querían regodearse con la idea de sus sufrimientos...

D **Expliquen el significado de la siguiente frase.**

Tita sabía que ella, más que su hermana Rosaura, era el centro de atención.

Dulcería, México

Actividades comunicativas

A **El banquete** Su mejor amigo(a) se casa y quiere que Ud. haga los preparativos para el banquete. Ud. tiene que tener alguna idea del número de invitados y de sus gustos. Pregúnteselo a su compañero(a). Después, prepare una lista de platos exquisitos y describa cada plato a su compañero(a) y pídale su opinión.

B **El restaurante** Un(a) amigo(a) es dueño(a) de un restaurante. Él (o ella) quiere que Ud. le prepare un anuncio para el periódico para clientes de habla española. El anuncio debe indicar las facilidades que tiene para bodas y banquetes y también debe hablar de su excelente cocina.

Jefa de cocina

LITERATURA

ciento uno 101

~Después de leer~

TEACHING TIPS

A. As you go over the *Comprensión* exercises, let students read their answers from their papers.

B. You may wish to do *Comprensión A* and *C* a second time and have students answer freely without referring to their papers.

ANSWERS
Comprensión

A 1. el carmín
  2. le preguntó si no le iba a poner el carmín
  3. las lágrimas de Tita
  4. el dedo
  5. la gran nostalgia que le entró

B 1. el fondant
  2. besos
  3. dormir

C Answers will vary.

D Answers will vary.

Actividades comunicativas

ANSWERS

A and B Answers will vary.

Learning From Photos

La dulcería de la foto es mexicana. Muchos de los dulces son de chocolate. Mucho antes de la llegada de los españoles los aztecas usaban el chocolate para preparar una bebida. Hasta el nombre chocolate viene de la palabra azteca chocolatl. Los españoles llevaron el chocolate a Europa en el siglo XVI.

Independent Practice

Assign any of the following:
1. Exercises, page 101
2. Workbook, *Literatura*

VISTAS DE BOLIVIA

OVERVIEW

The **Vistas de Bolivia** were prepared by National Geographic Society. Their purpose is to give students greater insight, through these visual images, into the culture and people of Bolivia. Have students look at the photographs on pages 102A-102B for enjoyment. If they would like to talk about them, let them say anything they can, using the vocabulary they have learned to this point.

National Standards

🏵 *Cultures*
The **Vistas de Bolivia** photos, and the accompanying captions, allow students to gain insights into the people of Bolivia.

Learning From Photos

1. **El pico de Illimani** Snow-capped **Illimani** towers over the city of La Paz at an altitude of 6,682 meters. It is part of the *Cordillera Real* of the Bolivian Andes.

2. **Festival de San Francisco, La Paz** The festivities in honor of the patron saint, San Francisco, take place in the enormous Plaza La Paz in downtown, La Paz. Note that part of the dress of the dancers is a derby-like hat.

3. **La Paz al anochecer** La Paz is the largest city in Bolivia with a population of about 2 million. It is the highest capital in the world at an altitude of 3,660 meters (12,000 feet).

4. **Mujer y niño aymarás a orillas del lago Titicaca** The Aymará peoples live in the Titicaca basin of Bolivia and Peru. Although they were

1

1. *El Illimani sobre La Paz*
2. *Festival, Plaza San Francisco, La Paz*
3. *Anochecer en La Paz*
4. *Mujer y niño aymaras, Lago Titicaca*
5. *Monolito preincaico, Tiahuanaco*
6. *Campanario de la Universidad San Francisco Javier, Chuquisaca, Sucre*
7. *Balsa de totora e hidrofoil, Lago Titicaca*

NATIONAL GEOGRAPHIC SOCIETY ## TEACHER'S CORNER

INDEX TO NATIONAL GEOGRAPHIC MAGAZINE

The following articles may be used for research relating to this chapter:

- "Simón Bolívar," by Bryan Hodgson, March 1994.
- "Sacred Peaks of the Andes," by Johan Reinhard, March 1992.
- "An Ancient Indian Herb Turns Deadly: Coca," by Peter T. White, January 1989.
- "The High Andes: South America's Island in the Sky," by Loren McIntyre, April 1987.
- "The Lost Empire of the Incas," by Loren McIntyre, December 1973.

NATIONAL GEOGRAPHIC

VISTAS DE BOLIVIA

Learning From Photos

(Continued from p. 102A)

subjugated by the Incas in the 15th century after a long struggle, they still dominate the region and continue to speak their languages.

5. **Monolito, Tiwanaku** The monolith is in the pre-Inca ruins of Tiwanaku or Tihuanaco in the region of Lake Titicaca and Lake Poopó. This region was the site of one of the great pre-Columbian civilizations.

6. **La Universidad de San Francisco Xavier de Chuquisaca** The bell tower belongs to this university in Sucre, in the department of Chuquisaca. The *Universidad de San Francisco Xavier,* founded in 1625, is the national university of Bolivia.

7. **Balsa y aerodeslizador en el lago Titicaca** Titicaca is high in the Andes on the border between Bolivia and Peru. It is the world's highest large lake at 3,810 meters (12,500 ft.) above sea level. The **balsa** in the photo is a flat-bottomed reed boat with reed sails.

PRODUCTS AVAILABLE FROM GLENCOE/MCGRAW-HILL

To order the following products call Glencoe/McGraw-Hill at 1-800-334-7344.

CD-ROMs
· Picture Altas of the World
· The Complete National Geographic: 109 Years of National Geographic Magazine

Software
· ZingoLingo: Spanish Diskettes

Transparency Set
· NGS PicturePack: Geography of South America

Videodisc
· STV: World Geography (Volume 3: "South America and Antarctica")

PRODUCTS AVAILABLE FROM NATIONAL GEOGRAPHIC SOCIETY

NATIONAL GEOGRAPHIC SOCIETY

To order the following products call National Geographic Society at 1-800-368-2728.

Books
· Exploring Your World: The Adventure of Geography
· National Geographic Satellite Atlas of the World

Video
· South America ("Nations of the World" Series)
· Mexico ("Nations of the World" Series)

Chapter 3 Overview ◆◆◆◆◆◆◆◆◆◆◆◆◆◆◆◆◆◆◆◆◆◆◆◆◆◆◆

SCOPE AND SEQUENCE pages 102C–102D

TOPICS	FUNCTIONS	STRUCTURE	CULTURE
◆ Leisure activities ◆ Cultural events ◆ Using formal and informal language	◆ How to handle a leisure time situation ◆ How to express opinions about leisure time activities ◆ How to use the verbs **importar, sorprender,** and **gustar** ◆ How to distinguish between **ser** and **estar** ◆ How to give commands ◆ How to express how long an activity has been going on ◆ How to relate opinions and emotions about past events ◆ How to read and discuss the poetic song «**Adiós muchachos**» and an excerpt from the play *Mi adorado Juan*	◆ **Verbos especiales con complemento indirecto** ◆ **Los verbos *gustar y faltar*** ◆ ***Ser y estar*** ◆ **Característica y condición** ◆ **Usos especiales de *ser* y *estar*** ◆ ***Ser de*** ◆ **El imperativo** ◆ **Hace y hacía** ◆ **Acabar de** ◆ **Imperfecto del subjuntivo** ◆ **Usos del imperfecto del subjuntivo** ◆ **Subjuntivo con expresiones indefinidas** ◆ **Subjuntivo en cláusulas relativas**	◆ Festivals in Spain and Latin America ◆ National Theater in San Jose, Costa Rica ◆ Expressing opinions in formal and colloquial language ◆ Attending a play: ***Don Juan Tenorio*** ◆ Spanish rock band, Mecano ◆ Windsurfing in Mexico ◆ The tango **Literatura** ◆ **El tango** ◆ **«Adiós muchachos»** ◆ *Mi adorado Juan,* **Miguel Mihura**

CHAPTER 3 RESOURCES

PRINT	MULTIMEDIA

Planning Resources

Lesson Plans Block Scheduling Lesson Plans	Interactive Lesson Planner

Reinforcement Resources

Writing Activities Workbook Student Tape Manual Video Activities Booklet Glencoe Foreign Language Web Site User's Guide	Transparencies Binder Audiocassette/Compact Disc Program Videocassette/Videodisc Program Online Internet Activities Electronic Teacher's Classroom Resources

Assessment Resources

Situation Cards Chapter Quizzes Testing Program	Testmaker Computer Software (Macintosh/Windows) Listening Comprehension Audiocassette/Compact Disc

Motivational Resources

Expansion Activities	Café Glencoe: **www.cafe.glencoe.com**

Enrichment

Fine Art Transparencies: F-1

Chapter 3 Planning Guide

SECTION	PAGES	SECTION RESOURCES
Cultura El tiempo libre *Algunos pasatiempos*	104–110	Transparencies 18–19 Audiocassette 5A/Compact Disc 3 Writing Activities Workbook, pages 53–55 Student Tape Manual, pages 34–35 Chapter Quizzes, page 29 Testing Program, pages 55–58
Conversación El teatro	111–114	Transparency 20 Audiocassette 5A/Compact Disc 3 Writing Activities Workbook, pages 56–57 Student Tape Manual, page 36 Chapter Quizzes, page 30 Testing Program, pages 59–60
Lenguaje Los gustos e intereses Antipatías Falta de interés o aburrimiento	115–119	Transparency 21 Audiocassette 5A/Compact Disc 3 Writing Activities Workbook, pages 58–59 Student Tape Manual, pages 36 Testing Program, pages 59–60
Repaso de estructura Verbos especiales con complemento indirecto Los verbos *gustar* y *faltar* *Ser* y *estar* Característica y condición Usos especiales de *ser* y *estar* *Ser de* El imperativo	120–128	Audiocassette 5B/Compact Disc 4 Writing Activities Workbook, pages 60–66 Student Tape Manual, pages 37–38 Chapter Quizzes, pages 31–37 Testing Program, pages 61–62
Periodismo El wind surf «Windsurf: agua, aire ¡y diversión!»	129–133	Transparencies 22A–22B Audiocassette 5B/Compact Disc 4 Writing Activities Workbook, pages 67–70 Student Tape Manual, pages 39–40 Chapter Quizzes, page 38 Testing Program, pages 63–64
Estructura *Hace* y *hacía* *Acabar de* Imperfecto del subjuntivo Usos del imperfecto del subjuntivo Subjuntivo con expresiones indefinidas Subjuntivo en cláusulas relativas	134–139	Audiocassette 6A/Compact Disc 4 Writing Activities Workbook, pages 71–75 Student Tape Manual, page 43 Chapter Quizzes, pages 39–43 Testing Program, pages 65–67
Literatura El tango «Adiós muchachos» *Mi adorado Juan,* Miguel Mihura	140–149	Transparencies 23A–23B, 24 Audiocassette 6A-6B/Compact Disc 4 Writing Activities Workbook, 76–78 Student Tape Manual, pages 44–46 Chapter Quizzes, pages 44–45 Testing Program, pages 68–73

OVERVIEW

In this chapter students will learn about the leisure activities of Spanish-speaking people. Students will also learn new vocabulary needed to discuss cultural events. They will talk about their interests and learn to express in formal and informal language why they do or do not like something. They will also learn how to express how long an action has been going on, as well as emotions and opinions about past events.

Students will read a newspaper article about a sporting event. They will learn the history of the tango, read "Adiós muchachos," a poetic song, and an excerpt from a play by Miguel Mihura.

National Standards

Communication
Students will engage in conversations, provide and obtain information, express feelings, and exchange opinions on the topic leisure time activities, including sports and fine and performing arts. They will listen to and read authentic language on the same topic.

Learning From Photos

Aquí se ve el interior del Teatro Nacional de Costa Rica, en San José. En 1997 el teatro celebró su centenario. Está situado en el centro de la ciudad y es una belleza, decorada con antiguos muebles europeos y maderas preciosas del país.

CAPÍTULO 3

Pasatiempos

Objetivos

In this chapter you will do the following:

- read about what Hispanics of all ages like to do during their free time
- handle such leisure time situations as getting tickets to a play, seeing and discussing it
- express opinions about leisure time activities
- review verbs like **importar**, **sorprender**, and **gustar**; uses of **ser** and **estar**; and commands
- read and discuss a magazine article about windsurfing
- learn to express how long an activity has been going on, and emotions and opinions about past events
- read and discuss the poetic song «Adiós muchachos», and an excerpt from the play *Mi adorado Juan* by Miguel Mihura

inter NET CONNECTION

The Glencoe Foreign Language Web site (http://www.glencoe.com/sec/fl) offers these options that enable you and your students to experience the Spanish-speaking world via the Internet:

- At **Café Glencoe**, the interactive "after-school" section of the site, you and your students can access a variety of additional online resources, including online newspapers, interactive games, and a send-a-postcard feature.
- The online **Proyectos** are correlated to the chapters and utilize Hispanic Web sites around the world.

 *ciento tres* 103

 103

 CAPÍTULO *3*

DIFFICULTY PLATEAUS

In all chapters, each reading selection in *Cultura*, *Periodismo*, and *Literatura*, as well as the *Conversación* and each structure topic, will be rated as follows:

◆ **Easy**
◆◆ **Intermediate**
◆◆◆ **Difficult**

The overall rating of this chapter is: ◆◆ **Intermediate.**

RANDOM ACCESS

You may either follow the exact order of the chapter or you may omit certain sections that you feel are not necessary for your students. Similarly, you may wish to present a literary selection without interruption or you may intersperse some material from the *Estructura* sections as you are presenting a literary or journalistic piece.

EVALUATION

Quizzes There is a quiz for every vocabulary presentation and every structure point.

Tests To accompany *¡Buen viaje! Level 3* there are global tests for both *Estructuras*, a combined *Conversación/Lenguaje* test, and one test for each reading in the *Cultura*, *Periodismo*, and *Literatura* sections. There is also a comprehensive chapter test.

Chapter Projects

1. **Los pasatiempos:** Antes de comenzar el capítulo, dígales a los alumnos que hagan una lista de todas las actividades que, en su opinión, son populares en el mundo hispano y otra lista para los Estados Unidos. Luego, compararán las dos listas con la información en la sección de *Cultura*.

2. **El teatro:** Elija algunas escenas de teatro español. Divida la clase en grupos y dé una escena a cada grupo para representar o para leer solamente. Dígales que escriban una escena imitando el estilo del autor que han leído. Ellos pueden también preparar un programa y distribuirlo a todos los alumnos antes de la representación.

103

Bell Ringer Review

Use the BRR Transparency 3-1, or write the following on the board: **Haga una lista de los deportes que se practican durante cada una de las cuatro estaciones.**

TEACHING TIPS

A. You may either read the *Introducción* to the students or have them read it silently.

B. Tell students to look for the following information: **¿Qué hace la gente con su tiempo libre? ¿Qué opinas? ¿Hacen los hispanos las mismas cosas que nosotros con su tiempo libre?**

RESOURCES

- Vocabulary Transparencies
- Audio Cassette 5A/Compact Disc 3
- Student Tape Manual
- Workbook
- Chapter Quizzes

FINE ART CONNECTION

Fernando Botero es un artista muy conocido. Nació en Medellín, Colombia, en 1932. En su obra combina lo mágico con lo real. Transforma retratos de grandes artistas e imágenes de las familias de la burguesía de Latinoamérica en cuadros y esculturas. Sus figuras son siempre grandes (gordas).

CULTURA
El tiempo libre

Introducción

¿Qué hace la gente con su tiempo libre en los países hispanos? Como aquí en los Estados Unidos, los pasatiempos favoritos varían según los gustos, intereses y preferencias personales. A algunos les gusta leer un buen libro, a otros les gusta ir al cine a ver un filme. Algunos prefieren dar una caminata mientras otros descansan en una hamaca. Hay quienes frecuentan los museos y los conciertos, y hay quienes prefieren escuchar un CD o una cinta en su propia sala.

«Niños ricos» de Fernando Botero

Vocabulario

la fiesta

la acera

el santo patrón

el desfile

Se oye el disparo de un cohete.

Cooperative Learning

1. Have students work in groups and describe their favorite pastimes. Then have them categorize the activities.
2. Have students work in groups as they look at and discuss *«Niños ricos»* by Botero. Have them give their impressions and reactions to the painting. Have those who like it, as well as those who don't like it, explain why.

Critical Thinking Activity

Thinking skills: supporting arguments with reasons **1. ¿Qué opinas? ¿Tiene la personalidad de una persona algo que ver con sus pasatiempos favoritos? ¿Cómo? ¿Por qué? Explica.
2. ¿Qué relación tiene tu personalidad con las actividades que te interesan?**

la plaza de toros

el cabestro

la boina

la faja

el toro

el encierro

el danzarín

la comparsa

el mozo   el joven, el muchacho, el chico

el varón   una persona de sexo masculino

el ayuno   el acto de no comer por motivos religiosos u otros

tranquilo(a)   calmo(a), quieto(a)

acabar   terminar

CULTURA

ciento cinco   **105**

TEACHING VOCABULARY

A. Have students repeat the new words in unison after you or Cassette 5A/Compact Disc 3.

B. To vary the procedure, give students a few minutes to peruse the definitions.

C. Then read the definitions aloud as students follow in their books.

D. You may wish to ask the following questions as you present the new words: **¿Cuántas horas por semana dedicas a los pasatiempos? ¿Cuáles son algunas fiestas típicas en los Estados Unidos? En tu escuela, ¿hay deportes de equipo y deportes individuales? ¿En qué deportes participas? ¿Tienes ganas de ver una buena película?**

ABOUT THE SPANISH LANGUAGE

◆ Note that the words **el film, el filme,** and **la película** are all used for "a film."

RECYCLING

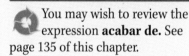

You may wish to review the expression **acabar de.** See page 135 of this chapter.

Additional Practice

Have students find words related to each of the following:

   disparar (el disparo)
   desfilar (el desfile)
   encerrar (el encierro)
   ayunar (el ayuno)

TEACHING TIPS

These exercises can be done in class with books open.

ANSWERS
Práctica

A 1. sí
 2. sí
 3. no
 4. sí
 5. sí
 6. no
 7. sí
 8. sí

B 1. a
 2. b
 3. c
 4. a

C 1. d
 2. f
 3. a
 4. g
 5. c
 6. h
 7. e
 8. b
 9. i

INFORMAL ASSESSMENT

Have students create original sentences using the new words.

Práctica

A. Las fiestas ¿Sí o no?

1. Durante muchas ferias y fiestas hay desfiles en las calles.
2. Un cohete estalla en el aire produciendo un gran ruido.
3. La corrida de toros es una función de música al aire libre.
4. Una comparsa es un grupo de danzarines y músicos en la calle.
5. El toro es un animal muy fuerte.
6. Se lleva una faja en la cabeza.
7. El santo patrón de San Juan de Puerto Rico es San Juan.
8. Los peatones andan o caminan sobre la acera.

B. Se divierten. Escojan.

1. Los ___ tocan un pasodoble.
   a. músicos
   b. cabestros
   c. danzarines
2. El ___ guía a los toros. Es un animal manso, no es feroz.
   a. encierro
   b. cabestro
   c. santo
3. La corrida tiene lugar en ___.
   a. el estadio
   b. la acera
   c. la plaza de toros
4. Los mozos llevan ___.
   a. faja y boina
   b. comparsas
   c. cohetes

C. ¿Cuál es la palabra? Escojan.

1. una fiesta
2. una boina
3. un toro
4. el mozo
5. tranquilo
6. un danzarín
7. acabar
8. un varón
9. ir a

a. un animal fuerte y bastante feroz
b. una persona de sexo masculino
c. quieto, calmo
d. una feria
e. lo contrario de «empezar»
f. un tipo de sombrero
g. un muchacho
h. un bailarín
i. acudir a

La Feria de Sevilla, España

Learning From Photos

Durante la Feria de Sevilla, la gente se regocija día y noche. En el real de la feria se levantan tiendas en las que la gente come, bebe, baila y escucha los artistas del flamenco. Por el real se pueden ver los preciosos caballos andaluces, jinetes vestidos de traje campero y las sevillanas con vestido de cola.

Independent Practice

Assign any of the following:
1. Exercises, page 106
2. Workbook, *Cultura*

Algunos pasatiempos

Cuando nosotros, los norteamericanos, pensamos en el tiempo libre, solemos pensar en el «weekend»—el fin de semana. El británico o norteamericano, desde hace muchos años, ha gozado del «weekend». Pero este concepto no es de invención hispana. En muchos países hispanos todavía no es común que un trabajador tenga dos días de descanso a la semana. Por eso, los obreros españoles lucharon por «la semana inglesa» de cinco días. Pero si el trabajador norteamericano tiene sus dos días feriados cada semana, el hispano vive en espera de sus ferias y fiestas. Algunas fiestas son puramente locales; otras son nacionales e internacionales. Todas, sin embargo, llevan la estampa del lugar donde se celebran.

Raro es el pueblo español o hispanoamericano que no rinda honor a su santo patrón: en Madrid, a San Isidro; en Puerto Rico, a San Juan; y en México, a la Virgen de Guadalupe. Estas fiestas patronales en las grandes ciudades pueden durar una semana o más. Hay música y bailes todas las noches. Vamos a mirar de cerca a algunas de estas fiestas.

Fiesta de la Virgen de Guadalupe, México

Una celebración en Venezuela

Critical Thinking Activity

Thinking skills: supporting arguments with reasons **¿Por qué son tan importantes algunos días de descanso para los que trabajan?**

Bell Ringer Review

Use the BRR Transparency 3-2, or write the following on the board:
1. **¿Adónde va Ud. para escuchar un concierto?**
2. **¿Adónde va Ud. para ver una obra de teatro?**
3. **¿Adónde va Ud. para ver una película?**
4. **¿Adónde va Ud. para ver una exposición de arte?**
5. **¿Adónde va Ud. para mirar la televisión?**

TEACHING THE READING

Algunos pasatiempos ◆◆

You may wish to call on individuals to read this section aloud since it contains some important general information. You may wish to intersperse some simple comprehension questions.

Paraphrasing Have students look at the reading and find how each of the following is stated.

Tenemos la costumbre de pensar en el «weekend».
El inglés ha disfrutado del «weekend».
Es bastante raro que un trabajador tenga dos días de reposo.
Esta idea no es de origen hispano.

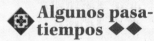

National Standards

Cultures
Students are helped to understand the relationship between the practices and perspectives of Hispanic cultures by learning about important festivals and their religious and historical connotations.

LITERATURE CONNECTION

You may ask students if they have read Hemingway's *The Sun Also Rises*. If they have, ask them if they remember some things about Pamplona.

TEACHING THE READING

A. *Las fiestas de San Fermín:* You may wish to intersperse some simple comprehension questions and/or ask volunteers to talk about the section.

B. *El Carnaval:* Have students read the section aloud. You may wish to make up some true/false statements as students read.

HISTORY CONNECTION

Navarra es una región muy interesante en la historia de España. Durante la dominación árabe, Navarra era uno de los cuatro reinos cristianos. Fue en el famoso pasaje de Roncesvalles en los Pirineos entre Francia y España donde murió Rolando en 778, mientras las tropas de Carlomagno trataban de regresar a Francia después de haber saqueado la ciudad de Pamplona. Y en 1813 las tropas napoleónicas tuvieron una de sus últimas batallas en Navarra antes de cruzar los Pirineos para escaparse a Francia.

Las fiestas de San Fermín

San Fermín, Pamplona, España, siete de julio. «Uno de enero, dos de febrero, tres de marzo, cuatro de abril, cinco de mayo, seis de junio, siete de julio, San Fermín. A Pamplona vamos ya, a Pamplona a ver el encierro, a Pamplona vamos ya, a Pamplona riáu riáu.» Ésa es una parte de la letra de una canción tradicional. El siete de julio es el día de San Fermín, santo patrón de Pamplona.

Para comprender la locura[1] que invade la ciudad durante la segunda semana de julio, hay que tener alguna idea de lo que es Pamplona. Capital de la provincia y del antiguo reino de Navarra, Pamplona es un lugar tranquilo durante cincuenta y una semanas del año. Si en algo se distingue Pamplona de las otras capitales de provincia es en ser quizás más quieta y soñolienta que las otras.

Pero comenzando el día siete de julio y por una semana o más, la ciudad se convierte en un manicomio[2]. Los mozos no duermen. Pasan la noche en la calle bailando y festejando. Bailan en grupos de varones o a solas. Cuando por fin se cansan, echan una siesta en la silla de algún café o en la misma acera.

A las seis de la madrugada, el disparo de un cohete anuncia que el encierro comienza. Los chicos se despiertan en seguida porque en pocos momentos por las calles pasarán los toros de la corrida de la tarde. Sí, corren a toda velocidad detrás de sus cabestros camino a la plaza.

Los mozos vestidos de blanco con faja y boina roja corren delante, desafiando[3] a aquellos monstruos negros. No tienen miedo porque saben que:

El que se levanta pa'[4] correr
delante los toros ya verá
como San Fermín que todo lo ve
y si tienes fe y si tienes fe
te levantará riáu, riáu.

Y en la última noche de feria se oye por todas partes el triste refrán: «Pobre de mí, pobre de mí, ya se acaban las fiestas de San Fermín. Pobre de mí, pobre de mí, ya se han acabado las fiestas de San Fermín».

Los sanfermines, Pamplona, España

[1] **locura** *craziness*
[2] **manicomio** *insane asylum*
[3] **desafiando** *daring*
[4] **pa'** *para*

Critical Thinking Activity

Thinking skills: making judgments

¿Cuáles son las ventajas y desventajas de los pasatiempos organizados y los que no están organizados desde el punto de vista de las personas siguientes?

a. los niños

b. los jóvenes

c. los adultos

d. los retirados

El Carnaval

El carnaval es una mezcla de lo sacro y lo profano, de tradiciones del Viejo Mundo con las del Nuevo Mundo.

Comenzando con el miércoles de ceniza[5], la cuaresma[6] imponía al buen cristiano cuarenta días de ayuno y de abstinencia. Cuarenta días sin música, ni baile, ni fiesta. Cuarenta días de solemnidad. Desde la Edad Media, se han utilizado los días anteriores al miércoles de ceniza para hartarse[7] de fiesta y para poder soportar mejor esos cuarenta días de cuaresma.

Esta fiesta se celebra en muchos países. En Nueva Orleans se conoce por su nombre francés, *Mardi Gras*. En los países hispanos se llama Carnaval. El de La Habana antes era de los mejores. Los verdaderos orígenes del carnaval están en la prehistoria. Es probable que las saturnales y bacanales romanas fueran sus antecedentes.

En los países del Caribe una nota típica de los carnavales es el desfile de las comparsas. Las comparsas son grupos de danzarines y músicos, todos vestidos igual, algunos con máscaras o caretas fantásticas, que desfilan por las avenidas de la ciudad. En el Caribe las comparsas se enriquecen con los ritmos de África.

[5] **miércoles de ceniza** Ash Wednesday
[6] **cuaresma** Lent
[7] **hartarse** to get one's fill of

Carnaval en Ponce, Puerto Rico

Carnaval en Puebla, México

Un baile en Chichicastenango, Guatemala

ciento nueve 〰 **109**

ABOUT THE SPANISH LANGUAGE

La palabra «carnaval» viene del latín «vale» que significa «adiós». Quiere decir «adiós carne», porque después del martes de carnaval comienzan los 40 días de cuaresma cuando no se come carne.

GEOGRAPHY CONNECTION

1. Ponce es la segunda ciudad de Puerto Rico. La más grande es la capital, San Juan. Ponce está en el sur de la isla, en la costa del Mar Caribe. Se le llama a Ponce el Cádiz de Puerto Rico porque tiene muchas casas blancas. Ponce tiene un museo muy bueno y en la plaza central hay una catedral bonita. En esta misma plaza se encuentra el parque de bombas pintado de muchos colores vivos.
2. Chichicastenango está a unos 140 kilómetros de la Ciudad de Guatemala. Es una ciudad que tiene mucha influencia indígena. Los jueves y los domingos por la mañana tiene lugar el mercado donde los habitantes de los pueblos remotos de las montañas vienen a vender lo que producen y a comprar lo que necesitan. En la plaza principal de la ciudad pequeña está la iglesia de Santo Tomás construida en 1540.

Critical Thinking Activity

Thinking skills: supporting statements with reasons **¿Deben ser una recompensa o un derecho los pasatiempos?**

Did You Know?

En la época de los romanos, las saturnales eran fiestas en las que reinaba el desorden. Las bacanales eran fiestas paganas celebradas en honor de Baco, el dios del vino. Baco era el hijo de Júpiter y Sémele.

TEACHING TIPS

You can assign the *Comprensión* exercises for homework. With more able groups, however, you may wish to go over the exercises immediately in class (upon completion of the reading) without previous preparation.

ANSWERS

Comprensión

A 1. sábado y domingo
2. cinco días laborales
3. un día libre
4. San Isidro
5. San Juan
6. La Virgen de Guadalupe
B 1. En la provincia de Navarra.
2. Es San Fermín.
3. Empiezan el 7 de julio.
4. Pamplona es tranquila y hasta soñolienta.
5. Los jóvenes bailan y festejan.
6. Se oye a las seis de la mañana.
7. Anuncia que el encierro comienza.
8. Pasan por la calle.
9. Los mozos corren delante de los toros.
10. Llevan faja y boina roja.
11. No tienen miedo porque los protegerá San Fermín.
C 1. el miércoles de ceniza
2. solemnidad
3. cuarenta días
4. el carnaval
5. grupos de danzarines y músicos
6. un desfile de comparsas

TEACHING TIPS

Actividad A can be done orally, or it can be written. You may wish to have a few of the most interesting ones presented to the class.

Actividades comunicativas

ANSWERS

A and B Answers will vary.

110

Comprensión

A ¿Qué es? Identifiquen.
1. el «weekend» o el fin de semana
2. la semana inglesa
3. un día feriado
4. el santo patrón de Madrid
5. el santo patrón de San Juan de Puerto Rico
6. la santa patrona de México

B Los sanfermines Contesten.
1. ¿Dónde está Pamplona?
2. ¿Quién es el santo patrón de Pamplona?
3. ¿Qué día empiezan las fiestas de San Fermín?
4. ¿Cómo es Pamplona?
5. ¿Qué hacen los jóvenes durante los sanfermines?
6. ¿A qué hora se oye el disparo de un cohete?
7. ¿Qué anuncia el disparo del cohete?
8. ¿Por dónde pasan los toros camino a la plaza de toros?
9. ¿Quiénes corren delante de los toros?
10. ¿Qué llevan?
11. ¿Por qué no tienen miedo? ¿Quién los protegerá?

C Los carnavales Completen.
1. La cuaresma comienza con ___.
2. Para muchos cristianos la cuaresma es un período de ___.
3. La cuaresma dura ___.
4. Es el *Mardi Gras* en Nueva Orleans pero en los países hispanos se llama ___.
5. Las comparsas son ___.
6. En los carnavales de los países del Caribe hay ___.

Una comparsa, Ponce, Puerto Rico

Fiesta de San Jerónimo, Masaya, Nicaragua

Actividades comunicativas

A La fiesta de... Describa una fiesta que tiene lugar cerca de donde Ud. vive. Dé todos los detalles posibles.

B Mi opinión ¿Preferiría Ud. trabajar cinco días a la semana con fin de semana libre, o trabajar los sábados y tener muchos días feriados al año? Explique por qué.

Did You Know?

Las **«caretas de cartón» son típicas de Ponce. Se usan solamente durante el carnaval. Hay artesanos especialistas en caretas.**

Independent Practice

Assign any of the following:
1. Exercises, page 110
2. Workbook, *Cultura*

Conversación

El teatro

Vocabulario

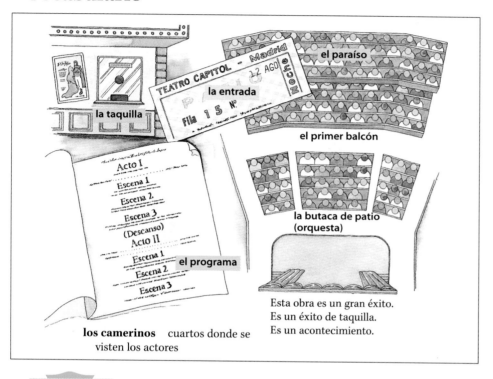

la taquilla

TEATRO CAPITOL — Madrid
PARAISO
Fila 1 5 Nº

la entrada

el paraíso

el primer balcón

Acto I
Escena 1
Escena 2
Escena 3
(Descanso)
Acto II
Escena 1
Escena 2
Escena 3

el programa

la butaca de patio
(orquesta)

Esta obra es un gran éxito.
Es un éxito de taquilla.
Es un acontecimiento.

los camerinos   cuartos donde se
visten los actores

Práctica

A **En el teatro**   Preguntas personales.

1. Si vas al teatro, ¿dónde prefieres sentarte?
2. ¿Qué butacas cuestan más, las butacas de patio o las del balcón?
3. ¿Te interesa mucho el mundo del espectáculo?
4. ¿Te gusta ir a los camerinos durante el descanso o después de la representación?

CONVERSACIÓN

ciento once 111

🔔 Bell Ringer Review

*Use the BRR Transparency 3-3, or
write the following on the board:*
**Haga una lista de las palabras
que se puede utilizar para
hablar del teatro o del cine.**

RESOURCES

- Vocabulary Transparencies
- Audio Cassette 5A/Compact Disk 3
- Student Tape Manual
- Workbook
- Chapter Quizzes

TEACHING VOCABULARY

A. Have students repeat the new words and sentences after you or Cassette 5A/Compact Disk 3.

B. You may want to ask students some additional questions to practice the vocabulary using the exercises on this page.

C. Definitions: Call on individuals to read each new word or phrase and its definition.

ANSWERS
Práctica
A Answers will vary.

Cooperative Learning

1. En grupos de tres o cuatro, preparen una ilustración que puede servir de publicidad para cualquier obra de teatro que conozcan, o si prefieren, una imaginaria.

2. Divida la clase en grupos de tres estudiantes. Cada grupo organiza un fin de semana en Madrid. El primero se encarga de organizar las actividades culturales; el segundo, las actividades deportivas; y el tercero, algunas actividades gastronómicas.

TEACHING THE CONVERSATION

 Escenas de la vida

A. Call on students to read the conversation aloud. Call on one pair to read *Una obra de teatro* and another pair to read *Durante el descanso*.

B. You can immediately ask the questions from the *Comprensión* exercise, page 114.

 ### LITERATURE CONNECTION

Don Juan Tenorio (1844) de José Zorilla se basa en el personaje original creado por el fraile Gabriel Téllez (1584-1648) cuyo pseudónimo es Tirso de Molina. El teatro de Tirso es muy abundante. Escribió más de 400 comedias. *El Burlador de Sevilla* trata del tema del famoso seductor, don Juan. Con la confianza de la juventud, de ninguna manera teme este don Juan la muerte. Siempre dice «*¡Qué largo me lo fiáis!*»

VOCABULARY EXPANSION

The word for "usher" in a theater is **el/la acomodador(a).**

Escenas de la vida

Una obra de teatro

ANDRÉS: Esta noche están presentando *Don Juan Tenorio* en el teatro Liceo. ¿Quieres ir?

MARA: Me estás tomando el pelo. No habrá más plazas. Esta obra es siempre un gran éxito.

ANDRÉS: No, es una obra antiquísima. Ya no acude todo Madrid.

MARA: Pues, vamos a la taquilla. Pero te aseguro que las entradas estarán agotadas. No quedará ni una.

ANDRÉS: Y si ya tengo entradas, ¿quieres ir?

MARA: ¿Tienes entradas?

ANDRÉS: Sí, las saqué ya hace unos quince días y no te lo quería decir. Sabía que te gustaría verlo. Tenemos dos butacas en el primer balcón.

Paired Activity

Have students work in pairs to make up a conversation about a movie. They can use the conversations on pages 112–113 as a guide.

Critical Thinking Activity

Thinking skills: identifying causes **¿Por qué tienen mucho éxito algunas representaciones y por qué fracasan otras?**

112

Durante el descanso

ANDRÉS: ¡Pues, bien! ¿Qué piensas?

MARA: ¡Qué tipo es este don Juan! Pero la verdad es que me hace reír. Y Joaquín Mellina que hace el papel de don Juan es fantástico.

ANDRÉS: ¿Quieres visitar los camerinos?

MARA: ¿Para qué? ¿Para ver a las estrellas y molestarlas? No, el mundo del espectáculo no me interesa tanto, pero la obra sí.

Did You Know?

When being seated in a theater in Spain and in some areas of Latin America, it is customary to tip the usher who seats you. Such is not the case in the United States.

Comprensión

A **Al teatro**   Contesten.

1. ¿Qué obra están presentando?
2. ¿Dónde?
3. ¿Cuándo?
4. ¿Por qué cree Mara que Andrés le está tomando el pelo?
5. ¿Por qué quiere ella ir a la taquilla?
6. ¿Cuál es la sorpresa que le tiene Andrés?
7. ¿Cuándo sacó las entradas?
8. ¿Quién hace el papel de don Juan?
9. ¿Tiene Mara ganas de visitar los camerinos?
10. ¿Cuándo hablaron los dos de la representación?

Teatro Colón, Buenos Aires, Argentina

Actividades comunicativas

A **El cine**   Indique si a Ud. le gusta o no le gusta el teatro o el cine. Explique.

B **Los títulos**   Prepare una lista de películas (filmes) que Ud. ha visto. Trate de ponerles títulos en español.

C **Una estrella de teatro**   ¿Quién es su estrella de cine o teatro favorita? Explique por qué.

El Teatro Nacional, San José, Costa Rica

Did You Know?

1. La zarzuela es una obra dramática española en la que se habla y se canta.
2. Dos de los teatros más importantes de Madrid son el Teatro Real, o la ópera, y el Teatro Nacional Lírico de la Zarzuela.

Learning From Photos

El Teatro Nacional de San José es una maravilla arquitectónica de estilo renacentista. Fue construido entre 1890 y 1897. Las esculturas que se ven aquí son del escultor italiano Pietro Balgarelli. En el Teatro Nacional se dan conciertos, ballets y sinfonías, y se presentan obras dramáticas, zarzuelas y óperas. Se usa el teatro también para conferencias y recepciones.

Lenguaje
Los gustos e intereses

Gustos

En español, como en inglés, hay varias expresiones para indicar lo que nos gusta, lo que queremos o adoramos y lo que apreciamos.

Es fantástico.

Me gusta mucho el regalo que me diste.
Me agrada mucho. Me da mucho placer.
Me encanta.

Quiero mucho a mi novio(a). Lo/La adoro.
Quiero mucho a mi perrito. Lo adoro.
Aprecio (Estimo) la generosidad de Pablo.

Hay razones por las cuales nos gusta algo. Algunas expresiones que podemos utilizar para describir lo que nos gusta o nos agrada son:

Es agradable.	Es fantástico.
Es formidable.	Es excepcional.
Es extraordinario.	Es genial.
Es maravilloso.	Es chévere. (en ciertas regiones)
Es sensacional.	Está muy bien.
Es estupendo.	

Intereses

Si queremos decir que algo nos interesa o que lo encontramos interesante, podemos decir:

El teatro me interesa.
Tengo mucho interés en el teatro.
El mundo del espectáculo me atrae.
Me atrae mucho. Me fascina.

Si queremos explicar por qué nos interesa o nos fascina algo, podemos decir:

Lo encuentro interesante.	Lo encuentro maravilloso.
Lo encuentro fascinante.	Me pica el interés.
Lo encuentro curioso.	Me pica la curiosidad.

Bell Ringer Review

Use the BRR Transparency 3-4, or write the following on the board:
1. Haga una lista de las actividades que le gustan y diga por qué.
2. Haga una lista de las actividades que no le agradan y diga por qué.

TEACHING TIPS

A. Read the explanatory information to the class and call on students to read the model sentences and expressions.
B. Since these are all very useful, high-frequency expressions, insist that students pronounce them with expression and with the most accurate intonation possible.

Cooperative Learning

Trabajen en pequeños grupos. Tema de debate: «¿Cuándo pueden ser obsesión los pasatiempos?» En cada grupo hagan Uds. una lista de las consecuencias buenas y malas que puedan resultar de la devoción excesiva a los pasatiempos. Presenten Uds. los resultados a los otros alumnos.

TEACHING TIPS

The exercises on this page can be gone over immediately without any previous preparation.

B. and **C.** If it is not too time-consuming, you may wish to have groups conduct surveys.

ANSWERS
Práctica

A **1.** aprecio
2. gusta
3. adoro

B and **C** Answers will vary.

Práctica

A **El agradecimiento** Completen.

1. —Quiero agradecerle a Emilio.
—¿Quieres agradecerle? ¿Por qué?
—Porque me ayudó mucho cuando estaba enfermo y quiero que sepa que yo ___ todo lo que ha hecho por mí.

2. —¿Te ___ esta pulsera?
—¡Sí! ¡Qué preciosa! ¿Acabas de comprártela?
—No, papá me la regaló para mi cumpleaños.

3. —Este perrito tuyo, ¡qué mono (precioso) es!
—¿Te parece? Yo lo ___.
—Comprendo por qué. Es adorable.

En la taquilla de un teatro, Buenos Aires, Argentina

B **¿Qué te gusta?** Contesten.

1. El libro que leíste, ¿te gustó? ¿Por qué? ¿Cómo lo encontraste?
2. La película que viste, ¿te gustó? ¿Por qué? ¿Cómo la encontraste?
3. La carta que recibiste, ¿te gustó? ¿Por qué? ¿Cómo la encontraste?
4. La obra teatral que viste, ¿te gustó? ¿Por qué? ¿Cómo la encontraste?
5. El concierto que oíste, ¿te gustó? ¿Por qué? ¿Cómo lo encontraste?
6. La canción que oíste, ¿te gustó? ¿Por qué? ¿Cómo la encontraste?

C **Lo encuentro interesante.** Preguntas personales.

1. De los cursos que tomas (sigues) este semestre, ¿cuáles te interesan? ¿Por qué te interesan tanto?
2. ¿En qué eventos culturales tienes interés? ¿Por qué?
3. ¿Qué deportes te atraen? ¿Por qué?
4. ¿Qué programas (emisiones) de televisión te pican el interés? ¿Por qué?
5. ¿Qué cosas que nunca has hecho te gustaría hacer porque te pican la curiosidad?

Learning From Photos

Los teatros más famosos de Buenos Aires son el Teatro Colón donde se presentan óperas, ballets y sinfonías y el Teatro Cervantes donde se presentan obras clásicas—en español y en inglés.

Independent Practice

Assign the exercises on page 116.

116

Antipatías

No me gusta esta música.

Para expresar lo que no nos gusta, podemos decir:

> **No me gusta este tipo de canción.**
> **No me gusta esta música.**
> **La aborrezco. La detesto.**
> **La odio.**

Como hay razones por las cuales nos gusta algo, hay también razones por las cuales no nos gusta algo.

> **Lo encuentro horrible.**
> **Lo encuentro detestable.**
> **Lo encuentro espantoso.**
> **Lo encuentro abominable.**
> **Lo encuentro repugnante.**
> **Lo encuentro asqueroso.**
> **¡Qué horror!**
> **Me da asco.**

Las palabras **asqueroso, asco** y **repugnante** indican repugnancia. Son palabras fuertes. De vez en cuando, hay algo o alguien que no podemos soportar ni tolerar por una razón u otra. En estos casos, podemos decir:

> **No puedo aguantar esta música.**
> **No aguanto esta música.**
> **No puedo aguantar a ese tío.**

Si ya no aguantamos más, podemos decir:

> **Es el colmo.**
> **No puedo más.**
> **Ya estoy harto(a).**

TEACHING TIPS

Follow the same suggestions as those given for *Los gustos e intereses* (page 115).

Students usually enjoy making these negative statements. For this reason you may wish to "seize the opportunity" and let them be creative and express their opinions on as many different topics as they can.

REGISTER

The word **tío** as used here is very familiar. In this context it does not mean "uncle" but "this guy."

TEACHING TIPS

Follow the same suggestions as those given for *Los gustos e intereses* (page 115).

All these exercises can be done without previous preparation.

ANSWERS
Práctica
A 1. **No la aguanto.**
   2. **Me gusta.**
   3. **Me gusta.**
   4. **No la aguanto.**
   5. **No la aguanto.**
   6. **Me gusta.**
   7. **No lo aguanto.**
   8. **Me gustan.**

Falta de interés o aburrimiento

Para expresar lo que no nos interesa, podemos decir:

> **No me interesa el teatro.**
> **No tengo interés en el teatro.**
> **Esta conferencia (Este discurso) me aburre. No lo/la encuentro interesante. Francamente lo/la encuentro muy aburrido/a.**

Para expresar la razón por nuestra falta de interés, podemos decir:

> **Es aburrido.**
> **Es monótono.**
> **Es pesado.**

Algunas expresiones más populares que indican una falta de interés son:

> **No me dice nada.**
> **No me hace nada.**
> **Me deja frío(a).**
> **No soy muy aficionado(a) al golf.**

A **No lo aguanto.** Indiquen si les gusta, no les gusta, no lo aguantan, les interesa o les aburre.

1. Esta música es horrible. ¡Una abominación! ¡Qué horror!
2. ¡Qué fabuloso es este disco!
3. Ella tiene una voz estupenda, divina, preciosa.
4. Esta ciudad es asquerosa. Me vuelve loco(a).
5. Esta comida es repugnante. No la puedo comer.
6. Pero el postre es delicioso. ¡Qué rico!
7. Yo encuentro asquerosos los modales de este tipo. ¡Qué tío!
8. Estos sonidos son agradables.

Cooperative Learning

Have students work in groups and make lists of their favorite cassettes or CDs, rock stars, actors, actresses, films, etc. Each student from each group will read an entry from his/her list and his/her partner will react using either the positive or negative expressions from the chapter. When they have finished, have them report to the class.

B Oraciones   Usen las siguientes palabras en una oración.

1. asqueroso   **3.** espantoso   **5.** repugnante
2. desagradable   **4.** horrible

C La historia   Completen.

1. —A mí no me gusta nada la historia.
  —¿El pasado no te interesa?
  —De ninguna manera. La encuentro ___.
  —No me digas. A mí me fascina.

2. —El amigo de Camila es un buen tipo pero el pobrecito habla y habla sin decir nada.
  —Es verdad lo que dices. Yo también lo encuentro muy ___. Es tan ___ que cuando me habla me adormezco.

D De otra manera   Expresen de otra manera.

1. No me gusta esta música.
2. Ese tipo de libro no me atrae. No me llama la atención.
3. Este artículo no me interesó.
4. No me gusta la obra de este pintor.
5. No puedo tolerar a este señor.

❧ Actividades comunicativas ❧

A Me interesa.   Haga dos listas: una de las cosas que le interesan, y otra de las cosas que no le interesan. Compare sus listas con las de un(a) compañero(a) de clase. Determinen los intereses que tienen en común. Expliquen por qué les interesa o no les interesa una cosa. Luego, determinen las actividades que a Uds. les gustaría hacer juntos.

B Compañeros de cuarto   Divídanse en grupos de tres. Imagínense que Uds. no se conocen bien. Sin embargo, el próximo año tienen que compartir un apartamento. Para evitar problemas, han decidido abrir un diálogo entre sí. Descríbanse a sí mismos(as) y comenten sus gustos, intereses, antipatías, enojos, etc.

Eurobuilding 2

APARTAMENTOS - SUITES SUPERLUJO EN ALQUILER CON TODOS LOS SERVICIOS DE UN HOTEL DE CINCO ESTRELLAS
RESERVAS DIRECTAS ALQUILERES: ☎ 270 21 56 - 51
CENTRALITA: ☎ 279 48 00 / DIRECCION: ☎ 270 25 08-09
Orense, 69 - 28020-MADRID
El Serpentín   CAFETERIA
BAR - RESTAURANTE
☎ 279 43 82

Departamentos Amoblados
1-2 - 3 Dormitorios, teléfono, piscina, servicio mucama. Estacionamiento.
DIAS - MESES
TURISTAS - EJECUTIVOS FAMILIAS
Riestrapart
☎ 344615 - 346534
FAX: 344615 - METRO TOBALABA - PROVIDENCIA
CASILLA 244 CORREO TAJAMAR - SANTIAGO - CHILE

ANSWERS

Práctica

B Answers will vary.
C 1. aburrida
  2. pesado, aburrido
D Some answers will vary.
  1. No me agrada esta música.
  2. Ese tipo de libro no me hace nada.
  3. Este artículo no me dijo nada.
  4. La obra de este pintor me deja frío(a).
  5. No puedo aguantar a este señor.

TEACHING TIPS

These *Actividades* allow students to work on their own and create situations in which they could find themselves when in a Spanish-speaking country. You may wish to have students select the activity or activities in which they take part.

Actividades comunicativas

ANSWERS

A and B Answers will vary.

ABOUT THE SPANISH LANGUAGE

◆ Note that the word for apartment varies from region to region. In Spain **apartamento** and **piso** are used. In many areas of South America **departamento** is used, as evidenced by the ad from a paper in Chile. In Puerto Rico and other areas **apartamento** is used.

◆ Note the use of **amoblado** in the ad. The word **amueblado** is more commonly used.

Learning From Realia

You may wish to ask the following questions:

¿Qué ofrece el «Eurobuilding»?
¿Dónde se encuentra?
¿A quiénes se les ofrece departamentos?
¿Cerca de qué estación de metro está Riestrapart?
¿De qué tamaños son los departamentos?

Independent Practice

Assign the exercises on pages 118–119.

Repaso de estructura

Expressing surprise, interest, and annoyance
Verbos especiales con complemento indirecto

1. The following verbs function the same in Spanish as in English.

asustar	*to scare*	**importar**	*to matter*
encantar	*to enchant, to delight*	**interesar**	*to interest*
enfurecer	*to infuriate, to anger*	**molestar**	*to bother*
enojar	*to annoy*	**sorprender**	*to surprise*

2. These verbs take an indirect object pronoun in Spanish. Look at the following:

> **Las películas policíacas me asustan (me molestan, me interesan, le enojan, les enfurecen, nos sorprenden).**

3. Note that the subject of the sentence often comes after the verb.

> **A Joaquín le sorprendieron mis ideas.**
> **La verdad es que me enojaron sus opiniones.**

 **Práctica**

A HISTORIETA Nunca están contentos.
Completen.
1. A Pepe ___ molest___ la música moderna.
2. Y a sus hermanas ___ encant___ la música moderna.
3. Pero a las hermanas ___ enoj___ la música clásica.
4. A nosotros no ___ molest___ los discos de Pepe.
5. A mí ___ sorprend___ sus reacciones.
6. Porque a nosotros siempre ___ interes___ toda clase de música.

Mecano, un conjunto español

B **Lo que me encanta.** Indiquen las cosas de la lista que les encantan a Uds.
1. ir al cine
2. los discos de rock
3. el helado
4. viajar
5. las películas de terror
6. los bailes
7. mirar la televisión
8. las clases
9. el chocolate
10. los blue jeans
11. los tenis

TEACHING STRUCTURE

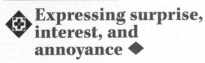

◆ Expressing surprise, interest, and annoyance ◆

A. Read the explanation to the students and call on individuals to read the model sentences.

B. Note that to start with the verbs that function the same in Spanish as in English makes the review of verbs such as **gustar** and **faltar** much easier. It helps students understand why the indirect object is used with these verbs.

VOCABULARY EXPANSION

◆ You may wish to give students the following noun forms of these verbs:

el susto
el encanto
el enfurecimiento
el enojo
el interés
la molestia
la sorpresa

ANSWERS
Práctica

A 1. le molesta
2. les encanta
3. les enoja
4. nos molestan
5. me sorprenden
6. nos interesa

B Answers will vary.

120

Independent Practice

Assign any of the following:
1. Exercises, pages 120–121
2. Workbook, *Repaso de estructura*

C Lo que le asusta a mi hermanito(a). ¿Cuáles son las cosas que le asustan a su hermano(a) menor?

D Lo que le enoja a mamá. ¿Cuáles son algunas cosas que le enojan a su mamá?

Expressing what you like or need
Los verbos **gustar** y **faltar**

The verb **gustar** is translated as "to like." **Faltar** is translated as "to need" or "to lack." The literal meaning of **gustar** is "to please" or "to be pleasing to." The literal meaning of **faltar** is "to be lacking." Note that in Spanish the verbs **gustar** and **faltar** function the same as **interesar** and **sorprender**.

> **A mí me gusta el fútbol.**
> **¿Qué deportes les gustan a Uds.?**
> **A mis hermanos les gustan todos los deportes.**
> **Me falta dinero.**

Práctica

A Los deportistas Contesten con **sí.**

1. ¿A Pablo le gusta el baloncesto?
2. ¿A Sandra le gusta jugar al tenis?
3. ¿A tus hermanos les gusta el fútbol?
4. ¿A las muchachas les gusta el vólibol?
5. ¿A tu hermana le gusta nadar?
6. ¿A tus padres les gusta el golf?

B HISTORIETA Las películas que nos gustan

Completen con las formas apropiadas de **gustar** y el pronombre.

A Jorge ___(1) las películas del oeste. A él no ___(2) las películas románticas. A mi hermana y a mí ___(3) todas las películas. Pero vimos una película anoche que no ___(4). Era una película de terror. A mi madre ___(5) las películas francesas e italianas. Y sé que a ti ___(6) el cine, pero no sé qué películas ___(7). A mí ___(8) mucho las películas documentales. ¿Y a ti?

C ¿Qué no tienes? Contesten según el modelo.

> **¿No tienes papel?**
> **No, me falta papel.**

1. ¿No tienes un bloc?
2. ¿No tienes una pluma?
3. ¿No tienes un lápiz?
4. ¿No tienes libros?

REPASO DE ESTRUCTURA

ciento veintiuno 121

ANSWERS
Práctica
C and **D** Answers will vary.

TEACHING STRUCTURE

◆ **Expressing what you like or need** ◆◆

Read the explanation to the students and have the entire class repeat the model sentences aloud.

RECYCLING

Have students look at the photograph and recall all the tennis vocabulary they have learned.

ANSWERS
Práctica
A 1. Sí, le gusta el baloncesto.
2. Sí, le gusta jugar al tenis.
3. Sí, les gusta el fútbol.
4. Sí, les gusta el vólibol.
5. Sí, le gusta nadar.
6. Sí, les gusta el golf.
B 1. le gustan
2. le gustan
3. nos gustan
4. nos gustó
5. le gustan
6. te gusta
7. te gustan
8. me gustan
C 1. No, me falta un bloc.
2. No, me falta una pluma.
3. No, me falta un lápiz.
4. No, me faltan libros.

Paired Activity

Have students do the following activity:
Trabaje con un(a) compañero(a). Hable de todo lo que le gustaba hacer y no le gustaba hacer cuando era joven.

Independent Practice

Assign any of the following:
1. Exercises, page 121
2. Workbook, *Repaso de estructura*

121

TEACHING STRUCTURE

◆ **Contrasting location and origin** ◆◆◆

A. Read the explanation to the students and have the entire class repeat the model sentences aloud.

B. Note: It is recommended that you not spend a great deal of time on this point. Students at this level usually understand the concepts, although they need constant reinforcement in order to use the correct verb.

TEACHING TIPS

These *Práctica* can be done without previous preparation.

ANSWERS

Práctica

A Some answers will vary.
1. Estoy...
2. Mi casa está...
3. Mi escuela está...
4. Mis padres están...
5. Mis amigos están...
6. Mi profesor(a) de español está...

B 1. Sí, sí. Son de España.
2. Sí, sí. Es de España.
3. Sí, sí. Es de España.
4. Sí, sí. Es de España.

C 1. son
2. está
3. está
4. es
5. está

Contrasting location and origin
Ser y estar

1. There are two verbs to express "to be" in Spanish. They are **ser** and **estar.** Each of these verbs has specific uses. They are not interchangeable. The verb **estar** is always used to express location, both temporary and permanent.

PERMANENT	TEMPORARY
Madrid está en España.	Mis primos están en Madrid ahora.
Mi casa está en los suburbios de Nueva York.	Mis amigos están en mi casa.

2. The verb **ser** is used to express origin, where someone or something is from.

> Yo soy de los Estados Unidos.
> Mi abuelo es de España y mi abuela es de Cuba.
> Este vino es de Chile.

3. Note that the following sentence illustrates both origin and location.

> El señor Rosas es de Colombia pero ahora está en Puerto Rico.

Práctica

A **¿Dónde está?** Preguntas personales.
1. ¿Dónde estás ahora?
2. ¿Dónde está tu casa?
3. Y tu escuela, ¿dónde está?
4. ¿Dónde están tus padres?
5. Y tus amigos, ¿dónde están?
6. ¿Dónde está tu profesor(a) de español?

B **¿De qué país es?** Contesten según el modelo.
> **¿Es español el señor Suárez?**
> **Sí, sí. Es de España.**
1. ¿Son españoles los Guzmán?
2. ¿Es español el jamón serrano?
3. ¿Es español el queso manchego?
4. ¿Es español el jabón Magno?

C **Unos primos** Completen con **ser** o **estar.**
1. Ángel y Guadalupe ___ de la Ciudad de México.
2. Su apartamento ___ en la calle Niza.
3. La calle Niza ___ en la colonia que se llama la Zona Rosa.
4. El primo de Ángel y Guadalupe ___ de Arizona.
5. Pero ahora él ___ en México porque está visitando a sus primos.

Learning From Realia

The food items shown here are **jamón serrano** and **queso manchego. Jamón serrano** is a type of Spanish cured ham. Eaten by itself it is one of the most popular **tapas** in Spain. Because of its delicious flavor, it is also used in many dishes.

Manchego is a well-cured cheese from **La Mancha.** It is made from sheep's milk.

Independent Practice

Assign any of the following:
1. Exercises, page 122
2. Workbook, *Repaso de estructura*

Expressing characteristics and conditions
Característica y condición

1. The verb **estar** is used to express a temporary state or condition.

> **El agua está muy fría.**
> **Y el té está muy caliente.**
> **No sé por qué estoy tan cansado.**

2. The verb **ser,** however, is used to express an inherent quality or characteristic.

> **El hermano de Juan es muy simpático.**
> **Y él es guapo.**
> **Y además es muy sincero.**

Práctica

A Yo Preguntas personales.

1. ¿Eres alto(a) o bajo(a)?
2. ¿Eres fuerte o débil?
3. ¿De qué nacionalidad eres?
4. ¿Eres simpático(a) o antipático(a)?
5. ¿Cómo estás hoy?
6. ¿Estás de buen humor o estás de mal humor?
7. ¿Estás bien o estás enfermo(a)?
8. ¿Estás contento(a) o triste?
9. ¿Estás cansado(a)?

Plaza Bolívar, Santafé de Bogotá, Colombia

B La capital de Colombia Completen con **ser** o **estar.**

1. La ciudad de Santafé de Bogotá ___ en Colombia.
2. La ciudad de Santafé de Bogotá ___ la capital de Colombia.
3. La ciudad de Santafé de Bogotá ___ muy bonita.
4. La ciudad ___ grande.
5. El tiempo en Santafé de Bogotá ___ muy frío hoy.
6. Los Andes ___ muy altos.
7. El barrio colonial de Santafé de Bogotá ___ muy viejo.
8. El barrio colonial ___ lleno de turistas en este momento.
9. Las plazas del barrio colonial ___ muy pintorescas.
10. No toda la ciudad de Santafé de Bogotá ___ antigua.
11. Muchas zonas de la ciudad ___ modernas.
12. Los rascacielos de los barrios modernos ___ impresionantes.
13. El Museo del Oro ___ cerrado debido a un accidente.

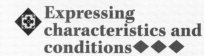

CAPÍTULO 3
Repaso de estructura

TEACHING STRUCTURE

◆ Expressing characteristics and conditions ◆◆◆

Read the explanation to the students and have the entire class repeat the model sentences aloud.

TEACHING TIPS

These exercises can be done without previous preparation.

ANSWERS

Práctica

A Some answers will vary.

1. **Soy alto(a) (bajo[a]).**
2. **Soy fuerte (débil).**
3. **Soy (americano[a]).**
4. **Soy simpático(a) (antipático[a]).**
5. **Estoy (bien).**
6. **Estoy de buen (mal) humor hoy.**
7. **Estoy bien (enfermo[a]).**
8. **Estoy contento(a) (triste).**
9. **Sí (No), (no) estoy cansado(a).**

B 1. **está**
2. **es**
3. **es**
4. **es**
5. **está**
6. **son**
7. **es**
8. **está**
9. **son**
10. **es**
11. **son**
12. **son**
13. **está**

Independent Practice

Assign any of the following:
1. Exercises, page 123
2. Workbook, *Repaso de estructura*

123

TEACHING STRUCTURE

More about *ser* and *estar*◆ ◆ ◆

Go over the explanatory material in steps 1–4 with the students and have them repeat the model sentences aloud. Ensure that they understand the differences in meaning. You may wish to give additional examples.

More about ser and estar
Usos especiales de **ser** y **estar**

1. As you have already learned, the verb **ser** is used to express origin, a characteristic, or an inherent quality. The verb **estar** is used to express a permanent or temporary location, a temporary state, or a condition. The speaker often chooses the verb **ser** or **estar** depending upon the meaning he or she wishes to convey. Observe and analyze the following.

> **Estas frutas son muy agrias.**
> **Estas frutas están muy agrias.**

The first sentence uses the verb **ser.** The meaning conveyed is that these fruits are supposed to be sour. The characteristic of these fruits is to be sour rather than sweet. The second sentence uses the verb **estar.** The meaning conveyed is that these particular fruits are sour but are supposed to be sweet.

2. Note the difference in meaning in the following pairs of sentences.

> **Carlos es guapo.**   *Charles is handsome (a handsome person).*
> **Carlos está muy guapo hoy.**   *Charles looks very handsome today.*
> **La sopa es buena.**   *Soup is (inherently) good (healthful).*
> **La sopa está buena.**   *The soup tastes good.*

3. Many words actually change meaning when used with **ser** or with **estar.** Study the following.

	WITH **ser**	WITH **estar**
aburrido	*boring*	*bored*
cansado	*tiresome*	*tired*
divertido	*amusing, funny*	*amused*
enfermo	*sickly*	*sick, ill*
listo	*bright, clever, smart, shrewd*	*ready*
triste	*dull*	*sad*
vivo	*lively, alert*	*alive*

Note that the verb **estar** with **vivo** means "to be alive." The verb **estar** is also used with **muerto** to mean "to be dead," even though death is permanent.

> **Su abuelo está muerto.**

4. The verb **ser** is used whenever the verb "to be" has the meaning of "to take place."

> **El concierto tendrá lugar mañana.**
> **El concierto será mañana.**
> **Tendrá lugar en el teatro.**
> **Será en el teatro.**

Additional Practice

1. Con su grupo discutan las oportunidades de trabajo en el futuro e indiquen cuáles son las cosas que más le importan a cada uno de Uds. en un oficio o profesión. Piensen en aspectos materiales y no materiales. Después preparen un resumen y preséntenlo a la clase.

2. Prepare una descripción de un personaje famoso. Lea su descripción a la clase y llame a alguien que identifique a su personaje famoso.

Práctica

A **¿Ser o estar?** Seleccionen el verbo apropiado.

1. Tienes que comer más verduras. Las verduras tienen muchas vitaminas y ___ muy buenas para la salud.
   a. son **b.** están

2. ¡Qué deliciosas! ¿Dónde compraste estas verduras? ___ muy buenas.
   a. Son **b.** Están

3. No sé lo que le pasa a la pobre Marta. Tiene que estar enferma porque ___ muy pálida.
   a. es **b.** está

4. No, no está enferma. Es su color. Ella ___ muy pálida.
   a. es **b.** está

5. Él ___ tan aburrido que cada vez que empieza a hablar, todo el mundo se duerme.
   a. es **b.** está

6. ¡Elena! Me encanta el vestido que llevas hoy. ¡Qué bonita ___!
   a. eres **b.** estás

7. El pobre Juanito ___ tan cansado que sólo quiere volver a casa para dormir un poco.
   a. es **b.** está

8. ¿___ listos todos? Vamos a salir en cinco minutos.
   a. Son **b.** Están

9. Ella ___ muy lista. Ella sabe exactamente lo que está haciendo y te aseguro que está haciéndolo a propósito.
   a. es **b.** está

10. Él ___ muy vivo y divertido. A mí, como a todo el mundo, me gusta mucho estar con él.
    a. es **b.** está

11. No, no se murió el padre de Josefina. Él ___ vivo.
    a. es **b.** está

B **¿Cuándo y dónde será?** Contesten según se indica.

1. ¿Dónde será el concierto? (en el parque central)
2. ¿Cuándo es la fiesta? (el domingo por la tarde)
3. ¿Dónde es la exposición de arte? (en el Museo de Arte Moderno)
4. ¿Cuándo será la exposición? (del 5 al 12 de este mes)
5. ¿A qué hora es la película? (a las ocho de la noche)

TEACHING TIPS

These exercises can be done without previous preparation.

ANSWERS

Práctica

A 1. **a**
2. **b**
3. **b**
4. **a**
5. **a**
6. **b**
7. **b**
8. **b**
9. **a**
10. **a**
11. **b**

B 1. **El concierto será en el parque central.**
2. **La fiesta es el domingo por la tarde.**
3. **La exposición de arte es en el Museo de Arte Moderno.**
4. **La exposición será del 5 al 12 de este mes.**
5. **La película es a las ocho de la noche.**

ABOUT THE SPANISH LANGUAGE

En México éstos son «chiles». En otras partes son «pimientos». Los que son pequeños y picantes también se llaman «ajíes» o «guindillas».

Additional Practice

Have students make up some of their own sentences using expressions or words that could be used with **ser** or **estar.** Have them explain in Spanish the meaning of their sentence and why the verb **ser** or **estar** is used.

125

TEACHING STRUCTURE

◆ **Expressing origin and ownership** ◆◆

Read the explanation to the students and have them repeat the model sentences aloud.

RECYCLING

Have students look at the photograph of the house and describe their own house or apartment.

TEACHING TIPS

This exercise can be done without any previous preparation.

ANSWERS
Práctica
C 1. es   5. Es
  2. está   6. es
  3. es   7. son
  4. es

TEACHING STRUCTURE

◆ **Giving commands** ◆◆◆

Note that in reviewing the commands, we have grouped all the subjunctive forms together. This allows for a succinct review of all commands, affirmative and negative. The only form that has to be dealt with separately is the affirmative **tú** command.

TEACHING TIPS

Guide the students through steps 1, 2, and 3, having them repeat the command forms after you for review practice.

Expressing origin and ownership
Ser de

The expression **ser de** is used to express origin, ownership, or source; for example, the material from which something is made.

Este reloj es de Suiza.   **No es de plata. Es de oro.**
El reloj es de Carlota.   **La casa es de los Amaral.**

❖ Práctica ❖

A **HISTORIETA** A la casa de los Amaral

Completen.

Aquí tenemos una foto de una casa bonita. La casa ___ de la familia Amaral. La casa ___ en el sur de
1 2

California. La casa de los Amaral no ___ de ladrillo. Tampoco ___ de
3 4

adobe. ___ de madera y estuco. El
5

techo ___ de tejas. Las tejas ___ de México.
6 7

Giving commands
El imperativo

1. Most commands are expressed by using the subjunctive. Review the following.

hablar	(no) hable Ud.	(no) hablen Uds.	no hables
comer	(no) coma Ud.	(no) coman Uds.	no comas
subir	(no) suba Ud.	(no) suban Uds.	no subas
volver	(no) vuelva Ud.	(no) vuelvan Uds.	no vuelvas
pedir	(no) pida Ud.	(no) pidan Uds.	no pidas
salir	(no) salga Ud.	(no) salgan Uds.	no salgas
conducir	(no) conduzca Ud.	(no) conduzcan Uds.	no conduzcas
ir	(no) vaya Ud.	(no) vayan Uds.	no vayas

Independent Practice

Assign any of the following:
1. Exercises, pages 125–126
2. Workbook, *Repaso de estructura*

2. The affirmative **tú** command is not expressed by the subjunctive. The affirmative **tú** command of regular verbs is the same as the **Ud.** form of the present indicative.

hablar	habla
comer	come
subir	sube
volver	vuelve
pedir	pide

3. The following verbs have irregular forms in the affirmative **tú** command.

decir	di
hacer	haz
salir	sal
poner	pon
tener	ten
venir	ven
ser	sé
ir	ve

Práctica

A **¿Qué debo hacer?** Contesten según el modelo.

> **¿Debo volver?**
> **Sí, vuelva Ud.**

1. ¿Debo esperar?
2. ¿Debo hablar?
3. ¿Debo comer?
4. ¿Debo leer?
5. ¿Debo escribir?
6. ¿Debo venir?
7. ¿Debo salir?
8. ¿Debo conducir
9. ¿Debo servir?
10. ¿Debo volver?

La Plaza de Armas, Santiago, Chile

B **¿Cómo se usa el teléfono?** Completen.

1. ___ (Descolgar) Ud. el auricular.
2. ___ (Esperar) la señal.
3. ___ (Introducir) la moneda en la ranura.
4. ___ (Marcar) el número.
5. ___ (Hablar) ahora.

TEACHING TIPS

As a review, these exercises can be done quickly without advance preparation. If the students seem to have difficulty, you may wish to have them write out some or all of the exercises (depending on where they have difficulty) and go over them again in class.

ANSWERS
Práctica

A **1. Sí, espere Ud.**
　2. Sí, hable Ud.
　3. Sí, coma Ud.
　4. Sí, lea Ud.
　5. Sí, escriba Ud.
　6. Sí, venga Ud.
　7. Sí, salga Ud.
　8. Sí, conduzca Ud.
　9. Sí, sirva Ud.
　10. Sí, vuelva Ud.
B **1. Descuelgue**
　2. Espere
　3. Introduzca
　4. Marque
　5. Hable

Learning From Photos

La Plaza de Armas es la plaza más antigua de Santiago. Aquí ven Uds. la catedral que data de 1780. Fue construida en el lugar que los conquistadores escogieron en 1541 como centro de la ciudad. De la Plaza de Armas sale el Paseo Ahumada que desde 1977 es un paseo peatonal. Se prohíbe el tráfico vehicular. Es un paseo adoquinado con jardines de flores, fuentes y tiendas elegantes.

ANSWERS

Práctica

C 1. Tome   6. vire
    2. doble   7. Tome
    3. Siga   8. Siga
    4. doble   9. salga
    5. Vaya

D 1. ve   5. sé
    2. haz   6. di
    3. pon   7. haz
    4. sirve   8. ve

E 1. Llama al restaurante.
    2. Reserva una mesa.
    3. Haz la reservación para las ocho.
    4. Pide una mesa para seis personas.
    5. Pregunta si tienen un menú fijo.
    6. Haz la reservación a tu nombre.

F 1. ¡Estudia!
    2. ¡Repasa!
    3. ¡Lee!
    4. ¡Escribe!
    5. ¡Ve!

G Pues, no hay problema.
    1. No cantes.
    2. No bailes.
    3. No estudies.
    4. No comas.
    5. No leas.
    6. No vuelvas.
    7. No duermas.
    8. No salgas.
    9. No vengas.
    10. No conduzcas.

Paired Activities

1. Hágale una entrevista a su compañero(a) de clase. Pregúntele cuáles son las actividades de la escuela que más le gustan y las que más le enojan. Después cambien de papel.
2. Explíquele a un(a) compañero(a) cómo ir de su casa a su escuela.
3. Explíquele a un(a) compañero(a) cómo ir de su casa al aeropuerto.

128

C **¡Perdone!** ¿Cómo salgo de la ciudad? Completen.

1. ___ (Tomar) Ud. la Alameda hasta el final.
2. Al final de la Alameda, ___ (doblar) a la izquierda.
3. ___ (Seguir) derecho hasta el tercer semáforo.
4. Al llegar al tercer semáforo, ___ (doblar) a la derecha.
5. ___ (Ir) a la tercera bocacalle, donde verá Ud. la casa de correos.
6. Después de pasar el correo, ___ (virar) a la derecha.
7. Es la calle Centauro. ___ (tomar) la calle Centauro.
8. ___ (Seguir) derecho hasta llegar a la entrada de la autopista.
9. Para ir a Torreblanca, ___ (salir) de la autopista en la primera salida después de pasar la segunda garita de peaje.

D **Pues, haz lo que te dé la gana.** Completen con el imperativo familiar.

1. Tengo que ir a casa. Pues, ___ a casa.
2. Tengo que hacer la comida. Pues, ___ la comida.
3. Tengo que poner la mesa. Pues, ___ la mesa.
4. Y luego tengo que servir la comida. Pues, ___ la comida.
5. Tengo que ser bueno(a). Pues, ___ bueno(a).
6. Tengo que decirles algo a mis padres. Pues, ___ algo.
7. Quiero hacer un viaje este verano. Pues, ___ un viaje si quieres.
8. Quiero ir al Perú. Pues, ___ al Perú.

E **Haz lo que debes hacer.** Contesten con el imperativo familiar.

1. ¿Debo llamar al restaurante?
2. ¿Debo reservar una mesa?
3. ¿Debo hacer la reservación para las ocho?
4. ¿Debo pedir una mesa para seis personas?
5. ¿Debo preguntar si tienen un menú fijo?
6. ¿Debo hacer la reservación a mi nombre?

F **Sí, sí. Es importante.** Contesten según el modelo.

> **No quiero estudiar.**
> **Pues, es importante, José. ¡Estudia!**

1. No quiero estudiar.
2. No quiero repasar la lección de biología.
3. No quiero leer el libro de historia.
4. No quiero escribir la composición.
5. No quiero ir a la clase de música.

G **No hay problema. No lo hagas.** Sigan el modelo.

> **No quiero hablar.**
> **Pues, no hay problema. No hables.**

1. No quiero cantar.
2. No quiero bailar.
3. No quiero estudiar.
4. No quiero comer.
5. No quiero leer.
6. No quiero volver.
7. No quiero dormir.
8. No quiero salir.
9. No quiero venir.
10. No quiero conducir.

Plaza Mayor, Madrid, España

Independent Practice

Assign any of the following:
1. Exercises, pages 127–128
2. Workbook, *Repaso de estructura*

Periodismo

El wind surf

Introducción

A mucha gente le gusta practicar un deporte durante sus horas libres. Puede ser un deporte divertido y a la vez una actividad muy sana porque los deportes nos hacen ejercitar el cuerpo. El *wind surf* o plancha de vela es una diversión relativamente nueva pero está haciéndose muy popular. Es un deporte que se puede practicar aun lejos del mar porque se puede hacer *wind surf* en un lago o en un río.

El artículo que sigue apareció en la revista mexicana *Eres.* Indica la popularidad del *wind surf* en ese país.

Vocabulario

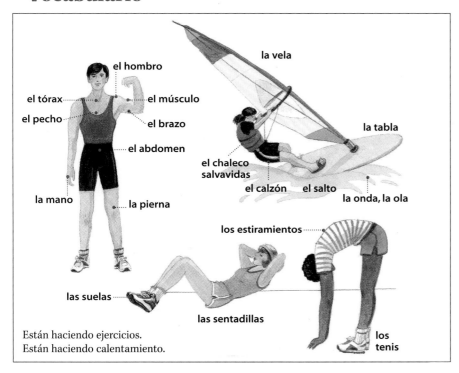

el hombro
el tórax
el músculo
el pecho
el brazo
el abdomen
la mano
la pierna
la vela
la tabla
el chaleco salvavidas
el calzón
el salto
la onda, la ola
los estiramientos
las suelas
las sentadillas
los tenis

Están haciendo ejercicios.
Están haciendo calentamiento.

TEACHING TIPS

You may wish to read the *Introducción* aloud or have the students read it silently.

RESOURCES

- Vocabulary Transparencies
- Audio Cassette 5B/Compact Disc 4
- Student Tape Manual
- Workbook
- Chapter Quizzes
- Testing Program

TEACHING VOCABULARY

You may wish to use some of the procedures suggested in previous chapters.

Cooperative Learning

Have students work in groups. They choose a leader and switch leaders every minute. They are in an aerobics or exercise class. The leader tells the group what to do. Other group members act it out. In addition to using the new vocabulary, this activity covers once again the commands just reviewed in *Repaso de estructura.*

ANSWERS

Práctica

A 1. los tenis
  2. la vela
  3. las sentadillas
  4. la onda, la ola
  5. la tabla
  6. el chaleco salvavidas
  7. el brazo (el músculo)
  8. la mano

B 1. La tabla tiene una vela.
  2. El joven salta la onda.
  3. Se cayó porque se resbaló.
  4. Sí, se volteó.
  5. Se volteó porque dio unos brincos fuertes.
  6. Hizo sentadillas y estiramientos.
  7. Lleva guantes para no lastimarse las manos.

El joven se resbaló.
La tabla dio unos brincos.
Se volteó.

ejercitar darle ejercicio a
lastimar hacerle daño, dañar, herir

los ligeros los que no pesan mucho, los que pesan pocos kilos
los pesados los que tienen mucho peso, lo contrario de «ligeros»
los novatos los principiantes, lo contrario de «expertos»

Práctica

A **¿Qué es?** Identifiquen.

1. 2. 3. 4.

5. 6. 7. 8.

B **¿Qué pasó?** Contesten según se indica.
  1. ¿Qué tiene la tabla? (una vela)
  2. ¿Qué salta el joven? (la onda)
  3. ¿Por qué se cayó de la tabla? (se resbaló)
  4. ¿Se volteó? (sí)
  5. ¿Por qué se volteó? (dio unos brincos fuertes)
  6. ¿Qué ejercicios hizo para hacer calentamiento? (sentadillas y estiramientos)
  7. ¿Por qué lleva guantes el/la *wind surfer*? (para no lastimarse las manos)

Independent Practice

Assign any of the following:
  1. Exercises, page 130
  2. Workbook, *Periodismo*

Wind surf: agua, aire ¡y diversión!

Para ti que te encanta pasártela súper con tus cuates[1] cerca del mar o de algún lago, haciendo deporte, ésta es una de las opciones con la que además de que te vas a sentir de maravilla, te vas a poner… ¡guauuuu!

Por Jorge Barajas Rocha

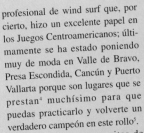

El wind surf es un deporte que no sólo es divertidísimo, sino que en él ejercitas muchísimas partes del cuerpo, además de que como se tiene que practicar en el agua, puedes echarte unas asoleadas[2] y nadadas, ¡otra onda!

Poco a poco ha ido agarrando[3] más fuerza en México, y desde hace unos años existe un equipo

profesional de wind surf que, por cierto, hizo un excelente papel en los Juegos Centroamericanos; últimamente se ha estado poniendo muy de moda en Valle de Bravo, Presa Escondida, Cancún y Puerto Vallarta porque son lugares que se prestan[4] muchísimo para que puedas practicarlo y volverte un verdadero campeón en este rollo[5].

Realmente, no necesitas de muchas cosas para poder hacer wind surf, sólo te hace falta una tabla con vela y, ¡listo! (Nada más no se te olvide el lago, ¿eh?) Eso sí, es básico estar protegido para que no te vayas a lastimar a las primeras de cambio[6], ¿no? Así, te conviene usar wetsuit, que son trajes color neón para que no te confundas con el agua (además de que guardan el calor de tu cuerpo), guantes especiales para que no te lastimes las manos, cinturón o arnés[7] (si es en forma de calzón, ¡mucho mejor!), chaleco salvavidas y tenis ligeros de suela blanda para que no te resbales.

Pero, ¿en qué consiste este deporte? El wind surf viene siendo algo así como una especialización del famosísimo "surfing", sólo que aquí tienes muchas más cosas de las que tienes que estar al pendiente porque a cada rato[8] andas en el aire dando unos brincos como para dejar a todo el mundo con el ojo cuadrado[9]. Lo fundamental del wind surf es aprender a controlar la vela para que el viento te lleve hacia donde tú quieras, así como aprovechar la fuerza del viento para tomar velocidad; obvio que también hay que saber manejar la tabla y mover tu cuerpo para que le hagas contrapeso[10] a la

---

PARA PRACTICARLO

Cerca del D.F.
Presa Escondida, Hgo.
Valle de Bravo, Edo. de Méx.
Atlangatepec, Tlax.

En la costa del Pacífico
Puerto Vallarta, Jal.
Puerto Escondido, Oax.
Puerto Ángel, Oax.
Huatulco, Oax.
Ensenada, B.C.
Cabo San Lucas, B.C.
La Paz, B.C.
Bahía Negra, B.C.
Acapulco, Gro.

En el Golfo de México
Cancún, Q. Roo

---

[1] **cuates** amigos (México)
[2] **echarte unas asoleadas** broncearte
[3] **agarrando** getting
[4] **se prestan** lend themselves
[5] **en este rollo** este deporte
[6] **las primeras de cambio** primera vez
[7] **arnés** harness
[8] **a cada rato** a cada momento
[9] **el ojo cuadrado** amazed
[10] **contrapeso** counterbalance

PERIODISMO

ciento treinta y uno 131

 Bell Ringer Review

Use the BRR Transparency 3-5, or write the following on the board: **Haga una lista de todas las actividades de verano que Ud. conoce.**

TEACHING THE READING

 Wind surf: agua, aire ¡y diversión!

It is suggested that you have students read the article silently. This article should be of some interest to the students as wind surfing is an increasingly popular pastime.

 GEOGRAPHY CONNECTION

Have students refer to a map of Mexico and locate the places mentioned under *Para practicarlo*.

Additional Practice

Have students reread the selection and make a list of all the parts of the body and a list of all the activities mentioned in the article.

vela y así evitar que te voltees a cada rato. Aunque al principio te la pasas en el agua, el chiste es que no te desesperes y vayas mejorando[11] poco a poco. Acuérdate que nadie nace siendo un campeón en ningún deporte, sino que se va aprendiendo con el tiempo y la experiencia.

Lo prendidísimo[12] es que cada fin de semana se organizan competencias en las que hay que recorrer un circuito en plan de carreras, así que además de ponerse súper listo para la onda de los saltos, también hay que tener rapidez para ganar.

La edad para practicarlo no tiene que ser una en específico, sólo que mientras más chico[13] empieces, vas adquiriendo más elasticidad, coordinación, control de la vela y sentido del equilibrio. De todos modos, no tengas miedo de hacer osos[14] si estás empezando y mejor concéntrate en este rollo; sólo hay que tener mucha disciplina. Además, la verdad, no es tan complicado como parece y, eso sí, es divertidísimo.

De cualquier forma, tienes que prepararte muy bien: primero, hay que tener una condición física excelente y, segundo, muchísima fuerza en tus piernas, brazos y abdomen, que es lo que más ejercitas. Para eso, antes de entrar al agua, es muy conveniente que hagas un poco de calentamiento para que no vayas a tener problemas con tus músculos, que sólo así estarán listos para ponerlos a prueba; puedes hacer sentadillas, abdominales, lagartijas[15], estiramientos y torsiones de tronco.

TIPS BÁSICOS

* Mantén el equilibrio en base a la velocidad y a la intensidad del viento.
* Conserva la ruta de la línea del viento.
* No luches contra el viento, sino ayúdate de él para ir en la dirección que quieras.
* Si no puedes pararte porque hay mucho viento, espérate a que baje un poco.
* Sé muy constante.

En México, hay varias asociaciones en las que puedes meterte para practicarlo más seguido dentro de diferentes categorías, por lo que igual encuentras un equipo de cuates que van desde los doce años hasta uno de gente mayor a los treinta años, además de que hay grupos de ligeros, pesados, masters y novatos. Como quien dice, ¡hay de todo para todos! Otra cosa de lo más padre[16] es que estás en pleno contacto con la natu-

sano porque hay un buen de gente que le está entrando[18] al wind surf y a la que también le encanta todo ese rollo, así es que siempre vas a conocer gente muy prendida[19].

Sobre las partes del cuerpo que ejercitas, te sirve muchísimo para los brazos, piernas y tórax, aunque igual te fortalece los hombros, el pecho y las pompas[20]. Como quien dice, ¡todo!

raleza porque siempre vas a estar rodeado de viento, agua, sol y con unos paisajes a tu alrededor que de plano ¡no te los acabas[17]!, además de que el ambiente es de lo más

Así que ya lo sabes, para pasarte unos fines de semana ¡otro rollo! en medio de un súper ambiente, haciendo ejercicio y agarrando un color envidiable, el wind surf es… ¡la mejor opción!

[11] **mejorando** *improving*
[12] **lo prendidísimo** más importante
[13] **chico** joven, pequeño
[14] **hacer osos** cometer errores
[15] **lagartijas** *push-ups*
[16] **padre** *nice (Mexico)*
[17] **no te los acabas** increíble
[18] **entrando** practicando
[19] **prendida** interesante
[20] **las pompas** *buttocks*

Comprensión

A ¿Es verdad? ¿Sí o no?

1. El *wind surf* ha ido agarrando (logrando) más fuerza (más popularidad) en México.
2. Desgraciadamente necesitas de muchas cosas para hacer *wind surf*.
3. Hay que pensar en más cosas cuando uno hace *wind surf* que cuando uno hace *surfing* (tabla).
4. Nadie nace siendo un campeón en ningún deporte. Hay que aprender, practicar y mejorar con el tiempo y la experiencia.
5. Hay una edad específica para practicar el *wind surf*.
6. El *wind surf* parece más complicado de lo que es.

B Agua, aire y diversión   Contesten.

1. ¿Cuáles son algunas ventajas del *wind surf*?
2. ¿Cuáles son algunas cosas esenciales para hacer *wind surf*?
3. ¿Por qué le conviene a uno llevar un *wet suit*?
4. ¿Por qué se debe llevar guantes?
5. ¿Cuál es lo fundamental del *wind surf*?
6. ¿Qué se organiza cada fin de semana?
7. ¿Qué dice el artículo sobre la gente que practica el *wind surf*?

C Le hace falta.   Hagan lo siguiente.

1. Den una lista de las cosas que hay que hacer para prepararse para el *wind surf*.
2. Preparen una lista de los grupos para quienes hay asociaciones de *wind surf*.

¡PURA Y SIMPLE!

Actividades comunicativas

A Para hacer *wind surf*   Imagínese que Ud. va a empezar a hacer *wind surf*. Prepare una lista de las cosas que necesitará y que comprará.

B Nos gustaría...   Trabaje con un(a) compañero(a) de clase. Decidan si Uds. creen que les gustaría el *wind surf*. ¿Por qué sí o por qué no?

TEACHING TIPS

A This exercise can be done without previous preparation.

B and C These exercises should be prepared first and then gone over in class.

ANSWERS

Comprensión

A 1. sí
   2. no
   3. sí
   4. sí
   5. no
   6. sí

B 1. No se necesitan muchas cosas para hacer *wind surf*.
   2. Se necesitan la tabla y la vela.
   3. Un *wet suit* guarda el calor del cuerpo.
   4. Se debe llevar guantes para no lastimarse las manos.
   5. Es aprender a controlar la vela.
   6. Se organizan competencias cada fin de semana.
   7. La gente que practica el *wind surf* es gente muy prendida.

C Answers will vary.

Actividades comunicativas

ANSWERS

A and B Answers will vary.

Cooperative Learning

Have students work in small groups and make up a story about a day at the beach.

Independent Practice

Assign any of the following:
   1. Exercises, page 133
   2. Workbook, *Periodismo*

133

Estructura

RESOURCES

- 📁 Workbook
- 📁 Student Tape Manual
- 🎧 Audio Cassette 6A/Compact Disc 4
- 💾 Computer Software: *Estructura*
- 📁 Chapter Quizzes
- 💾 Testing Program

TEACHING STRUCTURE

◈ **Expressing duration of time** ◆◆◆

Have the students read the explanations silently and then repeat the model sentences aloud after you or Cassette 6A/Compact Disc 4.

TEACHING TIPS

Students should be able to do these *Práctica* without advance preparation.

ANSWERS

Práctica

A Answers will vary.
1. **Hace... que vivo en la misma casa.**
2. **Hace... que conozco a mi mejor amigo(a).**
3. **Hace... que asisto a la misma escuela.**
4. **Hace... que estudio español.**
5. **Hace... que estudio con el mismo (la misma) profesor(a) de español.**

134

Expressing duration of time
Hace y hacía

1. The expression **hace** is used with the present tense to express an action that began sometime in the past but continues into the present. Observe and analyze the following examples.

> **¿Cuánto tiempo hace que tú estás aquí?**   *How long have you been here?*
> **Hace un año que estoy aquí.**   *I have been here for a year.*

2. Note that in English, the present perfect tense "has been" is used. But in Spanish, the present tense must be used. English uses the present perfect tense because the action began in the past. Spanish uses the present tense because the action actually continues into the present. Note too, that **desde hace** as well as **hace** can be used.

> **Hace un año que estoy aquí.**   *I have been here for a year.*
> **Estoy aquí desde hace un año.**   *I have been here for a year.*

3. The expression **hacía** is used with the imperfect tense to express an action that had been in effect until something else interrupted it. Observe and analyze the following sentence.

> **Hacía dos años que ellos vivían en México cuando la compañía los trasladó a Puerto Rico.**

✦Práctica✦

A **¿Cuánto tiempo hace?**   Contesten.
1. ¿Cuánto tiempo hace que Ud. vive en la misma casa?
2. ¿Cuánto tiempo hace que Ud. conoce a su mejor amigo(a)?
3. ¿Cuánto tiempo hace que Ud. asiste a la misma escuela?
4. ¿Cuánto tiempo hace que Ud. estudia español?
5. ¿Cuánto tiempo hace que Ud. estudia con el mismo (la misma) profesor(a) de español?

La Calle del Cristo en el Viejo San Juan, Puerto Rico

Learning From Photos

1. Have students describe the photo in their own words.
2. You may also wish to give them the following information: At the end of **Calle del Cristo** there is a small chapel and a delightful park, called **el Parque de las Palomas,** always crowded with thousands of pigeons that the children love to feed.

From the park there is a beautiful view of a part of the port of San Juan. The old section of San Juan, referred to as **el Viejo San Juan,** is an area of narrow cobble-stoned streets and picturesque plazas. Many of the old buildings have been restored. These buildings date from colonial times.

B **Actividades culturales** Contesten según se indica.

1. ¿Cuánto tiempo hace que están presentando la misma obra? (un año y medio)
2. ¿Cuánto tiempo hace que están poniendo (presentando) la misma película? (sólo cuatro días)
3. ¿Cuánto tiempo hace que están exhibiendo los cuadros impresionistas? (un mes)
4. ¿Cuánto tiempo hace que el equipo está jugando en este estadio? (un par de años)
5. ¿Cuánto tiempo hace que están construyendo el nuevo parque de atracciones? (más de un año)

C **HISTORIETA** **Mi hermano José**

Completen.

1. Hacía dos años que mi hermano José ___ (estudiar) francés cuando decidió que quería aprender el español.
2. Hacía mucho tiempo que él ___ (decir) que quería ir a Princeton cuando de repente decidió que quería ir a Harvard.
3. Hacía sólo dos días que él ___ (estar) de vacaciones cuando él conoció a Amalia.
4. Pero hacía un año entero que él ___ (salir) con Teresa cuando conoció a Amalia.
5. Y ahora, hace dos meses que él ___ (salir) con Amalia.
6. Hacía un mes que Teresa no le ___ (hablar) cuando ella decidió que no estaba enfadada con él.
7. Y ahora, hace un mes que Teresa ___ (salir) conmigo, el hermano mayor de Joselito.

Having just done something
Acabar de

The expression **acabar de** followed by an infinitive means "to have just." **Acabar de** is used in two tenses only, the present and the imperfect. Observe the following sentences.

Él acaba de salir.	*He has just left.*
Ellos acababan de salir.	*They had just left.*

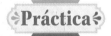

A **¡Qué confusión!** Contesten.

1. ¿Acabas de volver a casa?
2. ¿Acaba de volver María también?
3. ¿Acaban Uds. de hacer un viaje?
4. ¿Acaban Uds. de visitar a sus parientes?
5. ¿Acababan Uds. de entrar en la casa cuando sonó el teléfono?

ANSWERS
Práctica

B 1. Hace un año y medio que están presentando la misma obra.
2. Hace sólo cuatro días que están poniendo la misma película.
3. Hace un mes que están exhibiendo los cuadros impresionistas.
4. Hace un par de años que el equipo está jugando en este estadio.
5. Hace más de un año que están construyendo el nuevo parque de atracciones.

C 1. estudiaba
2. decía
3. estaba
4. salía
5. sale
6. hablaba
7. sale

TEACHING STRUCTURE

◆ **Having just done something** ◆

Since this is a review and a very simple concept, you may wish to have students read the explanation silently and then do the accompanying exercise.

ANSWERS
Práctica

A Answers can be negative.
1. Sí, acabo de volver a casa.
2. Sí, María acaba de volver también.
3. Sí, acabamos de hacer un viaje.
4. Sí, acabamos de visitar a nuestros parientes.
5. Sí, acabábamos de entrar en la casa cuando sonó el teléfono.

Independent Practice

Assign any of the following:
1. Exercises, pages 134–135
2. Workbook, *Estructura*

TEACHING STRUCTURE

 **Emotions and opinions about the past** ◆◆◆

A. Have students read the explanatory material silently.

B. Write the verb paradigms of **hablar, comer,** and **pedir** on the board and have the students repeat.

C. Have the class repeat the forms on the irregular verb chart in unison, making sure that their pronunciation is exact.

Emotions and opinions about the past
Imperfecto del subjuntivo

1. The imperfect subjunctive of all verbs is formed by dropping the **-on** ending of the third person plural, **ellos(as)**, form of the preterite tense of the verb.

PRETERITE	hablaron	comieron	pidieron	tuvieron	dijeron
STEM	hablar-	comier-	pidier-	tuvier-	dijer-

2. To this stem, you add the following endings: *-a, -as, -a, -amos, -ais, -an.*

INFINITIVE	hablar	comer	pedir	tener	decir
yo	hablara	comiera	pidiera	tuviera	dijera
tú	hablaras	comieras	pidieras	tuvieras	dijeras
él, ella, Ud.	hablara	comiera	pidiera	tuviera	dijera
nosotros(as)	habláramos	comiéramos	pidiéramos	tuviéramos	dijéramos
vosotros(as)	hablarais	comierais	pidierais	tuvierais	dijerais
ellos, ellas, Uds.	hablaran	comieran	pidieran	tuvieran	dijeran

IRREGULAR VERBS			
andar	anduvieron	anduvier-	anduviera
estar	estuvieron	estuvier-	estuviera
tener	tuvieron	tuvier-	tuviera
poder	pudieron	pudier-	pudiera
poner	pusieron	pusier-	pusiera
saber	supieron	supier-	supiera
querer	quisieron	quisier-	quisiera
venir	vinieron	vinier-	viniera
hacer	hicieron	hicier-	hiciera
leer	leyeron	leyer-	leyera
oír	oyeron	oyer-	oyera
decir	dijeron	dijer-	dijera
conducir	condujeron	condujer-	condujera
traer	trajeron	trajer-	trajera
ir	fueron	fuer-	fuera
ser	fueron	fuer-	fuera

Learning From Realia

You may wish to ask:
¿Qué obra dan?
¿Quién es el autor?
¿Es una obra moderna?
¿Cuántas representaciones dan cada día?

Emotions and opinions about the past
Usos del imperfecto del subjuntivo

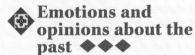
1. The same rules that govern the use of the present subjunctive govern the use of the imperfect subjunctive. It is the tense of the verb in the main clause that determines whether the present or imperfect subjunctive must be used in the dependent clause. If the verb of the main clause is in the present or future tense, the present subjunctive is used in the dependent clause.

> **Quiero que ellos me lo digan.**
> **Será necesario que nosotros lo sepamos para mañana.**

2. When the verb of the main clause is in the preterite, imperfect, or conditional, the imperfect subjunctive must be used in the dependent clause.

> **Yo insistí en que ellos estuvieran allí.**
> **Quería que ellos me lo dijeran.**
> **Sería necesario que nosotros lo supiéramos.**

A Los padres de Felipe   Contesten.

1. ¿Insistieron sus padres en que él continuara con sus estudios?
2. ¿Insistieron en que él aprendiera el español?
3. ¿Querían que él hiciera un viaje al graduarse?
4. ¿Preferían que él viajara con un grupo de estudiantes?
5. ¿Exigieron que él recibiera buenas notas para poder hacer el viaje?

B Ella quería que...   Sigan el modelo.

ir al teatro
Ella quería que yo fuera al teatro.

1. ir a la taquilla del teatro
2. comprar las entradas
3. seleccionar los asientos
4. pagar con mi tarjeta de crédito

C Nuestro querido profesor   Sigan el modelo.

hablarle en español
Nuestro profesor insistió en que le habláramos en español.

1. hablar mucho
2. pronunciar bien
3. llegar a clase a tiempo
4. aprender la gramática
5. escribir composiciones
6. leer novelas
7. trabajar mucho
8. hacer nuestras tareas

A. Have students read the explanation in steps 1 and 2.

B. Have the students repeat the model sentences in unison.

TEACHING TIPS

Many of these *Práctica* can be done without previous preparation. Depending on class ability, you may assign any or all exercises to be done for homework and go over them the following day in class. It is essential that the students pronounce the forms clearly.

ANSWERS
Práctica

A Answers can be negative.
1. **Sí, sus padres insistieron en que él continuara con sus estudios.**
2. **Sí, insistieron en que él aprendiera el español.**
3. **Sí, querían que él hiciera un viaje al graduarse.**
4. **Sí, preferían que él viajara con un grupo de estudiantes.**
5. **Sí, exigieron que él recibiera buenas notas para poder hacer el viaje.**

B Ella quería que yo...
1. **fuera...**
2. **comprara...**
2. **seleccionara...**
4. **pagara...**

C Nuestro profesor insistió en que...
1. **habláramos mucho.**
2. **pronunciáramos bien.**
3. **llegáramos a clase a tiempo.**
4. **aprendiéramos la gramática.**
5. **escribiéramos composiciones.**
6. **leyéramos novelas.**
7. **trabajáramos mucho.**
8. **hiciéramos nuestras tareas.**

Additional Practice

1. **Prepare Ud. una lista de las cosas que era necesario o importante que Ud. hiciera. Explique por qué era necesario o importante que Ud. las hiciera.**
2. **Para Ud., ¿quién sería la persona ideal? Dé todas las características y capacidades que Ud. quisiera encontrar en la persona ideal.**
   Busco un(a) amigo(a) que...

Learning From Photos

1. Have students describe the photo in their own words.
2. Have students make up a conversation they think the young couple is having.

TEACHING STRUCTURE

Expressing indefinite ideas ◆◆

A. After reading the explanation in step 1 aloud to the students, you may wish to put these expressions on the board and have the students repeat them aloud.

B. Have the students read the model sentence aloud in step 2 with its translation.

D | Las finanzas   Completen.

1. Ella quiere que yo cambie dinero.
   Ella quería que yo ___ dinero.
2. Ella te pide que hables con el cajero.
   Ella te pidió que ___ con el cajero.
3. Ella me aconseja que tenga cheques de viajero.
   Ella me aconsejó que ___ cheques de viajero.
4. Ella insiste en que el banco le haga cambio.
   Ella insistió en que el banco le ___ cambio.
5. Ella les dice que pongan su dinero en el banco.
   Ella les dijo que ___ su dinero en el banco.

E | Posiblemente   Hagan una sola oración.

1. Él aprendió la letra de la canción. (Era necesario...)
2. Él la cantó sin acompañamiento. (Era imposible...)
3. Alguien tocó la guitarra o el acordeón. (Era importante...)
4. Los otros bailaron. (Era mejor...)
5. Todos se divirtieron. (Era probable...)

F | Sería imposible.   Contesten según se indica.

> **¿Él te acompaña?**
> **Sería imposible que él me acompañara.**

1. ¿Él tiene bastante dinero?
2. ¿Él va a España?
3. ¿Él hace el viaje contigo?
4. ¿Él aprende el español?
5. ¿Él trabaja en España?

Expressing indefinite ideas
Subjuntivo con expresiones indefinidas

1. Many words can be made indefinite by adding the suffix **-quiera** to the word. Note the following.

quienquiera	whoever	**cuando quiera**	whenever
dondequiera	*wherever*	**como quiera**	*however*
adondequiera	*(to) wherever*	**cualquiera**	*whatever*

2. The subjunctive follows such indefinite expressions when uncertainty is implied. Observe and analyze the following.

> **Quienquiera que seas, adondequiera que vayas y cuando quiera que salgas, como quiera que vayas y dondequiera que estés, espero que tengas suerte y que te diviertas.**
> *Whoever you may be, wherever you may go and whenever you may leave, however you may go and wherever you may be, I wish you luck and hope you enjoy yourself.*

Independent Practice

Assign any of the following:
1. Exercises, page 138
2. Workbook, *Estructura*

Additional Practice

Have students make up original sentences using a word such as **quienquiera** or **dondequiera.**

Práctica

A **Dondequiera que vayas.** Completen.

1. Quienquiera que lo ___ (saber), nos lo debe decir.
2. Tú sabes que yo te ayudaré con cualquier problema que ___ (tener).
3. Dondequiera que tú ___ (estar), estaré a tu lado.
4. Cuando quiera que tú ___ (necesitar) mi ayuda, llámame.

Expressing the known and the unknown
Subjuntivo en cláusulas relativas

1. A relative clause modifies or describes a noun. If the noun refers to a definite person or thing, the indicative is used in the relative clause. If the noun refers to an indefinite person or thing, the subjunctive is used in the relative clause.

> **Donato tiene un amigo que habla español.**
> **Donato quiere un amigo que hable español.**
> **Yo tengo un amigo que juega bien al básquetbol.**

Note that the **a personal** is omitted when the noun is indefinite and after the verb **tener.**

2. The subjunctive is used in a relative clause that modifies a superlative statement or a negative expression.

> **Es el mejor libro que exista en el mundo.**
> **No hay nadie que lo haga como él.**

Práctica

A **¿A quién buscan?** Sigan el modelo.

> **hablar español**
> **El señor Salas busca una señora que hable español.**
> **La señorita Robles conoce a una señora que habla español.**

1. poder trabajar ocho horas al día
2. conocer varias computadoras
3. saber programar
4. tener experiencia

B **Opiniones** Contesten.

1. ¿Es Nueva York la ciudad más cosmopolita que exista en el mundo?
2. ¿Es el *Quijote* el mejor libro que haya en el mundo?
3. ¿Es verdad que él no tiene absolutamente nada que sea de valor?
4. ¿Dices que no hay nadie que tenga más talento que él?
5. ¿No hay ninguna capital de provincia que sea tan bonita como Pamplona?

ESTRUCTURA

ciento treinta y nueve 〜 **139**

Independent Practice

Assign any of the following:
1. Exercises, pages 139
2. Workbook, *Estructura*

B Answers can be negative.
1. Sí, Nueva York es la ciudad más cosmopolita que exista en el mundo.
2. Sí, el *Quijote* es el mejor libro que haya en el mundo.
3. Sí, es verdad que él no tiene absolutamente nada que sea de valor.
4. Sí, digo que no hay nadie que tenga más talento que él.
5. No hay ninguna capital de provincia que sea tan bonita como Pamplona.

TEACHING TIPS

The *Práctica* can be done immediately following the presentation.

ANSWERS
Práctica

A 1. sepa   3. estés
   2. tengas   4. necesites

🔔 Bell Ringer Review

Use the BRR Transparency 3-7, or write the following on the board:
Haga oraciones originales empleando cada una de las expresiones siguientes:
1. nada   3. mejor   5. ninguno
2. nadie   4. peor

TEACHING STRUCTURE

◆ Expressing the known and the unknown ◆◆

A. After reading the explanation with the students, have them repeat the model sentences.
B. Have the students give as many completions as possible:
Busco unos amigos que ___.
Espero encontrarme con alguien que ___.
Tengo unos amigos que ___.
He visto a alguien que ___.

ANSWERS
Práctica

A 1. busca... que pueda
    conoce a... que puede
2. busca... que conozca
    conoce a... que conoce
3. busca... que sepa
    conoce a... que sabe
4. busca... que tenga
    conoce a... que tiene

Bell Ringer Review

Use the BRR Transparency 3-8, or write the following on the board: **Haga una lista de palabras relacionadas con el campo de la música.**

TEACHING TIPS

Ask students to describe the illustrations on pages 140–141.

RESOURCES

- Vocabulary Transparencies
- Audio Cassette 6A/Compact Disc 4
- Student Tape Manual
- Workbook
- Chapter Quizzes
- Testing Program

TEACHING VOCABULARY

Have students repeat the new words, definitions, and sentences after you or Cassette 6A/Compact Disc 4.

RECYCLING

Have students review the names of musical instruments and dances they have already learned.

VOCABULARY EXPANSION

◆ For students interested in music you may wish to give the following additional vocabulary.

la cuerda *(string)*
el arco *(bow)*
la clavija *(tuning peg)*
el puente *(bridge)*
la mentonera *(chin rest)*

Literatura
El tango

Antes de leer

Ud. va a leer algo que parece poesía. Pero no es una poesía. Es la letra de una canción. Además es una canción a cuya música se puede bailar. Al leer la letra de la canción, decida Ud. si está hablando un joven o una persona mayor. ¿Le parece que el señor que está hablando es un poco nostálgico?

Vocabulario

la orquesta
el cantor, el cantante
el violín
el organillo
el bandoneón
la danza, el baile

La banda de amigos (La barra) está bailando.
Están bailando al compás de un organillo.
Están bailando en la esquina de la calle.

Did You Know?

When identifying strings in English, letters are used. Such is not the case in Spanish.

cuerda de sol = G
cuerda de re = D
cuerda de la = A
cuerda de mi = E

The keyboard octave in Spanish is: **do, C; re, D; mi, E; fa, F; sol, G; la, A; si, B; do, C.**

la boda

el recuerdo la memoria

alejarse ir lejos, distanciarse

acudir ir, venir

disfrutar gozar de, aprovechar

idolatrar adorar

Práctica

A **Bailes e instrumentos** Contesten.

1. ¿Son danzas el tango y el mambo?
2. ¿Cuáles son tres instrumentos musicales?
3. ¿Qué es un conjunto de músicos?
4. ¿Quién canta?
5. ¿Cuál es la ceremonia del casamiento?

B **¿Qué hace él?** Completen.

1. Él es un tipo muy bueno. Siempre quiere ___ de las tentaciones malas.
2. Él ___ adonde lo necesitan.
3. Él tiene ___ muy buenos de todo lo que ha hecho en su vida.
4. Él está muy contento y ___ de la vida.
5. Él ___ a sus hijos.

ANSWERS
Práctica
A **1. Sí, el tango y el mambo son danzas.**
2. Tres instrumentos musicales son el violín, el organillo y el bandoneón.
3. Un conjunto de músicos es una orquesta.
4. El cantante (el cantor) canta.
5. La boda es la ceremonia del casamiento.
B **1. alejarse**
2. acude
3. recuerdos
4. disfruta
5. idolatra

Independent Practice

Assign any of the following:
1. Exercises, page 141
2. Workbook, *Literatura*

141

TEACHING TIPS

A. It is suggested that you call on students to read this selection aloud. After one student has read one or two short paragraphs, you may wish to ask some of the following comprehension questions: **¿Cómo empezó el tango? ¿Dónde se practicaba? ¿Qué reputación tenía esta danza originalmente? ¿Cuándo se introdujo en Europa? ¿Quién es Carlos Gardel? ¿Qué instrumentos tienen importancia en la orquesta del tango? ¿Dónde se originó el tango? ¿Cuándo? ¿Dónde se bailaba? ¿Quiénes lo bailaban? ¿Cuándo pasaron a formar parte de la pareja las mujeres? ¿De dónde eran muchos de los inmigrantes que lo bailaban? ¿Dónde llegó a ser muy popular el tango?**

B. While the students continue reading individually, you may ask additional questions of your own.

CULTURAL CONNECTION

La Boca is the old port area of Buenos Aires where the Río Riachuelo empties into the Río de la Plata. In the section of **La Boca** called **el Caminito** there is a daily open-air exhibit of paintings, many depicting the tango.

Introducción

El tipo de tango que más fama tiene y ha tenido en el mundo es el tango rioplatense, o sea, el tango argentino. El tango empezó como una danza pero hoy es danza y canción. Sus primeras interpretaciones aparecieron a principios de este siglo. Tiene sus orígenes en las calles rioplatenses. Se practicaba en las esquinas de los barrios pobres al compás de° organillos. En aquel entonces, sólo los hombres bailaban el tango.

al compás de
to the rhythm of

El barrio italiano en Buenos Aires, Argentina, en 1936

Originalmente, esta danza tenía mala reputación porque los que la bailaban vivían en su gran mayoría al margen de la ley. Pero poco a poco, el tango se fue convirtiendo en un baile más popular. Se practicaba dentro de las familias, durante una boda, por ejemplo. Fue en esas celebraciones familiares que la mujer pasó a formar parte de la pareja. Al organillo se le añadió el bandoneón, como instrumento de acompañamiento. El bandoneón era un instrumento popular entre los inmigrantes italianos que en aquella época iban a la Argentina en busca de una vida mejor. Estos inmigrantes eran pobres, y durante sus pocas horas libres no les costaba nada tocar su viejo bandoneón y bailar un tango en una fiesta callejera.

El tango siguió siendo una diversión de los pobres hasta la Primera Guerra Mundial cuando se introdujo en Europa. En Europa tuvo mucho éxito. Logró una popularidad enorme en las «boîtes» o los «cabarets» de Montmartre en París. Llegó a ser popular también en las grandes salas de fiestas y en los espectáculos que se presentaban en muchas capitales europeas. Los de la alta sociedad europea se divertían bailando un buen tango.

Con el éxito del tango en las salas de fiestas y en los espectáculos, el cantor pasó a tener cada vez más importancia. La letra

fue revitalizada. La figura de Carlos Gardel, el famoso tanguista, se convirtió en el símbolo de una danza y de un canto. En la orquesta del tango tienen importancia el bandoneón y los violines. Aun los grandes compositores, como el ruso Igor Stravinski y el inglés William Walton, han empleado el tango en su obra.

La música es un arte, la danza es un arte y también lo es la literatura. Si la letra de una canción no es precisamente literatura, a veces se parece mucho a una poesía lírica. Fue del poeta argentino, Pascual Contursi, de origen italiano, que surgió la idea de adaptar versos a la música del tango. Lo que sigue es la letra de un tango famoso. A ver si Ud. cree que es poesía.

Did You Know?

La Boca es un barrio donde vivían muchos inmigrantes italianos—muchos de ellos oriundos de la región de Génova. En broma se le llama a este barrio la República Independiente de la Boca. Todavía hoy hay muchas cantinas donde sirven comidas italianas deliciosas. Todo el mundo se sienta a una mesa larga y mientras los meseros sirven, cantan.

Lectura

Adiós muchachos

Adiós muchachos, compañeros de mi vida
Barra querida, de aquellos tiempos
Me toca a mí hoy emprender° la retirada
Debo alejarme de mi buena muchachada°.

Adiós muchachos, ya me voy y me resigno:
Contra el destino nadie la talla°
Se terminaron para mí todas las farras°
Mi cuerpo enfermo no resiste más.

Acuden a mi mente°, recuerdos de otros tiempos
De los bellos momentos
Que antaño° disfruté
Cerquita de mi madre, santa viejita,
Y de mi noviecita
Que tanto idolatré.

emprender *to undertake*
muchachada *grupo de jóvenes*

nadie la talla *no one can win*
farras *revelry, sprees*

mente *mind*

antaño *en el pasado*

TEACHING THE READING

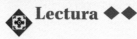 Lectura ◆◆

A. If possible, play a recording of this song.
B. Read the song aloud to the class or play the cassette/CD. The first time, have students listen only. The second time, have them open their books and follow along.
C. Give the students a few minutes to read the poem silently.

Paraphrasing Have students find the original wording for the following:
Adiós, amigos míos.
Mi grupo de amigos del pasado
Hoy es mi turno de retirarme.
Debo distanciarme.
Acepto lo que me va a pasar (suceder).
No se puede cambiar lo que le traerá a uno el futuro.
Para mí no hay más diversiones bulliciosas.
No puedo más.
Me acuerdo muy bien del pasado.
En el pasado gocé de momentos fabulosos.

National Standards

Communities
Students are encouraged to use the language for personal enjoyment by listening to a recording of «Adiós muchachos.»

Did You Know?

Hay algunos cabarets en Buenos Aires donde presentan espectáculos de tango. Estos cabarets no se encuentran en la Boca. Están en otro barrio de la ciudad, que se llama San Telmo, no muy lejos de la Boca.

143

TEACHING TIPS

Go over all the exercises orally.

ANSWERS

Comprensión

A 1. sí   6. sí
   2. no   7. sí
   3. no   8. no
   4. no   9. sí
   5. no

B 1. **El señor es viejo.**
   2. **Está hablando con sus amigos.**
   3. **Se está refiriendo a sus amigos.**
   4. **Se va a retirar.**
   5. **Debe alejarse de la buena muchachada (de sus amigos).**
   6. **Se terminaron todas las farras.**
   7. **Porque su cuerpo enfermo no resiste más.**
   8. **Los recuerdos de otros tiempos.**
   9. **Sus recuerdos son de bellos momentos.**
   10. **Sí, él disfrutó de la vida.**
   11. **Era feliz cerca de su madre y de su novia.**

INFORMAL ASSESSMENT

Have students share their reactions and emotions concerning *"Adiós muchachos."* This can be done as a whole-class activity or students can work in smaller groups.

TEACHING TIPS

Allow students to take part in the activity or activities that interest them.

Actividades comunicativas

ANSWERS

A **Su destino (final) es la muerte.**
B and C Answers will vary.

~Después de leer~

Comprensión

A El tango ¿Sí o no?

1. El tango famoso es el tango argentino.
2. El tango es sólo un baile.
3. El canto siempre era una parte importante del tango.
4. El tango tuvo su origen entre la gente acomodada (rica) de Buenos Aires.
5. El tango tuvo su origen en Europa.
6. A principios de este siglo, muchos italianos emigraron a la Argentina.
7. Al principio, sólo los hombres bailaban el tango.
8. El tango siempre gozó de buena reputación.
9. El tango argentino llegó a Europa durante la Primera Guerra Mundial.

B Adiós muchachos Contesten.

1. El señor que está hablando en la canción, ¿es joven o viejo?
2. ¿Con quiénes está hablando?
3. Cuando dice «barra querida», ¿a quiénes se está refiriendo?
4. ¿Qué va a hacer él?
5. ¿De quiénes debe alejarse?
6. Para él, ¿qué se terminó?
7. ¿Por qué?
8. ¿Qué acude a su mente?
9. ¿Cómo son sus recuerdos?
10. ¿Él disfrutó de la vida?
11. ¿Cerca de quiénes era feliz?

Actividades comunicativas

A Su destino En la canción, el señor habla de su destino. Explique qué puede ser su «destino».

B Otros bailes Hay danzas o cantos en los Estados Unidos que también tienen una historia interesante—«el jitter bug», «el charleston», «el rock», «los blues», «el jazz», «el break», por ejemplo. Escoja uno que le interesa a Ud. y prepare un informe corto sobre su historia.

C Carlos Gardel El más famoso cantante hispanoamericano según el libro *Récords y datos latinoamericanos*, publicado en Panamá, es Carlos Gardel. Él nació en Toulouse, Francia, en 1890 pero llegó a la Argentina a los dos años de edad. Fue en la Argentina donde él desarrolló su talento. Carlos Gardel grabó su primer disco en 1913, acompañándose con la guitarra. Fue una de las primeras grabaciones que utilizó un sistema acústico. El primer tango cantado fue *Mi noche triste* en 1917. Gardel lo estrenó en el famoso teatro Empire de Buenos Aires. Falleció en 1935 en Medellín, Colombia. Ahora, prepare una biografía corta sobre un(a) cantante norteamericano(a).

Carlos Gardel

Independent Practice

Assign any of the following:

1. Exercises, page 144
2. Workbook, *Literatura*

Mi adorado Juan

de Miguel Mihura

Antes de leer

Vamos a leer una escena de una comedia española. En la escena hay tres personajes: una muchacha joven, Irene; su padre y un amigo de su padre. Pero están hablando de un cuarto personaje, Juan. ¿Quién es este Juan? Pues, es un amigo de Irene. Vamos a ver si su padre lo conoce o no, y si le agrada el amigo de su hija.

Vocabulario

sonriente   que sonríe, que tiene una sonrisa en la cara
una temporada   un período de tiempo
un(a) holgazán(a)   una persona perezosa, no ambiciosa, que no hace nada
el oficio   la profesión, el empleo
el recado   el mensaje
los demás   los otros

de vuelta   de regreso, al volver

marcharse   irse, salir
rogar (ue)   pedir
callar(se)   no decir nada
casarse   contraer matrimonio
fastidiar   enfadar, molestar, enojar
dar un paseo   andar

el impermeable

la boina

la butaca

Práctica

A **Los sinónimos**   Expresen de otra manera.

1. Ella se sentó en una *silla grande y cómoda.*
2. Ella me *pidió* hacer algo.
3. Pero yo *no dije nada.*
4. Yo no dije nada a *los otros* tampoco.
5. Creo que el episodio le *enfadó.*
6. El novio no tiene *profesión.*
7. Le gusta *andar* por el parque.
8. Es *perezoso.*
9. Menos mal que *se va* el lunes.
10. Pero estará *de regreso* mañana.
11. Se marchó sin dejar *un mensaje.*

CAPÍTULO 3
Literatura

TEACHING TIPS

A. Call on a student to read the *Introducción* aloud as the others follow along.

B. Then ask: **¿Quién es el autor de la comedia? ¿Cómo se llama la comedia? ¿Quiénes son los personajes? ¿Quién es Juan?**

RESOURCES

- Vocabulary Transparencies
- Audio Cassette 6B/Compact Disc 4
- Student Tape Manual
- Workbook
- Chapter Quizzes
- Testing Program

TEACHING VOCABULARY

You may wish to follow some of the suggestions given for previous *Vocabulario* sections.

TEACHING TIPS

This *Práctica* can be done immediately after the *Vocabulario* has been presented.

ANSWERS
Práctica
A 1. **butaca**
   2. **rogó**
   3. **me callé**
   4. **los demás**
   5. **fastidió**
   6. **oficio**
   7. **dar un paseo**
   8. **holgazán**
   9. **se marcha**
   10. **de vuelta**
   11. **un recado**

Additional Practice

You may wish to ask the following personal questions using the new vocabulary:

¿Te gusta dar un paseo de vez en cuando?

¿Por dónde caminas?

Si das un paseo cuando llueve, ¿qué llevas?

De vuelta, ¿te gusta sentarte a descansar en una butaca cómoda en la sala?

Cuando tú no estás de acuerdo con algo o con alguien, ¿te callas o das tu opinión?

National Standards

Cultures
Students experience, discuss, and analyze an expressive product of the culture; the excerpt from the play *Mi adorado Juan,* by Miguel Mihura.

145

TEACHING TIPS

A. Present the information about Miguel Mihura as a mini-lecture. Write the important names and dates on the board.

B. After you present the information, ask: **¿Cuándo y dónde nació Mihura? ¿Qué era su padre? ¿Cuántas comedias escribió? ¿Qué más escribió? ¿Qué ganó esta comedia?**

TEACHING THE READING

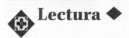 **Lectura** ◆

A. Have students close their books and listen to you or the recording of Cassette 6B/Compact Disc 4.

B. Read the scene once to the students as they follow along.

C. Call on three students to read the parts of Palacios, Irene, and Manríquez with as much expression as possible.

D. Do the *Comprensión* exercises that follow.

E. With more able groups you may wish to ask the more analytical questions in LITERARY ANALYSIS at the bottom of page 148.

Introducción

Cuando uno disfruta de una noche libre, es agradable y a veces informativo ir al teatro a ver una obra teatral. Pero, por lo general, no se puede esperar hasta el último momento porque frecuentemente las entradas están agotadas—es decir que no quedan más. Por consiguiente, es necesario ir a la taquilla a reservar las plazas de antemano, sobre todo en Madrid, una ciudad que ha tenido un resurgimiento fenomenal de actividades y eventos culturales. A Madrid se le llama la capital cultural de Europa.

El dramaturgo Miguel Mihura nació en esta ciudad en 1906. Hijo de un actor, Mihura conoció el teatro desde muy joven; de niño le encantaba ver ensayar a su padre.

Miguel Mihura

Durante su vida Mihura escribió dieciséis comedias, la mayoría de ellas después de 1950. Además de ser dramaturgo Mihura escribió cuentos, artículos para varios periódicos y los guiones de más de treinta películas. Miguel Mihura murió en 1977.

Su comedia *Mi adorado Juan* ganó el Premio Nacional de Teatro para la temporada teatral de 1955-56 en Madrid. La comedia está dividida en dos actos y cada acto está dividido en dos cuadros o escenas. Aquí tenemos un trozo del primer acto en que el padre de la protagonista, Irene, quiere saber más acerca del amigo de su hija, el adorado Juan.

Lectura

Mi adorado Juan

(Por la puerta del foro° aparece Irene. Es una muchacha de unos veinticinco años, bonita, sonriente, que viste con sencillez pero con gusto. Lleva puesto un impermeable y un sombrerillo o boina, que se empieza a quitar al entrar.)

foro *upstage*

    IRENE: Hola, buenas tardes.
    PALACIOS: ¡Ah! ¿Estás ya de vuelta?
    IRENE: Sí, papá… Acabo de volver. ¿Querías algo?
    PALACIOS: Te prohibí que salieras.
    IRENE: Creí que era una broma°…

broma *joke*

    PALACIOS: ¡Yo no gasto bromas, Irene!
    IRENE: ¡Qué lástima! ¡Con lo bien que se pasa°! (Y saluda a Emilio.) ¿Qué tal, Emilio?…

con lo bien que se pasa *considering all the fun it is*

    MANRÍQUEZ: Ya ves…
    PALACIOS: ¡Quiero hablar contigo seriamente!
    IRENE: ¿Más aun?
    PALACIOS: Más aun.
    IRENE: ¿Siempre de lo mismo?
    PALACIOS: Siempre de lo mismo.
    IRENE: Estoy a tu disposición, papá.
    (Y se sienta cómodamente en una butaca.)

Did You Know?

Durante toda su vida, el teatro le fascinó a Mihura. Era actor, director, diseñador de escenario y dramaturgo. Él se encargó personalmente de los ensayos de sus obras.

De vez en cuando él escribía sólo un acto de una obra de tres actos. Al terminar el primer acto lo ensayaba con los actores y las actrices. Durante los ensayos, él continuaba escribiendo. Así podía cambiar la dirección del argumento o la personalidad de los personajes.

MANRÍQUEZ: ¿Me marcho, profesor?

PALACIOS: No. Le ruego que se quede.

MANRÍQUEZ: Como usted quiera, profesor.

(El doctor Palacios se sienta en el sillón de su mesa, Irene en una butaca y Manríquez en otra. Hay una pausa.)

IRENE: Estoy preparada, papá. Puedes empezar cuando desees.

PALACIOS: Pues bien, Irene… Desde hace una temporada, en lugar de portarte° como lo que eres, como una señorita inteligente, juiciosa° y formal, hija de un científico famoso, te estás portando como una peluquera° de señoras.

portarte *behave*
juiciosa *mature*
peluquera *beautician*

MANRÍQUEZ: Exactamente.

IRENE: ¿Ah, sí? ¡Qué ilusión!

PALACIOS: ¿Por qué ilusión?

IRENE: Me encanta parecer una peluquerita de señoras… ¡Son tan simpáticas y tan alegres! ¡Tienen tantos temas distintos de conversación… !

PALACIOS: ¿Quieres callar?

IRENE: Sí, papá.

PALACIOS: Desde que tu pobre madre faltó°, tú has hecho sus veces° y has llevado la casa° y siempre he estado orgulloso° de ti… Por mi parte jamás te he negado nada… Ningún capricho°… Ningún deseo… Pero esto sí, Irene. Te prohíbo nuevamente, y esta vez muy en serio, que vuelvas a verte con ese hombre.

faltó *murió*
has hecho sus veces *have taken her place*
has llevado la casa *have managed the house*
orgulloso *proud*
capricho *whim*

IRENE: Pero, ¿quieres explicarme por qué?

PALACIOS: Porque ni siquiera sé quién es, ni lo que hace.

IRENE: No importa. Yo tampoco. Pero ya lo sabremos algún día.

PALACIOS: ¡No sabes aún de lo que vive!

IRENE: Él vive de cualquier manera… No tiene ambiciones ni necesidades… Su manjar° preferido es el queso y duerme mucho… Y como está casi siempre en el café, apenas necesita dinero para vivir…

manjar *comida*

MANRÍQUEZ: Entonces es un holgazán.

PALACIOS: Claro que sí.

IRENE: Nada de holgazán, papaíto… A él le gusta trabajar para los demás, pero sin sacar provecho de° ello… sin que se le note que trabaja°… Él dice que trabajar mucho, como comer mucho, es una falta de educación. ¡Son cosas de Juan!

sacar provecho de *beneficiarse de*
sin que se le note que trabaja *without anyone noticing that he works*
promoción *grupo*

PALACIOS: ¡Pero no tiene oficio!

IRENE: ¿Cómo que no? Es el número uno de su promoción°.

PALACIOS: ¿De qué promoción?

IRENE: ¡Cualquiera lo sabe°! A él no le gusta hablar nunca de promociones… Eso me lo dijo un amigo suyo, en secreto.

¡Cualquiera lo sabe! *¿Quién sabe?*

PALACIOS: ¡Pero con un hombre así serás desgraciada!

IRENE: Si estoy con él no me importa ser desgraciada… Estoy segura que ser desgraciada con él, debe ser la mayor felicidad.

PALACIOS: Me has dicho varias veces que iba a venir a hablarme y no ha venido, ¿por qué?

Critical Thinking Activity

Thinking skills: supporting arguments with reasons **¿Por qué le molesta tanto al padre de Irene que su amigo Juan no tenga trabajo? ¿Tiene razón su padre o no? Explique su opinión y defiéndala.**

Did You Know?

Mi adorado Juan se estrenó en el Teatro de la Comedia en Madrid la noche del 11 de enero de 1956.

IRENE: Es que se le olvida… Pero ya vendrá.

PALACIOS: Si se quiere casar contigo, ¿cómo se le puede olvidar una cosa así?

IRENE: Le fastidian las ceremonias y la formalidad.

PALACIOS: ¿Y cómo pretendes casarte con un hombre al que le fastidian el trabajo y la formalidad? ¡Vamos, contesta!

IRENE: ¿Quieres de verdad que te conteste?

PALACIOS: Sí, claro… Te lo exijo.

IRENE: Pues justamente porque vivo contigo y con Manríquez y estoy de formalidad hasta la punta del pelo… Justamente porque toda mi vida he sido formal, seria y respetuosa y he frenado° con mi educación todos mis sentimientos… Y ahora quiero sentir y padecer° y reír y hablar con la libertad de esa peluquerita de señoras a que tú antes te referías… Juan no es formal, no es, si quieres, trabajador; no tiene una profesión determinada; no se encierra en un laboratorio para hacer estudios profundos sobre biología; no es ambicioso, y el dinero y la fama le importan un pimiento°… Pero yo le adoro… Y quiero que tú se lo digas, papá, que hables con él, que le convenzas para que se case conmigo, porque la verdad es que no tiene ningún interés en casarse…

PALACIOS: ¿Pero ahora resulta que no quiere casarse contigo?

IRENE: No, papá… ¡Pero si ahí está lo malo! Él dice que no ha pensado en casarse en su vida, que no quiere echarse obligaciones, y que se encuentra muy a gusto en el bar jugando al dominó con sus amigos…

MANRÍQUEZ: Pero, ¿es que también juega al dominó?

IRENE: Es campeón de su barrio.

PALACIOS: ¡Pues qué maravilla de novio, hijita!

IRENE: Por eso, papá, tú tienes que ayudarme, para que si quiere seguir jugando al dominó, lo haga aquí, en nuestra casa, conmigo y contigo, después de cenar, y si Manríquez quiere, que haga el cuarto…

MANRÍQUEZ: Eso es una impertinencia, Irene.

IRENE: Perdóname… No he querido ofenderte.

PALACIOS: Entonces tú estás loca, ¿verdad?

IRENE: Sí, papá, estoy loca por él… ¿Qué quieres que le haga?

PALACIOS: Pues, muy bien. Quiero arreglar este asunto° inmediatamente. ¿Dónde estará ahora ese sujeto?

IRENE: No lo sé. Hemos ido juntos dando un paseo… Después me dejó y se fue… Cualquiera sabe dónde está.

PALACIOS: Pero después de veros, ¿no habéis quedado en nada?

IRENE: Él nunca queda en nada, papá.

PALACIOS: ¿No le puedes llamar por teléfono a ninguna parte?

IRENE: Sé el teléfono de una vecina de su casa que le da los recados… A lo mejor está allí.

(Y al decir esto ya ha empezado a marcar un número en el teléfono que hay sobre la mesa.)

frenado *held back, restrained*

padecer *sufrir*

le importan un pimiento *don't me… a thing*

asunto *matter*

Literary Analysis

1. Se dice que en la obra *Mi adorado Juan* hay un elemento autobiográfico. Se dice que Mihura mismo se parece bastante al protagonista Juan. Si esto es verdad, ¿cómo imagina Ud. el carácter o la personalidad de Mihura?

2. *Mi adorado Juan* es una sátira. ¿Qué estará satirizando o ridiculizando Mihura en esta obra?

3. Se caracterizan obras dramáticas como *Mi adorado Juan* con el nombre «teatro de evasión». Para Ud., ¿qué significa este término? ¿Por qué cabría *Mi adorado Juan* en esta categoría?

Después de leer

Comprensión

A **Irene** Contesten.

1. ¿Cómo es Irene?
2. ¿Qué lleva ella?
3. ¿Con quién está hablando ella?
4. ¿Cómo está su padre?
5. ¿De qué le quiere hablar?
6. ¿Cuál es la profesión del padre de Irene?
7. ¿Quién es el amigo de su padre?
8. Según el padre de Irene, ¿cómo es ella?
9. Pero, ¿cómo se está portando ahora?
10. ¿Está muerta la madre de Irene?
11. ¿Por qué ha estado orgulloso de Irene su padre?
12. Pero, ¿qué le prohíbe?

B **El amigo de Irene** Corrijan las oraciones falsas.

1. El padre de Irene ha conocido a su amigo.
2. El amigo sabe lo que hace.
3. Irene también sabe lo que hace su amigo.
4. El amigo pasa mucho tiempo en su oficina.
5. Al amigo le gusta trabajar para sí mismo.
6. El amigo quiere que todo el mundo sepa que trabaja.
7. El amigo dice que trabajar mucho es señal de educación.

C **Juan** Contesten.

1. ¿Por qué quiere Irene que su padre le diga a Juan que se case con ella?
2. En vez de casarse y tener obligaciones, ¿qué prefiere hacer Juan?
3. ¿Dónde quiere Irene que él juegue al dominó?
4. ¿Cómo quiere arreglar el asunto inmediatamente el padre de Irene?
5. ¿Sabe Irene dónde está su amigo?
6. ¿Dónde le puede llamar por teléfono?

Actividades comunicativas

A **Y Juan** Prepare una conversación telefónica entre Irene y la vecina de su amigo. ¿Qué le dice? ¿Qué le pregunta?

B **Lo que pasa.** Prepare una escena de la comedia. Por fin Irene ha hablado con su adorado Juan y él ha venido a su casa a conocer a su padre. ¿Qué pasa?

Independent Practice

Assign any of the following:
1. Exercises, page 149
2. Workbook, *Literatura*

ANSWERS

Comprensión

A 1. Es bonita y sonriente.
2. Lleva un impermeable y un sombrerillo.
3. Está hablando con su padre.
4. Él está enfadado.
5. Le quiere hablar de su amigo Juan.
6. Él es profesor.
7. Manríquez es el amigo del padre.
8. Ella es inteligente, juiciosa y formal.
9. Se está portando como una peluquera de señoras.
10. Sí, la madre de Irene está muerta.
11. El padre ha estado orgulloso de Irene por haber llevado bien la casa.
12. El padre le prohíbe que vuelva a verse con ese Juan.

B 1. El padre de Irene no ha conocido a su amigo.
2. El amigo no sabe lo que hace.
3. Irene tampoco sabe lo que hace su amigo.
4. El amigo pasa mucho tiempo en el café.
5. Al amigo le gusta trabajar para los demás, pero sin sacar provecho de ello.
6. No, él quiere que nadie sepa que él trabaja.
7. El amigo dice que trabajar mucho es falta de educación.

C 1. Irene quiere que su padre le convenza a Juan que se case con ella porque Juan no tiene ningún interés en casarse.
2. Él quiere estar en el bar y jugar al dominó.
3. Irene quiere que él juegue al dominó en la casa de ella.
4. El padre quiere hablar con Juan.
5. Irene no sabe dónde está su amigo.
6. Ella le puede llamar a casa de una vecina.

Actividades comunicativas

ANSWERS

A and **B** Answers will vary.

Chapter 4 Overview ◆◆◆◆◆◆◆◆◆◆◆◆◆◆◆◆◆◆

SCOPE AND SEQUENCE pages 150A–150B

TOPICS	FUNCTIONS	STRUCTURE	CULTURE
◆ Stages in life ◆ Social events ◆ Family celebrations	◆ How to discuss and contrast different stages in life from childhood to old age ◆ How to describe family ceremonies and events ◆ How to express future events and conditions ◆ How to make indirect statements ◆ How to refer to people and things already mentioned ◆ How to introduce information with expressions such as "so that," "unless," "perhaps," and "maybe" ◆ How to use time expressions ◆ How to read and discuss literary works by Ana María Matute, Ramón de Campoamor, and Amado Nervo	◆ **Futuro de los verbos regulares** ◆ **Futuro de los verbos irregulares** ◆ **El condicional o potencial** ◆ **Oraciones indirectas** ◆ **Pronombres de complemento directo e indirecto** ◆ **Dos complementos en la misma oración** ◆ **Subjuntivo en cláusulas adverbiales** ◆ **Subjuntivo con conjunciones de tiempo** ◆ **Subjuntivo con** *aunque, quizás, tal vez y ojalá* ◆ **Colocación de los pronombres de complemento** ◆ **Pronombres de complemento con el imperativo**	◆ Religious ceremonies in Spanish-speaking countries ◆ Points of interest in Cordoba, Spain ◆ The wedding of the Infanta Cristina of Spain ◆ Social announcements: the baptism of the first grandson of the king and queen of Spain ◆ El Centro de Bellas Artes, Puerto Rico **Literatura** ◆ **«El niño al que se le murió el amigo»**, Ana María Matute ◆ **«Cosas del tiempo»**, Ramón de Campoamor ◆ **«En paz»**, Amado Nervo

CHAPTER 4 RESOURCES

PRINT	MULTIMEDIA

Planning Resources

Lesson Plans Block Scheduling Lesson Plans	Interactive Lesson Planner

Reinforcement Resources

Writing Activities Workbook Student Tape Manual Video Activities Booklet Glencoe Foreign Language Web Site User's Guide	Transparencies Binder Audiocassette/Compact Disc Program Videocassette/Videodisc Program Online Internet Activities Electronic Teacher's Classroom Resources

Assessment Resources

Situation Cards Chapter Quizzes Testing Program	Testmaker Computer Software (Macintosh/Windows) Listening Comprehension Audiocassette/Compact Disc

Motivational Resources

Expansion Activities	Café Glencoe: **www.cafe.glencoe.com**

Enrichment

Fine Art Transparencies: F-2, F-3, F-4, F-5	

Chapter 4 Planning Guide

SECTION	PAGES	SECTION RESOURCES
Cultura **Eventos y ceremonias** *Pasajes*	152–156	Transparency 25 Audiocassette 7A/Compact Disc 5 Writing Activities Workbook, pages 89–90 Student Tape Manual, pages 51–52 Chapter Quizzes, page 46 Testing Program, pages 77–80
Conversación **Ceremonias familiares**	157–160	Transparency 26 Audiocassette 7A/Compact Disc 5 Writing Activities Workbook, page 91 Student Tape Manual, pages 53–54 Chapter Quizzes, page 47 Testing Program, pages 81–83
Lenguaje **Fórmulas**	161–162	Transparency 27 Audiocassette 7B/Compact Disc 5 Writing Activities Workbook, page 92 Student Tape Manual, page 54 Testing Program, pages 81–83
Repaso de estructura **Futuro de los verbos regulares** **Futuro de los verbos irregulares** **El condicional o potencial** **Oraciones indirectas** **Pronombres de complemento directo e indirecto** **Dos complementos en la misma oración**	163–171	Audiocassette 7B/Compact Disc 5 Writing Activities Workbook, pages 93–96 Student Tape Manual, pages 55–56 Chapter Quizzes, pages 48–53 Testing Program, pages 84–85
Periodismo **La boda y el nacimeinto** «El padre de la novia» «Bautizo del primer nieto de los reyes de España» **Anuncios sociales**	172–182	Transparencies 28, 29 Audiocassette 7B–8A/Compact Disc 5 Writing Activities Workbook, pages 97–99 Student Tape Manual, pages 57–58 Chapter Quizzes, pages 54–55 Testing Program, pages 86–90
Estructura **Subjuntivo en cláusulas adverbiales** **Subjuntivo con conjunciones de tiempo** **Subjuntivo con *aunque, quizás, tal vez* y *ojalá*** **Colocación de los pronombres de complemento** **Pronombres de complemento con el imperativo**	183–189	Audiocassette 8A/Compact Disc 5 Writing Activities Workbook, pages 100–102 Student Tape Manual, page 63 Chapter Quizzes, pages 56–61 Testing Program, pages 91–93
Literatura «El niño al que se le murió el amigo», Ana María Matute «Cosas del tiempo», Ramón de Campoamor «En paz», Amado Nervo	190–199	Transparencies 30, 31A–31B Audiocassette 8B/Compact Disc 6 Writing Activities Workbook, pages 103–106 Student Tape Manual, pages 64–65 Chapter Quizzes, pages 62–63 Testing Program, pages 94–98

OVERVIEW

In this chapter students will deal with the important topic of the different stages of life from birth to death. They will also discuss family ceremonies.

Students will read newspaper articles about social events, announcements, funerals, and other ceremonies. They will read three literary selections: one short story and two poems.

National Standards

Communication
Students will engage in conversations, provide and obtain information, express feelings, and exchange opinions on the topic of life passages: childhood to adolescence, adolescence to adulthood to old age; the rituals attendant to events such as birth, marriage, and death. They will listen to and read authentic language on the same topics.

Learning From Photos

Puede hacerles preguntas a los estudiantes basadas en la foto:
¿Quiénes son las dos personas?
¿Qué lleva ella en la mano?
¿Qué traje lleva ella?
¿Qué acaban de hacer?
Describa la ropa del hombre.

Pasajes

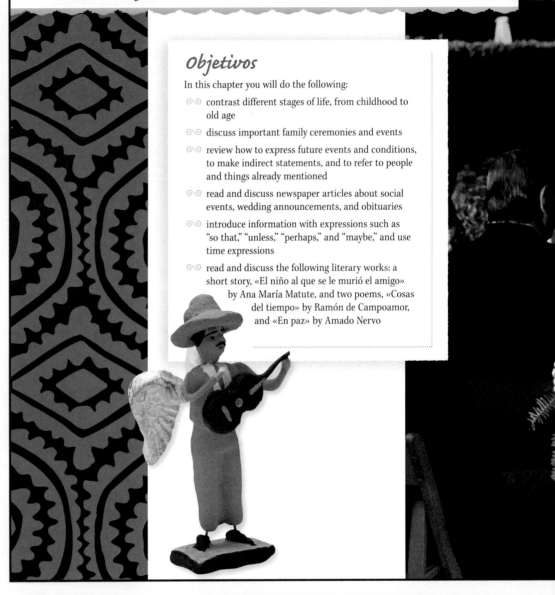

Objetivos

In this chapter you will do the following:

- contrast different stages of life, from childhood to old age
- discuss important family ceremonies and events
- review how to express future events and conditions, to make indirect statements, and to refer to people and things already mentioned
- read and discuss newspaper articles about social events, wedding announcements, and obituaries
- introduce information with expressions such as "so that," "unless," "perhaps," and "maybe," and use time expressions
- read and discuss the following literary works: a short story, «El niño al que se le murió el amigo» by Ana María Matute, and two poems, «Cosas del tiempo» by Ramón de Campoamor, and «En paz» by Amado Nervo

interNET CONNECTION

The Glencoe Foreign Language Web site (http://www.glencoe.com/sec/fl) offers these options that enable you and your students to experience the Spanish-speaking world via the Internet:

- At **Café Glencoe**, the interactive "after-school" section of the site, you and your students can access a variety of additional online resources, including online newspapers, interactive games, and a send-a-postcard feature.
- The online **Proyectos** are correlated to the chapters and utilize Hispanic Web sites around the world.

DIFFICULTY PLATEAUS

In all chapters, each reading selection in *Cultura, Periodismo,* and *Literatura,* as well as the *Conversación* and each structure topic, will be rated as follows:

◆ **Easy**
◆◆ **Intermediate**
◆◆◆ **Difficult**

Please note that the material in *¡Buen viaje! Level 3* does not become progressively more difficult. Each chapter has easy and difficult sections.

The overall rating of this chapter is: ◆◆ **Intermediate.**

RANDOM ACCESS

You may either follow the exact order of the chapter or omit certain sections that you feel are not necessary for your students.

Similarly, you may wish to present a literary selection without interruption or you may intersperse some material from the *Estructura.*

EVALUATION

Quizzes There is a quiz for every vocabulary presentation and every structure point.

Tests To accompany *¡Buen viaje! Level 3* there are global tests for both *Estructuras,* a combined *Conversación/Lenguaje* test, and one test for each reading in the *Cultura, Periodismo,* and *Literatura* sections. There is also a comprehensive chapter test.

ciento cincuenta y uno ∽ **151**

Chapter Projects

Las ocasiones grandes: Imagínese que Ud. es una persona vieja. Mire su álbum de fotos y describa varios eventos que recuerda de memoria. Haga unos anuncios sociales, unas tarjetas para los eventos más importantes de su vida. No olvide las ilustraciones. Si Ud. tiene abuelos, puede tener una entrevista con ellos para facilitar la creación de sus anuncios y tarjetas.

TEACHING TIPS

A. Call on students to read the *Introducción* aloud since it contains much useful vocabulary.

B. After they have read the *Introducción,* ask students to make a list of the seven stages of life.

C. Ask students to describe their feelings, both positive and negative, about their own family celebrations.

D. For each of the stages mentioned in the *Introducción,* you may also wish to ask students: **¿Quiénes participan en estas ocasiones? ¿Hay tradiciones con respecto a estas ocasiones? ¿Cómo se celebran estas ocasiones? ¿Depende de la región donde vive?**

RESOURCES

- Vocabulary Transparencies
- Audio Cassette 7A/Compact Disc 5
- Student Tape Manual
- Workbook
- Chapter Quizzes

TEACHING VOCABULARY

A. Have students repeat the new words in unison after you or Cassette 7A/Compact Disc 5.

B. Call on students to use the new words in original sentences.

CULTURA
Eventos y ceremonias

Introducción

Shakespeare habló de las siete edades del hombre. Los niños nacen. Luego, forman parte de la tradición religiosa de su gente. Llegan a la adolescencia. Aprenden un oficio o una profesión. Después se casan. Tienen hijos. Se jubilan o se retiran. Y, al final del viaje, mueren.

En todas las culturas hay ceremonias y eventos especiales para marcar el paso de la persona por las diferentes etapas de la vida. Las ceremonias pueden ser festivas y alegres, solemnes y majestuosas o tristes y sombrías. La religión frecuentemente juega un papel central en las ceremonias. Hasta las personas que no se consideran muy religiosas tienden a tomar parte en las ceremonias religiosas que acompañan a estos «pasajes» de la vida.

«El velorio» de Francisco Oller

Vocabulario

el marido   la esposa

el bautizo   los cónyuges

152 ∽ *ciento cincuenta y dos*   CAPÍTULO 4

Learning From Art

Francisco Oller y Cesteros (1833–1917), famoso pintor puertorriqueño, nació en Bayamón y murió en San Juan. Era impresionista. El cuadro representa un velorio en el campo de Puerto Rico. Entre los campesinos o «jíbaros» de Puerto Rico existía la costumbre del «baquiné».

Cuando se moría un bebé o un niño muy pequeño, la familia y los vecinos se reunían para celebrar con música, baile y comida. No era, insistían, razón para entristecerse sino para alegrarse, porque el niño estaría con Dios ya que había muerto inocente.

el velorio

el parto la acción de nacer, el nacimiento

la aparición la acción de aparecer, de estar presente

las amonestaciones el anuncio por la iglesia de los nombres de personas que van a casarse

la esquela el anuncio de la muerte en un periódico

el alma el espíritu, la esencia de una persona

hacerse cargo tomar el mando, la responsabilidad

parir, dar a luz producir un bebé

protagonizar tener, hacer el papel principal

pertenecer a ser parte integrante de, ser miembro de, ser posesión de

enterrar poner bajo tierra

librarse hacerse libre

 Práctica

A **HISTORIETA** El nacimiento

Expresen de otra manera.

1. La señora va a *tener su bebé* hoy mismo.
2. Esperamos que *el nacimiento* no sea difícil.
3. La doctora Morales va a *tomar el mando* del parto.
4. Todos esperan *la presentación* del bebé.
5. El bebé va a *tener el papel principal* en este evento.

B **Ceremonias** Completen.

1. El bebé está en la iglesia para su ___. Hoy lo van a cristianar.
2. Patricia y Julio se casan pronto, ya han publicado las ___.
3. Después de la boda, los ___ salen en su viaje de novios.
4. Ese coche ___ a los novios, es un regalo de los padres.
5. Don Elías murió anoche. Yo vi ___ en el periódico esta mañana.
6. Esta noche es ___, y yo voy a asistir.
7. Vamos a rezar por ___ del muerto.
8. Mañana lo van a ___.
9. Estuvo muy enfermo y sufrió mucho. Ahora puede ___ del dolor.

« Recuerdo »
de la
Primera Comunión
del niño
Alberto Luis
Puente Garduño
efectuada el día 12 de mayo
a las 8 horas, en la Iglesia de San
Juan Bautista, en (Coyoacán),
y recibida de manos de
Monseñor José Mercado Villalón.
Siendo su padrino el señor
Luis Gómez Puente

CULTURA   ciento cincuenta y tres 153

C. You may wish to ask the following questions as you present the new vocabulary: **¿Cuándo tienen lugar las amonestaciones? ¿Cuándo tiene lugar el bautizo? ¿Qué anuncia la esquela?**

TEACHING TIPS

You may wish to go over these *Práctica* without any previous preparation.

ANSWERS
Práctica

A 1. dar a luz (parir)
   2. el parto
   3. hacerse cargo
   4. la aparición
   5. protagonizar
B 1. bautizo
   2. amonestaciones
   3. cónyuges
   4. pertenece
   5. la esquela
   6. el velorio
   7. el alma
   8. enterrar
   9. librarse

ABOUT THE SPANISH LANGUAGE

◆ One of the most commonly mispronounced words among native speakers is **cónyuge**, erroneously pronounced **cónyugue**.

◆ **El verbo «parir» no se usa normalmente para describir el nacimiento de un bebé. Sí se usa cuando se habla de animales. «Dar a luz» es la expresión más común y más aceptable. No obstante, la palabra «parto», el acto de parir, es perfectamente aceptable, igual que «la partera», la mujer que asiste al parto y atiende a la madre, y «la parturienta», la señora que va a dar a luz.**

Learning From Realia

You may wish to ask these questions about the realia: **¿De qué es el recuerdo? ¿Quién recibió su primera comunión? ¿Cuándo y dónde fue la ceremonia? ¿Quién le dio la comunión? ¿Quién es el señor Gómez?**

Independent Practice

Assign any of the following:
1. Exercises, page 153
2. Workbook, *Cultura*

TEACHING THE READING

A. Call on students to read aloud.

B. Intersperse the following questions while students read:

¿Cuáles son algunas tradiciones religiosas en los países hispanos? ¿Cuál es el primer evento o «pasaje»? ¿Dónde tiene lugar en los países industrializados? ¿Y en las áreas rurales? ¿Quién es la comadrona o partera? ¿Cuál es la primera ceremonia para el recién nacido? ¿Qué papel hacen los padrinos? ¿Qué es la quinceañera? Explica la «endogamia». ¿Qué significa el compromiso? ¿Dónde tiene lugar el velorio?

C. Assign the selection to be reread at home and have students prepare the *Comprensión* exercises on page 156.

National Standards

Cultures
Students further their knowledge of sociology by learning about a number of the rituals and customs of Hispanic people: endogamy and exogamy.

Pasajes

En los países hispanos, la tradición religiosa es mayormente cristiana y predominantemente católica. No obstante, también hay significativas poblaciones judías e islamitas que observan sus propias tradiciones. Otro elemento importante es el indígena. Los primeros americanos también tienen sus propias costumbres y ceremonias para marcar los eventos principales de la vida.

Claro está que el primer evento o «pasaje» es el que nos trae al mundo—el nacimiento. En los países industrializados el nacimiento de un bebé casi siempre tiene lugar en un hospital, en la presencia y con la ayuda de un médico o una médica especialista en obstetricia. Pero en las áreas rurales, especialmente en los pueblos indígenas de Latinoamérica, la persona que ayuda a la madre a dar a luz es una «comadrona» o «partera», una señora con mucha experiencia en estos asuntos. Hoy día en los EE.UU., es bastante común que el padre acompañe a su esposa cuando ella da a luz al niño. En las culturas hispanas esto es menos frecuente y en las comunidades muy tradicionales, es rarísimo.

En los países hispanos la primera ceremonia para el recién nacido generalmente es el bautizo. Si la familia es pobre, el bautizo es poca cosa. Pero si la familia tiene dinero, entonces hay fiesta. Muy importantes son los padrinos. Muchas veces, los padrinos de bautizo son los mismos que sirvieron de padrinos en la boda de los padres. La selección de padrinos es, a veces, una decisión económica también. Se espera que los padrinos puedan ayudar al niño en el futuro si fuera necesario.

Pasan los años, y el o la joven pasa por otras etapas de la vida, marcadas por ceremonias. Si es católico, la primera comunión a los seis o siete años, y la confirmación entre los doce y los dieciocho años. Si es protestante, la confirmación a los doce o trece años, y si es judío, y es varón, la circuncisión a los ocho días, y el bar mitzvah para los muchachos y el bat mitzvah para las muchachas, a los trece años. Las muchachas hispanas, al cumplir los quince años, protagonizan un festejo en su honor, la fiesta de la quinceañera, que marca el pasaje de niña a mujer. Es parecido al «sweet sixteen» norteamericano, pero mucho más ceremonioso, o a la aparición de las «debutantes» entre las familias adineradas.[1]

[1] **adineradas**
wealthy

«La comunión o…»
de Jacobo Borges

Learning From Art

Have students describe the people and the setting of «La comunión o…» by Borges.

Did You Know?

Todavía es bastante común en las áreas rurales que una partera o comadrona sea la persona que asista al parto, y no un médico. Antes, las parteras eran mujeres sin preparación formal. Hoy muchas parteras son enfermeras especialistas con formación profesional.

«La boda» de Francisco de Goya

Un joven o una joven estudia, se prepara para un oficio o una profesión y, por lo general, se enamora, se compromete y se casa. En Norteamérica lo típico e ideal es el amor romántico que lleva al matrimonio. Pero no es así en todas las culturas. En muchas culturas los matrimonios suelen resultar de negociaciones entre familias en las que factores económicos y sociales tienen más importancia que el amor romántico entre los novios. Lo más común es que una pareja sea de la misma clase social, tenga la misma religión y pertenezca a la misma comunidad. Los sociólogos hablan de la «endogamia», la selección de cónyuges dentro de una comunidad pequeña y homogénea.

Normalmente, los novios anuncian su intención de contraer matrimonio con el compromiso. Se informa a los familiares y a los amigos. En algunas iglesias protestantes y en la católica, se publican las amonestaciones en la parroquia[2] durante tres domingos consecutivos.

Bat mitzvah en una sinagoga de México D.F., México

Finalmente se casan. Se casan por la iglesia o por lo civil. En algunos países hispanos hay que casarse por lo civil, no importa si se va a casar por la iglesia. Los padrinos, los pajes, las damas de honor y todos los invitados están allí para servir de testigos al enlace de los novios y de las dos familias. Los novios hacen el viaje de novios y pasan la luna de miel juntos. De esa manera comienza de nuevo el ciclo. Tienen hijos. Los hijos crecen y se casan. Algunos se divorcian (aunque sigue siendo menos frecuente el divorcio en los países hispanos). Los hijos tienen hijos. Los nietos crecen. Hay aniversarios de boda; las bodas de plata y las de oro, que marcan las décadas de la unión de la pareja. Y se llega por fin al final del viaje, al último pasaje, a la muerte.

Un funeral en Sipán, Perú

En los países hispanos el velorio en casa era tradicional, con el cuerpo presente. La familia y los amigos acompañaban al difunto en la sala de su casa, y el día después de la muerte lo enterraban. Las familias judías siguen enterrando a sus muertos un día después. En los periódicos se publican las esquelas. Si la persona es muy importante o famosa, las esquelas son grandes y numerosas. Y en los aniversarios de la muerte, aparecen en los periódicos recordatorios[3] que piden oraciones para el difunto.

[2] **parroquia** *parish*
[3] **recordatorios** *reminders*

FINE ART CONNECTION

«La boda» del cuadro de Francisco de Goya (1746–1828) tiene lugar durante la Guerra de la Independencia (1808–1814). Los españoles lucharon contra Napoleón y los franceses para echarlos de la península. De esta guerra vienen las palabras «guerrillas» y «guerrilleros», que se aplicaban a los grupos de paisanos que hacían la guerra contra los franceses.

Learning From Photos

1. Sigue la costumbre, especialmente en el campo, de llevar el ataúd en hombros hasta el cementerio. Los hombres de la familia y los buenos amigos lo llevan.

2. Los sefardíes o judíos españoles estuvieron en España durante siglos hasta 1492 (véase el Capítulo 8, Raíces). Muchos se establecieron después en Latinoamérica. En México y la Argentina hay importantes poblaciones judías.

TEACHING TIPS

Go over the *Comprensión* orally after the students have had the opportunity to prepare them for homework.

ANSWERS
Comprensión

A 1. la obstetricia
  2. ayuda a la madre a dar a luz
  3. los padrinos
  4. la fiesta quinceañera
  5. la selección de cónyuges de una comunidad pequeña y homogénea
  6. están para servir de testigos
  7. un día después
B 1. el bautizo, la primera comunión/confirmación, la boda, el velorio
  2. Se espera que los padrinos puedan ayudar al/a la niño(a).
  3. la quinceañera, la confirmación, el bar mitzvah, la bat mitzvah
  4. el aniversario de veinticinco años, el aniversario de cincuenta años

TEACHING TIPS

Expansion You may wish to have students make announcements for marriages, births, and deaths of famous people to be displayed in class.

Actividades comunicativas

ANSWERS
A–D Answers will vary.

VOCABULARY EXPANSION

You might wish to remind students that formal invitations include more elaborate language. Ask them to look at the invitation and figure out the meanings of: **jubiloso, el enlace matrimonial, su apreciable familia, que se llevará a efecto,** and **ubicada.**

156

Comprensión

A Las ceremonias   Contesten.
1. ¿Cómo se llama la especialización médica que trata del parto?
2. ¿Qué hace una comadrona o partera?
3. ¿Quiénes son muy importantes en el bautizo de un niño?
4. ¿Cuál es el equivalente hispano al «sweet sixteen» norteamericano?
5. ¿Qué es la «endogamia»?
6. ¿Cuál es la función de los pajes, las damas de honor y los invitados en una boda?
7. En la cultura judía, ¿cuándo entierran a los muertos?

B Los comentarios   Comenten.
1. En la lectura se mencionan cuatro tradiciones religiosas en los países hispanos. ¿Cuáles son?
2. Explique por qué la selección de los padrinos es, a veces, una decisión económica.
3. En la tradición judía y en la cristiana, existen ceremonias que coinciden con el comienzo de la adolescencia. ¿Cuáles son?
4. ¿Qué son las «bodas de plata» y las «bodas de oro»?

MANUEL CERVANTES RODRÍGUEZ y
CARMEN BARCENAS DE CERVANTES

EN SU 25o. ANIVERSARIO PARTICIPAN EL

XV ANIVERSARIO DE
MARÍA SALOMÉ

Y EL ENLACE MATRIMONIAL DE
CONCEPCIÓN y GENARO JOSÉ

Y tienen el honor de invitar a Usted y a su apreciable Familia a tan jubiloso acto Religioso que se llevará a efecto el día 22 del presente a las 18:30 horas en la Iglesia de Nuestra Señora del Carmen, ubicada en Plaza del Estudiante No. 8.

México, D. F. a 22 de Enero

✝
EL SEÑOR INGENIERO
Carlos Alberto Ariza Bernal
DESCANSÓ EN LA PAZ DEL SEÑOR

Sus padres Carlos Arturo Ariza Niño y Lucía Bernal de Ariza, y sus hermanos: Germán López, María Isabel Ariza, Ana María, Andrés Eduardo López Ariza, Jorge Enrique Ariza Bernal, Marta Cecilia Insignares e Isabella Ariza Insignares, agradecen a sus amigos y relacionados la asistencia a las exequias que se efectuarán hoy viernes 1 de mayo, a las 3:00 p.m., en la iglesia de San Juan de Ávila y luego acompañarlos a los Jardines del Recuerdo.
Velación: Capilla No. 2, San Juan de Ávila.

Actividades comunicativas

A El casamiento   La «exogamia», lo contrario de la «endogamia», es la práctica de escoger un cónyuge de afuera de su propio grupo o comunidad. Con su grupo, preparen una lista de las ventajas y desventajas de la endogamia y de la exogamia.

B El fallecimiento   Prepare Ud. una esquela para alguna persona famosa.

C El amor   En la lectura se habla del «amor romántico» y de los factores económicos y sociales que influyen en el matrimonio. Escriba sus ideas sobre el «amor romántico» y sobre los factores económicos y sociales que influyen en la selección de un esposo o una esposa.

D La endogamia   Algunos sociólogos dicen que la «endogamia» todavía existe en los EE.UU. ¿Qué cree Ud. que quieren decir? ¿Tienen razón? ¿Qué opina Ud.?

Critical Thinking Activity

Thinking skills: making inferences
¿Qué edad tendría Carlos Alberto Ariza Bernal cuando se murió? ¿Era un niño? ¿Era una persona muy vieja? ¿Qué nos da alguna idea de su edad?

Independent Practice

Assign any of the following:
1. Exercises, page 156
2. Workbook, *Cultura*

Conversación

Ceremonias familiares

Vocabulario

el entierro
la tumba familiar
el velo
el acompañamiento
la viuda
el ramo
la pila
el camposanto
el traje de novia

❖ Práctica ❖

A **¿Cuál es la palabra?** Completen.
1. Van a bautizar al niño con agua de la ___.
2. La novia lleva un precioso ___ blanco.
3. Ella también lleva un ___ de bellas flores.
4. Es díficil verle la cara a la novia porque lleva ___.

B **Definiciones** Den la palabra que se define.
1. el cementerio, el lugar del último descanso
2. la acción de enterrar a un muerto
3. la esposa de un muerto
4. el lugar en un cementerio dedicado a los restos de los miembros de una familia
5. el grupo de personas que acompaña al muerto en los funerales

CONVERSACIÓN

ciento cincuenta y siete 〰 **157**

Did You Know?

1. In many parts of the Hispanic world people are buried above ground in **nichos**. The **nichos** are recesses in a cemetery wall where the coffins are placed. The **nichos** are then sealed with cement. Village cemeteries are usually located just outside of town, close enough for the coffins to be carried on the shoulders of mourners.

2. **El luto:** En el pasado, las vuidas se vestían de negro para toda la vida. Si se le moría el padre o la madre, se llevaba negro por cierto número de años, luego se llevaba gris por otro tiempo específico.

CAPÍTULO 4
Conversación

🖌 **Bell Ringer Review**

Use the BRR Transparency 4-2, or write the following on the board: **¿Cuál es su ceremonia tradicional favorita? ¿Por qué?**

RESOURCES

- 🖐 Vocabulary Transparencies
- 🎧 Audio Cassette 7A/Compact Disc 5
- 📁 Student Tape Manual
- 📁 Workbook
- 📁 Chapter Quizzes

TEACHING VOCABULARY

A. Have students repeat the new words in unison after you or Cassette 7A/Compact Disk 5.
B. As you present the new vocabulary, you may wish to ask the following (or any additional) questions: **¿Has asistido alguna vez a un bautizo? ¿Una boda? ¿Un velorio?**

TEACHING TIPS

You can go over these *Práctica* with or without previous preparation.

ANSWERS
Práctica
A 1. pila
   3. ramo
   2. traje de novia
   4. velo
B 1. el camposanto
   2. el entierro
   3. la viuda
   4. la tumba familiar
   5. el acompañamiento

TEACHING THE CONVERSATION

A. Call on two students with good pronunciation to read the conversations aloud to the class with as much expression as possible. Allow the others to follow along in their books as they listen.

B. Have the students prepare the *Comprensión* exercises that follow on page 160.

Escenas de la vida

El bautizo

D. RUBÉN: Ésos son los padrinos, don Abelardo Sánchez y su esposa doña Marina. Él es el dueño del hipermercado Américas.

Dª. SARA: Ya están todos alrededor de la pila. Y ahora el cura le está echando agua bendita al bebé. Mira cómo llora, el pobrecito.

D. RUBÉN: Los padres están tan orgullosos de su príncipe.

Dª. SARA: ¿Qué nombre le han dado al niño?

D. RUBÉN: Abelardo, igual que el padrino.

Dª. SARA: No es ninguna coincidencia, ¿verdad?

Did You Know?

En el calendario católico romano hay uno o más santos para cada día del año. Es el «santoral». Muchas veces se le daba al/a la niño(a) el nombre del santo de su día. Se celebraba el «santo» de la persona, el día de su nombre, no el aniversario de su nacimiento.

Learning From Photos

You may wish to ask students: **¿Quiénes están vestidos de blanco? ¿Quién lleva al bebé en sus brazos? ¿Quiénes serán las otras personas? ¿Qué le está haciendo el cura al bebé?**

El matrimonio

RODRIGO: La novia es realmente preciosa.

ELENA: El traje que lleva habrá costado un dineral. Me gusta mucho el ramo de novia.

RODRIGO: ¿Quiénes son los pajes y las damas de honor?

ELENA: Todos son hermanos y hermanas de Diana y Nando.

RODRIGO: Mira, acaban de cambiar anillos.

ELENA: Nando le ha levantado el velo y la ha besado.

RODRIGO: Ya están casados. ¿Dónde es la recepción?

ELENA: En el Hotel Excélsior.

El velorio

MARTA: Allí está la viuda, doña Carmen.

FELIPE: Don Rafael se ve como dormido, ¿no crees?

MARTA Noventa y dos años. Una larga vida.

FELIPE: ¿Viste las esquelas en los periódicos esta mañana? Yo vi más de una docena.

MARTA: ¿A qué hora es el entierro mañana?

FELIPE: A las diez, en el camposanto del pueblo. Allí tienen la tumba familiar.

MARTA: Habrá cientos de personas en el acompañamiento, sin duda.

Critical Thinking Activity

Thinking skills: making judgments

1. ¿Vale la pena gastar tanto dinero en una boda? ¿Qué piensas?
2. Los funerales no deben ser ocasiones tristes sino felices. Defiende tu opinión.

Learning From Photos

For the upper photo you may wish to ask: **¿Quién es la muchacha? ¿Y el muchacho? ¿Cómo se visten ellos? ¿Qué hacen los dos?**

For the lower photo ask: **¿Quién está en el centro? ¿Cómo se visten ellos? Describa la expresión que tiene la señora. Describa el cuarto. ¿Qué hay en la mesa?**

Comprensión

A El bebito Corrijan las oraciones falsas.
1. Don Rubén y doña Sara asisten a una boda.
2. Los padres del bebé son los señores Sánchez.
3. El bebé es varón.
4. El bebé se llama Celsa.
5. Abelardo es el nombre del padre también.

B La ceremonia Completen.
1. El ___ probablemente ha costado mucho dinero.
2. Los hermanos y hermanas de los novios son ___ y ___.
3. Cada novio le pone un ___ en el dedo del otro.
4. El novio le dio un ___ a la novia.
5. Todos van al Excélsior para la ___.

C El entierro Escojan.
1. Don Rafael era el (esposo/hijo) de doña Carmen.
2. Él era muy (joven/viejo) cuando murió.
3. En los periódicos había (pocas/muchas) esquelas.
4. Mañana es el (funeral/velorio).
5. En el camposanto la familia tiene su (casa/tumba).
6. Muchas personas van a tomar parte en (el acompañamiento/la esquela).

Actividades comunicativas

A La boda del año Un canal de televisión en Latinoamérica les contrata a Ud. y a su compañero(a) para describir la boda de Rosa Treviño y Alfredo, dos famosos cantantes. Preparen Uds. la descripción para la tele.

B Los multimillonarios Ud. y su esposo(a) quieren que D. León Valladares y su esposa Dª. Josefa sean padrinos de su hijita Mercedes. (Los Valladares son multimillonarios.) Hable con los Valladares. Su compañero(a) es el Sr. Valladares o la Sra. Valladares. Después, cambien de papel.

C El ilustre científico Un periódico chileno le pide a Ud. un artículo con la descripción de los funerales de un ilustre científico norteamericano que vivía en su pueblo. Prepare el artículo. Incluya el día y la hora, quiénes asistieron, dónde fue el entierro, etc.

Abelardo Simón
Nació en la Ciudad de México, D. F., el día 13 de Diciembre, y fue bautizado el día 19 de Enero, en la Parroquia del Santo Niño de Praga.

Sus Padres:
Simón Lara Tejeda
y
Celsa Correa de Lara

Sus Padrinos:
Abelardo Sánchez García
y
Marina Cervantes de Sánchez

Padrino de Oleos:
Sr. Cura Pro. D. José Álvarez

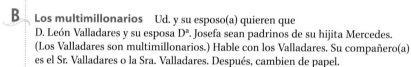

Marisela
y
Juan David

No existe nada más que para dos almas que sentir que han sido unidas para toda la vida, para fortalecerse el uno al otro en todo momento, para descansar el uno en el otro en toda tristeza, para asistirse mutuamente en todo dolor y para estar juntos en muchos y preciosos instantes...

RECUERDO DE NUESTRO MATRIMONIO
Parroquia de San José
Diciembre 11
Matagalpa, Nicaragua

Learning From Realia

You may wish to ask: **¿Qué se anuncia? ¿Cuánto tiempo pasó entre el nacimiento y el bautizo? ¿Cuándo y dónde nació? ¿Cómo se llama? ¿Quiénes son los padrinos? ¿Qué relación habrá entre el padrino y la madrina? ¿Qué querrá decir «Padrino de óleos»? ¿Qué son Marisela y Juan David? ¿Qué acaban de hacer? ¿Dónde y cuándo se casaron?**

Independent Practice

Assign any of the following:
1. Exercises, page 160
2. Workbook, *Conversación*

160

Lenguaje
Fórmulas

¡Enhorabuena!

Cuando nace un bebé, es normal felicitar a los padres diciéndoles:

> **¡Enhorabuena! ¡Felicitaciones!**

Y, claro, siempre se les dice que el bebé es bello, no importa lo feo que sea.
Se dice:

> **¡Qué bello!**
> **¡Ay, si es un ángel!**
> **¡Qué preciosidad!**

También se le hace caricias al bebé diciéndole cosas como:

> **Rico, dame una sonrisita.**
> **Preciosa, qué ojos tienes.**
> **Eres tan bella como tu mamá.**
> **Muñequita, eres adorable.**

Las bodas también tienen sus fórmulas. Las felicitaciones se les dan a los novios.
Se les dice:

> **Les deseamos mucha felicidad.**
> **¡Que sean siempre felices!**
> **¡Que tengan toda clase de dicha!**
> **¡Felicitaciones!**

LENGUAJE

ciento sesenta y uno 〜 **161**

TEACHING TIPS

A. Have the students read the explanatory material silently.
B. Call on individuals to read the expressions with the proper intonation.
C. Then have the entire class repeat them in unison.
D. Give students an expression and call on individuals to identify the occasion.

Additional Practice

After introducing the expressions, have students pretend they are seeing a new baby and saying something appropriate to the parents.

Have pairs of students play the roles of the baby and adult, with the adult saying "cute things" to the baby.

Cooperative Learning

Have six students play **los novios, los padres de la novia,** and **los padres del novio** in the receiving line after the wedding. Each student must go "through the line" and say something appropriate to each person. The "reception line" people will respond appropriately.

You may wish to let students select the activity or activities in which they wish to participate.

Actividades comunicativas

ANSWERS

A–D Answers will vary.

A los padres de los novios, especialmente durante los saludos formales o durante la recepción, se debe comentar sobre los deseos por la felicidad de los novios y sobre la belleza de la boda.

> ¡Qué bella pareja!
> Estarán Uds. muy orgullosos, y con razón.

La muerte tiene sus ceremonias y ritos. Uno debe dirigirse a la familia del difunto[1] con expresiones de dolor como:

> Sentido pésame.

> Sentido pésame.
> Le acompañamos en el dolor.
> Le expreso mi profunda condolencia.

Y la persona que recibe las felicitaciones o los pésames siempre los agradece diciendo personalmente o por escrito:

> Gracias.
> Se lo agradezco.
> Cuánto le agradezco su fina cortesía.

[1] **el difunto** el muerto

Actividades comunicativas

A **Muy diplomáticamente** Ud. está asistiendo a un bautizo. La madre del bebé le saluda. Responda apropiadamente.

B **Unas personas muy distinguidas** En la recepción después de la boda, le presentan a Ud. a los padres de la novia. Diga algo cortés y apropiado.

C **Que en paz descanse** Se murió el abuelo de su amigo. Después del funeral, Ud. se acerca a los padres de su amigo. Diga algo apropiado para la ocasión.

D **¡Qué honor!** Unos amigos hispanos le piden a Ud. que sea padrino o madrina de su hijo(a). Responda.

Additional Practice

Have pairs of students play the roles of the bereaved and the visitor to the wake or funeral. Each should use appropriate expressions of condolence and appreciation.

Did You Know?

It was customary in many Spanish-speaking countries to close the eyes of the dead and place coins over the eyelids and then to open the windows in the dead person's room to allow his or her spirit to escape.

Repaso de estructura

Expressing future events
Futuro de los verbos regulares

1. The future tense of regular verbs is formed by adding the personal endings to the entire infinitive of the verb. Review the forms of the future tense of regular verbs.

INFINITIVE	estudiar	beber	escribir
yo	estudiaré	beberé	escribiré
tú	estudiarás	beberás	escribirás
él, ella, Ud.	estudiará	beberá	escribirá
nosotros(as)	estudiaremos	beberemos	escribiremos
vosotros(as)	estudiaréis	beberéis	escribiréis
ellos, ellas, Uds.	estudiarán	beberán	escribirán

2. The future tense is used in the same way in Spanish as in English, to express an event or action that will take place in the future. Some adverbial expressions used to express future time are:

mañana (por la mañana, por la tarde, por la noche)
pasado mañana
de hoy en ocho días

la semana ⎤
el mes ⎥ que viene
el año ⎥
el verano ⎦

Ellos nos llamarán mañana por la noche.
Pero yo los veré mañana por la tarde.
Paco y yo iremos allá temprano.

3. There is another way to express future time. The expression **ir a** + *infinitive* is frequently used in Spanish instead of the future tense. It is used in the same way as the English expression "to be going to."

Ellos nos van a llamar mañana por la noche.
Pero yo los voy a ver mañana por la tarde.
Paco y yo vamos a ir allá temprano.

Para que la Información viaje con Usted...

...Sólo necesitará un computador portátil

COMPAQ
Contura Notebook
Procesador Intel 486-25sl,
Disco Duro de 120 MB,
Floppy de 3.5 (1.44MB),
Pantalla VGA Monocromática,
WINDOWS

3 AÑOS DE GARANTÍA

Y por Sólo
U.S.$ 1975*

En PC Price Club
El Computer Superstore
de Venezuela

* No incluye IVA
Promoción válida hasta agotarse las existencias

REPASO DE ESTRUCTURA

ciento sesenta y tres 〜 **163**

Learning From Realia

You may wish to ask the students: **¿Para qué es el anuncio? ¿De qué marca es el computador? ¿Qué tipo de computador es? ¿Qué tipo de garantía viene con la máquina? ¿Dónde la puede comprar?**

Critical Thinking Activity

Thinking skills: making inferences Ud. ya sabe lo que es la inflación y la hiperinflación. La moneda venezolana es «el bolívar», pero el precio se da en U.S.$. ¿Por qué será? Comente.

CAPÍTULO 4
Repaso de estructura

RESOURCES

- Workbook
- Student Tape Manual
- Audio Cassette 7B/Compact Disc 5
- Computer Software: *Estructura*
- Chapter Quizzes
- Testing Program

Bell Ringer Review

Use the BRR Transparency 4-3, or write the following on the board: **Cambie el verbo en cada frase al futuro.**
1. Llego a las ocho.
2. Veo a mis amigos.
3. Ellos están aquí.

TEACHING STRUCTURE

◆ Expressing future events ◆

A. Write the verb paradigm on the board and have students repeat the verb forms after you.
B. Call on students to repeat in unison all the model expressions and sentences.

ABOUT THE SPANISH LANGUAGE

En el anuncio se habla de un «computador». El anuncio viene de Venezuela. En Latinoamérica las palabras «computador» y «computadora» son las más frecuentes. Probablemente se debe a la influencia del inglés «computer». La palabra que se usa más en España es «ordenador». Es probable que esto se deba a la influencia del francés «ordinateur».

164

÷Práctica÷

A **Hoy, sí. Mañana, no.** Sigan el modelo.

Hoy estudio, pero mañana no estudiaré.

1. Hoy me levanto temprano, ___.
2. Hoy tomo el desayuno en casa, ___.
3. Hoy mamá nos lleva a la escuela, ___.
4. Hoy nos dan un examen en español, ___.
5. Hoy jugamos al baloncesto, ___.
6. Hoy recibimos uniformes, ___.
7. Hoy las clases terminan a las dos, ___.
8. Hoy cenamos en un restaurante, ___.
9. Hoy leo después de comer, ___.

Un colegio, La Paz, Bolivia

B **¿Adónde irás un día?** Preguntas personales.

1. ¿Adónde viajarás algún día?
2. ¿Cuánto tiempo pasarás allí?
3. ¿Qué cosas verás?
4. ¿Te quedarás en un hotel o con amigos?
5. ¿Qué monumentos o museos visitarás?
6. ¿Qué platos típicos comerás?

More future events
Futuro de los verbos irregulares

1. The following frequently used verbs have an irregular root in the future tense.

hacer	har-	venir	vendr-
decir	dir-	poner	pondr-
querer	querr-	salir	saldr-
saber	sabr-	tener	tendr-
poder	podr-	valer	valdr-

2. The future tense endings are the same for all verbs, regular or irregular.

INFINITIVE	decir	poder	salir
yo	diré	podré	saldré
tú	dirás	podrás	saldrás
él, ella, Ud.	dirá	podrá	saldrá
nosotros(as)	diremos	podremos	saldremos
vosotros(as)	*diréis*	*podréis*	*saldréis*
ellos, ellas, Uds.	dirán	podrán	saldrán

Práctica

A HISTORIETA ¿Qué hará el campeón?

Cambien en el futuro.

1. Él nunca dice nada.
2. Pero puede jugar.
3. El problema es que no quiere.
4. Tenemos que rogarle.
5. Le decimos que no ganamos sin él.
6. Y que todo el mundo viene a verle jugar.
7. Vale la pena intentarlo.
8. Si no, nunca sabemos.

El Estadio Santiago Bernabéu, Madrid, España

B HISTORIETA Hay que ser positivos.

Contesten con **sí** y el futuro.

1. ¿Se va a poner el uniforme?
2. ¿Va a estar en forma?
3. ¿Va a poder jugar?
4. ¿Todos van a venir al estadio?
5. ¿Van a tener entradas para todos?
6. ¿Le van a enseñar a jugar?
7. ¿Él va a hacer todo lo necesario?
8. ¿Va a ganar?
9. Y tú, ¿vas a estar contento(a)?

C HISTORIETA La boda

Cambien en el futuro.

1. Toda la familia asistió a la misa nupcial.
2. Todos los invitados fueron al banquete en honor de los recién casados.
3. Sirvieron una comida fabulosa.
4. Todos los invitados se divirtieron.
5. Después de la fiesta, la pareja salió de viaje.
6. Pasaron su luna de miel en México.
7. Después de quince días en México, volvieron a casa y abrieron todos sus regalos.
8. Tuvieron que agradecerles a todos sus familiares y a todos sus amigos por los regalos que les habían dado.

Luna de miel... perfecta

Es un programa de servicios ideado especialmente para las parejas que buscan opciones y requieren de una atención personalizada en la elección de un destino ideal para ese viaje tan especial.

Luna de Miel perfecta le brinda toda una gama de servicios sin ningún cargo adicional, poniendo a su disposición nuestra experiencia y afán de atenderle y sea ud. quien decida el destino, la estancia y el precio.

NAVHER
CORPORATIVO TURISTICO

Una Luna de Miel Perfecta

Viajes Montes de Oca

Llámenos
Tels. 208-53-42, 208-55-60
208-55-07, 208-56-97
208-57-58
Fax (915) 511-56-83 México D.F.

 Bell Ringer Review

Use the BRR Transparency 4-3, or write the following on the board:
Cambie al futuro.
1. Vamos a Puerto Vallarta.
2. Mi amigo va a tomar el sol.
3. Yo soy el guía.
4. Él compra algo.

TEACHING TIPS

You may go over these *Práctica* with books open.

ANSWERS
Práctica
A 1. dirá
2. podrá
3. querrá
4. Tendremos
5. diremos, ganaremos
6. vendrá
7. Valdrá
8. sabremos
B 1. se pondrá
2. estará
3. podrá
4. vendrán
5. tendrán
6. enseñarán
7. hará
8. ganará
9. estaré
C 1. asistirá
2. irán
3. Servirán
4. se divertirán
5. saldrá
6. Pasarán
7. volverán, abrirán
8. Tendrán

Learning From Photos

En el Estadio Santiago Bernabéu (130.000 espectadores) juega el «Real Madrid». Otro estadio importante en Madrid es el Estadio Vicente Calderón, donde juega el «Atlético de Madrid». El equipo de Barcelona juega en «Camp Nou» con una capacidad de 120.000 espectadores.

Independent Practice

Assign any of the following:
1. Exercises, pages 164–165
2. Workbook, *Repaso de estructura*

165

Repaso de estructura

TEACHING STRUCTURE

◈ Expressing conditions

A. You may wish to call on a student to read the explanatory material aloud.

B. Have the class repeat the verb forms and the model sentences.

🔔 Bell Ringer Review

Use the BRR Tranparency 4-5, or write the following on the board:
Complete en el futuro.
1. Yo ___ a España y mi amigo ___ a Francia. (ir, ir)
2. Nosotros ___ el mismo vuelo porque él ___ una semana en Madrid antes de ir a París. (tomar, estar)
3. En ocho días nosotros ___ visitar todos los lugares importantes. (poder)
4. Yo ___ muchos recuerdos pero mi amigo no ___ nada. (comprar, comprar)

TEACHING TIPS

This *Práctica* can be done without prior preparation.

ANSWERS
Práctica
Answers may vary.
A 1. Esquiaría (Patinaría) en la nieve.
2. Sí, tendría frío. Sí, me molestaría el frío.
3. Me quedaría en un hotel (una caravana).
4. Llevaría comida. Comería en un restaurante.
5. Haría el viaje en tren (en coche, en autobús).
6. Sí, sabría bajar por las pistas para expertos.
7. Podría esquiar... horas sin cansarme.
8. Saldría por la mañana (por la tarde).

166

Expressing conditions
El condicional o potencial

1. The conditional, like the future tense, is formed by adding the appropriate personal endings to the entire infinitive. The personal endings for the conditional are the same endings used for **-er** and **-ir** verbs in the imperfect tense. Review the following forms.

INFINITIVE	estudiar	beber	escribir
yo	estudiaría	bebería	escribiría
tú	estudiarías	beberías	escribirías
él, ella, Ud.	estudiaría	bebería	escribiría
nosotros(as)	estudiaríamos	beberíamos	escribiríamos
vosotros(as)	*estudiaríais*	*beberíais*	*escribiríais*
ellos, ellas, Uds.	estudiarían	beberían	escribirían

2. Verbs having an irregular root in the future tense have the same irregular root in the conditional.

hacer	haría	venir	vendría
decir	diría	poner	pondría
querer	querría	salir	saldría
saber	sabría	tener	tendría
poder	podría	valer	valdría

3. The conditional is used in Spanish as it is in English, to express what would or would not happen under certain circumstances or "conditions." The conditional in English is usually expressed by "would."

> **Yo lo llamaría, pero no tengo tiempo.**
> I would call him, but I don't have time.

❖ Práctica ❖

A HISTORIETA ¿Qué harías en las montañas?

Contesten.
1. ¿Esquiarías o patinarías en la nieve?
2. ¿Tendrías frío o no te molestaría el frío?
3. ¿Te quedarías en un hotel o en una caravana?
4. ¿Llevarías comida o comerías en un restaurante?
5. ¿Cómo harías el viaje, en tren, en coche o en autobús?
6. ¿Sabrías bajar por las pistas para expertos o no?
7. ¿Cuántas horas podrías esquiar sin cansarte?
8. ¿Saldrías para las pistas por la mañana o por la tarde?

Advanced Game

Conditional Game: ¿Qué harías?
Sample situation: Ud. lleva una bata *(robe)* **y sale de casa para buscar el periódico y la puerta de la casa se cierra. Nadie está en casa.** Write the situations on the board.
Set-up With students, brainstorm difficult or unusual situations people might find themselves in.

Game
1. Two students leave the room while the class picks a situation from the board.
2. The students return and take turns asking other students questions using the conditional to find out which situation the class has chosen. The first one to guess wins.

Expressing indirect discourse
Oraciones indirectas

1. Indirect discourse refers to indirect statements. Look at the following examples.

DIRECT DISCOURSE	INDIRECT DISCOURSE
Yo hablaré con Susana.	**Te digo que yo hablaré con Susana.**

2. When the verb of the main clause is in the present tense—**digo**, the verb in the dependent clause that follows is in the future—**hablaré.** If the verb of the main clause is in the preterite, the verb in the dependent clause is in the conditional.

MAIN CLAUSE	DEPENDENT CLAUSE
Present	Future
Preterite	Conditional

Yo te digo que hablaré con Susana.
Yo te dije que hablaría con Susana.

Digo que vendré mañana.
Dije que vendría mañana.

 **Práctica**

A **Siempre cumplo.** Sigan el modelo.

> **¿Vendrás mañana?**
> **Ya dije que vendría mañana.**

1. ¿Viajarás con el grupo?
2. ¿Irás en el coche?
3. ¿Tendrás bastante tiempo?
4. ¿Podrás conducir?
5. ¿Sabrás cómo ir?
6. ¿Pondrás los materiales en el coche?
7. ¿Volverás con el grupo?

TEACHING STRUCTURE

 Expressing indirect discourse ◆◆

Have the class read aloud the explanatory material together with the example sentences.

TEACHING TIPS

This *Práctica* can be done in class with books open.

ANSWERS
Práctica
Ya dije que…
A 1. viajaría con el grupo.
  2. iría en el coche.
  3. tendría bastante tiempo.
  4. podría conducir.
  5. sabría cómo ir.
  6. pondría los materiales en el coche.
  7. volvería con el grupo.

ABOUT THE SPANISH LANGUAGE

In Spanish, as in English, less educated speakers will often substitute "quotes" for indirect discourse. For example: "I told him: 'I'll go if you go with me.'" Instead of: "I told him I would go if he would go with me." **Yo le dije: —Iré si tú vas conmigo.** Instead of: **Yo le dije que iría si él fuera conmigo.**

Cooperative Learning

Have groups of three students create dialogues based on the scene in the photo. The roles are **la madre, el padre, la hija.** They should include information about "the trip." The more creative, the better.

Independent Practice

Assign any of the following:
1. Exercises, pages 166–167
2. Workbook, *Repaso de estructura*

Bell Ringer Review

Use the BRR Transparency 4-3, or write the following on the board:
Escriba:
1. tres cosas que le interesan
2. tres cosas que le divierten
3. tres cosas que no le gustan

TEACHING STRUCTURE

 Referring to people and things already mentioned ◆◆◆

A. Most students will probably need at least a quick review of this point.

B. Have students read the model sentences aloud in step 1.

C. As you go over step 2, write the sentences on the board. Draw a box around the noun that is the direct object and a circle around the object pronoun. Draw a line from the box to the circle to show that the pronoun replaces the noun.

D. When going over step 3, emphasize the fact that **le** and **les** replace both masculine and feminine nouns.

Referring to people and things already mentioned
Pronombres de complemento directo e indirecto

1. A direct object is the direct receiver of the action of a verb. An indirect object receives the action of the verb indirectly or secondarily. In Spanish, the pronouns **me, te,** and **nos** function as both direct and indirect object pronouns. Note that in Spanish the object pronoun precedes the conjugated form of the verb.

¿Te vio Teresa?	Sí, me vio.
¿Te dio un libro?	Sí, me dio un libro.

2. The third person singular and plural pronouns for direct and indirect objects are not the same. The direct object pronouns are **lo, la, los, las**. The direct object pronouns replace the names of persons, places, or things. Look at the following sentences.

Conozco el Museo Antropológico.	Lo conozco.
Conozco la playa de Luquillo.	La conozco.
Conocí a Ramón en el museo.	Lo conocí en el museo.
Conocí a Marta en la playa.	La conocí en la playa.

3. The third person indirect object pronouns are **le** and **les**. These pronouns replace both masculine and feminine nouns. Look at the following sentences.

Dorotea le dio un regalo a Pablo.
Y Pablo le dio un regalo a Dorotea.
Dorotea y Pablo les dieron regalos a sus padres.

4. Since **le** and **les** can refer to a number of different persons, they are often clarified by adding a prepositional phrase at the end.

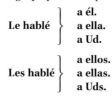

Le hablé ⎱ a él. / a ella. / a Ud.

Les hablé ⎱ a ellos. / a ellas. / a Uds.

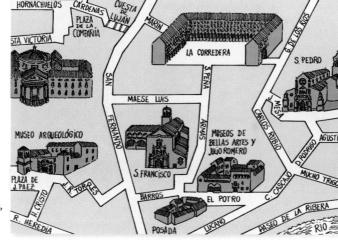

Puntos de interés,
Córdoba, España

Additional Practice

You may wish to have students practice giving directions using the "map." For example: **Ud. está en el Museo Arqueológico y quiere ir a La Corredera. Explique cómo llegar allí.**

✦Práctica✦

A HISTORIETA Una invitación

Contesten.

1. ¿Te llamó Teresa anoche?
2. ¿Teresa te invitó a la fiesta?
3. ¿Te invitó a ti y a Jorge también?
4. Ella me conoce, ¿verdad?
5. ¿Ella me va a invitar también?

¡Fiesta! ¡Fiesta!

Día: *31-5*

Hora: *20:00* Lugar: *Calle Suárez 25*

Firma: *Teresa Calderón*

B HISTORIETA En la fiesta

Completen.

Teresa ___ llamó a Luis y a mí. Ella ___ invitó a la fiesta. Ella ___ llamó a ti también, y ___ invitó, ¿no? Perdón, ahora tengo que tocar el piano, porque Teresa ___ lo pidió. A mí ___ gusta mucho la música latina. ¿Y a ti ___ gusta también?

C HISTORIETA ¡Al tren!

Contesten con el pronombre apropiado.

1. ¿Sara tiene su boleto?
2. ¿El mozo lleva las maletas?
3. ¿El revisor saluda a Sara?
4. ¿El revisor mira el boleto?
5. ¿Sara le pregunta al revisor dónde está el asiento?
6. ¿El revisor le dice donde está?
7. ¿Sara lleva los libros en la mochila?
8. ¿Sara ve a los amigos en el tren?
9. ¿Ellos le hablan a Sara?
10. Y Sara, ¿les habla a ellos?
11. Desde la ventanilla, ¿ve Sara el paisaje?
12. ¿Ella les dice a los amigos que el paisaje es bello?

Estación de RENFE, Jerez, España

D En el aeropuerto Completen.

El señor Sepúlveda llegó al mostrador de la línea aérea en el aeropuerto. Él ___ habló al agente. Él ___ habló en español. El señor Sepúlveda ___ dio las maletas al agente y el agente ___ puso en la báscula y ___ pesó. El agente ___ dijo al señor Sepúlveda cuánto pesaban. El pasajero ___ dio su boleto al agente. El agente ___ miró. Facturó el equipaje, y ___ dio el boleto y los talones al señor Sepúlveda. El agente ___ dio las gracias al pasajero y ___ deseó un feliz viaje.

REPASO DE ESTRUCTURA

ciento sesenta y nueve ∿ **169**

CAPÍTULO 4
Repaso de estructura

TEACHING TIPS

A. *Práctica A* and *C* can be done without any prior preparation. Have students close their books. Go over the exercises orally in class.
B. Give students two or three minutes to look over *Práctica B* and *D*. Then call on individuals to read them aloud.

ANSWERS
Práctica

A Answers can be negative.
1. **Sí, Teresa me llamó anoche.**
2. **Sí, me invitó a la fiesta.**
3. **Sí, nos invitó también.**
4. **Sí, ella te conoce.**
5. **Sí, ella te va a invitar también.**

B 1. nos 5. me
2. nos 6. me
3. te 7. te
4. te

C 1. lo 7. los
2. las 8. los
3. la 9. le
4. lo 10. les
5. le 11. lo
6. le 12. les

D 1. le 7. le
2. le 8. lo
3. le 9. le
4. las 10. le
5. las 11. le
6. le

Paired Activity

1. **Práctica C:** Have students work in pairs. One student reads the question, the other answers, then they reverse roles. You can circulate to listen, give grades, help, etc.
Hint: Set a time limit and use the timer to keep students focused on the task.
2. Have students work in pairs to make up their own invitations to a fiesta providing all the information indicated in the sample.

Independent Practice

Assign any of the following:
1. Exercises, page 169
2. Workbook, *Repaso de estructura*

169

TEACHING STRUCTURE

◈ Referring to people and things already mentioned ◆◆◆

This is one of those grammatical points that students learn better through examples than through explanation. In your presentation, it is recommended that you concentrate on the model sentences and use the actual answers to the exercises as examples rather than belabor the explanation of which pronoun goes where. The more students hear the correct order, the less frequently they will make errors.

With slower groups, you may wish to practice replacing only one object pronoun in each sentence and come back to this topic at another time.

ABOUT THE SPANISH LANGUAGE

Una «radiografía» es una foto o una imagen del interior del cuerpo. Se produce por medio de un tubo de «rayos X». Muchas veces se dice: «Me sacó unos rayos X».

Referring to people and things already mentioned
Dos complementos en la misma oración

1. Very frequently both a direct and an indirect pronoun appear in the same sentence. When they do, the indirect object pronoun is always placed before the direct object pronoun and both pronouns precede the conjugated form of the verb.

Alicia me dio el informe.	**Alicia me lo dio.**
Y ella me regaló las fotografías.	**Y ella me las regaló.**

2. The indirect object pronouns **le** and **les** change to **se** when used with the direct object pronouns **lo, la, los, las.** Because the pronoun **se** can mean **a él, a ella, a Ud., a ellos, a ellas,** and **a Uds.,** it is often clarified by a prepositional phrase.

La doctora le dio las radiografías a él.	**La doctora se las dio a él.**
La doctora les dio las radiografías a ellos.	**La doctora se las dio a ellos.**

Learning From Photos

Have students describe what they see in the photo. You may wish to ask: **¿Quién será la señora? ¿Qué es lo que mira? ¿Dónde estará ella?**

Práctica

A **¿Quién te lo regaló?** Contesten según el modelo.

¿Quién te regaló el saco de dormir?
Mi tía me lo regaló.

1. ¿Quién te regaló las esquís?
2. ¿Quién te regaló las sillas plegables?
3. ¿Quién te regaló el barquito?
4. ¿Quién te regaló la hamaca?
5. ¿Quién te regaló el billete?
6. ¿Quién te regaló la cámara?

B **¿Te gusta?** Contesten según el modelo.

¿Te gusta el traje?
Sí, mucho. ¿Quién te lo dio?

1. ¿Te gustan los tenis?
2. ¿Te gustan las pelotas?
3. ¿Te gusta la raqueta?
4. ¿Te gusta la camisa?
5. ¿Te gusta el traje de baño?
6. ¿Te gustan las gafas de sol?
7. ¿Te gusta la crema protectora?
8. ¿Te gustan los esquís acuáticos?
9. ¿Te gusta la toalla playera?

C **HISTORIETA** Una carta a la abuela

Contesten con los pronombres apropiados.

1. ¿Le escribiste la carta a abuelita?
2. ¿Le mandaste la carta hoy?
3. ¿Le diste una copia de tu artículo?
4. ¿Le mandaste las fotos de la familia?
5. ¿Le diste nuestros saludos también?
6. ¿Ella te contestará la carta?

D **HISTORIETA** En la taquilla

Completen con los pronombres.

Ayer fui a la taquilla para comprar entradas para unos amigos. Yo ___ compré. Pero
                                                                        1
cuando el taquillero ___ vendió, él me dijo que quedaban pocas. Yo llamé a Ramón y
                       2
___ dije. Ramón entonces ___ pidió que comprara una más. Volví a la taquilla y ___
3, 4   5   6
pedí otra entrada al taquillero. Pero el taquillero ya ___ había vendido. Él ___ vendió
                                                       7   8, 9
a una señora momentos antes de que yo regresara.

REPASO DE ESTRUCTURA   *ciento setenta y uno* 171

TEACHING TIPS

A. Go over *Práctica A* and *D* orally in class with no previous preparation.

B. *Práctica B* and *C* can be gone over orally in class then assigned for written homework. Have students read their answers aloud the next day.

ANSWERS
Práctica

A 1. me la
2. me las
3. me lo
4. me la
5. me lo
6. me la
7. me los

B 1. te los   6. te las
2. te las   7. te la
3. te la   8. te los
4. te la   9. te la
5. te lo

C 1. Se la escribí.
2. Se la mandé.
3. Se la di.
4. Se las mandé.
5. Se los di.
6. Me la contestará.

D 1. se las   5. le
2. me las   6. la
3. se lo   7. se la
4. me

ABOUT THE SPANISH LANGUAGE

There exists some controversy over the plural of **esquí**. The Real Academia accepts **esquís** as the term. However, most journalists use the term **esquíes**, a form that seems to correspond more closely to the usual plural ending for words ending in **í**, such as **rubí**, **marroquí**, etc. Some grammarians insist that the plural should be **esquíes**.

Independent Practice:

Assign any of the following:
1. Exercises, page 171
2. Workbook, *Repaso de estructura*

171

TEACHING TIPS

A. Call on a student to read the *Introducción* aloud.

B. After they have read the *Introducción*, ask students to make a list of the social occasions mentioned.

C. Ask students to describe their feelings, both positive and negative, about their own family celebrations.

D. For each of the occasions mentioned in the *Introducción*, you may also wish to ask students: **¿Quiénes participan en estos eventos? ¿Cómo se celebran? ¿Son iguales estos eventos en los EE.UU.? ¿Depende de la región?**

RESOURCES

- 🔖 Vocabulary Transparencies
- 🎧 Audio Cassette 7B/Compact Disc 5
- 📁 Student Tape Manual
- 📁 Workbook
- 📁 Chapter Quizzes
- 💾 Testing Program

TEACHING VOCABULARY

You may wish to ask the following questions as you present the new vocabulary:
¿Cuáles son los dos eventos que traen más alegría en todas las culturas?
¿Qué significa la expresión «Echan la casa por la ventana»?
¿Quiénes cubren los gastos de la boda?
¿Qué bodas son centro de atención para todos?

Periodismo
La boda y el nacimiento

Introducción

Las bodas y los nacimientos son los dos eventos que más alegría traen en todas las culturas. Las bodas se acompañan de mucha ceremonia y mucho festejo. Hay quienes «echan la casa por la ventana» cuando se trata de la boda de sus hijos. Por tradición, en la cultura hispánica y en la occidental en general, los gastos de las bodas los cubren los padres de la novia. Y hay bodas que cuestan muchísimo. La boda no es cuestión solamente del matrimonio de los novios, puede también representar para las familias una oportunidad de mostrar al mundo su posición social, su importancia y su rango.

Por eso, cuando se casan los hijos de personajes famosos, todo el mundo se interesa. Y cuando las bodas son de miembros de las familias reales, son centro de atención para todos. Recientemente la familia real española celebró dos eventos de gran alegría: la boda de su hija menor, la Infanta doña Cristina, y el nacimiento del primer nieto de los reyes.

Vocabulario

el trono

los novios

el brindis de los novios

ABOUT THE SPANISH LANGUAGE

You may wish to remind students that **el trono** is used in Spanish as in English with both the literal meaning of the seat of a monarch, and the metaphorical meaning of the monarchy or royal power.

VOCABULARY EXPANSION

You may wish to remind students that **novio(a)** has several meanings in Spanish. **Novios** are the rough equivalent of "boyfriend" and "girlfriend" but the word also has the meaning of "fiancée" or "betrothed" and can mean the same as **recién casados** or a "just married" couple.

la **Infanta**   hija de los Reyes de España
   nacida después del príncipe
el **primogénito**   el primer hijo
el **comunicado**   una comunicación oficial
el **parto**   el nacimiento
el **puro**   el cigarro

la **marcha**   la salida, la partida
entrañable   íntimo(a), afectuosísimo(a)
comedido(a)   discreto(a), moderado(a)
sensible   sensitivo, sentimental
desgraciado(a)   infeliz, miserable

Práctica

A Expresiones equivalentes   Pareen.

1. el comunicado
2. la madrugada
3. el primogénito
4. la Infanta
5. el parto
6. el trono

a. el asiento de los reyes
b. el momento de nacer
c. un informe oficial escrito
d. hija de los Reyes españoles
e. el hijo mayor
f. muy temprano por la mañana

Palacio de la Zarzuela, Madrid, España

B La boda   Completen.

1. El padrino levantó la copa y ofreció un ___ por los novios.
2. El padrino era amigo ___ del novio, era como un hermano.
3. Y como es un hombre muy ___ empezó a llorar.
4. Pero la madre fue más ___, más discreta y se controló.

ciento setenta y tres 173

ANSWERS
Práctica
A 1. c
  2. f
  3. e
  4. d
  5. b
  6. a
B 1. brindis
  2. entrañable
  3. sensible
  4. comedida

Learning From Photos

El Palacio de la Zarzuela queda a unos 15 kilómetros de Madrid. El palacio original era del siglo 17 pero fue totalmente destruido durante la Guerra Civil Española (1936-39). El palacio fue reconstruido en la década de 1950 y sirve hoy de residencia de los Reyes de España.

Did You Know?

El primer hijo de los Reyes lleva el título de Príncipe o Princesa. Pero todos los demás hijos legítimos son Infantes: Infante o Infanta. Quizás la más famosa de las Infantas de España es la Infanta Margarita, hija del Rey Felipe IV, la protagonista de la obra maestra de Velázquez, *Las meninas.*

Independent Practice

Assign any of the following:
1. Exercises, page 173
2. Workbook, *Periodismo*

173

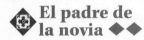 **El padre de la novia** ◆◆

A. Call on individual students to read this article aloud.

B. As each paragraph is read, you may wish to call on other students to answer the relevant questions in *Comprensión A* on page 175.

HISTORY CONNECTION

Don Juan Carlos is the grandson of the last king of Spain, Alfonso XIII. Alfonso abdicated in 1931 when elections were won by pro-republican parties. The Republic lasted until 1939 when General Franco's forces won the Civil War that had raged since 1936. The legitimate heir to the throne was Juan Carlos's father, Don Juan. Don Juan renounced his right to the throne and Juan Carlos became king upon the death of Franco in 1975.

El padre de la novia

de Jaime Peñafiel

El padre de la novia es, después de ésta, el protagonista más importante de la boda. Y no sólo porque es el pagano de la fiesta[1]—desde el vestido a los puros pasando por la dote[2] y el banquete—, sino porque, con la marcha de la hija, se suele ir un pedazo importante de su vida.

Don Juan Carlos, el pasado sábado día 4, fue más que Rey, fue padre y como tal se comportó. Nunca se le ha visto más entrañable y más grande.

Frente a la frialdad[3] de la Reina, siempre tan profesional, ella que a veces parece sobrehumana, la humanidad del Rey fue la única que se dejó sentir ¡y de qué manera! En tan solemne, comedida y controlada—por Doña Sofía—ceremonia.

Es la primera de mis 42 bodas reales en la que la novia, no es que no llorara, sino que ni siquiera se emocionó.

En la catedral gótica de Barcelona sólo se permitió, no esa debilidad, sino esa emoción incontenida[4], el padre de la novia. Pienso que llora porque es un hombre sensible y bueno. ¡Desgraciado del hombre que no llora el día que casa a su hija o entierra a su padre!

A millares de personas, sentadas ante el televisor, se les hizo un nudo en la garganta[5] cuando vieron al Rey tragar la saliva y bajar la cabeza para intentar ocultar las lágrimas. Cuando la levantó, las lágrimas habían formado dos visibles bolsas bajo sus ojos.

A los postres del banquete, Don Juan Carlos pudo hacer suyas las palabras de ese gran ausente, el Conde de Barcelona[6], otro padre, cuando en las mismas circunstancias y antes de alzar la copa para el brindis se dirigió a la novia en los siguientes términos: «Margarita, mi hija tan querida, sales de una casa donde fuiste polarización[7] de cariño y preocupaciones que hoy se mitigan[8] por verte caer en los brazos acogedores de Carlos, un hombre bueno y cariñoso… »

En esta hermosa historia de amor de hoy los novios se llaman Cristina e Iñaki. Y Juan Carlos, el padre de la novia.

La Infanta doña Cristina y su padre, Don Juan Carlos

[1] **el pagano de la fiesta** la persona que siempre paga
[2] **la dote** dinero u otros bienes que lleva la novia al matrimonio
[3] **la frialdad** *coldness*
[4] **incontenida** *uncontrollable*
[5] **un nudo en la garganta** *a lump in the throat*
[6] **El Conde de Barcelona** El Conde de Barcelona era el padre del Rey don Juan Carlos.
[7] **polarización** centro de atención
[8] **se mitigan** disminuyen, se suavizan

Additional Practice

You may wish to ask the following additional questions:

¿Quién no lloró ni se emocionó durante la boda?

¿Qué les ocurrió a las miles de personas que vieron al rey intentar ocultar las lágrimas?

¿De quién era hija Margarita?

Bautizo del primer nieto de los reyes de España

La Infanta Elena de España y su esposo, don Jaime de Marichalar, duques de Lugo, bautizaron este domingo a su primogénito. El niño recibió el nombre de Felipe Juan Froilán. Es el tercero en la línea de sucesión al trono después de su tío e hijo menor de los reyes, Felipe, y de su madre, la Infanta.

La Infanta Elena, de 34 años, se encontraba muy emocionada, igual que su esposo y todos los acompañantes.

La ceremonia se realizó en el Palacio de la Zarzuela. El rey fue el padrino de su primer nieto y la abuela paterna fue la madrina.

Comprensión

A **La Boda** Contesten.

1. Según el artículo, ¿quién es la persona más importante en la boda, y quién es la segunda más importante?
2. ¿Por qué le llaman al padre de la novia «el pagano de la fiesta»?
3. Dice el autor que alguien controlaba la ceremonia, ¿quién?
4. Hay dos ocasiones cuando el hombre es un desgraciado si no llora. ¿Cuáles son?
5. ¿Dónde tuvo lugar la boda de la Infanta doña Cristina?
6. ¿Qué es lo que les «hizo un nudo en la garganta» a las personas que miraban la televisión?
7. ¿Quiénes pudieron contener su emoción?
8. ¿Cómo se llama el esposo de la Infanta doña Cristina?

National Standards

Culture

Los padrinos juegan un papel muy importante en los bautizos. Se obligan a cuidar de la vida religiosa del bebé, pero también se comprometen a cuidar del bebé si por alguna razón faltaran los padres. Los padrinos de Felipe Juan Froilán son sus abuelos: el Rey don Juan Carlos, el padre de su madre, y la madre de su padre.

ANSWERS

Comprensión

A 1. la novia, el padre de la novia
2. porque paga para la fiesta
3. don Juan Carlos
4. el día que casa a su hija y entierra a su padre
5. en el catedral gótica de Barcelona
6. ver al Rey tragar la saliva y bajar la cabeza para intentar ocultar las lágrimas
7. la Reina y la novia
8. Iñaki Urdangarín

Learning From Photos

You may wish to ask these questions about the photo:

¿Quiénes son las personas en la foto? Describa el traje que lleva la Infanta Elena. Describa la ropa de don Jaime de Marichalar. ¿Qué ropa lleva el bebé?

Did You Know?

Although the Infanta Elena married a commoner, don Jaime de Marichalar, after the wedding the couple received a title of nobility, the Duques de Lugo. Their son, Felipe Juan Froilán, is third in the line of succession to the throne. His uncle, Prince Felipe, the first-born of the Royal Family, is first in the line of succession, followed by his own mother, the Infanta Elena.

ANSWERS

Comprensión

B 1. la Reina
2. el Rey
3. la Reina
4. la Reina
5. el Rey
6. la Reina
7. le Rey

C 1. Lugo
2. Felipe Juan Froilán
3. 34
4. esposo
5. Palacio de la Zarzuela
6. tercero

B **Los Reyes**   Según el artículo, ¿cuáles son los adjetivos que se aplican a la Reina doña Sofía, y cuáles al Rey don Juan Carlos?

1. sensible
2. afectuoso
3. controlado
4. profesional
5. entrañable
6. frío
7. cariñoso

Los reyes, doña Sofía y don Juan Carlos, doña Cristina e Iñaki Urdangarín

C **El primer nieto**   Completen.

1. La Infanta doña Elena y su esposo son los duques de ___.
2. Al hijo le dieron el nombre de ___.
3. La Infanta tiene ___ años.
4. Jaime de Marichalar es el ___ de la Infanta.
5. El bautizo tuvo lugar en el ___.
6. El niño Felipe es el ___ en la línea de sucesión al trono.

Learning From Photos

The king is wearing one of his military uniforms. The bride, the Infanta Cristina, wears **un traje de novia.** The groom is dressed in formal wear. He wears **un traje de etiqueta.**

Actividades comunicativas

A **La noticia**   Ud. es un(a) reportero(a) de televisión que tiene que anunciar el bautizo de Felipe Juan Froilán. Use la información del artículo, pero dé la noticia en sus propias palabras.

B **El novio**   El novio de la Infanta doña Cristina, Iñaki Urdangarín, es un atleta profesional. Ud. es Iñaki. Ud. tiene que hablar con uno de los Reyes (su compañero[a]) y convencerle que doña Cristina debe casarse con Ud.

Iñaki Urdangarín

Actividades comunicativas

ANSWERS

A and **B** Answers will vary.

Learning From Photos

Puede hacerles preguntas a los estudiantes basadas en la foto:

¿Quiénes son las dos personas?

¿Qué lleva ella en la mano?

¿Qué traje lleva ella?

¿Qué acaban de hacer?

Describa la ropa del hombre.

The husband of the Infanta Cristina is Iñaki Urdangarín. He is a professional player of **balonmano. Balonmano** or team handball is an Olympic sport, very popular in Spain and most of Europe, but it is virtually unknown in the United States. Team handball is an entirely different sport than the handball most Americans are familiar with. It has been described as a hybrid version of soccer, water polo, and lacrosse—11-man teams try to throw the ball into a guarded goal—with a bit of basketball thrown in—players must dribble the ball every few steps as they bring it down the court.

177

TEACHING TIPS

A. Call on a student to read the *Introducción* aloud since it contains much useful vocabulary.

B. After they have read the *Introducción*, ask students to make a list of the social occasions mentioned.

RESOURCES

- Vocabulary Transparencies
- Audio Cassette 8A/Compact Disk 5
- Student Tape Manual
- Workbook
- Chapter Quizzes
- Testing Program

TEACHING VOCABULARY

Present the new words and definitions and have students repeat them after you.

VOCABULARY EXPANSION

There are a number of terms used for the dead. Among them are: **el/la difunto(a), el/la muerto(a), el/la finado(a), el/la fenecido(a), el/la fallecido(a).**

Anuncios sociales

Introducción

Los pasajes de la vida se marcan con ceremonia. Por costumbre se espera que haya testigos. Se quiere informar a todas las personas que pudieran tener interés. Una manera de informar a un amplio público es por medio del periódico. Se anuncian los nacimientos, los cumpleaños, las bodas y las muertes.

Vocabulario

el ave picuda, la cigüeña   el festejo   las concurrentes   la cobijita

el marco   lo que rodea una cosa
el/la heredero(a)   el/la hijo(a)
el/la bisnieto(a)   el/la hijo(a) de un nieto o una nieta
el/la extinto(a)   el/la señor(a) que murió
el Magisterio Fiscal   los maestros de las escuelas públicas

participar   comunicar, notificar o informar
efectuar   hacer, realizar, tener lugar

obsequiar   dar, regalar
degustar   probar alimentos, especialmente alimentos finos y elegantes
lucir   brillar, ser espléndido
llevar a cabo   hacer, realizar

allegado(a)   cercano, próximo, se dice de los parientes e íntimos amigos
abnegado(a)   se dice de la persona generosa que hace sacrificios por los demás

Independent Practice

Assign any of the following:
1. Exercises, page 179
2. Workbook, *Periodismo*

⊹Práctica⊹

A **¿Qué es?** Contesten según los dibujos.

1. ¿Es un ave picuda o un canario?

2. ¿Es un festejo o un velorio?

3. ¿Son las concurrentes o las cobijitas?

4. ¿Es un marco o un festejo?

B **HISTORIETA** **¿Cuál es la palabra?**

Completen con la palabra apropiada.

1. Los nietos de doña Flor tienen hijos, así es que ella tiene ___.
2. Para su cumpleaños, le ___ a doña Flor exquisitos regalos.
3. Todas las personas ___ a doña Flor asistieron al festejo.
4. Y allí sirvieron deliciosos platos que todos los concurrentes ___.
5. Doña Flor siempre piensa en los demás y hace lo que puede por ellos. Es una persona muy ___.
6. Durante muchos años fue maestra en una escuela pública, y muchos amigos del ___ asistieron al festejo.
7. Doña Clara Calles, gran amiga de doña Flor, murió recientemente, y todas sus amigas pensaron en la ___.

C **Los sinónimos** Escojan.

1. participar   **a.** regalar
2. efectuar   **b.** probar
3. obsequiar   **c.** realizar
4. degustar   **d.** informar

TEACHING TIPS

Have students look for the information in *Práctica A, B,* and *C* before going over them in class.

ANSWERS
Práctica
A **1. un ave picuda**
    2. un velorio
    3. las cobijitas
    4. un festejo
B **1. bisnietos**
    2. obsequian
    3. allegadas
    4. degustaron
    5. abnegada
    6. Magisterio Fiscal
    7. extinta
C **1. d**
    2. c
    3. a
    4. b

Did You Know?

La cigüeña, o ave picuda, es un símbolo de fecundidad o fertilidad y, por consiguiente, de buena suerte. En muchos países se les animan a las cigüeñas a construir sus nidos en los tejados de las casas.

Learning From Photos

Have students answer questions about the photo: **¿Qué tipo de fiesta será? ¿Quiénes son los concurrentes? ¿Qué llevan en la cabeza? ¿Quiénes serán las señoras? ¿Dónde tiene lugar la fiesta?**

TEACHING TIPS

A. Have students take a look at the page to get an overall feel for it.

B. Have students read or scan these announcements as if they were browsing through a newspaper. It is not necessary that they be read aloud.

HISTORY CONNECTION

Los nombres de ciudades tienen interés histórico. En Latinoamérica hay varias ciudades que llevan el nombre de Santiago. Hay Santiagos en la Argentina, Chile, Costa Rica, Cuba, El Salvador, México, Panamá, el Perú y la República Dominicana. Cristóbal Colón llegó a la isla de Jamaica en 1494 y la nombró Santiago. En España hay varias ciudades con el nombre de Santiago además de la más importante, Santiago de Compostela, en Galicia. Santiago es el santo patrón de España. Durante las guerras contra los moros, los cristianos gritaban «¡Santiago, y cierra, España!» al comenzar cada lucha.

El Diario de Juárez se publica en Ciudad Juárez en el norte de México. Ciudad Juárez y El Paso, Tejas, en realidad forman una sola ciudad dividida por el Río Bravo o Río Grande. La ciudad lleva el nombre de Benito Juárez, héroe y presidente de México, quien luchó contra el Emperador Maximiliano y las tropas francesas por la independencia de México (1863–67).

EL MERCURIO   Santiago de Chile, 18 de abril

MATRIMONIO

Aspillaga Barros-Claverie Jaramillo

MICHEL Claverie Bartet, Marta Jaramillo de Claverie, Pedro Aspillaga Salas y Ana María Barros de Aspillaga participan a Ud. el matrimonio de sus hijos Rodrigo Aspillaga Barros y María Paz Claverie Jaramillo y le invitan a la ceremonia religiosa que se efectuará, con misa de precepto, en la Iglesia de los Sagrados Corazones de Alameda (Avda. Bernardo O'Higgins 2062), el día sábado 25 de abril a las 20.00 horas.

La feliz pareja, Rodrigo y María Paz

BODAS DE ORO

HOY celebran 50 años de matrimonio don Benjamín Saavedra Camus y la señora Inés Marchant de Saavedra, en compañía de sus hijos, nietos, bisnietos y hermanos.

4E   *El Diario de Juárez*   **30 de agosto**

Norma de Cardona Recibirá la Visita del Ave Picuda

En bonito festejo organizado por Yolanda M. de Téllez, fue felicitada por la espera de su primer bebé la señora Norma Téllez de Cardona.

Al baby shower asistieron amistades y familiares allegadas de Norma. La amplia estancia de la casa donde se llevó a cabo la celebración, lucía espléndidamente adornada de flores. Todo ello, sirvió de marco a la convivencia[1]. Posteriormente, Norma abrió cada uno de los regalos que le obsequiaron sus invitadas, los cuales iban desde zapatitos hasta cobijitas para cubrir a su frágil heredero.

Las distinguidas concurrentes degustaron deliciosos platillos, acompañados de refrescantes bebidas. Ya llegada la noche se retiraron a sus hogares.

Asistieron Adela González de Márquez, Alicia Salas, María de Jesús C. de Longoria, Escolástica V. de Solorio y Vicky de Guerrero.

Norma con su mamá

[1] **convivencia** reunión

EL DIARIO *Página 10*

8 de marzo

NECROLÓGICOS

SOF. 1ro. ESNA. OSWALDO MALDONADO JARJUIRI-ESPOSO, LIZ, PAMELA, WILLIAM, JESMY HIJOS, LOS PADRES POLÍTICOS, HERMANOS, HERMANOS POLÍTICOS, TÍOS, PRIMOS, SOBRINOS Y DEMÁS FAMILIARES DE LA QUE EN VIDA FUE QUERIDA ESPOSA Y ABNEGADA MADRE:

✝ SRA. PROF. EMMA ROJAS DE MALDONADO

(Q. E. P. D.) [1]

INVITAN AL MAGISTERIO FISCAL DE LA PAZ, ARMADA BOLIVIANA, RESIDENTES VALLEGRANDINOS, ORUREÑOS, PROVINCIA ALONZO DE IBÁÑEZ, HUANUNI, AMIGOS E INSTITUCIONES A LAS QUE PERTENECIÓ, SE DIGNEN ASISTIR A LA MISA DE RÉQUIEM QUE EN SUFRAGIO DEL ALMA DE LA EXTINTA Y RECORDANDO EL PRIMER AÑO DE SU LLORADO FALLECIMIENTO, SE MANDARÁ A OFICIAR EL DÍA MIÉRCOLES 10 DEL PTE. A HRS. 18:45 PM. EN LA CATEDRAL METROPOLITANA, NUESTRA SEÑORA DE LA PAZ (PLAZA MURILLO).

FAVOR DE COMPROMETER A LA GRATITUD DE LA FAMILIA DOLIENTE.

LA PAZ, MARZO 8

EL DUELO SE DESPIDE EN LA PUERTA DEL TEMPLO.

[1] **(Q.E.P.D.)** Que en paz descanse (R.I.P.)

Did You Know?

Las siglas Q.E.P.D. se encuentran frecuentemente en las lápidas *(headstones)* en los cementerios. Q.E.P.D. quiere decir: Que en paz descanse.

Critical Thinking Activity

Thinking skills: making inferences **Usando los detalles que aparecen en la esquela, determine la profesión del esposo de la Sra. Profesora Emma Rojas de Maldonado.**

Periodismo

TEACHING TIPS

Have students look for the information in *Práctica A, B,* and *C* before going over them in class.

ANSWERS
Comprensión

A 1. Rodrigo Aspillaga Barros y María Paz Claverie Jaramillo

2. sus padres

3. Rodrigo y María Paz

4. en la Iglesia de los Sagrados Corazones

5. religiosa

6. sábado, 25 de abril

7. Benjamín Saavedra Camus e Inés Marchant de Saavedra.

8. cincuenta años

9. sus hijos, nietos, bisnietos y hermanos

B 1. c   4. b

2. b   5. c

3. a   6. b

C 1. hace un año

2. Oswaldo Maldonado Jarjuiri

3. al Magisterio Fiscal de La Paz

4. el 10 de marzo en la Catedral Metropolitana, Nuestra Señora de la Paz

5. en la puerta del templo

EXPANSION You may wish to have students prepare announcements for births, deaths, marriages, etc., of people in the news.

ANSWERS

A and B Answers will vary.

FINE ART CONNECTION

Have students comment on the painting by Urteaga. You may wish to ask: **¿Cómo se sabe que es un entierro? ¿Tiene lugar en una gran ciudad, o no? ¿Qué lo indica?**

182

Comprensión

A Los anuncios sociales Contesten.

1. ¿Quiénes se casan?
2. ¿Quiénes anuncian la boda?
3. ¿Cómo se llaman los novios?
4. ¿Dónde tendrá lugar la boda?
5. ¿Será una ceremonia religiosa o civil?
6. ¿Cuál es la fecha de la boda?
7. ¿Quiénes celebran un aniversario?
8. ¿Cuántos años llevan de casados?
9. ¿Quiénes les acompañan en la celebración?

B La visita del ave picuda Escojan.

1. El segundo artículo es de un periódico ___.
   a. español **b.** chileno **c.** mexicano
2. La señora Norma de Cardona va a ___.
   a. casarse **b.** tener un bebé **c.** tener un cumpleaños
3. La casa donde se celebraba el evento estaba adornada de ___.
   a. flores **b.** cuadros **c.** fuentes
4. El «frágil heredero» se refiere a un ___.
   a. regalo **b.** bebé **c.** platillo
5. En la celebración les sirvieron a los invitados ___.
   a. zapatitos y cobijitas **b.** flores y marcos **c.** platillos y bebidas
6. Al llegar la noche, los invitados a la celebración ___.
   a. abrieron sus regalos **b.** regresaron a sus casas **c.** empezaron a comer

C El aniversario de la muerte Contesten.

1. ¿Cuándo murió la Sra. Rojas de Maldonado?
2. ¿Cómo se llama su esposo?
3. ¿A quiénes, en especial, invitan a la misa?
4. ¿Cuándo y dónde será la misa?
5. ¿Dónde terminará el evento?

Actividades comunicativas

A Una boda Un periódico español le ha pedido que prepare una descripción de una típica boda norteamericana. Escriba la descripción.

B Un «baby shower» Prepare una invitación a las amigas de Gloria Benavides a un «baby shower». En la invitación deben aparecer: el evento y la fecha, la hora y lugar del evento, los tipos de regalos que deben traer, que es un secreto.

«Entierro de un hombre ilustre» de Mario Urteaga

Additional Practice

You may wish to have students do the following writing activity: **Sus padres van a celebrar sus «bodas de plata». Prepare una invitación para mandar a todos los amigos y familiares en España y Latinoamérica.**

Independent Practice

Assign any of the following:
1. Exercises, page 182
2. Workbook, *Estructura*

Estructura

Subjunctive after certain conjunctions
Subjuntivo en cláusulas adverbiales

1. The subjunctive is always used after the following conjunctions because the information that follows is not necessarily real.

para que	so that	con tal de que	provided that
de modo que	so that, in such a way that	sin que	unless, without
de manera que	so that, in such a way that	a menos que	unless

Victoria no irá a menos que tú vayas.
Ella haría el viaje con tal de que fuéramos en tren.

2. The tense of the verb in the main clause determines the tense of the subjunctive in the dependent clause.

MAIN CLAUSE	DEPENDENT CLAUSE
Present Future	Present subjunctive
Preterite Imperfect Conditional	Imperfect subjunctive

Una clase universitaria, Madrid, España

A **La profesora** Completen.

1. La doctora Ramírez siempre presenta la lección de modo que todos nosotros ___ (comprender).
2. La doctora Ramírez presentó la lección ayer de modo que todos nosotros ___ (comprender).
3. Nadie entiende a menos que ella la ___ (presentar) claramente.
4. Nadie entendería a menos que ella la ___ (presentar) claramente.
5. Ella siempre nos explica todo de manera que ___ (estar) bien claro.
6. Ayer ella nos explicó todo de manera que ___ (estar) bien claro.

ESTRUCTURA

ciento ochenta y tres **183**

183

TEACHING STRUCTURE

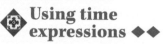 **Using time expressions** ◆◆

A. Have students read the explanation in step 1 aloud.
B. Have the class read the model sentences aloud.
C. Have the students repeat in unison the adverbial conjunctions of time in step 2.
D. Make certain that the students are aware of the exception to the rule in step 3. Have them repeat the model sentences aloud.

TEACHING TIPS

Have students prepare these *Práctica* before going over them in class.

ANSWERS
Práctica
A 1. llegó
   2. esté
   3. hablen
   4. acabemos
   5. expliquen

Using time expressions
Subjuntivo con conjunciones de tiempo

1. The subjunctive is used with adverbial conjunctions of time when the verb of the main clause is in the future, since it is uncertain if the action in the adverbial clause will really take place. When the verb in the main clause is in the past, the indicative is used since the action of the clause has already been realized.

   Ella nos hablará cuando lleguemos.
   Ella nos habló cuando llegamos.

2. Some frequently used adverbial conjunctions of time are:

cuando	*when*
en cuanto	*as soon as*
tan pronto como	*as soon as*
hasta que	*until*
después de que	*after*

3. The conjunction **antes de que**, "before," is an exception. **Antes de que** is always followed by the subjunctive. The imperfect subjunctive is used after **antes de que** when the verb of the main clause is in the past.

   Ellos saldrán antes de que nosotros lleguemos.
   Ellos salieron antes de que nosotros llegáramos.

 **Práctica**

A **HISTORIETA** ¿Cuándo la vieron?

Completen.

—¿Vieron Uds. a la senadora?

—Sí, la vimos en cuanto ella ___ (llegar) al aeropuerto.
                              1

—¿Y le hablaron?

—No, no pudimos. Pero le hablaremos tan pronto como ella ___ (estar) libre.
                                                              2

—Después de que Uds. ___ (hablar) con ella, vuelvan aquí en seguida.
                        3

—Bien, volveremos aquí cuando ___ (acabar) de hablar con ella.
                                 4

—Y no se olviden, no vuelvan aquí hasta que le ___ (explicar) la situación a la senadora.
                                                  5

Learning From Photos

You may wish to ask the students: **¿Dónde está toda esta gente? ¿Qué hacen ellos allí?**

B ¿En el futuro o en el pasado? Hagan los cambios necesarios.

1. Ella me vio cuando volví.
   _____ verá _____.
2. Yo le hablaré antes de que regrese.
   _____ hablé _____.
3. Ellos me llamaron en cuanto recibieron la noticia.
   _____ llamarán _____.
4. Y yo se lo agradeceré tan pronto como me informen.
   _____ agradecí _____.

Expressing *although*
Subjuntivo con **aunque**

1. The conjunction **aunque**, "although," may be followed by the subjunctive or the indicative depending upon the meaning of the sentence. Study the following sentences.

> **Ellos jugarán aunque haga mucho frío.**
> **Ellos jugarán aunque hace mucho frío.**

In the first sentence, the subjunctive is used to indicate that it is not very cold now but that they will play even if it gets very cold. The indicative is used in the second sentence because it is a fact that it is very cold and, although it is very cold, they will still play.

 **Práctica**

A  **HISTORIETA** *¿Lo hacemos o no?*

Contesten según el modelo.

> **Hace muchísimo frío. ¿Vas a jugar?**
> **Sí, voy a jugar aunque hace mucho frío.**

1. No tienes un boleto. ¿Vas al concierto?
2. No sé si el carro tiene bastante gasolina. ¿Vas a ir en el carro?
3. Podría llover. ¿Vendrá Diana con nosotros?
4. Subieron los precios de las entradas. ¿Todavía vamos?
5. Y si hay mucho tráfico, ¿qué? ¿Iremos o no?
6. No sé si Paco Mendes va a tocar. ¿Vas a ir?
7. Tito no tiene dinero. ¿Lo vas a llevar al concierto?
8. Y si la profesora nos da tarea, ¿todavía vamos a ir?

El Centro de Bellas Artes, San Juan, Puerto Rico

ANSWERS
Práctica

B 1. Ella me verá cuando vuelva.
 2. Yo le hablé antes de que regresara.
 3. Ellos me llamarán en cuanto reciban la notícia.
 4. Y yo se lo agradecí tan pronto como me informaron.

TEACHING STRUCTURE

◆ **Expressing *although*** ◆◆

Have the students read the explanatory material and model sentences aloud.

TEACHING TIPS

Have students prepare this *Práctica* before going over it in class.

ANSWERS
Práctica

A 1. Sí, voy al concierto aunque no tengo un boleto.
 2. Sí, voy a ir en el carro aunque no tenga bastante gasolina.
 3. Sí, Diana vendrá con nosotros aunque llueva.
 4. Sí, vamos aunque subieron los precios.
 5. Sí, iremos aunque haya mucho tráfico.
 6. Sí, voy a ir aunque Paco Mendes no vaya a tocar.
 7. Sí, lo voy a llevar al concierto aunque Tito no tiene dinero.
 8. Sí, vamos a ir aunque la profesora nos dé tarea.

Learning From Photos

You may wish to ask the students: **¿Qué se encontrará en este edificio? ¿Cuáles son las «bellas artes»? ¿Es moderno o antiguo el edificio?**

Independent Practice

Assign any of the following:
1. Exercises, pages 184–185
2. Workbook, *Estructura*

185

TEACHING STRUCTURE

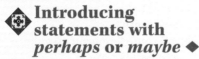 **Introducing statements with** *perhaps* or *maybe* ◆

Have the students read the explanation and model sentences aloud.

ABOUT THE SPANISH LANGUAGE

You may wish to ask students to do the following: **Busque el origen de la expresión «Ojalá» y explique por qué cree Ud. que siempre requiere el subjuntivo.**

TEACHING TIPS

Have students prepare these *Práctica* before going over them in class.

ANSWERS
Práctica
A **¡Ojalá que...**
  1. anuncien su compromiso.
  2. se casen.
  3. les sirvas de padrino (de dama de honor).
  4. tengan una recepción.
  5. hagan un viaje de novios.
  6. sean felices.
  7. tengan algunos niños.
B **No sé. Quizás...**
  1. vayamos en autobús.
  2. nos den de comer.
  3. sean baratas las entradas.
  4. estemos allí toda la tarde.
  5. veamos cosas interesantes.
  6. explique los detalles.
  7. vaya a hacer mucho calor.
  8. volvamos temprano.
  9. sea interesante la visita.

Statements with *perhaps* or *maybe*
Subjuntivo con **quizás, tal vez** y **ojalá**

1. The expressions **quizá(s)**, "perhaps," and **ojalá**, "I wish, would that," are always followed by the subjunctive.

> **Quizás nos llamen hoy.**
> **Ojalá nos inviten a la fiesta.**
> **Ojalá (que) nos invitaran a la fiesta.**

Note that **ojalá** can be followed by either the present or the imperfect subjunctive.

2. The expression **tal vez**, "perhaps," can be followed by either the subjunctive or the future indicative.

> **Tal vez lleguen hoy.**
> **Tal vez llegarán hoy.**

 **Práctica**

A **¡Ojalá!** Contesten según el modelo.

> **¿Se casarán?**
> **Ojalá que se casen.**

1. ¿Anunciarán su compromiso?
2. ¿Se casarán?
3. ¿Les servirás de padrino (de dama de honor)?
4. ¿Tendrán una recepción?
5. ¿Harán un viaje de novios?
6. ¿Serán felices?
7. ¿Tendrán algunos niños?

B **¿Nos acompañarán?** Contesten según el modelo.

> **¿Nos acompañarán los chicos?**
> **No sé. Quizás nos acompañen.**

1. ¿Iremos en autobús?
2. ¿Nos darán de comer?
3. ¿Serán baratas las entradas?
4. ¿Estaremos allí toda la tarde?
5. ¿Veremos cosas interesantes?
6. ¿Don Felipe explicará los detalles?
7. ¿Va a hacer mucho calor?
8. ¿Volveremos temprano?
9. ¿Será interesante la visita?

Additional Practice

You may wish to have students answer with **quizás, tal vez,** or **ojalá.**

1. **¿Podrás asistir a la universidad?**
2. **¿Estarán contentos tus padres?**
3. **¿La directora te escribirá una recomendación?**
4. **¿Tendrás bastante dinero?**

Cooperative Learning

Have groups of 4 students prepare a role play based on the photo. One student will be a newspaper reporter interviewing the other three. Find out what the group is, where they are from, the purpose of the trip, how long the trip will be, etc. The more creative the better!

Referring to people and things already mentioned
Colocación de los pronombres de complemento

1. The direct and indirect object pronouns precede a conjugated verb in Spanish.

Ella me lo dice.	**Ella me lo dijo.**
Ella se lo dirá.	**Ella se lo ha dicho.**

2. However, when a direct or indirect object pronoun is used with an infinitive, **-ar, -er, -ir,** or a present participle, **-ando, -iendo,** the pronoun or pronouns may either be attached to the infinitive or present participle, or they may precede the auxiliary verb that accompanies the infinitive or present participle. Look at the following sentences.

INFINITIVE

Ella me lo quiere decir.	**Ella quiere decírmelo.**
Ella me lo va a decir.	**Ella va a decírmelo.**
Ella me acaba de decir el nombre.	**Ella acaba de decirme el nombre.**

PRESENT PARTICIPLE

Ella me lo estaba diciendo.	**Ella estaba diciéndomelo.**
Ahora ella se lo está diciendo a ellos.	**Ahora ella está diciéndoselo a ellos.**
Ella les sigue hablando.	**Ella sigue hablándoles.**

3. Note that when two pronouns are attached to the infinitive, the infinitive carries a written accent mark to maintain the same stress. A present participle carries a written accent if either one or two pronouns is attached.

Práctica

A HISTORIETA **En el teatro**

Contesten con pronombres.

1. ¿Quiere ver la comedia Joaquín?
2. ¿Está diciendo a su amiga que la comedia es interesante?
3. ¿Joaquín va a comprar las entradas?
4. ¿Acaba de comprar las entradas en la taquilla?
5. ¿Está mostrando las entradas a la acomodadora?
6. ¿La acomodadora está llevando a los jóvenes a sus asientos?
7. ¿Los jóvenes pueden oír a los actores desde sus asientos?

Una sala de conciertos en el Teatro Colón, Buenos Aires, Argentina

TEACHING STRUCTURE

◆ Referring to people and things already mentioned ◆◆◆

This is one of those grammatical points that students learn better through examples than explanation. In your presentation, it is recommended that you concentrate on the model sentences and use the actual answers to the exercises as examples rather than belabor the explanation of which pronoun goes where. The more students hear the correct order, the less frequently they will make errors.

With slower groups, you may wish to practice replacing only one object pronoun in each sentence and come back to this topic at another time.

TEACHING TIPS

Go over *Práctica A* and *B* orally in class with no previous explanation. Then go over them a second time. Have students write the exercises at home.

ANSWERS
Práctica

A 1. Quiere verla.
    2. Está diciéndosela.
    3. Va a comprarlas.
    4. Acaba de comprarlas.
    5. Está mostrándoselas.
    6. Está llevándolos.
    7. Pueden oírlos.

Learning From Photos

El Teatro Colón es uno de los teatros más bellos del mundo. Allí se encuentra la Orquesta Sinfónica Nacional. El Teatro Colón tiene sus propias compañías de ballet y de ópera. La temporada comienza el 25 de mayo con una gala a la que asisten el Presidente de la República y su gabinete. Todos los artistas más importantes del mundo se pueden ver en los escenarios del Colón. Los argentinos, en particular los de la capital, son muy aficionados a la ópera. Esto se debe, probablemente, a la gran influencia italiana en Buenos Aires.

187

Bell Ringer Review

Use the BRR Transparency 4-8, or write the following on the board:
Escriba algunas órdenes que su profesor(a) de español le da siempre.

TEACHING STRUCTURE

Using commands ◆◆◆

Note It is a matter of teacher choice as to how thorough you wish to be in the presentation of this particular point, since one does not use the imperative a great deal until one is rather fluent. The only exception would be some fixed expressions such as: **dame, pásame, perdóname, dime.**

188

B HISTORIETA **En el mostrador del aeropuerto**

Sigan el modelo.

> **Ella está hablando al agente.**
> **Ella le está hablando.**
> **Ella está hablándole.**

1. El agente está atendiendo a la cliente.
2. Ella está hablando al agente.
3. Ellos están discutiendo su reservación.
4. Ella quiere pagar el boleto ahora.
5. Ella quiere reservar un asiento en el pasillo.
6. El agente puede reservarle el asiento.
7. El agente quiere ver su tarjeta de crédito.
8. La señora le está dando la tarjeta de crédito.
9. El agente acaba de mirar el boleto.
10. El agente está indicando la puerta de salida a la señora.

Aeropuerto, Santiago, Chile

Using commands
Pronombres de complemento con el imperativo

1. The direct and indirect object pronouns are always attached to affirmative commands, formal or familiar. The pronouns precede negative commands.

FORMAL

Hábleme Ud.	**No me hable Ud.**
Dígamelo ahora.	**No me lo diga ahora.**
Désela Ud. a Ramón.	**No se la dé Ud. a Ramón.**

FAMILIAR

Háblame.	**No me hables.**
Dímelo ahora.	**No me lo digas ahora.**
Dásela a Ramón.	**No se la des a Ramón.**

2. Note that the command carries a written accent when either one or two pronouns are added to it.

Did You Know?

El avión es un DC-10 de la Iberia. Este avión tiene asientos para unas 280 personas. Vuela a una velocidad de 488 millas por hora. Puede volar sin escala una distancia de 5.300 millas y consume más de 8.000 litros de combustible por hora de vuelo.

Independent Practice

Assign any of the following:
1. Exercises, pages 187–188
2. Workbook, *Estructura*

Práctica

A HISTORIETA El partido del domingo

Sigan el modelo.

> **Yo voy a organizar el partido**
> **¡Qué bien! ¡Organízalo!**

1. Yo voy a llamar a los jugadores.
2. Voy a preparar el campo.
3. Voy a comprar un balón.
4. Voy a arreglar las porterías.
5. Voy a buscar unos árbitros.
6. Voy a limpiar los uniformes.
7. Voy a darle un uniforme a Pablo.
8. Voy a pedirle zapatillas de deporte a don Braulio.
9. Voy a invitar a los maestros.

B ¡No, nunca! Contesten según el modelo.

> **¿Debo invitar a Emilio?**
> **No, no lo invites.**

1. ¿Debo invitar a las chicas?
2. ¿Debo hablarles?
3. ¿Debo decirles la verdad?
4. ¿Debo cambiar la fecha?
5. ¿Debo prepararles la merienda?
6. ¿Debo prestarles los discos?
7. ¿Debo servirles refrescos?
8. ¿Debo preocuparme?

C ¡No lo haga! Cambien del negativo al afirmativo.

1. No se la dé Ud.
2. No se lo diga Ud.
3. No lo compren Uds.
4. No me lo repita Ud.
5. No nos lo explique Ud. otra vez.
6. No le escriba Ud.
7. No se lo mencionen Uds.
8. No lo escuche Ud.

D Dice el director. Sigan el modelo.

> **Pienso recomendarlo.**
> **No estoy de acuerdo. No lo recomiende Ud.**

1. Pienso repararlas.
2. Pienso informarles.
3. Pienso contratarlos.
4. Pienso decírselo.
5. Pienso despedirlos.
6. Pienso cambiarlas.
7. Pienso telefonearlos.
8. Pienso preguntárselo.

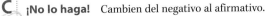

ESTRUCTURA

ciento ochenta y nueve 189

TEACHING TIPS

Have students prepare all of these *Práctica* before going over them in class.

ANSWERS

Práctica

A ¡Qué bien!...

1. ¡Llámalos!	6. ¡Límpialos!
2. ¡Prepáralo!	7. ¡Dáselo!
3. ¡Cómpralo!	8. ¡Pídeselas!
4. ¡Arréglalas!	9. ¡Invítalos!
5. ¡Búscalos!	

B No,...

1. no las invites.
2. no les hables.
3. no se la digas.
4. no la cambies.
5. no se la prepares.
6. no se los prestes.
7. no se los sirvas.
8. no te preocupes.

C 1. Désela.
2. Dígaselo.
3. Cómprenlo.
4. Repítamelo.
5. Explíquenoslo.
6. Escríbale.
7. Menciónenselo.
8. Escúchelo.

D No estoy de acuerdo...
1. No las repare Ud.
2. No les informe Ud.
3. No los contrate Ud.
4. No se lo diga Ud.
5. No los despida Ud.
6. No las cambie Ud.
7. No los telefonee Ud.
8. No se lo pregunte Ud.

Learning From Photos

Have students describe the articles of soccer clothing and equipment. They are: **el balón de fútbol, la bota de fútbol, el jersey/la camiseta de rayas, las medias, el pantalón (corto).** The cleats are called **tacos.**

Independent Practice

Assign any of the following:
1. Exercises, page 189
2. Workbook, *Estructura*

TEACHING TIPS

Have students do the pre-reading activity.

RESOURCES

- 🎙 Vocabulary Transparencies
- 🎧 Audio Cassette 8B/Compact Disc 6
- 📁 Student Tape Manual
- 📁 Workbook
- 📁 Chapter Quizzes
- 📙 Testing Program

TEACHING VOCABULARY

Have students repeat the new words and sentences after you or Cassette 8B/Compact Disc 6.

ABOUT THE SPANISH LANGUAGE

- ◆ The title of this short story is an example of what used to be called the "dative of interest." The indirect object pronoun **le** in the title refers to the **niño** of the title. Roughly translated, the title might be "The little boy whose friend died on him."

- ◆ There are a few idiomatic expressions you may wish to review with the students: **darse cuenta, de repente,** and **acabar con. Darse cuenta** is, of course, "to be aware of" or "to notice." **De repente** is "all of a sudden" or "suddenly." **Acabar con** is "to do away with" or "to destroy." Students may confuse **acabar con** and **acabar de** ("to have just").

Literatura
El niño al que se le murió el amigo
de Ana María Matute

Antes de leer

Uno de los pasajes que no se marca con ninguna ceremonia, y que a veces ocurre sin que nadie se dé cuenta en el momento, es el fin de la niñez. Algo ocurre, y de repente, el niño pasa a ser algo más, un ser más consciente, casi una persona mayor. Algunos dicen que es la pérdida de la inocencia. Es cuando ya no se cree en Santa Claus, o cuando las realidades de la vida acaban con las fantasías. El evento que marca este pasaje en la vida del niño en el cuento que sigue es dramático y triste.

Vocabulario

la valla, la cerca

el quicio de la puerta

el pozo

los juguetes

las canicas   el polvo

El niño estiró los brazos.   Y puso los codos en las rodillas.

Additional Practice

Ask students to describe the little boy and what he is wearing. They should be able to provide descriptions like: **Tiene el pelo castaño. Lleva una camiseta a rayas y un pantalón corto de color azul. Tiene calcetines blancos y unos tenis azules.**

Práctica

A **El niño**   Contesten según los dibujos.

1. ¿Qué juguetes son estos?   **2.** ¿Qué divide las propiedades?

3. ¿Dónde está el niño?   **4.** ¿Qué estiró el niño?

5. ¿De dónde sacan el agua?   **6.** ¿Qué tiene el niño en la ropa?   **7.** ¿Dónde puso el niño sus codos?

LITERATURA   *ciento noventa y uno*   **191**

TEACHING TIPS

This *Práctica* can be done without previous preparation and with books open.

ANSWERS
Práctica

A **1. las canicas**
  2. la cerca, la valla
  3. en el quicio de la puerta
  4. los brazos
  5. del pozo
  6. el polvo
  7. en las rodillas

LITERATURE CONNECTION

Han dicho Enrique Anderson Imbert y Lawrence B. Kiddle de la obra de Ana María Matute: «Ha escrito cuentos para niños y sobre niños. Son muy diferentes. El cuento para niños, «El país de la pizarra», es un viaje mágico, como el de Alicia en «*Through the Looking-Glass*», lleno de gracia, fantasía, lirismo y buen humor. Los cuentos sobre niños, en cambio, son terriblemente crueles. *Los niños tontos* son en verdad más poemas en prosa que cuentos. Son poemas crueles, de una belleza tan extraña, que a simple vista nos hieren como pedazos de fealdad.»

Independent Practice

Assign any of the following:
  1. Exercise, page 191
  2. Workbook, *Literatura*

TEACHING TIPS

You may call on a student to read the *Introducción* aloud as the others follow along.

TEACHING THE READING

Note You may wish to present this lovely story thoroughly using the following outline.

A. Give students a brief oral resumé of the selection in Spanish.

B. Ask some questions about your resumé.

C. Call on individuals to read about four or five sentences each, then ask comprehension questions of other students.

D. Upon completion of the reading, ask approximately 10 questions, the answers to which give a unified review of the story. Direct each question to a different student.

E. Call on a student to give a summary of the story in his/her own words.

F. With more able groups, you may wish to ask the analytical questions in LITERARY ANALYSIS at the bottom of this page.

ABOUT THE SPANISH LANGUAGE

Pure tin is **estaño**. **Hojalata** or **hoja de lata** is "tin-plated steel." **Lata** is the term for a tin (steel) can.

National Standards

Culture
Students experience, discuss, and analyze an expressive product of the culture: the excerpt from the short story «El niño al que se le murió el amigo» by Ana María Matute.

192

Introducción

Ana María Matute nació en la capital española en 1926. Hizo sus estudios en las dos principales ciudades de su país, Madrid y Barcelona. Su primera novela, *Los Abel*, se publicó en 1947. Diez años más tarde se publicó *Los niños tontos*, donde aparece «El niño al que se le murió el amigo».

Ana María Matute

Lectura

El niño al que se le murió el amigo

Una mañana se levantó y fue a buscar al amigo, al otro lado de la valla. Pero el amigo no estaba, y, cuando volvió, le dijo la madre: «El amigo se murió. Niño, no pienses más en él y busca otros para jugar». El niño se sentó en el quicio de la puerta, con la cara entre las manos y los codos en las rodillas.

«Él volverá», pensó. Porque no podía ser que allí estuviesen las canicas, el camión y la pistola de hojalata°, y el reloj aquel que ya no andaba, y el amigo no viniese a buscarlos. Vino la noche, con una estrella muy grande, y el niño no quería entrar a cenar. «Entra niño, que llega el frío», dijo la madre. Pero, en lugar de entrar, el niño se levantó del quicio y se fue en busca del amigo, con las canicas, el camión, la pistola de hojalata y el reloj que no andaba. Al llegar a la cerca, la voz del amigo no le llamó, ni le oyó en el árbol, ni en el pozo. Pasó buscándole toda la noche. Y fue una larga noche casi blanca, que le llenó de polvo el traje y los zapatos. Cuando llegó el sol, el niño, que tenía sueño y sed, estiró los brazos y pensó: «Qué tontos y pequeños son esos juguetes. Y ese reloj que no anda, no sirve para nada». Lo tiró al pozo, y volvió a la casa, con mucha hambre. La madre le abrió la puerta, y dijo: «Cuánto ha crecido este niño, Dios mío, cuánto ha crecido». Y le compró un traje de hombre, porque el que llevaba le venía muy corto.

hojalata *tin*

Literary Analysis

La autora describe emociones, sentimientos y estados mentales en poquísimas palabras. Busque en el cuento las frases que describen los siguientes estados de ánimo del niño:

Confusión: «‹El volverá›», pensó. Porque no podía ser que allí estuviesen...»

Comprensión: «Qué tontos y pequeños son esos juguetes...»
Resignación: «Lo tiró al pozo, y volvió a la casa, con mucha hambre.»
Madurez: «Cuánto ha crecido este niño...»

~Después de leer~

‹Comprensión›

A **¿Qué pasó?** Contesten.
1. Cuando se levantó el niño, ¿a quién fue a buscar?
2. ¿Adónde fue a buscarlo?
3. ¿Estaba el amigo?
4. ¿Qué le aconsejó la madre?
5. ¿Dónde se sentó el niño?

B **Lo que hizo el niño** Completen.
1. El niño creía que volvería su ___.
2. Creía que vendría a buscar sus ___.
3. El niño se quedó afuera y no entró a ___.
4. La madre le dijo que entrara porque hacía ___.
5. En lugar de entrar, el niño se fue ___ del amigo.

C **Opiniones y comentarios** Comenten.
1. Hay un momento en que el fin de la inocencia parece ocurrir. ¿Cuál es?
2. Hay una frase casi poética, que no tiene sentido literal. ¿Qué querrá decir: «Y fue una larga noche casi blanca, que le llenó de polvo el traje y los zapatos»?
3. Interprete la frase de la madre al final del cuento.
4. ¿Cree Ud. que el traje que llevaba el niño realmente le quedaba corto? Explique.

‹Actividades comunicativas›

A **El fin de la niñez** Para muchos de nosotros ha habido un evento que nos ha marcado el final de la niñez. Piense Ud. en el momento en que Ud. dejó de ser niño(a) y descríbalo en español.

B **Nos mudamos.** No es solamente la muerte de un amigo la que puede doler (*ache*) sino la separación. Lo más común es que nos mudamos de un pueblo y perdemos a los amigos, o que un buen amigo tiene que mudarse con la familia. ¿Esto le ha pasado a Ud.? Describa cómo se sintió.

C **Los juguetes** Los juguetes de los niños son a veces curiosos: el reloj que no anda, por ejemplo. Con un(a) compañero(a) comparen todos los «juguetes raros» que tenían cuando eran niños y presenten la lista a la clase.

LITERATURA

ciento noventa y tres ∽ **193**

ANSWERS
Comprensión
A 1. El niño fue a buscar al amigo.
  2. Fue al otro lado de la valla.
  3. El amigo no estaba.
  4. La madre le aconsejó que no pensara en el amigo, que buscara otros para jugar.
  5. El niño se sentó en el quicio de la puerta.
B 1. amigo
  2. juguetes
  3. cenar
  4. frío
  5. en busca
C Answers will vary.

TEACHING TIPS

A. Have students select the *Actividad* they would like to do.
B. These can be done individually or as a cooperative effort.
C. You may wish to have one student or group report to the class concerning each topic.

‹Actividades comunicativas›

ANSWERS
A–C Answers will vary.

Additional Practice

Have students complete the following phrases:
1. **Cuando fue a buscar al amigo, el niño llevaba ___.**
2. **Él fue andando hasta ___.**
3. **Aunque escuchaba con atención, no oía ___.**
4. **Por la mañana el niño tenía ___.**
5. **Él tiró todos los juguetes en ___.**

Independent Practice

Assign any of the following:
1. Exercises, page 193
2. Workbook, *Literatura*

Read the *Introducción* to the class or paraphrase it.

LITERATURE CONNECTION

Ramón de Campoamor se hizo famoso por sus poesías presentadas en tres colecciones—*Doloras* (1846), *Humoradas* (1886) y *Pequeños poemas* (1873–1892). «Cosas del tiempo» es una humorada. El mismo Campoamor dijo de estas poesías: «¿Qué es una humorada? Un rasgo intencionado. ¿Y dolora? Una humorada convertida en drama. ¿Y pequeño poema? Una dolora amplificada».

Las humoradas son todas muy cortas. Los temas de las humoradas son satíricos, amorosos y morales.

Varias humoradas tienen la forma de pareados, es decir, dos versos unidos y aconsonantados.

National Standards

Cosas del tiempo

de Ramón de Campoamor

Antes de leer

Se ha dicho que para los jóvenes, la juventud es eterna. Pero todos sabemos que los años pasan y dejan sus huellas. Lo que ocurre es que vemos las diferencias en otros pero no en nosotros mismos. Además de los pasajes dramáticos de la vida, también existe ese otro pasaje largo, inexorable, constante, que es el sencillo transcurso del tiempo que nos hace cambiar a todos, poco a poco, día tras día.

Introducción

Ramón de Campoamor (1817–1901) nació en Navia, un pueblecito de Asturias en el norte de España. Estudió latín y filosofía en la Universidad de Santiago de Compostela, y más tarde estudió medicina en Madrid y leyes, pero nunca terminó su carrera. Su verdadera vocación eran las letras.

Campoamor es un poeta que dice mucho con pocas palabras. Y casi siempre nos provee una moraleja. Las poesías de Campoamor han sido muy populares en todo el mundo hispano por su humor—un humor a veces dulce, pero también mordaz.

Ramón de Campoamor

Additional Practice

You may wish to have students read the **dolora, "¡Quién supiera escribir!"** It is probably the most well-known popular verse in Spanish. The **doloras**, although relatively short, are much longer than the **humoradas,** which are really epigrams.

Lectura

Cosas del tiempo

Pasan veinte años; vuelve él,
Y al verse, exclaman él y ella:
(—¡Santo Dios! ¿y éste es aquél?...)
(—¡Dios mío! ¿y ésta es aquélla?...)

 Después de leer

Comprensión

A **¿Quién vuelve?** Contesten.

1. ¿Quién vuelve?
2. ¿A quién ve?
3. ¿Cuánto tiempo hace que no se ven?
4. ¿Se reconocen?
5. ¿Han cambiado?
6. ¿Qué dice cada uno para indicar que el otro ha cambiado?

Actividades comunicativas

A **Un entremés** Un entremés es una pieza teatral corta y divertida de un solo acto. Los hermanos Quintero fueron dramaturgos españoles que escribieron un entremés titulado *Mañana de sol*. Este entremés está basado en el breve poema de Campoamor, *Cosas del tiempo*. Con su grupo busquen la obra de los Quintero y presenten una lectura dramática de la obra a la clase.

B **Un cuento** Con su grupo, traten de escribir un breve cuento en el que el personaje principal es un señor o una señora de edad avanzada. La persona ve a alguien que cree reconocer pero ya hace muchos años que no se ven. ¿Dónde se encuentran? ¿Cómo se reconocen? ¿Qué dicen? ¿Cómo se habían conocido antes? ¿Por qué hace tantos años que no se ven?

Additional Practice

You may wish to provide students with these two additional **humoradas** by Campoamor. «**En la guerra y en amor es lo primero el dinero, el dinero y el dinero**» and «**Todo en amor es triste; más triste y todo, es lo mejor que existe.**»

Have the students comment on both. You may wish to ask: **¿Por qué dice el poeta que el dinero es primero tanto en la guerra como en el amor? Dé algunos ejemplos. ¿Qué opina el autor del amor?**

TEACHING THE READING

A. Read the poem once aloud to the class or have the students listen to Cassette 8B/Compact Disc 6.

B. Call on a student to read aloud. Follow with the *Comprensión* activity.

 Después de leer

ANSWERS
Comprensión

A 1. **Él vuelve.**
   2. **Él la ve a ella.**
   3. **Hace veinte años que no se ven.**
   4. **Sí, se reconocen.**
   5. **Sí, han cambiado mucho.**
   6. **Ella dice «¿y éste es aquél?».**
     Él dice «¿y ésta es aquélla?».

TEACHING TIPS

A. You may wish to let students select the *Actividad* they would like to do.

B. These can be done individually or as a cooperative effort.

C. You may wish to have one student or group report to the class concerning each topic.

Actividades comunicativas

ANSWERS
A and B Answers will vary.

National Standards

Communities Students are encouraged to perform the **entremés, Mañana de sol** in Spanish for their own pleasure. They are also urged to use their Spanish for a creative writing experience: a short story based on «**Cosas del tiempo.**»

TEACHING TIPS

Have the students do the pre-reading activity.

TEACHING VOCABULARY

Have students repeat the new words, definitions, and sentences after you.

ABOUT THE SPANISH LANGUAGE

You may wish to remind students about the value of recognizing cognates. Have them identify the Spanish cognates of: destiny, existence, rancor, metaphor, extract, flowers, caress, face.

En paz

de Amado Nervo

Antes de leer

Hay quienes pueden morir conformes con lo que ha sido su destino en la vida. Ven acercarse el final de su existencia sin rencores, sin amargura. Saben que la vida ofrece de todo, de lo bueno igual que de lo malo, de lo bello y de lo feo. Busque en la siguiente poesía las bellas metáforas que emplea el poeta para describir las etapas de la vida.

Vocabulario

la miel

Las abejas extraen néctar de las flores.
Del néctar hacen miel.

la faz, la cara

El cura va a bendecir a todos.
El cura acaricia al bebé.
Él tiene una cara (faz) angelical.

Los labradores están cosechando los vegetales.

el ocaso   la puesta del sol, la decadencia, el final de la vida
la hiel   la amargura, los trabajos, las adversidades
las lozanías   los tiempos de vigor, la robustez, la fuerza

fallido(a)   frustrado(a), no logrado(a), no conseguido(a)
inmerecido(a)   injusto(a), no merecido(a)
rudo(a)   duro(a), tosco(a), riguroso(a)

Práctica

A   **HISTORIETA** El día se acaba.

Completen.

1. El día se acaba. Se pone el sol. Es el ___.
2. Y el camino a casa no es bueno. Es un camino ___.
3. Pero allí comeremos sabrosas tostadas con ___.
4. Esa miel que ___ las abejas de las flores es muy dulce.
5. ¡Mira! Los campesinos acaban de ___ las papas.
6. Ay, los últimos rayos del sol me ___ la cara.

B   **¡Se dice así!** Expresen de otra manera.

1. El religioso *consagra* la obra del filántropo.
2. Por poco se ve *frustrada* la obra.
3. Las quejas no son válidas; son *injustas*.
4. Si una ciudad tiene vida, éstas son *las épocas de vigor*.
5. Con estas renovaciones, la ciudad tiene una nueva *cara*.

ANSWERS
Práctica
A 1. ocaso
   2. rudo
   3. miel
   4. extraen
   5. cosechar
   6. acarician
B 1. bendice
   2. fallida
   3. inmerecidas
   4. las lozanías
   5. faz

**ABOUT THE
SPANISH LANGUAGE**

A **labrador** is not a "laborer." The definition of the word is: **Persona que posee hacienda de campo y la cultiva por su cuenta.** A labrador is really a "small farmer."

Independent Practice

Assign any of the following:
   1. Exercises, page 197
   2. Workbook, *Literatura*

Introducción

Amado Nervo (1870–1919) nació en México. Estudió para sacerdote en el Seminario de Jacona, pero en 1891 dejó la carrera religiosa. Entró en el servicio diplomático de su país a principios del siglo XX y pasó gran parte de su vida en Madrid, París, Buenos Aires y Montevideo, donde murió mientras servía de embajador de México en el Uruguay. Aunque el autor escribió en varios géneros, se destacó como poeta. En las poesías de su madurez se le nota una preocupación por la muerte y el amor.

Amado Nervo

Lectura

En paz

Muy cerca de mi ocaso, yo te bendigo, Vida,
porque nunca me diste ni esperanza fallida
ni trabajos injustos, ni pena inmerecida;

porque veo al final de mi rudo camino
que yo fui el arquitecto de mi propio destino;
que si extraje las mieles o la hiel de las cosas,
fue porque en ellas puse hiel o mieles sabrosas;
cuando planté rosales, coseché siempre rosas.

…Cierto, a mis lozanías va a seguir el invierno;
¡mas° tú no me dijiste que mayo fuese eterno!
Hallé sin duda largas las noches de mis penas;
mas no me prometiste tú sólo noches buenas;
y en cambio tuve algunas santamente serenas…

Amé, fui amado, el sol acarició mi faz.
¡Vida, nada me debes! ¡Vida, estamos en paz!

mas *but*

Literary Analysis

1. **La personificación es la atribución de vida o acciones o cualidades propias del ser racional a las cosas inanimadas, incorpóreas o abstractas. En este poema Amado Nervo se refiere a algo abstracto como si fuera persona. ¿Qué es lo que el poeta personifica?**

2. Ask the students to cite as many examples of figurative language used in the poem as they can. In addition to those in *Comprensión B* on page 199, they should cite: **mi ocaso; el final de mi rudo camino; arquitecto de mi propio destino.** Then have them interpret the terms.

▪Después de leer▪

Comprensión

A **La vida** Escojan.

1. ¿A quién se dirige el poeta en este poema?
   a. a Dios
   b. a la muerte
   c. a la vida
2. ¿Por qué dice el poeta «muy cerca de mi ocaso»?
   a. Habla por la tarde y se va a poner el sol.
   b. Se están acercando sus días finales.
   c. Él vive muy cerca de allí.
3. ¿Qué quiere decir el autor cuando dice que es «arquitecto de su propio destino»?
   a. Toma responsabilidad por lo bueno y lo malo de su vida.
   b. Está contento con los edificios que ha construido.
   c. Siempre ha sabido adonde dirigirse.

B **Otro significado** ¿Qué significa... ?

1. «si extraje las mieles o la hiel de las cosas, fue porque en ellas puse hiel o mieles sabrosas»
2. «cuando planté rosales, coseché siempre rosas»
3. «el invierno»
4. «mayo»
5. «a mis lozanías va a seguir el invierno»
6. «mas tú no me dijiste que mayo fuese eterno»

C **Lo que dice el poeta** Contesten.

1. ¿Tenía el autor noches de pena?
2. ¿Cómo las encontró?
3. ¿Tuvo sólo noches de pena?
4. ¿Qué dice el poeta en cuanto al amor?

▪Actividades comunicativas▪

A **Una feliz conclusión** Amado Nervo dice que la vida no le debe nada y que «estamos en paz». Explique por qué el poeta ha llegado a esa feliz conclusión.

B **Los embajadores** En España y Latinoamérica muchos autores y poetas han representado a su país como miembros del cuerpo diplomático. Busquen Ud. y su grupo algunos ejemplos.

LITERATURA

ciento noventa y nueve **199**

TEACHING TIPS

You may wish to have the students do the *Comprensión* exercises for homework before going over them in class.

ANSWERS
Comprensión

A 1. c
  2. b
  3. a

B 1. Saqué de las cosas—buenas o malas—lo que en ellas yo metí.
  2. Cuando hice cosas buenas, siempre tuve buenos resultados.
  3. Se refiere a la época final de la vida.
  4. Se refiere a la época de la juventud.
  5. La debilidad de la vejez sigue a los tiempos de vigor de la juventud.
  6. No me prometiste eterna juventud.

C 1. Sí, el autor tenía noches de pena.
  2. Él las encontró largas.
  3. No, también las tuvo serenas.
  4. Dice que amó y que fue amado.

Actividades comunicativas

ANSWERS

A and B Answers will vary.

Critical Thinking Activity

Thinking skills: making inferences

Los poetas con frecuencia utilizan la primavera y el invierno como metáfora. Usan estas estaciones del año para representar otra cosa. ¿Qué es lo que representan? ¿Por qué? Explique.

Independent Practice

Assign any of the following:
1. Exercises, page 199
2. Workbook, *Literatura*

VISTAS DE LA ARGENTINA

OVERVIEW

The **Vistas de la Argentina** were prepared by National Geographic Society. Their purpose is to give students greater insight, through these visual images, into the culture and people of Argentina. Have students look at the photographs on pages 200A-200B for enjoyment. If they would like to talk about them, let them say anything they can, using the vocabulary they have learned to this point.

National Standards

Cultures
The **Vistas de la Argentina** photos, and the accompanying captions, allow students to gain insights into the people of Argentina.

Learning From Photos

1. **El glaciar Moreno** This spectacular glacier, a 195 square kilometer of ice, is a major tourist attraction. It is in Patagonia in southeastern Argentina.

2. **Café al aire libre, Buenos Aires** This outdoor café is typical of Buenos Aires. Here customers can buy a cup of coffee and stay there virtually all day.

3. **Teatro Colón, Buenos Aires** This gem of a theater and opera house is one of the treasures of Buenos Aires. It boasts extraordinary acoustics. All the great opera singers have performed there.

4. **Iglesia de San Francisco, Salta** The city is the capital of the province of Salta in the northwest of Argentina. The city maintains a charming

1. Glaciar Moreno
2. Café, Buenos Aires
3. Teatro Colón, Buenos Aires
4. Iglesia de San Francisco, Salta
5. Uvas, Mendoza
6. Gaucho, Provincia de Entre Ríos
7. Lago Nahuel Huapi, Bariloche

200A

TEACHER'S CORNER

NATIONAL GEOGRAPHIC SOCIETY

INDEX TO NATIONAL GEOGRAPHIC MAGAZINE

The following articles may be used for research relating to this chapter:

NATIONAL GEOGRAPHIC

VISTAS

DE LA ARGENTINA

5

200B

Learning From Photos

(Continued from p. 200A) colonial atmosphere. Ruins of 17th century buildings abound in the surrounding countryside.

5. **Racimo de uvas, Mendoza** The grape variety is Lambrusco, a wine grape. Argentina is one of the five biggest wine producers in the world, with more than 490,000 acres of vineyards. Most of its production comes from the province of Mendoza.

6. **Gaucho, Entre Ríos** The gaucho is the symbol of the wide-open spaces of the Argentine Pampas. A superb horseman, the gaucho has been responsible for the care of the enormous herds of Argentine cattle. Argentina is one of the world's major beef producers.

7. **Lago Nahuel Huapí, Bariloche** San Carlos de Bariloche and the National Park of Nahuel Huapí are in Patagonia in the Andean foothills. Bariloche is one of the world's great ski resorts. The National Park of Nahuel Huapí offers rafting, horseback riding, trekking, and mountain biking.

PRODUCTS AVAILABLE FROM GLENCOE/MCGRAW-HILL

To order the following products call Glencoe/McGraw-Hill at 1-800-334-7344.

CD-ROMs
• Picture Altas of the World
• The Complete National Geographic: 109 Years of National Geographic Magazine

Software
• ZingoLingo: Spanish Diskettes

Transparency Set
• NGS PicturePack: Geography of South America

Videodisc
• STV: World Geography (Volume 3: "South America and Antarctica")

PRODUCTS AVAILABLE FROM NATIONAL GEOGRAPHIC SOCIETY

NATIONAL GEOGRAPHIC SOCIETY

To order the following products call National Geographic Society at 1-800-368-2728.

Books
• Exploring Your World: The Adventure of Geography
• National Geographic Satellite Atlas of the World

Video
• South America ("Nations of the World" Series)

Chapter 5 Overview ◆◆◆◆◆◆◆◆◆◆◆◆◆◆◆◆◆◆◆◆◆◆◆

TOPICS	FUNCTIONS	STRUCTURE	CULTURE
◆ The Spanish role in U. S. history ◆ Social problems in Spain and Latin America ◆ Reporting a minor nonviolent crime	◆ How to report a crime to the police ◆ How to express agreement or disagreement ◆ How to discuss subjects such as the news and social problems ◆ How to tell what you and others have done recently ◆ How to express affirmative and negative ideas ◆ How to use **sino** and **pero** ◆ How to talk about actions completed before other actions ◆ How to express what one would have done under certain circumstances ◆ How to describe what will happen before something else occurs ◆ How to describe people, things, and exceptional qualities ◆ How to discuss the ballad, **romance,** and **corrido** as important literary forms	◆ **El presente perfecto** ◆ **Palabras negativas y afirmativas** ◆ *Sino y pero* ◆ **El pluscuamperfecto** ◆ **El condicional perfecto** ◆ **El futuro perfecto** ◆ **Adjetivos apocopados** ◆ **El sufijo –ísimo(a)**	◆ Christopher Columbus' voyage to North America ◆ Spanish explorers in North America ◆ Reporting a crime at the police station ◆ Newspaper headlines ◆ Local news stories from Bogotá, Chihuahua, and Caracas **Literatura** ◆ **Un romance y un corrido** ◆ **«Abenámar»** ◆ **«En Durango comenzó»**

CHAPTER 5 RESOURCES

PRINT	MULTIMEDIA

Planning Resources

Lesson Plans Block Scheduling Lesson Plans	Interactive Lesson Planner

Reinforcement Resources

Writing Activities Workbook Student Tape Manual Video Activities Booklet Glencoe Foreign Language Web Site User's Guide	Transparencies Binder Audiocassette/Compact Disc Program Videocassette/Videodisc Program Online Internet Activities Electronic Teacher's Classroom Resources

Assessment Resources

Situation Cards Chapter Quizzes Testing Program	Testmaker Computer Software (Macintosh/Windows) Listening Comprehension Audiocassette/Compact Disc

Motivational Resources

Expansion Activities	Café Glencoe: **www.cafe.glencoe.com**

Enrichment

Fine Art Transparencies: F-6, F-7, F-8, F-9, F-10

Chapter 5 Planning Guide

SECTION	PAGES	SECTION RESOURCES
Cultura **Acontecimientos históricos** *Los españoles en la América del Norte*	202–208	🖐 Transparency 32 🎧 Audiocassette 9A/Compact Disc 6 📁 Writing Activities Workbook, pages 112–114 📁 Student Tape Manual, pages 72–73 📁 Chapter Quizzes, page 64 💾 Testing Program, pages 101–103
Conversación **Un crimen**	209–212	🖐 Transparency 33 🎧 Audiocassette 9A/Compact Disc 6 📁 Writing Activities Workbook, page 115 📁 Student Tape Manual, page 74 📁 Chapter Quizzes, page 65 💾 Testing Program, pages 104–105
Lenguaje **El acuerdo y el desacuerdo** **¿Sí o no?** **Una conversación que continúa**	213–215	🖐 Transparency 34 🎧 Audiocassette 9A/Compact Disc 6 📁 Writing Activities Workbook, page 116 📁 Student Tape Manual, page 74 💾 Testing Program, pages 104–105
Repaso de estructura **El presente perfecto** **Palabras negativas y afirmativas** *Sino y pero*	216–220	🎧 Audiocassette 9A/Compact Disc 6 📁 Writing Activities Workbook, pages 117–119 📁 Student Tape Manual, page 75 📁 Chapter Quizzes, pages 66–68 💾 Testing Program, pages 106–107
Periodismo **Los titulares** **Los sucesos**	221–229	🖐 Transparencies 35A–35B, 36 🎧 Audiocassette 9B/Compact Disc 6 📁 Writing Activities Workbook, pages 120–123 📁 Student Tape Manual, pages 76–79 📁 Chapter Quizzes, pages 69–70 💾 Testing Program, pages 108–112
Estructura **El pluscuamperfecto** **El condicional perfecto** **El futuro perfecto** **Adjetivos apocopados** **El sufijo** *-ísimo(a)*	230–235	🎧 Audiocassette 10A/Compact Disc 7 📁 Writing Activities Workbook, pages 124–126 📁 Student Tape Manual, page 81 📁 Chapter Quizzes, pages 71–75 💾 Testing Program, pages 113–114
Literatura **Un romance y un corrido** **«Abenámar»** **«En Durango comenzó»**	236–243	🖐 Transparency 37 🎧 Audiocassette 10A/Compact Disc 7 📁 Writing Activities Workbook, pages 127–129 📁 Student Tape Manual, pages 82–83 📁 Chapter Quizzes, page 76 💾 Testing Program, pages 115–118

OVERVIEW

In this chapter, students will read about Spain's role in the history of the United States, as well as typical social problems in Spain and Latin America. They will learn the vocabulary necessary to report a minor nonviolent crime. They will also learn expressions conveying agreement and disagreement as well as those used to continue or change the direction of a conversation. The latter are particularly useful when discussing current events. Students will learn to read and understand the importance of newspaper headlines. They will read newspaper articles about everyday local events such as accidents, minor mishaps, and human interest stories. They will also read a typical **romance** and a **corrido**.

National Standards

Communication
Students will engage in conversations, provide and obtain information, express feelings, and exchange opinions on a variety of topics, including history and current events in the Hispanic world. They will listen to and read authentic language on the same topics.

Learning From Photos

Esta estatua ecuestre de El Libertador, Simón Bolívar (1783–1830), está en Cartagena, Colombia. Bolívar liberó gran parte de Sudamérica del dominio español. La lucha contra los españoles duró desde 1810 hasta 1824.

Sucesos y acontecimientos

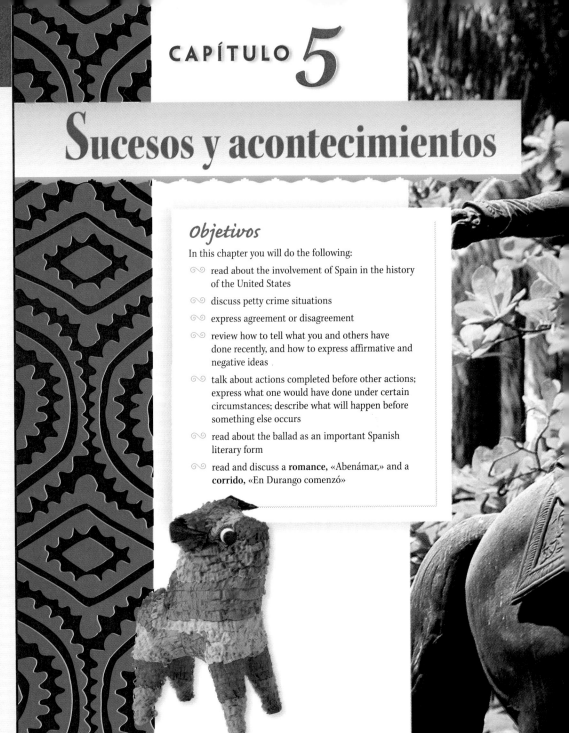

Objetivos

In this chapter you will do the following:

- read about the involvement of Spain in the history of the United States
- discuss petty crime situations
- express agreement or disagreement
- review how to tell what you and others have done recently, and how to express affirmative and negative ideas
- talk about actions completed before other actions; express what one would have done under certain circumstances; describe what will happen before something else occurs
- read about the ballad as an important Spanish literary form
- read and discuss a **romance**, «Abenámar,» and a **corrido**, «En Durango comenzó»

interNET CONNECTION

The Glencoe Foreign Language Web site (http://www.glencoe.com/sec/fl) offers these options that enable you and your students to experience the Spanish-speaking world via the Internet:

- At **Café Glencoe**, the interactive "after-school" section of the site, you and your students can access a variety of additional online resources, including online newspapers, interactive games, and a send-a-postcard feature.
- The online **Proyectos** are correlated to the chapters and utilize Hispanic Web sites around the world.

DIFFICULTY PLATEAUS

In all chapters, each reading selection in *Cultura, Periodismo,* and *Literatura,* as well as *Conversación* and each *Estrutura* will be rated as follows:

◆ **Easy**

◆◆ **Intermediate**

◆◆◆ **Difficult**

Please note that the material in *¡Buen viaje! Level 3* does not become increasingly difficult as the students progress.

Within each chapter there are easy and difficult sections. The overall rating of this chapter is: ◆◆ **Intermediate.**

RANDOM ACCESS

Because of the above type of rating, it is not necessary to follow the sequencing of the book exactly. You should feel free to omit any selection that does not interest you or that does not meet the needs of your students.

EVALUATION

Quizzes There is a quiz for every vocabulary section and every structure point.

Tests To accompany *¡Buen viaje! Level 3* there are global tests for both *Estructuras,* a combined *Conversación/Lenguaje* test, and one test for each reading in the *Cultura, Periodismo,* and *Literatura* sections. There is also a comprehensive chapter test.

doscientos uno ✿ **201**

Chapter Projects

Sucesos locales

A. Pida a los alumnos que seleccionen artículos de sucesos locales. Varios equipos deben preparar preguntas sobre estos sucesos.

B. Pida a los alumnos que escriban unos artículos para hacer un periódico. Pueden trabajar solos o en parejas. No olvide incluir todo lo que contiene un periódico: los titulares grandes, los sucesos, anuncios, etc.

C. Dígales a los alumnos que dibujen un mapa de los EE.UU. en el cual indican los lugares que hayan tenido influencia española.

TEACHING TIPS

A. You may either read the *Introducción* to the students or have them read it silently.

B. Ask students the following questions about the *Introducción:*
¿Qué son las actualidades? ¿Cuándo tienen lugar los sucesos históricos? Al estudiar nuestra historia, ¿qué es imprescindible tomar en cuenta? ¿Cuándo empezó?

HISTORY CONNECTION

Cristóbal Colón nació en 1446 en Génova, Italia. Entró al servicio de España en 1492. Obtuvo de Isabel la Católica tres carabelas: la Niña, la Pinta y la Santa María. Salió del puerto de Palos el 3 de agosto de 1492 en busca de una ruta más corta a las Indias. Llegó a tierra el 12 de octubre. En su primer viaje fue a Cuba y Haití dándole a esta isla el nombre de Hispaniola.

En su segundo viaje descubrió Puerto Rico y otras islas de las Antillas Menores y volvió otra vez a la Español (Hispaniola). En 1498 recorrió la costa de la América del Sur desde la desembocadura del río Orinoco hasta Caracas.

CULTURA
Acontecimientos históricos

Introducción

Las actualidades son acontecimientos o sucesos que tienen lugar en la actualidad—en el presente, hoy. Hay también acontecimientos importantes que tuvieron lugar en el pasado—acontecimientos o sucesos históricos. Al estudiar la historia de nuestro país, es imprescindible tomar en cuenta la enorme influencia española en ella—una influencia que empezó no años, sino siglos antes de la llegada de los ingleses.

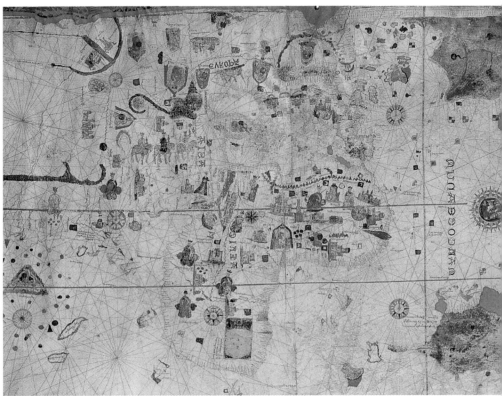

Detalle del mapa del mundo (1500), por Juan de la Cosa, cartógrafo de Cristóbal Colón

Did You Know?

Juan de la Cosa acompañó a Colón e hizo algunos mapas de las regiones descubiertas. Su mapa de 1500 (que vemos aquí) fue el primero en que se ve el nuevo continente descubierto por Colón. Este mapa se encuentra hoy día en el Museo Naval de Madrid. Juan de la Cosa murió en Tabasco, México, en 1510 en un encuentro con los indios.

Vocabulario

la corona

la bandera

el navegante

el marino

la flotilla

la tripulación

la desembocadura

las carabelas

redondo

el globo

Los conquistadores desembarcaron.

imprescindible absolutamente necesario
renombrado(a) famoso(a), muy conocido(a)

el apoyo la ayuda

CULTURA

doscientos tres ⌒ **203**

RESOURCES

- Vocabulary Transparencies
- Audio Cassette 9A/Compact Disc 6
- Student Tape Manual
- Workbook
- Chapter Quizzes

Bell Ringer Review

Use the BRR Transparency 5-1, or write the following on the board:
Haga una lista de:
1. **algunas cosas que se pueden leer**
2. **algunas cosas que se pueden escuchar**

TEACHING VOCABULARY

A. Have students repeat the new words in unison after you or Cassette 9A/Compact Disc 6.
B. Have students open their books and read the vocabulary for additional reinforcement.
C. You can immediately ask questions 1–5 of *Práctica A* on page 204, all of which relate to the illustrations.
D. You may wish to read the new words and definitions to the class or you may call on several individuals to read them aloud.
E. You may also wish to have students put each new word into a sentence.

RECYCLING

You may wish to review the ship vocabulary presented with «¡Al partir!» by Gertrudis Gómez de Avellaneda on page 44.

ABOUT THE SPANISH LANGUAGE

In addition to **el marino, el marinero** is also used for "sailor."

203

Additional Practice

Have students look at the new words on this page and identify cognates and false cognates.

TEACHING TIPS

A You can go over the questions of *Práctica A* as you present the vocabulary.

B and **C** Have students prepare *Práctica B* and *C* before going over them in class. Then call on students to read their answers.

EXPANSION After going over *Práctica B*, have students make up questions about each sentence.

ANSWERS
Práctica

A 1. Hay tres carabelas.
 2. Sí, el navegante está hablando con su tripulación.
 3. Sí, se ve la desembocadura del río.
 4. Sí, desembarcan los marinos.
 5. Hay cuatro banderas en las carabelas.

B 1. a
 2. b
 3. b
 4. a
 5. b
 6. b
 7. a
 8. b

C 1. d
 2. a
 3. i
 4. g
 5. j
 6. f
 7. h
 8. b
 9. e
 10. c

Práctica

A **La navegación** Contesten.
1. ¿Cuántas carabelas hay en la flotilla?
2. ¿Está hablando con su tripulación el navegante?
3. ¿Se ve la desembocadura del río?
4. ¿Desembarcan los marinos?
5. ¿Cuántas banderas hay en las carabelas?

B **¿Cuál es la palabra?** Escojan.
1. Los tres barcos de Cristóbal Colón eran ___.
   a. carabelas   **b.** caramelos
2. Hay ocho barcos en la ___ del almirante.
   a. pastilla   **b.** flotilla
3. La ciudad de Nueva York está en la ___ del río Hudson.
   a. boca   **b.** desembocadura
4. El capitán Nemo era ___.
   a. un gran navegante   **b.** una gran tripulación
5. El globo no es cuadrado; es ___.
   a. rectangular   **b.** redondo
6. Los conquistadores ___ en cuanto llegaron al puerto.
   a. despegaron   **b.** desembarcaron
7. ___ de España es amarilla y roja.
   a. La bandera   **b.** La corona
8. El rey y la reina llevan ___.
   a. banderas   **b.** coronas

C **Palabras derivadas** Escojan.
1. descubrir   **a.** la fundación, el fundador
2. fundar   **b.** la colonia, la colonización, el colono
3. desembarcar   **c.** la imaginación
4. navegar   **d.** el descubrimiento, el descubridor
5. llegar   **e.** la exploración, el explorador
6. viajar   **f.** el viaje, el viajero
7. entrar   **g.** la navegación, el navegante
8. colonizar   **h.** la entrada
9. explorar   **i.** el desembarque
10. imaginar   **j.** la llegada

Independent Practice

Assign any of the following:
1. Exercises, page 204
2. Workbook, *Cultura*

Los españoles en la América del Norte

Un acontecimiento histórico de transcendental importancia es la llegada de los españoles a las Américas y su exploración del Nuevo Mundo. Una parte vital de este Nuevo Mundo son los Estados Unidos de América. He aquí una lista de algunos de los sucesos más significativos de este importantísimo período en la historia de esta nación.

Todo el mundo sabe que los españoles descubrieron y colonizaron la mayor parte de Centro y Sudamérica. Menos conocido es el hecho de que los españoles también exploraron y colonizaron gran parte de la América del Norte. Al dar una ojeada[1] a los hechos históricos ya citados, aprendemos

[1] **ojeada** *quick glance*

1492 ÷ CRISTÓBAL COLÓN
al mando de una flotilla de tres carabelas—la Pinta, la Niña y la Santa María—sale de Palos de Moguer (Huelva) el 3 de agosto y llega a la isla de Guanahaní el 12 de octubre. Funda la primera colonia española, «Navidad», en La Española (Santo Domingo).

1513 ÷ JUAN PONCE DE LEÓN
el gobernador de Puerto Rico, llega a la Florida.

1526 ÷ LUCAS VÁZQUEZ DE AYLLÓN
establece una colonia, San Miguel de Guadalupe, en Carolina del Sur.

1533 ÷ FORTÚN JIMÉNEZ
llega a las costas de California.

1527–1534 ÷ ÁLVARO NÚÑEZ CABEZA DE VACA
explora el área desde Tampa, Florida, hasta el golfo de California.

1539–1542 ÷ HERNÁN DE SOTO
pasa por las Carolinas y llega hasta Coosa (Birmingham, Alabama).

1540–1542 ÷ FRANCISCO VÁZQUEZ DE CORONADO
viaja por el territorio de Arizona y Nuevo México.

1540 ÷ GARCÍA LÓPEZ DE CÁRDENAS
miembro de la expedición de Coronado, es el primer europeo que ve el Gran Cañón del Colorado.

1541 ÷ DE SOTO
cruza el río Misisipí y entra en Arkansas y, después, Oklahoma. **Coronado** llega hasta el centro de Kansas.

1542 ÷ JUAN RODRÍGUEZ CABRILLO
un portugués que navega bajo la bandera española, desembarca en San Diego, California.

1543 ÷ BARTOLOMÉ FERRELO
a cargo de la expedición de Rodríguez Cabrillo, quien murió en las islas del canal de Santa Bárbara, navega hasta la desembocadura del río Rogue en Oregón.

1607
Los ingleses fundan Jamestown en Virginia, la primera colonia británica en lo que hoy son los EE.UU.

1620
En Plymouth, Massachusetts, los ingleses fundan una colonia.

Juan Ponce de León

doscientos cinco ∞ **205**

Did You Know?

Ponce de León nació en España hacia 1460. Fue gobernador de Puerto Rico. Descubrió la Florida mientras buscaba la «Fuente de la juventud». Fundó la ciudad de San Agustín en 1513. Ponce de León murió en Cuba en 1521.

TEACHING THE READING

◆ **Los españoles en la América del Norte** ◆◆

A. Have students look at the title of the reading and the photos in the reading. Then, ask them what they think the reading is about.

B. Have students read this selection silently or call on individuals to read it aloud.

C. You can intersperse *Comprensión A* and *B* on page 207 as you are going over this section.

D. You may wish to assign *Comprensión A–E* on pages 207–208 for homework and go over them in class the following day.

GEOGRAPHY CONNECTION

Have students locate on a map the geographical areas mentioned in this reading.

National Standards

Connections
Students will reinforce and further their knowledge of the history of the U. S. with particular emphasis on the Hispanic contribution. They will see events through the distinctive viewpoint of the Spanish language and culture.

HISTORY CONNECTION

1. **El hijo de Cristóbal Colón, Bartolomé Colón, fundó la ciudad de Santo Domingo en 1496. Ésta es la ciudad más antigua de América. En la catedral de Santo Domingo hay un mausoleo donde se dice que se conservan los restos de Cristóbal Colón. En Sevilla se dice que sus restos están en la catedral de esta ciudad.**

2. **La réplica de la Santa María que aparece en la foto es una de las tres carabelas de Cristóbal Colón que están en el puerto de Barcelona.**

que en 1513, don Juan Ponce de León, el gobernador de Puerto Rico, llegó a la Florida en busca de la fuente de la juventud. Poco después, Lucas Vázquez de Ayllón fundó una colonia en Carolina del Sur, mientras Álvaro Núñez Cabeza de Vaca exploraba todo el sudoeste desde Tampa, Florida, hasta el golfo de California. Durante los años siguientes Hernán de Soto y Francisco Vázquez de Coronado viajaron por toda la región sur, sur-central y suroeste de lo que hoy son los Estados Unidos. Sólo hay que fijarse en las fechas para ver que había colonias españolas un siglo antes de la fundación de Jamestown por los ingleses.

Casa de Cristóbal Colón, República Dominicana

Réplica de la Santa María, España

Se ha dicho que quien escribe la historia determina la verdad. Durante muchos años, se les enseñaba a los estudiantes norteamericanos que la primera colonia europea en lo que hoy son los Estados Unidos fue Jamestown. La verdad es que en la Florida y en toda la zona del suroeste hasta e incluso California, los colonos eran hispanos y el primer idioma europeo que se habló en estas tierras fue el español, y no el inglés.

¡Otros hechos históricos interesantes sobre el descubrimiento y la colonización del Nuevo Mundo! Cristóbal Colón, el navegante genovés, tenía la idea revolucionaria de que el mundo era un globo, que era redondo, y presentó su teoría a Isabel la Católica, la reina de España. Ella le dio el apoyo[1] material y moral que necesitaba. El tres de agosto de 1492, Colón y los hermanos Pinzón salieron del puerto de Palos de Moguer en tres carabelas con tripulaciones de marinos españoles. Colón era el capitán de la *Santa María*, y los Pinzón, los capitanes de la *Pinta* y la *Niña*. Colón pensaba descubrir una ruta

[1] **apoyo** *help, support*

más rápida para llegar a la India y conseguir[2] especias. Cuando llegó a las Américas no creía haber llegado a un «Nuevo Mundo» sino a la India. Por eso, las islas adonde llegaron Colón y sus marinos españoles se nombraron, «las Indias». Colón hizo cuatro viajes a las Américas y fue él quien fundó la primera colonia europea en el Nuevo Mundo. La fundó durante su primer viaje, en la isla de La Española, hoy Santo Domingo.

El verdadero nombre del famoso navegante italiano Cristóbal Colón era Cristóforo Colombo. Pero, como hizo sus viajes con barcos y tripulaciones españolas, patrocinado[3] por la Corona española, decidió españolizar su nombre. Los historiadores ingleses y norteamericanos siempre han insistido en señalar la nacionalidad italiana del gran almirante.

No obstante, cuando los navegantes italianos Sebastiano y Giovanni Caboto exploraron las costas de Norteamérica y Groenlandia, patrocinados por la Corona inglesa, los historiadores olvidaron su nacionalidad italiana y hablaron de otra gran hazaña[4] británica. Los italianos Giovanni y Sebastiano Caboto se conocen en la historia por sus nombres anglicanizados, John y Sebastian Cabot. Los antepasados de los renombrados[5] Cabot de Massachusetts son Giovanni y Sebastiano Caboto.

Italianos y holandeses navegaban bajo la bandera británica, y portugueses e italianos bajo la española. La verdad es que la tremenda obra de descubrimiento y colonización del continente norteamericano se debe a la imaginación, a la dedicación y al valor de individuos de muchos países.

[2] **conseguir** *to get, obtain*
[3] **patrocinado** *sponsored*
[4] **hazaña** *deed*
[5] **renombrados** *famosos*

Critical Thinking Activity

Thinking skills: making inferences

1. **Explique por qué Colón nombró a las tierras que descubrió «las Indias».**
2. **¿Qué son las Indias Occidentales? Explique por qué en tiempos modernos se usa el término «las Indias Occidentales».**
3. **Explique el posible significado del cambio en los nombres de los hermanos Caboto.**

Cooperative Learning

Have students work in two groups of three. Each group prepares three descriptions of events in U.S. history. The group members read their descriptions to the members of the other group, who attempt to identify the event. If they cannot, they can ask for additional information.

Comprensión

A **Fechas** Completen.

1. Los españoles llegan a la costa del estado de Oregón en ___.
2. La primera colonia británica en los EE.UU. se establece en el año ___.
3. Un explorador español es el primer europeo que ve el Gran Cañón del Colorado en ___.
4. Los españoles llegan a lo que hoy es Alabama en ___.
5. Probablemente el primer europeo que toca tierra en los EE.UU. lo hace en la Florida, en ___.

B **Nombres** Escojan.

1. ___ estableció una colonia en Santo Domingo.
   a. Colón   **b.** Cabeza de Vaca   **c.** Coronado
2. ___ murió en la costa de California.
   a. De Soto   **b.** Cabrillo   **c.** Ferrelo
3. El primer gobernador de Puerto Rico fue ___.
   a. Ponce de León   **b.** Vázquez de Ayllón   **c.** Cabeza de Vaca
4. El primero de los exploradores que tocó tierra en California fue ___.
   a. De Soto   **b.** Colón   **c.** Cabrillo
5. El puerto de donde partió Colón en su primer viaje fue ___.
   a. Guadalupe   **b.** San Diego   **c.** Palos

C **Los colonizadores** Contesten.

1. ¿Qué saben todos acerca de la historia del Nuevo Mundo?
2. ¿Cuál es un hecho menos conocido?
3. ¿Por cuánto tiempo había habido colonias españolas en la América del Norte cuando se fundó Jamestown?
4. ¿Quiénes fueron los primeros colonos europeos de la América del Norte?
5. ¿Y cuál fue el primer idioma europeo que se habló en las Américas?

Fernando e Isabel, los Reyes Católicos

doscientos siete 〰 **207**

Learning From Art

Isabel la Católica (1451–1504) fue la reina de Castilla. Con la muerte de su suegro Juan II de Aragón, subió al trono Fernando de Aragón, el marido de Isabel, reuniendo las coronas de Aragón y Castilla. El reinado de Fernando e Isabel fue uno de los más importantes y más fecundos de la historia de España. Se dice que fue la reina Isabel quien gobernó y no su marido, Fernando. Ella apoyó la conquista de Granada y la expulsión de los árabes. Y fue ella la que le dio a Colón lo que necesitaba para realizar el descubrimiento del Nuevo Mundo.

ANSWERS

Comprensión

D 1. Colón tenía la idea revolucionaria de que la Tierra era redonda.

2. Colón hizo sus expediciones patrocinado por la Corona española.

3. Los hermanos Pinzón eran españoles.

4. Los hermanos Pinzón eran los capitanes de la Niña y la Pinta.

5. Los marinos a bordo de las carabelas de Colón eran españoles.

E 1. Colón hizo cuatro viajes.

2. Buscaba una ruta a las Indias.

3. Colón fundó la primera colonia europea en La Española (Santo Domingo o la República Dominicana) en 1492.

4. Cambió su nombre a Cristóbal Colón porque navegaba bajo la bandera española.

5. Los historiadores cambiaron los nombres a Sebastiano y Giovanni Caboto.

6. Los famosos navegantes italianos Sebastiano y Giovanni Caboto son antepasados de los renombrados Cabot de Massachusetts.

TEACHING TIPS

Actividad A may be of interest to those with both an artistic bent and an interest in history.

Actividades comunicativas

ANSWERS

A and **B** Answers will vary.

208

D El descubrimiento Corrijan.

1. Colón tenía la idea revolucionaria de que la Tierra era un rectángulo.

2. Colón hizo sus expediciones patrocinado por la Corona italiana.

3. Los hermanos Pinzón eran italianos.

4. Los hermanos Pinzón eran los capitanes de la Santa María.

5. Los marinos a bordo de las carabelas de Colón eran ingleses.

E Colón Contesten.

1. ¿Cuántos viajes hizo Colón al Nuevo Mundo?

2. ¿Qué buscaba?

3. ¿Dónde y cuándo fundó Colón la primera colonia europea del Nuevo Mundo?

4. ¿Por qué cambió Cristóforo Colombo su nombre a Cristóbal Colón?

5. ¿Quiénes les cambiaron los nombres a Sebastiano y Giovanni Caboto?

6. ¿De quiénes son antepasados los famosos navegantes italianos Sebastiano y Giovanni Caboto?

Actividades comunicativas

A Los viajes Aquí tiene Ud. el itinerario de los cuatro viajes de Cristóbal Colón. Sea Ud. cartógrafo(a) y dibuje un mapa de los viajes de Colón.

Primer viaje	1492–1493 Cuba y La Española (Haití y la República Dominicana)
Segundo viaje	1493–1496 Dominica, Guadalupe, Antigua, Puerto Rico
Tercer viaje	1498–1500 Trinidad y Tobago, Granada
Cuarto viaje	1502–1504 Honduras, Panamá

B Las colonias españolas En 1492, Colón llegó a las Américas. Con este viaje patrocinado por la reina Isabel la Católica, empezó la expansión española. Por unos cuatro siglos España dominó gran parte del mundo. Perdió sus últimas colonias (Cuba, Puerto Rico, Guam y las Filipinas) en 1898 durante su guerra contra los Estados Unidos.

Durante el reinado de Felipe II en el siglo XVI, se decía «En el imperio español nunca se pone el sol». Explique por qué.

Independent Practice

Assign any of the following:

1. Exercises, pages 207–208
2. Workbook, *Cultura*

Conversación

Un crimen

Vocabulario

el truco lo que se hace para engañar, alucinar o distraer a alguien

Práctica

A **Un robo** Contesten.

1. ¿Hay muchos robos donde tú vives?
2. ¿Hay carteristas?
3. ¿Hay que protegerse de los carteristas sobre todo cuando hay mucha gente, en una muchedumbre, por ejemplo?
4. ¿Cuál es el truco de los carteristas?
5. ¿Son agradables los trucos?
6. ¿Qué les quitan los carteristas a sus víctimas?
7. ¿Es cortés empujar a una persona cuando quieres avanzar?
8. ¿Adónde va uno(a) a denunciar un robo?

CONVERSACIÓN

doscientos nueve 209

RESOURCES

- Vocabulary Transparencies
- Audio Cassette 9A/Compact Disc 6
- Student Tape Manual
- Workbook
- Chapter Quizzes

TEACHING VOCABULARY

A. You may wish to follow the suggestions outlined in previous chapters.

B. After presenting the vocabulary, play the following in the form of a game. Have students give the word you are looking for: **el que roba la cartera, la persona que ha sido robada, el lugar donde se pone el dinero, el lugar donde se pone la cartera, el lugar adonde va la víctima para denunciar el robo.**

INFORMAL ASSESSMENT

Have students look at the illustrations and say whatever they can about them in their own words.

TEACHING TIPS

This Práctica can be done with books closed, open, or once each way. No previous preparation is necessary.

ANSWERS
Práctica
Some answers can be negative.
A 1. **Sí, hay muchos robos.**
   2. **Sí, hay carteristas.**
   3. **Sí, hay que protegerse.**
   4. **Ellos empujan a sus víctimas.**
   5. **No, no son agradables.**
   6. **Les quitan la cartera.**
   7. **No, no es cortés.**
   8. **Va a la comisaría.**

Independent Practice

Assign any of the following:
1. Exercise, page 209
2. Workbook *Conversación*

TEACHING THE CONVERSATION

◆ Escenas de la vida ◆

A. Give students a few minutes to read the *Conversación* silently.

B. Call on two students to read it aloud. Have them use as much expression as possible. Have the other members of the class close their books and listen.

C. Go over *Comprensión A* from page 212 orally. Then assign the exercises for homework.

Escenas de la vida

210

En la comisaría

MANUELA: Quiero denunciar un robo.

POLICÍA: ¿Cuál es el nombre de la víctima?

MANUELA: ¿La víctima? Soy yo, Manuela Contreras. Me robaron en el metro.

POLICÍA: ¿Cuándo?

MANUELA: Hace unos quince minutos.

POLICÍA: ¿Dónde?

MANUELA: En Independencia.

POLICÍA: ¿El ladrón llevaba algún arma?

MANUELA: No, que sepa yo. Era carterista. No me di cuenta de que me robaba.

POLICÍA: ¿Ud. puede explicar lo que pasó?

MANUELA: Sí, había mucha gente en el andén. Alguien me empujó. Creí que quería avanzar. Algunos momentos más tarde, cuando ya estaba en el metro, noté que alguien me había abierto el bolso.

POLICÍA: Claro. Es un truco de los carteristas. Trabajan en pares. Uno le empuja para distraerle mientras el otro le abre el bolso y le quita la cartera. ¿Cuánto dinero llevaba Ud.?

MANUELA: Unos 600 pesos y mis tarjetas de crédito.

POLICÍA: ¿Me podría dar una descripción del delincuente?

◆ El carterista es el que le quita la cartera a otro. También hay otros tipos de robo. El que roba es un ladrón. El hurto es el término legal para el robo. El hurto es quitarle ilícitamente la propiedad personal a una persona con la intención de robar. Se divide en hurto menor y hurto mayor.

◆ La categoría de hurto depende del valor de la propiedad robada. El desfalco es semejante al hurto. El desfalco consiste en quitarle la propiedad a una persona sobre cuyos bienes uno tiene cargo y control.

El latrocinio es el hurto de la propiedad ajena en contra de la voluntad de la persona por la fuerza, la violencia o la amenaza de la violencia. El escalamiento se define como «el abrir y entrar en un hogar con la intención de cometer un delito».

◆ La palabra «víctima» no cambia de género. Es siempre femenina—la víctima.

Cooperative Learning

Have students work in groups and discuss:
¿Qué está haciendo el gobierno municipal local para controlar o reducir el crimen?

TEACHING TIPS

A You can ask the questions from *Comprensión A* as you are going over the *Conversación*.

B *Comprensión B* is a word study exercise. You may wish to do it a second time. Have students cover the second column and see if they can come up with the related word.

ANSWERS

Comprensión

A 1. Manuela denunció un robo.
 2. Sí, fue a la comisaría.
 3. Un carterista le robó.
 4. Le robó en el metro.
 5. Había dos personas.
 6. La empujaron para distraerla.
 7. El otro le abría el bolso.
 8. Le quitaron dinero y sus tarjetas de crédito.
 9. Ella perdió 6.000 pesos.
 10. No, porque no se dio cuenta de que le robaban.

B 1. c
 2. e
 3. h
 4. a
 5. f
 6. g
 7. d
 8. b

Actividades comunicativas

ANSWERS

A and **B** Answers will vary.

Comprensión

A **En la comisaría** Contesten.

1. ¿Qué denunció Manuela?
2. ¿Fue a la comisaría?
3. ¿Quién le robó?
4. ¿Dónde le robó?
5. ¿Cuántas personas había?
6. ¿Por qué la empujaron?
7. Mientras un individuo la empujaba, ¿qué hacía el otro?
8. ¿Qué le quitaron?
9. ¿Cuánto dinero perdió?
10. ¿Podía dar una descripción de los carteristas?

B **Palabras derivadas** Escojan.

1. denunciar
2. robar
3. armar
4. empujar
5. distraer
6. describir
7. explicar
8. avanzar

a. el empuje
b. el avance
c. la denuncia
d. la explicación
e. el robo
f. la distracción
g. la descripción
h. el arma

Actividades comunicativas

A **El/La locutor(a)** Ud. es el/la locutor(a) del noticiero de un canal de televisión en Costa Rica. Acaban de cometer un crimen. Descríbalo y dé los siguientes detalles.

> el nombre de la víctima, su domicilio, el tipo de crimen, el lugar del crimen, cuándo tuvo lugar, cuántos criminales participaron, las consecuencias, una descripción del criminal o de los criminales

B **En la comisaría** Imagínese que Ud. está en Colombia y que ha sido el/la víctima de un crimen. Ud. va a la comisaría a denunciar el crimen. Un(a) compañero(a) de clase será el/la agente de policía. Preparen una conversación.

Cooperative Learning

1. *Actividad A,* page 212: For this activity, encourage students to be creative in their presentations. Have them decide who is the best anchorperson.
2. *Actividad B,* page 212: Have some groups present their skits from *Actividad B* to the class.

Learning From Photos

Have students make up a conversation between the police officer and the young woman.

Lenguaje
El acuerdo y el desacuerdo

Podemos usar las siguientes expresiones para indicar que estamos de acuerdo con algo o con alguien:

> Yo estoy de acuerdo con Ud. (con eso).
> Yo tengo la misma opinión que Ud.
> A mi parecer, Ud. tiene razón.

Estoy de acuerdo.

Para expresar que no estamos de acuerdo, podemos decir:

> No estoy de acuerdo con José Luis.
> Francamente estoy en contra de su idea.
> Yo tengo una opinión completamente contraria a la suya.
> No apruebo tal proyecto.
> No me convence nada.
> No estoy convencido(a).

Práctica

A **¿De acuerdo o no?** Indiquen si están de acuerdo o no.

1. Es mejor vivir en una región donde no hace ni mucho frío ni mucho calor.
2. Se debe reducir las horas de trabajo de 40 a 35 horas por semana.
3. El gobierno debe mantener o subvencionar todas las universidades para que no sea necesario pagar matrícula.
4. Se debe hacer todo lo posible para eliminar el hambre y la miseria en el mundo.
5. Se debe permitir a los jóvenes conseguir (obtener) su permiso de conducir antes de que cumplan los 15 años.
6. Debemos tener cursos obligatorios en el verano.
7. Deben exigirles a los estudiantes que tomen por lo menos seis cursos cada semestre.
8. Debemos tener clases seis días a la semana.
9. Se debe imponer la pena de muerte, o sea, la pena capital en todos los estados de los EE.UU.
10. Es necesario tener campañas o programas contra los conductores que conducen sus vehículos después de haber tomado (bebido) alcohol.
11. Se debe subir el límite de velocidad en las autopistas.
12. Los profesores deben recibir mayor sueldo que los atletas.

TEACHING TIPS

A. Read the explanatory information to the class and call on students to read the model sentences aloud.

B. Have one student read a statement and another student respond, using the expressions with the proper intonation. You may wish to call on a different pair of students for each statement. (If you want to expand upon this exercise, see CRITICAL THINKING ACTIVITY at the bottom of the page.)

ANSWERS
Práctica
A Answers will vary.

Critical Thinking Activity

Thinking skills: supporting statements with reasons With more able groups, have a student explain why he/she agrees or disagrees with each statement in the exercise.

All the statements in this exercise make excellent debate topics.

Cooperative Learning

Have students work in groups. Each group prepares a list of topics they think might be controversial thus causing both agreement and disagreement. Have groups exchange lists and state whether they agree or disagree that the topic is indeed controversial. Have them explain their reasons for their opinion.

ANSWERS

Práctica

A Answers will vary.

1. **No puede ser.**
2. **Imposible.**
3. **¡Cómo no!**
4. **No hay manera.**
5. **Absolutamente no.**
6. **Seguro.**
7. **Jamás.**
8. **De ninguna manera.**

¿Sí o no?

Si una persona le dice algo y Ud. quiere indicar que está de acuerdo, le puede decir:

Sí.	**Precisamente.**
Es verdad.	**Exactamente.**
Verdad.	**¡Cómo no!**
(Es) Cierto.	**Eso sí.**
Absolutamente.	**Efectivamente.**
Sin duda.	**Entendido.**
No hay duda.	**Ud. tiene razón.**
No cabe duda.	**De acuerdo.**
Seguro.	

Si Ud. quiere indicar que no sabe si está de acuerdo o no, puede decir:

Quizás.	**Si lo dice Ud. (dices tú).**
Puede ser.	**¿Ud. cree? (¿Crees?)**
Es posible.	**No sé si me convences.**
Ya veremos.	
Si Ud. quiere (tú quieres).	

Y si Ud. quiere indicar que no está de acuerdo, puede decir:

No.	**En mi vida.**
De ninguna manera.	**No puede ser.**
Jamás.	**No hay manera.**
Absolutamente no.	**¡Imposible!**

¡Imposible!

Práctica

A **¡Qué barbaridad!** Den una reacción personal.

1. El año que viene, habrá clases los sábados.
2. Van a eliminar las vacaciones de verano.
3. No habrá exámenes finales.
4. No habrá más bailes en la escuela.
5. Van a obligar a los muchachos a llevar saco y corbata a clase.
6. La primera clase será al mediodía.
7. No habrá más buses escolares y todos los alumnos tendrán que ir a la escuela a pie.
8. No habrá más escuelas mixtas. Las muchachas irán a una escuela y los muchachos a otra.

Una conversación que continúa

Cuando discutimos sobre los sucesos locales, los grandes acontecimientos o las actualidades mundiales, no es raro que la conversación que entablamos dure por un período de tiempo. Para comenzar una conversación, Ud. puede decir:

> **Oye, Josefa, ¿sabes que... ? o ¿qué piensas de... ?**
> **Pues, señor, ¿qué sabe de... ? o ¿qué piensa de... ?**

Si durante la conversación, Ud. quiere tomar la palabra, Ud. puede decir:

> **Yo pienso (creo) que...**
> **Escúchame... (informal)**
> **Permítame decir(le) algo. (más formal)**

Si Ud. quiere decir algo que tiene que ver con algo que otro acaba de decir, Ud. puede decir:

> **A propósito,...**
> **En cuanto a eso,...**

Y si Ud. quiere cambiar la conversación, Ud. puede decir lo siguiente antes de continuar con otro tema:

> **Cambiando de tema,...**

Práctica

A **Una conversación** ¿Qué dirían Uds.?

1. para comenzar una conversación
2. para tomar la palabra durante una conversación
3. para cambiar la dirección de la conversación
4. para añadir algo a lo que otro acaba de decir

Actividad comunicativa

A **Permítame decirle...** Trabajen en grupos de cuatro personas. Escojan temas un poco controversiales. Cada uno(a) de Uds. debe expresar su opinion.

TEACHING TIPS

A. Read the explanations to students.

B. Have students repeat the expressions after you.

C. Tell students you would like to have them continue to use the expressions from this chapter throughout the year. Explain to them that these expressions can "spice up" their answers and give them a real Spanish flair.

ANSWERS
Práctica
A Answers will vary.
1. Oye, ¿sabes que...?
2. Yo pienso que...
3. Cambiando el tema...
4. A propósito...

Actividades comunicativas

ANSWERS
A Answers will vary.

Independent Practice

Assign the exercises on pages 214–215.

Repaso de estructura

RESOURCES

- 📁 Workbook
- 📁 Student Tape Manual
- 🎧 Audio Cassette 9A/Compact Disc 6
- 💾 Computer Software: *Estructura*
- 📁 Chapter Quizzes
- 💾 Testing Program

TEACHING STRUCTURE

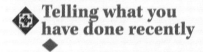

Telling what you have done recently

A. Most students will probably only need a quick review of this point.

B. Have students review the forms in steps 1–4.

C. Have students read the explanatory material in steps 1–6.

Telling what you have done recently
El presente perfecto

1. The present perfect tense is formed by using the present tense of the helping (auxiliary) verb **haber** and the past participle. Study the following forms of the present tense of the verb **haber.**

INFINITIVE	haber
yo	he
tú	has
él, ella, Ud.	ha
nosotros(as)	hemos
vosotros(as)	*habéis*
ellos, ellas, Uds.	han

2. The past participle of regular verbs is formed by dropping the infinitive ending -**ar**, -**er**, -**ir**, and adding -**ado** to -**ar** verbs, and -**ido** to both -**er** and -**ir** verbs.

hablar	habl-	hablado
comer	com-	comido
vivir	viv-	vivido

3. The following important verbs have irregular past participles.

abrir	abierto	freír	frito	poner	puesto
cubrir	cubierto	romper	roto	volver	vuelto
descubrir	descubierto	ver	visto	decir	dicho
escribir	escrito	morir	muerto	hacer	hecho

4. Study the forms of the present perfect tense of regular and irregular verbs.

INFINITIVE	hablar	pedir	hacer
yo	he hablado	he pedido	he hecho
tú	has hablado	has pedido	has hecho
él, ella, Ud.	ha hablado	ha pedido	ha hecho
nosotros(as)	hemos hablado	hemos pedido	hemos hecho
vosotros(as)	*habéis hablado*	*habéis pedido*	*habéis hecho*
ellos, ellas, Uds.	han hablado	han pedido	han hecho

Independent Practice

Assign any of the following:
1. Exercises, page 217
2. Workbook, *Repaso de estructura*

5. The present perfect tense is used to express a past action without reference to a particular time. It usually denotes an occurrence that continues into the present or relates closely to the present. Observe and analyze the following sentences.

Su madre ha estado enferma. *His mother has been ill.*

6. The adverb **ya** frequently accompanies a present perfect verb.

Ellos ya han salido. *They have already left.*

A HISTORIETA Un robo

Contesten según se indica.

1. ¿Le han robado? (Sí)
2. ¿Le han hecho daño (herido)? (No)
3. ¿Alguien ha llamado a la policía? (Sí)
4. ¿Él ha denunciado el robo en la comisaría? (Sí)
5. ¿Han llegado los policías al lugar del robo? (Sí)
6. ¿Han detenido a los maleantes? (No)
7. ¿Han identificado a los carteristas? (No)
8. ¿Roberto les ha dado una descripción de los carteristas? (Sí)

B HISTORIETA Viajes personales

Preguntas personales.

1. ¿Has hecho algunos viajes?
2. ¿Adónde has ido?
3. ¿Qué ciudades o países has visitado?
4. ¿Has conocido a mucha gente durante los viajes?
5. ¿Se han escrito?
6. ¿Se han visitado?
7. ¿Se han llamado por teléfono?

C HISTORIETA ¡Qué suerte!

Completen con el presente perfecto.

1. Nuestro amigo Ricardo no ___ (tener) muy buena suerte.
2. ¿No? ¿Qué le ___ (pasar)?
3. No sé exactamente. Pero sé que lo ___ (llevar) al hospital.
4. Pues, dime. ¿Se ___ (poner) enfermo o ___ (tener) un accidente?
5. No sé. Pregúntale a Teresa. Ella ___ (hablar) a su novia.

HOSPITAL SAN PABLO
NEUMOLOGÍA Y CIRUGÍA DEL TÓRAX
INFORMACIÓN:
20 401
DIRECCIÓN:
20 402
ADMINISTRACIÓN:
20 403
* Servicio de Rayos X
* Certificados Pulmonares
* Terapia Respiratoria
EL CONDOR
* Unidad de Salud Mental
* Farmacodependencia y Alcoholismo
20 543
COMUNIDAD HNAS. VICENTINAS
20 404
Barrio Zaragocilla • Apartado: 1279

Learning From Realia

1. You may wish to ask students the following questions about the realia:
   ¿Cómo se llama el hospital? ¿Trata la neumología de los pulmones o del corazón? ¿Es la cirugía del tórax, cirugía pulmonar u ortopédica?

2. Have students look at the ad and find the following:
   a. the term that indicates the hospital has a psychiatric division
   b. the term for drug addiction
   c. This hospital is run by an order of Roman Catholic nuns. Find the name of the order.
   d. What is **Hnas.** an abbreviation of?

TEACHING STRUCTURE

◆ **Affirmative and negative ideas** ◆

Note It may be possible to omit the review of this relatively easy point with some groups.

A. Guide students through the explanatory material in steps 1–5.

B. Have students read the model sentences aloud in steps 2–5.

National Standards

Comparisons Students will show an understanding of language as they contrast the use of the double negative in Spanish and discuss the absence of the construction in formal English, yet its presence in nonstandard English.

Affirmative and negative ideas
Palabras negativas y afirmativas

1. The most frequently used negative words in Spanish are:

nada	ni... ni
nadie	ninguno (ningún)
nunca	

2. Review and contrast the following affirmative and negative sentences.

AFFIRMATIVE	NEGATIVE
Yo sé que él tiene algo.	**Yo sé que él no tiene nada.**
Yo sé que alguien está allí.	**Yo sé que nadie está allí.**
Yo sé que él ve a alguien.	**Yo sé que él no ve a nadie.**
Yo sé que él siempre está.	**Yo sé que él nunca está.**
Yo sé que él tiene un perro o un gato.	**Yo sé que él no tiene ni un perro ni un gato.**
Yo sé que él tiene algún dinero.	**Yo sé que él no tiene ningún dinero.**

Note that **alguno** and **ninguno** shorten to **algún** and **ningún** before a masculine singular noun and carry a written accent.

3. In Spanish the placement of the negative word can vary and, unlike English, more than one negative word can be used in the same sentence.

Él nunca va allá.	**Él no va allá nunca.**
Nadie está.	**No está nadie.**
Él nunca dice nada a nadie.	

4. Note that the personal **a** must be used with **alguien** or **nadie** when either of these words is the direct object of the sentence.

Él vio *a* alguien.   **Él no vio *a* nadie.**

5. **Tampoco** is the negative word that replaces **también**.

Él lo sabe también.	**Él no lo sabe. (Ni) yo tampoco.**
A mí no me gusta.	**Ni a mí tampoco.**

SIEMPRE COMPARTIEND[O]

Independent Practice

Assign any of the following:
1. Exercises, page 219
2. Workbook, *Repaso de estructura*

Nunca tanto tan cerca.

Práctica

A **No lo he hecho yo.** Contesten en forma negativa.

1. ¿Has escrito algo?
2. ¿Has comprado algo?
3. ¿Has visto a alguien?
4. ¿Has llamado a alguien?
5. ¿Has viajado allí con frecuencia?
6. ¿Has estado allí muchas veces?

B **¡No, mil veces no!** Contesten.

1. ¿Estás haciendo algo?
2. ¿Estás leyendo algo?
3. ¿Estás llamando a alguien?
4. ¿Vas a hacerle una llamada a alguien?
5. ¿Vas a viajar algún día a la luna?
6. ¿Te vas a comprar un yate y una avioneta?

C **El pobre bebé** Den la forma negativa.

1. El bebé tiene algo en la boca.
2. El bebé está con alguien.
3. El bebé está jugando con el gato o con el perro.
4. El bebé tiene miedo de algo.
5. El bebé ve a alguien.
6. El bebé siempre quiere algo de alguien.
7. Alguien está con el bebé.

D **Los otros tampoco** Den la forma negativa.

1. Él lo sabe y yo lo sé también.
2. Ella quiere ir y yo quiero ir también.
3. A él le gusta y a mí me gusta también.
4. Yo voy a ir y ellos van también.
5. Uds. lo van a hacer y nosotros también.

VOCABULARY EXPANSION

Give students the names of the following breeds of dogs:
el cócker, el bóxer, el gran danés, el pequinés, el afgano, el galgo *(greyhound),* **el pastor alemán, el choco** *(poodle),* **el perro de San Bernardo, el perro de muestra** *(setter),* **el perro de aguas** *(spaniel)*

Critical Thinking Activity

Thinking skills: making inferences; evaluating information

1. Explique cómo o por qué un cachorro (un perrito joven) u otro animal doméstico puede mejorar la salud, sobre todo mental, de una persona.
2. Explique el significado de «Nunca tanto tan cerca».

TEACHING TIPS

These *Práctica* can be done without advance preparation, with books open or closed.

ANSWERS
Práctica

A No, no he...
 1. escrito nada.
 2. comprado nada.
 3. visto a nadie.
 4. llamado a nadie.
 5. viajado allí nunca.
 6. estado allí nunca.

B No, no...
 1. estoy haciendo nada.
 2. estoy leyendo nada.
 3. estoy llamando a nadie.
 4. voy a hacerle una llamada a nadie.
 5. voy a viajar a la luna nunca.
 6. voy a comprar ni un yate ni una avioneta.

C El bebé no...
 1. tiene nada en la boca.
 2. está con nadie.
 3. está jugando ni con el gato ni con el perro.
 4. tiene miedo de nada.
 5. ve a nadie.
 6. nunca quiere nada de nadie.
 7. Nadie está con el bebé.

D 1. Él no lo sabe y yo no lo sé tampoco.
 2. Ella no quiere ir y yo no quiero ir tampoco.
 3. A él no le gusta y a mí no me gusta tampoco.
 4. Yo no voy a ir y ellos no van tampoco.
 5. Uds. no lo van a hacer ni nosotros tampoco.

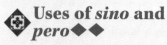

TEACHING STRUCTURE

◆ Uses of *sino* and *pero* ◆◆

Have students read the explanation and repeat the model sentences aloud in unison.

TEACHING TIPS

This *Práctica* can be done with books open or closed.

ANSWERS
Práctica

A 1. Él no es débil, sino fuerte.
   2. Él no es perezoso, sino ambicioso.
   3. Él no es gordo, sino flaco.
   4. Él no es interesante, sino aburrido.
   5. Él no es simpático, sino antipático.
   6. Él no es generoso, sino tacaño.

Uses of *sino* and *pero*
Sino y pero

1. **Sino** means "but" in the sense of "rather" or "on the contrary." It is used after a negative statement to contradict the negative statement.

   Él no es rico, sino pobre.
   José no es rubio, sino moreno.

2. **Pero** is used for "but" in all other cases.

   Trabaja mucho pero no gana dinero.

◆Práctica◆

A **No, todo lo contrario.** Formen oraciones negativas.

   alto / bajo
   Él no es alto, sino bajo.

   1. débil / fuerte
   2. perezoso / ambicioso
   3. gordo / flaco
   4. interesante / aburrido
   5. simpático / antipático
   6. generoso / tacaño

¡LA GORDURA PUEDE SER HEREDITARIA!

DESCUBRA CÓMO COMBATIRLA

Additional Practice

1. Trabajando con un(a) compañero(a) de clase, preparen, cada uno(a), una lista de cosas que han hecho recientemente. Luego comparen lo que han hecho.
   Yo he ___.
   Y... ha ___.
   Nosotros hemos ___.
   o
   Yo he ___.
   Pero... no ha ___.

2. Escoja a un(a) pariente suyo(a) que a su parecer (en su opinión) ha tenido una vida interesante. Prepare un párrafo indicando todo lo que él o ella ha hecho.

Periodismo

Los titulares

Introducción

Si uno quiere informarse de las últimas noticias o actualidades, ¿qué puede hacer? Pues, puede comprar un periódico y leer los titulares en letras grandes de la primera plana. Si un titular le interesa, seguirá leyendo el subtítulo. Si el artículo le parece interesante leerá el primer párrafo, y para enterarse de todos los detalles del acontecimiento leerá el artículo entero. Pero son los titulares los que le llaman a uno la atención primero. No se puede menospreciar la importancia de un titular bien escrito. He aquí varios titulares de periódicos de España y Latinoamérica.

Vocabulario

el colectivo

el reloj

el chófer

Advanced Game

Vocabulary Game: *El juego de Loto*
Set-up: Prepare two sets of index cards—one with the vocabulary words and the other with their definitions. Hand out the cards to the class.
Game: Call on different students to read their cards. The student with the matching card must read the corresponding word or definition.
Hint: You can also include vocabulary from previous chapters.

CAPÍTULO 5
Periodismo

🔔 Bell Ringer Review

Use the BRR Transparency 5-2, or write the following on the board: **Escriba una lista de los problemas sociales que el gobierno federal o municipal debe resolver.**

TEACHING TIPS

You may wish to read the *Introducción* aloud or have the students read it silently.

RESOURCES

- 🖐 Vocabulary Transparencies
- 🎧 Audio Cassette 9B/Compact Disc 6
- 📁 Student Tape Manual
- 📁 Workbook
- 📁 Chapter Quizzes
- 💾 Testing Program

TEACHING VOCABULARY

You may wish to use some of the procedures suggested in previous chapters.

ABOUT THE SPANISH LANGUAGE

- ◆ The term **colectivo** can vary from country to country. In some areas it is a public taxi that picks up passengers along a set route. In other areas, such as Argentina, **un colectivo** is a municipal bus.
- ◆ The term for "bus" varies from region to region. One will hear: **el autobús, el bus, el ómnibus, el autocar de larga distancia, de largo recorrido**

ANSWERS

Práctica

A 1. **el infarto**
  2. **el colectivo**
  3. **el reloj**
  4. **la demora**
  5. **reducir**
B 1. **un infarto**
  2. **el riesgo, otro infarto**
  3. **una tardanza o un retraso**
  4. **fracasar**
  5. **reducir, un infarto**
  6. **los colectivos**
  7. **El chófer**

FINE ART CONNECTION

Salvador Dalí nació en España en 1904. Se le consi-dera el más famoso de los surrealistas. En su célebre cuadro "La persis-tencia de la memoria", que vemos aquí, creó un mundo misterioso. El árbol muerto simboliza la muerte y el mon-struo marino en la playa desierta simboliza la descom-posición. El significado de este cuadro es que con el tiempo todo se descompone y muere con la excepción del tiempo mismo. A Dalí le gustaba la controversia que causaban sus obras y su comportamiento extraño. Decía «La diferencia entre un lunático y yo es que no estoy loco».

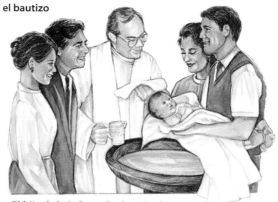

el bautizo

El hijo de la Infanta fue bautizado.

el infarto	el ataque cardíaco	**reducir**	disminuir, bajar
la demora	la tardanza, el retraso	**aprobar**	dar por bueno, autorizar
el riesgo	el peligro	**fracasar**	no tener éxito
el aumento	el incremento, lo contrario de «reducción»		

Práctica

A **¿Cuál es la palabra?** Identifiquen.
1. un ataque al corazón
2. un tipo de minibus o taxi público
3. aparato que indica la hora
4. el retraso
5. lo contrario de aumentar

B **De otra manera** Expresen de otra manera.
1. Su padre ha sufrido *un ataque al corazón.*
2. Existe *el peligro* de sufrir *otro ataque.*
3. La ambulancia llegó con *un retraso.*
4. Yo sé que no va a tener éxito y que va a *salir mal.*
5. No fumar *baja el peligro* de un *ataque cardíaco.*
6. No sé si pasan por aquí *los taxis públicos.*
7. *El conductor* maneja o conduce el carro.

«La persistencia de la memoria» de Salvador Dalí

Critical Thinking Activity

Thinking skills: **supporting arguments with reasons**
1. **¿Qué opina Ud.? ¿Está Ud. de acuerdo con la opinión de Dalí que el artista, y sólo el artista, puede conquistar el tiempo y alcanzar la inmortalidad por medio de su obra?**
2. **Explique en sus propias palabras por qué el tiempo es indestructible.**

Independent Practice

Assign any of the following:
1. Exercises, page 222
2. Workbook, *Periodismo*

Los titulares

El Clarín, Buenos Aires
sábado 29 de julio

Última hora

CONTRA EL RELOJ PARA APROBAR EL PRESUPUESTO

LaJornada

DIRECTOR FUNDADOR: CARLOS PAYAN VELVER • DIRECTORA GENERAL: CARMEN LIRA SAADE • MÉXICO, D.F. AÑO QUINCE • NÚMERO 5086

Tranquilas elecciones en Chiapas

Madrid, domingo 18 de junio — **El País**

SANIDAD

El consumo de cigarrillos bajos en nicotina no reduce el riesgo de infarto

☆☆☆☆

Buenos Aires, martes 3 de octubre

El Clarín

LOS CHOFERES TRABAJAN A CÓDIGO DESDE LA MEDIANOCHE

Demoras en el servicio de colectivos

Habrá inconvenientes hoy en el auto-transporte de pasajeros de corta y media distancia en esta Capital y en el Gran Buenos Aires. Los choferes aplican, desde la medianoche, el trabajo a código, que producirá demoras en el servicio. La protesta se debe al fracaso de las negociaciones salariales con los empresarios. Podrían funcionar también con dificultad los subterráneos.

Madrid, lunes 5 de octubre — **ABC DE SEVILLA**

Ayer fue bautizado en el Palacio de la Zarzuela el hijo de los Duques de Lugo

Madrid, lunes 17 de septiembre

EL MUNDO
(DEL SIGLO VEINTIUNO)

Muere Hugo Batalla, vicepresidente y presidente del Parlamento uruguayo

PERIODISMO

doscientos veintitrés ~ **223**

A. Have students read the headlines in a leisurely way, as they would in a real-life situation.

B. Have students arrange the headlines into the following topics: **Salud, Trabajo, Gobierno, Transporte, Eventos.**

ABOUT THE SPANISH LANGUAGE

El paro is different from **la huelga. El paro** is a work stoppage and **la huelga** is a strike. Those who are on strike are **huelguistas.**

Cooperative Learning

1. Have students read at home several articles that appear in today's local newspaper. The next day students give some information concerning what they read. They do not, however, give the precise details. Other members have to guess what news items they are referring to.

2. Have students work together in groups of four to write the headlines for the next edition of their school newspaper.

TEACHING TIPS

Have students select the *Actividad* that they would like to do.

Comprensión

A **Los titulares**   Contesten.

1. ¿Cómo trabajan los choferes?
2. ¿Qué habrá?
3. ¿A qué se debe la protesta?
4. ¿En qué ciudad habrá demoras?
5. ¿Por qué no se debe fumar cigarrillos bajos en nicotina?
6. ¿Cómo fueron las elecciones en Chiapas?
7. ¿Dónde tuvo lugar el bautizo del hijo de los Duques de Lugo?
8. ¿Quién fue el presidente del Parlamento uruguayo?

B **De otra manera**   ¿Cómo expresan los titulares las siguientes ideas?

1. Ayer tuvo lugar el bautizo del hijo de los Duques de Lugo.
2. Elecciones sin problemas en Chiapas.
3. Falleció Hugo Batalla.
4. Queda muy poco tiempo para aprobar el presupuesto.

Actividades comunicativas

A **Los editores**   Imagínese que Ud. trabaja para un periódico americano. Prepare una versión en inglés de cada titular.

B **En español**   Lea los titulares en la primera plana de su periódico local. Escoja tres titulares. Prepare una versión en español de cada titular.

12 COSAS QUE PODEMOS HACER EN LUGAR DE FUMAR CIGARILLOS.

Learning From Realia

Have students say as much as they can about the piece of realia.

Independent Practice

Assign any of the following:
1. Exercises, page 224
2. Workbook, *Periodismo*

Los sucesos

Introducción

En los periódicos leemos las noticias mundiales que tratan de asuntos económicos, políticos, etc., de gran importancia en la arena internacional. Pero en los periódicos aparecen también muchos artículos sobre sucesos locales que sólo tienen interés en la región donde ocurren. En casi todas partes del mundo estos sucesos o acontecimientos locales son muy parecidos: accidentes, robos, asaltos, catástrofes naturales.

Incendio forestal, Chile

TEACHING THE READING

 Los sucesos

Bring several copies of Hispanic newspapers to class. After students have read the *Introducción*, ask them to look at the newspapers and point out some examples of local news items.

VOCABULARY EXPANSION

You may wish to give students the following additional vocabulary about firefighting:

el bombero (*firefighter*)
la manguera (*hose*)
la boca de incendios (*fire hydrant*)
la boquilla (*nozzle*)
la escalera extensible (*ladder*)
el vehículo (el camión, el coche) de bomberos (*fire truck*)

Did You Know?

Los antiguos romanos tenían bomberos profesionales. En el siglo I d. C. había un cuerpo de unos 7.000 bomberos asalariados. Ellos también andaban por las calles de Roma e imponían castigos corporales a aquellas personas que violaban las ordenanzas contra incendios.

Vocabulario

un incendio

el naufragio

el/la maleante el/la delincuente
la madrugada las primeras horas de la mañana
los damnificados las víctimas, especialmente de una catástrofe

destruir causar la destrucción

sobrepasar exceder
ocasionar causar
fallecer morir
rescatar salvar, acudir al socorro (a la ayuda)
apoderarse de tomar, hacerse dueño de una cosa ajena (de otro)

Práctica

A **Los sucesos** Completen.

1. Un ___ o fuego tiene ___ y humo.
2. El ___ es un barco. Y otra palabra que significa ___ es ___.
3. Un delincuente es un ___.
4. Es un crimen ___ del dinero que le pertenece a otro.

5. Un ___ es un miembro de la tripulación (un tripulante).
6. Llegó otro barco para ___ a las víctimas del naufragio.
7. Un barco que se pierde es un ___.

B **Las noticias** Expresen de otra manera.

1. *El barco* se hundió.
2. Llevaron a *las víctimas* al hospital municipal.
3. El accidente tuvo lugar a las dos de *la mañana*.

4. Tenemos que ir a *salvar* a las víctimas.
5. Más de 100 personas *murieron*.
6. El número de damnificados *excedió* los mil.
7. El incendio *causó* mucha destrucción en la ciudad.

Incendio destruye 3 edificios

El Universo, Guayaquil

BOGOTÁ, (EFE).- Un incendio producido por un cortocircuito arrasó[1] ayer tres edificios de apartamentos en Fontibón, un suburbio de Santafé de Bogotá, y dejó 800 damnificados, informaron las autoridades.

La alcaldía de Fontibón, en el Distrito Capital, dijo que la conflagración se registró[2] en una cuadra formada por edificios de apartamentos, y que las llamas fueron controladas después de cinco horas.

La Oficina Nacional para la Prevención y Atención de Desastres anunció en Santafé de Bogotá que enviará alimentos y tiendas de campaña para atender a los damnificados, que se han refugiado provisionalmente en una iglesia local y en la sede de un colegio.

[1] **arrasó** *leveled*
[2] **registró** tuvo lugar

Comprensión

A **Un incendio** Den la siguiente información.

1. dónde se produjo el incendio
2. lo que causó el incendio
3. lo que el incendio destruyó
4. el número de damnificados
5. dónde se encuentra Fontibón
6. cuántas horas tomó para controlar las llamas

TEACHING THE READING

◈ Incendio destruye 3 edificios ◆◆

A. Have students read this selection silently as if they were actually reading the newspaper.

B. Tell students to read the article once. Tell them to read it a second time as they look for the information in the *Comprensión* exercise on page 227. It is recommended that this be done as a homework assignment.

ANSWERS
Comprensión

A 1. **Fontibón**
   2. **un cortocircuito**
   3. **tres edificios de apartamentos**
   4. **800**
   5. **en las afueras de Santafé de Bogotá**
   6. **cinco horas**

Critical Thinking Activity

Thinking skills: identifying consequences

¿Cuáles son las consecuencias de un incendio?

Independent Practice

Assign any of the following:
1. Exercise, page 227
2. Workbook, *Periodismo*

227

TEACHING THE READING

✦ Víctimas por ola de calor en México ✦

A. Have the students read this selection as if they were actually reading the newspaper.

B. Tell the students to read the article once. Tell them to read it a second time as they look for the information in the *Comprensión* exercise on page 228. It is recommended that this be done as a homework assignment.

ANSWERS
Comprensión

1. una ola de calor
2. 40 grados centígrados
3. al menos seis
4. Tamaulipas y Chihuahua
5. niños
6. 44 grados centígrados

GEOGRAPHY CONNECTION

Chihuahua es la capital del estado de Chihuahua, México. El estado de Chihuahua tiene una frontera con los estados de Tejas y Arizona. Ciudad Juárez, al otro lado del Río Grande (Río Bravo) de El Paso, Tejas, está en el estado de Chihuahua.

Buenos Aires ☆☆☆☆ **El Clarín**

Víctimas por ola de calor en México

CHIHUAHUA, (EFE).- Una ola de calor, con temperaturas que sobrepasan los 40 grados, ocasionó la muerte de al menos 6 personas y la deshidratación de varias decenas en los estados mexicanos de Tamaulipas y Chihuahua, informaron las autoridades. La mayoría de las víctimas del intenso calor son niños, uno de los cuales, de 11 meses, falleció cuando se alcanzaron los 44 grados centígrados en el municipio de Bachiniva, Chihuahua.

Una anciana murió el jueves pasado por el calor en Chihuahua, capital del estado del mismo nombre.

Comprensión

A **Una ola de calor** Den la siguiente información.

1. lo que ocasionó víctimas en México
2. la temperatura que se sobrepasó
3. el número de personas que murieron
4. los estados mexicanos donde hubo víctimas
5. quiénes fueron la mayoría de las víctimas
6. la temperatura que se alcanzó en Bachiniva, Chihuahua

Independent Practice

Assign any of the following:
1. Exercise, page 228
2. Workbook, *Periodismo*

Dos ecuatorianos mueren en naufragio

CARACAS, (EFE).- Dos marinos ecuatorianos y un costarricense murieron el lunes al hundirse en aguas venezolanas el navío La Mafia, de bandera dominicana, informaron ayer las autoridades de Puerto Cabello, 250 kilómetros al oeste de Caracas.

El navío, que llevaba 600 toneladas de cemento del puerto de Chichiriviche (Venezuela) al de San Juan de Puerto Rico, se hundió la madrugada del lunes al abrírsele una vía de agua cuando capeaba un temporal[1].

Los cinco supervivientes del naufragio, que estuvieron catorce horas a la deriva[2], sujetos a unas tablas, identificaron a las víctimas como Jorge Macías, ecuatoriano y capitán del barco, y su compatriota y cocinero Fiolvi Macías.

El hundimiento fue tan rápido que los dos ecuatorianos no tuvieron tiempo de abandonar la nave, mientras que el costarricense Quizano Palacios desapareció cuando una ola lo lanzó de la tabla que lo mantenía a flote.

Pulovio Moreno y Alicio Otero, maquinistas del buque siniestrado[3], indicaron que fueron rescatados por la motonave Cavaliere Star, que venía de Port Everglades (EE.UU.) y los dejó en el puerto venezolano de Tucacas.

[1] **capeaba un temporal** _weathering a storm_ [3] **siniestrado** _involved in the accident_
[2] **a la deriva** _adrift_

Comprensión

A Un naufragio Contesten.

1. ¿De qué nacionalidad eran los tres marinos que murieron en el naufragio?
2. ¿Cómo se llamaba el navío?
3. ¿Qué carga llevaba?
4. ¿De dónde salió?
5. ¿Adónde iba?
6. ¿A qué hora ocurrió el naufragio?
7. ¿Cuántos supervivientes hubo?
8. ¿Cuántas horas estuvieron a la deriva?
9. ¿Por qué no tuvieron tiempo de abandonar la nave los dos tripulantes ecuatorianos?
10. ¿Cómo fueron rescatados los dos maquinistas?

Actividades comunicativas

A
Los periodistas En grupos de cuatro, escriban varios titulares sobre cosas que han ocurrido en el colegio o en la ciudad. Luego, den los titulares a otro grupo para que escriban un artículo corto para cada titular.

B
Un acontecimiento Prepare Ud. un artículo para un periódico sobre un acontecimiento local o nacional.

Did You Know?

There was a time when crew members of a ship were all of the same nationality—usually of the country of the flag the ship flew. Today most ships sail under flags of convenience (Panama, Liberia, etc.) and have a multinational crew.

Independent Practice

Assign any of the following:
1. Exercise, page 229
2. Workbook, _Periodismo_

CAPÍTULO 5
Periodismo

TEACHING THE READING

Dos ecuatorianos mueren en naufragio ◆◆

To vary the procedure, you may wish to call on individuals to read the article aloud in class.

TEACHING TIPS

Have students prepare the _Comprensión_ exercise before going over it in class.

ANSWERS
Comprensión

A 1. Eran dos ecuatorianos y un costarricense.
   2. El navío se llamaba La Mafia.
   3. Llevaba cemento.
   4. Salió del puerto venezolano Chichiriviche.
   5. Iba a San Juan de Puerto Rico.
   6. El naufragio ocurrió en la madrugada.
   7. Hubo cinco supervivientes.
   8. Estuvieron a la deriva catorce horas.
   9. No tuvieron tiempo de abandonar la nave los dos tripulantes ecuatorianos porque el hundimiento fue muy rápido.
   10. Los dos maquinistas fueron rescatados por la motonave Cavaliere Star que venía de Port Everglades.

TEACHING TIPS

Actividades A and _B_ can be done as individual or group assignments.

Actividades comunicativas

ANSWERS
A and B Answers will vary.

Estructura

An action completed prior to another action
El pluscuamperfecto

1. The pluperfect tense is formed by using the imperfect tense of the auxiliary verb **haber** and the past participle. Study the following forms of the pluperfect tense.

INFINITIVE	llegar	salir	hacer
yo	había llegado	había salido	había hecho
tú	habías llegado	habías salido	habías hecho
él, ella, Ud.	había llegado	había salido	había hecho
nosotros(as)	habíamos llegado	habíamos salido	habíamos hecho
vosotros(as)	habíais llegado	habíais salido	habíais hecho
ellos, ellas, Uds.	habían llegado	habían salido	habían hecho

2. The pluperfect tense is used the same way in Spanish as it is in English. The pluperfect describes a past action completed before another past action. Observe and analyze the following sentence.

> **Ellos ya habían salido cuando**   *They had already left when*
> **yo llegué.**   *I arrived.*

Note that both actions of the above sentence took place in the past. The action that took place first, "they had left," is in the pluperfect. The action that followed it, "I arrived," is in the preterite.

Práctica

A   **Ya lo habían hecho.**   Completen según el modelo.

> **terminar**
> **Cuando yo salí, ellos ya ___.**
> **Cuando yo salí, ellos ya habían terminado.**

1. cantar
2. bailar
3. ver el espectáculo
4. abrir los regalos
5. volver
6. servir la comida
7. comer
8. acostarse

RESOURCES

- Workbook
- Student Tape Manual
- Audio Cassette 10A/Compact Disc 7
- Computer Software: *Estructura*
- Chapter Quizzes
- Testing Program

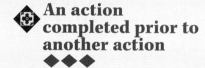

Bell Ringer Review

Use the BRR Transparency 5-3, or write the following on the board:
Ponga las oraciones siguientes en el presente perfecto.
- **Yo ___ (terminar) mis tareas.**
- **Yo le ___. (hablar)**
- **Él me ___ (devolver) las tareas.**

Note Of the tenses presented in this section, the one most frequently used is the conditional perfect. You may wish to go over the pluperfect and the future perfect very quickly.

TEACHING STRUCTURE

◆ An action completed prior to another action
◆◆◆

A. Write the verb forms on the board and have the students repeat them.

B. The easiest way to have students understand this concept is to imagine two events that took place last week. One took place on Thursday and the other one the previous Tuesday. The event on Tuesday occurred before the event on Thursday.

C. Call on students to read the model sentences.

Additional Practice

Con un(a) compañero(a) de clase preparen listas individuales de cosas que Uds. ya habían hecho antes de matricularse en la escuela superior. Comparen sus listas e identifiquen las cosas que Uds. habían hecho en común.
Él (Ella) había ___ y yo había ___.
Yo había ___ y (pero) (name) (no) había ___.

Independent Practice

Assign any of the following:
1. Exercises, pages 230–231
2. Workbook, *Estructura*

B **Ya lo habían hecho.** Contesten según el modelo.

¿Escribirlo?
Pero ya lo habían escrito.

1. ¿Escribirlo?
2. ¿Devolverlo?
3. ¿Romperlo?
4. ¿Verlo?
5. ¿Abrirlo?
6. ¿Cubrirlo?
7. ¿Descubrirlo?
8. ¿Ponerlo?
9. ¿Decirlo?
10. ¿Hacerlo?

C **Y yo después...** Formen oraciones según el modelo.

Ellos salieron antes. Yo salí después.
Ellos ya habían salido cuando yo salí.

1. Ellos llegaron antes. Yo llegué después.
2. Ellos volvieron antes. Yo volví después.
3. Ellos lo vieron antes. Yo lo vi después.
4. Ellos le hablaron antes. Yo le hablé después.
5. Ellos lo hicieron antes. Yo lo hice después.
6. Ellos terminaron antes. Yo terminé después.

D **HISTORIETA** Él había estado en España.

Completen.

1. Roberto ___ (estar) en España antes de ir a Francia.
2. Él ___ (conocer) a Madrid antes de conocer a París.
3. Él ___ (aprender) el español antes de estudiar el francés.
4. Él ___ (estudiar) en la Universidad de Madrid antes de matricularse en la Sorbona.

Palacio de Oriente, Madrid, España

Expressing what one would have done
El condicional perfecto

1. The conditional perfect is formed by using the conditional of the auxiliary verb **haber** and the past participle. Study the following forms.

INFINITIVE	estudiar	recibir	decir
yo	habría estudiado	habría recibido	habría dicho
tú	habrías estudiado	habrías recibido	habrías dicho
él, ella, Ud.	habría estudiado	habría recibido	habría dicho
nosotros(as)	habríamos estudiado	habríamos recibido	habríamos dicho
vosotros(as)	habríais estudiado	habríais recibido	habríais dicho
ellos, ellas, Uds.	habrían estudiado	habrían recibido	habrían dicho

ESTRUCTURA

doscientos treinta y uno 231

CAPÍTULO 5
Estructura

ANSWERS
Práctica
A Cuando yo salí, ellos ya...
1. habían cantado.
2. habían bailado.
3. habían visto el espectáculo.
4. habían abierto los regalos.
5. habían vuelto.
6. habían servido la comida.
7. habían comido.
8. se habían acostado.

B Pero ya lo habían...
1. escrito.   6. cubierto.
2. devuelto.   7. descubierto.
3. roto.   8. puesto.
4. visto.   9. dicho.
5. abierto.   10. hecho.

C 1. habían llegado
2. habían vuelto
3. lo habían visto
4. le habían hablado
5. lo habían hecho
6. habían terminado

D 1. había estado
2. había conocido
3. había aprendido
4. había estudiado

TEACHING STRUCTURE

◆ Expressing what one would have done ◆◆

A. Have students read the explanatory material aloud.
B. Have them repeat the verb forms and model sentences.

Did You Know?

1. **Delante del Palacio de Oriente hay jardines preciosos. Son obra de Francisco Sabatini, arquitecto español de origen italiano. Nació en Palermo, Sicilia. Él contribuyó a la planificación de la ciudad de Madrid bajo órdenes de Carlos III. La Puerta de Alcalá es otra obra de Sabatini. Los jardines del Palacio de Oriente llevan su nombre— los jardines de Sabatini.**

2. **El rey Juan Carlos vive actualmente en el Palacio de la Zarzuela en las afueras de la capital, no muy lejos de la ciudad universitaria. El primer ministro vive en el Palacio de la Moncloa en el mismo barrio.**

2. The conditional perfect is used in Spanish, as it is in English, to state what would have taken place had something else not interfered or made it impossible. Observe and analyze the following sentences.

Él habría hecho el viaje pero tenía que trabajar.	*He would have taken the trip but he had to study.*
Yo habría salido pero empezó a llover.	*I would have gone out but it started to rain.*

Práctica

A **HISTORIETA** **Durante el accidente**

Preguntas personales.

1. ¿Habrías salvado a las víctimas?
2. ¿Habrías arriesgado (*risked*) tu vida?
3. ¿Les habrías dado primeros auxilios a las víctimas?
4. ¿Les habrías pedido ayuda a otras personas?
5. ¿Habrías hablado con los socorristas?
6. ¿Habrías llevado a las víctimas al hospital?
7. ¿Habrías ayudado a los damnificados?

Destrucción causada por el huracán Mitch, Tegucigalpa, Honduras

B **Yo lo habría hecho pero…** Completen.

1. Yo ___ (comer) pero no tenía hambre.
2. Yo lo ___ (tomar) pero no tenía sed.
3. Yo ___ (dormir) pero no tenía sueño.
4. Yo lo ___ (comprar) pero la verdad es que no tenía bastante dinero.
5. Yo lo ___ (hacer) pero francamente tenía miedo.
6. Yo lo ___ (decir) pero me daba vergüenza.

C **Yo sé que ellos lo habrían hecho.** Completen.

1. Ellos ___ (salir) pero no salieron porque empezó a llover.
2. Nosotros ___ (ir) a la playa pero no fuimos porque hacía mal tiempo.
3. Él me ___ (dar) el dinero pero no me lo dio porque no lo tenía.
4. Yo te lo ___ (decir) pero no te lo dije porque yo no tenía los resultados.
5. Él ___ (vivir) en la ciudad pero no vivía en la ciudad porque era imposible hallar un apartamento.

232

Describing events at different times in the future
El futuro perfecto

1. The future perfect tense is formed by using the future tense of the auxiliary verb **haber** and the past participle. Study the following forms of the future perfect.

INFINITIVE	hablar	ir	ver
yo	habré hablado	habré ido	habré visto
tú	habrás hablado	habrás ido	habrás visto
él, ella, Ud.	habrá hablado	habrá ido	habrá visto
nosotros(as)	habremos hablado	habremos ido	habremos visto
vosotros(as)	habréis hablado	habréis ido	habréis visto
ellos, ellas, Uds.	habrán hablado	habrán ido	habrán visto

2. The future perfect tense is used to express a future action that will be completed prior to another future action. Observe and analyze the following sentences.

Desgraciadamente ellos no estarán. Habrán salido antes de nuestra llegada.

Note in the above sentences that the people will not be present at some time in the future. They will not be present because they will have already left before our arrival. Their departure precedes our arrival even though both actions will be in the future. This tense is seldom used.

ꙮ Práctica ꙮ

A  **H**ISTORIETA **¿Qué habrás hecho antes de verme?**

Contesten.
1. Antes de verme, ¿habrás hablado con Juan?
2. Antes de verme, ¿lo habrás invitado?
3. Antes de verme, ¿habrás comprado las entradas para el teatro?
4. Antes de verme, ¿habrás llamado al restaurante?
5. Antes de verme, ¿habrás hecho una reservación?

 Bell Ringer Review

Use the BRR Transparency 5-4, or write the following on the board:
Cambie al futuro.
1. **Vamos a las Islas Canarias.**
2. **Mi amigo quiere bañarse en el mar.**
3. **Yo soy el guía.**
4. **Él compra algo en una tienda.**

TEACHING STRUCTURE

◆ **Describing events at different times in the future**◆

A. Since this tense is used rarely, it is recommended that you not spend a great deal of time on it.
B. To have students understand the concept of the future perfect, tell them that two or more events can happen in the future. One will take place next Tuesday and the other, next Thursday. By the time the Thursday event takes place, the Tuesday one will have already taken place. For this reason it is expressed in the future perfect.

TEACHING TIPS

You may go over this *Práctica* with books open.

ANSWERS
Práctica
A Answers can be negative.
1. **Sí, habré hablado con Juan.**
2. **Sí, lo habré invitado.**
3. **Sí, las habré comprado.**
4. **Sí, habré llamado al restaurante.**
5. **Sí, habré hecho una reservación.**

233

TEACHING STRUCTURE

◆ **Shortened forms of adjectives** ◆

A. It is recommended that you go over this point quickly. It is a rather easy point but one that needs frequent reintroduction until it "sounds right."

B. Read the explanation to students and have the entire class repeat the model expressions and adjective forms aloud.

Shortened forms of adjectives
Adjetivos apocopados

1. Several adjectives in Spanish have a shortened form when they precede a masculine singular noun. They drop the **-o** ending. Observe the following.

bueno	**Roberto es un buen tipo.**
malo	**No es un mal tipo.**
primero	**Él vive en el primer piso de una casa de apartamentos.**
tercero	**Sus abuelos viven en el tercer piso.**

2. The adjective **grande** becomes **gran** when it precedes either a masculine or feminine noun in the singular. The shortened form, **gran,** conveys the meaning "great" or "famous" rather than "big" or "large." Observe the following.

un hombre grande	*a big man*
un gran hombre	*a great man*
una mujer grande	*a big woman*
una gran mujer	*a great woman*

3. The number **ciento** is shortened to **cien** before a masculine or feminine noun.

Él tiene cien libros en su biblioteca.
Cada uno de sus cien libros tiene más de cien páginas.

4. The word **Santo** is shortened to **San** before a masculine saint's name unless the name of the saint begins with **To-** or **Do-**.

San Pedro	**Santo Domingo**	**Santa María**
San Alfonso	**Santo Tomás**	**Santa Teresa**

Biblioteca Nacional, Madrid, España

Additional Practice

Lea un artículo en el periódico sobre un acontecimiento que ha tenido lugar recientemente. Dé una descripción del protagonista o de los protagonistas del acontecimiento.

Learning From Photos

La biblioteca española más importante es la Biblioteca Nacional de Madrid que antes era la Biblioteca Real. Fue fundada por Felipe V en 1712. La biblioteca contiene más de tres millones de libros.

234

Práctica

A **Miguel de Cervantes Saavedra** Completen.

1. Cervantes es más que un ___ (bueno) novelista. Es un ___ (grande) novelista.
2. En el ___ (primero) capítulo de su novela *El Ingenioso hidalgo don Quijote de la Mancha*, Cervantes describe al ___ (grande) caballero andante, don Quijote.
3. Cuando don Quijote salió de su pueblo la ___ (primero) vez, salió sin escudero. La segunda vez salió con un vecino, Sancho Panza. Sancho le sirvió de escudero. Don Quijote sabía que un ___ (grande) caballero andante como él no podía viajar por el mundo sin escudero.
4. El pobre Sancho no tenía ___ (ninguno) deseo de conquistar todos los males del mundo. Él quería volver a casa.
5. Esta ___ (grande) novela de Cervantes es muy larga. Tiene más de ___ (ciento) páginas. La verdad es que tiene casi ___ (ciento) capítulos.

Don Quijote y Sancho Panza

Expressing exceptional qualities
El sufijo -ísimo(a)

1. The suffix **-ísimo(a)** can be added to adjectives to convey the meaning "most," "very," or "extremely."

guapo(a)	Aquel señor es guapísimo.	Aquella señora es guapísima.
simpático(a)	Es simpatiquísimo.	Es simpatiquísima.

2. If the adjective ends in a consonant, add **-ísimo(a)** directly to the singular form. If it ends in a vowel, drop the vowel before adding **-ísimo(a).**

fácil	El examen es facilísimo.
bueno(a)	La profesora es buenísima.

Práctica

A **Es fabuloso** Contesten según el modelo.

Él es muy alto, ¿no?
Sí, es altísimo.

1. Él es guapo, ¿no?
2. Y es interesante también, ¿no?
3. Me parece que es rico, ¿no?
4. Y su novia es muy guapa, ¿no?
5. Ella es muy simpática, ¿no?

REPASO DE ESTRUCTURA

doscientos treinta y cinco ✤ **235**

Learning From Photos

Esta estatua de don Quijote y Sancho Panza se encuentra en la Plaza de España en el centro de Madrid. Esta plaza placentera tiene una fuente bonita. Muchos madrileños pasan unos momentos libres leyendo, descansando o tomando un refresco en la Plaza de España.

Independent Practice

Assign any of the following:
1. Exercises, page 235
2. Workbook, *Estructura*

CAPÍTULO 5
Estructura

TEACHING TIPS

This *Práctica* can be done orally without previous preparation.

ANSWERS
Práctica

A 1. buen, gran
   2. primer, gran
   3. primera, gran
   4. ningún
   5. gran, cien, cien

TEACHING STRUCTURE

◆ **Expressing exceptional qualities**◆

A. Give the students a few minutes to read the explanation silently.
B. Then call on individuals to read the model sentences. This is the type of grammar point that students learn better through examples than explanations.

TEACHING TIPS

This *Práctica* can be done without previous preparation.

ANSWERS
Práctica

A 1. guapísimo
   2. interesantísimo
   3. riquísimo
   4. guapísima
   5. simpatiquísima

PAIRED ACTIVITY

Trabaje con un(a) compañero(a) de clase. Imagínese que él/ella es un(a) modelo famoso(a). Dé una descripción detalladísima de todo lo que lleva puesto. Luego cambien de papel.

235

Literatura
Un romance y un corrido

TEACHING TIPS

Have students read the introduction silently. You may wish to ask the following questions: **¿Cómo es la influencia árabe en la península ibérica? ¿Quiénes son unos líderes revolucionarios muy conocidos?**

HISTORY CONNECTION

El general Victoriano Huerta traicionó al presidente mexicano Madero en 1913. Pero su gobierno duró sólo un año. El pueblo se levantó en armas. El caudillo revolucionario más popular del sur de México fue Emiliano Zapata, un indio analfabeto. En el norte del país, había tres caudillos: Pancho Villa, Venustiano Carranza y Álvaro Obregón.

National Standards

Connections
Students will reinforce and further their knowledge of the history of Spain and Mexico. They will see events through the distinctive viewpoint of the Spanish language.

Antes de leer

Vamos a leer dos poemas que tratan de acontecimientos históricos—uno en España y el otro en México; uno en el siglo XV y el otro en el siglo XX. Pero antes, un poco de historia.

España: En 711, los moros invadieron a España. Vinieron del norte de África y no salieron hasta 1492, cuando el último rey moro, Boabdil, fue expulsado de Granada. Durante la conquista de España, los árabes construyeron mezquitas y palacios bellísimos, sobre todo en Andalucía: en Sevilla, Córdoba y Granada. La influencia cultural árabe en la península ibérica es enorme. En la lengua española hay muchas palabras que comienzan en **al; el alcázar,** por ejemplo, es un palacio. Estas palabras son todas de origen árabe: **alcázar, almohada, alhambra.**

México: En México, a principios del siglo XX, precisamente en 1910, estalló una revolución. Esta revolución fue una reacción contra la dictadura de Porfirio Díaz que duró 33 años. Desde 1906 los obreros organizaban huelgas. En 1910, diversos grupos se pusieron bajo el mando de Francisco I. Madero y se levantaron contra Porfirio Díaz. El 25 de mayo de 1911 el dictador renunció al poder y huyó del país. Madero fue elegido presidente fácilmente, pero no logró satisfacer los deseos de las distintas facciones. En el mismo año de 1911, Emiliano Zapata se levantó con un grupo de campesinos en Morelos, gritando «¡Tierra y Libertad!» Madero murió asesinado y Victoriano Huerta tomó el poder.

Venustiano Carranza, el gobernador del estado de Coahuila, no reconoció al nuevo gobierno. Consiguió el apoyo de viejos líderes como Francisco (Pancho) Villa, Emiliano Zapata y Álvaro Obregón. En julio de 1914, Huerta dejó el poder. Pancho Villa y Emiliano Zapata entraron en la Ciudad de México con el deseo de establecer un gobierno favorable a los obreros y campesinos. Carranza consiguió el apoyo de Obregón, quien derrotó a Villa y obtuvo la presidencia del país. El amigo de ayer llegó a ser el enemigo de hoy.

Emiliano Zapata fue asesinado durante la revolución por el coronel Jesús Guajardo. Pancho Villa murió asesinado en 1923, después de la revolución.

«Campamento zapatista» de Fernando Leal

Additional Practice

You may wish to ask the following questions about the *Antes de leer* section:

1. **¿Quiénes invadieron a España en 711?**
2. **¿De dónde vinieron ellos?**
3. **¿Cuándo salieron?**
4. **¿Quién fue el último rey de los moros en España?**
5. **¿Qué construyeron los árabes durante su ocupación de España?**
6. **¿Cuándo empezó la Revolución mexicana?**
7. **¿Qué fue esta revolución?**
8. **¿Por cuántos años había gobernado Porfirio Díaz y cómo?**
9. **¿Quiénes se levantaron contra Porfirio Díaz?**
10. **¿Cuándo renunció al poder Porfirio Díaz?**
11. **¿Quién fue elegido presidente?**
12. **¿Qué no pudo hacer?**

Vocabulario

El sargento gritó.

nacer venir al mundo	**la mentira** lo contrario de «la verdad»
labrar trabajar la tierra	**el/la cautivo(a)** el/la prisionero(a), el/la preso(a)
casarse contraer matrimonio	**la huerta** el huerto, el jardín
la vida el tiempo que vive una persona	**la viuda** la mujer cuyo esposo (marido) ha muerto
la muerte el final de la vida	**el golpe** el choque entre dos cuerpos
el/la moro(a) el/la árabe	

RESOURCES

- Vocabulary Transparencies
- Audio Cassette 10A/Compact Disc 7
- Student Tape Manual
- Workbook
- Chapter Quizzes
- Testing Program

TEACHING VOCABULARY

A. Have students repeat the new words and expressions after you or Cassette 10A/Compact Disc 7.

B. Since this reading selection is longer than most and since these definitions are not very difficult, you may wish to have students study the words as a homework assignment and prepare the *Práctica* on page 238.

Additional Practice

Have students find a word related to each of the following:

morir
mentir
golpear
el casamiento
el nacimiento
el grito
la labor

ANSWERS

Práctica

A 1. rey
2. alcázar
3. mezquita
4. la muerte
5. nace, muere
6. gritó
7. los moros
8. labran
9. la huerta
10. golpe
11. viuda

B 1. El rey moro estaba en el alcázar.
2. El sargento llevaba provisiones en la bolsa.
3. No dijo la verdad; dijo una mentira.
4. La huerta está a orillas de la laguna.

C 1. gritar
2. el alcázar
3. la huerta
4. el/la cautivo(a)
5. el monte
6. la laguna
7. la mentira
8. labrar
9. la mezquita

FINE ART CONNECTION

Francisco de Zurbarán nació en Badajoz en 1598. Murió en Madrid en 1662. Sus cuadros más famosos son de temas religiosos.

⟨ Práctica ⟩

A **¿Cuál es la palabra?** Completen.

1. El ___ de España es Juan Carlos de Borbón.
2. El ___ es un palacio árabe.
3. La ___ es un edificio religioso islámico (mahometano).
4. La vida siempre termina con ___.
5. Cada persona ___, vive y ___.
6. El sargento ___ algo y todos lo oyeron.
7. Los árabes del norte de África eran conocidos como ___.
8. Los campesinos ___ la tierra.
9. En ___ crecen flores y legumbres.
10. El niño se cayó y se dio un ___ fuerte en la cabeza.
11. Ella se casó en 1950 y su marido murió hace poco. Ella es ___.

B **Los soldados del rey**

Contesten según se indica.

1. ¿Dónde estaba el rey moro? (en el alcázar)
2. ¿Qué llevaba el sargento en la bolsa? (provisiones)
3. ¿Dijo la verdad? (no, una mentira)
4. ¿Dónde está la huerta? (a orillas de la laguna)

C **Expresiones equivalentes**

Den otra palabra.

1. hablar en voz muy alta
2. el palacio
3. el jardín
4. el preso
5. la montaña
6. el lago pequeño
7. lo contrario de «la verdad»
8. trabajar
9. un edificio religioso mahometano

«La batalla contra los moros en Jerez» de Francisco de Zurbarán

---

Independent Practice

Assign any of the following:
1. Exercises, page 238
2. Workbook, *Literatura*

Introducción

Durante la Edad Media en España, la gente se informaba de lo que pasaba por medio de los juglares que iban de castillo en castillo y transmitían las noticias en forma de verso. Recitaban cantares de gesta. Éstos casi siempre trataban de hazañas guerreras. El romance, o lo que llamamos *ballad* en inglés, se deriva de los antiguos cantares de gesta. Algunos romances «juglarescos» fueron compuestos por los juglares a partir del siglo XIV. Muchos de ellos narraban acontecimientos que acababan de ocurrir y estimulaban la imaginación de quienes los escuchaban. Ciertos romances juglarescos llamados «moriscos» tratan de la vida árabe en España. Otros llamados «fronterizos» tratan de las relaciones guerreras entre caballeros cristianos y moros. El romance que sigue, «Abenámar», es un romance fronterizo. En este romance el rey Juan II, el padre de Isabel la Católica, le habla al moro,

Abenámar. Abenámar le muestra al rey los edificios importantes de la ciudad de Granada. Esta ciudad ya había sido sitiada por los españoles. Luego, el rey le habla a la ciudad de Granada como si fuera una señora con quien él quisiera casarse. Es interesante notar la respuesta de Granada y el significado de su respuesta.

El corrido es una composición popular mexicana. Se deriva, y sigue la tradición, del antiguo romance español que los conquistadores trajeron a América. El corrido tiene un carácter muy descriptivo. Hay muchos tipos de corridos. Algunos hablan de hechos y eventos locales. Otros de personajes legendarios y de momentos históricos. Los más famosos cuentan relatos de la Revolución mexicana. El corrido que sigue, «En Durango comenzó», trata de Pancho Villa, una figura importante de la Revolución mexicana.

Juglares de la Edad Media

LITERATURA   *doscientos treinta y nueve* **239**

TEACHING THE READING

 Abenámar ◆◆◆

A. Give students a brief oral resumé in Spanish.

B. Ask a few comprehension questions about the resumé you gave.

C. Call on students with good pronunciation to read the poem as a conversation.

D. With more able groups, ask the more analytical questions in LITERARY ANALYSIS at the bottom of the page.

 **FINE ART CONNECTION**

La gloriosa Alhambra domina toda la ciudad de Granada. Su construcción se comenzó en el siglo XIII. La arquitectura y la decoración son de una belleza incomparable. Uno de sus patios más famosos es el Patio de los Leones al que dan los apartamentos privados.

National Standards

Cultures
Students experience, discuss, and analyze an expressive product of the culture the medieval ballad «**Abenámar**».

Lectura

Abenámar

Patio de los Leones, La Alhambra, Granada, España

¡Abenámar, Abenámar,
moro de la morería,
el día que tú naciste
grandes señales° había!   **señales** *signs*
Estaba la mar en calma,
la luna estaba crecida°:   **crecida** *full*
moro que en tal signo nace,
no debe decir mentira.—
Allí respondiera el moro,
bien oiréis lo que decía:
—Yo te lo diré, señor,
aunque me cueste la vida,
porque soy hijo de un moro
y una cristiana cautiva;
siendo yo niño y muchacho
mi madre me lo decía:
que mentira no dijese,
que era grande villanía°:   **villanía** *cosa no honrada ni honesta*
por tanto pregunta, rey,
que la verdad te diría.
—Yo te agradezco, Abenámar,
aquesa° tu cortesía.   **aquesa** *aquella*
¿Qué castillos son aquéllos?
¡Altos son y relucían!
—El Alhambra era, señor,
y la otra la Mezquita;
los otros los Alixares,
labrados a Maravilla.
El moro que los labraba
cien doblas° ganaba al día,   **doblas** *monedas antiguas*
y el día que no los labra
otras tantas se perdía;
desque° los tuvo labrados,   **desque** *desde que*
el rey le quitó la vida,
porque no labre otros tales
el rey del Andalucía.
El otro es Generalife,
huerta que par no tenía;
el otro Torres Bermejas,
castillo de gran valía°.—   **valía** *valor*
Allí habló el rey don Juan,
bien oiréis lo que decía:

Literary Analysis

¿Qué le dijo el rey a Granada? ¿Qué le daría? ¿Cómo le contesta Granada? ¿Es ella casada o viuda? ¿Con quién está casada? ¿Qué significa la respuesta de Granada? ¿Por qué menciona el término «viuda»?

References to the poem:

Abenámar: príncipe que le pidió ayuda al rey Juan II contra sus rivales de Granada

La morería: territorio de los moros

La mezquita: templo de los mahometanos

Los Alixares: un palacio

El Generalife: palacio de verano de los califas

Torres Bermejas: palacio cerca de la Alhambra

—Si tú quisieses°, Granada,
contigo me casaría;
daréte en arras°y dote°
a Córdoba y a Sevilla.
—Casada soy, rey don Juan,
casada soy, que no viuda;
el moro que a mí me tiene,
muy grande bien me quería.

quisieses quisieras

arras *thirteen coins the groom gives to the bride*
dote *dowry*

EN
DURANGO
COMENZÓ

En Durango comenzó
su carrera de bandido
En cada golpe que daba
Se hacía el desaparecido°

Cuando llegó a La Laguna
Robó la estación de Horizonte
Del entonces lo seguían
Por los pueblos y los montes

Un día ya en el nordeste
Entre Tirso y la Boquilla
Se encontraban acampanadas°
Las fuerzas de Pancho Villa

Gritaba Francisco Villa
El miedo no lo conozco
Que viva Pancho Madero
Y que muera Pascual Orozco

Gritaba Francisco Villa
En su caballo tordillo°
En la bolsa traigo plata
Y en la cintura casquillo°.

«Emiliano Zapata» de Diego Rivera

se hacía el desaparecido *played a disappearing act*

acampanadas
in great danger

tordillo *dapple-gray*

Pancho Villa (en el centro)

casquillo *empty
shells, cartridges*

LITERATURA

doscientos cuarenta y uno ∾ **241**

TEACHING THE READING

❖ **En Durango
comenzó** ❖❖

You may wish to have students take
turns reading portions of the **corrido.** The more able students may wish
to try to contrast the romance
«Abenámar» with the **corrido.**

FINE ART CONNECTION

**Diego Rivera nació en 1886. Es
el primero y más conocido del
grupo de tres pintores mexicanos de murales: él, José
Clemente Orozco y David
Alfaro Siqueiros. Las pinturas
murales de Rivera son de tema
revolucionario. Él pintaba para
educar al pueblo. Los temas de
sus obras son la vida, la historia y los problemas sociales del
peón mexicano.**

National Standards

Cultures
Students experience, dis-
cuss, and analyze an expressive
product of the culture: the
Mexican **corrido,** «**En Durango
comenzó**».

Critical Thinking Activity

Thinking skills: evaluating information
Emiliano Zapata continued fighting in the
South even after Pancho Villa was forced to
retire from politics in the North. Zapata
said, **«Es preferible morir de pie que vivir
de rodillas.»** Explain the meaning of this
sentence.

Did You Know?

Zapata's slogan «**Es preferible morir de
pie que vivir de rodillas**» was adopted as a
watchword by the Republicans during the
Spanish Civil War.

TEACHING TIPS

A. You might want to use *Comprensión A* and *D* as the students read the selections aloud.

B. *Comprensión B, C, E,* and *F* may be done as a homework assignment.

ANSWERS

Comprensión

A 1. **Se llama Abenámar.**
2. **Había grandes señales.**
3. **La mar estaba en calma.**
4. **La luna estaba crecida.**
5. **No debe decir mentiras.**
6. **Es hijo de un moro y una cristiana cautiva.**
7. **Su madre le dijo que no mintiera nunca.**
8. **Le muestra los castillos al rey.**
9. **El Generalife tiene una huerta que no tiene par.**
10. **El rey habla con Granada.**
11. **Le contesta negativamente.**

B **la Alhambra, la Mezquita, los Alixares, el Generalife, las Torres Bermejas**

C Answers will vary.

D 1. **Él comenzó su carrera en Durango.**
2. **Comenzó la carrera de bandido.**
3. **Robó la estación de Horizonte al llegar a La Laguna.**
4. **Las autoridades lo seguían.**
5. **Lo seguían por los pueblos y los montes.**
6. **Se encontraban acampadas entre Tirso y la Boquilla.**
7. **Pancho Villa gritó que él no conocía el miedo, que viva Pancho Madero y que muera Pascual Orozco.**
8. **Estaba montado en un caballo tordillo.**
9. **Tenía plata en la bolsa.**
10. **Tenía casquillo en la cintura.**

Después de leer

Comprensión

A **Abenámar** Contesten.
1. ¿Cómo se llama el moro con quien está hablando el rey Juan II?
2. ¿Qué había en el cielo el día que nació el moro?
3. ¿Cómo estaba la mar?
4. ¿Y la luna?
5. ¿Qué no debe decir el moro?
6. ¿De quién es hijo el moro?
7. ¿Por qué no mentía nunca?
8. ¿Qué le muestra Abenámar al rey?
9. ¿Qué tiene el Generalife?
10. ¿Con quién, o con qué, habla el rey?
11. ¿Le contesta negativa o afirmativamente?

B **Edificios árabes** Den la siguiente información.

Prepare una lista de los edificios que el moro Abenámar le mostró al rey Juan II.

C **La respuesta de Granada** Analicen.

¿Cuál es el significado de la respuesta negativa que le dio la ciudad de Granada al rey Juan II?

D **El corrido** Contesten.
1. ¿Dónde comenzó Pancho Villa su carrera?
2. ¿Qué carrera comenzó?
3. ¿Qué robó al llegar a La Laguna?
4. ¿Quiénes lo seguían?
5. ¿Dónde lo seguían?
6. ¿Dónde se encontraban acampanadas las fuerzas de Pancho Villa?
7. ¿Qué gritó Pancho Villa?
8. ¿En qué estaba montado?
9. ¿Qué tenía en la bolsa?
10. ¿Y en la cintura?

El Generalife, palacio moro, Granada, España

Patio de la acequia en el Generalife

Learning From Photos

El Generalife fue construido como residencia de verano para los califas que buscaban el fresco. Está situado en una colina no muy lejos de la Alhambra. Es un palacio blanco rodeado de jardines bonitos y numerosas fuentes.

E **De otra manera** ¿Cómo se expresa lo siguiente en el corrido?

1. Pancho Villa les causaba daño a sus enemigos, las autoridades del gobierno.
2. Pero las autoridades no lo pudieron encontrar.
3. Yo no tengo miedo de nada ni temo a nadie.

F **Buscando información** Hagan lo siguiente.

1. Prepare una lista de los lugares mencionados en el corrido y búsquelos en un mapa de México.
2. Dé el nombre de un amigo y el de un enemigo de Pancho Villa.

Actividades comunicativas

A **Un edificio moro** Mire las fotografías de los edificios moros que aparecen en este capítulo. Escoja una y descríbala.

B **Los árabes en España** Prepare un informe sobre la influencia de los árabes en España.

C **El moro Abenámar** Escriba un párrafo dando un resumen de lo que sucedió en el romance «Abenámar».

D **Pancho Villa** En un párrafo, escriba lo que Ud. aprendió sobre Pancho Villa al leer el corrido «En Durango comenzó».

Pancho Villa, Emiliano Zapata y sus seguidores

E 1. **En cada golpe que daba...**
   2. **Se hacía el desaparecido.**
   3. **El miedo no lo conozco.**
F 1. **Answers will vary.**
   2. **Emiliano Zapata, amigo; Pascual Orozco, enemigo**

TEACHING TIPS

These *Actividades* may be done as individual assignments or as a cooperative group effort.

Actividades comunicativas

ANSWERS
A–D Answers will vary.

National Standards

Communities Students are encouraged to use the language for personal enrichment by independent reading of a biography of the Mexican revolutionary, Francisco Villa.

Independent Practice

Assign any of the following:
1. Exercises, pages 242–243
2. Workbook, *Literatura*

Chapter 6 Overview

SCOPE AND SEQUENCE pages 244A–244B

TOPICS	FUNCTIONS	STRUCTURE	CULTURE
◆ The Hispanic value system ◆ Proper forms of politeness	◆ How to discuss values that are important to Hispanics and how they compare with American values ◆ How to use the definite and indefinite article in special cases ◆ How to use prepositional pronouns ◆ How to read and discuss a letter to the editor published in a Spanish newspaper ◆ How to explain what one hopes has happened and what one hopes would have happened ◆ How to discuss contrary-to-fact situations ◆ How to indicate ownership ◆ How to point out people and things ◆ How to read and discuss literary works by Pío Baroja and Manuel del Toro	◆ **Usos especiales del artículo** ◆ **El artículo** ◆ **El artículo con los días de la semana** ◆ **El artículo con los verbos reflexivos** ◆ **Artículo indefinido** ◆ **Pronombres con preposición** ◆ **El presente perfecto del subjuntivo** ◆ **Pluscuamperfecto del subjuntivo** ◆ **Cláusulas con** *si* ◆ *El mío, el tuyo, el suyo, el nuestro y el vuestro El suyo, la suya, los suyos, las suyas* ◆ **Los prombres demostrativos**	◆ Hispanic values: family, generosity, and dignity ◆ "The one who invites pays" ◆ The game of «**las monedas**» ◆ "The Charge of the Rough Riders" by Fredric Remington ◆ A letter to the editor ◆ Spanish bullfighters Paquirri, Francisco Rivera Ordóñez, and Antonio Ordóñez ◆ The importance and influence of family **Literatura** ◆ ***Zalacaín el aventurero,*** Pío Baroja ◆ «**Mi padre**», Manuel del Toro

CHAPTER 6 RESOURCES

PRINT	MULTIMEDIA

Planning Resources

Lesson Plans Block Scheduling Lesson Plans	Interactive Lesson Planner

Reinforcement Resources

Writing Activities Workbook Student Tape Manual Video Activities Booklet Glencoe Foreign Language Web Site User's Guide	Transparencies Binder Audiocassette/Compact Disc Program Videocassette/Videodisc Program Online Internet Activities Electronic Teacher's Classroom Resources

Assessment Resources

Situation Cards Chapter Quizzes Testing Program	Testmaker Computer Software (Macintosh/Windows) Listening Comprehension Audiocassette/Compact Disc

Motivational Resources

Expansion Activities	Café Glencoe: **www.cafe.glencoe.com**

Enrichment

Fine Art Transparencies: F-11, F-12	

SECTION	PAGES	SECTION RESOURCES
Cultura **Los valores culturales** **Los valores en común**	246–250	🖌 Transparency 38 🎧 Audiocassette 11A/Compact Disc 7 📁 Writing Activities Workbook, pages 137–139 📁 Student Tape Manual, pages 88–89 📁 Chapter Quizzes, page 77 💾 Testing Program, pages 121–123
Conversación **El que invita paga**	251–254	🖌 Transparency 39 🎧 Audiocassette 11A/Compact Disc 7 📁 Writing Activities Workbook, page 139 📁 Student Tape Manual, page 89 📁 Chapter Quizzes, page 78 💾 Testing Program, pages 124–126
Lenguaje **Invitaciones**	255	🖌 Transparency 40 🎧 Audiocassette 3B/Compact Disc 7 📁 Writing Activities Workbook, page 139 📁 Student Tape Manual, page 90 💾 Testing Program, pages 124–126
Repaso de estructura **Usos especiales del artículo** **El artículo** **El artículo con los días de la semana** **El artículo con los verbos reflexivos** **Artículo indefinido** **Pronombres con preposición**	256–261	🎧 Audiocassette 11A/Compact Disc 7 📁 Writing Activities Workbook, pages 140–144 📁 Student Tape Manual, pages 91–93 📁 Chapter Quizzes, pages 79–84 💾 Testing Program, pages 127–128
Periodismo **Una carta al director** **«Cartas al director»** **La influencia de la familia** **«La muerte de Paquirri»**	262–272	🖌 Transparencies 41A–41B, 42 🎧 Audiocassette 11B/Compact Disc 8 📁 Writing Activities Workbook, pages 145–147 📁 Student Tape Manual, pages 94–95 📁 Chapter Quizzes, pages 85–86 💾 Testing Program, pages 129–133
Estructura **El presente perfecto del subjuntivo** **Pluscuamperfecto del subjuntivo** **Cláusulas con *si*** ***El mío, el tuyo, el suyo, el nuestro y el vuestro*** ***El suyo, la suya, los suyos, las suyas*** **Los prombres demostrativos**	273–280	🎧 Audiocassette 12A/Compact Disc 8 📁 Writing Activities Workbook, pages 148–150 📁 Student Tape Manual, page 98 📁 Chapter Quizzes, pages 87–92 💾 Testing Program, pages 134–136
Literatura ***Zalacaín el aventurero*, Pío Baroja** **«Mi padre», Manuel del Toro**	281–293	🖌 Transparencies 43A–43B, 44A–44B 🎧 Audiocassette 12A–12B/Compact Disc 8 📁 Writing Activities Workbook, pages 151–156 📁 Student Tape Manual, pages 99–101 📁 Chapter Quizzes, pages 93–94 💾 Testing Program, pages 137–142

CAPÍTULO 6

OVERVIEW

In this chapter students will acquire some insight into the Hispanic value system, which they can then compare and contrast with their own. Students will learn the proper forms of politeness regarding invitations. They will read items from a Spanish newspaper. They will also read an excerpt from a novel by Pío Baroja and a short story by Manuel del Toro.

National Standards

Communication
Students will engage in conversations, provide and obtain information, express feelings, and exchange opinions on a variety of topics, especially the values important to Hispanics and to themselves. They will listen to and read authentic language on the same topics.

Learning From Photos

La foto es de una familia mexicana de la capital. Puede preguntarles a los estudiantes:
¿Esta familia sería típica en los EE.UU.? ¿Por qué sí o por qué no?
¿Quién será el señor del pelo blanco?
¿Quién será su esposa? ¿Por qué?
¿Tienen animales? ¿Qué son?
¿Quiénes son los más jóvenes?

Los valores

Objetivos

In this chapter you will do the following:

- tell what values are important to Hispanics, both young and old, and compare them with yours
- identify other uses of the definite and indefinite articles, and of the prepositional pronouns
- read and discuss a letter to the editor published in a Spanish newspaper, and an article about bullfighter Francisco Rivera Ordóñez
- explain what you hope has happened and what you hoped would have happened, discuss contrary-to-fact situations, indicate ownership, and point out people and things
- read and discuss an excerpt from *Zalacaín el Aventurero* by Pío Baroja, and a short story, «Mi padre», by Manuel del Toro

interNET CONNECTION

The Glencoe Foreign Language Web site (http://www.glencoe.com/sec/fl) offers these options that enable you and your students to experience the Spanish-speaking world via the Internet:

- At **Café Glencoe**, the interactive "after-school" section of the site, you and your students can access a variety of additional online resources, including online newspapers, interactive games, and a send-a-postcard feature.
- The online **Proyectos** are correlated to the chapters and utilize Hispanic Web sites around the world.

DIFFICULTY PLATEAUS

In all chapters, each reading selection in *Cultura, Periodismo,* and *Literatura,* as well as the *Conversación* and each structure topic, will be rated as follows:

◆ **Easy**
◆◆ **Intermediate**
◆◆◆ **Difficult**

The overall rating of this chapter is: ◆◆◆ **Difficult.**

RANDOM ACCESS

You may either follow the exact order of the chapter or omit certain sections that you feel are not necessary for your students. Similarly, you may wish to present a literary selection without interruption or you may intersperse some material from the *Estructura* section as you are presenting a literary piece.

EVALUATION

Quizzes There is a quiz for every vocabulary presentation and every structure point.

Tests To accompany *¡Buen viaje! Level 3* there are global tests for both *Estructuras,* a combined *Conversación/Lenguaje* test, and one test for each reading in the *Cultura, Periodismo,* and *Literatura* sections. There is also a comprehensive chapter test.

Chapter Projects

Los valores: **Antes de comenzar el capítulo, pídales a los alumnos que preparen una lista de los diez rasgos de carácter más importantes en nuestra sociedad. Pídales también que preparen una lista de cinco rasgos de carácter que han perdido su valor. Después de leer los valores pueden comparar sus resultados.**

CULTURA
Los valores culturales

Introducción

Los valores son ideas abstractas que los miembros de una cultura aceptan sobre lo que se considera bueno, deseable y apropiado, o, por lo contrario, malo, indeseable e inapropiado. Cada persona desarrolla sus propias metas y ambiciones, pero la cultura provee normas generales a sus miembros. Los valores no indican específicamente lo que el individuo debe hacer, pero sí dan una guía para evaluar a las personas, las ideas y los eventos en cuanto a su mérito, su moral o su «valor». Los valores de una cultura no cambian de repente. Rara vez cambian durante la vida de un solo individuo.

Con ciertas variantes y grados o niveles de importancia, algunos de los valores predominantes en la cultura occidental son: la importancia de la familia, el honor, la dignidad, el individualismo, la generosidad, la comodidad material, la igualdad de todas las personas, el nacionalismo, la eficiencia, la fe en la ciencia. Ahora bien, una cultura puede tener ciertos valores a pesar de que no se respeten. Se puede hablar del valor de la igualdad al mismo tiempo que se cree que su propio grupo es superior a otros. Se puede hablar del honor y portarse de forma deshonrada. Lo importante es que las culturas y las sociedades tienen sus propios valores, y esos valores no son siempre los mismos. Al no conocer los valores de una cultura podemos cometer errores graves cuando tratamos con sus miembros.

«Tamalada» de Carmen Lomas Garza

246

Vocabulario

el/la desconocido(a)   una persona a quien uno no conoce
el parentesco   la relación, conexión familiar
el ascenso   una promoción en el empleo
los recursos   los bienes, medios de subsistencia
el eje   una persona, cosa o circunstancia que constituye el centro de algo
la deshonra   el deshonor, descrédito

lanzarse   tirarse, como se lanza una pelota
girar   dar vueltas
compartir   dividir, repartir algo entre varias personas
recoger   dar protección a un niño, recolectar, juntar
hacerse cargo de   tomar la responsabilidad

la gota

el mendigo

los trapos

Práctica

A **Los valores**   Completen.

1. La familia de Joselito es muy pobre y no tiene los ___ para mantener al niño.
2. Vamos a ___ al pequeño y traerlo a vivir con nosotros. Mira la ropa que tiene, el pobrecito se viste de ___. Parece un ___.
3. Y yo me ___ de ayudarle con sus estudios.
4. Joselito es de nuestra familia, no es un ___.
5. Su madre es la sobrina de mi cuñado, así es que existe un ___.
6. No importa, aunque no tuviera una ___ de nuestra sangre, todavía lo recogeríamos.
7. Tenemos bastante para ___ con el niño.
8. Y no nos vamos a preocupar del dinero, ganaré más porque acabo de recibir un ___.
9. No, tenemos que traerlo aquí, proteger el nombre de la familia y evitar la ___.
10. La familia es el ___ en torno al cual gira nuestra vida.

B **Palabras afines**   Pareen.

1. la deshonra   **a.** reflection
2. suntuosamente   **b.** hierarchy
3. el reflejo   **c.** dishonor
4. la jerarquía   **d.** sumptuously

CULTURA

doscientos cuarenta y siete   **247**

RESOURCES

- Vocabulary Transparencies
- Audio Cassette 11A/Compact Disc 7
- Student Tape Manual
- Workbook
- Chapter Quizzes

TEACHING VOCABULARY

A. Have students repeat the new words in unison after you or Cassette 11A/Compact Disc 7.
B. Call on students to use the new words in an original sentence.
C. Assign the *Práctica* on page 247 for homework.

TEACHING TIPS

Have students open their books and go over the *Práctica* with them.

ANSWERS
Práctica

A 1. **recursos**
  2. **recoger, trapos, mendigo**
  3. **haré cargo**
  4. **desconocido**
  5. **parentesco**
  6. **gota**
  7. **compartir**
  8. **ascenso**
  9. **deshonra**
  10. **eje**
B 1. **c**   3. **a**
  2. **d**   4. **b**

VOCABULARY EXPANSION

Hay varios sinónimos de «mendigo»—mendicante, menesteroso y pordiosero. El nombre de «pordiosero» viene de «por Dios» que es lo que decían los mendigos: «Una limosna, por amor de Dios». La limosna es el dinero que se le da al mendigo.

Additional Practice

You may wish to ask these questions to check comprehension of the *Introducción:*
1. ¿Son los valores ideas concretas o abstractas?
2. ¿Cuál es la fuente de los valores? ¿Quién o quiénes los provee?
3. ¿Con qué frecuencia cambian los valores?

Independent Practice

Assign any of the following:
1. Exercises, page 247
2. Workbook, *Cultura*

TEACHING THE READING

Los valores ◆◆

Note This *Cultura* selection is more difficult than those in other chapters. If you have the students read this silently, they can use the *Comprensión* exercises as a comprehension guide. If you present this section to them, you may wish to follow the suggestions below.

A. La familia: You may wish to ask the following questions: **¿Qué quiere decir «la sangre llama»? ¿Qué diferencias de significado existen en las denominaciones de los parientes en las culturas hispanas y anglosajonas? ¿Qué sabe Ud. de la familia nuclear?**

B. La generosidad: Ask: **¿Es el orgullo o la generosidad el valor hispano?**

C. La dignidad: Compare la posición de un director de una empresa en los Estados Unidos con la de uno en un país hispano.

Los valores en común

La verdad es que no debemos hablar de la cultura hispánica, sino de las culturas hispánicas. España y la veintena de repúblicas hispanoamericanas no comparten todas los mismos valores. En algunos países hispanos la población mayoritaria es indígena, sin una gota de sangre española. En otros, hay tanta herencia italiana, alemana y africana como española. No obstante, hay muchos valores que todos tienen en común.

La familia

La familia es, ha sido siempre y probablemente seguirá siendo el eje en torno al cual gira la vida del hispano. El viejo refrán dice que «la sangre llama». Esto quiere decir que el parentesco impone obligaciones. Estas obligaciones pueden parecer muchas veces injustas y hasta inmorales. Por ejemplo, si soy dueño de una fábrica o un comercio, ¿a quién voy a emplear primero? ¿A alguien que viene de la calle o a un pariente? ¿Y a quién le voy a dar un ascenso? ¿Al hijo de mi primo o a un desconocido? Por otra parte, esta obligación requiere que yo haga todo lo necesario para defender el buen nombre de la familia. Si un hijo de mi primo ha hecho algo que puede traernos deshonra, y si sus padres no tienen los recursos, yo tomo la responsabilidad de proteger nuestro nombre.

Como ya se sabe, la familia nuclear era antes casi desconocida en los países hispanos. La familia hispana consistía en tíos, abuelos, primos, cuñados, nietos y biznietos, muchos de ellos, a veces, viviendo en la misma casa.

Hoy, como tantas otras cosas, la estructura familiar también está cambiando. La familia nuclear ya no es tan rara en España y Latinoamérica. No obstante, en una fiesta familiar todavía se ve, con mucha frecuencia, a cuatro generaciones alrededor de la mesa, gozando del calor humano que provee una familia numerosa.

Existen diferencias de significado en las denominaciones de los parientes en las culturas hispanas y anglosajonas. Para los hispanos, es más importante la generación que el parentesco exacto. Los hijos de los tíos son «primos hermanos». No hay primos terceros o cuartos. Si los primos son de la generación de los padres, se les llama «tíos». Y al hermano del abuelo, se le llama «tío abuelo».

Learning From Photos

Have students describe the people in each of the photos. You may wish to ask: **¿Cómo será el clima en el lugar de la foto de arriba? ¿De qué grupo étnico son los dos jóvenes? En la foto de la derecha, ¿de qué grupo serán los niños? ¿Qué nos indica su grupo? ¿Cómo será el clima allí? Describa a los jóvenes en la foto del centro. ¿De qué grupo étnico serán ellos? ¿Vivirán en un área rural o urbana? La señora de la foto de la izquierda, ¿qué hace (teje)? ¿Cómo lleva el pelo? ¿De dónde será ella? ¿Cuál será su grupo étnico?**

Es muy común, especialmente en áreas rurales, que se «recoja» a los hijos de parientes pobres. Si los padres no pueden mantener a sus hijos, los parientes se hacen cargo de ellos. A veces, los niños recogidos no son realmente parientes, sino sólo vecinos. Aunque, a decir verdad, muchas veces se les trata como algo menos que un hijo y algo más que servidumbre[1].

La importancia de la familia se nota también en la costumbre de llevar los apellidos de la familia de la madre al igual que los del padre. Todos quieren saber quiénes son «tu gente». Y también se nota en el máximo tabú de faltarle el respeto a la madre. El insulto mayor en la cultura hispana es el insulto a la madre. Ha llegado a tal extremo que a veces se evita mencionar a la familia, y mucho menos a la madre.

La generosidad

La generosidad es un valor común a muchas culturas. El norteamericano es famoso por la manera en que se abre las puertas de su casa al extraño; el árabe, el chino, el africano, todos valoran la generosidad. ¿Quién no ha oído de la costumbre del «potlatch», según la cual el indígena de Norteamérica, el Kwakiutl, regala todos sus bienes a sus vecinos, quedándose sin nada?

La generosidad del hispano es también un reflejo del orgullo. El español, por ejemplo, lucha sinceramente por pagar la cuenta en un café o restaurante. El anglosajón echa los dados[2], y si gana, no tiene que pagar la cuenta. El español también juega. Juega a las monedas, y si gana, paga. Es que no quiere «quedar mal». Sin tener dinero para sus propias necesidades, da una limosna al mendigo en la calle. ¿Es generosidad o es orgullo?

La dignidad

Legendario es el exagerado sentido de «dignidad» del castellano viejo. En los cuentos antiguos abundan ejemplos, como el caso del hidalgo[3] «venido a menos[4]» que, aunque esté pasando hambre, anda por la calle con un palillo[5] en la boca para que todos crean que acaba de comer suntuosamente. La dignidad también tiene que ver con el rol que la persona hace en la sociedad. El rol que asume la persona requiere ciertos modales y comportamiento. El norteamericano suele ser bastante flexible en cuanto a jerarquías. El director de una gran empresa se pone trapos para trabajar en su jardín, juega al sóftbol con los empleados, va a la pizzería con la familia, todos en blue jeans y tenis, deja que todos lo llamen por su nombre de pila. El director hispano suele ser siempre mucho más formal, conforme con la importancia de su posición. Su posición le indicará cómo debe vestirse, dónde puede comer, con quiénes puede divertirse y el respeto con que los demás deben tratarlo.

[1] **servidumbre** sirviente
[2] **echa los dados** throws the dice
[3] **hidalgo** nobleman
[4] **venido a menos** having lost status
[5] **un palillo** a toothpick

Zapatería, México D.F.

doscientos cuarenta y nueve 〜 **249**

> ### ABOUT THE SPANISH LANGUAGE
>
> ◆ You may wish to remind students that **parientes** are relatives. **Los padres** are parents. Review the rule for plurals: **hermano y hermana = hermanos; tío y tía = tíos**; etc.
>
> ◆ **Un hidalgo es una persona de linaje o ascendencia noble. Un ejemplo es** *El ingenioso hidalgo don Quijote de la Mancha.* **El significado literal de la palabra es «hijo de algo».**

Critical Thinking Activity

Thinking skills: supporting arguments with reasons

1. **El nepotismo, el dar preferencia exagerada a los parientes en el trabajo, especialmente el trabajo público, es muy mal visto en muchas culturas, e ilegal en varias. ¿Cree Ud. que es peor visto en los países hispanos o en los anglosajones? ¿Por qué?**

2. **En la cultura hispana la gente lleva los apellidos de las familias de los dos padres. En los EE.UU. es frecuente que las mujeres lleven el apellido de soltera como nombre. ¿Qué ventajas y desventajas tiene el sistema hispano de dos apellidos?**

TEACHING TIPS

Have students look up the answers as they are reading the selection. You may tell them to scan the *Comprensión* exercises before reading. The exercises will help the students determine what to look for as they are reading.

ANSWERS
Comprensión

A 1. **Hay diferencias entre las varias culturas hispanas.**
2. **Los indígenas son la mayoría en algunos países hispanos.**
3. **La familia tiende a ser el centro de la vida hispana.**
4. **«La sangre llama» se refiere a las obligaciones familiares.**
5. **La familia hispana tradicional antes consistía en tíos, abuelos, primos, cuñados, nietos y bisnietos.**

B 1. **generaciones**
2. **generación**
3. **hijo**
4. **recoge**
5. **vecinos**
6. **orgullo**
7. **hermano**
8. **dos**

C 1. **no**
2. **sí**
3. **sí**
4. **no**
5. **no**
6. **no**

TEACHING TIPS

A, B, and C These *Actividades* may be done as cooperative group activities or individual efforts.

Actividades comunicativas

ANSWERS
A, B, and C Answers will vary.

Comprensión

A **La familia**   Contesten.
1. ¿Por qué dice el autor que debemos pensar en «las culturas hispánicas»?
2. ¿Cuál es el grupo mayoritario en algunos países hispanos?
3. ¿Qué tiende a ser el centro de la vida hispana?
4. ¿Cuál es el refrán que se refiere a las obligaciones familiares?
5. ¿En qué consistía antes la familia hispana tradicional?

B **El parentesco**   Completen.
1. En una fiesta hispana podría haber parientes de varias ___.
2. Para los hispanos, llamar a uno «tío» o «primo» depende de la ___ de la persona.
3. Un primo hermano es el ___ de un tío.
4. A veces se ___ a los hijos de parientes pobres que no los pueden mantener.
5. Los niños recogidos no son siempre de la familia, a veces, son sólo ___.
6. La generosidad del hispano puede ser reflejo del ___.
7. Un tío abuelo es el ___ del abuelo.
8. Los hispanos suelen llevar ___ apellidos.

C **Más costumbres**   Contesten con **sí** o **no**.
1. El español echa los dados para no tener que pagar la cuenta.
2. El hispano da una limosna hasta cuando necesita el dinero.
3. Los norteamericanos suelen ser más flexibles que los hispanos en cuanto a jerarquías.
4. La familia nuclear no existe en los países hispanos.
5. A los niños recogidos se les trata siempre como si fueran hijos de la familia.
6. El «potlatch» es una costumbre de los indígenas de Centroamérica.

Atlixco, Puebla, México

Actividades comunicativas

A **El potlatch**   Busque información sobre la costumbre del «potlatch». Prepare un breve informe para presentar a la clase.

B **Un tabú**   En la cultura hispana el insulto a la madre es un tabú. ¿Existe este tabú en otras culturas? Con su grupo discuta la existencia de este tabú.

C **¿Quién paga?**   El juego para determinar quien paga o no paga existe en la cultura norteamericana y la hispana. Describa las diferencias y diga lo que Ud. opina. ¿Cuál de las costumbres, la hispana o la americana, prefiere Ud. y por qué?

Additional Practice

You may wish to assign this "research project": **Busque información sobre los Niños Héroes de México y prepare un breve informe. Lo que ellos hicieron aparece en las historias de México y de los EE.UU. La historia de los Niños Héroes tiene lugar durante la guerra entre los EE.UU. y México (1846–48).**

Independent Practice

Assign any of the following:
1. Exercises, page 250
2. Workbook, *Conversación*

Conversación

El que invita paga

Vocabulario

el pelado

las monedas

Los dos señores están jugando a las monedas.

adivinar	predecir, descubrir	**dar vergüenza**	hacer sentir la
agradar	dar gusto, gustar		humillación, ponerse roja la cara

Práctica

A **Se dice así** Exprese de otra manera.

1. ¿Puedes *descubrir* lo que tengo en la mano?
2. Es algo que te va a *gustar*.
3. No quiero nada de ti. No soy un *pobre*.
4. Eso me *humilla*.

CONVERSACIÓN

doscientos cincuenta y uno 251

Did You Know?

El juego de las monedas se hace más
complicado cuando hay más jugadores.
¿Por qué? (Porque hay más combinaciones y posibilidades.)

RESOURCES

- Vocabulary Transparencies
- Audio Cassette 11A/Compact Disc 7
- Student Tape Manual
- Workbook
- Chapter Quizzes

Bell Ringer Review

Use the BRR Transparency 6-2, or write the following on the board: **Para vivir en armonía en la familia, ¿qué debe hacer cada miembro de la familia?**

TEACHING VOCABULARY

You may wish to follow the procedures from previous chapters.

TEACHING TIPS

Have students refer to the illustrations as they do this *Práctica*. After going over this *Práctica*, have students use the new words in original sentences.

ANSWERS
Práctica
A 1. adivinar
   2. agradar
   3. pelado
   4. da vergüenza

ABOUT THE SPANISH LANGUAGE

The word **vergüenza** has various meanings: shame, bashfulness, embarrassment, honor, dignity. An honorable person **tiene vergüenza**. Something that shames or embarrasses **da vergüenza**. A supreme insult is to call someone **un sinvergüenza**.

Use the BRR Transparency 6-3, or write the following on the board: **En cuanto a pagar la cuenta, ¿cuáles son algunas costumbres entre los jóvenes de nuestra sociedad?**

TEACHING THE CONVERSATION

 Escenas de la vida
◆◆ ◆◆

Call on two students to read the *Conversación* aloud with as much expression as possible.

VOCABULARY EXPANSION

Synonyms Have students find synonyms in the *Conversación* for the following words and expressions: **permitir, absolutamente no, no me gusta, un pobre.**

Escenas de la vida

GERARDO: Insisto. Dame la cuenta.
MAURICIO: De ninguna manera. Yo te invité. El que invita paga.
GERARDO: Pero tú nunca dejas que nadie pague. No puedo permitirlo.
MAURICIO: Pues, ¿por qué no jugamos a las monedas? Cada uno se pone de cero a tres monedas en la mano. Entonces adivinamos por turnos el total de monedas. El que gana, paga.
GERARDO: Bueno. Pero no me agrada nada. Esto me está dando vergüenza. Van a creer que soy un pelado.

Advanced Game

Gemelos
Set-up Your class is made up of sets of identical twins who have never met each other. (You could have one set of triplets if you have an uneven number of students.) Prepare two sets of identical index cards that describe each twin in detail. List his/her likes and dislikes, and describe his/her family and family customs. Distribute the cards to the class and have students circulate as if they were at a party.

Game The students must find out things about each other and locate their identical twin within a certain time limit.

Learning From Photos

Have students describe in detail the clothing worn by the two young men. Then, have them prepare a conversation between the two.

ANSWERS

Comprensión

A 1. sí

  2. no

  3. sí

  4. no

  5. no

  6. sí

  7. Mauricio sugiere que ellos jueguen a las monedas.

  8. no

Actividad comunicativa

ANSWERS

A Answers will vary.

ABOUT THE SPANISH LANGUAGE

Una repostería es una tienda donde se preparan y se venden tortas, pasteles y bizcochos. Normalmente no se vende pan en una reposteria.

Comprensión

A **¿Verdad o no?** Contesten con **sí** o **no.**

1. Gerardo quiere pagar la cuenta.
2. Mauricio no tiene ningún inconveniente en que Gerardo pague.
3. Mauricio dice que él tiene que pagar porque él invitó.
4. Gerardo dice que está bien que Mauricio pague.
5. A Gerardo le gusta mucho la idea del juego.
6. Gerardo está muy molesto con esta situación.
7. ¿A Gerardo le gusta la alternativa?

Actividad comunicativa

A **El juego de las monedas** Explique en sus propias palabras el «juego de las monedas».

Critical Thinking Activity

Thinking skills: comparing and contrasting, supporting statements with reasons

1. ¿Cuál es la diferencia entre una familia muy tradicional y una familia muy moderna?
2. ¿Qué prefieres, una familia moderna o una familia tradicional? ¿Por qué?

Learning From Realia

Ask the following questions about the restaurant bill: **¿Qué es este papel? ¿Cómo se llama el restaurante? ¿Qué tipo de comida sirven? ¿Quién es el/la dueño(a)? ¿En qué ciudad está? ¿Cuál es la dirección? ¿Para cuántas personas será la cuenta? ¿Cuánto pagaron en total? ¿Hubo algún impuesto en la cuenta? ¿En qué fecha estuvieron allí?**

Lenguaje
Invitaciones

Te invito a tomar café.

Para invitar a una persona a comer o a tomar algo, se dice:

> **Te invito a tomar...**
> **Quiero convidarte a un...**

Esto quiere decir que Ud. va a pagar.
Para evitar un problema como el de Mauricio, hay que contestar:

> **Te acompaño pero esta vez yo te invito, o no voy.**

Para sólo sugerir que vayan a tomar algo, se puede decir:

> **¿Te apetece tomar algo?**
> **Tengo mucha sed (hambre), voy a tomar algo.**
> **¿Qué te parece si entramos al café (la cafetería, etc.)?**

Si realmente quieres pagar, sin que haya mucho teatro, lo más fácil es decirle al camarero en voz baja:

> **Me trae Ud. la cuenta a mí y a nadie más, por favor.**

Actividad comunicativa

A **Mire, quiero...** Ud. está en un café con sus amigos y no quiere que ninguno de ellos pague la cuenta. Escriba una nota para el camarero. Indíquele quién es Ud. y lo que quiere.

LENGUAJE

TEACHING TIPS

A. Call on individuals to read the expressions with the proper intonation.
B. Then have the entire class repeat them in unison.
C. Give students an expression and call on individuals to identify the circumstances.

Actividad comunicativa

ANSWERS
A Answers will vary.

Additional Practice

Have pairs of students role-play. The first student will give the following invitations with the intention of paying:

a tomar un refresco
a comer un sándwich
a tomar un helado

The second student will suggest, without intending to pay, having the same things.

TEACHING STRUCTURE

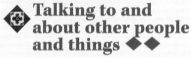 **Talking to and about other people and things** ◆◆

A. Students are familiar with this construction and should have little difficulty with it.

B. Read the explanations to students and call on individuals (or the whole class) to read the model sentences.

TEACHING TIPS

You may wish to go over this *Práctica* without prior preparation.

ANSWERS

Práctica

A	1. las	5. las	8. el
	2. la	6. los	9. la
	3. las	7. El	10. la
	4. los		

TEACHING STRUCTURE

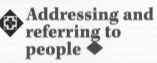 **Addressing and referring to people** ◆

Follow the same procedures as in the presentation above.

256

Repaso de estructura

Talking to and about other people and things
Usos especiales del artículo

In English, when we use an abstract noun or a noun in a generic or general sense, we do not use an article. In Spanish, the definite article is required before nouns used in a general sense and before abstract nouns. Compare the following Spanish and English sentences.

Los mendigos son pobres.	*Beggars are poor.*
Los cobardes tienen miedo.	*Cowards are afraid.*
La gente tiene que trabajar.	*People have to work.*
La bondad es una virtud.	*Kindness is a virtue.*

✦Práctica✦

A **Las clases de ciencias** Completen.

En ___(1) clases de ciencias aprendemos mucho. En ___(2) clase de biología, por ejemplo, estudiamos ___(3) amebas y ___(4) paramecios. En la clase de química aprendemos algo sobre ___(5) sustancias químicas y cómo afectan a ___(6) seres humanos. ___(7) hidrógeno y ___(8) oxígeno son necesarios para la vida humana. En la clase de física estudiamos ___(9) materia y ___(10) energía.

Addressing and referring to people
El artículo

1. The definite article must be used with titles in Spanish when speaking about someone.

> **El señor Antúnez es abogado.**
> **Su esposa, la doctora Antúnez, es médica.**

2. The article is not used with a person's title when speaking directly to the person.

> —**Buenos días, señor Antúnez.**
> —**Hasta mañana, doctora Antúnez.**

Critical Thinking Activity

Thinking skills: supporting arguments with reasons **Hoy, en las Américas como en Europa, se encuentran músicos que tocan en la calle. Ellos viven de las monedas que el público les da. ¿Daría Ud. dinero al músico callejero? ¿Es buena idea o no? ¿Por qué?**

Independent Practice

Assign any of the following:
1. Exercise, page 256
2. Workbook, *Repaso de estructura*

256

Práctica

A **HISTORIETA** En el consultorio de la médica

Completen con el artículo cuando sea necesario.

—Buenos días, ___ señor Gaona.
₁

—Buenos días, ___ señorita Flores.
₂

—¿Cómo se siente Ud. hoy?

—Bastante bien, gracias. ¿Está ___ doctora
₃
Antúnez?

—Lo siento. En este momento ___ doctora
₄
Antúnez no está. Tuvo que ir a la clínica para
una reunión con ___ doctor Cela.
₅

—¿Sabe Ud. a qué hora va a volver?

—Por lo general, ___ doctora Antúnez vuelve de la reunión a las dos y media. Voy a
₆
llamarla por teléfono.

—¡Aló! ___ señorita Vélez, ¿me puede hacer un favor? Cuando salga ___ doctora
₇   ₈
Antúnez, dígale que me llame. Ah, está allí. Le hablaré. Soy yo, Marta Flores, ___
₉
doctora Antúnez. Estoy con ___ señor Gaona. Quiere saber cuándo Ud. vuelve...
₁₀
Bien. Se lo diré. Lo siento, ___ señor Gaona, pero ___ doctora Antúnez no vuelve
₁₁   ₁₂
esta tarde. Pero lo puede atender mañana a las dos.

—Entonces vuelvo mañana. Muchas gracias, ___ señorita Flores.
₁₃

—Hasta mañana, ___ señor Gaona.
₁₄

B ¿Qué hace la doctora Antúnez?
Contesten.

1. ¿Quién busca a la doctora?
2. ¿Quién le habla al señor en el consultorio?
3. ¿Está la doctora o no?
4. ¿Dónde está la doctora?
5. ¿Con quién está ella?
6. ¿Quién llama por teléfono?
7. ¿Quién contesta el teléfono?
8. ¿Quién volverá mañana?

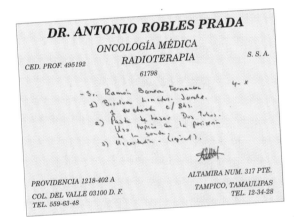

REPASO DE ESTRUCTURA

CAPÍTULO 6
Repaso de estructura

TEACHING TIPS

Have students open their books and do *Práctica A* and *B*. If you perceive that the majority of the class experiences difficulty, assign the exercises for homework and go over them again the next day.

ANSWERS
Práctica

A 1. —   8. la
  2. —   9. —
  3. la   10. el
  4. la   11. —
  5. el   12. la
  6. la   13. —
  7. —   14. —

B 1. El Sr. Gaona busca a la doctora.
  2. La señorita Flores le habla al señor en el consultorio.
  3. No, la doctora no está.
  4. La doctora está en una reunión.
  5. Ella está con el doctor Cela.
  6. La señorita Flores llama por teléfono.
  7. La señorita Vélez contesta el teléfono.
  8. La doctora Antúnez volverá mañana.

ABOUT THE SPANISH LANGUAGE

◆ You may wish to remind students that **la receta** means both a medical prescription and a recipe for food preparation. The verb is **recetar**.

◆ «Ced. Prof.» quiere decir «cédula profesional». ¿Qué será una «cédula profesional» (*professional license*)? ¿Quiénes tendrán que tener este tipo de documento?

Learning From Realia

Ask the following questions about the realia: **¿Qué es este papel? ¿Cómo se llama el médico? ¿Cuáles son sus especialidades? ¿Qué se emplea en la radioterapia? ¿Dónde tiene sus consultas? ¿En qué estado está Tampico? ¿Por qué el número de teléfono del Dr. Robles en el D.F. tiene siete dígitos, y en Tampico sólo seis?**

Independent Practice

Assign any of the following:
1. Exercises, page 257
2. Workbook, *Repaso de estructura*

Repaso de estructura

TEACHING STRUCTURE

 Talking about days of the week ◆

Since this is a review of a simple concept, you may wish to have the students read the explanation and model sentences silently and do the accompanying exercise with books open without prior preparation.

ANSWERS
Práctica
A Answers will vary.

ABOUT THE SPANISH LANGUAGE

The word for "homework" varies from region to region. **Tareas** and **deberes** are the most common terms.

Cross-Cultural Comparison

You may wish to remind students that Spanish calendars begin with Monday, not Sunday. You may also wish to remind them of the origins of the names of the days of the week:
lunes: la Luna
martes: Marte *(Mars),* **el dios romano de la guerra**
miércoles: Mercurio *(Mercury),* **dios romano**
jueves: Iovis *(Jove/Jupiter),* **dios romano**
viernes: veneris, día dedicado a Venus, diosa romana
sábado: del hebreo *shabbath,* **séptimo día de la semana**
domingo: del latín *domenicus die,* **día de Dios**

Talking about days of the week
El artículo con los días de la semana

In Spanish, the definite article is used with the days of the week to convey the meaning "on." Observe the following examples.

Tengo clases los lunes.	*I have classes on Mondays.*
El domingo voy al campo.	*On Sunday I'm going to the country.*

◆Práctica◆

A **¿Durante qué días?** Contesten.
1. ¿Qué días tienes clase de español?
2. ¿Y qué días no tienes clases?
3. ¿Qué haces los sábados?
4. ¿Adónde vas los domingos?
5. Y esta semana, ¿qué haces el sábado?
6. Y, ¿adónde vas el domingo?
7. Algunas personas dicen que deben tener clases los sábados. Tú, ¿qué crees?

LECCIONES Y DEBERES

	ASIGNATURAS	Exponer o Redactar	TEMAS
LUNES	Matemáticas		Ejercicios en la página 235.
MARTES	Historia		Leer el capítulo 9 y contestar las preguntas.
MIÉRCOLES	Inglés		Estudiar para el examen el jueves.
JUEVES	Química		Ir al laboratorio.
VIERNES	Lenguaje		Escribir una composición sobre mis metas personales.
SÁBADO	Geografía		Dibujar un mapa.
DOMINGO			

258 ∽ *doscientos cincuenta y ocho*   CAPÍTULO 6

Learning From Realia

You may wish to ask the following questions about the realia: **¿En cuántas asignaturas tiene deberes el estudiante? ¿En cuál de las ciencias tiene un curso? ¿Qué lengua extranjera estudia? ¿En qué asignatura va a tener una prueba? ¿Cuándo la va a tener?**

Independent Practice

Assign any of the following:
1. Exercise, page 258
2. Workbook, *Repaso de estructura*

Articles of clothing and parts of the body
El artículo con los verbos reflexivos

1. In Spanish when you refer to parts of the body and articles of clothing, you use the definite article with the reflexive pronoun. Observe the following examples.

Yo me lavo las manos antes de comer.	*I wash my hands before eating.*
Después de comer, me cepillo los dientes y me lavo la cara.	*After eating, I brush my teeth and wash my face.*

2. Note also that the object noun is usually in the plural in English when the subject is plural. In Spanish, the noun is in the singular. Observe the following sentences.

Nosotros nos ponemos el casco para trabajar.	*We put on our hardhats to work.*
Y nos quitamos la corbata y la gorra.	*And we take off our ties and caps.*

Since each person has only one hardhat, one tie, and one cap, the singular form is used, not the plural.

 **Práctica**

A **Por la mañana** Completen.

1. Cuando me levanto, me lavo ____.
2. Y me cepillo ____.
3. Cuando hace frío, todos nos ponemos ____ para salir.
4. Cuando llegamos a la escuela, mi hermano y yo nos quitamos ____.
5. El profesor Pérez no ve muy bien y tiene que ponerse ____.

TEACHING STRUCTURE

◆ **Articles of clothing and parts of the body** ◆

A. Have individual students read the explanation aloud in steps 1 and 2.
B. Call on individuals to repeat the model sentences aloud.

TEACHING TIPS

This *Práctica* can be done with books open.

ANSWERS
Práctica
A Some answers will vary.
1. **la cara**
2. **los dientes**
3. **el abrigo, el suéter**
4. **la gorra, el abrigo**
5. **los anteojos**

ABOUT THE SPANISH LANGUAGE

You may wish to remind students of the various words for sweater: **jersey** (Spain), **suéter** (México, Central America, Caribbean), **chompa** (Colombia, Perú, Bolivia), **pulóver** (Argentina).

Independent Practice

Assign any of the following:
1. Exercise, page 259
2. Workbook, *Repaso de estructura*

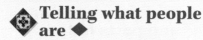

TEACHING STRUCTURE

◆ **Telling what people are** ◆

You may wish to have the students read the explanation silently, then read the model sentences aloud in unison.

TEACHING TIPS

This *Práctica* can be done without previous preparation.

ANSWERS
Práctica

A **1.** Es electricista. Y es un electricista excelente.
2. Es bióloga. Y es una bióloga excelente.
3. Es contable. Y es un contable excelente.
4. Es ingeniera. Y es una ingeniera excelente.
5. Es periodista. Y es una periodista excelente.
6. Es secretario. Y es un secretario excelente.

VOCABULARY EXPANSION

La computadora también se llama computador y ordenador. El «monitor» tiene una «pantalla» igual que el cine. Para «entrar» datos se usa el «teclado» igual que el de la máquina de escribir. Muchas computadoras tienen un «disco duro» interno, y también usan «disquetes». Hay que usar «sofware» para hacer funcionar la computadora. Las computadoras modernas tienen mucha «memoria».

260

Telling what people are
Artículo indefinido

1. The indefinite article is omitted in Spanish when the verb **ser** is followed by an unmodified noun that denotes a profession or nationality. In English, the indefinite article is used. Observe the following sentences.

La señorita Valladares es abogada.	*Ms. Valladares is a lawyer.*
La señora Herrera es viuda.	*Mrs. Herrera is a widow.*
José Romero es viudo.	*José Romero is a widower.*

2. The indefinite article must be used whenever the noun that follows the verb **ser** is modified.

La señorita Valladares es una abogada muy hábil.	*Ms. Valladares is a very able lawyer.*
La señora Herrera es una viuda muy joven.	*Mrs. Herrera is a very young widow.*

A **¿Qué y cómo?** Sigan el modelo.

¿Qué es la doctora Rosas? (médica)
Es médica. Y es una médica excelente.

1. el señor Garcés (electricista)
2. la señorita Bernales (bióloga)
3. el señor Martín (contable)
4. la señora Robles (ingeniera)
5. la señorita Chávez (periodista)
6. el señor Marcos (secretario)

Sala de redacción de un periódico, México D.F.

Did You Know?

Despite the popularity of TV news, newspapers continue to be a major source of information in Spain and Latin America, even for young people. Hispanic newspapers tend to be closely associated with political parties. Often a person's party affiliation can be determined from the newspaper he or she regularly reads. In Spain, for example, the *ABC* is monarchist, *El País* is liberal.

A pronoun after a preposition
Pronombres con preposición

1. A prepositional pronoun follows a preposition, **a, de, en, con, sin,** etc. In Spanish, the prepositional pronouns are the same as the subject pronouns except for **mí** and **ti** (**yo** and **tú**).

SUBJECT PRONOUNS	PREPOSITIONAL PRONOUNS	SUBJECT PRONOUNS	PREPOSITIONAL PRONOUNS
yo	mí	nosotros(as)	nosotros(as)
tú	ti	*vosotros(as)*	*vosotros(as)*
él	él	ellos	ellos
ella	ella	ellas	ellas
Ud.	Ud.	Uds.	Uds.

> **Fernando vive cerca de mí.**
> **Ellos siempre salen con nosotros.**
> **Allí está Josefina. ¿Quién está con ella?**

2. With the preposition **con, mí** becomes **conmigo,** and **ti** becomes **contigo.**

> **Yo quería ir al centro contigo, pero saliste muy temprano.**
> **¿Quieres ir conmigo mañana?**

Una carpa

A **¿Para quién es todo esto?**   Contesten con **sí** y el pronombre apropiado.

1. Esta mochila, ¿es para Gabriela?
2. ¿Para quién es la linterna? ¿Para ti?
3. ¿La carpa es para los muchachos?
4. ¿Es para mí el botiquín?
5. Los sacos de dormir son para Uds., ¿verdad?
6. ¿Esas botas son para Eduardo?
7. La mesita es para nosotros, ¿no?
8. ¿Es para las chicas ese bote?
9. ¿Para quién es el hornillo? ¿Para Ud.?

B **¿Quién va con quién?**   Contesten según se indica. Usen pronombres.

1. ¿Quién va con Ud.? (Antonia)
2. ¿Y quién va a ir conmigo? (Fernando)
3. ¿Los niños van con Uds.? (sí)
4. ¿Quién va contigo? (Ernesto)
5. ¿Las chicas van con Teresa? (no)
6. ¿Pepe va con los muchachos? (sí)

Independent Practice

Assign any of the following:
1. Exercises, pages 260–261
2. Workbook, *Repaso de estructura*

TEACHING STRUCTURE

 A pronoun after a preposition ◆

You may continue in the same fashion as with previous grammatical points in this chapter.

TEACHING TIPS

These *Práctica* can be done with books open or closed without prior preparation.

ANSWERS
Práctica

A 1. Sí, esta mochila es para ella.
  2. Sí, la linterna es para mí.
  3. Sí, la carpa es para ellos.
  4. Sí, el botiquín es para ti.
  5. Sí, los sacos de dormir son para nosotros.
  6. Sí, las botas son para él.
  7. Sí, la mesita es para Uds.
  8. Sí, ese bote es para ellas.
  9. Sí, el hornillo es para mí.
B 1. Antonia va conmigo.
  2. Fernando va a ir contigo.
  3. Sí, los niños van con nosotros.
  4. Ernesto va conmigo.
  5. No, las chicas no van con ella.
  6. Sí, Pepe va con ellos.

RECYCLING

Have the students review vocabulary associated with camping: **la tienda de campaña/la carpa, el hornillo, la silla plegable, el saco de dormir, la caravana, el botiquín, la linterna, la mochila.**

261

TEACHING TIPS

A. Call on a student to read the *Introducción* aloud.

B. After the students have read pages 262–264, have them make a list of differences and similarities between Hispanic and American traditions.

RESOURCES

- Vocabulary Transparencies
- Audio Cassette 11B/Compact Disc 8
- Student Tape Manual
- Workbook
- Chapter Quizzes
- Testing Program

TEACHING VOCABULARY

You may wish to follow previous procedures for vocabulary presentation.

HISTORY CONNECTION

The charge of the Rough Riders ocurrió durante la Guerra de Cuba, entre los EE.UU. y España (1898). Los famosos *Rough Riders* tenían como jefe el Coronel Teodoro Roosevelt, el mismo que llegó a ser presidente de los EE.UU. España perdió la guerra y con ella sus últimas posesiones en las Américas, Cuba y Puerto Rico, y las Islas Filipinas en Asia.

Frederic Remington (1861–1909) sirvió de corresponsal para los periódicos de Hearst durante la Guerra de Cuba. Remington fue pintor y escultor. Sus cuadros y esculturas del *far west* son famosísimos.

262

Periodismo
Una carta al director

Introducción

A veces, hay conflictos porque los valores de una cultura se oponen a los de otra cultura. El resultado puede ser tan grave como una guerra, o puede ser relativamente insignificante, solamente un malentendido entre individuos. Se ha comentado desde hace siglos sobre «el orgullo y la dignidad» del hispano. Estos valores probablemente hicieron que España entrara en guerra contra los Estados Unidos en 1898. Todo el mundo, incluso los españoles, sabía que España jamás podría ganar. Pero rendirse sin luchar hubiera sido deshonroso e indigno.

La carta que sigue la escribió un profesor norteamericano a un periódico español. En la carta, se nota que el profesor no necesariamente comparte los mismos valores que el guía español.

«The Charge of the Rough Riders at San Juan Hill», de Frederic Remington

Vocabulario

el carné

el presupuesto

la bondad

Ella está perpleja.

Critical Thinking Activity

Thinking skills: supporting arguments with reasons Todos los españoles tienen que llevar un carné de identidad oficial del gobierno. Casi todos los países de Europa requieren un carné de identidad. En la Comunidad Europea los ciudadanos de los países miembros sólo tienen que pre-sentar su carné en lugar de un pasaporte para cruzar las fronteras. ¿Se debe requerir un carné de identidad en los EE.UU.? ¿Qué ventajas y desventajas hay en obligar a todos a tener un carné de identidad? Comente.

El guía cobró 4.000 pesetas.
Era inflexible.
Rehusó bajar su precio.

El señor se marchó.

el afecto   la devoción, la amistad
el cargo   la responsabilidad
el trayecto   la distancia, el camino
autorizar   dar la autorización, permitir

proponer   hacer una propuesta
terminantemente   categóricamente,
   de manera concluyente

Práctica

A **¿Cuál es la palabra?**   Completen.

1. Yo los quiero mucho. Les tengo mucho ___.
2. Han sido tan buenos conmigo. Siempre me han tratado con ___.
3. Y hoy yo soy responsable por ellos. Yo estoy a ___ de ellos.
4. Yo pago lo que sea necesario. Lo pagaré de mi propio ___.

B **Expresiones equivalentes**   Expresen de otra manera.

1. Su jefe es *muy rígido*.
2. Ella le *expuso* un plan excelente.
3. Y él lo *rechazó*.
4. Él se negó a estudiarlo *de manera concluyente*.

C **Más expresiones equivalentes**   Pareen.

1. autorizar
2. cobrar
3. el trayecto
4. el carné
5. perplejo

a. hacer pagar
b. el documento de identidad
c. dar permiso
d. la distancia
e. confuso

ABOUT THE SPANISH LANGUAGE

El carné, que es un documento oficial como una licencia de conductor o una tarjeta de identidad, recibe su nombre de la palabra francesa *carnet*.

   «Marcharse» es una expresión muy española. En casi todos los otros países se diría «irse». Una expresión más popular para irse es«largarse», que se aproxima al inglés, *take off, get out of here.*

TEACHING TIPS

You may wish to go over these *Práctica* without any previous preparation.

ANSWERS
Práctica

A 1. **afecto**
   2. **bondad**
   3. **cargo**
   4. **presupuesto**
B 1. **inflexible**
   2. **propuso**
   3. **rehusó**
   4. **terminantemente**
C 1. **c**
   2. **a**
   3. **d**
   4. **b**
   5. **e**

Independent Practice

Assign any of the following:
1. Exercises, page 263
2. Workbook, *Periodismo*

263

TEACHING THE READING

◆ Cartas al director ◆◆

A. You may wish to call on students to read this selection aloud.

B. You may wish to intersperse *Comprensión A, B, C,* and *D* on pages 265–266 as the students read.

C. You may ask volunteers to summarize the letter.

D. You may ask these additional questions about the letter:
¿Qué puede hacer una persona trilingüe? ¿Qué clase de carné tenía el guía? ¿Cuánto tiempo había pasado el guía con los estudiantes?

E. The more able students may have some ideas as to the curious behavior of the guide, in light of Hispanic culture.

Paraphrasing Have students paraphrase the following:

1. **...quiero decirles que siempre he tenido mucho cariño por España...** They may say:
...quiero indicarles que siempre he tenido gran afecto por España...

2. **Durante los quince años que enseño español...** They may say:
Durante los quince años que llevo enseñando español...

3. **Soy guía que habla tres idiomas y ése es el precio.** They may say:
Soy guía trilingüe y ésa es la tarifa.

National Standards

❀ Cultures
Students will gain an understanding of the practices and perspectives of Hispanic culture as they become familiar with the concept of **orgullo y dignidad** illustrated by the reading.

CARTAS
AL DIRECTOR

Sr. Director:
Primero, quiero indicarles a Ud. y a sus lectores que siempre he tenido gran afecto por España y los españoles. Durante los quince años que llevo enseñando español en mi país, he llevado grupos de estudiantes a España casi cada año. Los españoles siempre nos han tratado con cortesía y bondad.

Pero el verano pasado ocurrió algo que me ha dejado un poco confuso. Se lo explicaré.

Yo tenía a mi cargo un grupo de veintidós estudiantes de secundaria. Todos los muchachos hablaban español bastante bien. Fuimos a visitar un monumento importante. Yo tenía un presupuesto bastante limitado. Me habían indicado que las visitas con guías costaban cierta cantidad. Como llegamos tarde, el último grupo de la mañana ya había comenzado su visita. Un señor se nos acercó. Nos dijo que era guía oficial y nos mostró su carné. Él dijo que era «guía trilingüe» y que cobraba una cantidad bastante por encima de la tarifa por visitas oficiales. Yo le dije que me parecía mucho. Él me contestó que era porque los guías de las visitas oficiales sólo hablaban español, y él era «guía trilingüe» y estaba autorizado a cobrar la cantidad que había mencionado. Yo le dije que sí, que entendía, pero que no queríamos que hablara ni inglés ni francés, sólo español, como los guías para las visitas oficiales. Iban a cerrar pronto, y el tiempo se nos iba. Yo le dije que llevara a los muchachos y que hablaríamos después.

Después de la visita el señor vino a cobrar. Yo le dije que me parecía justo que él cobrara más, pero que lo que él quería era mucho. Le propuse que dividiéramos en dos la diferencia entre la tarifa «oficial» y lo que él quería, y yo lo pagaría con mucho gusto. Él rehusó terminantemente.

—Soy guía trilingüe, y ésa es la tarifa.

—Pero sólo me autorizan a pagar la tarifa oficial.

—Entonces, es un regalo. Adiós.

Yo no pude creerlo. El señor dio la vuelta y empezó a marcharse. Yo fui detrás de él, tratando de pagarle. Y él repitió:

—Es un regalo.

Así estuvimos durante un trayecto de cien metros. Yo, con el dinero en la mano, ofreciéndoselo. Y él repitiendo aquello del «regalo». Yo todavía no lo entiendo. Ese señor había pasado hora y media con los estudiantes. Ellos estuvieron muy contentos con la visita. Yo quise ser justo con el señor. La diferencia entre las dos tarifas saldría de mi propio bolsillo.[1]

Yo les pregunto, ¿por qué fue tan inflexible ese señor? Lo que yo le propuse me parece sumamente razonable. ¿No les parece a Uds.?

Sigo perplejo. Espero que alguien me explique la curiosa conducta del guía.
Filadelfia, Pensilvania EE.UU.

[1] **bolsillo** *pocket*

Cooperative Learning Activity

In groups of five, three students will be the panel of judges, one will be the **"guía"** and the other the **"profesor."** The guide and the teacher will present his or her "case" to the panelists who will ask questions and prepare a "judgment" **(un juicio)** regarding who is right **(tiene razón).**

Independent Practice

Assign any of the following:
1. Exercises, pages 265–266
2. Workbook, *Periodismo*

⚜ Comprensión ⚜

A   **El guía**   Contesten.

1. ¿Cuál es la profesión de la persona que escribe?
2. ¿Qué actitud muestra hacia España?
3. ¿Qué ha hecho muchas veces durante los últimos años?
4. ¿A quiénes han tratado los españoles con bondad?
5. ¿Cuándo ocurrió el incidente que cuenta el escritor?
6. ¿Qué eran las 22 personas que iban con el señor?
7. ¿Qué iban a visitar?

B   **Un incidente**   Escojan.

1. El incidente le dejó al escritor ___.
   a. confuso   **b.** inflexible   **c.** autorizado
2. La habilidad de hablar español de los estudiantes era ___.
   a. casi nada   **b.** muy poca   **c.** bastante buena
3. Todos fueron a visitar ___.
   a. una universidad   **b.** un teatro   **c.** un monumento
4. Lo que era «limitado» era ___ que tenía el profesor.
   a. el tiempo   **b.** la paciencia   **c.** el dinero
5. El último grupo de la mañana ya había ___ la visita.
   a. comenzado   **b.** cancelado   **c.** terminado

Cúpula del Mihrab, Gran Mezquita de Córdoba, España

Ruinas de Medina Azara, Córdoba, España

Real Monasterio de San Lorenzo de El Escorial, España

CAPÍTULO 6
Periodismo

TEACHING TIPS

Have students look for the information in *Comprensión A, B, C,* and *D* before going over them in class. If you don't think this information is important, you can omit the exercises and just have students scan the letter.

ANSWERS
Comprensión

A 1. Él es profesor de español.
    2. Él tiene afecto hacia España.
    3. Ha llevado grupos de estudiantes a España muchas veces.
    4. Los españoles lo han tratado a él y a los estudiantes con cortesía y bondad.
    5. El incidente ocurrió el verano pasado.
    6. Las 22 personas eran estudiantes.
    7. Iban a visitar un monumento importante.

B 1. a
    2. c
    3. c
    4. c
    5. a

Learning From Photos

1. El mihrab es el lugar más sagrado de una mezquita, hacia donde todos deben mirar cuando están rezando. La foto es del Mihrab de la Mezquita de Córdoba, construida en el siglo VIII.
2. Las ruinas del palacio de Medina Azara quedan a unos once kilómetros de Córdoba. El califa de Córdoba hizo construir el palacio en el siglo X para su favorita.
3. El Real Monasterio de San Lorenzo está en El Escorial (the Ash Heap) a unos 50 kilómetros de Madrid. El rey Felipe II lo mandó construir en memoria de su padre, el emperador Carlos V.

265

Periodismo

C **Un guía trilingüe**   Corrijan las oraciones falsas.

1. El guía le enseñó su dinero al señor.
2. El guía hablaba dos idiomas.
3. El guía cobraba menos que la tarifa oficial para grupos.
4. Además del español, el guía hablaba italiano y alemán.
5. El profesor quería que el guía hablara solamente inglés.
6. Los guías para las visitas oficiales hablaban inglés y francés.
7. Después de la visita, el guía vino a pagar.
8. El guía aceptó la propuesta del señor.

D **Análisis**   Expliquen.

1. ¿Por qué tenía prisa el profesor en comenzar la visita?
2. ¿Qué quería decir el profesor con «le dije que llevara a los muchachos y que hablaríamos después»?
3. ¿Cuál fue la proposición que le hizo el profesor al guía?
4. ¿Qué quería decir el guía con «es un regalo»?
5. Explique por qué el profesor no quería pagar la cantidad que quería cobrar el guía.

Monasterio Abadía de Montserrat, Barcelona, España

Actividades comunicativas

A **Un asunto personal**   Con su grupo, discutan y determinen si la propuesta del profesor fue «razonable» o no.

B **Un malentendido**   Escriba lo que Ud. considera el problema fundamental al que se refiere la carta del profesor. ¿Cuál ha sido el conflicto de valores?

C **Un lugar interesante**   Describa a la clase, en detalle, un lugar de interés turístico en su pueblo o ciudad.

D **Un anuncio**   Con su grupo, prepare un anuncio ofreciendo sus servicios como guía para turistas hispanos que visitan su estado. Incluya los lugares de interés, las horas y los días de visita y las tarifas.

Ávila, España

CAPÍTULO 6

Learning From Photos

El monasterio de Montserrat, en las montañas cerca de Barcelona, se fundó en 880 d. C. Miles de peregrinos visitan el monasterio cada año para ver a la Virgen Negra de Montserrat que, según la tradición, fue labrada en madera por San Lucas, el evangelista.

GEOGRAPHY CONNECTION

La ciudad de Ávila es famosa por ser uno de los mejor preservados pueblos amurallados de la Edad Media. Las murallas fueron levantadas por orden del rey Alfonso I en 1090. Las murallas con sus 88 torres encierran completamente la ciudad con una extensión de más de dos kilómetros y medio.

La influencia de la familia

Introducción

En una cultura donde tanta influencia tiene la familia y donde el respeto a los padres es un valor universal, no es raro que un hijo siga los pasos del padre y del abuelo. Y si añadimos la importancia que tiene la valentía en la jerarquía de valores, es casi de esperar que Francisco Rivera Ordóñez, hijo de «Paquirri» y nieto de Antonio Ordóñez, se hiciera torero.

Hoy Francisco Rivera Ordóñez es uno de los toreros más famosos de España. La siguiente entrevista apareció en la revista *Hola* cuando él comenzaba su carrera y sólo tenía 19 años.

Antonio Ordóñez

«Paquirri», padre de Francisco Rivera Ordóñez

doscientos sesenta y siete ∽ **267**

TEACHING TIPS

◆ **La influencia de la familia** ◆◆◆

Have the students read the *Introducción* silently.

ABOUT THE SPANISH LANGUAGE

The English word "respect" has two equivalents in Spanish, **respeto** and **respecto**. "Respect" in the sense of "esteem" or "honor" is **respeto**. "Respect" in the sense of "reference to" or "regarding" is **respecto**, i.e., «Con *respecto* a los documentos...» «Siempre le tratamos con enorme *respeto* porque es una persona muy honrada.»

Did You Know?

1. La foto de Antonio Ordóñez fue tomada en la Plaza de Toros de Ronda, la plaza de toros más antigua del mundo (1784). Pedro Romero, el padre del toreo moderno, era rondeño, igual que Antonio Ordóñez. *Antonio Ordóñez murió en 1998.*

2. Paquirri era el apodo de Francisco Rivera, torero español. Nació en Azahara de los Atunes (Cádiz) en 1948 y murió de una cornada en la Plaza de Toros de Pozoblanco (Córdoba) en 1984.

3. Ernest Hemingway pasó la temporada taurina de 1958 con Antonio Ordóñez, lo que resultó en el libro titulado *The Dangerous Summer.*

RESOURCES

- Vocabulary Transparencies
- Audio Cassette 11B/Compact Disc 8
- Student Tape Manual
- Workbook
- Chapter Quizzes
- Testing Program

TEACHING VOCABULARY

A. Present the new words and have students repeat them after you or Cassette 11B/Compact Disc 8.

B. You may wish to go over the words and definitions on this page in the usual way.

TEACHING TIPS

Have the students prepare the *Práctica* and then go over them in class.

ANSWERS
Práctica

A 1. extraña
2. el toreo
3. taurino
4. venas
5. ha heredado
6. afición

B 1. meta
2. casta
3. asemeja
4. está dispuesto
5. fluye

268

Vocabulario

el toreo

el torero

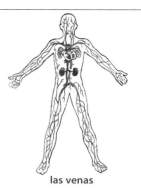
las venas

la casta la clase, la calidad
la meta el gol, el objetivo, el fin
la tontería una cosa estúpida, una estupidez
el poder la fuerza, la energía
la afición la inclinación, el amor por alguien o algo

elegir seleccionar, escoger
vengar tomar venganza, vindicar

fluir correr un líquido como el agua o la sangre
heredar recibir de los padres, abuelos, etc.
estar dispuesto(a) estar listo(a) o preparado(a) para hacer algo
asemejarse ser parecido a
extrañar sorprender, asombrar
aportar dar, contribuir

taurino(a) que tiene relación con el toreo

Práctica

A **HISTORIETA** **Expresiones equivalentes**

Expresen de otra manera.

1. A mí me *sorprende* mucho que sea torero.
2. Sé que siempre le ha interesado *el arte de torear*.
3. Pero no creía que iba a meterse en el mundo *de los toros*.
4. Ya sé que corre por sus *arterias* sangre taurina.
5. Y que *ha recibido* de su padre y su abuelo el deseo de torear.
6. Tiene una gran *inclinación* al toreo.

B **¿Cuál es la palabra?** Completen.

1. La ___ del torero es llegar a ser el número uno.
2. El muchacho es muy valiente, tiene mucha ___ de torero.
3. En eso se ___ mucho a su padre, es igual que él.
4. El chico ___ ___ a hacer cualquier cosa para triunfar.
5. Por sus venas ___ sangre de grandes toreros.

Antonio Ordóñez

Independent Practice

Assign any of the following:
1. Exercises, page 268
2. Workbook, *Periodismo*

LA MUERTE DE PAQUIRRI

Cuando se cumplen nueve años de la trágica muerte de Paquirri

FRANCISCO RIVERA ORDÓÑEZ

«Nunca elegí ser torero para vengar la muerte de mi padre, aquéllo fue un accidente.»

Ya han pasado nueve años desde la trágica muerte de Francisco Rivera, «Paquirri», en el coso[1] de Pozoblanco. Su hijo mayor, Francisco Rivera Ordóñez, a sus diecinueve años, ha heredado la afición familiar y está dispuesto a continuar con éxito la tradición.

Por sus venas fluye sangre taurina, pues es nieto, hijo y sobrino de toreros. Tras dos años como novillero, en los que fue dirigido por su apoderado[2] y abuelo, Antonio Ordóñez, Francisco nos habla ahora del pasado, del presente y del futuro.

—¿En qué momento te diste cuenta de que querías ser torero?

—Desde muy pequeño, pero cuando me decían «torea» sentía miedo y no quería. Ya a los dieciséis años comencé a ir al campo y a prepararme, hasta que mi abuelo me dijo: «Vas a debutar».

Desde que recuerdo he oído hablar de mi padre, de mi abuelo, de mi tío, de toda la familia. Por tanto, era normal que sintiera curiosidad.

—¿A quién crees que te asemejas en el ruedo[3]?

—No sé si me parezco más a mi padre o a mi abuelo, porque no les he visto torear. Lo que sí he visto han sido videos, pero no es igual. Creo que tengo mi propio estilo.

—¿Qué recuerdas del día que debutaste en Ronda?

—Ese día me di cuenta de la responsabilidad que tenía, porque la plaza estaba llena, y eso, allí, nunca había ocurrido en una novillada sin picadores[4]. El paseíllo[5] fue muy duro.

—¿Cuáles han sido los consejos[6] que has recibido de tu abuelo?

—Que esto es muy difícil, que lo más fácil es que yo no sea torero. Mi abuelo conoce esto bien y sabe lo difícil que es.

---

[1] **el coso** la plaza de toros
[2] **apoderado** manager
[3] **el ruedo** the bullring
[4] **una novillada sin picadores** a novice bullfight
[5] **el paseíllo** el desfile de toreros
[6] **los consejos** advice

Did You Know?

Una novillada sin picadores is a bullfight for novice matadors with small bulls. **Picadores** are used only when the bulls are above a certain size and weight. Bullfighters have entered the professional ranks when they appear in **novilladas con picadores.**

National Standards

Cultures
Students will gain further understanding of the practices and perspectives of Hispanic culture as they increase their knowledge of the role of the family while reading about a family of famous bullfighters.

TEACHING THE READING

◈ La muerte de Paquirri ◆◆◆

A. Before assigning the reading for homework, have students look at the title of the article, as well as the interview questions, and ask them to tell you briefly what the article is about.

B. Have students look for the information from the *Comprensión* on pages 271–272 and write the answers as they read the interview at home. Go over the exercises in class.

ABOUT THE SPANISH LANGUAGE

◆ You may wish to point out the use of **les** for **los** when Francisco says, **"...porque no les he visto torear"**. It is very common in Spain to use the indirect object pronoun **le** as a direct object pronoun instead of **lo** when referring to a person. This **"leísmo"** is considered acceptable. The use of **les** for **los** is less acceptable.

◆ Both pronunciations and spellings—**video** and **vídeo**—are accepted. **Vídeo** is more common in Spain; **video,** in parts of Latin America.

◆ **Debutar** is derived from the French **debut.** The appropriate Spanish word is **presentar. Debutar** is almost always used when referring to a bullfighter's first appearance in the plaza.

> «Mi abuelo ha sido siempre mejor torero que mi padre, pero mi padre era más valiente, tenía más poder y mucha casta.»

—Vuestras relaciones actuales parecen no ser todo lo buenas que se desearía.

—No. Lo que ocurre es que he cambiado de apoderado. Mi abuelo me había dicho que cuando creyera que estaba preparado para volar me dejaría. Y es lo que ha pasado. En la última época, él me protegía demasiado, sufría mucho cuando me veía torear y pasaba malos ratos. Mi abuelo es mi amigo, mi consejero[7] y ha sido casi mi padre, aunque también tengo a mi madre, claro.

—Si tuvieras que elegir entre dos toreros: Paquirri y Antonio Ordóñez, ¿con cuál te quedarías?

> «La separación de mi abuelo y mía tenía que ocurrir; él me dijo que cuando estuviera preparado me dejaría volar.»

—Considero más bonito el toreo que hacía mi abuelo. Creo que es la forma de torear adecuada. Mi abuelo ha sido mejor torero que mi padre. Sin embargo, mi padre tenía más poder, era más valiente y, además, tenía mucha casta. Mi abuelo ha sido el número uno de todos los tiempos. No hay más vuelta de hoja[8]. Por eso no es de extrañar que diga que mi abuelo es mejor que mi padre.

—¿A qué aspiras en la vida?

—Lo que me motiva y a lo que aspiro es a ser más que mi abuelo. Es difícil, casi imposible, pero ésa es mi meta.

—¿Se puede pensar que elegiste este camino quizá para vengar la muerte de tu padre en el ruedo?

—Cuando tenía diez años y murió mi padre decidí ser torero. Pero que yo sea torero para vengar la muerte de mi padre es una tontería. En ese caso sería exterminador de toros. La muerte de mi padre me ha afectado y marcado en la misma medida que puede afectar a cualquier niño al que se le muera su padre. La muerte de mi padre no ha tenido nada que ver en mi decisión de torear. Al contrario. Yo nunca he pensado en ello, sino en la gloria que aportó mi padre al toreo... ¿Y si mi padre hubiese perdido la vida en un coche, entonces ya nunca me hubiera podido montar en uno?

[7] **consejero** *advisor*
[8] **No hay más vuelta de hoja.** *No ifs, ands, or buts.*

Critical Thinking Activity

Thinking skills: evaluating information

You may wish to ask students to identify and interpret the metaphor in "**...él me dijo que cuando estuviera preparado me dejaría volar**".

You may also wish to have them explain the seeming contradiction in: «**Mi abuelo ha sido siempre mejor torero que mi padre, pero mi padre era más valiente, tenía más poder y mucha casta.**»

Una corrida de toros

Comprensión

A **Paquirri** Contesten.

1. ¿Cuál era el verdadero nombre de «Paquirri»?
2. ¿Cuál era su profesión?
3. ¿Dónde murió Paquirri?
4. ¿Qué relación existe entre Paquirri y Francisco Rivera Ordóñez?
5. ¿Cuántos años tenía Francisco Rivera Ordóñez cuando lo entrevistaron?
6. ¿Qué ha heredado él de su padre?
7. ¿Qué parientes de Francisco han tenido la misma profesión?
8. ¿Cuántos años hace que Francisco es torero?

B **El joven Francisco** Completen.

1. Antonio Ordóñez es el ___ del joven Francisco.
   a. padre   **b.** tío   **c.** abuelo
2. El joven comenzó a prepararse para su profesión cuando tenía ___ años.
   a. nueve   **b.** dieciséis   **c.** diecinueve
3. El joven Francisco cree que su estilo es ___.
   a. como el de su padre   **b.** como el de su abuelo   **c.** original en él mismo
4. Francisco se dio cuenta de su responsabilidad cuando ___.
   a. debutó en Ronda   **b.** su abuelo se lo dijo   **c.** murió su padre
5. El primer apoderado de Francisco era también su ___.
   a. padre   **b.** tío   **c.** abuelo
6. «Vuestras relaciones» son las relaciones entre ___.
   a. Paquirri y su hijo   **b.** el joven Francisco y su abuelo
   c. Paquirri y Antonio Ordóñez
7. Más que nada, el joven Francisco quiere ___.
   a. ser mejor que su abuelo   **b.** vengar a su padre   **c.** no ser torero

PERIODISMO   *doscientos setenta y uno* 〰 **271**

ANSWERS
Comprensión
A 1. El verdadero nombre de «Paquirri» era Francisco Rivera.
   2. Él era torero.
   3. Paquirri murió en Pozoblanco.
   4. Ellos son padre e hijo.
   5. Francisco Rivera Ordóñez tenía diecinueve años.
   6. Él ha heredado la sangre taurina de su padre.
   7. El padre y el abuelo de Francisco han tenido la misma profesión.
   8. Hace tres años que Francisco es torero.
B 1. c
   2. b
   3. c
   4. a
   5. c
   6. b
   7. a

Additional Practice

Have pairs of students role-play the parts of young Francisco and his grandfather. Francisco wants to strike out on his own. His grandfather disagrees. Pairs should prepare short conversations.

TEACHING TIPS

Both *Actividades A* and *B* should be of maximum interest to students. Those not wishing to enter the debate in *Activity B* might want to do a cooperative report on Hemingway and his work on bullfighting.

Actividades comunicativas

272

C **¿Sí o no?** Corrijan las oraciones erróneas.

1. El padre, el tío y el abuelo de Francisco han sido todos toreros.

2. Paquirri murió en la plaza de toros de Ronda.

3. Francisco se preparaba para su profesión en la ciudad.

4. Francisco debutó en la plaza de toros de Pozoblanco.

5. Su abuelo le decía que el toreo era muy fácil.

6. El abuelo pasaba malos ratos cuando veía torear a su nieto.

7. El joven cree que su padre era mejor torero que su abuelo.

8. Francisco tenía dieciséis años cuando se murió su padre.

9. La muerte de su padre no influyó en su decisión de torear.

D **¿Dónde dice... ?** Busquen.

1. quién fue su primer apoderado

2. cómo fue su debut como torero

3. lo que el joven piensa del toreo de su padre

4. lo que dice del toreo de su abuelo

5. cuándo decidió hacerse torero

6. lo que lo motivó a hacerse torero

Ronda, España

Actividades comunicativas

A **Hemingway** El famoso autor norteamericano Ernest Hemingway escribió mucho sobre los toros. Una de sus últimas obras fue *The Dangerous Summer*, en la que habla de una temporada taurina con Antonio Ordóñez. Lea la obra y prepare un resumen en español.

B **Debate** Muchas personas creen que la corrida de toros es salvaje y que se debe prohibir. Muchos españoles dicen lo mismo del boxeo. Dividan su grupo en dos y preparen un debate sobre el tema: ¿Prohibir el boxeo o la corrida? ¿Por qué o por qué no?

Did You Know?

Ronda es un pueblo antiquísimo. Allí se escondían los bandidos y contrabandistas de los siglos XVIII y XIX. Ronda era casi inaccesible hasta que se construyó el Puente Nuevo en 1761. Sólo se podía llegar al pueblo por un estrecho y peligroso camino, fácil de proteger. Artistas desde Goya hasta Hemingway se han enamorado de la espectacular belleza de este pueblo andaluz.

Independent Practice

Assign any of the following:

1. Exercise, pages 271–272

2. Workbook, *Periodismo*

Estructura

Feelings about what has happened
El presente perfecto del subjuntivo

1. The present perfect subjunctive is formed by using the present subjunctive of the auxiliary verb **haber** and the past participle. Study the following forms of the present perfect subjunctive.

INFINITIVE	hablar	comer	vivir
yo	haya hablado	haya comido	haya vivido
tú	hayas hablado	hayas comido	hayas vivido
él, ella, Ud.	haya hablado	haya comido	haya vivido
nosotros(as)	hayamos hablado	hayamos comido	hayamos vivido
vosotros(as)	*hayáis hablado*	*hayáis comido*	*hayáis vivido*
ellos, ellas, Uds.	hayan hablado	hayan comido	hayan vivido

2. The present perfect subjunctive is used when the action in the dependent clause occurred before the action in the main clause.

Me alegro mucho de que tú hayas venido.   *I'm very glad that you have come.*
Dudo que ellos lo hayan visto.   *I doubt that they have seen it.*

A   **Un buen estudiante**   Contesten según el modelo.

> **¿Luis ha recibido una nota alta?**
> **Es posible que haya recibido una nota alta.**

1. ¿El profesor le ha felicitado?
2. ¿Ha ganado Luis un premio?
3. ¿Le han dado una beca?
4. ¿Tú también has recibido un sobresaliente?
5. ¿Yo he sacado una nota buena también?
6. ¿Hemos sido los mejores de la escuela?

RESOURCES

- Workbook
- Student Tape Manual
- Audio Cassette 12A/Compact Disc 8
- Computer Software: *Estructura*
- Chapter Quizzes
- Testing Program

TEACHING STRUCTURE

◈ Feelings about what has happened ◆◆

Note You may wish to intersperse the grammar points as you are doing other sections of the chapter.

A. Have students read the explanatory material in steps 1 and 2.

B. Have students repeat the forms in step 1 aloud.

C. Have the students read the model sentences aloud in step 2.

TEACHING TIPS

A. Have students open their books and do the exercises without prior preparation.

B. For added reinforcement, if necessary, assign the *Práctica* for homework.

C. Go over them once again the following day in class.

ANSWERS

Práctica

A **Es posible que...**
1. él le haya felicitado...
2. haya ganado...
3. le hayan dado...
4. yo también haya recibido...
5. tú hayas sacado...
6. hayamos sido...

Learning From Photos

Have students describe the scene in the photo. This is a good opportunity to reinforce location: **a la izquierda, en frente de, la segunda a la derecha,** etc. You may wish to ask: **¿Dónde están estos jóvenes? ¿Qué están haciendo? ¿Dónde está sentado el muchacho a quien todos miran? ¿Qué les estará diciendo? ¿Cómo reaccionan las muchachas? ¿Quién parece que no le está prestando atención?**

273

B **No, no lo creo.**   Contesten con **no, no creo.**

1. ¿La viuda ha llegado?
2. ¿Ella llamó?
3. ¿El hijo ha ido a buscarla?
4. ¿Los parientes la vieron salir?
5. ¿Ella ha indicado cómo viene?
6. ¿Uds. la han conocido?
7. ¿Se habrá perdido?
8. ¿Yo le di malas direcciones?

C **HISTORIETA El informe**

Completen con el presente perfecto del subjuntivo.

Aunque es posible que ellos ___(1)___ (terminar) la obra, nosotros lo dudamos. Primero, es difícil que los materiales ___(2)___ (llegar) a tiempo. Y, segundo, no es posible que ___(3)___ (poder) pagar a todos los empleados a tiempo. Los bancos se negaron a ayudarlos, y es probable que ___(4)___ (tener) que vender alguna maquinaria. Quizás ellos ___(5)___ (encontrar) dinero en otra parte, pero es dudoso.

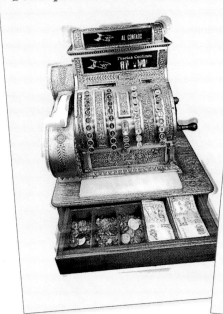

Para que su negocio funcione...

Cuente con todo nuestro apoyo.

El Banco Bilbao Vizcaya le ofrece toda una serie de soluciones para que usted consiga los mejores resultados en su negocio.
Productos financieros, equipos tecnológicos y servicios especializados para el comercio, con el eficaz complemento de nuestra experiencia en el servicio a la pequeña y mediana empresa.
Toda una línea de apoyo para que su negocio funcione.

BBV

BANCO BILBAO VIZCAYA

Learning From Realia

You may wish to ask these questions about the realia: **¿Para qué compañía es el anuncio? ¿A quién se dirige el anuncio? ¿Qué se les ofrece a los clientes? ¿Qué es la máquina que aparece en la foto? (Es una caja registradora.)**

Independent Practice

Assign any of the following:
1. Exercises, pages 273–274
2. Workbook, *Estructura*

Feelings about what had happened
Pluscuamperfecto del subjuntivo

1. The pluperfect subjunctive is formed with the imperfect subjunctive of the auxiliary verb **haber** and the past participle. Study the forms of the pluperfect subjunctive.

INFINITIVE	hablar	comer	vivir
yo	hubiera hablado	hubiera comido	hubiera vivido
tú	hubieras hablado	hubieras comido	hubieras vivido
él, ella, Ud.	hubiera hablado	hubiera comido	hubiera vivido
nosotros(as)	hubiéramos hablado	hubiéramos comido	hubiéramos vivido
vosotros(as)	hubierais hablado	hubierais comido	hubierais vivido
ellos, ellas, Uds.	hubieran hablado	hubieran comido	hubieran vivido

2. The pluperfect subjunctive is used after a verb in a past tense that requires the subjunctive, when the action of the verb in the subjunctive occurred prior to the action of the verb in the main clause.

Me sorprendió que ellos hubieran hecho tal cosa.
It surprised me that they had (would have) done such a thing.

✦Práctica✦

Una guardia civil

A **La Guardia Civil** Completen con el pluscuamperfecto del subjuntivo.
1. Temíamos que ellos ___ (volver).
2. Pero nos alegramos de que la Guardia Civil ___ (venir).
3. Yo dudaba que ellos ___ (poder) regresar a casa.
4. Nadie creía que los guardias civiles ___ (arrestar) a los ladrones.
5. Era increíble que ellos ___ (encontrar) a todos.

B **Lo dudaba.** Contesten con **Dudaba que** y el pluscuamperfecto del subjuntivo.
1. ¿Ellos habían conseguido muchos clientes nuevos?
2. ¿Ramírez había recibido un contrato?
3. ¿La empresa había vendido todo el producto?
4. ¿Tú habías conocido al director?
5. ¿El tesorero había pedido dinero prestado al banco?
6. ¿Nosotros habíamos comprado sus acciones (*stocks*)?
7. ¿Yo había recibido su informe anual?

ESTRUCTURA doscientos setenta y cinco **275**

TEACHING STRUCTURE

◆ **Discussing contrary-to-fact situations** ◆◆◆

A. Have the students read the explanatory material in steps 1 and 2.

B. Have the students repeat the model sentences.

TEACHING TIPS

Have students prepare these *Práctica* for homework before going over them in class the following day.

ANSWERS
Práctica
A Answers will vary.

Discussing contrary-to-fact situations
Cláusulas con **si**

1. **Si** (*If*) clauses are used to express contrary-to-fact conditions. **Si** clauses conform to a specific sequence of tenses. Study these examples.

Si tengo tiempo, iré al cementerio.	*If I have time, I will go to the cemetery.*
Si tuviera tiempo, iría al cementerio.	*If I had time, I would go to the cemetery.*
Si hubiera tenido tiempo, habría ido al cementerio.	*If I had had time, I would have gone to the cemetery.*

2. The sequence of tenses for *si* clauses is as follows.

MAIN CLAUSE	SI CLAUSE
Future	Present indicative
Conditional	Imperfect subjunctive
Conditional perfect	Pluperfect subjunctive

Práctica

A **¿Qué harías?**   Contesten.

1. Si cierran la escuela la semana que viene, ¿qué harás?
2. Si te dieran un carro nuevo, ¿adónde irías?
3. Si tú fueras un gran atleta, ¿con qué equipo jugarías?
4. Si tú hubieras podido hablar con Abraham Lincoln, ¿qué le habrías dicho?
5. Si tú no hubieras decidido estudiar español, ¿qué otra asignatura habrías escogido?
6. Si cualquier persona aceptara tu invitación a un baile, ¿a quién invitarías?
7. Si encuentras un millón de dólares en la calle, ¿qué harás?

La Recoleta, cementerio en Buenos Aires, Argentina

Learning From Photos

En el cementerio «Recoleta» en Buenos Aires, cada cripta contiene los restos de generaciones de la misma familia. Los muertos no se entierran. Se ponen en unas grandes «cajas» de granito o mármol dentro de la cripta.

Independent Practice

Assign any of the following:
1. Exercises, pages 276–277
2. Workbook, *Estructura*

B **Lo que haré, haría o habría hecho si...**
Completen.

1. **pagar** Yo trabajaré en la muralla si ellos me ___.
   Juana también trabajaría si le ___.
   Y el sábado pasado, tú habrías trabajado si te ___.

2. **pedir** Yo visitaré el cementerio si mi abuela me lo ___.
   Paco también iría si su abuela se lo ___.
   Y la semana pasada, todos nosotros habríamos ido
   si abuela nos lo ___.

3. **ir** Yo recogeré las flores si ___ al campo.
   Ella también recogería las flores si ___ al campo.
   Y sé que Uds. habrían recogido las flores si ___
   al campo.

4. **recibir** Yo asistiré a la corrida si ___ una entrada.
   Y tú también asistirías a la corrida si ___ una entrada.
   El domingo pasado todos los chicos habrían asistido a
   la corrida si ___ una entrada.

5. **hacer** Yo saldré del caserío si ___ un esfuerzo.
   Tú saldrías del caserío también si ___ un esfuerzo.
   Los chicos habrían salido del caserío si ___ un esfuerzo.

Expressing ownership
El mío, el tuyo, el suyo, el nuestro y el vuestro

1. A possessive pronoun replaces a noun that is modified by a possessive adjective. The possessive pronoun must agree in number and gender with the noun it replaces. Possessive pronouns are accompanied by definite articles.

   Yo tengo mi mochila, no la tuya.   *I have my knapsack, not yours.*

POSSESSIVE ADJECTIVE	POSSESSIVE PRONOUN
mi, mis	el mío, la mía, los míos, las mías
tu, tus	el tuyo, la tuya, los tuyos, las tuyas
nuestro, nuestra, nuestros, nuestras	el nuestro, la nuestra, los nuestros, las nuestras
vuestro, vuestra, vuestros, vuestras	el vuestro, la vuestra, los vuestros, las vuestras
su, sus	el suyo, la suya, los suyos, las suyas

2. Note that the definite article is often omitted after the verb **ser**.

   Estos libros son de Marta. Son suyos. No son míos.

   To emphasize whose they are, the article can be used.

   Éstos son los míos y aquéllos son los tuyos.

ESTRUCTURA   *doscientos setenta y siete* 〰️ **277**

ANSWERS
Práctica

B 1. **pagan, pagaran, hubieran pagado**
   2. **pide, pidiera, hubiera pedido**
   3. **voy, fuera, hubieran ido**
   4. **recibo, recibieras, hubieran recibido**
   5. **hago, hicieras, hubieran hecho**

TEACHING STRUCTURE

◆ **Expressing ownership** ◆◆

A. Write the chart forms of step 1 on the board while an individual student reads step 1 aloud.
B. Have students read step 2 silently.

ABOUT THE SPANISH LANGUAGE

◆ Manuel Benítez lleva el apodo de «El Cordobés». ¿Por qué será? Muchos toreros llevan apodos. Un apodo muy común es uno que viene del nombre de su pueblo: «El Cordobés», «El Madrileño», «El Sanluqueño», «El Jerezano», «El Rondeño». ¿De dónde son ellos?

◆ El nombre de uno de los toreros es José Ma. Manzanares. «Ma.» es la abreviatura de «María». Es muy común que los hombres tengan «María» como parte de su nombre, especialmente «José María» y «Jesús María». Es interesante que en las culturas anglosajonas no se les da el nombre de Jesús a los niños. En las culturas hispanas Jesús es un nombre muy común.

Learning From Realia

El cartel de toros es típico de los anuncios para las corridas de toros. Se ponen en las paredes. Este cartel es interesante porque es para una corrida «mano a mano». Se llama «mano a mano» porque solamente figuran dos matadores. En una corrida normal hay tres matadores y seis toros. En una corrida «mano a mano» cada uno de los dos toreros tiene que matar a tres toros.

You may wish to ask: **¿Dónde tiene lugar la corrida? ¿Quiénes son los toreros? ¿De qué ganadería son los toros? ¿A qué hora comienza la corrida?**

TEACHING TIPS

Have students prepare these *Práctica* for homework before going over them the following day in class.

ANSWERS
Práctica

A 1. el mío
2. la nuestra
3. los suyos
4. los míos
5. la mía
6. la tuya

B el tuyo
la tuya
las mías
las tuyas
las mías
la tuya
La mía
Las tuyas
las mías

C Answers will vary.

D 1. la nuestra
2. el mío
3. el mío (el tuyo)
4. los míos
5. las mías

Práctica

A **¿Suyos o míos?** Cambien al pronombre posesivo.

1. Carlos viajó en su carro y yo viajé en *mi carro*.
2. Llegamos a la fiesta en casa de Nilda. Su casa está muy cerca de *nuestra casa*.
3. Nilda tocó sus discos y Carlos tocó *sus discos*.
4. Yo también toqué *mis discos*.
5. Los chicos dejaron sus mochilas en el suelo y yo dejé *mi mochila* allí también.
6. Nilda quería escribir algo pero no tenía una pluma y tú le diste *tu pluma*.

B **HISTORIETA En la estación de ferrocarril**

Completen.

NORA: Sara, no tengo mi boleto. ¿Tú tienes ___₁?

SARA: Claro que sí. Yo lo puse en mi bolsa, y tú lo pusiste en ___₂.

NORA: Ay, ¿y mis maletas? No sé dónde están ___₃.

SARA: Allí están mis maletas, ¿ves? Y ___₄ están al lado de ___₅, cerca del mostrador.

NORA: Ah, sí. ¿Dónde está tu mochila? Mi mochila no es tan grande como ___₆. ___₇ es muy pequeña.

SARA: Sí, pero mira mis maletas y tus maletas. Mis maletas son pequeñas. ___₈ son enormes comparadas con ___₉.

C **El exagerado** Escriban una oración. Usen la imaginación.

Mi carro es grande.
El tuyo es grande, pero el mío es ___.

1. Mis padres son ricos.
2. Mi profesora es excelente.
3. Mis amigas son inteligentes.
4. Mi madre es senadora.

D **Porque son así.** Completen.

1. Es nuestra maleta, porque ___ es grande y verde.
2. Es mi boleto, porque ___ lleva mi nombre.
3. Es tu anorak, porque ___ es viejo.
4. Son mis patines, porque ___ son grises.
5. Son mis botas, porque ___ son así.

278 ～ *doscientos setenta y ocho*

Independent Practice

Assign any of the following:
1. Exercises, page 278
2. Workbook, *Estructura*

Expressing ownership
El **suyo**, la **suya**, los **suyos**, las **suyas**

1. The possessive pronouns **el suyo, la suya, los suyos,** and **las suyas** replace a noun that is modified by the possessive adjective **su**. Whenever it is unclear to whom the possessive pronoun is referring, a prepositional phrase is substituted for clarification.

el suyo	la suya	los suyos	las suyas
el de él	la de él	los de él	las de él
el de ella	la de ella	los de ella	las de ella
el de Ud.	la de Ud.	los de Ud.	las de Ud.
el de ellos	la de ellos	los de ellos	las de ellos
el de ellas	la de ellas	los de ellas	las de ellas
el de Uds.	la de Uds.	los de Uds.	las de Uds.

2. In a sentence such as **Elena lleva el suyo,** the intended meaning is "Elena is wearing hers," since the subject of the sentence is the person who is wearing her own garment. If the intended meaning were "Elena is wearing his (sweater, etc.)," it would be stated as **Elena lleva el de él,** in order to avoid confusion.

Práctica

A **Él tiene la suya.** Sigan los modelos.

Ramón tiene su entrada.
Ramón tiene la entrada de Elena.

Ramón tiene la suya.
Ramón tiene la de ella.

1. Ramón está en su asiento.
2. Él está guardando el asiento de Elena.
3. Ahora, ella tiene su entrada.
4. Los amigos buscan sus asientos.
5. Ellos tienen el programa de Elena y el de Ramón.
6. Y Ramón no tiene su programa.

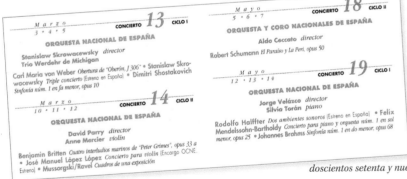

doscientos setenta y nueve 279

TEACHING STRUCTURE

◆ Expressing ownership ◆ ◆

Note You may wish to point out the following to students: When a possessive pronoun immediately follows the verb **ser,** the definite article is usually omitted.

Este asiento es mío.
¿Es tuyo ese asiento?

The article can be used for emphasis, however.

Este asiento es el mío.
No es el tuyo.

Have the students read the explanatory material in steps 1 and 2 and study the chart of step 1.

TEACHING TIPS

You may wish to have the students do this *Práctica* with books open after they have been given a minute or two to look it over.

ANSWERS
Práctica
A 1. Ramón está en el suyo.
  2. Él está guardando el de ella.
  3. Ahora, ella tiene la suya.
  4. Los amigos buscan los suyos.
  5. Ellos tienen el de ella y el de él (el de ellos).
  6. Y Ramón no tiene el suyo.

Learning From Realia

Fíjense que las artes son realmente universales. Los artistas que aparecen en Madrid vienen de todas partes del mundo.

¿De dónde viene el director del concierto número 13? ¿De qué nacionalidad será el director del concierto número 18?

TEACHING STRUCTURE

◆ **Pointing out people and things** ◆

Have the students read through the explanation silently, after which you may wish to have them repeat the model sentences in step 1 aloud in unison.

TEACHING TIPS

This *Práctica* can be done with books open without prior preparation.

ANSWERS
Práctica
A 1. aquél
2. ésa
3. aquél
4. éste
5. este

Paired Activity

Have pairs of students play the roles of the two people in the photo. One is the mechanic, the other the customer. Provide time for development of the dialogue.

Pointing out people and things
Los pronombres demostrativos

1. The demonstrative pronouns are the same as the demonstrative adjectives, except that they often carry a written accent mark to distinguish them from the adjectives.

ADJECTIVES	PRONOUNS
este, esta, estos, estas	éste, ésta, éstos, éstas
ese, esa, esos, esas	ése, ésa, ésos, ésas
aquel, aquella, aquellos, aquellas	aquél, aquélla, aquéllos, aquéllas

> **Este libro es excelente, me gusta mucho éste.**
> **Ese libro es aburrido, no me gusta ése para nada.**

2. Remember **ése, ésa,** etc., refer to things near the person spoken to and not very far from the speaker. **Aquél, aquélla,** etc., refer to things distant from both the speaker and the person spoken to.

❖Práctica❖

A HISTORIETA *¿Este coche o aquél?*

Completen con pronombres o adjetivos demostrativos.

1. Este coche es más caro que ___ (allá).
2. Pero esta camioneta no es tan buena como ___ que tú tienes.
3. El mecánico ___ (allá) me dijo que el motor es excelente.
4. Pero otro mecánico, ___ aquí, dice que usa mucho aceite.
5. También me gusta ___ modelo aquí.

280 ∾ *doscientos ochenta*

CAPÍTULO 6

Learning From Photos

This is an opportunity to review automobile vocabulary: **el capó, el motor, la batería, el radiador, la transmisión, el freno, el acelerador, el aceite, el tanque, las gomas/llantas/los neumáticos, el parabrisas, el volante.**

Independent Practice

Assign any of the following:
1. Exercise, page 280
2. Workbook, *Estructura*

Literatura
Zalacaín el Aventurero

de Pío Baroja

Antes de leer

El filósofo y académico español Salvador de Madariaga
(1886–1978) escribió que «la clave de sus emociones y el motor
de sus actos puros... son, respectivamente: para el inglés, *fair play,*
para el francés, *le droit*°; para el español, *el honor.*»

    Mucho se ha escrito sobre el
sentido del honor del español.
Ese sentido del honor que se
refleja en el orgullo. Dijo un
francés que en España siempre
habría una monarquía porque
cada español se considera un
rey. Además de su natural
orgullo y su sentido del honor
siente una tremenda lealtad
hacia la familia y el buen nombre
de la familia. El honor de la
familia se defiende hasta la
muerte. No importa que se trate
de una familia de nobles o de la
más pobre de las familias.

    El trozo que sigue es de la
novela *Zalacaín el Aventurero*
de Pío Baroja. El protagonista,
Martín Zalacaín, nace en un
caserío cerca de un pueblo del
norte de España. Es de una familia
muy pobre. Su padre muere joven
en una epidemia de viruelas°. Martín es un niño pequeño cuando
muere el padre. Mientras los demás niños se educan en la escuela,
Martín aprende en la calle. Un día, el hijo de una familia rica lo
llama «ladrón». Y es verdad, porque Martín robaba fruta de los
árboles de esa familia. Pero el niño, no contento con llamar ladrón
a Martín, dice: —Toda tu familia es de ladrones. —Lo demás nos
lo cuenta Pío Baroja.

le droit *right*

> **PÍO BAROJA**
>
> # ZALACAÍN
> ## EL
> ## AVENTURERO

viruelas
smallpox

LITERATURA

doscientos ochenta y uno **281**

TEACHING VOCABULARY

A. Have students repeat the new words and expressions after you or Cassette 12A/Compact Disc 8.

B. To vary the procedure you may wish to read the definitions to the students. To help the students better understand the words being defined, you may wish to use them in sentences.

ABOUT THE SPANISH LANGUAGE

◆ La terminación «-azo» se usa para describir un golpe. Un puñetazo es un golpe con el puño. ¿Qué serán, entonces, un rodillazo y un codazo? Por su semejanza al coco, se llama coco a la cabeza. ¿Qué será un «cocotazo»?

◆ En español hay un verbo derivado de «viudo» y «viuda» que es «enviudar». ¿Qué significará este verbo? El verbo «adivinar» tiene una palabra cognada en inglés. ¿Cuál es? *(to divine)*

Vocabulario

la villa   la ciudad

el/la soltero(a)   una persona no casada

el/la viudo(a)   una persona cuyo(a) esposo(a) está muerto(a)

el odio   la aversión, la antipatía, la animosidad, la hostilidad

el/la ladrón(a)   el/la que roba

atravesar   cruzar

adivinar   tratar de descubrir alguna cosa ignorada, descubrir el futuro

soñar (ue)   representar en la fantasía, lo que sucede mientras dormimos

habitar   vivir, residir

pertenecer a   ser posesión de

asustar   causar miedo

matar   quitarle la vida a alguien

Did You Know?

La palabra «tejado»: viene de «tejas» que son cada una de las piezas de barro *(clay)* cocido con que se cubren los techos. El tejado todavía se llama tejado aunque no esté cubierto de «tejas».

Práctica

A **El cementerio** Contesten.

1. ¿Es grande el cementerio?
2. ¿Hay estrellas de David en el cementerio?
3. ¿Hay una muralla alrededor del cementerio?
4. Al lado del cementerio, ¿hay un caserío?
5. ¿Es humilde o elegante el caserío?
6. ¿Está en malas condiciones el tejado del caserío?
7. ¿Están en malas condiciones las paredes del caserío?
8. ¿Hay un cartel en la pared del caserío?
9. ¿Es de piedra la muralla?
10. ¿Hay gallinas y patos en el patio del caserío?
11. ¿Ponen huevos las gallinas?

B **Unas definiciones** Identifiquen.

1. un golpe dado con el puño
2. un golpe dado en la cara con la mano abierta
3. la mano cerrada
4. un golpe brusco que causa movimiento
5. lo contrario de «el amor» o «el cariño»

C **¿Cuál es la palabra?** Completen.

1. Cuando no sabes algo por cierto, a veces tienes que ____.
2. Ese caserío ____ a una familia pobre.
3. Una familia pobre ____ este caserío.
4. La madre tiene cinco hijos. Era ____ hasta los 25 años y luego se casó. Su marido murió hace poco. Hace unos meses que la pobre señora es ____.
5. La pobre mujer ____ cada noche con una vida mejor, menos penosa, con menos miseria.
6. El ____ cuando roba casi siempre le ____ a su víctima.
7. El ladrón le roba a su víctima. El asesino la ____.

CAPÍTULO 6
Literatura

TEACHING TIPS

You may wish to go over these *Práctica* with or without previous preparation.

ANSWERS
Práctica

A 1. no
  2. no
  3. sí
  4. sí
  5. Es humilde.
  6. sí
  7. sí
  8. no
  9. sí
  10. sí
  11. sí

B 1. un puñetazo
  2. una bofetada
  3. un puño
  4. un empujón
  5. el odio

C 1. adivinar
  2. pertenece
  3. habita
  4. soltera, viuda
  5. sueña
  6. ladrón, asusta
  7. mata

Independent Practice

Assign any of the following:
1. Exercises, page 283
2. Workbook, *Literatura*

Introducción

Pío Baroja nació en San Sebastián en el País Vasco en 1872. Estudió para médico, carrera que ejerció por poco tiempo en un pueblo muy pequeño. Fue también propietario de una panadería. Finalmente, se dedicó a lo que quería hacer—escribir. Escribió más de cien novelas. Cuando Hemingway recibió el Premio Nóbel de literatura dijo que Baroja, y no él, lo debía recibir.

En sus novelas Baroja ha creado millares de personajes, algunos inolvidables. Le encantan los vagabundos, los aventureros, los hombres cínicos y resentidos que desprecian la sociedad. Critica tanto en su obra que se ha dicho que no cree en nada. Nadie ha escapado su censura—ni los políticos, ni los militares, ni los religiosos, ni los aristócratas. Sin embargo, hay en su obra cierta simpatía hacia los oprimidos, los no conformistas, los miserables. Baroja viajó mucho y durante sus viajes observó, sobre todo, la vida de los de la clase baja.

Pío Baroja

El trozo que sigue de su novela famosa *Zalacaín el Aventurero* describe la juventud de un muchacho pobre y oprimido en el norte de España.

Lectura

Zalacaín el Aventurero

CÓMO VIVIÓ Y SE EDUCÓ MARTÍN ZALACAÍN ◆ Un camino en cuesta baja° de la Ciudadela pasa por encima del cementerio y atraviesa el portal de Francia. Este camino, en la parte alta, tiene a los lados varias cruces de piedra° que terminan en una ermita° y por la parte baja, después de entrar en la ciudad, se convierte en calle. A la izquierda del camino, antes de la muralla, había hace años un caserío viejo, medio derruido° con el tejado terrero° lleno de pedruscos y la piedra arenisca de sus paredes desgastada° por la acción de la humedad y del aire. En frente de la decrépita y pobre casa, un agujero° indicaba donde estuvo en otro tiempo el escudo°, y debajo de él se adivinaban, más bien que se leían, varias letras que componían una frase latina: *Post funera virtus vivit.*

En este caserío nació y pasó los primeros años de su infancia Martín Zalacaín de Urbia, el que más tarde había de ser llamado Zalacaín, el Aventurero; en este caserío soñó sus primeras aventuras y rompió los primeros pantalones.

en cuesta baja	*going downhill*
cruces de piedra	*stone crosses*
una ermita	*a hermitage*
derruido	*pulled down*
terrero	*mud, earthen*
desgastada	*dilapidated*
un agujero	*hole*
el escudo	*coat-of-arms*

Pueblo del norte de España

Los Zalacaín vivían a pocos pasos de Urbia, pero ni Martín ni su familia eran ciudadanos; faltaban a su casa unos metros para formar parte de la villa.

El padre de Martín fue labrador, un hombre oscuro y poco comunicativo, muerto en una epidemia de viruelas; la madre de Martín tampoco era mujer de carácter; vivió en esta oscuridad psicológica normal entre la gente del campo, y pasó de soltera a casada a viuda en absoluta inconsciencia. Al morir su marido quedó con dos hijos, Martín y una niña menor llamada Ignacia.

El caserío donde habitaban los Zalacaín pertenecía a la familia de Ohando, familia la más antigua, aristocrática y rica de Urbia.

Vivía la madre de Martín casi de la misericordia de los Ohando.

En tales condiciones de pobreza y de miseria, parecía lógico que, por herencia y por la acción del ambiente, Martín fuese como su padre y su madre, oscuro, tímido y apocado°, pero el muchacho resultó decidido, temerario° y audaz°.

apocado cobarde
temerario *reckless, bold*
audaz *bold*

En esta época los chicos no iban tanto a la escuela como ahora, y Martín pasó mucho tiempo sin sentarse en sus bancos. No sabía de ella más sino que era un sitio oscuro, con unos cartelones blancos en las paredes, lo cual no le animaba a entrar. Le alejaba también de aquel modesto centro de enseñanza el ver que los chicos de la calle no le consideraban como uno de los suyos a causa de vivir fuera del pueblo y de andar siempre hecho un andrajoso°.

andrajoso *in rags*

Por este motivo les tenía odio; así que cuando algunos chiquillos de los caseríos de extramuros entraban en la calle y comenzaban a pedradas° con los ciudadanos, Martín era de los más encarnizados° en el combate; capitaneaba las hordas bárbaras, las dirigía y hasta las dominaba.

a pedradas *throwing stones*
encarnizados furiosos

Tenía entre los demás chicos el ascendiente de su audacia y de su temeridad. No había rincón del pueblo que Martín no conociera. Para él Urbia era la reunión de todas las bellezas, el compendio de todos los intereses y magnificencias.

LITERATURA

doscientos ochenta y cinco ∾ **285**

ABOUT THE SPANISH LANGUAGE

El padre de Zalacaín había sido labrador. El «labrador» en España es una persona que posee su propia tierra, aunque poca, y la cultiva por su propia cuenta. No es uno que normalmente trabaja para otro.

GEOGRAPHY CONNECTION

El pueblo de este cuento está en el País Vasco. Esta comunidad autónoma del norte de España consta de las provincias de Vizcaya, Guipúzcoa y Álava. Sus importantes ciudades son Bilbao y San Sebastián. Los vascos tienen su propio idioma, el vascuence o, en vascuence, el euskera. El euskera es un idioma que aparentemente no se parece a ningún otro en el mundo. Históricamente, los vascos han gozado de gran autonomía salvo durante la dictadura de Francisco Franco (1939–1975). Algunos antropólogos creen que los vascos son los descendientes de los iberos originales.

LITERATURE CONNECTION

Pío Baroja pertenece a la llamada «Generación del '98», un grupo de autores que se preocupaban profundamente por la reforma social y moral de España después del desastre de la guerra de Cuba. Dos características del estilo de los escritores del '98 son su uso de un lenguaje natural, sin adorno, y una reafirmación de los valores nacionales. Otros importantes autores del '98 son Miguel de Unamuno, Antonio Machado y Azorín (José Martínez Ruiz).

286

VOCABULARY EXPANSION

Las poblaciones llevan diferentes nombres según su tamaño y lugar. Una «metrópoli» es la ciudad más grande de la nación. Una «capital» es normalmente una capital de provincia. Un «caserío» —excepto en el País Vasco— es una agrupación de casas. Una «aldea» es un pueblo pequeño de campo. Una «villa» es una aldea que por alguna razón se distingue. Un «burgo» es una aldea dependiente de otra. Un «municipio» es una demarcación geográfica de un pueblo. Los pueblos grandes y las ciudades tienen sus «barrios», sus «arrabales», que son barrios apartados del centro, y sus suburbios.

LITERATURE CONNECTION

El estilo de Pío Baroja es sobrio, sencillo y directo. Las obras de los rusos Tolstoi y Dostoievski influyeron en su obra, igual que el filósofo alemán Nietzsche. Pío Baroja deja que sus ideas se expresen en boca de sus personajes. Sus «héroes» generalmente son hombres cínicos y resentidos. Ellos desprecian la sociedad. Pío Baroja fue crítico y enemigo del tradicionalismo español.

Nadie se ocupaba de él, no compartía con los demás chicos la escuela y huroneaba° por todas partes. Su abandono° le obligaba a formarse sus ideas espontáneamente y a templar la osadía° con la prudencia.

Mientras los niños de su edad aprendían a leer, él daba la vuelta a la muralla, sin que le asustasen las piedras derrumbadas° ni las zarzas° que cerraban el paso.

Sabía donde había palomas torcaces° e intentaba coger sus nidos, robaba fruta y cogía moras y fresas silvestres°.

A los ocho años Martín gozaba de una mala fama, digna ya de un hombre. Un día al salir de la escuela Carlos Ohando, el hijo de la familia rica que dejaba por limosna° el caserío a la madre de Martín, señalándole con el dedo gritó:

—¡Ése! Ése es un ladrón.

—¿Yo? —exclamó Martín.

—Tú, sí. El otro día te vi que estabas robando peras en mi casa. Toda tu familia es de ladrones.

Martín, aunque respecto a él no podía negar la exactitud del cargo, creyó que no debía permitir este ultraje° dirigido a los Zalacaín y abalanzándose° sobre el joven Ohando le dio una bofetada morrocotuda°. Ohando contestó con un puñetazo, se agarraron los dos y cayeron al suelo; se dieron de trompicones°, pero Martín, más fuerte, tumbaba° siempre al contrario. Un alpargatero° tuvo que intervenir en la contienda y a puntapiés° y a empujones separó a los dos adversarios. Martín se separó triunfante y el joven Ohando, magullado y maltrecho° se fue a su casa.

La madre de Martín, al saber el suceso, quiso obligar a su hijo a presentarse en casa de Ohando y a pedir perdón a Carlos, pero Martín afirmó que antes lo mataría. Ella tuvo que encargarse de dar toda clase de excusas y explicaciones a la poderosa familia.

Desde entonces, la madre miraba a su hijo como a un réprobo°.

—¿De dónde ha salido este chico así? —decía, y experimentaba al pensar en él un sentimiento confuso de amor y de pena, sólo comparable con el asombro y la desesperación de la gallina cuando empolla° huevos de pato y ve que sus hijos se zambullen° en el agua sin miedo y van nadando valientemente.

huroneaba exploraba
abandono neglect
la osadía daring

derrumbadas fallen
las zarzas brambles
palomas torcaces wild doves
moras y fresas silvestres wild blackberries and strawberries
dejaba por limosna gave as charity

ultraje abuso
abalanzándose rushing, falling upon
morrocotuda dura, fuerte
trompicones golpes
tumbaba knocked down
un alpargatero a shoemaker
puntapiés kicking
magullado y maltrecho bruised and battered

un réprobo a criminal

empolla hatch
se zambullen dive

Aldea del norte de España

Literary Analysis

Al final del trozo, Pío Baroja compara los sentimientos de la madre con los de una gallina. En sus propias palabras, explique esta comparación de la madre con la gallina.

Additional Practice

Have pairs of students reenact the conversation between Zalacaín's mother and one of the parents of Carlos Ohando. Allow time to prepare the dialogs.

Después de leer

Comprensión

A **Martín** Contesten.

1. ¿Por qué no eran ciudadanos de Urbia los Zalacaín?
2. ¿A quiénes pertenecía el caserío donde habitaban los Zalacaín?
3. ¿Cómo era la familia de los dueños?
4. ¿Qué sabía Martín de la escuela?
5. ¿Por qué los muchachos de la escuela no consideraban a Martín como uno de los suyos?
6. ¿De qué fama gozaba Martín cuando sólo tenía ocho años?
7. ¿Quién lo llamó «ladrón»? ¿Por qué?
8. ¿Qué pasó cuando lo llamó «ladrón»?
9. ¿Fue a su casa a pedir perdón Martín?
10. ¿Quién lo hizo? ¿Cómo?

Vejer de la Frontera, Andalucía, España

B **La familia de Martín** Hagan lo siguiente.

1. Dé una descripción de la casa de los Zalacaín.
2. Describa a la familia de Martín.
3. Describa a Martín. Mencione sus características.
4. Describa la reacción de la madre de Martín ante su carácter y su comportamiento.

Actividades comunicativas

A **La biografía** Escriba la biografía de Zalacaín el Aventurero.

B **El reportero** Imagínese que Ud. es reportero(a) del periódico en el pequeño pueblo de Urbia. Ud. está encargado(a) de escribir un artículo para la edición de mañana sobre este suceso o acontecimiento.

C **Soy sociólogo(a).** Imagínese que trabaja como sociólogo(a). Analice la influencia del ambiente en que vivía Zalacaín sobre el desarrollo de su carácter.

D **Le aconsejo que…** Imagínese que trabaja como psicólogo(a) y dígale a Martín lo que debe hacer. Dele consejos.

LITERATURA

Learning From Photos

You may wish to ask questions about the photo, such as: **¿Quiénes están en la calle? ¿Qué están haciendo? ¿De qué edad, más o menos, son ellas? ¿Cómo se visten? ¿Cómo es la calle? Describa la calle y las casas.**

Independent Practice

Assign any of the following:
1. Exercises, page 287
2. Workbook, *Literatura*

Después de leer

TEACHING TIPS

You may wish to intersperse in the reading questions from *Comprensión A.*

ANSWERS
Comprensión

A 1. Porque faltaban a su casa unos metros para formar parte de la ciudad.
2. El caserío pertenecía a la familia Ohando.
3. Era una familia antigua, aristócrata y rica.
4. Sabía que era un sitio oscuro, con unos cartelones blancos en las paredes.
5. Porque él vivía fuera del pueblo y andaba siempre hecho un andrajoso.
6. Gozaba de una mala fama digna de un hombre.
7. Carlos Ohando lo llamó «ladrón» porque Martín estaba robando peras en casa de Carlos.
8. Martín le dio una bofetada morrocotuda a Carlos.
9. Martín se negó a pedir perdón.
10. La madre fue a pedir perdón, y ella dio toda clase de excusas a la poderosa familia.

B Answers will vary.

TEACHING TIPS

Allow students to select the *Actividad* in which they wish to participate.

Actividades comunicativas

A–D Answers will vary.

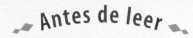
Antes de leer

TEACHING TIPS

A. Have students read the *Antes de leer* silently.

B. Ask if they agree with the following: **No se puede tener confianza siempre en las apariencias.**

C. Ask students if they can think of a proverb in English that suggests that one shouldn't judge others by their outward appearance. (You can't judge a book by its cover.)

RESOURCES

- Vocabulary Transparencies
- Audio Cassette 12B/Compact Disc 8
- Student Tape Manual
- Workbook
- Chapter Quizzes
- Testing Program

TEACHING VOCABULARY

You may wish to use some suggestions from previous chapters.

Mi padre

Manuel del Toro

Antes de leer

La valentía o la bravura, es un valor que se estima en la cultura hispana como en todas las culturas. Pero hay una gran diferencia entre la persona valiente y el «bravucón», el tipo que constantemente muestra su fuerza y su falta de miedo. El bravucón es, casi siempre, valiente en apariencia solamente. En el cuento que sigue veremos a un «guapo», un típico bravucón, tratando de impresionar a los demás con su fanfarronería. Y veremos a un valiente de verdad. El niño del cuento aprende una importante lección sobre la verdad y las apariencias.

El campo, Puerto Rico

Vocabulario

la sien
el mentón
la cicatriz
el barril de macarelas
Los hombres tallaban con una baraja.

Learning From Photos

Puerto Rico es una isla relativamente pequeña. En forma más o menos rectangular, tiene menos de 200 kilómetros de largo y unos 60 de ancho. La población es de unos 3.5 millones. La isla es bastante montañosa. Una cordillera atraviesa el centro de Puerto Rico del este al oeste. El tabaco fue, durante muchos años, uno de los productos más importantes de Puerto Rico.

¡GULP!

el escalofrío   una sensación de frío, a veces debido al terror
el temor   el miedo
el/la cobarde   una persona sin valentía
la virtud   una cualidad moral
la hazaña   una acción importante o heroica
el aliento   la respiración

envidiar   querer algo que tiene otra persona

aturdido(a)   lento(a) por el efecto del alcohol o similar
a hurtadillas   furtivamente, a escondidas

El joven tragó algo.

Práctica

A **¿Cuál es la palabra?**   Completen.
1. Rogelio tiene miedo de todo, es un ___.
2. Se le ve el ___ en los ojos.
3. Y le dan ___ como si hiciera mucho frío.
4. Ni puede respirar, le falta el ___.
5. Le gusta escuchar los cuentos de las ___ de los héroes.
6. Pobre Rogelio, les ___ a los héroes porque no puede ser como ellos.

B **Unas definiciones**   Den la palabra que se define.
1. un conjunto de pedazos de cartón que se usa para el póker y otros juegos
2. un objeto grande, de madera, que se usa para guardar vinos, pescado, etc.
3. la marca que queda después de curarse una herida
4. en estado confuso, sin todas sus facultades
5. la fuerza o el valor moral, la integridad
6. de manera furtiva, sin dejar que se note
7. hacer que una cosa pase por la boca

ANSWERS
Práctica
A 1. cobarde
   2. temor
   3. escalofríos
   4. aliento
   5. hazañas
   6. envidia
B 1. una baraja
   2. un barril
   3. la cicatriz
   4. aturdido
   5. la virtud
   6. a hurtadillas
   7. tragar

LITERATURA

Did You Know?

La baraja de póker tiene 52 naipes. La española tiene 48. La baraja de póker tiene «corazones», «diamantes», etc. La española tiene «bastos», «copas», «espadas» y «oros». Hay nueve naipes por cada uno de los cuatro «palos» (suits) de la baraja española.

Independent Practice

Assign any of the following:
1. Exercises, pages 289
2. Workbook, *Literatura*

TEACHING TIPS

Call on students to read the
Introducción aloud.

TEACHING THE READING

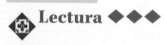

Lectura ◆◆◆

A. You may wish to call on students to read this selection aloud.
B. After every few sentences you may wish to have a student summarize the main idea.

ABOUT THE SPANISH LANGUAGE

La palabra «manso» significa benigno, suave, apacible y pacífico. Cuando se aplica a un animal, quiere decir dócil, sin bravura ni valentía. En las corridas de toros el toro «manso» es devuelto a los corrales porque no es valiente, y no se le puede torear. ¿Qué querrá decir el autor cuando habla de la «mansa habilidad» de su padre?

National Standards

Cultures
Students experience, discuss, and analyze an expressive product of the culture: the short story, «Mi padre», by the Puerto Rican author, Manuel del Toro.

Introducción

En el mundo hispano ha habido grandes figuras literarias que sobresalieron en otros campos también. Pío Baroja era médico y panadero. Salvador de Madariaga era estadista. Gabriela Mistral era maestra de escuela rural. Alonso de Ercilla era soldado. Rómulo Gallegos, Manuel Azaña y Juan Bosch fueron presidentes de sus repúblicas. José Martí era héroe nacional. Docenas de literatos hispanos han servido en el cuerpo diplomático.

El cuento que sigue, «Mi padre», del puertorriqueño Manuel del Toro, apareció en *Asomante*, la revista literaria de la facultad de graduados de la Universidad de Puerto Rico en Río Piedras. Muchos poetas, dramaturgos, cuentistas y críticos importantes han contribuido a *Asomante*.

La obra literaria de Manuel del Toro no es abundante. Como tantos otros intelectuales hispanos, el señor del Toro se ha dedicado a otra profesión, pero ha mantenido su vocación de escritor.

En «Mi padre» el autor evoca un Puerto Rico rural casi desaparecido. Es el Puerto Rico del «jíbaro», el campesino sencillo que se dedicaba al cultivo del tabaco y a la agricultura.

Lectura

Mi padre

De niño siempre tuve el temor de que mi padre fuera un cobarde. No porque le viera correr seguido de cerca por un machete como vi tantas veces a Paco el Gallina y a Quino Pascual. ¡Pero era tan diferente a los papás de mis compañeros de clase! En aquella escuela de barrio donde el valor era la virtud suprema, yo bebía el acíbar° de ser el hijo de un hombre que ni siquiera usaba cuchillo. ¡Cómo envidiaba a mis compañeros que relataban una y otra vez sin cansarse nunca de las hazañas de sus progenitores°! Nolasco Rivera había desarmado a dos guardias insulares. A Perico Lugo le dejaron por muerto en un zanjón° con veintitrés tajos de perrillo°. Felipe Chaveta lucía una hermosa herida desde la sien hasta el mentón.

Mi padre, mi pobre padre, no tenía ni una sola cicatriz en el cuerpo. Acababa de comprobarlo con gran pena mientras nos bañábamos en el río aquella tarde sabatina° en que como de costumbre veníamos de voltear las talas de tabaco°. Ahora seguía yo sus pasos hundiendo mis pies descalzos en el tibio polvo del camino y haciendo sonar mi trompeta. Era ésta un tallo de amapola° al que mi padre con aquella mansa habilidad para todas las cosas pequeñas había convertido en trompeta con sólo hacerle una incisión longitudinal.

Al pasar frente a La Aurora me dijo:

—Entremos aquí. No tengo cigarros para la noche.

el acíbar *bitterness*

sus progenitores *sus padres*
un zanjón *a ditch*
tajos de perrillo *los cortes con un cuchillo*

sabatina *del sábado*
las talas de tabaco *tobacco stalks*

un tallo de amapola *a poppy stem*

Did You Know?

Salvador de Madariaga (1886–1978) ensayista y filósofo español, sirvió a la República Española de embajador ante la Liga de las Naciones y en distintos países. Gabriela Mistral (1889–1957), gran poeta chilena y ganadora del Premio Nóbel de Literatura, sirvió de cónsul de Chile en Nápoles, Lisboa, Río de Janeiro y Los Ángeles. Alonso de Ercilla y Zúñiga (1533–1594), autor de *La Araucana*, quizás el poema épico de las Américas, luchó valientemente de día contra los **indios de Chile y de noche escribió el poema alabándolos. Rómulo Gallegos (1884–1969), gran novelista venezolano (*Doña Bárbara, Canaima*), fue senador, ministro de Instrucción Pública y presidente de la República. Manuel Azaña (1880–1940), novelista y ensayista español, sirvió de Ministro de Guerra y después de presidente de la Segunda República Española. Juan Bosch (1909–), novelista, fue elegido presidente de la República Dominicana en 1963. José**

Del asombro por poco me trago la trompeta. Porque papá nunca entraba a La Aurora, punto de reunión de todos los guapos del barrio. Allí se jugaba baraja, se bebía ron y casi siempre se daban tajos. Unos tajos de machete que convertían brazos nervudos en cortos muñones°. Unos tajos largos de navaja que echaban afuera intestinos y se entraba la muerte.

Después de dar las buenas tardes, papá pidió cigarros. Los iba escogiendo uno a uno con fruición° de fumador, palpándolos° entre los dedos y llevándolos a la nariz para percibir su aroma. Yo, pegado al mostrador forrado de zinc, trataba de esconderme entre los pantalones de papá. Sin atreverme a tocar mi trompeta, pareciéndome que ofendía a los guapetones hasta con mi aliento, miraba a hurtadillas de una a otra esquina del ventorrillo°. Acostado sobre la estiba de arroz° veía a José el Tuerto comer pan y salchichón echándole los pellejos al perro sarnoso° que los atrapaba en el aire con un ruido seco de dientes. En la mesita del lado tallaban con una baraja sucia Nolasco Rivera, Perico Lugo, Chus Maurosa y un colorado que yo no conocía. En un tablero colocado sobre un barril se jugaba dominó. Un grupo de curiosos seguía de cerca las jugadas. Todos bebían ron.

Fue el colorado el de la provocación. Se acercó a donde estaba papá alargándole la botella de la que ya todos habían bebido.

—Dése un palo, don.

—Muchas gracias, pero yo no puedo tomar.

—Ah, ¿conque me desprecia porque soy un pelao?

—No es eso, amigo. Es que no puedo tomar. Déselo usted en mi nombre.

—Este palo se lo da usted o ca... se lo echo por la cabeza.

Lo intentó pero no pudo. El empellón° de papá lo arrojó contra el barril de macarelas. Se levantó aturdido por el ron y por el golpe y palpándose el cinturón con ambas manos dijo:

—Está usted de suerte, viejito, porque ando desarmao.

—A ver, préstenle un cuchillo. —Yo no podía creer pero era papá el que hablaba.

Todavía al recordarlo un escalofrío me corre por el cuerpo. Veinte manos se hundieron en las camisetas sucias, en los pantalones raídos, en las botas enlodadas, en todos los sitios en que un hombre sabe guardar su arma. Veinte manos surgieron ofreciendo en silencio de jíbaro encastado°el cuchillo casero, el puñal de tres filos, la sevillana corva°...

—Amigo, escoja el que más le guste.

—Mire, don, yo soy un hombre guapo pero usté es más que yo.

Así dijo el colorado y salió de la tienda con pasito lento.

Pagó papá sus cigarros, dio las buenas tardes y salimos. Al bajar el escaloncito escuché al Tuerto decir con admiración:

—Ahí va un macho completo.

Mi trompeta de amapola tocaba a triunfo. ¡Dios mío que llegue el lunes para contárselo a los muchachos!

LITERATURA

doscientos noventa y uno ◎ **291**

---

muñón lo que queda de un brazo o pierna amputada

fruición el placer, la anticipación de un placer

palpándolos tocar algo con las manos para saber cómo es

ventorrillo bodega

la estiba de arroz el montón de sacos de arroz

sarnoso *mangy*

el empellón *shove*

jíbaro encastado un puro y legítimo campesino puertorriqueño

el cuchillo casero, el puñal de tres filos, la sevillana corva tres tipos de cuchillo

---

ABOUT THE SPANISH LANGUAGE

◆ El «jíbaro» en muchas partes de Latinoamérica se refiere al campesino, sus costumbres, etc. En Puerto Rico, el «jíbaro» es un campesino blanco, generalmente del interior, de la montaña. En la región del Amazonas en la América del Sur, el «jíbaro» o «jívaro» es miembro de una tribu indígena conocida por su costumbre de preparar como trofeo las cabezas de sus enemigos, reduciéndolas al tamaño de un puño.

◆ Es bastante común «comerse» la «d» del participio pasado de los verbos de la primera conjugación, los que terminan en -*ar*: «hablao» por «hablado», «desarmao» por «desarmado». En algunas regiones como Madrid, por ejemplo, esto no es mal visto. En otras partes se considera inculto. Entre los madrileños «castizos», se le considera «cursi» (pretencioso) a la persona que pronuncia esta «d». Se burlan de ellos, diciendo: «Sí, y ha comido bacalado en Bilbado» (bacalao/ Bilbao). El tragar la «d» del participio pasado de los verbos en -*er* e -*ir* es considerado inculto en todas partes; «comío» por «comido», «salío» por «salido», etc.

◆ En la línea 3, el hijo dice: «...por poco me trago la trompeta». Aunque la narración está en el pasado, después de la expresión «por poco» siempre se usa el presente del verbo.

◆ Un «palo» en Puerto Rico es una porción de una bebida alcohólica. También se dice un «trago» en Puerto Rico y toda Latinoamérica.

Did You Know? cont.

Martí (1853–1895), el máximo héroe cubano, fue gran poeta, uno de los iniciadores del movimiento modernista y murió en batalla luchando contra España por la independencia de Cuba.

.•Después de leer•.

TEACHING TIPS

Have students read the selection at home and write the answers to the *Comprensión* exercises. Go over them in class.

ANSWERS
Comprensión

A 1. **cobarde**
   2. **machete**
   3. **diferente**
   4. **valor**
   5. **cuchillo**

B 1. **Nolasco Rivera había desarmado a dos guardias insulares.**
   2. **En el cuerpo de Perico Lugo dejaron veintitrés tajos de perrillo.**
   3. **Felipe Chaveta tenía una hermosa cicatriz entre la sien y el mentón.**
   4. **No tenía ni una sola cicatriz.**
   5. **Este incidente ocurrió un sábado.**
   6. **Padre e hijo acababan de voltear las talas de tabaco.**

C 1. **a**   6. **a**
   2. **b**   7. **c**
   3. **c**   8. **b**
   4. **a**   9. **a**
   5. **b**   10. **b**

National Standards

✿ *Communities*
Students will use the language beyond the school setting by creating faxes to be sent to the political parties in Puerto Rico seeking information.

Students are also encouraged to arrange interviews with older Puerto Rican residents of their community to find out their feelings toward independence, statehood, and commonwealth status for the island.

✤ Comprensión

A No era cobarde.   Completen.
1. El niño creía que posiblemente su padre fuera un ___.
2. A Paco el Gallina y a Quino Pascual muchas veces les corrían detrás con un ___.
3. El padre del niño era muy ___ a los padres de sus amigos.
4. La virtud más importante para los niños de la escuela era el ___.
5. Y el padre del niño no usaba ___.

B Las cicatrices   Contesten.
1. ¿Qué les había quitado Nolasco Rivera a unos guardias insulares?
2. ¿Qué dejaron en el cuerpo de Perico Lugo?
3. ¿Qué tenía Felipe Chaveta entre la sien y el mentón?
4. ¿Cuántas cicatrices llevaba el padre del niño?
5. ¿En qué día de la semana ocurrió este incidente?
6. ¿Qué acababan de hacer padre e hijo antes de bañarse?

C Lo que pasó   Escojan.
1. ¿De qué era la trompeta del niño?
   a. De parte de una planta.   **b.** De madera y metal.   **c.** De papel.
2. ¿Dónde consiguió el niño la trompeta?
   a. La compró en La Aurora.   **b.** Su padre se la hizo.
   c. El niño la encontró en la escuela.
3. ¿Por qué entró el padre en La Aurora?
   a. Para jugar baraja.   **b.** Para tomar ron.   **c.** Para comprar cigarros.
4. ¿Quiénes se reunían en La Aurora?
   a. Los bravucones del barrio.   **b.** Los alumnos de la escuela.
   c. Los músicos del pueblo.
5. ¿Qué es lo que palpaba y olía el padre?
   a. Las talas de tabaco.   **b.** Los cigarros.   **c.** Las macarelas.
6. ¿Con qué frecuencia entraba el padre a La Aurora?
   a. Nunca entraba.   **b.** De vez en cuando.   **c.** Todas las noches.
7. ¿Qué hacía José el Tuerto?
   a. Jugaba baraja.   **b.** Dormía.   **c.** Comía.
8. ¿Cuántas personas jugaban baraja?
   a. Tres.   **b.** Cuatro.   **c.** Cinco.
9. ¿Qué le ofrece uno de los hombres al padre?
   a. Un trago de ron.   **b.** Un cigarro.   **c.** Un árbol.
10. ¿Por qué no acepta el padre?
   a. Porque no fuma.   **b.** Porque no bebe.   **c.** Porque no tiene hambre.

Cooperative Learning

Puerto Rico is a commonwealth of the United States. Various nonbinding plebiscites have been held in Puerto Rico to help determine its future status, i.e., independence, statehood, or continued commonwealth status. Have groups of students carry out the following activities:

1. Develop faxes in Spanish for each of the major political parties in Puerto Rico—**Partido Popular** (commonwealth), **Partido Nuevo Progresista** (statehood), **Partido Independentista** (independence)—requesting information about their party and its position on Puerto Rico's status.

2. Try to arrange for interviews with older Puerto Ricans to find out their feelings regarding independence, statehood, and commonwealth. The group should prepare questions beforehand and check them for correctness.

D **Quiere decir.** ¿Qué querrá decir...?

1. Dése un palo.
2. ... ando desarmao.
3. ... usté es más guapo que yo.
4. Ahí va un macho completo.
5. Mi trompeta de amapola tocaba a triunfo.

E **¿Qué es?** Comenten.

1. La palabra «colorado» normalmente quiere decir «con color o rojo». En Puerto Rico el inglés ha tenido mucha influencia en el habla. ¿Qué quiere decir «colorado» en el cuento cuando se refiere a una persona?
2. Describa «La Aurora» en sus propias palabras.
3. ¿Cuál habrá sido el oficio del padre?

Actividades comunicativas

A **Mi papá** Imagínese que Ud. es el niño del cuento. ¿Qué le va a decir a los amiguitos cuando vuelva a la escuela?

B **No es cobarde.** Este tema de la persona que parece ser cobarde, pero que no lo es, es bastante frecuente en la literatura, el teatro y el cine. Piense en un ejemplo y escriba un resumen en español del cuento, drama o película.

Niños puertorriqueños

ANSWERS

Comprensión

D 1. ¡Tómese un trago!
  2. Ando sin arma.
  3. Ud. es más valiente que yo.
  4. Ahí va un hombre valiente.
  5. El hijo estaba orgulloso del padre.

E 1. una persona de ascendencia africana
  2. Era un centro de reunión de todos los «guapos» del barrio.
  3. El padre habrá sido agricultor.

TEACHING TIPS

B. Have students work in groups of four. Give each group four minutes to come up with the best "moral." Each group reads its "moral" to the others, who decide which one is the best.

Actividades comunicativas

ANSWERS

A and B Answers will vary.

Learning From Photos

You may wish to ask these questions about the photo: **¿Quiénes serán los niños? Describa el lugar donde ellos están. ¿Qué tipo de clima habrá allí? ¿Por qué? Comente sobre la ropa que llevan los niños.**

Independent Practice

Assign any of the following:
1. Exercises, pages 292–293
2. Workbook, *Literatura*

VISTAS DE COLOMBIA

OVERVIEW

The **Vistas de Colombia** were prepared by National Geographic
Society. Their purpose is to give students greater insight, through these
visual images, into the culture and
people of Colombia. Have students
look at the photographs on pages
294A–294B for enjoyment. If they
would like to talk about them, let
them say anything they can, using
the vocabulary they have learned to
this point.

National Standards

Cultures
The **Vistas de Colombia**
photos, and the accompanying
captions, allow students to gain
insights into the people of
Colombia.

Learning From Photos

1. **Selva, serranía del Darién**
   The *serranía* is within the
   Choco region of Columbia,
   which stretches from the
   western slopes of the Andes
   mountains to the Pacific
   Ocean. It encompasses a wide
   range of forest habitats,
   including this tropical forest.

2. **Indígenas guambianos,
   Cauca** The indigenous
   population of Colombia is
   quite small, estimated at 1%.
   The *mestizo* population,
   however, is the largest, at 58%.
   The *Guambianos* of the Cauca
   valley are probably descendents
   of the *Chibcha*, a very
   advanced culture.

3. **Pueblo cerca de Bogotá** A
   typical hillside village near the
   capital city of Bogotá. The
   traditional center of village life
   has been the church.

1. Selva tropical, serranía del Darién
2. Indio guambiano leyendo a sus hijos,
   provincia de Cauca
3. Pueblo cerca de Bogotá
4. Guitarrista, Cartagena
5. Aeropuerto, Medellín
6. Bogotá, centro
7. Playa Boca Grande, Cartagena

NATIONAL GEOGRAPHIC SOCIETY **TEACHER'S CORNER**

INDEX TO NATIONAL GEOGRAPHIC MAGAZINE

The following articles may be used for research relating to this chapter:

- "Eruption in Colombia," by Bart McDowell,
  May 1986.
- "The Gauchos, Last of the Breed," by Robert
  Laxalt, October 1980.

NATIONAL GEOGRAPHIC
VISTAS
DE COLOMBIA

(Continued from p. 294A)

4. Guitarrista, Cartagena
Cartagena is a Caribbean port in northwestern Colombia. It was founded by the Spaniards in 1533 and became the treasure city of the Spanish Main.

5. Aeropuerto, Medellín
Medellín is the capital of the department of Antioquia. It is also the major manufacturing center of Colombia with textiles, steel, automobiles, and chemicals produced there. Gold and silver are mined nearby.

6. Bogotá, centro de la ciudad
Skyscrapers blend with old colonial buildings in Santafé de Bogotá, Colombia's capital and major city with a population of 5 million. Bogotá is situated in central Colombia in the department of Cundinamarca.

7. Playa de Boca Grande, Cartagena The beaches of Cartagena have become quite popular with tourists. Cruise ships regularly stop there to allow passengers time to enjoy the warm Caribbean waters.

PRODUCTS AVAILABLE FROM GLENCOE/MCGRAW-HILL

To order the following products call Glencoe/McGraw-Hill at 1-800-334-7344.

CD-ROMs
• Picture Altas of the World
• The Complete National Geographic: 109 Years of National Geographic Magazine

Software
• ZingoLingo: Spanish Diskettes

Transparency Set
• NGS PicturePack: Geography of South America

Videodisc
• STV: World Geography (Volume 3: "South America and Antarctica")

PRODUCTS AVAILABLE FROM NATIONAL GEOGRAPHIC SOCIETY

NATIONAL GEOGRAPHIC SOCIETY

To order the following products call National Geographic Society at 1-800-368-2728.

Books
• Exploring Your World: The Adventure of Geography
• National Geographic Satellite Atlas of the World

Video
• South America ("Nations of the World" Series)

Chapter 7 Overview ◆◆◆◆◆◆◆◆◆◆◆◆◆◆◆◆◆◆◆◆◆◆◆

SCOPE AND SEQUENCE pages 294C-294D

TOPICS	FUNCTIONS	STRUCTURE	CULTURE
◆ Good health habits ◆ Staying in shape ◆ Going for a physical exam ◆ Health care systems in Latin American countries	◆ How to handle health care situations such as having a medical check-up ◆ How to discuss physical and mental health ◆ How to use irregular comparative and superlative adjectives ◆ How to compare people and things ◆ How to use reflexive verbs ◆ How to discuss reciprocal actions ◆ How to combine sentences using the relative pronoun **que** ◆ How to specify who or what is being referred to ◆ How to refer to previously stated ideas ◆ How to use **por** and **para** ◆ How to express durations ◆ How to read and discuss literary works by Gabriel García Márquez and Mario Vargas Llosa	◆ **Formas irregulares del comparativo y del superlativo** ◆ **Comparativo de igualdad** ◆ **Formas regulares de los verbos reflexivos** ◆ **Sentido recíproco** ◆ **Pronombre relativo** *que* ◆ *El que, la que, los que y las que* ◆ *Lo que, cuyo* ◆ *Por y para* ◆ *Por y para* **con expresiones de tiempo** ◆ *Por y para* **con el infinitivo** ◆ **Otros usos de** *por* **y** *para*	◆ Health statistics in Latin America ◆ Medical check-ups ◆ Map of Mexico City ◆ Student health: prohibiting smoking in schools ◆ Health column in *Vanidades* magazine: *Dieta* ◆ Noise pollution ◆ Las Ramblas in Barcelona **Literatura** ◆ «**Un día de éstos**», Gabriel García Márquez ◆ *La tía Julia y el escribidor*, Mario Vargas Llosa

CHAPTER 7 RESOURCES

PRINT	MULTIMEDIA

Planning Resources

Lesson Plans
Block Scheduling Lesson Plans

Interactive Lesson Planner

Reinforcement Resources

Writing Activities Workbook
Student Tape Manual
Video Activities Booklet
Internet Activities Booklet
Glencoe Foreign Language Web Site User's Guide

Transparencies Binder
Audiocassette/Compact Disc Program
Videocassette/Videodisc Program
Online Internet Activities
Electronic Teacher's Classroom Resources

Assessment Resources

Situation Cards
Chapter Quizzes
Testing Program

Testmaker Computer Software (Macintosh/Windows)
Listening Comprehension Audiocassette/Compact Disc

Motivational Resources

Expansion Activities

Café Glencoe: **www.cafe.glencoe.com**

SECTION	PAGES	SECTION RESOURCES
Cultura **Estadísticas sobre la salud** **Algunas estadísticas médicas y alimentarias interesantes**	296–300	Transparency 45 Audiocassette 13A/Compact Disc 9 Writing Activities Workbook, pages 166–168 Student Tape Manual, pages 105–106 Chapter Quizzes, page 95 Testing Program, pages 145–146
Conversación **La salud**	301–304	Transparency 46 Audiocassette 13A/Compact Disc 9 Writing Activities Workbook, page 169 Student Tape Manual, pages 107–108 Chapter Quizzes, page 96 Testing Program, pages 148–150
Lenguaje **La salud** **El estado mental**	305–308	Transparency 47 Audiocassette 13A/Compact Disc 9 Writing Activities Workbook, pages 169–170 Student Tape Manual, pages 109–110 Testing Program, pages 148–150
Repaso de estructura **Formas irregulares del comparativo y del superlativo** **Comparativo de igualdad** **Formas regulares de los verbos reflexivos** **Sentido recíproco**	309–313	Audiocassette 13B/Compact Disc 9 Writing Activities Workbook, pages 171–174 Student Tape Manual, pages 111–112 Chapter Quizzes, pages 97–100 Testing Program, pages 151–152
Periodismo **Salud estudiantil** **«Libreta salud estudiantil y no se fumará en colegios»** **La dieta** **«Dieta»** **La contaminación por el ruido** **«Cómo protegernos...de la contaminación por el ¡Ruido!»**	314–326	Transparencies 48A–48B, 49, 50 Audiocassette 13B–14A/Compact Disc 9 Writing Activities Workbook, pages 175–179 Student Tape Manual, pages 113–117 Chapter Quizzes, pages 101–103 Testing Program, pages 153–159
Estructura **Pronombre relativo** *que* *El que, la que, los que* **y** *las que* *Lo que, cuyo* *Por* **y** *para* *Por* **y** *para* **con expresiones de tiempo** *Por* **y** *para* **con el infinitivo** **Otros usos de** *por* **y** *para*	327–336	Audiocassette 14A/Compact Disc 9 Writing Activities Workbook, pages 180–182 Student Tape Manual, page 120 Chapter Quizzes, pages 104–110 Testing Program, pages 160–161
Literatura **«Un día de éstos», Gabriel García Márquez** *La tía Julia y el escribidor,* **Mario Vargas Llosa**	337–351	Transparencies 51, 52A–52B Audiocassette 14B/Compact Disc 10 Writing Activities Workbook, pages 183–188 Student Tape Manual, pages 121–124 Chapter Quizzes, pages 111–112 Testing Program, pages 162–168

OVERVIEW

In this chapter students will learn to talk about health and well-being. Topics covered include good health habits and diets, staying in shape, and going for a physical.

Students will also learn about the healthcare systems and health related statistics in Latin American countries. They will learn expressions that convey physical and mental states as well as those used when cheering up a sick person.

They will also learn the uses of the relative pronouns and of **por** and **para**. They will read magazine articles about noise pollution and its effect on hearing, and about student health. In the *Literatura* section they will read "Un día de éstos" by Gabriel García Márquez, and an excerpt from Mario Vargas Llosa's *La tía Julia y el escribidor*.

National Standards

⚜ *Communication*
Students will engage in conversations, provide and obtain information, express feelings, and exchange opinions on a variety of topics, especially health and fitness. They will listen to and read authentic language on the same topics.

Learning From Photos

Es el río Futaleufu en la Patagonia chilena. Es uno de los ríos más difíciles para el *rafting* o los *kayac*. El río es famoso por sus rápidos. Queda en una zona bastante remota pero de gran belleza natural.

La salud y el bienestar

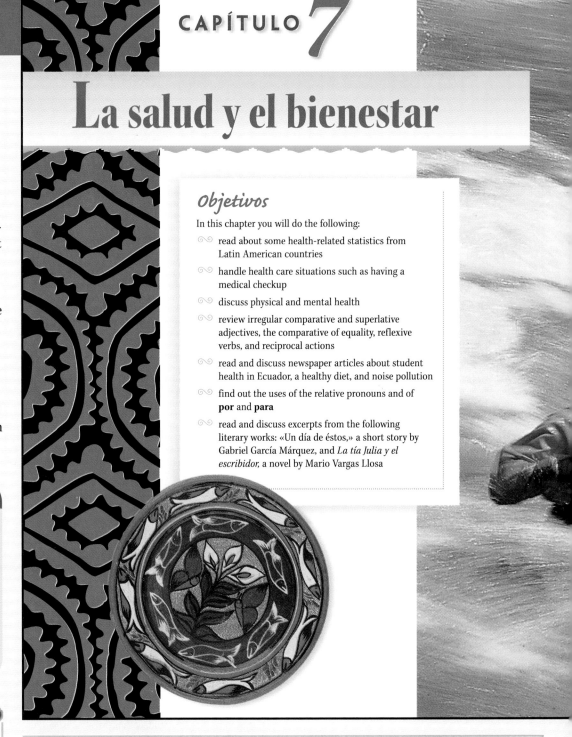

Objetivos

In this chapter you will do the following:

- read about some health-related statistics from Latin American countries
- handle health care situations such as having a medical checkup
- discuss physical and mental health
- review irregular comparative and superlative adjectives, the comparative of equality, reflexive verbs, and reciprocal actions
- read and discuss newspaper articles about student health in Ecuador, a healthy diet, and noise pollution
- find out the uses of the relative pronouns and of **por** and **para**
- read and discuss excerpts from the following literary works: «Un día de éstos,» a short story by Gabriel García Márquez, and *La tía Julia y el escribidor*, a novel by Mario Vargas Llosa

 *inter*NET
CONNECTION

The Glencoe Foreign Language Web site (http://www.glencoe.com/sec/fl) offers these options that enable you and your students to experience the Spanish-speaking world via the Internet:

- At **Café Glencoe**, the interactive "after-school" section of the site, you and your students can access a variety of additional online resources, including online newspapers, interactive games, and a send-a-postcard feature.
- The online **Proyectos** are correlated to the chapters and utilize Hispanic Web sites around the world.

DIFFICULTY PLATEAUS

In all chapters, each reading selection in *Cultura, Periodismo,* and *Literatura,* as well as the *Conversación* and each structure topic, will be rated as follows:

◆ **Easy**
◆◆ **Intermediate**
◆◆◆ **Difficult**

The overall rating of this chapter is: ◆◆ **Intermediate.**

RANDOM ACCESS

You may either follow the exact order of the chapter or omit certain sections that you feel are not necessary for your students. Similarly, you may wish to present a literary selection without interruption or you may intersperse some material from the *Estructura* sections as you are presenting a literary piece.

EVALUATION

Quizzes There is a quiz for every vocabulary presentation and every structure point.

Tests To accompany *¡Buen viaje! Level 3* there are global tests for both *Estructuras,* a combined *Conversación/Lenguaje* test, and one test for each reading in the *Cultura, Periodismo,* and *Literatura* sections. There is also a comprehensive chapter test.

doscientos noventa y cinco ∽ **295**

Chapter Projects

1. *La salud:* Todos juntos, imaginen que van a abrir un gimnasio. Escojan el sitio, los ejercicios, las máquinas, la alimentación, etc. Hagan una publicidad para su club.

2. Pídales a los alumnos que preparen una grabación describiendo la rutina diaria.

3. Pídales a los alumnos que entrevisten a los deportistas y los entrenadores de su escuela sobre cómo se mantienen en forma.

Bell Ringer Review

Use the BRR Transparency 7-1, or write the following on the board:
Haga una lista de cinco cosas que Ud. hace para ponerse en forma o para mantenerse en forma.

TEACHING TIPS

A. You may either read the *Introducción* to the students or have them read it silently.

B. Ask students the following questions about the *Introducción:*
¿Hay diferencias entre las 19 repúblicas de América Latina en los servicios médicos disponibles? ¿Hay diferencias entre las zonas rurales y las grandes ciudades? ¿Por qué?

RESOURCES

- Vocabulary Transparencies
- Audio Cassette 13A/Compact Disc 9
- Student Tape Manual
- Workbook
- Chapter Quizzes

TEACHING VOCABULARY

A. Have students repeat the new words in unison after you or Cassette 13A/Compact Disc 9.

B. You can immediately do *Práctica A* and *B* on page 297 without previous preparation.

CULTURA
Estadísticas sobre la salud

Introducción

En la América Latina hay 19 repúblicas. Hay grandes diferencias entre ellas, hasta en el nivel de su desarrollo industrial y económico. No cabe duda que el nivel del desarrollo influye en los servicios médicos disponibles para los ciudadanos. En la mayoría de las grandes ciudades hay hospitales modernos con el equipo más avanzado. Pero en muchas zonas rurales y aisladas hay una falta de personal y servicios médicos.

Hospital, Buenos Aires, Argentina

Vocabulario

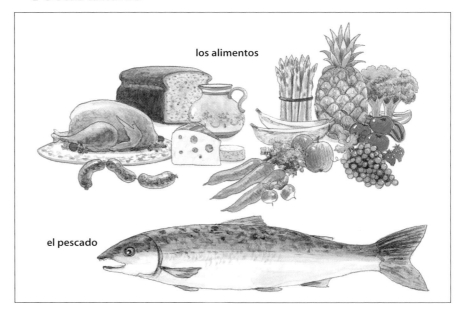

los alimentos

el pescado

Did You Know?

In many cities of Europe and Latin America, hospitals and schools were established to serve a particular ethnic community: **alemán, francés, americano, británico,** etc. This hospital, **Hospital alemán**, would have a German—as well as a Spanish—speaking staff. Today, many of these institutions tend to serve the entire community, not just the particular ethnic group.

el enfermero   la médica   el médico   la enfermera

inscribir matricular
estatal del estado, del gobierno
médico(a) de la medicina

diario(a) de cada día
alimenticio(a), alimentario(a) de los alimentos
pesquero(a) del pescado

✦Práctica✦

A **¿Cuál es la palabra?** Completen.
1. El cirujano es un ___ especialista.
2. El ___ ayuda o asiste al médico.
3. Los cereales, la carne y los huevos son todos ___.
4. El atún y las sardinas son ___.
5. La industria ___ es importante en los países que tienen mucha costa.
6. Es importante tener una buena dieta ___.
7. No es un hospital privado. Es ___.
8. Los que están gravemente enfermos necesitan de mucha atención ___.

B **Palabras derivadas** Escojan.
1. asistir
2. consumir
3. contener
4. caracterizar
5. extraer
6. exportar
7. inscribir

a. la inscripción
b. la extracción
c. la asistencia, el/la asistente(a)
d. el consumo, el consumidor
e. la característica
f. la exportación
g. el contenido

REPLANTEE EL PRESUPUESTO DE SU ACTUAL SERVICIO MEDICO Y SOLO LE RESTARA INGRESAR A

MEDICORP
Argentina

En medicina privada, todo mejor, nada parecido.

Cerrito 836 7° Piso (1010) Buenos Aires
Tel. 46-1271/1272/3969/3809 - 49-2547/8251 - 40-4607

ANSWERS
Práctica
A 1. médico
  2. enfermero
  3. alimentos
  4. pescados
  5. pesquera
  6. alimenticia (alimentaria)
  7. estatal
  8. médica
B 1. c
  2. d
  3. g
  4. e
  5. b
  6. f
  7. a

RECYCLING

1. Have students give words they know related to the following topics: doctor's office, hospital, physical exam, minor accident.
2. Then have students make up sentences using the words and expressions they have given.

Learning From Realia

Have students read the ad and answer:
¿Cuál es el mensaje de este anuncio?

Independent Practice

Assign any of the following:
1. Exercises, page 297
2. Workbook, *Cultura*

297

TEACHING THE READING

Algunas estadísticas médicas y alimentarias interesantes ◆

You may wish to have students read aloud and go over some paragraphs orally in class.

Algunas estadísticas médicas y alimentarias interesantes

Dentistas

México es el país latinoamericano con el mayor número de dentistas.

Uruguay es el país con la mayor proporción de dentistas: 8 por cada mil habitantes.

Guatemala es el país con el menor número de dentistas.

Honduras es el país con el menor número de dentistas por cada mil habitantes.

Médicos y enfermeros

Argentina es el país latinoamericano con el mayor número de médicos. También cuenta con la mayor proporción de médicos por cada mil habitantes: 26,7.

Guatemala es el país que cuenta no sólo con el menor número de médicos pero también con el menor número por cada mil habitantes: 1,2.

México es el país con el mayor número de enfermeras.

Uruguay es el país con el mayor número de enfermeras por cada mil habitantes.

La República Dominicana es el país que cuenta con el menor número de enfermeras. Y también es el país que tiene el menor número de enfermeras por cada mil habitantes: 0,9.

Estudiantes de medicina

México es el país latinoamericano con el mayor número de estudiantes de medicina.

El Salvador es el país con el menor número de estudiantes matriculados en medicina.

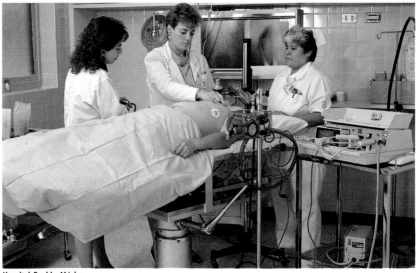

Hospital, Puebla, México

Cooperative Learning

1. Have students work in groups of four to discuss the health care system in the United States.
2. Have students prepare a debate: **Es aconsejable que el Estado asuma la responsabilidad de asegurar el cuidado médico para todos sus ciudadanos. ¿Ud. está a favor o en contra?**

Learning From Photos

Have students say as much about the photograph on page 298 as they can.

Hospital, Puebla, México

Argentina es el país cuyos habitantes tienen el mayor consumo diario de proteínas; con un régimen alimenticio de 112,8 g. por habitante, de los cuales el 67% es de origen animal.

La República Dominicana es el país donde la dieta de la población tiene el menor contenido de proteínas: 46,3 g. por habitante, de los cuales el 38% es de origen animal.

Clínica rural, México

Hospitales

Argentina es el país con el mayor número de hospitales.

Honduras es el país que tiene el menor número de hospitales.

En Hispanoamérica existen dos países en los que el Estado ha asumido el control total de los hospitales: Uruguay y Cuba. Es decir, en esas naciones el 100% de los centros de asistencia médica son estatales.

La República Dominicana es el país con la menor proporción de hospitales del gobierno; sólo el 40,7% de los hospitales existentes son propiedad del Estado.

Argentina es el país que cuenta con el mayor número de camas por hospital.

Paraguay es el país con el menor número de camas por hospital.

Alimentos

Argentina es el país cuya dieta alimenticia tiene el más alto contenido de calorías: 3.368 calorías diarias, promedio aritmético anual.

Ecuador es el país con el menor número de calorías consumidas: 2.081 calorías diarias, promedio aritmético anual.

Producción agropecuaria

Argentina es el país con la mayor producción de carne y siempre se ha caracterizado por ofrecerle al mundo productos de este tipo de una calidad extraordinaria.

Chile es el país con mayor producción pesquera. Sus volúmenes de extracción lo han colocado en el séptimo lugar de la producción mundial.

Argentina es el país que tradicionalmente ha exportado la mayor cantidad de productos comestibles.

México es el país con el mayor volumen de productos comestibles importados.

Learning From Photos

Preparen Uds. una conversación entre las dos enfermeras que aparecen en la foto en esta página.

Critical Thinking Activity

Thinking skills: evaluating information

Explique el significado de lo siguiente: «En Latinoamérica existen dos países en los que el Estado ha asumido el control de los hospitales.»

ANSWERS
Comprensión
A Answers will vary.

TEACHING TIPS

Actividad A can be done as an individual project, while *Actividades B* and *C* work well as paired activities.

Actividades comunicativas

ANSWERS

A–C Answers will vary.

ABOUT THE SPANISH LANGUAGE

◆ The word **hacienda** is probably the most common one used today to express "country estate." However, in Argentina one will often hear **la estancia**. Once upon a time **la estancia** was a "cattle station," but today it more commonly means "country estate." Other terms that can mean a country estate or farm are: **la finca, la granja, el rancho** (Mexico), **el cortijo** (cattle farm in Spain). A country house is often called **la quinta**. In some areas, however, this word is used in a more general sense for a suburban house.

◆ The word **rancho** in most instances does not convey the meaning of "ranch" except in Mexico. The original meaning of this word is a "hut" and the shantytowns around Caracas are called **ranchos**.

◆ The word for "cowboy" also varies from region to region. **Los vaqueros** is a rather generic term. Others are **los gauchos** (Argentina and Uruguay), **los charros** (Mexico), **los llaneros** (Venezuela), and **los huasos** (Chile).

Hacienda, las Pampas, Argentina

Botes pesqueros, Antofagasta, Chile

Comprensión

A **En Latinoamérica** Den algunos datos sobre los siguientes países.

1. Argentina
2. Honduras
3. Cuba
4. Uruguay
5. Ecuador
6. Chile
7. la República Dominicana
8. México

Actividades comunicativas

A **Los comestibles** Prepare Ud. una lista de todos los alimentos o comestibles que pueda identificar en español. De esta lista, decida cuáles son altos en calorías y cuáles son bajos en calorías. Decida cuáles son buenos para la salud y cuáles no son muy buenos para la salud.

B **¡Qué mal me siento!** Ud. se siente mal. Vaya a la farmacia. Descríbale los síntomas al/a la farmacéutico(a) (un[a] compañero[a] de clase) y pregúntele qué le puede recetar. El/La farmacéutico(a) le va a hacer algunas preguntas sobre su salud y le va a recomendar algo para aliviar sus síntomas.

C **En la consulta** Trabajando con un(a) compañero(a) de clase, imagínense que están en la sala de consulta de un(a) médico(a). Uno será el/la médico(a) y el/la otro(a) será el/la paciente. Preparen una conversación.

Independent Practice

Assign any of the following:
1. Exercises, page 300
2. Workbook, *Cultura*

Conversación

La salud

Vocabulario

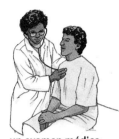

un examen médico

tomar una radiografía de los pulmones

tomar el pulso

caminar

la jeringa

tomar una muestra de sangre

tomar la tensión arterial

exigir   pedir, necesitar
estar en (de) buena salud, gozar de buena salud   estar bien

pulmonar   de los pulmones
cardíaco(a)   del corazón

Práctica

A   **Cosas de la salud**   ¿Sí o no?

1. La tensión arterial crónicamente alta o elevada es peligrosa.
2. Hay que introducir una jeringa para tomar una muestra de sangre.
3. Los rayos equis son una radiografía.
4. Caminar es una actividad física.
5. Comer entre comidas es bueno para la salud.

B   **¿Cuál es la palabra?**   Den la palabra apropiada.

1. de los pulmones
2. del corazón
3. andar a pie
4. la presión arterial

CONVERSACIÓN

Bell Ringer Review

Use the BRR Transparency 7-3, or write the following on the board:
Describa Ud. su última visita a la consulta del médico.

RESOURCES

- Vocabulary Transparencies
- Audio Cassette 13A/Compact Disc 9
- Student Tape Manual
- Workbook
- Chapter Quizzes

TEACHING VOCABULARY

You may wish to follow the suggestions outlined in previous chapters.

ANSWERS
Práctica
A 1. sí   4. sí
   2. sí   5. no
   3. sí
B 1. pulmonar   4. la tensión
   2. cardíaco   arterial
   3. caminar

ABOUT THE SPANISH LANGUAGE

- **Caminar** conveys the physical activity of walking. **Dar un paseo** or **pasear** means "to take a walk" or "to go for a walk."
- In addition to **la tensión arterial,** one will also hear **la tensión sanguínea** and **la presión arterial (sanguínea).**

Additional Practice

1. Have students describe a typical physical exam.
2. Skit: Have students make up funny skits about going to the nurse's office in their school.

Independent Practice

Assign any of the following:
1. Exercises, page 301
2. Workbook, *Conversacíon*

301

TEACHING THE CONVERSATION

◆ Escenas de la vida ◆

A. Have students listen to the recording of the *Conversación* on Cassette 13A/Compact Disc 9.

B. Call on two students to read the *Conversación* aloud.

C. Have students make up questions about the conversation. They may call on whomever they want to answer their questions.

Escenas de la vida

Un examen médico

MARCOS: Acabo de hacerme un examen médico.

CRISTINA: ¿Por qué?

MARCOS: Porque quiero jugar al fútbol con el equipo de la escuela y exigen un examen físico completo.

CRISTINA: ¿Qué te hizo el médico?

MARCOS: Pues, me tomó el pulso y la tensión.

CRISTINA: ¿Y?

MARCOS: Todo normal. Sabes, el médico me dijo que muchos adolescentes también tienen una tensión arterial elevada. Es algo que yo no sabía.

CRISTINA: ¿Te tomó una muestra de sangre?

MARCOS: Sí, y no me gustó nada, pero quería hacerme un análisis de sangre.

CRISTINA: ¿Tienes los resultados?

MARCOS: Sí, me dijo que todo está normal—el nivel de colesterol, de azúcar, etc.

CRISTINA: ¿Te tomó una radiografía de los pulmones?

MARCOS: Sí. Salió negativa, ningún problema pulmonar. Y el electrocardiograma, también normal. No tengo problemas cardíacos.

CRISTINA: Entonces, mi amor, estás muy bien de salud.

MARCOS: Sí. Estoy muy bien de salud y de forma.

Did You Know?

In some Latin American cities there has been an active campaign to lower cholesterol levels. Medical vans have been set up on some major streets to conduct tests for cholesterol.

302

¡Estoy en forma!

CRISTINA: Siempre estás en forma porque haces ejercicios. Nunca en mi vida he visto a nadie que haga tanto ejercicio como tú.

MARCOS: Sí, me gusta caminar y hacer jogging. Y escojo con mucho cuidado los alimentos que como. Sigo una dieta buena.

CRISTINA: Me imagino que comienzas el día con un buen desayuno.

MARCOS: Ah, sí. Yogur, cereales. Tomo tres comidas al día y no como entre comidas.

CRISTINA: ¿Nunca?

MARCOS: Casi nunca.

CRISTINA: Pues, estoy de acuerdo contigo. La salud personal es muy importante. Estar en forma está muy de moda.

ABOUT THE SPANISH LANGUAGE

◆ Other terms used for **hacer jogging** are **hacer footing, hacer el trote,** and **trotar.**
◆ One often wears **una sudadera** (*sweat suit*) for jogging.

VOCABULARY EXPANSION

You may wish to give students the following vocabulary so that they are able to describe a typical American breakfast in Spanish:

los huevos: pasados por agua, fritos, revueltos
el tocino, el jamón, la salchicha
los panqueques, el jarabe
el pan tostado, la mermelada
los cereales, el yogur

CONVERSACIÓN

trescientos tres 〜 **303**

Independent Practice

Assign any of the following:
1. Exercises, page 304
2. Workbook, *Conversacíon*

TEACHING TIPS

A You can ask the questions from *Comprensión A* as you are going over the *Conversación*.

B You may allow students to look up the information if they can't recall it.

ANSWERS
Comprensión

A 1. Marcos acaba de hacerse un examen físico.
  2. Él quiere jugar al fútbol.
  3. El médico le tomó el pulso y la tensión.
  4. Sí, ya los recibió.
  5. Todo está normal.
  6. No, no tiene problemas.
  7. Sí, está siempre en forma.
  8. Hace ejercicios y come bien.
  9. Toma tres comidas al día.
  10. Casi nunca come entre comidas.

B 1. tensión arterial normal
  2. colesterol normal
  3. radiografía pulmonar negativa
  4. electrocardiograma normal
  5. fútbol
  6. caminar y hacer jogging
  7. tres comidas

Actividades comunicativas

ANSWERS

A–D Answers will vary.

Comprensión

A **Un examen físico** Contesten.
  1. ¿Qué acaba de hacerse Marcos?
  2. ¿Por qué?
  3. ¿Qué le ha hecho el médico?
  4. ¿Ha recibido Marcos los resultados?
  5. ¿Cuáles son los resultados?
  6. ¿Tiene problemas o trastornos?
  7. ¿Está siempre en forma Marcos?
  8. ¿Qué hace para mantenerse en forma?
  9. ¿Cuándo come?
  10. ¿Come entre comidas?

B **La salud de Marcos** Den la siguiente información.
  1. la tensión arterial de Marcos
  2. su nivel de colesterol
  3. el resultado de su radiografía pulmonar
  4. el resultado de su electrocardiograma
  5. el deporte que quiere practicar
  6. los ejercicios que le gustan
  7. el número de comidas que come cada día

Actividades comunicativas

A **La consulta** En sus propias palabras, describa una consulta con el médico.

B **Me pongo en forma.** Explique todo lo que Ud. hace para mantenerse en forma.

C **La higiene personal** Converse con un(a) compañero(a) de clase sobre la importancia de la higiene personal. Expliquen lo que Uds. hacen para mantener una buena higiene personal.

D **Un formulario médico** Complete el siguiente formulario médico. Escriba en otro papel.

CLÍNICA SAN BERNARDO

ORDEN DE INGRESO   Número
Documento: _____
Historia Clínica: _____
Registro Movimiento Enfermos: _____

Asegurado
Beneficiario

NOMBRE Y APELLIDOS: _____
DIAGNÓSTICO PROVISIONAL _____
FACULTATIVO QUE ORDENÓ EL INGRESO: _____
PLANTA: _____ HABITACIÓN: _____ CAMA NÚMERO: _____
SERVICIO: _____
Compañía de Seguros _____
Nº de Póliza □□□□□□□□□□□ PROCEDENCIA { URGENCIA / CONSULTA / OTRAS }

INGRESO
Día ___ de _____ de 1.9___ hora _____
MOTIVO: _____
El Médico de guardia.

ALTA
Día ___ de _____ de 1.9___ hora _____
CAUSA: _____
El Jefe de la Clínica.

Learning From Realia

1. Ask: **¿Qué es el documento?**
2. Have students find the Spanish equivalent for each of the following:
   temporary, initial **(provisional)**
   admittance **(el ingreso)**
   release **(dar de alta)**
   doctor **(el médico, el facultativo)**
   doctor on duty **(el médico de guardia)**

Cooperative Learning

Have students work in pairs. One asks questions based on the **Orden de ingreso** (realia). The other responds. Together they will fill out the document on a separate sheet of paper.

Lenguaje

La salud

Si quiere saber cómo está alguien, le puede preguntar:

¿Cómo está Ud.?	**¿Cómo te sientes?**
¿Cómo le va?	**¿Cómo estás?**
¿Cómo se siente Ud.?	**¿Cómo te va?**
	¿Qué tal?

¿Cómo está Ud.?

Si alguien le hace una de estas preguntas a Ud., puede contestar de varias maneras:

POSITIVO	NEGATIVO
Estoy muy bien, gracias.	**Así, así.**
Muy bien.	**No me siento bien.**
	Estoy enfermo(a).
	Tengo ___.

Sin embargo, hay que señalar que por lo general uno contesta que está bien hasta cuando no sea verdad. Solemos discutir nuestro verdadero estado de salud sólo con gente que conocemos bien.

Si Ud. se despide de alguien que está enfermo, le puede decir:

¡Cuídese bien!
¡Cuídate bien!

Hay muchas expresiones que podemos usar para describir nuestro estado físico. Algunas son:

Tengo hambre.
Él no tiene mucho apetito.
Ella está cansada (agotada, rendida, molida).
Yo no duermo bien.
No puedo dormirme.
No puedo conciliar el sueño.
Tengo un hambre que me mata.
Come como un pájaro.
Paso la noche dando vueltas en la cama.

Tengo hambre.

Bell Ringer Review

Use the BRR Transparency 7-4, or write the following on the board: **¿Cómo estás? Dé varias respuestas a esta pregunta.**

TEACHING TIPS

Read the explanatory information to the class. Call on individuals or have the class repeat the various expressions in unison. Insist that they repeat with expression and the proper intonation.

VOCABULARY EXPANSION

Some additional vocabulary you may wish to give that is useful when traveling is:
Me duele el estómago.
Me siento mareado(a).
Tengo diarrea.
Estoy estreñido(a).
(constipated)

ABOUT THE SPANISH LANGUAGE

There are some false cognates related to health and emotional states that nonnative speakers of Spanish should be made aware of.

◆ **Estoy constipado(a)** does not mean constipated but rather "I have a cold." **Estar constipado(a)** is a synonym of **tener catarro, tener un resfriado,** or **estar resfriado(a). Estoy estreñido(a)** is "I am constipated."

◆ **Embarazada** means "pregnant," not embarrassed. It is a synonym for **estar encinta.** "To be embarrassed" is **estar avergonzado(a).**

Advanced Game

Vocabulary Game: Create Your Own Story Set-up Prepare (or have students in pairs prepare) cards with vocabulary words from the current chapter, one word per card. Include verbs (verbs might be on colored cards since each group needs to have some). Students can work in small groups (3–4) or with a partner. Shuffle the cards and distribute 10–20 per group.

Game The object of the game is to come up with a story using as many of the cards as possible. Tell students what tense the story is to be in. Each team gets 1 point for every word they use correctly. They can use words twice. One point is deducted for every unused card. Stories can be put on butcher paper for the others to read.

TEACHING TIPS

Have students close their books. Do these *Práctica* orally. Encourage students to answer in as much detail as possible.

ANSWERS
Práctica
A and **B** Answers will vary.

◈ Práctica ◈

A **¿Estás enfermo(a)?** Preguntas personales.

1. ¿Cómo estás hoy?
2. ¿Estás en forma?
3. ¿Qué haces para mantenerte en forma?
4. ¿Conoces a alguien que esté enfermo? ¿Qué tiene?
5. ¿Cómo te sientes cuando tienes un resfriado?
6. ¿Estás cansado(a)?
7. ¿Duermes bien o no?
8. ¿Te duermes en cuanto te acuestas o no?
9. ¿Te gusta comer?
10. ¿Siempre tienes apetito?
11. ¿Te gusta comer entre comidas?

B **¿Cómo se dice?** Expresen de otra manera.

1. ¿Qué tal?
2. Muy bien.
3. No estoy muy bien.
4. Tengo mucha hambre.
5. ¡Qué sueño tengo!
6. No duermo bien.
7. No puedo dormirme.

Learning From Photos

Saltar a la cuerda (soga) is the expression for "to jump rope."

Independent Practice

Assign the exercises on page 306.

El estado mental

Estoy triste.

Estoy contenta.

Estoy enojada.

El estado mental tiene mucho que ver con nuestra salud y nuestro bienestar. Hay cosas que nos ponen contentos y otras que nos ponen tristes o deprimidos. Para expresar nuestra felicidad o nuestra tristeza, podemos decir:

> **Estoy contento(a).**
> **Estoy alegre.**
> **Estoy (Soy) feliz.**
> **Estoy de buen humor.**
> **Estoy de mal humor.**
> **Estoy triste.**
> **Estoy deprimido(a).**
> **Estoy nervioso(a), preocupado(a).**

Hay muchas cosas que nos pueden hacer infelices, que nos afectan negativamente porque nos molestan.

> **Esto me molesta. Me fastidia.**
> **Esto me enfada, me enoja, no me alegra.**
> **Esto me da rabia, me pone furioso(a).**

TEACHING TIPS

Have students repeat the model sentences after you. Be sure that they say these expressions with the proper intonation as they speak.

ABOUT THE SPANISH LANGUAGE

- Other expressions for "to be angry" or "to get mad" are **estar bravo(a), ponerse bravo(a).**
- It is no longer necessary to use the verb **ser** with **feliz.** The old grammar rule states that one must use **ser** with **feliz** and **estar** with **contento.** One will very frequently hear and read **estar feliz,** even in the works of such authors as Gabriel García Márquez and Isabel Allende.

Advanced Game

Divide the class into two teams. Give each student an index card. Have all students make up possible situations that would elicit any of the positive or negative expressions on page 307. (They can model the situations in *Práctica B* on page 308.) Each team takes turns reading their situations to the other team. A point is given for an appropriate response or deducted for an inappropriate one. The team being questioned should continue until someone makes an error.

Alumno(a) 1: Tú has salido mal en el examen de matemáticas.
Alumno(a) 2: Estoy deprimido(a).

307

⟐Práctica⟐

A **¿Cómo estás?** Preguntas personales.
1. Hoy, ¿estás contento(a) o triste?
2. ¿Estás siempre contento(a)?
3. Hoy, ¿estás de buen humor o de mal humor?
4. ¿Siempre estás de buen humor?
5. ¿Estás enfadado(a) o enojado(a) ahora? Si contestas que sí, ¿por qué? ¿Qué o quién te ha enojado o enfadado?

B **¿Cómo te sientes?** Expliquen.
1. Tu hermanito(a) siempre está haciendo cositas que a ti no te gustan.
2. Tu amigo(a) te pidió prestada la bicicleta. Se la prestaste y la perdió. La dejó en alguna parte pero no se acuerda dónde.
3. Un(a) buen(a) amigo(a) está muy enfermo(a).
4. Acabas de recibir una noticia muy buena.
5. Acabas de recibir una noticia muy mala.
6. Has ganado la lotería.
7. Has recibido tres notas muy malas.
8. Una persona a quien conoces acaba de morir.

C **Me molesta.** Completen.
1. Él me enfada cuando ___.
2. Me molesta saber que ___.
3. Ella me da rabia cuando ___.
4. Yo estaba furioso(a) porque ___.
5. Mis padres se ponen furiosos cuando yo ___.
6. Estoy deprimido(a) porque ___.

⟐Actividades comunicativas⟐

A **Estoy alegre.** Con un(a) compañero(a) de clase, comenten sobre las cosas que les molestan, les ponen contentos, les dan rabia y los deprimen. Luego digan lo que cada uno(a) hace cuando siente estas emociones. Indiquen si se comportan de la misma manera o no.

B **Mauricio y Mayela** Mauricio y Mayela descubren que mañana van a tener un examen de historia importantísimo. La profesora de historia es bastante exigente y nunca avisa cuando va a dar un examen. ¿Cómo se sienten Mauricio y Mayela? Con un(a) compañero(a) de clase, preparen una conversación entre Mayela y Mauricio en la que describen sus reacciones.

Repaso de estructura

Making comparisons
Formas irregulares del comparativo y del superlativo

1. Review the comparative and superlative forms of the following adjectives.

bueno(a)	**mejor**	**el/la mejor**
malo(a)	**peor**	**el/la peor**
grande	**mayor**	**el/la mayor**
pequeño(a)	**menor**	**el/la menor**

2. **Menor** and **mayor** are used to refer to age and quantity. For size, **más grande** or **más pequeño** are usually used.

> **Si no me equivoco, su hermana es la mayor de la familia.**
> **La mayor parte de sus parientes vive(n) en Los Ángeles.**
> **Su familia es más grande que la nuestra.**

3. **Mejor** and **peor** are also used as adverbs.

bien	**mejor**	**el mejor**
mal	**peor**	**el peor**

> **El médico dice que estará mejor mañana.**
> **El enfermo está peor hoy.**

Práctica

A HISTORIETA La familia Ugarte

Contesten.

1. Emilio tiene 18 años y su hermana Pepita tiene 16. ¿Quién es menor? ¿Quién es mayor?
2. Emilio y Pepita tienen muchos primos. Su prima Lupita tiene sólo ocho meses, mientras que su primo Paco tiene unos 25 años. De todos sus primos, ¿quién es la menor? ¿Quién es el mayor?
3. Emilio no se siente muy bien hoy. Tiene catarro. ¿Cómo estará mañana?

RESOURCES

- Workbook
- Student Tape Manual
- Audio Cassette 13B/Compact Disc 9
- Computer Software: *Estructura*
- Chapter Quizzes
- Testing Program

Bell Ringer Review

Use the BRR Transparency 7-5, or write the following on the board: **¿Cómo te va? Contesta con todas las expresiones que acabas de aprender.**

TEACHING STRUCTURE

◆ Making comparisons ◆

Guide the students through the review in steps 1, 2, and 3 and have the class repeat the forms and model sentences in unison.

TEACHING TIPS

These *Práctica* can probably be done with books closed without previous preparation.

ANSWERS
Práctica

A 1. **Pepita es menor. Emilio es mayor.**
2. **Lupita es la menor. Paco es el mayor.**
3. **Mañana estará mejor (peor).**

310

ANSWERS

Práctica

B Answers will vary.

TEACHING STRUCTURE

✦ Comparing people and things ✦

Since this is a review of a relatively simple concept, have the students read through steps 1–3 and repeat the model sentences in unison.

TEACHING TIPS

This *Práctica* can be done immediately following the explanatory material with books closed or open.

ANSWERS

Práctica

A 1. tantos, como
   2. tantas, como
   3. tan, como
   4. tantas, como
   5. tan, como
   6. tanta, como
   7. tan, como

B **¿El mayor o el menor?** Preguntas personales.

1. ¿Cómo estás hoy? Y mañana, ¿estarás mejor o peor?
2. En tu escuela, ¿cuál es la mejor nota que se puede recibir?
3. ¿Y cuál es la peor?
4. ¿En qué curso recibes la mejor calificación?
5. ¿Y la peor?
6. ¿Quién es menor, tu madre o tu padre?
7. ¿Quién es el/la mayor de tu familia?
8. ¿Y quién es el/la menor de tu familia?
9. ¿Vive la mayor parte de tus parientes en la misma región o no?

Comparing people and things
Comparativo de igualdad

1. Very often we compare two items that have the same characteristics. Such a comparison is called the comparison of equality. In English we use the expression *as... as.* In Spanish **tan... como** is used with either an adjective or an adverb.

> **José es tan deportista como su hermana.**
> **Él juega tan bien como ella.**

2. The comparison of equality can also be used with nouns. In English we use *as much as, as many as.* In Spanish the expression **tanto... como** is used with nouns. **Tanto** must agree with the noun it modifies.

> **Ella tiene tanta fuerza como él.**
> **Ella ha ganado tantos campeonatos como él.**

3. Note that when a pronoun follows a comparative construction either the subject pronoun or a negative word is used.

> **Ella juega mejor que yo. Tiene más trofeos que nadie.**

⬦ Práctica ⬦

A **Los dos son iguales.** Completen.

1. Él hace ___ ejercicios ___ ella.
2. Ella ha corrido en ___ carreras ___ él.
3. Ella es ___ ágil ___ él.
4. El bróculi tiene ___ vitaminas ___ las judías verdes.
5. Las verduras son ___ buenas para la salud ___ las frutas.
6. Estos cigarrillos contienen ___ nicotina ___ los otros.
7. Estos cigarrillos son ___ dañinos para la salud ___ los otros.

Learning From Photos

In order to describe the photo, you may wish to give students the following words about track and field events: **correr en una carrera, el/la corredor(a), el pelotón** (pack of runners), **la pista, el campo, la salida, la llegada, la línea de llegada, el/la primer(a) corredor(a), el/la corredor(a) que va a la cabeza, ir parejos** (to be tied for position), **ganar por una cabeza.**

Independent Practice

Assign any of the following:
1. Exercises, page 310
2. Workbook, *Repaso de estructura*

What people do for themselves
Formas regulares de los verbos reflexivos

1. A reflexive verb is one in which the action of the verb is both executed and received by the subject.

> **Me lavo.**   *I wash myself.*

2. Since the subject also receives the action of the verb, an additional pronoun is used. This pronoun is called a reflexive pronoun. Review the following forms.

INFINITIVE	lavarse	bañarse
yo	me lavo	me baño
tú	te lavas	te bañas
él, ella, Ud.	se lava	se baña
nosotros(as)	nos lavamos	nos bañamos
vosotros(as)	*os laváis*	*os bañáis*
ellos, ellas, Uds.	se lavan	se bañan

3. The following verbs have a stem change in both the present and preterite tenses.

> **despedirse (i, i)**
> **vestirse (i, i)**
> **divertirse (ie, i)**
> **sentirse (ie, i)**
> **dormirse (ue, u)**

4. Remember that a reflexive pronoun is used only when the subject also receives the action of the verb. If a person or object other than the subject receives the action of the verb, no reflexive pronoun is used. Look at the following sentences.

> **María se lava.**
> **María lava el carro.**
>
> **Papá se acuesta.**
> **Papá acuesta al bebé.**
>
> **Ella se mira en el espejo.**
> **Ella mira al niño.**

 Bell Ringer Review

Use the BRR Transparency 7-6, or write the following on the board: **Escriba una lista de todo lo que Ud. hace por la mañana antes de salir de casa.**

TEACHING STRUCTURE

 What people do for themselves ◆

Note It is quite possible that students will not need much review on this particular point.

A. Write the forms of one of the verbs on the board. Circle the subject and the reflexive pronoun. Draw a line from the reflexive pronoun to the subject pronoun to indicate that they are the same.

B. As students read the sentences in step 4, they can dramatize washing themselves vs. washing something else. These dramatizations help students visualize and, therefore, understand the concept.

Learning From Photos

Have students say as much as they can about the photo.

Did You Know?

Aunque los blue jeans y las camisetas son muy populares entre los jóvenes hispanos, todavía es costumbre vestir a las niñas pequeñas en vestidos femeninos, y a los varoncitos en ropa masculina.

311

TEACHING TIPS

A. *Práctica A* can be done with books closed without previous preparation.

B. You may wish to assign *Práctica B* and *C* for homework and go over them in class the next day.

ANSWERS

Práctica

A Answers will vary.

B 1. se acostó

2. se durmió

3. no me dormí

4. se acostaron Uds.

5. se levantaron

6. nos desayunamos

7. te desayunaste

8. se despidió

9. se divirtieron

C 1. me

2. me

3. (no reflexive, no reflexive)

4. (no reflexive), se

5. (no reflexive)

A HISTORIETA **Algunas costumbres mías**

Contesten.

1. ¿A qué hora te acuestas?
2. ¿Te duermes en seguida o pasas la noche dando vueltas en la cama?
3. ¿A qué hora te levantas?
4. ¿Te despiertas fácilmente?
5. ¿Te bañas o te duchas antes de acostarte o después de levantarte?
6. ¿Te desayunas antes de salir para la escuela?
7. ¿Te cepillas los dientes después de tomar el desayuno?
8. ¿Te pones un uniforme para ir a la escuela?
9. ¿Te vistes elegantemente para ir a la escuela?
10. ¿Te diviertes con tus amigos en la escuela?
11. ¿Te despides de tus amigos cuando sales de la escuela?

B **No me dormí.** Escriban las siguientes oraciones en el pretérito.

1. Juan se acuesta a las diez y media.
2. Se duerme en seguida.
3. Desgraciadamente, yo no me duermo en seguida.
4. ¿A qué hora se acuestan Uds.?
5. ¿Y a qué hora se levantan?
6. Nosotros nos desayunamos en casa.
7. ¿Te desayunas en casa o en la escuela?
8. Juan se despide de sus padres antes de salir para la escuela.
9. Juan y sus amigos se divierten mucho en la escuela.

C **¿Reflexivo o no?** Completen con el pronombre reflexivo cuando sea necesario.

1. Yo ____ acuesto a las once de la noche.
2. Yo ____ baño antes de acostarme.
3. Mamá ____ lava al bebé y luego papi ____ acuesta al bebé.
4. Cada mañana yo ____ despierto a mi hermano. Si no lo hiciera yo, él no ____ despertaría nunca.
5. Mi perrito tiene el pelo muy largo. Yo ____ cepillo al perrito tres o cuatro veces a la semana.

Learning From Photos

You may call on students to compare their room with the room of the young woman in the photo. Students may want to use the words **ordenado, desordenado, cuidadoso.**

Independent Practice

Assign any of the following:
1. Exercises, page 312
2. Workbook, *Repaso de estructura*

Reciprocal actions
Sentido recíproco

A reciprocal verb expresses a mutual action or relationship. In English you use "each other" or "one another." In Spanish, you use a reflexive pronoun.

Ellos se vieron pero no se hablaron.
They saw one another but they didn't speak to one another.

Nos besamos en la mejilla.
We kissed each other on the cheek.

Los dos hermanos se parecen mucho.
The two brothers look a lot like each other.

Práctica

A **Se conocieron en la fiesta.** Completen.

1. Él me vio y yo lo vi. Nosotros ___ ___ en la tienda por departamentos.
2. Ella me conoció y yo la conocí. Nosotros ___ ___ en la fiesta de Alejandro.
3. Ella le escribió a él y él le escribió a ella. Ellos ___ ___ la semana pasada.
4. Él la quiere y ella lo quiere. Ellos ___ ___.
5. El niño ayuda a la niña y la niña ayuda al niño. Los niños ___ ___ mucho.
6. Carlos encontró a María y María encontró a Carlos. Ellos ___ ___ por casualidad en la esquina de Madero y Correo.

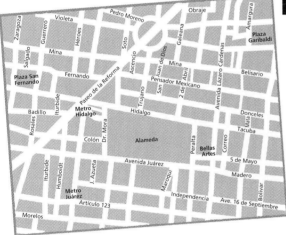

trescientos trece 〜 **313**

TEACHING STRUCTURE

◆ Reciprocal actions ◆◆

It should not be necessary to spend much time on the review of the reciprocal construction. You may wish to have the students read the model sentences aloud and then proceed directly to the *Práctica* on page 313.

ANSWERS
Práctica

A 1. nos vimos
2. nos conocimos
3. se escribieron
4. se quieren
5. se ayudan
6. se encontraron

Additional Practice

Have students do the following activities:
1. **Prepare Ud. el horario de su rutina diaria. Compárelo con el de un(a) compañero(a) de clase.**
2. **Prepare Ud. un informe sobre los mejores alimentos para la salud. Explique por qué son tan buenos.**

Learning From Realia

Have students try to guess by the names of the streets what city this is. **(la Ciudad de México)**

313

Periodismo
Salud estudiantil

Introducción

Recientemente el Ministerio de Educación del Ecuador ha tomado varias medidas relacionadas con la salud de los alumnos en las instituciones educativas del país. Han prohibido el uso (el consumo) y la venta (el expendio) de cigarrillos en las escuelas. Han establecido reglamentos respecto a los alimentos que se permiten consumir en las escuelas y también sobre cómo deben ser manipulados estos alimentos.

El artículo que sigue apareció en un periódico de Quito.

Vocabulario

el aula

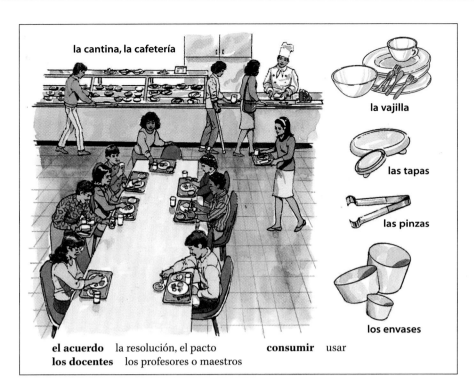

la cantina, la cafetería
la vajilla
las tapas
las pinzas
los envases

el acuerdo la resolución, el pacto   **consumir** usar
los docentes los profesores o maestros

TEACHING TIPS

Práctica A and *B* can be done orally with books closed after the vocabulary has been presented.

ANSWERS
Práctica
A 1. docentes
   2. aula
   3. pinzas
   4. tapa
   5. la vajilla
B 1. un acuerdo
   2. Los docentes
   3. el aula
   4. consumen

Práctica

A **En la escuela** Completen.

1. Los ___ enseñan y los alumnos aprenden.
2. Los alumnos están sentados en filas en el ___.
3. Sirven el almuerzo en la cafetería. Para no tocar los sándwiches con las manos, las señoras los sirven con ___.
4. El envase tiene una ___ para cerrarlo.
5. Las tazas, los platos, etc. son ___.

B **Se dice así.** Expresen de otra manera.

1. Han llegado a *una resolución*.
2. *Los maestros* enseñan a los alumnos.
3. Enseñan a los alumnos en *la sala de clase*.
4. En la escuela *usan* mucho papel.

PERIODISMO   *trescientos quince* ∾ **315**

Independent Practice

Assign any of the following:
1. Exercises, page 315
2. Workbook, *Periodismo*

TEACHING THE READING

◆ Libreta Salud estudiantil y no se fumará en colegios ◆

A. You may wish to call on students to read some paragraphs aloud. You may have them read others silently. Or, you may wish to have students read the entire article silently.

B. You may wish to intersperse the reading with the following questions: **¿Cuáles son los tres acuerdos que el Ministerio de Educación ha expedido? En cuanto a cigarrillos y alcohol, ¿qué se prohíbe? ¿De qué habla el tercer decreto?**

ABOUT THE SPANISH LANGUAGE

1. Note the use of the word **bar** in this article: **los bares en los establecimientos educativos.** In some areas, **el bar** does not necessarily have to serve alcoholic beverages.

2. The word **local** can mean "local" but as a noun **el local** means "place" or "establishment" as in the expression used here, **los locales educativos.**

3. Note the use of the word **fundas** for "wrappers." **Funda** also means "pillow case" and in the Dominican Republic it is used for a "bag" or "sack."

Libreta Salud estudiantil y no se fumará en colegios

QUITO—El Ministerio de Educación expidió tres acuerdos mediante los cuales se procurará[1] mejorar[2] la calidad de vida de miles de estudiantes de los diferentes establecimientos educativos del país.

Mediante el Decreto 2368, se regula y establece oficialmente la Libreta de Salud Integral en todo el país, la misma que tendrá un costo de 1.000 sucres y servirá como único documento legal para la matrícula de primer año en los tres niveles del sistema educativo; con el respectivo seguimiento de los 5 a los 18 años de edad.

Prohibido fumar

El segundo acuerdo tiene relación con la prohibición de consumir cigarrillos y alcohol en los establecimientos de todos los niveles educativos del país, dentro y fuera del aula. Para este efecto, se mantendrá en los locales educativos un estricto control del uso y abuso del cigarrillo y alcohol, por parte de los docentes.

Igualmente, se prohíbe el expendio[3] de cigarrillos y alcohol en los establecimientos y se responsabilizará a las autoridades de los mismos, por el fiel cumplimiento de esta norma.

Reglamento

El tercer Decreto, Nº 2371, habla de la expedición del reglamento para el manejo y administración de bares en establecimientos educativos del país; el mismo establece que los alimentos y bebidas que se expendan deben ser naturales y frescos, sin fermentación, cuyas características físicas, químicas y biológicas, no atenten contra la salud de los consumidores.

Los alimentos procesados industrialmente, deben poseer el Registro Sanitario con fecha de preparación y caducidad[4]. Los alimentos deben transportarse en envases limpios y con tapa de seguridad. Deben ser manipulados para su expendio con pinzas limpias, inoxidables[5] y servido en vajillas desechables[6] o fundas[7] plásticas originales.

[1] **se procurará** *will try*
[2] **mejorar** *to improve*
[3] **el expendio** *sale, distribution*
[4] **caducidad** *expiration*
[5] **inoxidables** *rustproof*
[6] **desechables** *disposable*
[7] **fundas** *wrappers*

Learning From Photos

Prepare a list of topics the women in the photo may be discussing.

Comprensión

A Última noticia Contesten.

1. ¿Qué expidió el Ministerio de Educación?
2. ¿Dónde?
3. ¿Qué prohíbe el segundo acuerdo?
4. ¿Qué se mantendrá en las escuelas?
5. ¿Cómo deben ser los alimentos que se sirven en las escuelas?
6. ¿Qué deben poseer los alimentos procesados industrialmente?
7. ¿Cómo deben transportarse?
8. ¿Cómo deben ser servidos?

B Los reglamentos ¿Sí o no?

1. Se puede fumar fuera de las aulas pero no dentro de ellas.
2. Se prohíbe la venta de los cigarrillos en las escuelas.
3. Los envases para los alimentos no tienen que tener tapa de seguridad.
4. En las escuelas tienen que servir los alimentos en envases.
5. Tienen que servir los alimentos en vajillas desechables o fundas plásticas originales.

Actividades comunicativas

A Debe tener... Prepare Ud. una lista de las reglas que debe tener su escuela para mejorar la calidad de vida de los estudiantes.

B Yo creo que... Escriba un párrafo en el que explica por qué son buenos o malos los nuevos decretos del gobierno ecuatoriano.

PERIODISMO

ANSWERS
Comprensión

A 1. El Ministerio de Educación expidió tres acuerdos para tratar de mejorar la vida de los estudiantes.
2. Los acuerdos cubrirán los diferentes establecimientos educativos del país.
3. El segundo acuerdo prohíbe el consumo de cigarrillos y alcohol.
4. Se mantendrá en las escuelas un estricto control.
5. Los alimentos que se sirven en las escuelas deben ser naturales y frescos.
6. Los alimentos procesados industrialmente deben poseer el Registro Sanitario.
7. Se deben transportar en envases limpios y con tapa de seguridad.
8. Deben ser servidos en vajillas desechables o fundas plásticas originales.

B 1. no
2. sí
3. no
4. no
5. sí

Actividades comunicativas

ANSWERS
A and B Answers will vary.

Learning From Realia

Have students look for the Spanish equivalent of the following expressions:
precooked (**precocinado**)
flash frozen (**ultracongelado**)
white meat tuna (**atún claro**)

Independent Practice

Assign any of the following:
1. Exercises, page 317
2. Workbook, *Periodismo*

317

TEACHING TIPS

A. Have students read the *Introducción* silently.

B. Ask students if they agree or disagree with the following statement and why: **Para mantenerse en forma hay que comer bien.**

RESOURCES

- Vocabulary Transparencies
- Audio Cassette 14A/Compact Disc 9
- Student Tape Manual
- Workbook
- Chapter Quizzes
- Testing Program

TEACHING VOCABULARY

A. You may wish to use some of the suggestions given for previous vocabulary sections.

B. Have students answer the following questions using the new words: **¿Te gustan los camarones? ¿el pescado? ¿el pavo? ¿el pollo?**, etc.

VOCABULARY EXPANSION

You may wish to give students the words to identify some chicken parts they may want to order:
la pechuga *(breast)*
el muslo *(thigh)*
el (las) ala(s) *(wings)*

La dieta

Introducción

Hoy en día a mucha gente le gusta mantenerse en forma y gozar de buena salud. Para conservarse en forma hay que mantener un peso apropiado y comer bien. Hay que comer alimentos que contienen vitaminas, minerales, hidratos de carbono (carbohidratos), proteínas, etc.

En la revista *Vanidades*, en una columna titulada *Dieta—Buenos consejos*, escrita por la doctora Estrella Mederos-Sibila, apareció una pregunta importante con las correspondientes respuestas de la doctora Mederos-Sibila.

Vocabulario

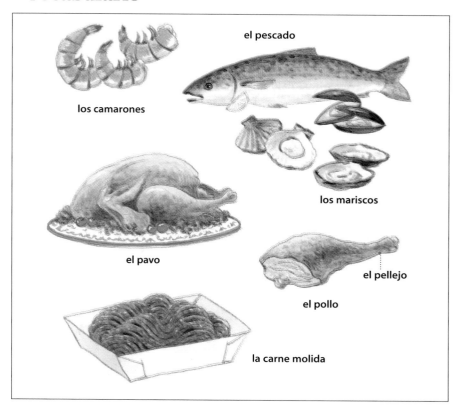

los camarones

el pescado

los mariscos

el pavo

el pellejo

el pollo

la carne molida

Independent Practice

Assign any of the following:
1. Exercise, page 319
2. Workbook, *Periodismo*

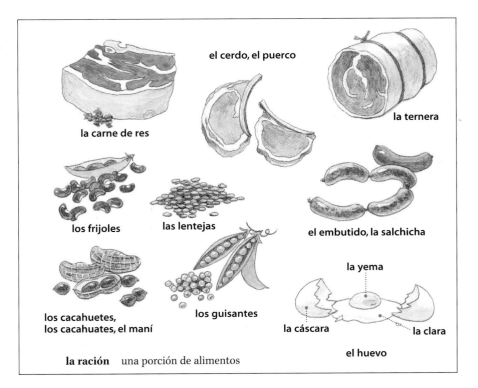

el cerdo, el puerco

la carne de res

la ternera

los frijoles

las lentejas

el embutido, la salchicha

los cacahuetes,
los cacahuates, el maní

los guisantes

la yema

la cáscara

la clara

el huevo

la ración   una porción de alimentos

Práctica

A   **Las comidas**   ¿Sí o no?

1. El pollo y el pavo son aves.
2. La ternera es un pescado.
3. Los camarones y la langosta son mariscos.
4. Las sardinas y el atún son pescados.
5. La carne de res es del puerco.
6. Se preparan hamburguesas con carne molida.
7. La salchicha es un embutido.
8. Los frijoles son legumbres.
9. Los guisantes son verdes y redondos.
10. Los cacahuetes tienen cáscara.
11. El huevo contiene una yema y una clara.
12. El huevo tiene pellejo.

PERIODISMO

trescientos diecinueve   **319**

Periodismo

TEACHING THE READING

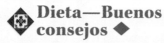

Dieta—Buenos consejos ◆

You may wish to have students read this short, easy selection aloud since it contains some good advice.

ABOUT THE SPANISH LANGUAGE

- There are many words for "beans": **los frijoles, las habichuelas, los porotos, las judías, los fríjoles.**
- **Los guisantes** are also called **las arvejas, los petits-pois,** and **los chícharos.**
- **Los cacahuetes** is used in Spain, **los cacahuates** throughout most of Latin America, and **el maní** in the Caribbean.

dieta
BUENOS CONSEJOS
LAS MEJORES PROTEÍNAS

¿Cuáles son las proteínas mejores, más sanas?

Sin duda las que contienen menos grasa. En ese caso, trate de dar preferencia a las siguientes:

- pescados y mariscos
- pollo y pavo sin pellejo
- pavo molido (sólo 15% de grasa)
- carne de res (vacuno), ternera, carnero y cerdo (puerco) sin grasa

Coma raciones pequeñas, de 7 oz o menos al día. Coma también proteínas vegetales, como la contenida en las legumbres: frijoles, lentejas, guisantes, mantequilla de maní (cacahuete) o tofú. Y sólo dos yemas de huevo a la semana (incluyendo las que necesite para hornear[1] o preparar platos mixtos).

Por otra parte, restrinja el consumo de: camarones, pollo frito, pato, carne molida con su grasa, embutidos e hígado[2] y otras vísceras[3].

[1] **hornear** to bake
[2] **hígado** liver
[3] **vísceras** organ meats

Cooperative Learning

Divida la clase en grupos de tres: un(a) dietista y dos clientes, uno que quiere perder peso y el otro, aumentar de peso. Los dos clientes explican su caso y el/la dietista les da una dieta apropiada.

❖ Comprensión

A **Los buenos alimentos** Contesten.

1. ¿Contienen grasa algunas proteínas?
2. ¿Es mejor comer las proteínas que contienen más o menos grasa?
3. ¿Cómo se debe comer el pollo?
4. ¿Contienen grasa las carnes como la carne de res y de cerdo?
5. ¿Es aconsejable comer raciones grandes o pequeñas?
6. ¿Cuáles son algunas legumbres que contienen proteínas?
7. ¿Se debe comer muchas o pocas yemas de huevo a la semana?
8. ¿Para qué se usan mucho las yemas de huevo?
9. ¿Cuáles son algunos alimentos que se deben evitar o por lo menos comer muy poco?

B **¿Cuál es otra palabra?** Escojan.

1. la carne molida	**a.** el bife
2. la carne de res	**b.** la salchicha, el chorizo
3. el cerdo	**c.** el maní, el cacahuate
4. el cacahuete	**d.** la carne picada
5. el embutido	**e.** el puerco

❖ Actividades comunicativas

A **Una comida sana** Con dos compañeros(as), planifiquen una comida buena y sana para la clase. Presenten el menú a la clase.

B **Una encuesta** Entreviste a cuatro compañeros(as) para descubrir sus comidas y bebidas preferidas. Tome apuntes y escriba un resumen de los resultados. Luego, dígale a la clase quién, en su opinión, sigue la mejor dieta, la más sana. También indique quién, en su opinión, sigue la peor dieta, la menos sana. Defienda sus opiniones.

LAS COMBINACIONES ALIMENTICIAS

La asociación correcta de los alimentos en la comida natural: base de una verdadera y sana dieta

Gudrun Dalla Via

2ª edición ampliada

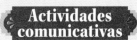

EDICIONES DESNIVEL
Pablo Bueno
COCINA de MONTAÑA
RECETAS Y DIETÉTICA

PERIODISMO

trescientos veintiuno 〜 **321**

TEACHING TIPS

These *Comprensión* exercises can be done orally after the students have completed the reading.

ANSWERS
Comprensión
A 1. sí
  2. menos
  3. sin pellejo
  4. sí
  5. pequeñas
  6. frijoles, lentejas, guisantes, mantequilla de maní, tofú
  7. pocas
  8. para hornear o para platos mixtos
  9. camarones, pollo frito, pato, carne molida con su grasa, embutidos, hígado y otras vísceras
B 1. d
  2. a
  3. e
  4. c
  5. b

TEACHING TIPS

Have students select the activity in which they wish to participate.

Actividades comunicativas

ANSWERS
A and B Answers will vary.

Independent Practice

Assign any of the following:
1. Exercises, page 321
2. Workbook, *Periodismo*

Bell Ringer Review

Use the BRR Transparency 7-8, or write the following on the board:

Busque la palabra que corresponde:

1. los dedos   a. la vista
2. la nariz   b. tocar
3. los ojos   c. oír
4. las orejas   d. oler
5. la lengua   e. el sabor

TEACHING TIPS

You may wish to read the *Introducción* aloud or have the students read it silently.

RESOURCES

- Vocabulary Transparencies
- Audio Cassette 14A/Compact Disc 9
- Student Tape Manual
- Workbook
- Chapter Quizzes
- Testing Program

TEACHING VOCABULARY

A. Have students repeat the new vocabulary after you.
B. Call on students to read the new words and definitions.
C. After reading the *Introducción*, you may wish to ask the following questions: **¿Quiénes están expuestos a la contaminación por el ruido? ¿Hay mucha o poca gente que sufre de trastornos auditivos? ¿Quiénes pueden sufrir de una pérdida de audición? ¿Cuál es una advertencia *(warning)* para los jóvenes? ¿De qué revista fue tomado el artículo? ¿A quiénes se dedica la revista?**

La contaminación por el ruido

Introducción

Se habla mucho de la contaminación del ambiente. Desgraciadamente, todos estamos expuestos a la contaminación por el ruido. Muchísima gente sufre de trastornos auditivos. Todos los que trabajan en lugares ruidosos pueden sufrir una pérdida de audición. Muchos jóvenes, sobre todo los que tocan su música a todo volumen, sufren de problemas auditivos.

El artículo que sigue apareció en la revista *Eres* de México. Es una revista dedicada en particular a la juventud.

Vocabulario

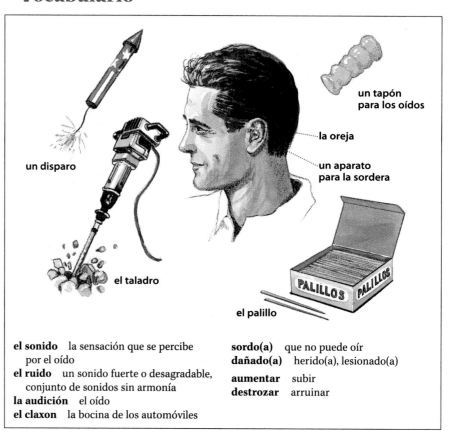

un disparo

el taladro

un tapón para los oídos

la oreja

un aparato para la sordera

PALILLOS PALILLOS

el palillo

el sonido   la sensación que se percibe por el oído
el ruido   un sonido fuerte o desagradable, conjunto de sonidos sin armonía
la audición   el oído
el claxon   la bocina de los automóviles

sordo(a)   que no puede oír
dañado(a)   herido(a), lesionado(a)
aumentar   subir
destrozar   arruinar

Advanced Game

To practice the vocabulary words and definitions, you may wish to play **Vocabulary Game III: *El juego de Loto,*** which was explained in Chapter 5, page 221.

TEACHING TIPS

Práctica A and *B* can be done orally with books closed after the vocabulary has been presented.

ANSWERS
Práctica

A **1.** sordo, un aparato para la sordera
  2. sonido, ruido
  3. tapón para los oídos
  4. disparo, destrozar
  5. taladro
  6. cláxones
  7. palillo
  8. grita

B **1.** b
  2. c
  3. f
  4. a
  5. d
  6. e

VOCABULARY EXPANSION

You may wish to give students the following additional vocabulary so that they can talk about the photo:
el casco (*hard hat*)
el bache (*pothole*)
el pico
la pala

Práctica

A **¿Cuál es la palabra?** Completen.

1. Él ha sufrido una pérdida de audición casi total. Es ___ y tiene que llevar ___.
2. Un ___ puede ser agradable pero el ___ es casi siempre desagradable.
3. Un ___ nos puede proteger contra ruidos peligrosos y dañinos.
4. Un sonido fuerte como el del ___ de una pistola cerca de la oreja puede ___ el oído.
5. El ___ es una máquina ruidosa que se usa en lugares de construcción.
6. En las ciudades el ruido que causan los ___ de muchos coches puede ser muy desagradable.
7. Un ___ es para los dientes, no para los oídos.
8. Él no habla, sino que ___.

B **Una expresión equivalente** Escojan.

1. aumentar	**a.** levantar mucho la voz
2. un aparato	**b.** subir, elevar
3. el claxon	**c.** la máquina
4. gritar	**d.** derrotar, destruir, arruinar
5. destrozar	**e.** el oído
6. la audición	**f.** la bocina

PERIODISMO · · · · · · · · · · · · · *trescientos veintitrés* 〜 **323**

Did You Know?

1. The expression **el trabajo de pico y pala** means "manual labor."
2. The sign you will see in Spanish-speaking countries to indicate that construction or repair work is being done will state **En obras** or **Hombres trabajando.**

Independent Practice

Assign any of the following:
1. Exercises, page 323
2. Workbook, *Periodismo*

TEACHING THE READING

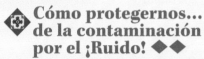

**Cómo protegernos...
de la contaminación
por el ¡Ruido! ◆◆**

A. You may wish to call on students
to read some paragraphs aloud.
You may have them read others
silently. Or, you may wish to have
students read the entire article
silently.

B. You may wish to intersperse the
following questions in the reading: **¿Cuál es el resultado de la
pérdida del oído? ¿Cuáles son
algunas cosas que causan la
pérdida inmediata del oído?
¿Cuáles son algunos ruidos que
nos afectan? ¿Cómo debe uno
protegerse? ¿Qué más provoca
la contaminación por el ruido?**

National Standards

Connections Students will reinforce
and/or further their knowledge
of health and hygiene as they
learn about the effects of excessive noise on hearing and learn
of ways to avoid or decrease their
exposure to such noises.

Cómo protegernos...
de la contaminación por el
¡Ruido!

Por Pilar Obón

Por si no lo sabes, hoy
somos 20% más sordos,
en general, que hace
algunos años. No sólo ha
aumentado grueso la contaminación por ruido, sino que
somos mucho más ruidosos
que antes, posiblemente
debido al estrés que nos hace
gritar, pegarnos al claxon,
poner el estéreo o el compact a
todo volumen, etcétera.

La pérdida del oído, ya sea
parcial o total, es el resultado
más común del acto casi suici-
da de exponernos a altos volúmenes de sonido, igual si éstos
proceden de una motoconformadora[1] que de un walkman al
tope[2]. Algunas cosas te causan
pérdida inmediata del oído,
como por ejemplo un disparo
que suene a unos cuantos cen-
tímetros de tu tímpano, que es
súper delicado. Pero la mayoría
de los ruidos que nos afectan,
van causando una pérdida gradual de la audición que para
colmo[3], es difícil detectar,

porque ocurre tan lentamente
que casi no te das cuenta.

Las primeras que se afectan,
son las frecuencias que están
en la parte superior de la
escala. Probablemente necesitas ir a checarte la audición si
eres incapaz de escuchar el tic-
tac de un reloj, palabras aisladas en una conversación o una
música tocada a bajo volumen.
Otros signos de alarma son
dolor, un zumbido[4] en el oído,
o una sensación de embotamiento[5] después de escuchar
ruidos muy fuertes. A veces, lo
que se pierde es la capacidad
para escuchar algunos sonidos
que vibran en una frecuencia
específica. Así como tu lengua[6]
tiene papilas especializadas
para captar el sabor amargo o
el dulce, tu oído posee también
células específicas para ruidos

determinados, más graves o
más agudos[7]. Si algunas de esas
células son dañadas, entonces
perderás la capacidad de escuchar en la frecuencia en la que
ellas están especializadas en
captar.

NO SÓLO SORDO SINO...
La contaminación por ruido no
solamente puede causar que
te quedes sordo o sorda como
una tapia[8], fíjate. Checa que
también puede provocarte una
notable elevación en la presión
sanguínea[9], acrecentar tu
neura[10], disminuir tus reflejos y
tu capacidad para el trabajo e,
incluso, producirte una elevación de los niveles de colesterol, de azúcar en la sangre y de
la producción de ácidos en el
estómago, con ulcerosas consecuencias.

[1] **motoconformadora** *road grader*
[2] **al tope** *at the highest level*
[3] **para colmo** *to make matters worse*

[4] **un zumbido** *a buzzing, ringing*
[5] **embotamiento** *dullness, drowsiness*
[6] **lengua** *tongue*

[7] **agudos** *sharp*
[8] **una tapia** *a wall*
[9] **la presión sanguínea** *la tensión arterial*
[10] **acrecentar tu neura** *ponerse nervioso*

Cooperative Learning

**Pídales a los alumnos que hagan una
investigación de la contaminación por el
ruido y que presenten sus resultados a la
clase.**

Learning From Photos

The type of truck pictured here is **un tractor con remolque.** Other words you may
wish to familiarize students with are: **el
camión, la camioneta** (pick-up truck), **el
tractor, el remolque, el camión cisterna**
or **el camión tanque,** and **el camión bas-
culante** (dump truck).

Y todavía no terminamos. Según varios estudios realizados en Estados Unidos, se ha comprobado que los niños y jóvenes que se encuentran en escuelas ubicadas en zonas muy ruidosas, son lentos para aprender, no entienden nada y tienen muchas dificultades para concentrarse. Si los niños son pequeños y los ruidos muy fuertes, pueden incluso confundir el sonido de algunas letras y tener problemas de lenguaje. ¿Qué tal?

CÓMO PROTEGERTE

A menos que quieras terminar usando un aparatito para sordera o un cono pegado a tu oreja, tienes que comenzar a protegerte de la contaminación por ruido, sobre todo si vives en una ciudad muy poblada y sonorífera. Aquí tienes algunos tips:

➤ Favor de no traer el walkman a todo volumen pegado en los oídos. Perderás tu audición antes de mucho tiempo.

➤ Cuando vayas a la disco procura salirte a ratos o irte a descansar a un sitio menos ruidoso (el baño, por ejemplo) de cuando en cuando. Se supone que uno no debe soportar un ruido de ese tamaño por más de dos horas seguidas.

➤ El programa de la televisión no va a ser más interesante si le subes todo el volumen, así que trata de escucharlo a su volumen normal.

➤ El estéreo, compact y demás artilugios[11] de sonido se hicieron para que los disfrutes, no para que destroces tu tímpano y el de los demás. Muchos se sienten ¡importantísimos! yendo en un coche cuyo estéreo puede escucharse a tres cuadras. En realidad, están demostrando terrible tontería. No sólo corren el peligro de quedarse sordos, sino también de hacer más

lentos sus reflejos y atontarse a tal grado que se estrellarán sin remedio a la primera emergencia. ¡Bájenle!

➤ Si estás expuesto o expuesta a una gran cantidad de ruido, lo mejor es irte a checar más o menos cada seis meses con un especialista.

➤ Y hablando del oído, favor de no andarse metiendo palillos ni pasadores con el objeto de limpiarse la cerilla[12], porque en una de ésas, te llevas el tímpano y para qué quieres. Si sientes tapados[13] los oídos ver con el doctor para que te haga una limpieza.

➤ Si vas a ir a un lugar con ruido excesivo (una fábrica con maquinaria pesada, por ejemplo), unos tapones para los oídos pueden serte de gran utilidad.

➤ Finalmente…

¡NO GRITEN!

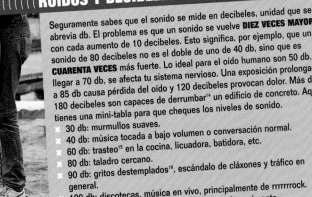

(((((RUIDOS Y DECIBELES)))))

Seguramente sabes que el sonido se mide en decibeles, unidad que se abrevia db. El problema es que un sonido se vuelve **DIEZ VECES MAYOR** con cada aumento de 10 decibeles. Esto significa, por ejemplo, que un sonido de 80 decibeles no es el doble de uno de 40 db, sino que es **CUARENTA VECES** más fuerte. Lo ideal para el oído humano son 50 db. Al llegar a 70 db, se afecta tu sistema nervioso. Una exposición prolongada a 85 db causa pérdida del oído y 120 decibeles provocan dolor. Más de 180 decibeles son capaces de derrumbar[14] un edificio de concreto. Aquí tienes una mini-tabla para que cheques los niveles de sonido.

- ✘ 30 db: murmullos suaves.
- ✘ 40 db: música tocada a bajo volumen o conversación normal.
- ✘ 60 db: trasteo[15] en la cocina, licuadora, batidora, etc.
- ✘ 80 db: taladro cercano.
- ✘ 90 db: gritos destemplados[16], escándalo de cláxones y tráfico en general.
- ✘ 100 db: discotecas, música en vivo, principalmente de rrrrrrock.
- ✘ 120 db: motoconformadoras, perforadoras de pavimento.
- ✘ 150 db: despegue de un avión.
- ✘ 180 db: lanzamiento de terrible cohete espacial

[11] **artilugios** gadgets
[12] **la cerilla** wax
[13] **tapados** clogged
[14] **derrumbar** to knock down
[15] **trasteo** bustle
[16] **destemplados** excesivos

Critical Thinking Activity

Thinking skills: supporting arguments with reasons **El artículo dice: «Somos mucho más ruidosos que antes, posiblemente debido al que nos hace gritar, pegarnos al claxon, poner el estéreo o el compact a todo volumen, etc.» ¿Qué opina Ud.? ¿Nos hace hacer estas cosas el estrés?**

ABOUT THE SPANISH LANGUAGE

El uso del verbo «checarte» o «checar» es un mexicanismo derivado del inglés *to check.*

National Standards

Connections
Students further their knowledge of science as they learn about the functioning of the ear.

INTERDISCIPLINARY CONNECTION

As students look at the drawing of the ear on page 326, you may wish to explain the following: **La manera en que funciona el oído es impresionante. Las ondas sonoras son captadas por la oreja y hacen vibrar el tímpano que comunica con los tres huesos del oído medio, los huesillos que amplifican las vibraciones. Estas vibraciones amplificadas se transmiten al oído interno y se convierten en impulsos eléctricos. Estos impulsos se transmiten al cerebro por el nervio auditivo y el cerebro hace inteligible el mensaje sonoro. Aunque no se conoce bien la manera en que las ondas sonoras se convierten en mensaje, hoy día se puede ayudar a la mayoría de la gente que sufre de trastornos auditivos.**

Comprensión

A 1. sí
2. sí
3. no
4. sí
5. no
6. sí
7. no
B 1. Está aumentando.
2. gritar, pegarnos al claxon, poner el estéreo a todo volumen
3. la pérdida del oído
4. una pérdida gradual de la audición
5. el dolor, un zumbido en el oído o una sensación de embotamiento
6. la elevación en la presión sanguínea, acrecentar la neura, disminuir los reflejos y la capacidad de trabajar
7. el decibel
8. Un sonido de 80 decibeles es cuarenta veces más fuerte que uno de 40.
C Answers will vary.
D 1. 120
2. 50
3. 70

Actividades comunicativas

A and B Answers will vary.

Comprensión

A **El ruido y la sordera** ¿Sí o no?

1. Hoy hay más sordos que antes.
2. Somos más ruidosos que antes.
3. Es imposible sufrir una pérdida inmediata de la audición.
4. El tímpano es una membrana tensa situada en el interior del oído.
5. Es difícil herir o dañar el tímpano.
6. El oído posee células específicas para ciertos ruidos.
7. Un sonido de 80 decibeles es el doble de uno de 40 db.

B **Los ruidos** Contesten.

1. ¿Está aumentando o bajando la contaminación por ruido?
2. ¿Qué nos hace hacer el estrés?
3. ¿En qué resulta la exposición a altos volúmenes de sonido?
4. ¿Qué causan la mayoría de los ruidos?
5. ¿Cuáles son algunos síntomas que indican la pérdida de la audición?
6. Además de la sordera, ¿cuáles son otras condiciones que pueden provocar la contaminación por ruido?
7. ¿Qué unidad se usa para medir el sonido?
8. ¿Cuántas veces más fuerte es un sonido de 80 decibeles que uno de 40?

C **Un análisis** Expliquen.

¿Cómo y por qué es posible perder la capacidad de oír ciertos sonidos?

D **¿Cuál es la palabra?** Completen.

1. Los sonidos de ___ decibeles provocan dolor.
2. Lo ideal para el oído humano son sonidos de ___ decibeles.
3. Los sonidos que llegan a ___ decibeles afectan el sistema nervioso.

Actividades comunicativas

A **Protección** Prepare Ud. una lista de precauciones que puede tomar para protegerse contra la contaminación por ruido.

B **¿Es malo el ruido?** Trabajando con un(a) compañero(a) de clase, preparen una lista de ruidos. Luego, determinen cuáles son agradables/desagradables, inofensivos/peligrosos.

Additional Practice

Explique en español lo que es:
la pérdida total del oído
la pérdida parcial del oído
una pérdida gradual del oído

Independent Practice

Assign any of the following:
1. Exercises, page 326
2. Workbook, *Periodismo*

Estructura

Combining sentences
Pronombre relativo que

1. Relative pronouns replace nouns or pronouns and are used to join two short sentences. The most common relative pronoun is **que.** It can be used as a subject or an object. It can refer to a person or thing.

   SUBJECT
   La señora está hablando. La señora ganó el concurso.
   La señora que está hablando ganó el concurso.

   El trofeo está en la mesa. El trofeo es para ella.
   El trofeo que está en la mesa es para ella.

   OBJECT
   El concurso es importantísimo. Ella ganó el concurso.
   El concurso que ella ganó es importantísimo.

   Tú conociste a la señora. La señora ganó el concurso.
   Tú conociste a la señora que ganó el concurso.

2. The relative pronoun **que** is used after a short preposition when it refers to a place or thing.

   Es el concurso de que yo te hablaba el otro día.
   Es el concurso en que participó.

3. **Quien** and **quienes** refer only to people. They are usually used as the object of a preposition. When used as a direct object, **quien(es)** must be preceded by the preposition **a.**

   La señora que tú conociste es la tía de Jaime.
   La señora a quien tú conociste es la tía de Jaime.

   El señor de quien tú me hablas es periodista.
   Las señoras con quienes yo trabajé eran mexicanas.

RESOURCES

- 📁 Workbook
- 📁 Student Tape Manual
- 🎧 Audio Cassette 14A/Compact Disc 9
- 💾 Computer Software: *Estructura*
- 📁 Chapter Quizzes
- 💾 Testing Program

TEACHING STRUCTURE

 **Combining sentences** ◆◆

A. Have students read through the explanation in steps 1–3.
B. Have students repeat the model sentences in steps 1–3 aloud in unison.

TEACHING TIPS

Expansion Have students make up their own sentences using **que, quien, el que, la que, los que,** and **las que.**

ANSWERS
Práctica

A 1. **El señor que está haciendo ejercicios es médico.**
2. **Los ejercicios que hace el señor son rigurosos.**
3. **Él va al gimnasio que tiene el mejor equipo.**
4. **Él sigue un régimen alimenticio que es muy estricto.**
5. **Él sigue un régimen que es rico en carbohidratos y fibra.**
6. **El libro que él está leyendo trata de la nutrición y la forma física.**
7. **Ese señor que está hablando ahora escribió el libro.**

B 1. **que**
2. **que**
3. **que**
4. **quien**

Práctica

A **HISTORIETA** El señor que se mantiene en forma

Formen una sola oración.

> **El señor es médico. El señor se mantiene en forma.**
> **El señor que se mantiene en forma es médico.**

1. El señor es médico. El señor está haciendo ejercicios.
2. El señor hace ejercicios. Los ejercicios son rigurosos.
3. Él va al gimnasio. El gimnasio tiene el mejor equipo.
4. Él sigue un régimen alimenticio. El régimen es muy estricto.
5. Él sigue un régimen. El régimen es rico en carbohidratos y fibra.
6. Él está leyendo un libro. El libro trata de la nutrición y la forma física.
7. Ese señor escribió el libro. Ese señor está hablando ahora.

B **HISTORIETA** ¿De quién o de qué hablas?

Completen.

1. El libro del ____ tú me hablas es de ella.
2. Ella es la señora ____ vino a la fiesta anoche, ¿no?
3. Sí, es la señora ____ tú conociste en la fiesta.
4. ¿Es la misma señora con ____ yo hablaba?

Independent Practice

Assign any of the following:
1. Exercises, page 328
2. Workbook, *Estructura*

Specifying who or what is being referred to
El que, la que, los que y las que

1. The longer pronouns, **el que, la que, los que,** and **las que,** are used to add emphasis. They mean "who," "the one(s)," or "that" in English.

De todos los libros, el que estoy leyendo ahora es el más interesante.	*Of all the books, the one (that) I am reading now is the most interesting.*
De todas mis hermanas, la que tiene más talento es mi hermana mayor.	*Of all my sisters, the one who has the most talent is my older sister.*

Note that these pronouns agree in gender and number with the word they refer to.

2. The pronouns **el que, la que, los que,** and **las que** often begin a sentence. Observe the following.

El que habla ahora es mi hermano.	*The one who is talking now is my brother.*
La que hablará mañana es mi hermana.	*The one who will speak tomorrow is my sister.*
Los que hablaron ayer fueron mis padres.	*The ones who spoke yesterday were my parents.*

3. Note the sequence of tenses in the above sentences. If the verb following **el que** is in the present or future, the present tense of **ser** is used in the main clause. If the verb that follows **el que** is in the preterite, the preterite of **ser** is used in the main clause.

 **Práctica**

A **¿Quién es el que lo hace?** Contesten según el modelo.

> **¿Quién está haciendo calentamiento? (mi primo)**
> **El que está haciendo calentamiento es mi primo.**

1. ¿Quién está haciendo ejercicios? (mi amigo)
2. ¿Quién hizo los ejercicios aeróbicos? (su novia)
3. ¿Quién ganó la carrera? (José)
4. ¿Quién salió primero? (José)
5. ¿Quiénes ganarán el campeonato? (los Tigres)
6. ¿Quiénes recibirán la Copa Mundial? (ellos)
7. ¿Quién presentará (otorgará) el trofeo? (la directora)

Learning From Photos

El ciclismo es un deporte muy popular en España y en Sudamérica, sobre todo en Colombia. La carrera de ciclismo más famosa es el Tour de France. Ha sido ganado varias veces por españoles. En los años 90, el vasco Miguel Induráin lo ha ganado por lo menos cuatro veces.

CAPÍTULO 7
Estructura

TEACHING STRUCTURE

◆ **Specifying who or what is being referred to** ◆◆

Note Although this grammatical point is not overly difficult, students do have trouble with it. Since it is of relatively low frequency, they do not have a great deal of practice in using it. It is recommended that you present this point but that you not expect all students to use it with relative ease.

Go over the explanation, emphasizing the model sentences. Students will learn this point more easily through examples than explanation.

TEACHING TIPS

A. It is suggested that you have students close their books and listen as you read the completed *Práctica.* The purpose of this is to give students more opportunities to hear these pronouns used in sentences.

B. Then have students open their books and do the *Práctica* without prior preparation. Correct as necessary.

C. For additional reinforcement, assign the *Práctica* for homework.

D. Go over it once again the following day in class.

ANSWERS
Práctica

A 1. **El que está haciendo ejercicios es mi amigo.**
2. **La que hizo los ejercicios aeróbicos fue su novia.**
3. **El que ganó la carrera fue José.**
4. **El que salió primero fue José.**
5. **Los que ganarán el campeonato son los Tigres.**
6. **Los que recibirán la Copa Mundial son ellos.**
7. **La que presentará (otorgará) el trofeo es la directora.**

Previously stated ideas
Lo que, cuyo

1. The neuter relative pronoun **lo que** is used to refer to a previously stated idea, situation, or event, or to one that will be stated later. It is equivalent to the English "what."

Lo que necesito es más dinero.	*What I need is more money.*
Lo que me encanta es leer un buen libro.	*What I like is to read a good book.*
Lo que me gustaría hacer es ir al cine.	*What I'd like to do is go to the movies.*

2. The relative pronoun **cuyo** expresses possession and corresponds to the English "whose" or "of which." Note that **cuyo** agrees with the noun it modifies.

El señor cuya hija está hablando ahora es el director de la compañía.	*The man whose daughter is speaking now is the director of the company.*
Tiene una gran compañía cuyo nombre he olvidado.	*He has a large company, the name of which I have forgotten.*

 Práctica

A **Lo que te hace falta**   Sigan el modelo.

> **Necesito dinero.**
> **Lo que necesito es dinero.**

1. Digo la verdad.
2. Necesito más dinero.
3. Tengo que comprarme un carro.
4. Dices la verdad.
5. Te hace falta dinero.

B **HISTORIETA**   El señor rico cuyo dinero...

Completen.

1. El señor ____ tienda acabamos de visitar es muy rico.
2. Es un señor ____ recursos económicos son increíbles.
3. Es el señor ____ esposa conduce un Rolls.
4. Perdón. Su esposa es la señora ____ chófer conduce un Rolls.
5. Es el matrimonio ____ hijos tienen un Jaguar.
6. Es una familia ____ riqueza es increíble.

Contrasting *por* and *para*
Por y para

1. The prepositions **por** and **para** have very specific uses in Spanish. They are not interchangeable. These two prepositions are often translated into English as "for." Such a translation is quite restrictive, because these two words express many ideas in addition to "for."

The preposition **para** is used to indicate destination or purpose.

El avión salió para Bogotá.	*The plane left for Bogotá.*
Este regalo es para María.	*This gift is for Mary.*
Ella estudia para abogada.	*She is studying to be a lawyer.*

2. The preposition **por**, in contrast to **para**, is more circuitous. Rather than expressing a specific destination, **por** conveys the meanings "through," "by," and "along."

Ellos viajaron por la América del Sur.	*They traveled through South America.*
Su barco pasó por las costas de las Galápagos.	*Their boat passed by the shores of the Galápagos.*
El ladrón entró en la casa por la ventana.	*The thief entered the house through the window.*

3. **Por** also has the meanings "in behalf of," "in favor of," and "instead of." Observe and analyze the difference in meaning in the following sentences.

Compré el regalo para mi madre.	*I bought the gift for my mother. (I am going to give the gift to my mother.)*
Compré el regalo por mi madre.	*I bought the gift for my mother. (The gift is for another person, but my mother could not go out to buy it so I went for her.)*

4. The preposition **por** is used after the verbs **ir, mandar, volver,** and **venir** in order to show the reason for the errand.

El joven fue a la tienda por pan.	*The young man went to the store for bread.*
Ellos mandaron por el médico.	*They sent for the doctor.*

DR. FAUSTO LÓPEZ INFANTE

OTORRINOLARINGOLOGÍA
CIRUGÍA RECONSTRUCTIVA FUNCIONAL DE LA NARIZ

CONSULTAS: LUNES, MIÉRCOLES Y VIERNES
DE 10:30 A 13:30 HRS.

393·05·50   393·48·31   572·02·52

BULEVARD DEL CENTRO Nº 205 COL. BULEVARES EDO. MEX. C.P. 53140

REG. S.S. 22739   REG. DGP. 87687

trescientos treinta y uno 〰 **331**

TEACHING STRUCTURE

◆ Contrasting *por* and *para* ◆◆◆

A. Have the students read through the explanation in steps 1–4 once silently.

B. Call on individuals to read the explanatory material aloud and have all students repeat the model sentences aloud in unison.

Learning From Realia

1. Have students pronounce the tongue twister **otorrinolaringología.**

2. Give a definition of **la otorrinolaringología: Es la parte de la patología que trata de las enfermedades del oído, de la nariz y de la laringe.**

3. Ask the following questions about the realia: **¿Cómo se llama el médico? ¿Cuál es su especialidad? ¿Qué tipo de cirugía hace? ¿Qué días tiene consultas? ¿Cuáles son sus horas de consulta?**

TEACHING TIPS

You may wish to have students prepare these *Práctica* for homework and then go over them in class the following day.

ANSWERS

Práctica

A Answers can be negative.
1. **Sí, va a salir para Barcelona.**
2. **Sí, va a viajar por Cataluña.**
3. **Sí, va a estudiar para enfermera en Barcelona.**
4. **Sí, Teresa va a andar por las Ramblas.**
5. **Sí, va a comprar regalos para sus parientes.**
6. **Sí, ella va a comprar las cositas por ellos.**

B 1. **para**
2. **por**
3. **por**
4. **por**
5. **para**
6. **por**

TEACHING STRUCTURE

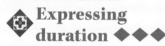 **Expressing duration** ◆◆◆

Have students read the explanation silently and then have them repeat the model sentences aloud.

Práctica

Las Ramblas, Barcelona, España

A HISTORIETA Salen para Barcelona.
Contesten.
1. ¿Va a salir para Barcelona Teresa?
2. ¿Va a viajar por Cataluña?
3. ¿Va a estudiar para enfermera en Barcelona?
4. ¿Va a andar por Las Ramblas Teresa?
5. ¿Va a comprar regalos para sus parientes?
6. Algunos amigos quieren que ella les compre algunas cositas y le dieron el dinero. ¿Va a comprar las cositas por ellos?

B HISTORIETA Al mercado
Completen.
1. Hoy yo salí ___ el mercado a las ocho de la mañana.
2. Natalia no pudo ir así que yo fui ___ ella.
3. Cuando salí del mercado, di un paseo ___ el centro de la ciudad.
4. Pasé ___ las elegantes tiendas de la calle Serrano.
5. Entré en una de las tiendas y compré un regalo ___ mi madre. Se lo voy a dar mañana.
6. Cuando volví a casa, el hijo de Natalia vino ___ las cosas que yo le había comprado en el mercado.

Expressing duration
Por y para con expresiones de tiempo

1. The preposition **para** is used to indicate a time deadline.

   Ellos tienen que estar aquí para el día ocho.   *They have to be here by the eighth.*

2. **Por**, in contrast to **para**, is used to define a period of time.

   Van a estar aquí por una semana.   *They are going to be here for a week.*

3. **Por** is also used to express an indefinite time.

   Creo que ellos van a volver por diciembre.   *I think they are going to return around December.*

Learning From Photos

Las Ramblas es un paseo famoso en el centro de Barcelona. Bordeado de árboles, las Ramblas tiene muchas librerías, floristerías, etc. A todas horas del día y de la noche los peatones andan por las Ramblas. En la Rambla de las Flores las piedras pintadas fueron diseñadas por el famoso artista catalán Joan Miró.

A pesar de ser un solo paseo, se llama las Ramblas, porque cada sección lleva un nombre distinto, como «la Rambla de las Flores».

✦Práctica✦

A **¿Para cuándo y por cuánto tiempo?** Contesten.

1. ¿Pueden Uds. llegar para las ocho?
2. ¿Y pueden tener los resultados para mañana?
3. Cuando vienen Uds. mañana, ¿pueden quedarse aquí por una semana?
4. La última vez que vinieron, Uds. estuvieron por dos semanas, ¿no?
5. ¿Piensan Uds. volver otra vez por Navidad?

B **HISTORIETA Los árabes**

Completen.

Los árabes salieron del Norte de África __1__ España en el siglo ocho. Invadieron a España en el año 711, y estuvieron en el país __2__ unos ocho siglos. Viajaron __3__ toda la Península Ibérica. Por eso, si uno hace un viaje __4__ España, verá la influencia de los árabes en casi todas partes del país. Pero si uno viaja __5__ Andalucía en el sur del país, visitará sin duda la famosa Alhambra de Granada, el Alcázar de Sevilla y la Mezquita de Córdoba, tres monumentos famosos de los árabes. __6__ mañana yo tengo que preparar un informe sobre la influencia musulmana en España __7__ mi clase de español. Así que yo fui hoy a la biblioteca __8__ los libros que necesitaba __9__ hacer mis investigaciones.

La Alhambra, Granada, España

ESTRUCTURA

TEACHING TIPS

A. *Práctica A* can be done orally without prior preparation.
B. You may wish to have students collaborate on *Práctica B* in pairs, giving them time in class to prepare it.
C. Call on pairs to offer their choices for *Práctica B* and ask them to defend their position.

ANSWERS

Práctica

A Answers can be negative.
1. **Sí, podemos llegar para las ocho.**
2. **Sí, podemos tener los resultados para mañana.**
3. **Sí, podemos quedarnos aquí por una semana.**
4. **Sí, estuvimos por dos semanas.**
5. **Sí, pensamos volver otra vez por Navidad.**

B 1. **para**
2. **por**
3. **por**
4. **por**
5. **por**
6. **Para**
7. **para**
8. **por**
9. **para**

Learning From Photos

See notes on page 240 of *¡Buen viaje! Level 3* about the Alhambra.

Independent Practice

Assign any of the following:
1. Exercises, page 333
2. Workbook, *Estructura*

333

TEACHING STRUCTURE

 **Por** and *para* with the infinitive ◆◆◆

You may wish to use procedures suggested elsewhere in this chapter.

TEACHING TIPS

A. These exercises can be done orally with books closed immediately after the reading of steps 1–4.

B. Give students a few minutes to look over these exercises and then call on individuals to go over them orally.

ANSWERS
Práctica

A Answers can be negative.
1. Sí, quiero ir a mi cuarto para estudiar.
2. Sí, tengo que preparar un informe para obtener una buena nota.
3. Estoy para trabajar (divertirme).
4. Sí, me queda mucho por hacer.
5. Sí, fui a la biblioteca por los libros que me hacían falta.
6. Sí, estoy para salir también.

VOCABULARY EXPANSION

You may wish to give students the following library terms:

el fichero *(card catalog, also used for computer)*
las fichas *(index cards)*
los depósitos *(stacks)*
las estanterías *(shelves)*

Por and *para* with the infinitive
Por y **para** con el infinitivo

1. When followed by an infinitive, **para** expresses purpose and means "in order to."

Tengo que ir a la biblioteca para hacer mis investigaciones.	*I have to go to the library (in order) to do my research.*

2. When **por** is followed by an infinitive, it expresses what remains to be done.

No he terminado mi informe. Me queda mucho por hacer.	*I haven't finished my report. There is still a lot to do.*

3. The expression **estar para** means "to be about to" or "to be ready to."

Ellos están para salir pero no sé lo que van a hacer porque está para llover.	*They are about (ready) to leave, but I don't know what they are going to do because it is about to rain.*

4. The expression **estar por** means "to be inclined to." It does not mean that the action will immediately take place.

Estoy por salir porque hace buen tiempo.	*I'm in the mood to go out because the weather is nice.*

◆Práctica◆

A ¿Estás listo(a) o dispuesto(a)... ? Contesten.

1. ¿Quieres ir a tu cuarto para estudiar?
2. ¿Tienes que preparar un informe para obtener una buena nota?
3. ¿Estás para trabajar o para divertirte?
4. Para el informe, ¿te queda mucho por hacer?
5. ¿Fuiste a la biblioteca por los libros que te hacían falta?
6. Yo estoy para salir. ¿Estás para salir también?

Biblioteca del Congreso, Buenos Aires, Argentina

Learning From Photos

You may wish to ask students: **¿De qué es la foto? En los Estados Unidos, ¿hay una Biblioteca del Congreso? ¿Dónde está? ¿Quién puede usarla?**

Independent Practice

Assign any of the following:
1. Exercises, pages 334–335
2. Workbook, *Estructura*

B HISTORIETA ¿Listo(a) o dispuesto(a)?

Completen.

1. Ya me bañé y me vestí y estoy ___ salir.
2. ¡Ay, pero mira! Está ___ llover.
3. Tendré que subir ___ mi paraguas.
4. Quiero ir al teatro. ___ ir al teatro tendré que tomar un taxi porque no hay bus que pase ___ el teatro.
5. Me pregunto si tendré que hacer cola ___ comprar las entradas.
6. Estoy ___ divertirme. Al salir del teatro voy a visitar uno de los mesones de Cuchilleros.
7. Trabajé todo el día y todavía me queda mucho ___ hacer.

LAS CUEVAS
DE
LUIS CANDELAS

HORNO DE ASAR

CUCHILLEROS, 1
Teléfono 366 54 28
28005 MADRID

Other uses of *por* and *para*
Otros usos de **por** y **para**

1. Para is used to express a comparison.

Para cubano él habla muy bien el inglés.	*For a Cuban, he speaks English very well.*
Y para americano Roberto habla muy bien el español.	*And for an American, Robert speaks Spanish very well.*

2. Por is used to express means, manner, or motive.

La carta llegó por correo aéreo.	*The letter arrived by air mail.*
Los soldados lucharon por la libertad de su país.	*The soldiers fought for the freedom of their country.*

3. Por is used to express "in exchange for."

Él me pagó cien dólares por el trabajo que hice.	*He paid me a hundred dollars for the work I did.*
Él cambió pesos por dólares.	*He exchanged pesos for dollars.*

4. Por is also used to express an opinion or estimation.

Yo lo tomé por francés pero es español.	*I took him for French but he is Spanish.*

5. Por is used to indicate measure or number.

Las papas se venden por kilo.	*They sell potatoes by the kilo.*
Este avión vuela a mil kilómetros por hora.	*This plane flies 1,000 kilometers per hour.*

ESTRUCTURA

trescientos treinta y cinco ～ **335**

ANSWERS
Práctica
B 1. para/por
2. para
3. por
4. Para, por
5. para
6. para
7. por

TEACHING STRUCTURE

◆ **Other uses of *por* and *para*** ◆◆◆

Have students read through steps 1–5. Then have the class repeat the model sentences aloud in unison.

Learning From Realia

Las Cuevas de Luis Candelas está en la calle Cuchilleros, una calle famosa del viejo Madrid. En Cuchilleros hay muchos mesones que frecuentan los universitarios. Los mesones son muy conocidos por sus tapas.

Las Cuevas de Luis Candelas es uno de los mesones más viejos. Lleva el nombre del bandido legendario Luis Candelas.

TEACHING TIPS

You may wish to assign these *Práctica* for homework before going over them the following day. Be sure students are able to defend their selections.

ANSWERS

Práctica

A 1. Para
2. Para
3. por
4. por
5. por
6. por
7. por

B 1. El tren va para Barcelona.
2. Los dulces son para el niño.
3. Me dieron mil dólares por el carro.
4. Si, para mexicano habla muy bien el inglés.
5. Pienso venir para abril.
6. Me queda mucho (poco) trabajo por hacer.
7. Lo terminaré para mañana.
8. Si, ellos pasaron mucho tiempo viajando por Cataluña.
9. Lo mandaron por corréo aéreo.

C 1. por
2. para
3. para
4. para
5. Para
6. por
7. por
8. por
9. por
10. por
11. para
12. Para
13. por
14. por

·❧Práctica❧·

A **¿Comparado con quién?** Completen.

1. ___ español, el señor Chaval habla muy bien el francés.
2. ___ argentina, la señora Filitti sabe mucho de los Estados Unidos.
3. Ella vino a Miami en avión. Dijo que el avión volaba a unos mil kilómetros ___ hora.
4. Ella cambió sus pesos ___ dólares antes de salir de la Argentina.
5. La primera vez que yo conocí a la señora Filitti, yo la tomé ___ italiana. La verdad es que ella es de ascendencia italiana pero hace años que su familia vive en la Argentina.
6. La señora Filitti sabe que a mí me gustan mucho los zapatos argentinos. Ella me trajo dos pares. No quería que yo le pagara pero yo le di el dinero ___ los zapatos.
7. Hoy llegó un paquete para la señora Filitti. El paquete llegó ___ correo aéreo.

B **Un resumen** Contesten con **por** o **para**.

1. ¿Cuál es el destino del tren? ¿Barcelona?
2. ¿A quién vas a dar los dulces? ¿Al niño?
3. Cuando vendiste el carro, ¿te dieron mil dólares?
4. Es mexicano pero habla muy bien el inglés, ¿verdad?
5. ¿Cuándo piensas venir? ¿En abril?
6. ¿Te queda mucho o poco por hacer?
7. ¿Cuándo lo terminarás? ¿Mañana?
8. Ellos pasaron mucho tiempo en Cataluña, ¿verdad?
9. ¿Cómo mandaron el paquete que acabas de recibir? ¿Correo aéreo?

C **Un resumen** Escriban las oraciones con **por** o **para**.

1. Andan *en* el parque.
2. Mañana salen *con destino a* Barcelona.
3. Los chicos van ahora *en la dirección de* la ciudad.
4. Tengo que estar allí *no más tarde de* las tres.
5. *A pesar de que es* viejo, viaja mucho.
6. Hay un montón de trabajo *que tengo que* terminar.
7. Papá no podía asistir, así que yo fui *en lugar de* él.
8. Los chicos corrieron *en* la calle.
9. Voy al mercado *en busca de* carne.
10. Mis padres lo pagaron *en vez de* mí.
11. Subimos al tren *con destino a* Granada.
12. *A pesar de que es* rico, no es generoso.
13. Nos gusta viajar *en* Colombia.
14. Estaremos en Cali *durante* siete días.

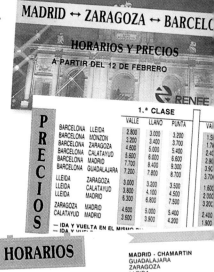

Independent Practice

Assign any of the following:
1. Exercises, page 336
2. Workbook, *Estructura*

Literatura
Un día de éstos

de Gabriel García Márquez

Antes de leer

«Un día de éstos» del famoso autor colombiano Gabriel García Márquez tiene lugar en el gabinete o consulta de un dentista. Ud. verá por la descripción que es un gabinete viejo. El hijo del dentista le dice que le duele un diente (una muela) al alcalde y que éste quiere que el dentista se lo saque. El dentista detesta al alcalde. Lea lo que el dentista le hace.

Vocabulario

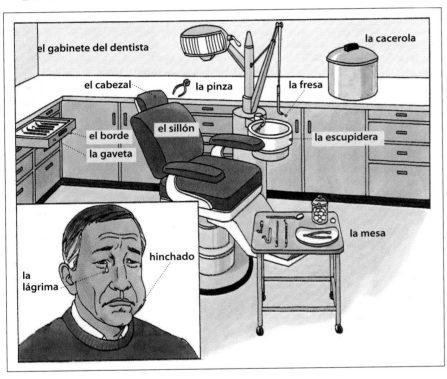

el gabinete del dentista
la cacerola
el cabezal
la pinza
la fresa
el borde
el sillón
la gaveta
la escupidera
la mesa
hinchado
la lágrima

TEACHING TIPS

A. Call on a student to read the introduction aloud as the others follow along.

B. Then ask: **¿Quién es el autor? ¿Cuál es el título? ¿De qué país es el autor? ¿Dónde tiene lugar este cuento?**

RESOURCES

- Vocabulary Transparencies
- Audio Cassette 14B/Compact Disc 10
- Student Tape Manual
- Workbook
- Chapter Quizzes
- Testing Program

TEACHING VOCABULARY

You may wish to follow some of the suggestions given for previous vocabulary sections.

VOCABULARY EXPANSION

You may wish to give students the following additional dental vocabulary:

el puente
la corona
la ortodoncia
la banda
los tirantes *(braces)*
el soporte ortodóntico

TEACHING TIPS

A. You may wish to call on volunteers to contribute to the description asked for in *Práctica A*.

B. *Práctica B* and *C* can be done orally immediately following the presentation of the vocabulary.

ANSWERS

Práctica

A and B Answers will vary.

C 1. c

   2. b

   3. c

   4. b

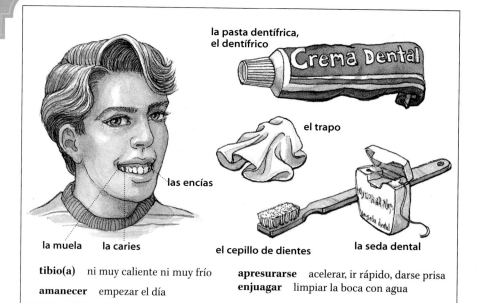

la pasta dentífrica, el dentífrico

el trapo

las encías

la muela   la caries

el cepillo de dientes

la seda dental

tibio(a)   ni muy caliente ni muy frío

amanecer   empezar el día

apresurarse   acelerar, ir rápido, darse prisa

enjuagar   limpiar la boca con agua

⇒Práctica⇐

A   **El gabinete del dentista**   Describan lo que Uds. ven en el gabinete del dentista.

B   **La higiene dental**   Preguntas personales.

1. ¿Cómo se llama su dentista?
2. ¿Cuántas veces al año tiene Ud. una consulta con el dentista?
3. ¿Le hace un examen dental?
4. ¿Le limpia los dientes?
5. ¿Tiene Ud. muchas caries?
6. ¿Cuántas veces al día se cepilla Ud. los dientes?
7. ¿Tiene un cepillo de dientes suave?
8. ¿Usa Ud. una pasta dentífrica antitártaro?
9. ¿Utiliza Ud. la seda dental?

C   **¿Cuál es la palabra?**   Escojan la palabra.

1. Se debe enjuagar la boca con agua ___.
   a. helada   **b.** muy caliente   **c.** tibia
2. ___ es un diente.
   a. La caries   **b.** La muela   **c.** La encía
3. Amanece ___.
   a. por la noche   **b.** por la tarde   **c.** por la mañana
4. Él tiene que ___ porque tiene que ver al dentista a las nueve en punto.
   a. cepillarse los dientes   **b.** apresurarse   **c.** amanecer

Independent Practice

Assign any of the following:

1. Exercises, page 338
2. Workbook, *Literatura*

Introducción

Gabriel García Márquez es indudablemente uno de los más importantes escritores de la literatura hispánica. Es el más brillante exponente de la tendencia literaria contemporánea denominada «realismo mágico».

García Márquez nació en Aracataca, Colombia, en 1928. Estudió periodismo en la Universidad Nacional de Colombia en Bogotá y leyes en la Universidad de Cartagena. Ha sido periodista en Barranquilla, Bogotá y Cartagena. Ha trabajado también en Italia, España y México.

Inicialmente, Gabriel García Márquez escribió cuentos cortos para los periódicos donde trabajaba. Ahora escribe novelas. Ya ha escrito muchas. Una de las más famosas es *Cien años de soledad*, publicada en 1967. Otra novela popularísima de García Márquez es *El amor en los tiempos del cólera*. En 1982, García Márquez recibió el premio Nóbel de Literatura.

«Un día de éstos» es un cuento de su obra *Los funerales de la Mamá Grande*. Para comprender esta selección hay que conocer el fondo histórico. La lucha entre liberales y conservadores en Colombia fue acompañada de mucha violencia. Comenzó en 1948 con el asesinato del candidato liberal y laborista José Eliecer Gaitán. Este suceso produjo un clima de terror por todo el país. En una sola década, murieron trágicamente más de 300.000 personas. García Márquez se ocupa de esta lucha fratricida en «Un día de éstos». El dentista le tiene tanto odio y rencor al alcalde que poder hacerle sufrir le da una gran satisfacción.

Gabriel García Márquez

TEACHING TIPS

A. Present the information on Gabriel García Márquez as a mini-lecture. Write the important names and dates on the board.

B. After you present the information, ask: **¿García Márquez es el más brillante exponente de qué tendencia literaria? ¿Dónde y cuándo nació? ¿Qué estudió? ¿Qué premio recibió? ¿De qué obra viene esta selección? ¿Cuál es el fondo histórico de este cuento?**

Additional Practice

You may wish to ask the following questions about the *Introducción*:

¿Qué estudió y dónde estudió García Márquez?

¿Cómo ha trabajado y dónde?

¿Cuáles son las dos novelas más famosas de García Márquez?

¿De qué obra es «Un día de éstos»?

¿Dónde tiene lugar la historia? ¿Quiénes estaban luchando?

¿De qué fue acompañada la lucha entre liberales y conservadores?

En esta obra, ¿qué le da una gran satisfacción al dentista?

¿Por qué le da mucha satisfacción?

TEACHING THE READING

◆ Lectura ◆◆

A. Have students close their books and listen to the recording on Cassette 14B/Compact Disc 10

B. Read the beginning paragraphs to the students as they follow along.

C. Call on three students to read the parts of the **dentista,** his son, and the **alcalde** with as much expression as possible.

D. As you go over the reading, you may wish to ask some rather general questions that have students seek the main ideas without having to give minute and unnecessary detail. Some questions you may want to ask are: **¿Cómo estaba el tiempo? ¿Adónde fue el dentista? ¿Cómo estaba vestido? ¿Por qué parecía que el dentista no pensaba en lo que hacía? ¿Quién vino a hablarle? ¿Qué le dijo su hijo? ¿Qué le contestó el dentista?**

E. Then do *Comprensión A* on page 343.

F. With more able groups, you may wish to ask the more analytical question in LITERARY ANALYSIS at the bottom of page 342.

National Standards

Cultures

Students experience, discuss, and analyze an expressive product of the culture: the short story, «Un día de estos», by the Nobel Prize-winning Colombian author, Gabriel García Márquez.

Lectura

Un día de éstos

El lunes amaneció tibio y sin lluvia. Don Aurelio Escovar, dentista sin título y buen madrugador°, abrió su gabinete a las seis. Sacó de la vidriera una dentadura postiza° montada aún en el molde de yeso° y puso sobre la mesa un puñado de instrumentos que ordenó de mayor a menor, como en una exposición. Llevaba una camisa a rayas, sin cuello, cerrada arriba con un botón dorado, y los pantalones sostenidos con cargadores° elásticos. Era rígido, enjuto°, con una mirada que raras veces correspondía a la situación, como la mirada de los sordos.

Cuando tuvo las cosas dispuestas sobre la mesa rodó la fresa hacia el sillón de resortes y se sentó a pulir la dentadura postiza. Parecía no pensar en lo que hacía, pero trabajaba con obstinación, pedaleando en la fresa incluso cuando no se servía de ella.

Después de las ocho hizo una pausa para mirar el cielo por la ventana y vio dos gallinazos° pensativos que se secaban al sol en el caballete° de la casa vecina. Siguió trabajando con la idea de que antes del almuerzo volvería a llover. La voz destemplada de su hijo de once años lo sacó de su abstracción.

—Papá.

—¿Qué?

—Dice el Alcalde que si le sacas una muela.

—Dile que no estoy aquí.

Estaba puliendo° un diente de oro. Lo retiró a la distancia del brazo y lo examinó con los ojos a medio cerrar. En la salita de espera volvió a gritar su hijo.

—Dice que sí estás porque te está oyendo.

El dentista siguió examinando el diente. Sólo cuando lo puso en la mesa con los trabajos terminados, dijo:

—Mejor.

Volvió a operar la fresa. De una cajita de cartón donde guardaba las cosas por hacer, sacó un puente° de varias piezas y empezó a pulir el oro.

—Papá.

madrugador *early riser*

una dentadura postiza *a set of false teeth*
yeso *plaster*

cargadores *suspenders*

enjuto *lean*

gallinazos *buzzards*
el caballete *chimney cowl*

puliendo *polishing*

un puente *a dental bridge*

340

—¿Qué?

Aún no había cambiado de expresión.

—Dice que si no le sacas la muela te pega un tiro°.

Sin apresurarse, con un movimiento extremadamente tranquilo, dejó de pedalear en la fresa, la retiró del sillón y abrió por completo la gaveta inferior de la mesa. Allí estaba el revólver.

—Bueno —dijo. —Dile que venga a pegármelo.

Hizo girar° el sillón hasta quedar de frente a la puerta, la mano apoyada en el borde de la gaveta. El Alcalde apareció en el umbral°. Se había afeitado la mejilla izquierda, pero en la otra, hinchada y dolorida, tenía una barba de cinco días. El dentista vio en sus ojos marchitos muchas noches de desesperación. Cerró la gaveta con la punta de los dedos y dijo suavemente:

—Siéntese.

—Buenos días —dijo el Alcalde.

—Buenos —dijo el dentista.

Mientras hervían los instrumentos, el Alcalde apoyó el cráneo en el cabezal de la silla y se sintió mejor. Respiraba un olor glacial. Era un gabinete pobre: una vieja silla de madera, la fresa de pedal y una vidriera con pomos de loza°. Frente a la silla, una ventana con un cancel de tela° hasta la altura de un hombre. Cuando sintió que el dentista se acercaba, el Alcalde afirmó los talones y abrió la boca.

te pega un tiro *he'll shoot you*

girar *turn around*
el umbral *the doorway*

pomos de loza *small porcelain bottles*
cancel de tela *cloth screen*

LITERATURA

trescientos cuarenta y uno ∞ **341**

CAPÍTULO 7
Literatura

LITERATURE CONNECTION

Cien años de soledad es la obra más famosa de Gabriel García Márquez. La primera edición apareció en mayo de 1967. Ha sido traducida a muchos idiomas. Para el latinoamericano, la historia del pueblo de Macondo y la de la familia Buendía son una alegoría de su continente. La novela trata de siete generaciones de esta familia—pero no en orden cronológico. La novela es una serie tras otra de episodios y eventos inesperados—todos contados con el sentido de humor genial y singular de García Márquez.

La novela es una alegoría trágica sobre la condición humana. Es la historia de toda una familia que pasa de la inocencia a la destrucción. El autor ha creado un lugar mítico—Macondo—donde tiene lugar la historia mágica de la familia Buendía, que simboliza la explotación y la corrupción de un pueblo concreto de Hispanoamérica. Dice Ramón Xiaru en su ensayo «Crisis del realismo»: «*Cien años de soledad* es la novela de una tierra y de una familia, de la tierra y de los hombres. La magia predomina en la novela; una magia hecha de tierra y sueño que es también mito y leyenda más que historia. Acaso lo más extraordinario de *Cien años de soledad* sea la capacidad de narrar con un realismo preciso y hasta transformar la realidad en leyenda sin que la leyenda pierda bulto de realidad».

Critical Thinking Activity

Thinking skills: evaluating information After giving students the information concerning *Cien años de soledad*, have them express in their own words what they think **realismo mágico** is.

341

TEACHING TIPS

A. Have students explain in their own words the italicized elements:

El alcalde trató de sonreír. El dentista *no le correspondió.*

Hizo todo sin mirar al alcalde. Pero el alcalde *no lo perdió de vista.*

Sus ojos se llenaron de lágrimas.

B. Have students look for the original wording of the following:

El alcalde agarró las barras de la silla.

No suspiró.

Estaba sudando (transpirando).

Tenía dificultad en respirar.

LITERATURE CONNECTION

Otra novela famosa de Gabriel García Márquez es *El amor en los tiempos del cólera,* **publicada en 1985. Florentino Ariza está enamorado de Fermina Daza pero ella decide casarse con uno de los hombres más ricos de su ciudad, el doctor Juvenal Urbino. Por más de cincuenta años Fermina Daza y el doctor Urbino llevan su vida juntos. Y Florentino Ariza tiene su vida también pero en su corazón se queda fiel a Fermina y no se casa. Cuando muere el doctor Urbino, se reúnen Florentino y Fermina a bordo de un barco llamado** *Nueva Fidelidad.*

Don Aurelio Escovar le movió la cara hacia la luz. Después de observar la muela dañada, ajustó la mandíbula con una cautelosa presión de los dedos.

—Tiene que ser sin anestesia —dijo.

—¿Por qué?

—Porque tiene un absceso.

El Alcalde lo miró a los ojos. —Está bien —dijo, y trató de sonreír. El dentista no le correspondió. Llevó a la mesa de trabajo la cacerola con los instrumentos hervidos y los sacó del agua con unas pinzas frías, todavía sin apresurarse. Después rodó la escupidera con la punta del zapato y fue a lavarse las manos en el aguamanil°. Hizo todo sin mirar al Alcalde. Pero el Alcalde no lo perdió de vista.

Era un cordal inferior°. El dentista abrió las piernas y apretó la muela con el gatillo° caliente. El Alcalde se aferró° a las barras de la silla, descargó toda su fuerza en los pies y sintió un vacío helado en los riñones°, pero no soltó un suspiro. El dentista sólo movió la muñeca. Sin rencor, más bien con una amarga ternura, dijo:

—Aquí nos paga veinte muertos°, teniente.

El Alcalde sintió un crujido° de huesos en la mandíbula y sus ojos se llenaron de lágrimas. Pero no suspiró hasta que no sintió salir la muela. Entonces la vio a través de las lágrimas. Le pareció tan extraña a su dolor, que no pudo entender la tortura de sus cinco noches anteriores.

Inclinado sobre la escupidera, sudoroso°, jadeante°, se desabotonó la guerrera° y buscó a tientas° el pañuelo en el bolsillo del pantalón. El dentista le dio un trapo limpio.

—Séquese las lágrimas —dijo.

El Alcalde lo hizo. Estaba temblando. Mientras el dentista se lavaba las manos, vio el cielo raso desfondado° y una telaraña° polvorienta con huevos de araña° e insectos muertos. El dentista regresó secándose las manos. —Acuéstese —dijo—y haga buches de agua de sal. El alcalde se puso de pie, se despidió con un displicente saludo militar, y se dirigió a la puerta estirando las piernas, sin abotonarse la guerrera.

—Me pasa la cuenta —dijo.

—¿A usted o al municipio?

El Alcalde no lo miró. Cerró la puerta, y dijo, a través de la red° metálica:

—Es la misma vaina°.

aguamanil *washstand*

un cordal inferior *a bottom wisdom tooth*
el gatillo *forceps*
se aferró *clung to, grasped*
los riñones *kidneys*

muertos *deaths (you have caused)*
un crujido *a crackle, creak*

sudoroso *sweaty*
jadeante *panting*
la guerrera *military jacket*
a tientas *groping*

el cielo raso desfondado *the broken ceiling*
una telaraña *a spider web*
araña *spider*

la red *the screen*

la misma vaina *la misma cosa*

Literary Analysis

¿Qué puede simbolizar la telaraña polvorienta con huevos de araña e insectos muertos?

⊷Después de leer⊷

⦿ Comprensión ⦿

A **El dentista**   Contesten.

1. ¿Qué le dice al dentista su hijo?
2. ¿Qué quiere el dentista que su hijo le diga al alcalde?
3. ¿Qué le va a hacer el alcalde si no le saca la muela?
4. ¿Qué tomó el dentista de la gaveta inferior de su mesa?
5. Según el dentista, ¿cómo tenía que sacarle la muela?
6. ¿Qué le dijo el dentista al alcalde que hiciera?

B **Descripciones**   Hagan lo siguiente.

1. Describa al dentista.
2. Describa el gabinete del dentista.
3. Describa al alcalde mientras el dentista le sacaba la muela.

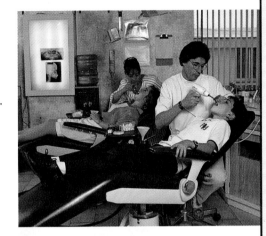

C **¿Qué quiere decir?**   Expliquen el significado.

1. Aquí nos paga veinte muertos, teniente.
2. El dentista le dio un trapo limpio.
   —Séquese las lágrimas —dijo.
3. —Me pasa la cuenta —dijo (el alcalde).
   —¿A Ud. o al municipio?
   —Es la misma vaina.

⦿ Actividades comunicativas ⦿

A **El tema principal**   En sus propias palabras, explique lo que Ud. considera el tema principal de este cuento.

B **¡Qué tensión!**   Entre el dentista y el alcalde hay mucha tensión. Prepare Ud. una lista de las acciones que introduce el autor para indicar esta tensión.

C **La corrupción**   En un párrafo corto, explique cómo García Márquez critica la corrupción que existe en el gobierno.

D **Un debate**   Con un(a) compañero(a) de clase preparen un debate. ¿Son justos y aceptables los deseos de venganza y el comportamiento del dentista o no? ¿Por qué?

LITERATURA

trescientos cuarenta y tres ⟋⟍ **343**

Independent Practice

Assign any of the following:
1. Exercises, page 343
2. Workbook, *Literatura*

CAPÍTULO 7
Literatura

TEACHING TIPS

A. You may wish to intersperse questions from *Práctica A* while the reading is taking place.

B. Volunteers may be called upon to do *Práctica B* and *C*. For reinforcement, you may wish to assign these exercises for homework.

ANSWERS
Comprensión

A 1. Le dice que el alcalde quiere que le saque una muela.
  2. El dentista quiere que le diga al alcalde que no está.
  3. El alcalde le va a pegar un tiro.
  4. El dentista tomó el revólver.
  5. Tenía que sacarle la muela sin anestesia.
  6. Le dijo que se secara las lágrimas.

B 1. Era rígido, enjuto y con una mirada rara.
  2. Era un gabinete pobre: tenía una vieja silla de madera, la fresa de pedal y una vidriera con pomos de loza.
  3. El alcalde se aferró a las barras de la silla, descargó toda su fuerza en los pies, pero no soltó un suspiro.

C Answers will vary.

TEACHING TIPS

Allow students to select the activities in which they wish to participate.

⦿ Actividades comunicativas ⦿

ANSWERS
A–D Answers will vary.

TEACHING TIPS

You may wish to read *Antes de leer* aloud to the class.

RESOURCES

- 🔊 Vocabulary Transparencies
- 🎧 Audio Cassette 14B/Compact Disc 10
- 📁 Student Tape Manual
- 📁 Workbook
- 📁 Chapter Quizzes
- 💾 Testing Program

TEACHING VOCABULARY

You may wish to use some suggestions from previous chapters.

La tía Julia y el escribidor

de Mario Vargas Llosa

Antes de leer

El trozo de la novela *La tía Julia y el escribidor* del famoso autor peruano Mario Vargas Llosa trata de un médico, el doctor Alberto de Quinteros. La acción tiene lugar en San Isidro, un suburbio de la clase acomodada de Lima, la capital del Perú. Al médico le interesa mucho estar en forma. Por consiguiente, frecuenta el Gimnasio Remigius que está a unas cuadras de su casa. En el gimnasio ve a su sobrino, Richard, un joven muy guapo. Esta tarde la sobrina del doctor, la hermana de Richard, va a casarse. Ella es una muchacha bellísima. Uds. descubrirán si su familia está satisfecha o no con el joven a quien ella ha escogido como marido.

Vocabulario

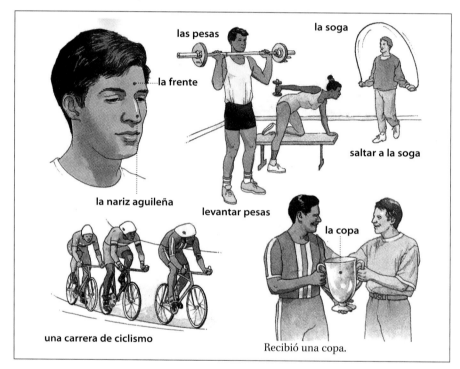

las pesas
la soga
la frente
saltar a la soga
la nariz aguileña
levantar pesas
la copa
una carrera de ciclismo
Recibió una copa.

el azulejo

la ducha   el casillero

El joven anuda
los cordones.

el ladrido

los visillos   la valla

el césped

El señor palmeó
al perro.
El perro ladra.

el perro

el galeno el/la médico(a)

el vientre el estómago

el/la ciego(a) el/la que no tiene vista, no puede ver

cotidiano(a) de todos los días

apuesto(a) muy guapo(a) y elegante

flaco(a) delgado(a), lo contrario de gordo

regar darle agua a una planta

podar cortar ramas de plantas o árboles

✦Práctica✦

A **HISTORIETA** En el gimnasio

Contesten.

1. ¿Vas a un gimnasio?
2. Antes de hacer ejercicios fuertes, ¿calientas?
3. ¿Te gusta levantar pesas?
4. ¿Te gusta saltar a la soga?
5. ¿Te gusta el ciclismo?
6. Cuando vas al gimnasio, ¿pones tu ropa en un casillero?
7. ¿Anudas los cordones de tus tenis?
8. Después de hacer ejercicios, ¿tomas una ducha?

B **Una casa bonita**   Completen.

1. Los ___ cubren las ventanas.
2. Delante de la casa hay un ___ que hay que ___ para que esté verde.
3. Es una lástima que el ___ no pueda ver el jardín.
4. Alrededor del jardín hay una ___ de madera.
5. Ellos tienen un perro en el jardín. El perro no ___ mucho.

LITERATURA

ABOUT THE SPANISH LANGUAGE

◆ Other words that mean "tile" are: **el mosaico, la baldosa, el baldosín, la loseta.**

◆ **Los visillos** are sheer curtains. Other types of window coverings are **las cortinas** (*curtains*), **los colgantes** (*drapes*), and **las persianas** (*blinds*).

◆ Another word for **los cordones** is **los pasadores.**

TEACHING TIPS

A. Have students close their books and answer the questions orally.

B. You may wish to have students complete this exercise with books open.

ANSWERS

Práctica

A Answers will vary.

B 1. **visillos**
   2. **césped, regar**
   3. **ciego**
   4. **valla**
   5. **ladra**

Independent Practice

Assign any of the following:
1. Exercises, page 345
2. Workbook, *Literatura*

345

Literatura

TEACHING TIPS

Read the *Introducción* aloud to the students. Ask: **¿Quién es Mario Vargas Llosa? ¿Dónde y cuándo nació? ¿Dónde hizo sus estudios? ¿Para qué fue candidato en 1990? ¿Ganó las elecciones?**

TEACHING THE READING

Lectura ◆◆

A. Have the students read the selection at home.

B. The next day, go over the *Lectura* in class.

C. You may wish to paraphrase the paragraphs after the students have read them aloud in class. You may also call on one student to give a brief synopsis after each paragraph is read.

D. You may also wish to ask comprehension questions during the reading.

E. Call on individuals to read the roles of the narrator and the other participants.

F. With more able groups, you may wish to ask the analytical question in LITERARY ANALYSIS at the bottom of page 347.

GEOGRAPHY CONNECTION

Arequipa está situada a 7.590 pies sobre el nivel del mar. Es una de las pocas ciudades que goza de la «primavera eterna». El sol sale casi todos los días. A Arequipa se le llama la Ciudad Blanca porque muchas de las casas e iglesias, sobre todo las de la época colonial, son de «sillar», una piedra volcánica de color blanco. La Plaza de Armas de Arequipa es una de las más bonitas de todo el país.

346

Introducción

Mario Vargas Llosa, uno de los más famosos escritores hispanoamericanos de hoy, nació en Arequipa, Perú, en 1936. Hizo sus estudios primarios en Cochabamba, Bolivia, y los secundarios en Lima. Se licenció en letras en la Universidad de San Marcos de Lima. Recibió su doctorado de la Universidad de Madrid. Vargas Llosa ha residido en París, Barcelona y Londres. Recibió el Premio Internacional de Literatura Rómulo Gallegos en 1967.

Durante un período turbulento en su país, Vargas Llosa fue candidato para la presidencia (1990). Casi todo el mundo creyó que él ganaría las elecciones pero al último momento salió victorioso Alberto Fujimori, el primer presidente de origen japonés de un país hispanoamericano.

Mario Vargas Llosa

Lectura

La tía Julia y el escribidor

Era una de esas soleadas mañanas de la primavera limeña, en que los geranios amanecen más arrebatados°, las rosas más fragantes y las buganvilias más crespas°, cuando un famoso galeno de la ciudad, el doctor Alberto de Quinteros—frente ancha, nariz aguileña, mirada penetrante, rectitud y bondad en el espíritu— abrió los ojos y se desperezó° en su espaciosa residencia de San Isidro. Vio, a través de los visillos, el sol dorando el césped del cuidado jardín que encarcelaban vallas de crotos, la limpieza del cielo, la alegría de las flores, y sintió esa sensación bienhechora° que dan ocho horas de sueño reparador y la conciencia tranquila.

Era sábado y, a menos de alguna complicación de último momento con la señora de los trillizos°, no iría a la clínica y podría dedicar la mañana a hacer un poco de ejercicio y a tomar una sauna antes del matrimonio de Elianita. Su esposa y su hija se hallaban en Europa, cultivando su espíritu y renovando su vestuario°, y no regresarían antes de un mes. Otro, con sus medios de fortuna y su apostura°—sus cabellos nevados en las sienes° y su porte distinguido, así como su elegancia de maneras, despertaban miradas de codicia incluso en señoras incorruptibles—, hubiera aprovechado la momentánea soltería° para echar algunas canas° al aire. Pero Alberto de Quinteros era un hombre al que ni el juego, ni las faldas ni el alcohol atraían más de lo debido, y entre sus conocidos—que eran legión—circulaba este apotegma°: «Sus vicios son la ciencia, su familia y la gimnasia».

arrebatados	*flushed*
crespas	*curled*
se desperezó	*stretched*
bienhechora	*kind*
los trillizos	*the triplets*
vestuario	*ropa*
apostura	*bearing*
las sienes	*temples*
soltería	*single life*
echar canas	*have some fun*
apotegma	*refrán*

Did You Know?

Durante las elecciones de 1990 había muchos que creían que Mario Vargas Llosa las ganaría y que sería presidente del Perú. Pero al último momento salió victorioso Alberto Fujimori. Desde 1990 muchos compatriotas de Vargas Llosa lo han criticado por haber vivido fuera del Perú durante las muchas crisis económicas y políticas de las que ha sufrido el país. En años recientes Vargas Llosa estaba viviendo en Madrid.

Ordenó el desayuno y, mientras se lo preparaban, llamó a la clínica. El médico de guardia le informó que la señora de los trillizos había pasado una noche tranquila y que las hemorragias de la operada del fibroma habían cesado. Dio instrucciones, indicó que si ocurría algo grave lo llamaran al Gimnasio Remigius, o, a la hora de almuerzo, donde su hermano Roberto, e hizo saber que al atardecer se daría una vuelta° por allá. Cuando el mayordomo le trajo su jugo de papaya, su café negro y sus tostadas con miel de abeja°, Alberto de Quinteros se había afeitado y vestía un pantalón gris de corduroy, unos mocasines sin taco° y una chompa° verde de cuello alto. Desayunó echando una ojeada° distraída a las catástrofes e intrigas matutinas° de los periódicos, cogió su maletín deportivo y salió. Se detuvo unos segundos en el jardín a palmear a Puck, el engreído° fox-terrier que lo despidió con afectuosos ladridos.

El Gimnasio Remigius estaba a pocas cuadras, en la calle Miguel Dasso, y al doctor Quinteros le gustaba andarlas. Iba despacio, respondía a los saludos del vecindario, observaba los jardines de las casas que a esa hora eran regados y podados, y solía parar un momento en la Librería Castro Soto a elegir algunos best-sellers. Aunque era temprano, ya estaban frente al Davory los infalibles muchachos de camisas abiertas y cabelleras alborotadas°. Tomaban helados, en sus motos o en los guardabarros° de sus autos sport, se hacían bromas y planeaban la fiesta de la noche. Lo saludaron con respeto, pero apenas los dejó atrás, uno de ellos se atrevió° a darle uno de esos consejos que eran su pan cotidiano en el Gimnasio, eternos chistes° sobre su edad y su profesión, que él soportaba con paciencia y buen humor: «No se canse mucho, doctor, piense en sus nietos». Apenas lo oyó pues estaba imaginando lo linda que se vería Elianita en su vestido de novia diseñado para ella por la casa Christian Dior de París.

No había mucha gente en el Gimnasio esa mañana. Sólo Coco, el instructor, y dos fanáticos de las pesas, el Negro Humilla y Perico Sarmiento, tres montañas de músculos equivalentes a los de diez hombres normales. Debían de haber llegado no hacía mucho tiempo, estaban todavía calentando:

—Pero si ahí viene la cigüeña° —le estrechó la mano Coco.

—¿Todavía en pie, a pesar de los siglos? —le hizo adiós el Negro Humilla.

Perico se limitó a chasquear° la lengua y a levantar dos dedos, en el característico saludo que había importado de Texas. Al doctor Quinteros le agradaba esa informalidad, las confianzas que se tomaban con él sus compañeros de Gimnasio, como si el hecho de verse desnudos y de sudar° juntos los nivelara en una fraternidad donde desaparecían las diferencias de edad y posición. Les contestó que si necesitaban sus servicios estaba a sus órdenes, que a los primeros mareos o antojos° corrieran a su consultorio donde tenía listo el guante de jebe° para auscultarles la intimidad.

se daría una vuelta *he would stop by*
miel de abeja *honey*

taco *heel*
una chompa *a jersey*
ojeada *glance*
matutinas *de la mañana*
el engreído *spoiled*

cabelleras alborotadas *rumpled hair*
los guardabarros *the fenders*

se atrevió *dared*

chistes *jokes*

la cigüeña *the stork*

chasquear *click*

sudar *to sweat*

antojos *cravings*
jebe *elastic, rubber*

TEACHING THE READING

A. After reading the first two paragraphs, you may wish to ask the following questions: **¿Tenía que ir el doctor al hospital o no? ¿Por qué? ¿Qué hizo el médico antes de salir? ¿Para dónde salió?**

B. Discusión: **En el segundo párrafo hay algunos elementos sociológicos. ¿Cuáles son?**

ABOUT THE SPANISH LANGUAGE

◆ Ask students what word they have already learned that means taco. **(tacón)**

◆ Have students scan the first paragraph and tell where the doctor is going to be at lunch time. **¿Dónde va a estar el médico a la hora del almuerzo?** Note the use of donde: **donde su hermano Roberto,** meaning **en casa de su hermano Roberto.**

Critical Thinking Activity

Thinking skills: evaluating information
Vargas Llosa ha dicho que mientras mayor sea el patriotismo, mayor deberá ser la crueldad. Explique lo que está diciendo el autor y comente si Ud. está de acuerdo o no.

Literary Analysis

En el trozo que hemos leído, ¿cuáles son algunas cosas que indican que los protagonistas son de la clase acomodada?

TEACHING TIPS

Have the students do the following:
1. Preparen una lista de actividades que tenían lugar en el gimnasio.
2. Describan al sobrino del médico.

VOCABULARY EXPANSION

Have students give other words they know for the following glosses:

tablista (el súrfer)
el buzo (la sudadera)
bruñido (bronceado)
churro (hermoso)

—Cámbiate y ven a hacer un poco de warm up —le dijo Coco, que ya estaba saltando en el sitio otra vez.

—Si te viene el infarto, no pasas de morirte, veterano —lo alentó Perico, poniéndose al paso de Coco.

—Adentro está el tablista° —oyó decir al Negro Humilla, cuando entraba al vestuario.

el tablista *the surfer*

Y, en efecto, ahí estaba su sobrino Richard, en buzo° azul, calzándose las zapatillas. Lo hacía con desgano°, como si las manos se le hubieran vuelto de trapo, y tenía la cara agria y ausente. Se quedó mirándolo con unos ojos azules totalmente idos y una indiferencia tan absoluta que el doctor Quinteros se preguntó si no se había vuelto invisible.

buzo *jogging suit*
con desgano *reluctantly*

—Sólo los enamorados se abstraen así —se acercó a él y le revolvió los cabellos. Baja de la luna, sobrino.

—Perdona, tío —despertó Richard, enrojeciendo° violentamente, como si lo acabaran de sorprender haciendo algo sucio—. Estaba pensando.

enrojeciendo *blushing*

—Me gustaría saber en qué maldades —se rió el doctor Quinteros, mientras abría su maletín, elegía un casillero y comenzaba a desvestirse—. Tu casa debe ser un desbarajuste° terrible. ¿Está muy nerviosa Elianita?

un desbarajuste *a mess*

Richard lo miró con una especie de odio súbito y el doctor pensó qué le ha picado a este muchacho. Pero su sobrino, haciendo un esfuerzo notorio por mostrarse natural, esbozó° un amago de sonrisa:

esbozó *outlined*

—Sí, un desbarajuste. Por eso me vine a quemar un poco de grasa°, hasta que sea hora.

El doctor pensó que iba a añadir: «de subir al patíbulo°». Tenía la voz lastrada por la tristeza, y también sus facciones y la torpeza° con que anudaba los cordones y los movimientos bruscos de su cuerpo revelaban incomodidad, malestar íntimo, desasosiego°. No podía tener los ojos quietos: los abría, los cerraba, fijaba la vista en un punto, la desviaba, la regresaba, volvía a apartarla, como buscando algo imposible de encontrar. Era el muchacho más apuesto de la tierra, un joven dios bruñido° por la intemperie— hacía tabla aun en los meses más húmedos del invierno y descollaba también en el basquet, el tenis, la natación y el fulbito—, al que los deportes habían modelado un cuerpo de esos que el Negro Humilla llamaba «locura de todos»: ni gota de grasa, espaldas anchas que descendían en una tersa línea de músculos hasta la cintura de avispa y unas largas piernas duras y ágiles que habrían hecho palidecer de envidia al mejor boxeador. Alberto de Quinteros había oído con frecuencia a su hija Charo y a sus amigas comparar a Richard con Charlton Heston y sentenciar que todavía era más churro°, que lo dejaba botado en pinta°. Estaba en primer año de arquitectura, y según Roberto y Margarita, sus padres, había sido siempre un modelo: estudioso, obediente, bueno con ellos y con su

grasa *fat*
patíbulo *scaffold*
la torpeza *slowness*

desasosiego *uneasiness*

bruñido *tanned*

churro *guapo*
botado en pinta *better looking*

Did You Know?

In comparison to many of the contemporary writers of Latin America, such as Gabriel García Márquez and Isabel Allende, the political views of Vargas Llosa are much more conservative. Whereas the other writers are of the left in their political orientation, Vargas Llosa leans to the right.

hermana, sano, simpático. Elianita y él eran sus sobrinos preferidos y por eso, mientras se ponía el suspensor, el buzo, las zapatillas—Richard lo esperaba junto a las duchas, dando unos golpecitos contra los azulejos—el doctor Alberto de Quinteros se apenó al verlo tan turbado.

—¿Algún problema, sobrino? —le preguntó, como al descuido, con una sonrisa bondadosa—. ¿Algo en que tu tío pueda echarte una mano?

—Ninguno, qué ocurrencia —se apresuró a contestar Richard, encendiéndose de nuevo como un fósforo—. Estoy regio° y con unas ganas bárbaras de calentar.

regio *super*

—¿Le llevaron mi regalo a tu hermana? —recordó de pronto el doctor—. En la Casa Murguía me prometieron que lo harían ayer.

—Una pulsera bestial —Richard había comenzado a saltar sobre las losetas° blancas del vestuario—. A la flaca° le encantó.

las losetas *the tiles*
la flaca *the thin one*

—De estas cosas se encarga tu tía, pero como sigue paseando por las Europas, tuve que escogerla yo mismo. —El doctor Quinteros hizo un gesto enternecido:— Elianita, vestida de novia, será una aparición.

Porque la hija de su hermano Roberto era en mujer lo que Richard en hombre: una de esas bellezas que dignifican a la especie y hacen que las metáforas sobre las muchachas de dientes de perla, ojos como luceros, cabellos de trigo y cutis de melocotón, luzcan mezquinas. Menuda, de cabellos oscuros y piel muy blanca, graciosa hasta en su manera de respirar, tenía una carita de líneas clásicas, unos rasgos que parecían dibujados por un miniaturista del Oriente. Un año más joven que Richard, acababa de terminar el colegio, su único defecto era la timidez —tan excesiva que, para desesperación de los organizadores, no habían podido convencerla de que participara en el Concurso Miss Perú —y nadie, entre ellos el doctor Quinteros, podía explicarse por qué se casaba tan pronto y, sobre todo, con quien. Ya que el Pelirrojo Antúnez tenía algunas virtudes —bueno como el pan, un título de Business Administration por la Universidad de Chicago, la compañía de fertilizantes que heredaría y varias copas en carreras de ciclismo—pero, entre los innumerables muchachos de Miraflores y San Isidro que habían hecho la corte a Elianita y que hubieran llegado al crimen por casarse con ella, era, sin duda, el menos agraciado y (el doctor Quinteros se avergonzó por permitirse este juicio sobre quien dentro de pocas horas pasaría a ser su sobrino) el más soso° y tontito.

soso *dull, inane*

—Eres más lento para cambiarte que mi mamá, tío —se quejó Richard, entre saltos.

Cuando entraron a la sala de ejercicios, Coco, en quien la pedagogía era una vocación más que un oficio, instruía al Negro Humilla, señalándole el estómago, sobre este axioma de su filosofía:

—Cuando comas, cuando trabajes, cuando estés en el cine..., en todos los momentos de tu vida, y, si puedes, hasta en el féretro°: ¡hunde la panza°!

el féretro *the coffin*
hunde la panza *pull in the belly*

LITERATURE CONNECTION

Una novela famosa de Vargas Llosa es *La ciudad y los perros*. *La ciudad y los perros* es el lugar donde tiene lugar la novela, el colegio militar Leoncio Prado de Lima.

Los estudiantes ingresan en este colegio porque tienen interés en una carrera militar o porque sus padres los quieren castigar. Los jóvenes son procedentes de todos los niveles económicos, sociales, étnicos y geográficos del Perú.

La novela es un alegato en contra de la brutalidad y la falsa virilidad que ese colegio militar trata de inculcar en los jóvenes. En vez de fabricar héroes, su entrenamiento resulta en la anulación de toda sensibilidad.

VOCABULARY EXPANSION

Have students give other words they know for the following glosses:

las losetas (las baldosas)
la flaca (la delgada)
soso (sin gracia, sin ánimo)
el féretro (el ataúd)
hunde la panza (hunde el estómago)

National Standards

Communities
Students are encouraged to read other works in Spanish by the authors Gabriel García Márquez and Mario Vargas Llosa for their own personal enjoyment and enrichment.

—Diez minutos de warm ups para alegrar el esqueleto, Matusalén —ordenó el instructor.

Mientras saltaba a la soga junto a Richard, y sentía que un agradable calor iba apoderándose interiormente de su cuerpo, el doctor Quinteros pensaba que, después de todo, no era tan terrible tener cincuenta años si uno los llevaba así. ¿Quién, entre los amigos de su edad, podía lucir un vientre tan liso y unos músculos tan despiertos? Sin ir muy lejos, su hermano Roberto, pese a ser tres años menor, con su rolliza° y abotagada° apariencia y la precoz curvatura de espalda, parecía llevarle diez. Pobre Roberto, debía de estar triste con la boda de Elianita, la niña de sus ojos. Porque, claro, era una manera de perderla. También su hija Charo se casaría en cualquier momento —su enamorado, Tato Soldevilla, se recibiría dentro de poco de ingeniero— y también él, entonces, se sentiría apenado° y más viejo. El doctor Quinteros saltaba a la soga sin enredarse ni alterar el ritmo, con la facilidad que da la práctica, cambiando de pie y cruzando y descruzando las manos como un gimnasta consumado. Veía, en cambio, por el espejo, que su sobrino saltaba demasiado rápido, con atolondramiento°, tropezándose. Tenía los dientes apretados, brillo de sudor en la frente y guardaba los ojos cerrados como para concentrarse mejor. ¿Algún problema de faldas, tal vez?

—Basta de soguita°, flojonazos° —Coco, aunque estaba levantando pesas con Perico y el Negro Humilla, no los perdía de vista y les llevaba el tiempo—. Tres series de sit ups. Sobre el pucho°, fósiles.

Los abdominales eran la prueba de fuerza del doctor Quinteros. Los hacía a mucha velocidad, con las manos en la nuca, en la tabla alzada a la segunda posición, aguantando la espalda a ras del suelo y casi tocando las rodillas con la frente. Entre cada serie de treinta dejaba un minuto de intervalo en que permanecía tendido, respirando hondo. Al terminar los noventa, se sentó y comprobó, satisfecho, que había sacado ventaja a Richard. Ahora sí sudaba de pies a cabeza y sentía el corazón acelerado.

—No acabo de entender por qué se casa Elianita con el Pelirrojo Antúnez —se oyó decir a sí mismo, de pronto—. ¿Qué le ha visto?

Fue un acto fallido y se arrepintió° al instante, pero Richard no pareció sorprenderse. Jadeando°—acababa de terminar los abdominales— le respondió con una broma:

—Dicen que el amor es ciego, tío.

—Es un excelente muchacho y seguro que la hará muy feliz— compuso las cosas el doctor Quinteros, algo cortado—. Quería decir que, entre los admiradores de tu hermana, estaban los mejores partidos de Lima. Mira que basurearlos° a todos para terminar aceptando al Pelirrojo, que es un buen chico, pero tan, en fin...

—¿Tan calzonudo°, quieres decir? —lo ayudó Richard.

—Bueno, no lo hubiera dicho con esa crudeza —aspiraba y

rollizo *roly-poly*
abotagada *hinchada*

apenado *triste*

atolondramiento *confusion*

soguita *jump rope*
flojonazos *perezosos*

sobre el pucho *enseguida*

se arrepintió *was sorry*
jadeando *panting*

basurearlos *throw them away like trash*

calzonudo *estúpido*

expulsaba el aire el doctor Quinteros, abriendo y cerrando los brazos—. Pero, la verdad, parece algo caído del nido. Con cualquier otra sería perfecto, pero a Elianita, tan linda, tan viva, el pobre le llora. —Se sintió incómodo con su propia franqueza—. Oye, no lo tomes a mal, sobrino.

—No te preocupes, tío —le sonrió Richard—. El Pelirrojo es buena gente y si la flaca le ha hecho caso por algo será.

~Después de leer~

Comprensión

A **Un día en la vida del doctor** Contesten.

1. ¿Qué tiempo hacía?
2. ¿Qué día era?
3. ¿Tenía que pasar el doctor Quinteros la mañana en la clínica?
4. ¿Cómo podría pasar la mañana?
5. ¿Dónde estaban su esposa y su hija?
6. ¿Qué tipo de hombre era el doctor Quinteros?
7. ¿Qué comió para el desayuno?
8. ¿Cómo fue al gimnasio?
9. ¿A quién encontró el médico en el gimnasio?
10. ¿Parecía estar de buen humor Richard?
11. ¿Quién iba a casarse? ¿Cuándo?
12. ¿Por qué no participó ella en el concurso de Miss Perú?
13. ¿Quién es Charo?
14. ¿Qué le dijo el doctor a su sobrino?
15. ¿Por qué no comprende el médico por qué su sobrina haya escogido al joven con quien se va a casar?
16. ¿Cómo le contesta Richard a su tío?

B **¿Cómo son?** Den una descripción de los siguientes personajes.

1. Alberto de Quinteros
2. Richard
3. Elianita
4. Roberto de Quinteros

Actividades comunicativas

A **En el gimnasio** Prepare Ud. una lista de todo lo que hizo el doctor Quinteros en el gimnasio.

B **San Isidro** San Isidro es un barrio elegante entre el centro de Lima y el océano Pacífico. ¿Cómo alude el autor a la elegancia o al nivel de vida de los residentes de San Isidro? Cite algunos ejemplos.

LITERATURA *trescientos cincuenta y uno* 351

Independent Practice

Assign any of the following:
1. Exercises, page 351
2. Workbook, *Literatura*

TEACHING TIPS

A. After going over the selection in class, assign it for homework again and have the students write the answers to the *Comprensión* questions.

B. Go over the exercises the following day in class.

ANSWERS
Comprensión

A 1. **Hacía un sol primaveral.**
2. **Era sábado.**
3. **No, no tenía que ir a la clínica.**
4. **Podría pasar la mañana en el gimnasio.**
5. **Ellas estaban en Europa.**
6. **Era un hombre serio y elegante.**
7. **Él comió tostadas con miel de abeja.**
8. **Fue a pie.**
9. **Él encontró a Coco, al Negro Humilla y a Perico Sarmiento.**
10. **No, Richard no parecía estar de buen humor.**
11. **La hermana de Richard iba a casarse esa tarde.**
12. **Porque ella es muy tímida.**
13. **Charo es la hija del médico.**
14. **¿Algún problema, sobrino?**
15. **Él no comprende por qué su sobrina haya escogido al joven con quien se va a casar porque ella tiene muchos pretendientes.**
16. **Richard le dice que el amor es ciego.**

B Answers will vary.

Actividades comunicativas

ANSWERS
A–C Answers will vary.

SCOPE AND SEQUENCE pages 352A-352B

TOPICS	FUNCTIONS	STRUCTURE	CULTURE
◆ Racial and ethnic backgrounds in Spain and Latin America ◆ Native groups in the Americas ◆ Politeness in conversation	◆ How to discuss the ethnic background of people in Latin America and Spain ◆ How to talk about indigenous groups in Spanish America ◆ How to express oneself politely ◆ How to read and discuss a magazine article about the Mayan civilization ◆ How to read and discuss letters written by indigenous people of Latin America ◆ How to read and discuss a magazine article about Jewish migration to the Caribbean during the 17th and 18th centuries ◆ How to express actions in progress ◆ How to describe how actions are carried out ◆ How to tell someone what was done ◆ How to use the passive voice ◆ How to conjugate verbs ending in *–ir* ◆ How to suggest group activities ◆ How to read and discuss literary works by Rigoberta Menchú, Nicolás Guillén, Federico García Lorca, and José Santos Chocano	◆ **El participio presente** ◆ **Adverbios en** *-mente* ◆ **La voz pasiva** ◆ **La voz pasiva con** *se* ◆ **Verbos que terminan en** *–uir*	◆ Racial and ethnic diversity in Spanish-speaking countries ◆ Native languages ◆ Miguel de Cervantes ◆ Maya civilization ◆ The language «**guaraní**» in Paraguay and Bolivia ◆ Jewish migration in the Caribbean ◆ Jorge Luis Borges **Literatura** ◆ **Costumbres quichés** ◆ *me llamo Rigoberta Menchú y así me nació la conciencia,* Rigoberta Menchú ◆ «**Búcate plata**», Nicolás Guillén ◆ «**El prendimiento de Antoñito el Camborio en el camino de Sevilla**», Federico García Lorca ◆ «**¡Quién sabe!**», José Santos Chocano

CHAPTER 8 RESOURCES

PRINT	MULTIMEDIA
Planning Resources	
Lesson Plans Block Scheduling Lesson Plans	Interactive Lesson Planner
Reinforcement Resources	
Writing Activities Workbook Student Tape Manual Video Activities Booklet Glencoe Foreign Language Web Site User's Guide	Transparencies Binder Audiocassette/Compact Disc Program Videocassette/Videodisc Program Online Internet Activities Electronic Teacher's Classroom Resources
Assessment Resources	
Situation Cards Chapter Quizzes Testing Program	Testmaker Computer Software (Macintosh/Windows) Listening Comprehension Audiocassette/Compact Disc
Motivational Resources	
Expansion Activities	Café Glencoe: **www.cafe.glencoe.com**
Enrichment	
Fine Art Transparencies: F-13	

SECTION	PAGES	SECTION RESOURCES
Cultura *La fusión del Viejo Mundo y el Nuevo Mundo*	354–359	Transparency 53A–53B Audiocassette 15A/Compact Disc 10 Writing Activities Workbook, pages 193–194 Student Tape Manual, pages 127–128 Chapter Quizzes, page 113 Testing Program, pages 171–174
Conversación **Las lenguas indígenas**	360–364	Transparency 54A–54B Audiocassette 15A/Compact Disc 10 Writing Activities Workbook, page 195 Student Tape Manual, pages 129–130 Chapter Quizzes, page 114 Testing Program, pages 175–177
Lenguaje **Para continuar una conversación**	365–366	Transparency 55 Audiocassette 15A/Compact Disc 10 Writing Activities Workbook, pages 195–196 Student Tape Manual, page 130 Testing Program, pages 175–177
Repaso de estructura **El participio presente** **Adverbios en *-mente***	367–370	Audiocassette 15B/Compact Disc 11 Writing Activities Workbook, pages 197–198 Student Tape Manual, page 131 Chapter Quizzes, pages 115–116 Testing Program, pages 178–179
Periodismo **Los mayas** **«Descifrando un enigma... ¿qué pasó realmente con la civilización maya?»** **Unas cartas** **Los judíos en el Caribe** **La nación**	371–386	Transparencies 56, 57, 58 Audiocassette 15B–16A/Compact Disc 11 Writing Activities Workbook, pages 199–201 Student Tape Manual, pages 132–134 Chapter Quizzes, pages 117–119 Testing Program, pages 180–187
Estructura **La voz pasiva** **La voz pasiva con *se*** **Verbos que terminan en *-uir***	387–390	Audiocassette 16A/Compact Disc 11 Writing Activities Workbook, pages 202–205 Student Tape Manual, page 137 Chapter Quizzes, pages 120–123 Testing Program, pages 188–189
Literatura **Costumbres quichés** *me llamo Rigoberta Menchú y así me nació la conciencia,* **Rigoberta Menchú** **«Búcate plata», Nicolás Guillén** **«El prendimiento de Antoñito el Camborio en el camino de Sevilla», Federico García Lorca** **«¡Quién sabe!», José Santos Chocano**	391–407	Vocabulary Transparencies 59, 60, 61, 62 Audiocassette 16A–16B/Compact Discs 11–12 Writing Activities Workbook, pages 206–211 Student Tape Manual, pages 138–141 Chapter Quizzes, pages 124–127 Testing Program, pages 190–199

OVERVIEW

In this chapter, students will learn about the racial and ethnic backgrounds of the Spanish-speaking people in Spain and Latin America. In addition, they will learn about some of the native groups in the Americas.

Students will read articles about various ethnic and indigenous groups in the Hispanic world.

The *Literatura* section includes several poems by well-known literary figures.

National Standards

✿ *Communication*
Students will engage in conversations, provide and obtain information, express feelings, and exchange opinions on a variety of topics, especially the ethnic background of the many Hispanic peoples, with emphasis on the contributions of the Arabs, the Jews, the Africans, and the indigenous people of the Americas. Students will listen to and read authentic language on the same topics.

National Standards

✿ *Connections*
Students will increase their understanding of sociology as they do their research and prepare a detailed report on their own ethnic background or that of a person of their choosing.

Raíces

Objetivos

In this chapter you will do the following:

- ∞ discuss the ethnic background of the people of Latin America and Spain
- ∞ express yourself politely
- ∞ read and discuss a magazine article about the Mayan civilization, letters written by indigenous people of Latin America, and a magazine article about Jewish migration to the islands of the Caribbean during the seventeenth and eighteenth centuries
- ∞ tell what was done by someone, describe what is done in general, and talk about activities in the present and the past
- ∞ read and discuss the following literary works: a selection from the autobiography of Rigoberta Menchú; «Búcate plata,» a poem by Nicolás Guillén; «El prendimiento de Antoñito el Camborio en el camino de Sevilla,» a poem by Federico García Lorca; and «¡Quién sabe!,» a poem by José Santos Chocano

*inter*NET CONNECTION

The Glencoe Foreign Language Web site (http://www.glencoe.com/sec/fl) offers these options that enable you and your students to experience the Spanish-speaking world via the Internet:

- At **Café Glencoe**, the interactive "after-school" section of the site, you and your students can access a variety of additional online resources, including online newspapers, interactive games, and a send-a-postcard feature.
- The online **Proyectos** are correlated to the chapters and utilize Hispanic Web sites around the world.

DIFFICULTY PLATEAUS

In all chapters, each reading selection in *Cultura, Periodismo,* and *Literatura,* as well as the *Conversación* and each structure topic, will be rated as follows:

◆ **Easy**
◆◆ **Intermediate**
◆◆◆ **Difficult**

The overall rating of this chapter is: ◆◆ **Intermediate.**

RANDOM ACCESS

You may either follow the exact order of the chapter or omit certain sections that you feel are not necessary for your students. Similarly, you may wish to present a literary selection without interruption or you may intersperse some material from the *Estructura* sections as you are presenting a literary piece.

EVALUATION

Quizzes There is a quiz for every vocabulary presentation and every structure point.

Tests To accompany *¡Buen viaje! Level 3* there are global tests for both *Estructuras,* a combined *Conversación/Lenguaje* test, and one test for each reading in the *Cultura, Periodismo,* and *Literatura* sections. There is also a comprehensive chapter test.

trescientos cincuenta y tres ◦◦ **353**

Learning From Photos

Es el famosísimo mercado de Chichicastenango, en Guatemala. Al mercado acuden los indígenas de la zona todos los jueves y domingos; las mujeres están vestidas en sus trajes tradicionales de vivos colores tejidos a mano.

Chapter Projects

1. Divida la clase en grupos de dos. Cada pareja debe escoger un país y presentar un informe sobre el país al resto de la clase—geografía, población, historia, economía, lenguas, composición étnica, etc.

2. «Mis raíces»: Haga que los estudiantes preparen un informe sobre sus propias raíces étnicas. Deben también acompañar su informe con un mapa que trace los viajes que llevaron a sus antepasados de sus países de origen a los EE.UU. Ud. debe proveerles la opción de preparar un informe sobre alguna figura famosa si así lo desean.

TEACHING TIPS

A. Have students read the *Introducción* aloud.

B. Ask students the following questions: **¿Quién es Alberto Fujimori? ¿Qué recibió Rigoberta Menchú en 1992? ¿Quién fue el libertador de Chile? ¿Cómo murió Antonio Maceo?**

HISTORY CONNECTION

1. **Bernardo O'Higgins (1776–1842), de ascendencia irlandesa, fue militar y político. Luchó, junto con San Martín, por la independencia de Chile y la Argentina. Fue el primer jefe del Estado chileno.**

2. **Antonio Maceo (1845–1896) fue uno de los principales líderes en la lucha por la independencia cubana. Murió en batalla.**

CULTURA
La herencia etnocultural de los hispanos

Introducción

En Hispanoamérica hay una gran diversidad étnica y racial. En 1992, los peruanos eligieron presidente de la República a don Alberto Fujimori, peruano de ascendencia japonesa. Y fue reelecto en 1995. Rigoberta Menchú, maya guatemalteca, recibió el Premio Nóbel de la Paz en 1992. El libertador de Chile y héroe nacional es el general Bernardo O'Higgins. Antonio Maceo, patriota y gran héroe militar cubano, era de ascendencia africana. Murió luchando contra los españoles en la Guerra de la Independencia cubana. Los españoles también son producto de diversas culturas y etnias.

Bernardo O'Higgins

Rigoberta Menchú

Alberto Fujimori

Antonio Maceo

Learning From Photos

1. **Rigoberta Menchú (1959–) nació en la aldea de Chimel, Guatemala. Ha luchado por los derechos de los indígenas de las Américas, especialmente por los de su gente, los mayas, en Guatemala. Ella siempre se viste en ropa tradicional maya.**

(An excerpt from Rigoberta Menchú's biography appears in the Workbook.)

2. **Alberto Fujimori (1938–), hijo de inmigrantes japoneses, fue elegido presidente del Perú en 1992.**

Vocabulario

la raíz

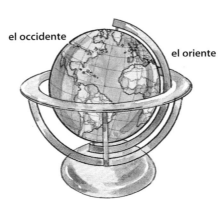

el occidente

el oriente

la ascendencia una serie de antecesores de una persona

la voz la palabra

el genio el carácter, el temperamento

el conocimiento las nociones, las ideas, el saber

el quechua, el aymará pueblos indígenas y sus lenguas

la mezcla la mixtura, la composición, la combinación

el esfuerzo el empleo de la fuerza, el impulso, el trabajo

la política la doctrina y la actividad de un gobierno

el impulso el estímulo, la motivación

el/la traficante el que trafica, el que compra y vende

el maltrato el abuso, el trato duro o cruel

la norma el modelo, lo típico

el/la esclavo(a) la persona sin libertad que tiene que trabajar para otro

la antigüedad el tiempo antiguo

expulsar echar, expeler, desterrar

enriquecerse hacerse rico

musulmán (musulmana) islámico(a), mahometano(a)

grato(a) agradable, placentero(a)

forzado(a) obligatorio(a), obligado(a) por la fuerza

RESOURCES

- Vocabulary Transparencies
- Audio Cassette 15A/Compact Disc 10
- Student Tape Manual
- Workbook
- Chapter Quizzes
- Testing Program

TEACHING VOCABULARY

A. Have students repeat the new words in unison after you.

B. Have students open their books and read the vocabulary for additional reinforcement.

C. You may wish to call on one or two students to read the definitions and on other students to give the word being defined.

D. Call on students to use the new words in an original sentence.

ABOUT THE SPANISH LANGUAGE

◆ Debido a que los nombres de las lenguas quechua y aymará son nombres indígenas, en lengua indígena, los nombres en español son sólo una aproximación a la pronunciación auténtica. Además, la pronunciación indígena varía también de región en región. Por eso, se ve aymará, aimará, aimara, aymara; quechua, quichua, kechua, igual que otras varantes.

◆ «Antigüedad» significa tiempo antiguo, pero también significa un artefacto o una cosa de gran edad. Hay tiendas de «antigüedades» (antiques) que venden tales cosas.

◆ Muchos estudiantes no saben que «occidente» tiene un cognado en inglés—occident—que también quiere decir «oeste». Pregúnteles en qué estado estará «Occidental College» (California).

Cooperative Learning

Divida la clase en grupos. Cada grupo debe escoger uno de los siguientes grupos: los negros, los judíos, los indígenas, los hispanos. Si algunos prefieren, pueden escoger otro grupo. Deben indicar la contribución del grupo a los Estados Unidos. Deben indicar las palabras que han traído al idioma, las comidas y las ideas. Además, deben informarse sobre las contribuciones de individuos específicos que son miembros del grupo. Sus investigaciones deben resultar en un informe—en español—acompañado de fotografías.

TEACHING TIPS

Have students do these *Práctica* for homework and go over them the next day in class. Call on students to read their answers.

ANSWERS
Práctica

A 1. impulso
2. esfuerzo
3. maltrato
4. política
5. lo normal
6. voces
7. mezcla

B 1. esclavo
2. grato
3. enrique-cerse
4. expulsar
5. conocimiento

C 1. traficantes
2. forzado
3. maltrato
4. esfuerzo
5. política
6. mezcla
7. ascendencia

D 1. Las raíces de los españoles están en Europa y en el Medio Oriente.
2. España, Francia y los EE.UU. son países de occidente.
3. El Japón, la China y las Filipinas son países de oriente.
4. sí
5. sí
6. sí
7. El quechua y el aymará son lenguas indígenas.

HISTORY CONNECTION

Hernán Cortés (1485–1547) nació en Medellín, Extremadura. Fue a La Española en 1504 y después a Cuba con Diego Velázquez. En 1519 salió para México donde comenzó la conquista del Imperio Azteca. La conquista de los aztecas y la toma de Tenochtitlán tuvieron lugar después de tres meses de sitio en agosto de 1521.

❖ Práctica ❖

A HISTORIETA **Sinónimos**

Expresen de otra forma.

1. El oro sirvió de *estímulo* a muchos conquistadores.
2. Ellos tuvieron que hacer un *trabajo* enorme para conquistar a los aztecas.
3. Después, vino el *abuso* de los indígenas.
4. La *doctrina* del gobierno era de defender a los indios.
5. No obstante, el abuso de los indígenas era *lo típico*.
6. En el español moderno hay varias *palabras* indígenas.
7. El mestizaje es la *fusión* de sangre española con la indígena.

B Lo contrario   Den los antónimos de las siguientes palabras.

1. voluntario
2. desagradable
3. empobrecer
4. admitir
5. ignorancia

C HISTORIETA **¿Cuál es la palabra?**

Completen cada oración con una palabra apropiada.

1. Los ___ en esclavos buscaban a sus víctimas en África.
2. A los esclavos se les obligaba al trabajo ___.
3. El ___ de los indios y negros por los conquistadores era típico.
4. Algunos religiosos hicieron un gran ___ por proteger a los indígenas.
5. También la ___ oficial era bastante benévola, aunque en la práctica no siempre se respetó.
6. Los hijos de españoles e indígenas son mestizos; el mestizaje es la ___ de la sangre española con la indígena.
7. Hay latinoamericanos de ___ europea, indígena, negra y asiática.

D ¿Sí o no?   Corrijan las oraciones falsas.

1. Las raíces de los españoles están en las Américas.
2. España, Francia y los EE.UU. son países de oriente.
3. El Japón, la China y las Filipinas son países de occidente.
4. Los conquistadores se enriquecieron con el oro de América.
5. Los esclavos no gozan de la libertad.
6. La religión de los musulmanes es el islám.
7. El quechua y el aymará son lenguas europeas.

Hernán Cortés y los aztecas

Critical Thinking Activity

Thinking skills: supporting arguments with reasons **En su opinión, ¿cuál ha sido el resultado de la fusión de sangre española con la de los indígenas en varias partes del mundo hispano? Defienda su opinión.**

Did You Know?

La ciudad con mayor número de personas de ascendencia japonesa fuera del Japón es São Paulo, Brasil.

   El Barrio Chino de Lima se estableció en 1872 cuando vinieron al Perú miles de inmigrantes de la China. Hoy viven allí medio millón de peruanos de ascendencia china.

La fusión del Viejo Mundo y el Nuevo Mundo

El español tiene sus raíces en Iberia, en Grecia, en Roma, en el norte de Europa y en África. Los árabes llegaron del norte de África en el año 711. En poco tiempo, conquistaron casi toda la Península Ibérica. No fue hasta 1492 que los cristianos pudieron expulsarlos de su último reino, el reino de Granada.

Los árabes estuvieron en la Península por casi ochocientos años. Eran dueños de todas las tierras entre Bagdad y Córdoba. Su influencia en España ha sido profunda. Dejaron incomparables monumentos artísticos, como la Alhambra y el Generalife de Granada, la Giralda de Sevilla y la Mezquita de Córdoba. Dejaron la lengua castellana enriquecida de voces árabes: *alcázar*, *almohada*, *alcalde*, *ojalá* y muchas más. Dejaron costumbres y tradiciones. Y dejaron su sangre y su genio.

La Giralda, Sevilla, España

Sobre todo en «al Andalus», Andalucía, donde por más tiempo estuvieron.

Durante ocho siglos, los árabes y los cristianos se encontraron en una interminable, si bien intermitente, lucha para dominar la Península. Los cristianos conquistaron Jaén en 1246 y Sevilla en 1248, dejando muy reducido el territorio musulmán. A pesar de estas victorias, la lucha continuó hasta 1492.

Fernando e Isabel conquistaron el reino de Granada en 1492. Boabdil, el último rey moro, lloró de pena al abandonar su querida Granada. Y hoy, en la poesía árabe todavía se lamenta la pérdida de la riqueza y belleza de «al Andalus».

Fernando e Isabel expulsaron no solamente a los árabes sino también a los judíos que habían residido en España durante siglos. Tanto cristianos como judíos vivían en paz en los reinos árabes de España. El gran filósofo judío, Maimónides, por ejemplo, nació en Córdoba en 1135.

1492. Esta fecha, aunque para los españoles y los árabes recuerda la conquista de Granada, para casi todo el resto del mundo recuerda el viaje de Cristóbal Colón al Nuevo Mundo. Y para millones de negros africanos e indígenas americanos, el recuerdo de la llegada de europeos a las Américas no es nada grato.

Grandes grupos de indígenas vivían en las Américas, desde Alaska y el Canadá hasta la Tierra del Fuego. En el norte vivían los dakota, apaches y seminoles. En las Antillas vivían los caribes y taínos; en México y Centroamérica, los aztecas y mayas. Y en Sudamérica estaban los quechuas, incas, guaraníes, araucanos, aymarás, patagones y muchos más. Las culturas de algunos de estos grupos, los aztecas, incas y mayas en particular, fueron bastante avanzadas. Los conocimientos de los mayas en la arquitectura, la escultura y la astronomía fueron realmente extraordinarios.

trescientos cincuenta y siete 〰 **357**

Did You Know?

Los azulejos son un ejemplo de los bellos diseños islámicos que se encuentran en la Alhambra y los otros monumentos árabes. El islám no permite la reproducción de figuras humanas en el arte. Por eso predominan los diseños con figuras geométricas.

TEACHING THE READING

◈ La herencia etnocultural de los hispanos ◆◆

A. Call on individuals to read this section aloud.

B. You can intersperse questions from the *Comprensión A–D* on page 359 as you are going over this section.

C. Or, you may prefer to have students read this section for homework and prepare the *Comprensión* exercises that follow.

D. After completing the reading, have a few students answer in their own words: **El hispanoamericano es el fruto de una rica variedad de razas y culturas. Explica.**

National Standards

◉ Connections
Students will reinforce and/or further their knowledge of anthropology as they read about the various ethnic groups that contributed to the modern cultures of Spain and Latin America.

ABOUT THE SPANISH LANGUAGE

La mayoría de las palabras que comienzan con «al» en español son de origen árabe—alcázar, almohada y alcalde. Lo curioso es que el prefijo «al» es el artículo en árabe que corresponde a «el» o «la» en español. Por eso, cuando uno dice «la almohada», es como si dijera *the, the pillow*. Otras palabras comunes de origen árabe son alambre, alhaja, albañil, almendra. La palabra «ojalá» viene del árabe. Invoca la ayuda de Dios-Alá.

358

ABOUT THE SPANISH LANGUAGE

◆ «Quisqueya» es el nombre que los indígenas dieron a la isla de Santo Domingo, hoy Haití y la República Dominicana. El significado del nombre es «madre de todas las tierras». El nombre dado a Puerto Rico por sus indígenas era «Borinquén» o «Boriquén».

◆ Los santos varones se llaman «San»—San Felipe, San Antonio, San Francisco, San Isidro, San Diego. Las santas mujeres se llaman «Santa»—Santa Marta, Santa Teresa, Santa Bárbara, etc. La excepción son los santos varones cuyos nombres comienzan con «To...» o «Do...». A éstos se les llama «Santo»—Santo Tomás, Santo Domingo, Santo Tomé, Santo Toribio. Una curiosa excepción se nota en Puerto Rico donde la gente llama a *Saint Thomas*, de las Islas Vírgenes, «San Tomás».

A diferencia de la América del Norte, en Latinoamérica la influencia indígena es significativa. En Bolivia, por ejemplo, la mayor parte de la población actual (54%) es indígena. Los pueblos quechua y aymará son los más numerosos. En Bolivia el español, aunque lengua oficial, es una lengua minoritaria.

Los europeos llegaron en el siglo XV y conquistaron los pueblos indígenas de toda la América. Pero hubo una diferencia importante entre las colonizaciones de Angloamérica y Latinoamérica. Mientras que hubo poca mezcla de las razas blanca e indígena en Norteamérica, en Latinoamérica era casi la norma. En varios países hispanos la población más numerosa hoy día es la mestiza (México, 55%), o sea, la población de sangre europea e indígena.

A pesar de los esfuerzos de religiosos como Fray Bartolomé de las Casas y la política benévola de la corona, los abusos y el maltrato de los indígenas eran (y, lamentablemente, siguen siendo), en muchas partes, muy común. No obstante, es importante notar que la política española con respecto a los indígenas fue mucho más benévola y justa que la política de los otros países colonizadores.

Durante cuatro siglos, catorce millones de negros fueron sacados de África por ingleses, portugueses, holandeses y españoles, y traídos a las Américas como esclavos. Es probable que los españoles trajeran a los primeros esclavos africanos para trabajar en las minas de La Española por el año 1502. Fray Bartolomé de las Casas, el gran defensor de los indios, dio impulso al horrible tráfico de esclavos negros cuando sugirió que ellos sustituyeran a los indios en el trabajo forzado, ya que, según él, eran más fuertes y resistían mejor el calor y las fatigas. En 1517, el Emperador Carlos V les concedió a varias casas comerciales un monopolio para la importación de esclavos de África a las Antillas. Así fue que los primeros negros llegaron a Cuba, Puerto

Los indios de Quisqueya

Rico, Santo Domingo y Jamaica.

Los traficantes en esclavos recogían su carga humana en las costas de África entre Ghana y Angola. Muchos esclavos eran del interior. En luchas entre tribus eran tomados prisioneros y vendidos en la costa a los traficantes blancos.

Las poblaciones de ascendencia africana en Latinoamérica se concentran en ciertas áreas: en las Antillas, en las costas del Caribe de México y Centroamérica, Colombia, Venezuela y sobre todo en el Brasil. Así como la mezcla de la sangre indígena con la española dio el mestizo, la fusión de la sangre española con la negra dio el mulato. Y de estas combinaciones han resultado muchas otras.

En Latinoamérica también hay importantes poblaciones europeas no españolas: italianos y rusos, serbocroatas, alemanes, ingleses e irlandeses. Y no solamente de Europa, sino del Medio Oriente y Asia han venido inmigrantes—libaneses y sirios, chinos, coreanos y japoneses.

El hispanoamericano es el fruto de toda esta rica variedad de razas y culturas, desde los romanos y fenicios de la antigüedad, los mayas, incas y aztecas precolombinos, los conquistadores españoles, hasta los inmigrantes de ayer y hoy, salidos de los viejos mundos de oriente y occidente en busca de una vida nueva en un nuevo mundo.

Did You Know?

La esclavitud se abolió en los EE.UU. con el fin de la Guerra Civil (1865). En España no se abolió la esclavitud hasta 1870. En las colonias españolas del Caribe la esclavitud se abolió en Cuba en 1870, el mismo año que en la Península, y no hasta más tarde en Puerto Rico— 1873.

Independent Practice

Assign any of the following:
1. Exercises, page 359
2. Workbook, *Cultura*

✦Comprensión✦

A **¿Quiénes son los hispanos?** Contesten según la lectura.

1. ¿Cuánto tiempo estuvieron los árabes en España?
2. ¿Cuál fue la extensión del territorio árabe?
3. ¿Cuáles son algunos monumentos árabes en España?
4. Además de monumentos, ¿qué dejaron los árabes en España?
5. ¿En qué región de España estuvieron por más tiempo los árabes?
6. ¿A quiénes expulsaron Fernando e Isabel además de los árabes?

B **La conquista árabe** Completen.

1. Los cristianos lucharon contra los ___ para dominar a España.
2. La lucha duró unos ___ años.
3. En 1248, los cristianos conquistaron ___.
4. Antes de 1200, Jaén y Sevilla formaban parte del territorio ___.
5. En 1492, la lucha entre cristianos y musulmanes ___.
6. El nombre que los árabes dan a Andalucía es ___.
7. El último rey moro fue ___.

C **¿Sí o no?** Corrijan según la lectura.

1. Cristóbal Colón viajó desde España al Viejo Mundo.
2. Los dakota vivían en Sudamérica.
3. En el Caribe estaban los taínos.
4. Los guaraníes, araucanos y mayas son grupos europeos.
5. Los patagones sabían mucho de arquitectura.

Fray Bartolomé de las Casas

D **El Nuevo Mundo** Contesten según la lectura.

1. ¿Por qué no es grato para muchos el recuerdo del viaje de Colón?
2. ¿Qué trató de hacer Fray Bartolomé de las Casas?
3. ¿Cuál era la política de la Corona respecto a los indígenas?
4. ¿Quiénes traficaban en esclavos?
5. ¿En qué regiones de Latinoamérica se concentra la población negra?
6. ¿De dónde han venido inmigrantes a Latinoamérica?

✦Actividades comunicativas✦

A **Las poblaciones indígenas** Durante la conquista de las Américas las poblaciones indígenas del Caribe casi desaparecieron. Explique por qué.

B **Fray Bartolomé de las Casas** Ud. y su grupo, escriban la carta de las Casas a Carlos V en defensa de los indios.

Learning From Photos

Fray Bartolomé de las Casas (1474–1566), sacerdote dominicano, estudió en Salamanca, fue a México con los conquistadores y fue obispo de Chiapas. Gran defensor de los indígenas de América, escribió y luchó contra los abusos de los conquistadores.

Additional Practice

You may give students this exercise:

1. el/la mestizo(a)
2. el quechua
3. el/la traficante
4. el Medio Oriente
5. los indígenas

a. los nativos de un lugar
b. uno que se dedica a la compraventa
c. una lengua de las Américas
d. el Líbano, Siria, Egipto
e. el/la hijo(a) de europeo e indígena

ANSWERS

Comprensión

A 1. casi ocho siglos
2. todas las tierras entre Bagdad y Córdoba
3. la Alhambra, el Generalife de Granada, la Giralda de Sevilla y la Mezquita de Córdoba
4. Los árabes dejaron costumbres y tradiciones además de influir en la lengua española.
5. en Andalucía
6. a los judíos

B 1. árabes   5. terminó
2. ochocientos   6. al Andalus
3. Sevilla   7. Boabdil
4. árabe

C 1. Cristóbal Colón viajó desde España al Nuevo Mundo.
2. Los dakota vivían en la América del Norte.
3. sí
4. Los guaraníes, araucanos y mayas son grupos indígenas.
5. Los mayas sabían mucho de arquitectura.

D 1. por los abusos y el maltrato que recibieron los indígenas
2. Fray Bartolomé de las Casas trató de mejorar el trato de los indígenas.
3. La política era más benévola y justa que la de otros países colonizadores.
4. los ingleses, los portugueses, los holandeses
5. Se concentra en las Antillas, las costas del Caribe, de México y Centroamérica, Colombia, Venezuela y Brasil.
6. Han venido de Europa, del Medio Oriente y de Asia.

You may wish to have students do these activities in pairs or small groups.

Actividades comunicativas

ANSWERS

A and B Answers will vary.

RESOURCES

- 🖊 Vocabulary Transparencies
- 🎧 Audio Cassette 15A/Compact Disc 10
- 📁 Student Tape Manual
- 📁 Workbook
- 📁 Chapter Quizzes

TEACHING VOCABULARY

Follow the presentation suggestions
outlined in other chapters.

ABOUT THE SPANISH LANGUAGE

**Una «vivienda» es cualquier
tipo de casa donde se vive. Las
casas, chabolas, mansiones, los
palacios, apartamentos, pisos,
chalets, condominios, todos
son «viviendas». Un sinónimo
de vivienda es «domicilio».**

VOCABULARY EXPANSION

**Otras palabras que significan
«entrenamiento» son:
preparación, perfecciona-
miento y adiestramiento.**

Conversación

Las lenguas indígenas

Vocabulario

la vivienda

Es una vivienda humilde.

el entrenamiento

Los jóvenes están recibiendo entrenamiento.

En esta escuela rural alfabetizan a los indígenas.
Les enseñan a leer y a escribir el español.

Additional Practice

You may wish to give students the following
matching activity to reinforce the cognate
vocabulary in the *Escenas de la vida.*

1.	**preservar**	**a.**	techniques
2.	**proteger**	**b.**	preserve
3.	**bilingüe**	**c.**	population
4.	**metodología**	**d.**	protect
5.	**técnicas**	**e.**	bilingual
6.	**población**	**f.**	methodology
7.	**voluntario**	**g.**	majority
8.	**mayoría**	**h.**	volunteer

el maya-quiché una lengua de los mayas guatemaltecos
los bisabuelos los padres de los abuelos
el/la opresor(a) el/la dominador(a), déspota, tirano(a)
Limón/Puerto Limón una provincia y ciudad de Costa Rica

reconocer considerar y aceptar
influir tener influencia

étnico(a) con relación a una nación o raza
autóctono(a) indígena, natural, originario(a), aborigen
culpable responsable, que tiene la culpa

británico

⟡ Práctica ⟡

A **No hablan español.** Completen.

1. El programa de ___ les enseñará a todos a leer.
2. Son mayas y no hablan español. Hablan ___.
3. Ellos hablan una lengua ___.
4. Ellos forman parte del grupo ___ más grande del país.

B **HISTORIETA El puesto de Andrés**

Expresen de otra manera.

1. Antes de tomar el puesto le darán *una preparación* especial.
2. Ellos *se dan cuenta* que el trabajo es difícil.
3. Tendrá que vivir en el campo en *una residencia* humilde.
4. Él habla inglés bastante bien, ya que es de ascendencia *inglesa*.
5. Los ingleses siempre *han tenido influencia* en este país.
6. Algunos han sido *responsables por* algunas injusticias.
7. Han sido libertadores y también *déspotas*.
8. Uno de ellos era el *padre del abuelo* de Andrés.

TEACHING TIPS

Assign the *Práctica* and then go over them in class.

ANSWERS
Práctica
A **1. alfabetización**
  2. maya-quiché
  3. autóctona
  4. étnico
B **1. un entrenamiento**
  2. reconocen
  3. una vivienda
  4. británica
  5. han influido
  6. culpables de
  7. opresores
  8. bisabuelo

Independent Practice

Assign any of the following:
1. Exercises, page 361
2. Workbook, *Conversación*

Conversación

TEACHING THE CONVERSATION

◆ Escenas de la vida ◆◆

A. Divide the *Conversación* into three parts. Call on different pairs of students to read each section aloud. Have them use as much expression as possible.

B. As each segment of the conversation is read, go over the corresponding exercise on page 364 orally.

C. Assign the exercises for homework.

Escenas de la vida

El voluntario y la directora del Cuerpo de Paz

DAVID: ¿En qué tipo de programa voy a trabajar?

PILAR: Es un programa de alfabetización en lenguas indígenas para personas mayores. Se trata de alfabetizar a la gente en su propio idioma.

DAVID: Y los que vamos a participar en el programa tenemos que aprender esas lenguas, ¿verdad?

PILAR: Claro. En tu caso, como vas a trabajar con unos grupos mayas, tienes que aprender el maya-quiché. Pero no te preocupes, aquí en el centro lo aprenderás.

DAVID: Pero yo creía que Guatemala era un país de habla española. ¿No es así?

PILAR: El español es la lengua oficial, pero se reconoce la importancia de las lenguas autóctonas y la necesidad de preservarlas y protegerlas. Además, en muchas escuelas hay programas de educación bilingüe.

DAVID: ¿Hay muchas personas de origen indígena en Guatemala?

PILAR: ¿Que si hay? El 50% de la población es indígena. Los indígenas son el mayor grupo étnico del país. Y muchos no hablan español.

DAVID: Pues, no lo sabía. Interesante. Y, ¿qué hacemos mañana?

PILAR: Mañana comienza el entrenamiento. Tendrás clases en maya-quiché por la mañana, de 7 a 12. Después del almuerzo, de 1 a 3, es el curso sobre cultura maya. Y de las 3:30 hasta las 5:30, metodología y técnicas de enseñar.

DAVID: Dos preguntitas: ¿Cómo llegaré al pueblo donde voy a trabajar, y dónde voy a vivir?

PILAR: Bueno, la única forma de llegar a tu lugar es tomar el bus al pueblo más cercano y después caminar. En cuanto a la vivienda, tendrás una casita como la de la gente de allí. Ya te lo explicaremos todo. Ahora debes conocer al equipo del centro y a los demás voluntarios.

Did You Know?

El Cuerpo de Paz (a veces llamado Los Cuerpos de Paz) fue creado en 1961 por decreto del presidente John F. Kennedy. Los voluntarios del Cuerpo de Paz sirven por un período de dos años. Ahora, hay voluntarios trabajando con programas en sesenta países. Hay programas en agricultura, la enseñanza de idiomas, especialmente el inglés, matemáticas y ciencias, preparación vocacional, administración pública y de empresas y el desarrollo de recursos naturales.

Los africanos en Latinoamérica

LUCIO: Yo no sabía que había tanta gente de ascendencia africana en Latinoamérica.

CELIA: Pues, sí. Hay mucha gente, y han influido mucho en las culturas de casi todos los países, especialmente en el Caribe, Centroamérica y el norte de Sudamérica.

LUCIO: Y tú, Celia. Eres costarricense, pero tu apellido es Taylor. ¿De dónde son tus padres?

CELIA: Mis padres son de aquí. Y mis abuelos también. Pero mis bisabuelos eran de Barbados. Vinieron a Centroamérica durante la construcción del canal de Panamá. Cuando terminó la construcción, se quedaron.

LUCIO: ¿Tú hablas inglés, pues?

CELIA: Sí, hombre. Casi todos los que vivimos en Limón somos bilingües. Hablamos inglés y español. Y muchas de las costumbres y los gustos en comida, por ejemplo, nos vienen de Barbados, Jamaica, Trinidad y las otras islas.

LUCIO: Esto es interesantísimo. ¿Todos los negros latinoamericanos vienen de las islas británicas, entonces?

CELIA: No, no, no. Hay otros lugares en Centroamérica, como Limón, Bluefields en Nicaragua, y por supuesto, Belice, un país independiente, donde la lengua oficial es el inglés. La mayoría de la gente allí es de ascendencia africana. Sus antepasados vinieron con los ingleses. Pero, acuérdate que las poblaciones negras de Cuba, la República Dominicana, Puerto Rico, Venezuela, Colombia y otros países hispanoamericanos son importantes. Y ellos no tienen nada que ver con los ingleses.

LUCIO: Claro. El horrible tráfico en esclavos africanos. Los ingleses, portugueses, holandeses y españoles, todos fueron culpables. Llevaron a los africanos a trabajar en sus colonias.

CELIA: Y no te olvides de los franceses. Ellos llevaron esclavos a Haití. Fue en Haití donde por primera vez en la historia, los esclavos negros se levantaron contra sus opresores y establecieron una república independiente.

LUCIO: ¡Qué poco sé de todo esto!, Celia. Me parece que tengo mucho que aprender.

HISTORY CONNECTION

Bluefields es la capital del departamento de Zelaya en Nicaragua. Es el puerto caribeño más importante del país. Durante los siglos XVI y XVII Bluefields fue el centro de reunión de piratas británicos y holandeses. Durante varios años sirvió de capital del protectorado inglés sobre la Costa de los Mosquitos (1678). Durante las intervenciones norteamericanas (1912–15, 1926–33) las tropas de la infantería marina (marines) fueron destinadas a Bluefields.

TEACHING TIPS

You can go over these exercises without prior preparation as students are doing the *Conversación* in class, or you may assign them for homework and then go over them in class.

ANSWERS

Comprensión

A 1. a
   2. b
   3. b
   4. c
   5. c

B 1. leer, escribir
   2. bilingües
   3. el bus
   4. vivienda
   5. voluntarios

C 1. **La influencia africana se nota mucho en el Caribe, en Centroamérica y en el norte de Sudamérica.**
   2. **El apellido de Celia viene de Barbados (de los ingleses).**
   3. **Celia es costarricense.**
   4. **Sus bisabuelos trabajaron en el Canal de Panamá.**
   5. **En Limón hablan inglés y español.**
   6. **Limón, Bluefields en Nicaragua y Belice son tres lugares donde la gente habla inglés.**

D 1. africana
   2. británicas
   3. negras (africanas)
   4. esclavos
   5. Haití

Comprensión

A   Trabajando en Guatemala   Escojan.

1. En su trabajo, David va a ___.
   a. enseñar a leer y a escribir   **b.** construir viviendas   **c.** conducir un bus
2. Antes de comenzar a trabajar, David tiene que aprender ___.
   a. a conducir   **b.** una lengua autóctona   **c.** el español
3. El 50 por ciento de la población guatemalteca es ___.
   a. española   **b.** indígena   **c.** africana
4. La lengua oficial de Guatemala es el ___.
   a. maya-quiché   **b.** inglés   **c.** español
5. David va a tener ___ horas diarias de clase en maya-quiché.
   a. 2   **b.** 3   **c.** 5

B   Cuestión de lenguas   Completen.

1. Ellos creen que es importante ___ y ___ las lenguas indígenas.
2. En varias escuelas enseñan en español y otra lengua. Son programas ___.
3. Para ir al pueblo donde va a vivir, David va a tomar ___.
4. Él va a vivir en una ___ como las de los indígenas.
5. No les pagan mucho a David y a sus colegas porque son ___.

C   La influencia africana   Contesten.

1. ¿En qué partes de Latinoamérica se nota mucho la influencia africana?
2. ¿De dónde viene el apellido de Celia?
3. ¿Cuál es la nacionalidad de Celia?
4. ¿En qué trabajaron los bisabuelos de Celia?
5. ¿En qué parte de Costa Rica hablan inglés y español?
6. ¿Cuáles son tres lugares en Centroamérica donde la gente habla inglés?

D   Diferentes poblaciones   Completen.

1. En Belice, mucha gente es de ascendencia ___.
2. Muchas personas que se establecieron en Bluefields, Limón y Belice vinieron de las islas ___.
3. Cuba, la República Dominicana y Puerto Rico tienen importantes poblaciones ___.
4. Los ingleses, portugueses, holandeses, españoles y franceses eran traficantes de ___.
5. La primera república negra, fundada por esclavos, fue ___.

Camareras del restaurante La Caña, República Dominicana

Learning From Photos

Have students describe the dresses of the waitresses in as much detail as possible.

Independent Practice

Assign any of the following:
1. Exercises, page 364
2. Workbook, *Conversación*

Lenguaje

Para continuar una conversación

Cuando Ud. quiere cambiar de tema de una
conversación, debe decir algo como:

Una cosa…

> Muy interesante. Ajá. Eh, quería hacerle una pregunta…
> Pues, no lo sabía. A propósito, ¿qué le parece si…
> No me digas. Interesante. Una cosa,…
> Ud. sabe mucho de eso. Ah, antes de que se me olvide…

Lo importante es que le indique a la persona
que Ud. estaba escuchando y que tenía
interés en lo que decía.

También es cortés decir algo antes de hacer
una pregunta, como, por ejemplo:

> Eh, quería preguntarle, ¿cómo…?
> Por favor, una preguntita. ¿Qué…?
> Si me permite. ¿Cuál es…?

Las siguientes recomendaciones sobre la conversación vienen de *El libro de los buenos
modales* por F.Y.R. Torralva Tomás:

> Es más importante saber escuchar que saber hablar.
> Escuchar con comprensión, tolerancia y amabilidad; no estar al acecho[1]
> para cortar el hilo de la conversación.
> Podemos interrumpir y hacer una observación, pero con oportunidad, de
> vez en cuando.
> Resulta molesto y grosero no parar de hablar, impidiendo que intervengan
> los demás.
> El que habla debe dar la sensación de que quien escucha es un personaje
> importante para él.
> No poner en primer término el «yo» y los propios problemas, o cuestiones
> que sólo a nosotros pueden interesar.
> Saber cambiar el tema de la conversación cuando se aborden cuestiones
> inoportunas.
> Hay que decir lo que se piensa, pero se debe pensar lo que se dice.

[1] **estar al acecho** *to be on the alert*

LENGUAJE

trescientos sesenta y cinco 〜 **365**

TEACHING TIPS

Read the explanatory information to
the class. Have the class repeat in
unison or call on individuals to read
the expressions. Insist that they read
them with proper intonation and
animated expression.

ABOUT THE SPANISH LANGUAGE

**Hay un viejo refrán que dice: El
burro por delante, para que no
se espante. En el campo se le
pone al burro delante de las
mulas o caballos porque es más
dócil. En el refrán se alude a la
costumbre de siempre ponerse
a uno mismo en primera plana,
de ser demasiado egoísta.
También se les dice a los niños
que no pongan el «yo» antes de
la otra persona en una oración.
Por ejemplo: «Yo y María
fuimos a la escuela» en lugar
de «María y yo fuimos a la
escuela».**

Advanced Games

Vocabulary Game I: *Create Your Own Story*
Set-up Prepare (or have students in pairs
prepare) cards with vocabulary words from
the current chapter—one word per card.
Include verbs (verbs might be on colored
cards since each group needs to have some).
Students can be in small groups (3–4) or
with a partner. Shuffle the cards and distribute 10–20 per group.

Game The object of the game is to come up
with a story using as many of the cards as
possible. Tell students what tense the story
is to be in. Each team gets one point for
every word they use correctly. They can use
words twice. One point is deducted for every
unused card. Stories can be put on butcher
paper for the other students to read.

TEACHING TIPS

You may wish to have students choose the *Actividad* in which they wish to take part. These reports may be incorporated into a special bulletin board project.

Actividades comunicativas

ANSWERS
A–D Answers will vary.

HISTORY CONNECTION

Belice ganó su independencia de Gran Bretaña en 1981. Antes se conocía como Honduras Británica. Aunque se dice que Colón llegó a las costas de Belice en 1502, la primera colonización europea ocurrió en 1638 cuando unos marineros ingleses llegaron a las costas, víctimas de un naufragio. Desde 1763 hasta 1798 Belice estuvo bajo la soberanía de España. En 1798 los colonos ingleses, con el apoyo naval británico, se apoderaron del territorio. Guatemala, durante muchos años, no reconocía a la Honduras Británica ni a Belice, considerándolo territorio guatemalteco. En los mapas guatemaltecos Belice figuraba como parte de Guatemala. En 1981, a cambio de importantes concesiones, Guatemala renunció su reclamación sobre el territorio.

Actividades comunicativas

A | **Los buenos modales** Dé Ud. ejemplos de personas que no siguieron las recomendaciones de *El libro de los buenos modales*. Indique como reaccionó Ud. ¿Cuáles de estas recomendaciones considera Ud. las más importantes?

B | **Belice y Haití** En la conversación entre Celia y Lucio se habló de Belice y de Haití. Escoja uno de los dos y prepare un breve informe sobre el país.

C | **El canal de Panamá** Mucha gente salió de Trinidad, Jamaica, Barbados y las otras islas británicas para trabajar en la construcción del canal de Panamá. Busque datos y prepare un informe sobre la mano de obra que construyó el canal.

D | **Los esclavos** Se ha hablado mucho del trato de los indígenas de las Américas por los españoles y por los ingleses. Con su grupo, estudien las colonizaciones de las dos Américas y preparen un informe contrastándolas. Los profesores de historia y de estudios sociales les podrán ayudar.

La Habana, Cuba

Construcción del canal de Panamá

Did You Know?

El gran ingeniero francés Ferdinand de Lesseps, el que construyó el canal de Suez, comenzó a construir el canal en Panamá en 1881. Este intento fracasó. Los norteamericanos compraron los derechos de los franceses. Comenzaron la nueva obra en 1906 y la terminaron en 1914.

Repaso de estructura

Describing actions in progress
El participio presente

1. The present participle "-ing" in English is formed by dropping the ending of the infinitive and adding **-ando** to **-ar** verbs, and **-iendo** to **-er** or **-ir** verbs.

bailar	comer	vivir
bail-	com-	viv-
bailando	comiendo	viviendo

2. Many stem-changing verbs have a stem change in the present participle.

sentir	sintiendo	decir	diciendo
preferir	prefiriendo	venir	viniendo
pedir	pidiendo	dormir	durmiendo

3. The following verbs have a **y** in the present participle.

creer	creyendo	oír	oyendo
leer	leyendo	construir	construyendo
traer	trayendo	distribuir	distribuyendo

4. The present participle is used with the verb **estar** to form the progressive tenses. Review the forms of the present and imperfect progressive.

INFINITIVE	PRESENT PROGRESSIVE		
	hablar	comer	vivir
yo	estoy hablando	estoy comiendo	estoy viviendo
tú	estás hablando	estás comiendo	estás viviendo
él, ella, Ud.	está hablando	está comiendo	está viviendo
nosotros(as)	estamos hablando	estamos comiendo	estamos viviendo
vosotros(as)	estáis hablando	estáis comiendo	estáis viviendo
ellos, ellas, Uds.	están hablando	están comiendo	están viviendo

TEACHING STRUCTURE

 **Actions in progress**◆

Have students read the explanatory material and the model sentences in steps 1–6.

Note You may wish to remind students that while the gerund is used as a verbal noun in English—"Skiing is my favorite sport"; "I don't like playing the piano"—the infinitive is used in Spanish: **El esquiar es mi deporte favorito. No me gusta tocar el piano.**

367

TEACHING TIPS

Give students the opportunity to prepare these *Práctica* before going over them in class.

ANSWERS
Práctica

A 1. **Están presentando** *Mi adorado Juan.*

2. **Sí, está teniendo muchísimo éxito.**

3. **Víctor Salinas está haciendo el papel de Juan.**

4. **Susana Cordiel está haciendo el papel de Irene.**

5. **Sí, me está picando el interés. Quiero ir a verla.**

INFINITIVE	hablar	comer	vivir
		IMPERFECT PROGRESSIVE	
yo	estaba hablando	estaba comiendo	estaba viviendo
tú	estabas hablando	estabas comiendo	estabas viviendo
él, ella, Ud.	estaba hablando	estaba comiendo	estaba viviendo
nosotros(as)	estábamos hablando	estábamos comiendo	estábamos viviendo
vosotros(as)	*estabais hablando*	*estabais comiendo*	*estabais viviendo*
ellos, ellas, Uds.	estaban hablando	estaban comiendo	estaban viviendo

5. A progressive tense is used to describe an action that is actually taking place at the time in question. The most commonly used progressive tenses are the present and imperfect, and sometimes the future. The present progressive indicates what is taking place right now and the imperfect progressive is used to indicate what was actually taking place at the past time in question.

> PRESENT PROGRESSIVE
>
> **En este momento, Susana está tocando el piano.**
> **Ella está tocando el piano y su amigo está cantando.**

> IMPERFECT PROGRESSIVE
>
> **Mientras Susana estaba tocando el piano y su amigo estaba cantando, su hermano menor estaba comiendo un helado.**

6. Note that the progressive tenses can also be formed with the verbs **ir, venir, andar, continuar,** and **seguir.**

> **Él va caminando.**
> **Él viene cantando.**
> **Ellos andan estudiando.**
> **Ella continúa luchando.**
> **Ellas siguen trabajando.**

Práctica

A **HISTORIETA En el teatro**

Contesten según se indica.

1. ¿Qué obra están presentando? (*Mi adorado Juan*)
2. ¿Está teniendo mucho éxito. (sí, muchísimo)
3. ¿Quién está haciendo el papel de Juan? (Víctor Salinas)
4. ¿Y quién está haciendo el papel de Irene? (Susana Cordiel)
5. ¿Te está picando el interés? ¿Quieres ir a verla? (sí)

Learning From Realia

La obra es *La Gran Sultana* de Miguel de Cervantes. Cervantes basó la obra en sus experiencias en el cautiverio en Argel. Después de la batalla de Lepanto, Cervantes fue tomado prisionero por piratas (1575) y llevado a Argel en el norte de África. Cervantes estuvo allí como prisionero durante cinco años. En 1580 su familia pagó el rescate, una cantidad de dinero que arruinó a la familia.

B HISTORIETA Una fiesta

Contesten.

1. ¿Está dando Marcos una fiesta?
2. ¿Están bailando sus amigos?
3. ¿Están escuchando discos y cintas?
4. ¿Todos se están divirtiendo mucho?
5. ¿Está sirviendo Marcos refrescos?
6. ¿Están comiendo todos?
7. ¿Están charlando juntos?
8. ¿Lo están pasando bien?

C El surf y el wind surf
Completen con el imperfecto progresivo.

1. El viento ___ (soplar).
2. Todos ___ (hacer) calentamiento.
3. Ellos ___ (ejercitar).
4. Los windsurfers ___ (llevar) guantes.
5. Pero los surfers no ___ (llevar) guantes.
6. Algunos ___ (esperar) las olas.
7. Otros ___ (correr) las olas.

D HISTORIETA Lo que estaba haciendo en aquel entonces

Cambien en el imperfecto progresivo.

1. En aquel entonces, José vivía en el dormitorio de la universidad.
2. Estudiaba medicina en la Facultad de Medicina.
3. Cuando no asistía a clases, trabajaba en el hospital.
4. Trabajaba mucho pero no ganaba mucho dinero.
5. En aquel entonces, él salía con Yolanda.
6. Ella seguía cursos en la Facultad de Filosofía y Letras.
7. Cuando ella no estudiaba, daba clases de inglés.

E HISTORIETA Están celebrando.

Contesten según se indica.

1. ¿Qué están bailando? (el tango)
2. ¿Quiénes lo están bailando? (un grupo de amigos)
3. ¿Qué instrumento está tocando el señor? (el organillo)
4. ¿Dónde están bailando? (en la calle)
5. ¿Qué están celebrando? (una fiesta patronal)

ANSWERS

Práctica

B 1. Sí, Marcos está dando una fiesta.
  2. Sí, están bailando sus amigos.
  3. Sí, están escuchando discos y cintas.
  4. Sí, todos se están divirtiendo mucho.
  5. Sí, Marcos está sirviendo refrescos.
  6. Sí, están comiendo todos.
  7. Sí, están charlando juntos.
  8. Sí, lo están pasando bien.
C 1. estaba soplando
  2. estaban haciendo
  3. estaban ejercitando
  4. estaban llevando
  5. estaban llevando
  6. estaban esperando
  7. estaban corriendo
D 1. estaba viviendo
  2. Estaba estudiando
  3. estaba asistiendo, estaba trabajando
  4. Estaba trabajando, estaba ganando
  5. estaba saliendo
  6. estaba siguiendo
  7. estaba estudiando, estaba dando
E 1. Están bailando el tango.
  2. Un grupo de amigos lo están bailando.
  3. El señor está tocando el organillo.
  4. Están bailando en la calle.
  5. Están celebrando una fiesta patronal.

Did You Know?

Por lo general, los estudiantes universitarios en España y Latinoamérica tienen que encontrar su propia vivienda cuando asisten a la universidad. Claro está que los que viven en las grandes ciudades pueden dormir en casa. Los que vienen de afuera se alojan en «pensiones» o en «casas de huéspedes» cerca de las universidades. En España hay «colegios mayores» que son residencias para universitarios, muchas veces patrocinados por grupos religiosos.

ABOUT THE SPANISH LANGUAGE

You may wish to remind students that **una facultad** is a "school" within the university, for example, medical school: **la facultad de medicina**; law school: **la facultad de derecho (leyes)**. The "faculty" is **el profesorado** or, at the secondary level, **los docentes.**

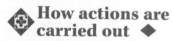

TEACHING STRUCTURE

Have students read the explanatory material and the model sentences.

TEACHING TIPS

These *Práctica* can be done without prior preparation.

ANSWERS
Práctica

A 1. tristemente
  2. puntualmente
  3. elegantemente
  4. rápidamente
  5. respetuosamente
  6. humildemente
  7. locamente
  8. discretamente
  9. ricamente
 10. posiblemente
B 1. sincera y honestamente
  2. clara y cuidadosamente
  3. sencilla y elegantemente
  4. rápida y peligrosamente
  5. cortés y respetuosamente

Telling how actions are carried out
Adverbios en -mente

1. An adverb modifies a verb, an adjective, or another adverb. In Spanish, many adverbs end in **-mente.** To form an adverb from an adjective that ends in **e** or a consonant, you simply add **-mente** to the adjective. Study the following.

ADJECTIVE	+ *mente*	ADVERB
decente		**decentemente**
reciente		**recientemente**
principal		**principalmente**
general		**generalmente**

2. To form an adverb from an adjective that ends in **-o**, add **-mente** to the feminine **-a** form of the adjective.

FEMININE ADJECTIVE	+ *mente*	ADVERB
sincera		**sinceramente**
cariñosa		**cariñosamente**

3. When more than one adverb ending in **-mente** modifies a verb, only the last adverb carries the **-mente** ending. Study the following.

    Él habló lenta y claramente.
    Yo se lo digo honesta y sinceramente.

Práctica

A **Los adverbios** Formen adverbios con los siguientes adjetivos.

1. triste		**6.** humilde	
2. puntual		**7.** loco	
3. elegante		**8.** discreto	
4. rápido		**9.** rico	
5. respetuoso		**10.** posible	

B **¿Cómo lo hacen?** Contesten según el modelo.

    ¿Cómo habla Ramón? (lento/claro)
    Ramón habla lenta y claramente.

1. ¿Cómo responde Luisa? (sincero/honesto)
2. ¿Cómo enseña la profesora? (claro/cuidadoso)
3. ¿Cómo se viste ella? (sencillo/elegante)
4. ¿Cómo conduce Pepe? (rápido/peligroso)
5. ¿Cómo se porta el niño? (cortés/respetuoso)

Learning From Photos

Have students describe the young woman and man in detail. You may wish to review the future of probability with questions such as: **¿Por qué se vestirá así el joven? ¿Adónde irá él hoy? ¿Qué será el joven? ¿Por qué se vestirá así la joven? ¿Adónde irá ella?**

Independent Practice

Assign any of the following:
  1. Exercises, page 370
  2. Workbook, *Repaso de estructura*

Periodismo
Los mayas

Introducción

Los mayas eran oriundos de Guatemala. De Guatemala pasaron a la península de Yucatán en México, a Belice y Honduras. La cultura de los mayas era aun más avanzada que la de los aztecas a quienes encontró Cortés cuando llegó a México. La arquitectura de los mayas era notable como atestiguan las famosas ruinas de templos y pirámides en Palenque, Uxmal, Tikal y Copán. Se sitúa el apogeo de su cultura y civilización en el año 250 después de Jesucristo. Poco antes del año 900 D. de J.C. desaparecen. Su desaparición ha sido un enigma. No se sabe precisamente cómo ni por qué desaparecieron. El artículo que sigue es de la revista *Mundo 21*. Nuevos descubrimientos arqueológicos indican que existe la posibilidad de que los mayas quisieron lograr una gran expansión territorial y que las confrontaciones bélicas que acompañaban esa expansión fueran la causa más importante de la decadencia del Imperio Maya.

Vocabulario

el soberano, el rey

el auge el apogeo, la cima	**lograr** obtener, conseguir
la tarea el trabajo, la labor	**soler (ue)** tener la costumbre
la meta el objetivo	**enfatizar** dar énfasis a
señalar indicar	**pacífico(a)** lo contrario de guerrero(a)
desarrollar aumentar, perfeccionar	o bélico(a)

Cooperative Learning

Have students who are interested in archaeology work in groups to prepare reports on the Mayan civilization.

TEACHING TIPS

A. Ask the students what they know about the Mayas and write a synopsis of the information on the board.
B. Read the *Introducción* aloud to the students or call on individual students to read.
C. After reading the *Introducción*, you may wish to ask the following questions: **¿De dónde eran oriundos los mayas? ¿A qué otras partes pasaron los mayas? ¿Dónde están los templos y pirámides construidos por los mayas? ¿Cuándo desaparecieron? ¿Qué indican los nuevos descubrimientos arqueológicos?**

ABOUT THE SPANISH LANGUAGE

You may wish to have students find the cognates of the following English words in the *Introducción*: advanced, attest, is situated, apogee (highest point), disappear/disappearance, discoveries, confrontations, decadence, empire.

RESOURCES

- Vocabulary Transparencies
- Audio Cassette 15B/Compact Disc 11
- Student Tape Manual
- Workbook
- Chapter Quizzes
- Testing Program

TEACHING VOCABULARY

Have students repeat the words and definitions after you or Cassette 15B/Compact Disc 11.

ANSWERS

Práctica

A 1. señalar, se desarrolló
   2. auge
   3. soberano
   4. La meta
   5. una tarea
   6. enfatizar
   7. solían

B 1. d
   2. a
   3. b
   4. c

❖Práctica❖

A **HISTORIETA** Expresiones equivalentes

Expresen de otra manera.

1. Es necesario *indicar* a los mayas cuya cultura *se formó y se perfeccionó* en Centroamérica.
2. El período de verdadero *apogeo* del imperio maya empezó alrededor del año 250 después de Jesucristo.
3. El imperio empezó a decaer durante el reinado del *rey* Regidor.
4. *El objetivo* del equipo de arqueólogos es tratar de explicar la decadencia del imperio.
5. No es *un trabajo* fácil.
6. Hay que *dar énfasis al hecho de* que hay teorías diferentes para explicar la desaparición y destrucción del Imperio Maya.
7. Ellos *tenían la costumbre de* hacer la guerra.

B **Palabras derivadas**   Pareen.

1. señalar   a. el desarrollo
2. desarrollar b. el logro
3. lograr   c. el énfasis
4. enfatizar   d. la señal

Copán
HONDURAS

Learning From Realia

Copán se sitúa en Honduras. Allí se ven las ruinas de una ciudad maya. Las estelas y la escritura jeroglífica son notables. La Escalera Jeroglífica tiene más de 2.000 ejemplos de esta escritura. Se cree que Copán fue un centro intelectual maya donde se especializaban en la astronomía. Durante las décadas de 1930 hasta 1950 se llevaron a cabo muchas obras de investigación y restauración en Copán.

372

DESCIFRANDO UN ENIGMA...

¿QUÉ PASÓ REALMENTE CON LA CIVILIZACIÓN MAYA?

por EULALIA DÍAZ   Ilustraciones: ARMANDO ESTÉVEZ

Los hallazgos[1] de las excavaciones realizadas en Guatemala parecen indicar que un rey maya—cuya tumba y pertenencias han sido descubiertas en las selvas de Petén—trató de lograr una gigantesca expansión territorial que llegó a convertirse en una verdadera catástrofe bélica[2] y ecológica... ¡Posiblemente ésta sea una de las causas más importantes de la inexplicable decadencia del Imperio Maya!

El Dr. Arthur A. Demarest

S in duda alguna, entre las grandes civilizaciones precolombinas de nuestra América, es imprescindible señalar a los mayas, cuya cultura se desarrolló en Centroamérica, dejando muestras impresionantes de los logros alcanzados en diversos órdenes del conocimiento y el arte.

Precisamente a partir del estudio de los restos que han llegado hasta nuestros días de toda esta grandeza, desde hace mucho tiempo los historiadores han definido que el período de verdadero auge del imperio maya comenzó alrededor del año 250 D. de J.C. con el surgimiento de grandes ciudades y centros destinados a ceremonias rituales. Igualmente, los estudiosos concluyen que este desarrollo formidable terminó—al menos en el sur de Guatemala—poco antes del año 900 D. de J.C., de forma inexplicable...

¿Qué factores abalanzaron[3] a este imperio floreciente[4], y en pleno auge, a la desintegración total? Hasta ahora los especialistas no habían podido formular una hipótesis

Vasijas polícromas

sólida que fundamentase una respuesta lógica a esta incógnita[5]... pero los estudios realizados recientemente, han dado un giro[6] total a las investigaciones.

¡UN AMBICIOSO PROYECTO DE INVESTIGACIONES SE HA PUESTO EN MARCHA! SU OBJETIVO: ¡DEMOSTRAR QUE LOS MAYAS FUERON AUDACES[7] GUERREROS!

Un equipo de arqueólogos—bajo la dirección del doctor Arthur A. Demarest, de la Universidad de Vanderbilt, en Tennessee (Estados Unidos)—se ha dado a la tarea de desentrañar[8] los misterios de la civilización maya, como parte de las investigaciones del Proyecto Arqueológico Regional de Petexbatún, un programa que comenzó hace algunos años y en el que participan especialistas de diferentes disciplinas científicas.

---

[1] **los hallazgos**   los descubrimientos
[2] **bélica**   hostil, guerrero
[3] **abalanzaron**   *pushed*
[4] **floreciente**   *flourishing*
[5] **incógnita**   *unknown*
[6] **un giro**   *a turn*
[7] **audaces**   *bold*
[8] **desentrañar**   *get to the bottom of*

PERIODISMO

trescientos setenta y tres 373

CAPÍTULO 8
Periodismo

TEACHING THE READING

◆ Descifrando un enigma...

¿Qué pasa realmente con la civilización maya? ◆◆◆

A. It is suggested that you have students read this selection silently as if they were browsing through the magazine.

B. You may wish to have the students reread this article for homework.

C. You may wish to assign the *Comprensión* on page 377 for homework before going over them the following day in class.

National Standards

Connections
Students will increase their knowledge of archeology as they learn of a major archeological project undertaken in Guatemala to discover the factors that led to the decline of Mayan civilization.

HISTORY CONNECTION

Los historiadores y arqueólogos dividen la prehistoria de la región maya en tres períodos: la formativa (1500 a. C.–300 d. C.), la clásica (300–900) y la posclásica (900–1500). La civilización maya floreció durante la época «clásica». Nadie sabe por qué, alrededor de 1100 d. C., la región de los mayas, con excepción de Yucatán, perdió un 90% de su población. Éste es el «misterio de los mayas».

HISTORY CONNECTION

La región del Petén donde trabaja el Dr. Demarest es un área enorme de unos 39.000 kilómetros cuadrados. Está en medio de una densa selva tropical. El Petén fue el centro del antiguo Imperio Maya. A pesar de que los españoles habían conquistado esta región bajo Cortés en 1524–25, no fue hasta 1697 cuando cayó realmente bajo el dominio español.

La Plaza de Dos Pilas antes del año 670 D. de J.C.

El objetivo central del proyecto consiste, precisamente, en demostrar que la naturaleza bélica de los mayas y sus esfuerzos expansionistas condujeron a la caída[9] y desaparición de la civilización, al menos en esa región de Guatemala... ¡y ya los científicos han comenzado a arribar[10] a las primeras conclusiones fundamentadas en el hallazgo de fosos, paredes y zanjas[11] construidos por los mayas como obras militares o para la defensa!

Lograr esto no ha sido fácil; se han necesitado abundantes recursos humanos y materiales. Por ejemplo, hace algún tiempo se sumaron a estas tareas más de veinte arqueólogos y técnicos, incluyendo catedráticos y estudiantes, tanto guatemaltecos como extranjeros, además de unos noventa trabajadores que colaboran con el equipo de expertos.

El amplio programa de estudios con que cuenta este magno empeño[12], se ha dividido para su mejor organización en unos seis subproyectos, cada uno de los cuales tiene sus propias metas, metodologías, equipos de investigación y codirectores. Toda esta organización cuenta con el respaldo[13] de prestigiosas instituciones, como son la propia Universidad de Vanderbilt y el Instituto de Antropología e Historia de Guatemala, patrocinados[14] por la Sociedad Geográfica Nacional de los Estados Unidos, la Funda-ción Guggenheim y el Museo Smithsonian, entre otras organizaciones.

LA IMPORTANCIA DE LOS JEROGLÍFICOS, PARA DESCIFRAR LA HISTORIA DE LOS MAYAS

Los Reyes mayas solían mandar a grabar[15] en jeroglíficos, inscritos en estelas[16] o monumentos públicos, todos los acontecimientos que ocurrían durante su reinado; asimismo, datos tales como su nacimiento, su matrimonio, los hijos que tenían, sus conquistas, adquisiciones, derrotas y hasta su muerte. La estela encontrada—grabada sobre piedra caliza[17]—seguramente encierra valiosos secretos sobre la historia de este pueblo, los que serán develados[18] por los expertos en escritura maya una vez que los jeroglíficos se descifren.

UN HALLAZGO TRASCENDENTAL PARA EL CURSO DE LAS INVESTIGACIONES: ¡UNA TUMBA REAL!

Adentrándose en la selva de Petén, (en Dos Pilas), el Dr. Demarest y su equipo hallaron recientemente lo que ellos mismos clasifican como «un tesoro arqueológico de valor incalculable.» Se trata de una tumba al parecer de un personaje importante entre los antiguos mayas... de un rey cuyo nombre aún se desconoce hasta que sea revelado por la lectura de los jeroglíficos que aparecen en los objetos que le acompañaban, y al que los científicos han llamado Regidor II. La antigüedad de los restos hallados se estima en unos 1.200 años.

La tumba real fue encontrada a más de 9,5 metros de profundidad, bajo las ruinas de la pirámide o templo funeral que se halla en la Gran Plaza de Dos Pilas, antigua capital de la región de Petexbatún. En su interior se encontró una osamenta[19]

[9] **la caída** *downfall*	[13] **el respaldo** *backing, support*	[17] **piedra caliza** *limestone*
[10] **arribar** *llegar*	[14] **patrocinados** *sponsored*	[18] **develados** *revealed*
[11] **zanjas** *trenches*	[15] **grabar** *engrave*	[19] **una osamenta** *un esqueleto, unos huesos*
[12] **empeño** *undertaking*	[16] **estelas** *inscribed stone slabs*	

Additional Practice

You may wish to ask additional comprehension questions:

1. ¿Qué quiere decir «la naturaleza bélica» de los mayas?
2. ¿De dónde vinieron los catedráticos y estudiantes que trabajaron en el proyecto?
3. ¿Para qué servían las estelas?
4. Para entender lo que está escrito en las estelas, ¿qué hay que hacer primero?
5. ¿Qué había encima de la tumba real?

Fortificaciones alrededor de Dos Pilas

Sin embargo, no todos los estudiosos están de acuerdo con esta hipótesis, y aunque muchos arqueólogos estiman que el reciente descubrimiento es un gran aporte a los estudios sobre los mayas, otros no están del todo dispuestos a aceptar la posibilidad de que la decadencia de ese imperio se debió a una rápida escalada bélica y a una desmedida[22] expansión terri-

El campamento científico

perfectamente conservada que—según el Dr. Demarest—«tiene puesta una bellísima cofia[20] y un collar hecho de conchas, madreperlas y jade, montado en una máscara». También fue hallada la estela real, cuchillas de obsidiana (que se cree que se utilizaban en ceremonias de sacrificios humanos y rituales mágicos) y piezas de cerámica—verdaderas obras de arte—adornadas con jeroglíficos, entre las que están hermosas vasijas policromas con escenas de episodios en la historia maya.

LOS CIENTÍFICOS OPINAN QUE EL REGIDOR II FUE UNA FIGURA IMPORTANTE EN LA CULTURA MAYA

Según estima el Dr. Demarest, «todo parece indicar que el Regidor II fue una figura clave[21] en toda una secuencia de eventos catastróficos para los mayas, en los cuales el gobierno central del imperio maya se dividió en una docena de estados guerreros, que militarizaron la región durante un período de cincuenta años». Si las teorías del destacado especialista son ciertas, el Regidor II fue, sin duda, uno de los reyes más importantes en la cultura maya, cuya ambición expansionista lo llevó a conquistar los estados vecinos y a obtener el control de diversas rutas de comercio con un activo intercambio comercial en la zona.

torial, que provocó el desequilibrio, el empobrecimiento y la pérdida de la fe[23] del pueblo maya en su soberano.

MUCHOS CIENTÍFICOS DE PRESTIGIO SE MUESTRAN CAUTELOSOS[24] ANTE LOS DESCUBRIMIENTOS... ¡PERO LAS INVESTIGACIONES SIGUEN AVANZANDO!

El doctor Jeremy A. Sabloff, experto en arqueología maya (de la Universidad de Pittsburgh, Estados Unidos), estima que el hallazgo del doctor Demarest es muy importante, pero expresa dudas de que un solo factor, como una destructiva guerra, haya sido la causa principal de la decadencia de la civilización maya.

El Dr. Sabloff enfatiza el hecho de que «esa civilización no desapareció de repente, al final de su período clásico, pues mientras

[20] **cofia** *headgear*
[21] **una figura clave** *a key figure*
[22] **desmedida** *excesiva*

[23] **la fe** *faith*
[24] **cautelosos** *cautious, wary*

Critical Thinking Activity

Thinking skills: supporting arguments with reasons, evaluating information

1. **Muchas personas, y especialmente algunos grupos indígenas, se quejan de que las obras arqueológicas constituyen una ofensa ya que profanan las tumbas de sus antepasados. ¿Se debe permitir este tipo de excavaciones o no? ¿Por qué sí, o por qué no?**

2. **¿Cuál es, precisamente, la hipótesis del Dr. Demarest? ¿Por qué no están todos de acuerdo con su hipótesis?**

Paraphrasing Have students paraphrase the following:

1. ...distinguido especialista en el tópico maya... They may say: ...destacado especialista en el tema maya...

2. No obstante todas las opiniones halladas... They may say: A pesar de todas las opiniones encontradas...

3. ...las investigaciones... indican que los mayas pasaron por un período de excesiva violencia... They may say: ...las investigaciones... muestran que los mayas atravesaron por un período de extrema violencia...

ABOUT THE SPANISH LANGUAGE

«Lítico» quiere decir «de piedra». Todos los objetos que se ven en las fotos fueron hechos de piedra. La palabra inglesa *lithium,* uno de los elementos, viene de la misma raíz griega—*lithikos* (piedra).

---

que las ciudades del sur de Guatemala se encontraban ya en decadencia, todavía en el norte los mayas edificaban grandes centros ceremoniales... en el área de Yucatán, por ejemplo».

Por su parte, el doctor David Webster (Arqueólogo de la Universidad Estatal de Pennsylvania, Estados Unidos, y destacado especialista en el tema maya), considera que «los descubrimientos realizados en las excavaciones de Dos Pilas tienden a crear una nueva visión *revisionista* dentro de la historia conocida de este pueblo, pues hasta hace muy poco se consideraba que éste había sido pacífico y laborioso».

A pesar de todas las opiniones encontradas sobre este tema fascinante, los hallazgos de fosas, máscaras de guerra, sacrificios humanos y rituales—además de la tumba y las extensas fortificaciones excavadas en Dos Pilas—evidencian una gran actividad bélica y parecen indicar que los mayas fueron mucho más militaristas y guerreros que lo que se pensaba anteriormente.

¿SE ENCONTRARÁ EN LA TUMBA DEL REGIDOR II LA VERDAD HISTÓRICA SOBRE LA DECADENCIA DEL PUEBLO MAYA Y SU CULTURA?

El Dr. Demarest estima que los descubrimientos realizados y los conocimientos recopilados por su equipo hasta el presente, indican que aunque el expansionismo maya inicialmente produjo riqueza y bienestar al lugar—principalmente bajo los reinados de los Regidores II y III—posteriormente el reino de Petexbatún empezó a debilitarse a causa de tantas y tan seguidas guerras.

Según este experto, los mayas construyeron viviendas, centros ceremoniales y campos de cultivo, pero llegó un momento

en que empezaron a vivir bajo la continua amenaza[25] de la violencia, por lo cual se vieron precisados a emplear tiempo, energía y fuerza de trabajo en la construcción de empalizadas[26] (como la descubierta en Dos Pilas), y kilómetros de murallas de piedra (en la cercana región de Aguateca), un gran sistema de fosos (en Punta de Chimino) y otras murallas en torno a campos cercanos... Y como las guerras causaron la muerte de muchos de los hombres que trabajaban como

Objetos líticos encontrados en Dos Pilas

agricultores en tiempo de paz, esto trajo como consecuencia dificultades desde el punto de vista económico, al reducirse las cosechas[27] y el intercambio comercial. La vida se convirtió en un perenne estado de sitio[28], y el pueblo se vio obligado a vivir amurallado para poder protegerse.

CONCLUSIÓN

Aunque los conceptos e hipótesis planteados por el Dr. Demarest son aún controversiales y no han sido plenamente demostrados, las investigaciones actuales indudablemente muestran que los mayas atravesaron por un período de extrema violencia y completo caos social antes de su derrumbe[29]...

¿Cuál será, en definitiva, la verdad histórica? Los científicos que trabajan en Dos Pilas se esfuerzan por encontrarla.

[25] **amenaza** *threat*
[26] **empalizadas** *stockades, palisades*
[27] **las cosechas** *harvests*
[28] **sitio** *siege*
[29] **derrumbe** *collapse*

Critical Thinking Activity

Thinking skills: evaluating information, making inferences

1. **El Dr. David Webster habla de una «nueva visión revisionista». ¿Cuál es esta «visión revisionista»? ¿Qué es lo que trata de revisar o contradecir?**

2. **¿Cómo y por qué fue afectada la agricultura por las guerras?**

Comprensión

A **Los mayas** Contesten.

1. ¿Cuál es una posible causa de la desaparición del Imperio Maya?
2. ¿Cómo se supone que los mayas construían sus ciudades inicialmente?
3. ¿Cuándo se vieron obligados a construir empalizadas y murallas?
4. ¿Qué quiere demostrar el equipo del doctor Demarest?
5. ¿Qué solían mandar a grabar en jeroglíficos los reyes mayas?
6. ¿Dónde descubrieron la tumba del Regidor II?
7. ¿Qué se encontró en la tumba?
8. ¿En qué se dividió el Imperio Maya?
9. Según el doctor Demarest, ¿qué quería hacer el Regidor II?
10. ¿Qué cree el doctor Sabloff?
11. Sin embargo, ¿qué evidencian los hallazgos de fosas y máscaras de guerra y las fortificaciones excavadas?
12. Según el doctor Demarest, ¿qué produjo el expansionismo maya inicialmente?
13. ¿Y qué causó la decadencia?
14. ¿Cuál es la conclusión de este artículo?

Chac-mool, el portador de ofrendas a los dioses

B **¿Qué es?** Identifiquen.

1. Petén
2. el doctor Arthur Demarest
3. Dos Pilas

C **Información** Den la siguiente información.

1. dónde se desarrolló la cultura maya
2. el período de auge del imperio en el sur de Guatemala

Actividad comunicativa

A **El derrumbe final** Explique en sus propias palabras cómo el expansionismo militar hubiera podido resultar en la decadencia y el derrumbe final del imperio maya.

Did You Know?

El Museo Antropológico en México, D.F. tiene una extensa colección de artefactos del México precolombino. Enormes figuras talladas en piedra semejantes a la de Chac-mool, figuras en jade, obsidiana, oro y plata abundan. Es uno de los más importantes museos del mundo.

Independent Practice

Assign any of the following:
1. Exercises, page 377
2. Workbook, *Periodismo*

ANSWERS

Comprensión

A 1. la naturaleza bélica de los mayas y sus esfuerzos expansionistas
2. como obras militares o para la defensa
3. después del reino de Petexbatún
4. que la naturaleza bélica de los mayas y sus esfuerzos expansionistas condujeron a la caída y desaparición de la civilización
5. Grababan todos los acontecimientos que ocurrían durante su reinado.
6. en la selva de Petén
7. una osamenta perfectamente conservada, la estela real, cuchillas de obsidiana y piezas de cerámica
8. en una docena de estados guerreros
9. conquistar los estados vecinos y obtener el control de diversas rutas de comercio
10. Duda que un solo factor haya sido la causa principal de la decadencia de la civilización maya.
11. una gran actividad bélica y parecen indicar que los mayas fueron más bélicos que lo que se pensaba
12. riqueza y bienestar
13. la continua amenaza de la violencia
14. que los mayas atravesaron por un período de extrema violencia y caos social antes de su derrumbe

B 1. una región selvática guatemalteca
2. el arqueólogo de la Universidad de Vanderbilt
3. la antigua capital de la región de Petexbatún

C 1. Se desarrolló la cultura maya en Centroamérica.
2. El período de auge del imperio en el sur de Guatemala es 250 d. C.

Actividad comunicativa

ANSWERS

A Answers will vary.

You may wish to present this *Introducción* by having students read it aloud, or you may wish to have the students read the *Introducción* silently. You may then call on one or two individuals to explain it in a few sentences.

Unas cartas

Introducción

Después de siglos de persecución y marginación, los grupos indígenas en Latinoamérica empiezan a luchar por sus derechos y por su cultura. Una manera de mantener la cultura es por medio del idioma. En Bolivia y en otros países hay programas de alfabetización para grupos indígenas. En estos programas los participantes aprenden a escribir en su propio idioma, ya sea el quechua, el aymará, el guaraní o cualquier otro.

Éstas son traducciones al español de cartas escritas originalmente en lengua guaraní. El guaraní se habla en Paraguay y también en partes de Bolivia.

Una muchacha boliviana

Tamaraeme
Asamblea del Pueblo Guaraní

Did You Know?

Más de 2.000.000 de personas hablan guaraní. Ellos viven mayormente en el Paraguay y en áreas contiguas de Brasil, Bolivia y la Argentina. La lengua guaraní es una de las dos lenguas oficiales de la República del Paraguay; la otra es el español.

Vocabulario

la cartilla

La alumna anotó las letras del alfabeto en su cuaderno.

la voluntad   el ánimo, el deseo, la intención   **comunicar**   decir, informar

engañar   dar a la mentira la apariencia de la verdad

A **Expresiones equivalentes** Expresen de otra manera.

1. Quiero *decir* a todo el mundo lo que estoy aprendiendo.
2. Primero, aprendemos *el alfabeto*.
3. Todos tenemos mucha *intención* de aprender.
4. *Apuntamos* todo en el papel.
5. Ahora nadie nos va a *explotar* en el mercado.

Independent Practice

Assign any of the following:
1. Exercise, page 379
2. Workbook, *Periodismo*

RESOURCES

- Vocabulary Transparencies
- Audio Cassette 15B/Compact Disc 11
- Student Tape Manual
- Workbook
- Chapter Quizzes
- Testing Program

TEACHING VOCABULARY

Have students repeat the vocabulary words and definitions after you or Cassette 15B/Compact Disc 11.

TEACHING TIPS

This *Práctica* can be done immediately after the new vocabulary has been presented.

ANSWERS
Práctica

A 1. comunicar
   2. la cartilla
   3. voluntad
   4. Anotamos
   5. engañar

ABOUT THE SPANISH LANGUAGE

El cuaderno que usa el estudiante para escribir tiene varios nombres además de «cuaderno». En España se llama un «bloc» o un «bloque». En Puerto Rico es una «libreta».

379

TEACHING THE READING

 Cartas ◆

Tell students to read the letters once. Have them read them a second time as they look for the information in the *Comprensión* on page 382. It is recommended that this be done as a homework assignment.

Rodeo, 7 de agosto

Les comunico que estoy aprendiendo. A todos nos gusta esta enseñanza porque nos da fuerza. Nosotros sabemos escribir, al comienzo no podía leer la cartilla, pero ahora ya leo de a poquito.

Termino en estas letras.

Mi nombre
Félix Romero Vaca

Rodeo, 7 de julio

Antes, yo no sabía escribir en nuestro idioma, ahora ya estoy aprendiendo algo.

Estoy estudiando con voluntad para que cuando venda mi producto ya no sea engañada.

Estoy en el grupo de Marciano Cuéllar, me llamo Teófila Segundo y tengo 33 años.

A las autoridades del TEKO les mando saludos.

Teófila Segundo

Additional Practice

You may wish to select students to attempt to read aloud the letters in **guaraní.**

380

Urundeiti, 15 de junio

Saludos a todos.

Ya sabemos leer y escribir un poco en guaraní.

Eso les puedo contar a ustedes jefes.

Ahora anotaré mi nombre, para que sepan que yo, Marina Curinda, ya sé escribir mi nombre. El que me enseña tiene un buen carácter.

Marina Curinda
22 años

Critical Thinking Activity

Thinking skills: supporting arguments with reasons En varios países con grandes poblaciones de indígenas, existe una controversia sobre si se debe enseñar a los niños en su idioma nativo o en español. Algunos dicen que se aprenden las materias mejor en su propio idioma. **Otros** dicen que los niños tienen que dominar el idioma nacional—el español—para tener éxito, y que el aprender en su propio idioma retarda su progreso. ¿Qué opina Ud.? ¿Quiénes tienen razón y por qué?

381

TEACHING TIPS

A. This activity can be done as an individual assignment.
B. Volunteers may be solicited to form a debate team on this subject.

Comprensión

A La carta de Félix Romero Escojan.
1. Félix Romero es de ___.
   a. Urundeiti   b. Rodeo   c. TEKO
2. Él dice que la enseñanza les da ___.
   a. fuerza   b. voluntad   c. autoridad
3. Al principio él no sabía leer ___.
   a. las instrucciones   b. el alfabeto   c. la comunicación

B La carta enviada el 7 de julio Completen.
1. El siete de julio ___ escribió una carta.
2. Ella estudia mucho para que nadie la pueda ___.
3. Ella está aprendiendo a ___ su propio idioma.
4. La persona que enseña a su grupo es ___.

C La carta de Marina Curinda Contesten.
1. ¿Dónde vive Marina Curinda?
2. ¿A quiénes saluda ella?
3. ¿Qué puede hacer ella ahora?
4. ¿A quién se lo puede contar?
5. ¿Qué piensa ella de la persona que le enseña?
6. ¿Cuál es el idioma de Marina Curinda?

D Ideas principales ¿De qué tratan estas cartas? Escriba un párrafo explicando lo que Ud. cree que es. También indique su reacción.

Indios guaraníes

Actividades comunicativas

A Un grupo indígena Escoja un grupo de la lista y prepare un breve informe sobre el grupo.

los aztecas	**los taínos**	**los aymarás**	**los quechuas**
los mayas	**los araucanos**	**los guaraníes**	**los incas**

B Debate En varios países se celebra la llegada de Cristóbal Colón al Nuevo Mundo el doce de octubre. Muchos indígenas protestan, diciendo que esta fecha conmemora un evento terrible para ellos. Preparen y presenten un debate sobre el tema: «Cristóbal Colón y la llegada de los europeos: ¿para bien o para mal?».

Learning From Photos

Describa el cuadro. ¿Qué se puede ver en el cuadro? ¿Quiénes lo habrán hecho, españoles o indígenas? ¿Por qué?

Independent Practice

Assign any of the following:
1. Exercises, page 382
2. Workbook, *Periodismo*

Los judíos en el Caribe

Introducción

El artículo que sigue apareció en un folleto publicado por el Museo de Arte Moderno de Bogotá para una exposición de fotografías tomadas por los miembros de una expedición enviada al Caribe por el Museo Beth Hatefutsuth en Israel. El propósito de la expedición fue localizar y tomar fotografías de las ruinas de las comunidades judías en el Caribe, sobre todo en Surinam; Coro, Venezuela; Barranquilla, Colombia; Panamá; Santo Tomás y San Eustaquio.

Los judíos que fueron al Caribe habían sido expulsados de España en 1492.

Vocabulario

la sinagoga

el pilar

el rabino

los judíos   los hebreos, los israelitas
el hogar   la casa

perseguir   seguir a uno que huye
expulsar   echar de una región

Práctica

A **¿Cuál es la palabra?**   Completen.
1. La ___ es un templo de los judíos.
2. El ___ es el maestro del culto hebreo o judío.
3. Las sinagogas se construían alrededor de cuatro ___.
4. Los españoles ___ a los judíos en 1492.
5. Los ___ fueron expulsados de España durante la Inquisición.

TEACHING TIPS

You may wish to read the *Introducción* aloud or have the students read it silently.

RESOURCES

- Vocabulary Transparencies
- Audio Cassette 16A/Compact Disc 11
- Student Tape Manual
- Workbook
- Chapter Quizzes
- Testing Program

TEACHING VOCABULARY

Have students repeat the vocabulary after you. Then call on students to read the new words and definitions.

TEACHING TIPS

This *Práctica* can be done orally with books closed after the vocabulary has been presented.

ANSWERS
Práctica
A **1. sinagoga**
   2. rabino
   3. pilares
   4. expulsaron
   5. judíos

Independent Practice

Assign any of the following:
1. Exercise, page 383
2. Workbook, *Periodismo*

TEACHING THE READING

Los judíos españoles y portugueses en la zona del Caribe ◆◆

A. You may wish to have students read this selection once silently and then aloud.

B. You may wish to intersperse the *Comprensión* questions on page 386 as the students read.

HISTORY CONNECTION

La «Inquisición» o «Santo Oficio» no originó en España. Fue creada por el Papa Gregorio IX para combatir las «herejías» de los albigenses en el sur de Francia durante la Edad Media. La Inquisición española se estableció en 1242. En el siglo XV se reestableció bajo los Reyes Católicos centrándose en la represión del judaísmo y después de la expulsión de los judíos, en la persecución de los falsos conversos. Carlos V y Felipe II emplearon la Inquisición también como instrumento político. La Inquisición fue suprimida por las Cortes de Cádiz en 1813.

National Standards

Connections
Students will increase their knowledge of the history of the Americas as they read about the expulsion of the Jews from Spain in the XV century and their subsequent settlements in Latin America.

LA NACIÓN

Los judíos españoles y portugueses en la zona del caribe

LA NACIÓN

✡ Alrededor de 200.000 judíos fueron expulsados de España en 1492. Cerca de 50.000 se dirigieron a países del Mediterráneo pero la gran mayoría cruzó la frontera hacia Portugal. Cinco años después fue promulgada la ley para expulsar de Portugal a los judíos, pero cuando se dieron cuenta del daño económico que esto causaría al país, decretaron en su lugar que los judíos portugueses estaban, por ley, obligados a bautizarse. Aquéllos que lo hicieron fueron conocidos como «Nuevos Cristianos» o «Miembros de la Nación Hebrea en Portugal» («La Nación»). Vivieron a la sombra de la Inquisición, la cual perseguía a los que seguían observando el judaísmo en secreto. Los «Nuevos Cristianos» de Portugal aprovecharon cualquier oportunidad para salir del país. Encontraron refugio en Bayona y Burdeos (Francia), en Hamburgo y especialmente en Amsterdam. En sus nuevos hogares gozaron, en gran medida, de libertad religiosa, podían regresar al judaísmo y establecer comunidades. Algunos de ellos se dedicaron al comercio que estaba desarrollándose a comienzos del siglo XVII y vinieron al Nuevo Mundo. Allí se reunieron con los miembros de «La Nación» que lograron emigrar directamente de Portugal.

Los judíos que llegaron a la región del Caribe se encontraron con un

La sinagoga Mikve Israel, la más antigua de Sudamérica, Willemstad, Curazao

---

Did You Know?

Curazao pertenece a Holanda y es una de las Antillas Holandesas. Está cerca de la costa de Venezuela. Curazao fue colonizada por los españoles en 1527. Los holandeses la capturaron en 1634. Sirvió de centro del comercio en esclavos hasta la abolición de la esclavitud en 1863.

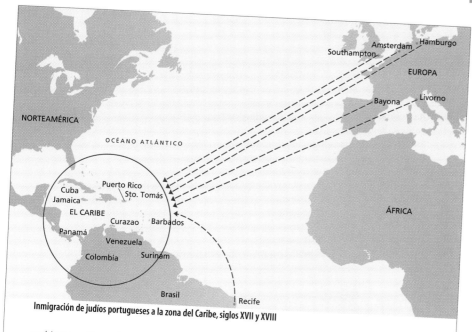

Inmigración de judíos portugueses a la zona del Caribe, siglos XVII y XVIII

ambiente análogo al de Europa. La Ley Católica de España y Portugal había sido desplazada por las fuerzas protestantes de Holanda, Bretaña y Dinamarca. Eran tolerantes con colonizadores de otras religiones y se les otorgó privilegios, garantizándoles una gran libertad. Algunas comunidades judías gozaron de autonomía y en Surinam tenían una milicia.

Los judíos fueron pioneros en varios campos de la economía. Muchos eran propietarios de plantaciones de caña de azúcar y café. Algunos estuvieron entre los primeros en refinar azúcar en la zona.

Miembros de «La Nación» establecieron comunidades en Surinam, Barbados, Curazao, Jamaica, las Islas Vírgenes, San Eustaquio, Venezuela, Colombia, Panamá y en otras zonas del Caribe. Conservaron sus privilegios y trataron de gozar de los mismos derechos que tenían los judíos en otras partes. Existía un sentimiento de mutua responsabilidad que trascendió fronteras y estados. Rabinos líderes, procedentes de comunidades más grandes visitaban regularmente las islas que no tenían rabinos para realizar servicios religiosos. Aspectos materiales unían también a los miembros de «La Nación», tales como la arquitectura común de sus sinagogas, construidas alrededor de 4 pilares centrales (que llamaban las 4 madres) o la costumbre de cubrir el piso de la sinagoga con arena.

Los judíos también desempeñaron un rol dentro de los movimientos de liberación de la zona, durante el siglo XIX. Simón Bolívar, Libertador de Venezuela, Colombia, el Ecuador y el Perú encontró refugio y ayuda entre los judíos de Curazao cuando planeó su lucha contra los españoles.

Did You Know?

Algunas de las familias judías más ilustres de los EE.UU. son de ascendencia sefardí. Ellos salieron de España en el siglo XV y se fueron a Holanda para escaparse de la persecución de la Inquisición. Cuando Nieuw Amsterdam (Nueva York) fue colonia holandesa, ellos se establecieron allí durante los primeros años del siglo XVII. Entre las renombradas familias sefardíes de Nieuw Amsterdam figuran los Baruch y los Cardozo. Bernard Baruch fue multimillonario y consejero del Presidente Franklin Roosevelt. Benjamín Cardozo sirvió de juez en la Corte Suprema de los Estados Unidos.

ANSWERS

Comprensión

A 1. Alrededor de 200.000 judíos fueron expulsados de España.

2. La mayoría fue a Portugal.

3. Estaban obligados a bautizarse.

4. Se llamaban Nuevos Cristianos o «La Nación».

5. Muchos judíos encontraron refugio en Bayona, Burdeos, Hamburgo y Amsterdam.

6. En sus nuevos hogares podían regresar al judaísmo.

7. Algunos de ellos se dedicaron al comercio.

8. Sí, en el Caribe eran tolerantes con las personas de otras religiones.

9. En Surinam ellos tenían una milicia.

10. Ellos eran propietarios de plantaciones de azúcar y café.

11. Sus sinagogas estaban construidas alrededor de cuatro pilares.

12. Cubrían el piso con arena.

13. Ellos le ayudaron a Simón Bolívar a planear su lucha contra los españoles.

TEACHING TIPS

This *Actividad* should be interesting as well as entertaining for the students. You may wish to divide the class into groups of four and have them do the translation.

ABOUT THE SPANISH LANGUAGE

Noten algunas de las transformaciones del español moderno al ladino. En español, ¿qué será la «k» que se usa en ladino? ¿Qué son la «ce» y «ci» españolas en ladino? ¿En qué se convierte la «ll»? ¿Cómo se escriben en español las palabras con «f» como «ferido»? ¿Qué otros cambios pueden encontrar?

386

Comprensión

A **Los emigrantes judíos**   Contesten.

1. ¿Cuántos judíos fueron expulsados de España en 1492?
2. ¿Adónde fue la mayoría de ellos?
3. ¿Qué estaban obligados a hacer los judíos en Portugal?
4. ¿Cómo se llamaban?
5. ¿Dónde encontraron refugio muchos judíos que salieron de Portugal?
6. ¿Qué podían hacer en sus nuevos hogares?
7. ¿A qué se dedicaron algunos de ellos?
8. En el Caribe, ¿eran tolerantes los colonizadores con personas de otras religiones?
9. ¿Qué tenían los judíos en Surinam?
10. ¿Qué trabajo hacían muchos judíos?
11. ¿Cómo estaban construidas sus sinagogas?
12. ¿De qué cubrían el piso de la sinagoga?
13. ¿Cómo desempeñaron los judíos un rol dentro del movimiento de liberación?

Actividad comunicativa

A **El ladino**   Una lengua interesante derivada del español es el ladino. ¿Qué es el ladino? Es el idioma que hablan los descendientes de los judíos de origen español que huyeron de España durante la Inquisición. La mayoría de los judíos que fueron expulsados de España se establecieron en los países del sur, como por ejemplo, en el norte de África y en la Península de los Balcanes. Estos judíos se llaman sefardíes y su lengua es el ladino. El ladino que hablan los sefardíes se parece mucho al español que se hablaba en el siglo XV. Incluye también algunas importaciones turcas, árabes y griegas. Se escribe con un alfabeto parecido al alfabeto hebreo.

El Tiempo es un semanario que se edita actualmente en Tel Aviv-Jaffa en lengua judeoespañola. El aviso al lado del nombre del periódico dice: «Sobre la rogativa (la petición) de muchos lectores de cultura no latina, nuestro semanario adoptó la ortografía fonética».

Lea el siguiente artículo en ladino y tradúzcalo al español.

ANIO 18 No 841
30 Agorot
Sobre la rogativa de muchos lectores de cultura no latina, nuestro semanario adopto la ortografía fonetica.

EL TIEMPO
SEMANAL-POLITICO Y LITERARIO

Un traktorista ferido gravemente por un akto de sabotaje de los sirianos

«Un miembro del kibutz Chamir, Nadav Beler, de 24 anios, fue ferido gravemente viernes pasado kuando su traktor trompezo kon una mina siriana.

El traktor salto por la fuerte detonasion del explosivo y el traktorista fue gravemente ferido. Los primeros kuydos le fueron dados sobre el lugar por los medikos y ambulansia que yegaron de prisa.

Despues el ferido fue transportado kon elikoptero al hospital Poris, el mas serkano al lugar.»

Echkol: vamos a fixar nuestra propia politika en lo ke konserna nuestra seguridad

---

Independent Practice

Assign any of the following:
1. Exercises, page 386
2. Workbook, *Periodismo*

Estructura

Telling what was done
La voz pasiva

1. The true passive voice is used much less in Spanish than in English. In Spanish, the active voice is almost always preferred. Compare these sentences that illustrate the active and passive voice in English.

ACTIVE
The Arabs conquered Spain.

PASSIVE
Spain was conquered by the Arabs.

2. The true passive in Spanish is formed by using the verb **ser** with the past participle.

ACTIVE
Los árabes conquistaron a España.

PASSIVE
España fue conquistada por los árabes.

Remember that the past participle agrees with the subject. The agent or performer of the action is introduced by the preposition **por.** Note that **por** is replaced by **de** if emotion is expressed.

El soberano fue admirado de todos.

3. The true passive is frequently used in an elliptical (shortened) form for newspaper headlines.

Costa destruida por huracán

A HISTORIETA **El rey moro**

Cambien las oraciones en la voz pasiva según el modelo.

El rey moro mandó un ultimátum.
Un ultimátum fue mandado por el rey moro.

1. Las tropas moras invadieron a España.
2. El Califa dirigió la campaña árabe.
3. Los árabes tomaron Granada.
4. Los árabes ganaron la guerra.
5. Siglos después, los españoles reconquistaron a Granada.
6. Los defensores defendieron la ciudad durante muchos meses.

La Alhambra, Granada, España

ESTRUCTURA

trescientos ochenta y siete ∞ **387**

RESOURCES

- Workbook
- Student Tape Manual
- Audio Cassette 16A/Compact Disc 11
- Computer Software: *Estructura*
- Chapter Quizzes
- Testing Program

 Bell Ringer Review

Use the BRR Transparency 8-3, or write the following on the board:
Complete en el pretérito:
1. Los árabes ___ (conquistar) a España.
2. Todos ___ (admirar) al soberano.
3. El huracán ___ (destruir) la costa.

TEACHING STRUCTURE

◆ **Telling what was done** ◆◆

A. Have students read the explanatory material aloud.
B. Have them repeat the verb forms and the model sentences.

ANSWERS
Práctica
A 1. **España fue invadida por las tropas moras.**
2. **La campaña árabe fue dirigida por el Califa.**
3. **Granada fue tomada por los árabes.**
4. **La guerra fue ganada por los árabes.**
5. **Siglos después, Granada fue reconquistada por los españoles.**
6. **La ciudad fue defendida por los defensores durante muchos meses.**

TEACHING STRUCTURE

◆ **What is done in general** ◆◆

Have students read the explanatory material aloud, then repeat the model sentences aloud.

TEACHING TIPS

These *Práctica* can be done orally with books closed after the explanatory material has been presented.

ANSWERS
Práctica

A 1. **Se prepara**   6. **se ponen**
  2. **se hierve**   7. **Se sirve**
  3. **se echa**   8. **se come**
  4. **Se agregan**   9. **se recomienda**
  5. **se cocinan**

B 1. **Se vende fruta en la frutería.**
  2. **Se vende leche en la lechería.**
  3. **Se venden mariscos en la pescadería.**
  4. **Se venden tomates en la verdulería.**
  5. **Se vende carne en la carnicería.**
  6. **Se vende lechuga en la verdulería.**
  7. **Se venden chuletas en la carnicería.**
  8. **Se vende pan en la panadería.**
  9. **Se venden muebles en la mueblería.**
  10. **Se vende ropa en la tienda de ropa (la tienda por departamentos).**
  11. **Se venden pasteles en la pastelería.**
  12. **Se vende perfume en la perfumería (la tienda por departamentos).**
  13. **Se venden aspirinas en la farmacia.**
  14. **Se venden zapatos en la zapatería (la tienda por departamentos).**
  15. **Se venden flores en la florería.**
  16. **Se vende jabón en la tienda por departamentos.**

388

What is done in general
La voz pasiva con se

1. In Spanish, the true passive is often replaced by the reflexive pronoun **se** and the third person singular or plural of the verb, especially when the agent or person carrying out the action is not expressed.

Se prohíbe fumar.	*Smoking is prohibited.*
Aquí se venden periódicos.	*Newspapers are sold here.*

Note that the subject often follows the verb in this construction.

2. The **se** construction is also used when the subject is indefinite.

Se dice que él no puede ganar.	*They say (It is said) that he can't win.*

Práctica

A **HISTORIETA** La paella

Completen usando **se.**

1. ___ (Preparar) la paella a base de arroz.
2. Primero ___ (hervir) el agua para el arroz.
3. Cuando el agua está hirviendo, ___ (echar) el arroz.
4. ___ (Agregar) también azafrán y sal.
5. Aparte, ___ (cocinar) el chorizo y el pollo.
6. Para presentarla ___ (poner) encima pimientos y varios mariscos.
7. ___ (Servir) la paella en una gran paellera.
8. Es un plato que ___ (comer) con gusto.
9. Después de comerla ___ (recomendar) echar una siesta.

B ¿Dónde se vende(n)... ?

Contesten.

1. fruta	9. muebles
2. leche	10. ropa
3. mariscos	11. pasteles
4. tomates	12. perfume
5. carne	13. aspirinas
6. lechuga	14. zapatos
7. chuletas	15. flores
8. pan	16. jabón

AGATHA RUIZ DE LA PRADA

Cooperative Learning

Have students work in pairs. The first student begins a sentence in the active voice and the partner responds with the passive voice.

Independent Practice

Assign any of the following:
1. Exercises, pages 387–388
2. Workbook, *Estructura*

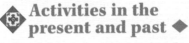
Activities in the present and past
Verbos que terminan en -uir

1. Verbs that end in **-uir** have a **y** in all forms of the present tense except **nosotros** and **vosotros,** and in the third person singular and plural, **él, ella, Ud., ellos, ellas, Uds.,** of the preterite. Study these forms of the verb **construir.**

	PRESENT	PRETERITE
yo	construyo	construí
tú	construyes	construiste
él, ella, Ud.	construye	construyó
nosotros(as)	construimos	construimos
vosotros(as)	construís	construisteis
ellos, ellas, Uds.	construyen	construyeron

El señor Garcés construye casas
    de campo.
Él construyó la casa de los Romero.
Los señores Romero distribuyen
    libros de texto.

2. Other verbs ending in **-uir** are:

destruir	*to destroy*
disminuir	*to diminish, to lessen*
distribuir	*to distribute*
huir	*to flee, to escape*
incluir	*to include*
sustituir	*to substitute*

3. Note that the verb **oír** follows the same pattern as the verbs above except for the **yo** form in the present tense, **oigo.**

oír	oigo	oyes	oye	oímos	oís	oyen

4. The verbs **leer, oír,** and **caer** follow the pattern of the **-uir** verbs in the preterite tense.

leer	leí	leíste	leyó	leímos	leísteis	leyeron
oír	oí	oíste	oyó	oímos	oísteis	oyeron
caer	caí	caíste	cayó	caímos	caísteis	cayeron

◈ Activities in the present and past ◆

A. Read the explanatory material aloud.

B. Call on students to read the verb forms and model sentences aloud.

LITERATURE CONNECTION

Los libros que se ven son de Jorge Luis Borges (1899–1986). A este autor argentino se le considera quizás el más destacado escritor hispanoamericano contemporáneo. Residió algún tiempo en España donde tuvo contacto con los movimientos de vanguardia y colaboró en varias revistas. Introdujo el ultraísmo en América. Recibió el premio Cervantes en 1979. Escribió ensayos, cuentos y poesía. Algunos de sus libros más importantes son *Historia universal de la infamia, El Aleph, Ficciones, Fervor de Buenos Aires, Luna de enfrente, Inquisiciones* y *Otras inquisiciones.*

La familia de la madre de Borges era inglesa y él hablaba inglés perfectamente. Durante sus últimos años Borges no podía ver, pero seguía escribiendo.

389

TEACHING TIPS

Go over these *Práctica* in class as soon as the grammar point has been presented, then assign them for homework.

ANSWERS
Práctica

A 1. construye
2. construyeron
3. oímos
4. cayeron
5. destruyó
6. huyó
7. distribuyen
8. incluyen

B 1. oyes   5. oyen
2. oigo   6. oye
3. oyes   7. oye
4. oímos   8. oyes

C 1. oíste   5. oyeron
2. oí   6. oyó
3. oíste   7. oyó
4. oímos   8. oíste

D 1. oíste   6. huyeron
2. oí   7. cayó
3. leyeron 8. destruyeron
4. leyó   9. huyó
5. oyó   10. cayeron

PAIRED ACTIVITY

Have pairs of students create continuing dialogs based on *Práctica B* and/or the photo. Ask them to be as creative as possible.

ABOUT THE SPANISH LANGUAGE

With regard to the realia on this page, you may wish to ask the following: **Un «polígono» es una unidad de terreno delimitada dedicada a un uso particular, comercial, residencial, industrial, etc. ¿Para qué uso es el Polígono Urtinsa?**

Práctica

A HISTORIETA Los constructores
Completen.

1. La compañía ___ (construir) fábricas.
2. El año pasado, ellos ___ (construir) solamente dos.
3. Nosotros ___ (oír) hablar de ellos con frecuencia.
4. Parece que sus ganancias ___ (caer) bastante el año pasado.
5. Una explosión ___ (destruir) una de las fábricas en construcción.
6. El responsable de la explosión ___ (huir).
7. Hoy ___ (distribuir) los dividendos de fin de año.
8. Los cheques no ___ (incluir) nada extra para nadie.

B HISTORIETA ¿Qué oyes?
Completen con el presente de **oír.**

—Rosa, ¿qué ___₁ tú?

—¿Yo? No ___₂ nada.

—¿Que tú no ___₃ nada? Pero Ramón y yo sí que ___₄ algo.

—Es que Uds. ___₅ algo que nadie más ___₆.

—Pues todo el mundo ___₇ algo, y tú no ___₈ nada. Y tú tienes razón, ¿no?

C ¿Qué oíste?
Completen la conversación de la Práctica B con el pretérito de **oír.**

D HISTORIETA Ayer en clase
Completen con el pretérito.

1. ¿Tú ___ (oír) lo que pasó en clase?
2. No, no ___ (oír) nada.
3. Pues, Carlos y Tina ___ (leer) un artículo.
4. Paco entonces ___ (leer) otro.
5. En ese momento, todo el mundo ___ (oír) un ruido tremendo.
6. Unos criminales que ___ (huir) de la policía entraron en la clase.
7. Paco se ___ (caer) al suelo de miedo.
8. Los criminales ___ (destruir) mucho en la clase.
9. Pero esta vez no ___ (huir) ni uno de ellos.
10. Todos ___ (caer) en manos de la policía.

CONDENSADORES

FÁBRICA ESPAÑOLA DE COMPONENTES ELECTRÓNICOS S.A.

28095 ALCORCÓN (Madrid)
Las Industrias, s/n (Pol. Urtinsa)

☎ *641 54 12
Télex 48153 FACE-E
Fax: ☎ 641 68 56

Learning From Realia

You may wish to ask the following questions based on the ad: **¿A qué se dedica la compañía? ¿Cuál es el «logo» de la compañía? ¿Qué significará el «logo»? ¿Qué será Alcorcón? ¿Qué quiere decir «s/n»? (sin número) ¿Qué significará «Pol.»? (polígono)**

Independent Practice

Assign any of the following:
1. Exercises, page 390
2. Workbook, *Estructura*

Literatura
Costumbres quichés

Antes de leer

En muchas partes de Latinoamérica la población indígena es significativa, y en algunos países, mayoritaria. A pesar de lo numerosa que es la población indígena, su participación en la vida económica y social nacional es frecuentemente muy limitada. Las poblaciones indígenas se ven marginadas. Muchas veces son víctimas de pobreza y discriminación. Siempre ha habido defensores de los indígenas, como Fray Bartolomé de las Casas en el México del siglo XVI. Pero hoy, desde México hasta Tierra del Fuego, son los mismos indígenas que luchan por la justicia y por sus derechos.

Vocabulario

la cosecha del maíz

la candela

la milpa

TEACHING TIPS

Before they read *Antes de leer*, ask students what they know about the Mayas and if they have heard of Rigoberta Menchú. Select a student to read *Antes de leer* aloud.

RESOURCES

- 🔖 Vocabulary Transparencies
- 🎧 Audio Cassette 16A/Compact Disc 11
- 📁 Student Tape Manual
- 📁 Workbook
- 📁 Chapter Quizzes
- 💾 Testing Program

TEACHING THE VOCABULARY

Have students repeat the new words after you.

391

el cultivo

sembrar

el/la ladino(a) mestizo(a), indio(a) que habla castellano

el antepasado abuelo, ancestro

desperdiciar perder, malgastar

herir causar daño, lastimar

compuesto(a) hecho(a), producido(a)

sagrado(a) venerable, santo(a), con valor religioso

Práctica

A **La naturaleza** Completen.

1. Los recursos naturales son limitados, no se deben ___.
2. Los indígenas respetan el agua y la tierra porque creen que son cosas ___.
3. Los indígenas también respetan a sus abuelos y otros ___.
4. Ellos prefieren los productos naturales, no los productos ___ por máquinas.
5. No puedo ver sin la luz que nos da ___.
6. Nunca debemos ___ o lastimar a nadie.
7. Los campesinos tienen que ___ bien los campos si quieren una cosecha buena.
8. El ___ del maíz es importante para los indígenas.

Introducción

Rigoberta Menchú pertenece a los quichés, grupo indígena de Guatemala, descendientes de los mayas. Ella nació en 1959 en la pequeña aldea de Chimel en el estado guatemalteco de El Quiché en el norte del país.

A los veintitrés años de edad Rigoberta Menchú contó la historia de su vida a Elizabeth Burgos quien la redactó tal como se la contó Rigoberta. Dice Burgos:

«La historia de su vida es más un testimonio sobre la de Guatemala. Por ello es ejemplar, puesto que encarna la vida de todos los indios del continente americano. Lo que ella dice a propósito de su vida, de su relación con la naturaleza, de la vida, la muerte, la comunidad, lo encontramos igualmente entre los indios norteamericanos, los de América Central y los de Sudamérica.»

Rigoberta Menchú ha luchado por los derechos de los indígenas, no sólo de Guatemala, sino de toda la América. En 1992 ella recibió el Premio Nóbel de la Paz.

En la selección de su libro *me llamo Rigoberta Menchú y así me nació la conciencia* ella nos habla de la importancia de la naturaleza en la vida de los quichés.

La selección comienza con unas frases del *Popol Vuh*, el libro sagrado de los quichés de Guatemala que data del siglo XVI.

Lectura

me llamo Rigoberta Menchú y así me nació la conciencia

Capítulo X *La naturaleza* (fragmento)

Tojil, en la oscuridad que le era propicia, con una piedra golpeó el cuero de su sandalia, y de ella, al instante, brotó una chispa, luego un brillo y en seguida una llama y el nuevo fuego lució esplendoroso. (Popol Vuh)

Entonces también desde niños recibimos una educación diferente de la que tienen los blancos, los ladinos. Nosotros, los indígenas, tenemos más contacto con la naturaleza. ... respetamos una serie de cosas de la naturaleza. Las cosas más importantes para nosotros. Por ejemplo, el agua es algo sagrado. La explicación que nos dan nuestros padres desde niños es que no hay que desperdiciar el agua, aunque haya. El agua es algo puro, es algo limpio y es algo que da vida al hombre. Sin el agua no se puede vivir, tampoco hubieran podido vivir nuestros antepasados... Tenemos tierra. Nuestros padres nos dicen «Hijos, la tierra es la madre del hombre porque es la que da de comer al hombre.» Y más nosotros que nos basamos en el cultivo, porque nosotros los indígenas comemos maíz, frijol y yerbas del campo y no sabemos comer, por ejemplo, jamón o queso, cosas compuestas con aparatos, con máquinas. Entonces se considera que la tierra es la madre del hombre. Y de hecho nuestros padres nos enseñan a respetar esa tierra. Sólo se puede herir la tierra

Aldea quiché, Guatemala

Lectura ◆◆

A. Have students read the questions in *Comprensión A* on page 394 so that they can look for the information as they read the selection.

B. Select students to read portions of the selection aloud to the class. Remind them that this is a first person narrative.

C. After each student has read his or her portion of the text, call on another student to tell in his or her own words what was read to them.

National Standards

Cultures

Students increase their understanding of the concept of culture by learning of the customs and traditions of the Quiché peoples of Guatemala, as described by Rigoberta Menchú, and contrasting these customs and traditions with their own.

CULTURE CONNECTION

The *Popol Vuh*, the sacred book of the Quiché, is the most important document of the religion, mythology, and history of the Quiché. The conquistador Pedro de Alvarado destroyed the original. It was rewritten in Spanish by a converted Quiché shortly after the conquest.

Did You Know?

In Mesoamerica land was not owned by anybody. Lands were cultivated communally. The Aztec and Mayan concept was that the earth was a goddess, a divine being, superior to any human and could not be owned. The **milpa** system of cultivation led to the development of village community government under the leadership of elders or headmen. The needs of agriculture also dictated the need to watch the stars. A proper study of the seasons was necessary for efficient cultivation of food crops. This brought about the extraordinary calendars of the Aztecs and the Maya.

LITERATURE CONNECTION

Rigoberta Menchu's book is an example of an "as told to" work. Elizabeth Burgos transcribed and edited the work by Ms. Menchú. It should be noted, however, that she tried to maintain the original flavor and feeling of the narrative provided by Ms. Menchú.

ANSWERS

Comprensión

A Answers will vary but must indicate:

1. **las cosas de la naturaleza**
2. **la tierra, da de comer al hombre**
3. **los representantes de la tierra, del agua y del maíz**
4. **las personas están hechas de maíz**

B Answers will vary.

Actividades comunicativas

ANSWERS

A and **B** Answers will vary.

National Standards

Comparisons
Ask the students to compare the attitudes of Americans and indigenous peoples such as the Quiché toward the cultivation of the land and the use of natural resources such as water.

394

---

cuando hay necesidad. Esa concepción hace que antes de sembrar nuestra milpa, tenemos que pedirle permiso a la tierra.

Cuando se pide permiso a la tierra, antes de cultivarla, se hace una ceremonia…. En primer lugar se le pone una candela al representante de la tierra, del agua, del maíz, que es la comida del hombre. Se considera, según los antepasados, que nosotros los indígenas estamos hechos de maíz. Estamos hechos del maíz blanco y del maíz amarillo, según nuestros antepasados. Entonces, eso se toma en cuenta. Y luego la candela, que representa al hombre como un hijo de la naturaleza, del universo. Entonces, se ponen esas candelas y se unen todos los miembros de la familia a rezar. Más que todo pidiéndole permiso a la tierra, que dé una buena cosecha. También se reza a nuestros antepasados, mencionándoles sus oraciones, que hace tiempo, hace mucho tiempo, existen.

Después de leer

Comprensión

A **Tradiciones**   Contesten.

1. Según Rigoberta Menchú, ¿cuáles son las cosas más importantes para los indígenas?
2. ¿Quién es la *madre del hombre*, y por qué se le considera así?
3. En la ceremonia que describe Rigoberta Menchú se pone una candela ante tres cosas, ¿cuáles son?
4. ¿Qué importancia tiene el maíz blanco y el amarillo en la tradición de los indígenas?

B *El Popol Vuh*   Expliquen.

El capítulo X comienza con unas frases del *Popol Vuh*. ¿A qué cree usted que se refieren?

Actividades comunicativas

A **Una entrevista**   Ud. es un voluntario del Cuerpo de Paz en Guatemala. Su compañero(a) es un miembro del grupo quiché. Ud. le hace una entrevista y le pregunta sobre su vida diaria, sus costumbres y tradiciones.

B **Los quichés**   Hoy día más de 300.000 quichés viven en Guatemala. Sus tradiciones y costumbres son únicas. Busque información sobre los quichés y prepare un informe para presentar a la clase.

Did You Know?

In 1998 an American anthropologist questioned a number of assertions found in Rigoberta Menchú's book. He accused her of fabricating or seriously exaggerating many of the episodes in the book. Her claim that she only learned Spanish as an adult, for example, seemed to be refuted by nuns who claimed to have taught her as a child in church schools. Nevertheless, the conditions and descriptions of village life related by her are, it is agreed, accurate.

National Standards

Cultures
Students experience, discuss, and analyze an expressive product of the culture: the selection from *me llamo Rigoberta Menchú y así me nació la conciencia* by Rigoberta Menchú and Elizabeth Burgos.

Búcate plata

de Nicolás Guillén

Antes de leer

Ilustres poetas latinoamericanos como el cubano Nicolás Guillén han tomado la experiencia negra para crear maravillosas poesías. En el poema «Búcate plata», de Nicolás Guillén, se nota que el poeta ha imitado el habla de los negros cubanos. Al leer el poema, piensen en la difícil situación en que se encuentra la mujer. Y noten que le molesta mucho el «¿qué dirán?» En las Antillas, y en Cuba en particular, decirle a uno «mi negro» o «mi negra» es expresarle cariño.

Vocabulario

la plata, el dinero   las galletas   correr

dar un paso

Un joven dio un paso atrás. El otro corrió.

Práctica

A **Unas definiciones** Den la palabra.

1. un tipo de pan duro
2. irse de prisa, abandonar un sitio
3. moverse sin ir muy lejos
4. otro término para «el dinero»

B **¿Cómo se pronuncia?** Pareen.

1. arroz   **a.** búcate
2. nada más   **b.** arró
3. búscate   **c.** tó
4. está   **d.** na má
5. después   **e.** etá
6. todo   **f.** depué

Did You Know?

La población negra de Cuba siempre ha sido importante igual que su influencia en la cultura cubana. Además de la poesía afrocubana ha habido una tradición de música afrocubana muy popular en las dos Américas y en Europa.

RESOURCES

- Vocabulary Transparencies
- Audio Cassette 16A/Compact Disc 11
- Student Tape Manual
- Workbook
- Chapter Quizzes
- Testing Program

TEACHING VOCABULARY

Follow the presentation suggestions outlined in other chapters.

ANSWERS
Práctica

A 1. **las galletas**
   2. **correr**
   3. **dar un paso**
   4. **la plata**

B 1. **b**
   2. **d**
   3. **a**
   4. **e**
   5. **f**
   6. **c**

ABOUT THE SPANISH LANGUAGE

La «galleta» *(cracker/biscuit)* es un tipo de pan duro. También significa una bofetada o golpe a la cara con la mano abierta. En algunas partes de Latinoamérica «colgar la galleta» quiere decir despedir a alguien de su empleo.

TEACHING TIPS

TEACHING TIPS

Call on students to read the *Introducción* aloud. You can have the other students listen with books closed or follow along in their books.

TEACHING THE READING

Lectura ◆◆

Before going over the selection, have students read the *Comprensión* questions on page 397 so that they can look for the information as they read the poem.

FINE ART CONNECTION

El cuadro representa «la zafra» en Cuba. La zafra es la cosecha de la caña de azúcar. Notarán a la niña en el cuadro. Ella está masticando un trozo de caña para sacarle el jugo. El jugo de la caña es muy dulce. El gran cuchillo que llevan los hombres es un machete, que se usa para cortar la caña.

National Standards

🍀 **Cultures**
Students experience, discuss, and analyze an expressive product of the culture: the poem «Búcate plata», by the Cuban poet Nicolás Guillén.

Introducción

Nicolás Guillén nació en Camagüey, Cuba, en 1902. Muy temprano, introdujo en sus versos el folklore negro de su país. Es el mejor cultivador de la poesía afrocubana. Su poesía a la vez nos ofrece magníficas escenas costumbristas y un fervoroso ataque contra la explotación del negro antillano. En «Búcate plata» la mujer lamenta no poder gozar de las comodidades que tienen otros. Ella siente pena por el hombre, pero «hay que comer».

Nicolás Guillén

Lectura

Búcate plata

Búcate plata,
búcate plata,
porque no doy un paso má;
etoy a arró con galleta,
na má.

Yo bien sé como etá tó,
pero viejo, hay que comer:
búcate plata,
búcate plata,
porque me voy a correr.

Depué dirán que soy mala,
y no me querrán tratar°,
pero amor con hambre, viejo,
¡qué va!
Con tanto zapato nuevo,
¡qué va!
Con tanto reló, compadre,
¡qué va!
Con tanto lujo°, mi negro,
¡qué va!

Cosecha de la caña de azúcar, Cuba

tratar tener alguna relación con una persona

lujo opulencia

Additional Practice

You may wish to ask these questions to help students understand the poem: **¿Qué es lo que la mujer quiere que el hombre busque? ¿Qué es lo que ella no va a dar? (un paso más) ¿Qué es lo que la mujer ha estado comiendo con la galleta? (arroz) ¿Qué más come? (nada) Si ella abandona al hombre, ¿qué va a decir la gente?**

Después de leer

Comprensión

A **No está contenta.** Contesten.

1. ¿Qué es lo que le pide la mujer al hombre?
2. ¿Qué es lo único que ella come ahora?
3. ¿Qué va a hacer ella si las cosas no cambian?
4. ¿Qué ve ella que la hace sentir mal?

B **¿Qué quiere decir... ?** Expliquen el significado.

1. ... no doy un paso má;
2. Depué dirán que soy mala, y no me querrán tratar,
3. pero amor con hambre, viejo, ¡qué va!
4. Yo bien sé como etá tó.

C **¿Dónde dice?** Busquen dónde indica...

1. que ella comprende que las cosas son difíciles
2. que ella va a abandonar a «su viejo»
3. que la gente hablará mal de ella
4. que otros tienen mucho

Trinidad, Cuba

Actividades comunicativas

A **Un resumen** Prepare un resumen del poema en sus propias palabras.

B **Debate** Divida su grupo en dos y debatan el tema: ¿Tiene razón la mujer o no en abandonar al hombre en «Búcate plata»?

C **La influencia africana** Con su grupo, busquen información sobre la influencia africana en las Antillas. ¿De qué parte de África vino la mayoría de los negros? ¿Cuándo llegaron? ¿Cuál es el tamaño de la población negra en los distintos países?

LITERATURA

397

Ask the following questions about the *Antes de leer* section: **¿Qué es un romance?** (un tipo de poema, como la balada inglesa) **¿Qué es el «prendimiento»?** (la captura, el tomar prisionero) **¿Cómo se llama la familia de Antoñito?** (Camborio) **¿Cuál es una diferencia entre los gitanos españoles y los otros gitanos? ¿Cuál es el idioma de los gitanos? ¿De dónde vinieron originalmente los gitanos? ¿En qué campos o profesiones han tenido gran éxito los gitanos españoles?**

El prendimiento de Antoñito el Camborio en el camino de Sevilla

Antes de leer

El romance que sigue, «El prendimiento de Antoñito el Camborio en el camino de Sevilla», es obra del gran poeta español Federico García Lorca. García Lorca era andaluz y es en Andalucía donde se encuentra la mayoría de los gitanos españoles. El Antoñito del poema es gitano, del clan de los Camborio.

Los gitanos se encuentran en Irlanda, Hungría, Rumania y en toda Europa. Se cree que los gitanos tienen su origen en el norte de la India. Los gitanos europeos están siempre en camino de un lugar a otro. Los gitanos españoles, no. Los gitanos tienen sus propias costumbres y hasta su propia lengua, *el caló*. A pesar de haber vivido en España desde hace siglos, siempre se les considera «diferentes». Los gitanos siempre han sufrido del prejuicio racial. Hay quienes los acusan de ladrones, de traficantes en droga, etc. Al mismo tiempo, los gitanos españoles tienen fama de ser los mejores intérpretes del cante y del baile flamencos, y de producir algunos de los mejores y más finos toreros. Los gitanos también contribuyen a esa mezcolanza de razas y culturas que ha formado al español.

La Guardia civil española es el cuerpo destinado a mantener el orden en el campo y en los caminos. Hasta hace poco los guardias civiles llevaban un tricornio, un sombrero de tres picos. Al leer el poema, trate de determinar dónde residen las simpatías del poeta, ¿con el gitano o con los guardias civiles?

Gitanas, Córdoba, España

Learning From Photos

1. Las gitanas se visten siempre de falda larga de vivos colores. Los gitanos abundan en las grandes capitales de Andalucía: Córdoba, Sevilla, Granada.
2. Estos gitanos viajan en caravanas tiradas por caballos, mulas o burros. Noten los perros. Cuando hace mucho calor, los perros andan debajo de las caravanas para protegerse del sol.

Vocabulario

los toros

el tricornio

la aceituna

el oro

el hombro

el codo

el arroyo

el guardia civil

Tiró el limón al agua.

la sangre   el líquido rojo que corre por las venas

el calabozo   la prisión

el potro   un caballo joven

redondo(a)   de forma circular

❖Práctica❖

A **¿Cuál es la palabra?** Completen.

1. Los —— y los —— son animales.
2. El —— y el —— son partes del cuerpo humano.
3. El —— es una fruta.
4. El —— es un metal precioso.
5. La —— es la fruta del olivo.
6. El —— es un río pequeño.
7. Un miembro de la policía nacional española es un —— ——.
8. El sombrero que lleva es un ——.
9. Le sale —— de la herida causada por un cuchillo.
10. Los policías lo llevan al ——.

LITERATURA

trescientos noventa y nueve ∞ **399**

TEACHING VOCABULARY

Have students repeat the new words and expressions after you.

ABOUT THE SPANISH LANGUAGE

En todas las lenguas romances la fruta del olivo se llama oliva, olive, etc. La raíz es latina. En español «aceituna» viene del árabe «al zeitun». No obstante, el árbol es «el olivo», el lugar donde crece es «el olivar». «Aceite» viene de aceituna. Así es que decir «aceite de oliva» es decir «aceite de oliva de oliva».

VOCABULARY EXPANSION

You may wish to review the names of shapes: **redondo, cuadrado** *(square)*, **rectangular, triangular, elipsoide, esférico.**

Independent Practice

Assign any of the following:
1. Exercise, page 399
2. Workbook, *Literatura*

ANSWERS
Práctica

A 1. toros, potros
  2. hombro, codo
  3. limón
  4. oro
  5. aceituna
  6. arroyo
  7. guardia civil
  8. tricornio
  9. sangre
  10. calabozo

TEACHING TIPS

Call on students to read the *Introducción* aloud.

Introducción

Federico García Lorca (1898–1936) nació en una aldea de la provincia de Granada, en Andalucía. Hijo de una familia acomodada, pasó una infancia feliz en el campo. Estudió derecho y filosofía y letras en la Universidad de Granada, y también en la Universidad de Madrid. Desde muy joven, García Lorca tenía afición a la pintura, al teatro y a la música. Manuel de Falla, el famoso compositor español, dijo de él «si hubiera querido ser músico, hubiera sido tan bueno como el poeta que es».

Federico García Lorca

Durante su corta vida, García Lorca viajó por Europa, la América del Sur, el Canadá y los Estados Unidos. En algunos países trabajó como director de teatro. En 1929 y 1930, pasó una temporada en Nueva York, donde se matriculó en una clase de inglés en la Universidad de Columbia. Durante su estadía en Nueva York, dio conferencias sobre música, folklore y poesía. Escribió una colección de poesías titulada *Poeta en Nueva York*. En 1936, al comenzar la Guerra Civil española, García Lorca murió misteriosa y trágicamente, asesinado en su querida Granada.

A pesar de haber muerto muy joven, García Lorca dejó una producción caudalosa de poesía y teatro. En la poesía de García Lorca hay teatro y en su teatro hay poesía. Toda su obra combina lo lírico con lo dramático. De todos los poetas de habla española de este siglo, es García Lorca quien ha cruzado con mayor éxito las fronteras de la lengua. Su obra se ha traducido en muchos idiomas.

El poema que sigue es de su *Romancero gitano*, publicado en 1928. Un romancero es una colección de romances. Ud. verá al leer este romance que la poesía de García Lorca está llena de imágenes, de formas, de sonidos, de sensaciones y de misterio. Su obra es como teatro poético. Al leer «El prendimiento de Antoñito el Camborio en el camino de Sevilla», trate de formarse una imagen mental de lo que está pasando.

Andalucía, España

Additional Practice

You may wish to ask: **¿Dónde y qué estudió García Lorca? ¿Era pobre su familia? ¿Dónde y cómo murió el poeta? ¿En qué dos géneros literarios se destacó García Lorca? ¿Qué quiere decir «ha cruzado con mayor éxito las fronteras de la lengua»?**

Learning From Photos

El señor en la foto es un «cabrero» o pastor de cabras. La carne de cabra, especialmente de cabrito, es muy popular en España y Latinoamérica, igual que la leche de cabra.

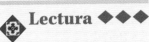
Lectura

*El prendimiento de
Antoñito el Camborio
en el camino de
Sevilla*

«La gitana» de Isidro Nonell

Antonio Torres Heredia,
hijo y nieto de Camborios,
con una vara de mimbre°
va a Sevilla a ver los toros.
Moreno de verde luna,
anda despacio y garboso°.
Sus empavonados bucles°
le brillan entre los ojos.
A la mitad del camino
cortó limones redondos,
y los fue tirando al agua
hasta que la puso de oro.
Y a la mitad del camino,
bajo las ramas de un olmo°,
guardia civil caminera
lo llevó codo con codo.

El día se va despacio,
la tarde colgada° a un hombro
dando una larga torera°
sobre el mar y los arroyos.
Las aceitunas aguardan
la noche de Capricornio,
y una corta brisa, ecuestre°,
salta los montes de plomo°.
Antonio Torres Heredia,
hijo y nieto de Camborios,
viene sin vara de mimbre
entre los cinco tricornios.

—Antonio, ¿quién eres tú?
Si te llamaras Camborio,
hubieras hecho una fuente
de sangre con cinco chorros°.
Ni tú eres hijo de nadie,
ni legítimo Camborio.
¡Se acabaron los gitanos
que iban por el monte solos!
Están los viejos cuchillos
tiritando° bajo el polvo.

A las nueve de la noche
lo llevan al calabozo,
mientras los guardias civiles
beben limonada todos.
Y a las nueve de la noche
le cierran el calabozo,
mientras el cielo reluce
como la grupa° de un potro.

una vara de mimbre *a reed stick*

garboso *gracefully*
empavonados bucles *carefully combed (slick) curls*

un olmo *an elm*

colgada *hanging on*
una larga torera *a pass with a cape in a bullfight*

ecuestre *relativo al caballo*
plomo *lead*

chorros *spurts*

tiritando *shivering*

grupa *flank*

TEACHING TIPS

Lectura ◆◆◆

A. Before going over the selection, have students read the *Comprensión* questions on pages 402–403 so that they can look for the information as they read the poem.

B. You may wish to assign some of the *Comprensión* questions for homework.

C. You may wish to ask these questions to aid in comprehension of the poem: **¿Adónde iba Antonio? ¿Qué iba a hacer en Sevilla? Describa a Antonio. ¿Qué le puso al agua «de oro»? ¿Qué quiere decir «codo con codo»? ¿Cómo describe García Lorca el anochecer? ¿Qué son los cinco tricornios? ¿El tricornio es una metáfora que representa qué? ¿Cuál es «la fuente con cinco chorros»? ¿Cómo brilla el cielo al final del poema?**

LITERATURE CONNECTION

El romancero gitano es una colección de unos 18 poemas en forma de romance. Los gitanos o Andalucía figuran en todos. Junto con «El prendimiento de Antoñito el Camborio en el camino de Sevilla» está «La muerte de Antoñito el Camborio», en el que figura el poeta mismo cuando dice Antoñito: «¡Ay Federico García, llama a la Guardia Civil! Ya mi talle se ha quebrado como caña de maíz.»

Did You Know?

Se cree que los gitanos originaron en el norte de la India y que fueron a Persia antes del año 1.000 d. C. Allí se supone que se dividieron en tres grupos: los Kalderash, los Manush y los Gitanos. Los primeros gitanos llegaron a la Europa Occidental en el siglo XV. Mientras que los Kalderash y los Manush son mayormente nómadas, no es así con los gitanos españoles, que tienden a mudarse con menos frecuencia.

National Standards

Cultures
Students experience, discuss, and analyze an expressive product of the culture: the poem, «El prendimiento de Antoñito el Camborio en el camino de Sevilla», by the Spanish poet Federico García Lorca.

401

ANSWERS

Comprensión

A 1. El gitano se llama Antonio Torres Heredia.
   2. Lleva una vara de mimbre en la mano.
   3. Él va a Sevilla.
   4. Quiere ver los toros.
   5. Él es moreno.
   6. Anda despacio y garboso.
   7. Lleva el pelo empavonado.
   8. Entre sus ojos brillan sus bucles.
   9. Corta limones de los árboles.
  10. Los tira al agua.
  11. Los guardias civiles van caminando por la mitad del camino.
  12. Llevan a Antoñito codo con codo.

B 1. Antoñito viene sin vara de mimbre.
   2. El poeta habla de los cinco tricornios.
   3. El poeta le habla a Antonio. (Antonio se habla a sí mismo.)
   4. El poeta le dice que es cobarde. Si fuera un verdadero Camborio, habría atacado a sus perseguidores (a los guardias civiles).
   5. Los guardias lo llevan al calabozo y beben limonada.

C 1. c
   2. b
   3. b
   4. c
   5. a
   6. b

✎ Después de leer ✎

❧ Comprensión ❧

A   **El gitano**   Contesten.

1. ¿Cómo se llama el gitano?
2. ¿Qué lleva en la mano?
3. ¿Adónde va?
4. ¿Qué quiere ver?
5. ¿Cómo es la piel del gitano?
6. ¿Cómo anda?
7. ¿Cómo lleva el pelo?
8. ¿Qué brilla entre sus ojos?
9. ¿Qué corta de los árboles?
10. ¿Dónde los tira?
11. ¿Por dónde van caminando los guardias civiles?
12. ¿Cómo llevan a Antoñito?

B   **¿Cómo se sabe?**   Expliquen.

1. A Antoñito lo han tomado preso los guardias. ¿Cómo viene ahora?
2. Hay más de un guardia civil. ¿Cúantos hay? ¿Cómo se sabe?
3. En el poema alguien dice: «Antonio, ¿quién eres tú?» ¿Quién le está hablando a quién?
4. ¿Quién le está diciendo que es cobarde? ¿Por qué? Si fuera un verdadero Camborio, ¿qué habría hecho?
5. ¿Qué pasa a las nueve de la noche? ¿Qué hacen los guardias?

C   **Los símbolos**   Escojan.

1. ¿Qué significa «moreno de verde luna»?
   a. El gitano camina de noche.
   b. El gitano tiene el pelo negro, la piel morena y los ojos verdes.
   c. El gitano de piel morena es joven.

2. ¿Qué significa «la tarde colgada a un hombro»?
   a. El gitano tiene algo que le cubre el hombro.
   b. El tiempo pasa despacio y el gitano está preocupado y pensativo.
   c. Van a colgar a Antoñito durante la tarde.

3. ¿Qué significa «hubieras hecho una fuente de sangre»?
   a. Hubieras recibido una herida.
   b. Hubieras apuñalado (herido con un cuchillo) a los guardias.
   c. Le hubiera salido mucha sangre de su herida.

Guardias civiles

Learning From Photos

Los guardias civiles ya no llevan tricornio. Hoy llevan un «kepis» estilo francés. La Guardia Civil fue fundada en 1844. El primer director fue el duque de Ahumada. El cuerpo se estableció para mantener el orden en el campo. En esa época los bandidos dominaban los caminos, especialmente en Andalucía. Los guardias civiles tradicionalmente andan en parejas—antes, a caballo, hoy en coches de patrulla.

4. ¿Qué significa «una corta brisa ecuestre»?
  a. una brisa fría
  b. un viento fuerte de invierno
  c. una brisa repentina como la que surge cuando pasa rápido un caballo

5. ¿Qué significa «salta los montes de plomo»?
  a. Los montes de esta región contienen mucho plomo.
  b. Los montes y los olivos que crecen allí son grises.
  c. Los montes tienen piedras que saltan cuando pasan los caballos.

6. ¿Qué significa «están los viejos cuchillos tiritando bajo el polvo»?
  a. Los cuchillos brillan tanto que es imposible verlos.
  b. Los gitanos ya no usan cuchillo, han perdido su bravura.
  c. Los cuchillos están enterrados en un cementerio.

D **Los significados** ¿Qué cree Ud. que significa… ?

1. la vara de mimbre
2. Las aceitunas aguardan la noche de Capricornio.

Actividades comunicativas

A **Una descripción** García Lorca nos da una descripción bastante completa del aspecto físico de Antoñito. Describa al joven.

B **La marcha del día** ¿Cuál es la imagen que García Lorca usa para describir la marcha del día?

C **Una crítica** En un párrafo, describa como Antoñito se critica a sí mismo.

D **Los gitanos** Según la voz que le habla a Antoñito, ¿cómo han cambiado los gitanos?

E **Prosa en verso** Muchos críticos literarios dicen que la obra de García Lorca es siempre teatro poético, sea en prosa o en verso. Lea una vez más el poema. Luego, trabajando con un(a) compañero(a) de clase, preparen una escena dramática basándola en lo que sucedió en el poema.

Un gitano, Granada, España

ANSWERS

Comprensión
D Answers will vary.

TEACHING TIPS

You may wish to allow students to choose the *Actividad* in which they wish to participate.

Actividades comunicativas

ANSWERS

A **Antoñito es moreno y garboso y tiene empavonados bucles.**
B **la tarde colgada a un hombro**
C–E Answers will vary.

Did You Know?

Las cuevas del Sacromonte, en Granada, han servido de domicilio a familias gitanas desde hace siglos. Algunas cuevas tienen electricidad, televisión, etc. Para los turistas hay espectáculos de cante y baile flamencos.

Independent Practice

Assign any of the following:
  1. Exercises, pages 403
  2. Workbook, *Literatura*

403

RESOURCES

- Vocabulary Transparencies
- Audio Cassette 16B/Compact Disc 12
- Student Tape Manual
- Workbook
- Chapter Quizzes
- Testing Program

TEACHING VOCABULARY

Have the students repeat the new words, definitions, and sentences after you.

ABOUT THE SPANISH LANGUAGE

La palabra «sudar» equivale al inglés *to sweat.* «Transpirar» es un poco más fino, es como *perspire.* El sustantivo *sweat* es «el sudor» y *perspiration* es «la transpiración».

¡Quién sabe!

de José Santos Chocano

Antes de leer

El fragmento que sigue es del poema «Tres notas del alma indígena» del conocido poeta peruano, José Santos Chocano. Aquí Chocano le habla al indio de hoy. Le pregunta si se ha olvidado de la grandeza del pasado, cuando los indios eran dueños de las Américas. La respuesta del indio, «¡Quién sabe, señor!», significa que se niega a opinar. Esa contestación es muy típica del habla del indio.

Vocabulario

la frente
el sudor
labrar

El indio está labrando la tierra.
Tiene una mirada taciturna, melancólica.
Está sudando (transpirando).

ignorar   no saber, no conocer   **el amo**   el jefe, el patrón, el dueño

Did You Know?

La papa o patata se cultivó por primera vez en la región andina. Los antiguos incas la cultivaban. Hoy los científicos y agrónomos se preocupan por la falta de variedad en la papa que se cultiva en Europa y América. Ellos van al Perú y Bolivia para asegurar que otras variedades antiguas se conserven en caso de alguna plaga que pudiera acabar con las pocas variedades que se están cultivando.

❧Práctica❧

A **La tierra** Contesten.

1. ¿Qué hace el indio?
2. ¿Qué expresión tiene en la cara?
3. ¿Por qué está sudando?
4. ¿Dónde tiene el sudor?

B **Una expresión equivalente** Expresen de otra manera.

1. El indio está *trabajando en el campo*.
2. Su *patrón* es bastante cruel.
3. El indio trabaja duro y está *transpirando*.
4. Tiene *una expresión* triste.
5. Él *no conoce* las grandezas pasadas de su gente.

Indígenas mayas

Indígena boliviana

Indígena peruano

TEACHING TIPS

These *Práctica* can be done orally with books closed immediately following the presentation of the vocabulary.

ANSWERS
Práctica

A 1. El indio está labrando la tierra.
  2. Tiene una mirada taciturna, melancólica.
  3. Está sudando porque está trabajando mucho.
  4. Tiene el sudor en la frente.
B 1. labrando la tierra
  2. amo
  3. sudando
  4. una mirada
  5. ignora

Learning From Photos

La señora en la foto a la izquierda lleva un sombrero de «hongo». Según la tradición, un fabricante británico llevó unos cuantos sombreros de este tipo a Bolivia y al Perú. A las «cholas», o señoras mestizas, les gustaron enormemente, y el comerciante inglés los vendió todos. Hoy se fabrican localmente, y las señoras todavía los llevan. El bilingüismo es más frecuente entre las mujeres que los hombres ya que son ellas las que se dedican a la compra y venta en los mercados donde tienen que usar el español.

TEACHING TIPS

Read the *Introducción* aloud to the class.

TEACHING THE READING

 Lectura ◆◆

A. Have students close their books, then read this selection aloud to them. Tell students to try to get the general idea.

B. Read the poem again as students follow along.

C. Give the students a few minutes to read the selection silently.

National Standards

Cultures
Students experience, discuss, and analyze an expressive product of the culture: the poem, «¡Quién sabe!» by the Ecuadorean poet, José Santos Chocano.

Introducción

José Santos Chocano (1875–1934) nació en el Perú. Durante su vida tumultuosa viajó por muchos países de Hispanoamérica y vivió varios años en Madrid. En sus poesías Chocano cantó las hazañas de su gente y describió la naturaleza americana: los volcanes, la cordillera andina y las selvas misteriosas.

Chocano se sentía inca. Él quería ser indio y español a la vez. Esa fusión de lo indígena y lo español la sentía en sus venas porque una de sus abuelas descendía de un capitán español y la otra era de una familia inca. La voz del poeta era la de un mestizo que conocía a su gente y su tierra. Se declaró a sí mismo cantor «autóctono y salvaje» de la América de habla española.
—Walt Whitman tiene el Norte, pero yo tengo el Sur, —dijo Chocano.

José Santos Chocano

Lectura

¡Quién sabe!

—Indio que labras con fatiga
tierras que de otros dueños son:
¿Ignoras tú que deben tuyas
ser, por tu sangre y tu sudor?
¿Ignoras tú que audaz codicia°,
siglos atrás te las quitó?
¿Ignoras tú que eres el Amo?
—¡Quién sabe, señor!

—Indio de frente taciturna
y de pupilas sin fulgor°.
¿Qué pensamiento es el que escondes
en tu enigmática° expresión?
¿Qué es lo que buscas en tu vida?
¿Qué es lo que imploras a tu Dios?
¿Qué es lo que sueña tu silencio?
—¡Quién sabe, señor!

audaz codicia *bold greed*

sin fulgor *without spark or brightness*

enigmática *puzzling*

Cultivo del maíz en el altiplano

Independent Practice

Assign any of the following:
1. Exercises, pages 407
2. Workbook, *Literatura*

Después de leer

Comprensión

A **El indio** Contesten.
1. ¿Qué hace el indio hasta estar rendido (muy cansado)?
2. ¿Cuáles son tres cosas que es posible que el indio no sepa?
3. ¿Cómo contesta el indio?
4. ¿Sabemos si el indio tiene las respuestas a las preguntas?

B **Sus tierras** Expliquen.
1. ¿Por qué le dice el autor al indio que las tierras deben ser suyas por su sangre y su sudor?
2. El autor le pregunta al indio si sabe que ya hace siglos una audaz codicia le quitó sus tierras. ¿A qué o a quiénes se refiere el autor?
3. ¿Por qué habrá escrito el autor *el amo* con letra mayúscula?

C **Chocano dice...** Contesten.
1. ¿Cómo describe José Santos Chocano a los indios?
2. ¿Cómo dice Chocano... ?
   El indio parece melancólico.
   Parece que no tiene alegría ni esperanza.
   Tiene una mirada vaga.
   Parece que está pensando en algo pero no se lo revela a nadie.

Actividades comunicativas

A **Latinoamérica** Ernest Lewald dice en su libro *Latinoamérica: Sus culturas y sociedades*: «Según los investigadores antropológicos, el indio latinoamericano añadió a su estoicismo y rutina de tiempos precolombinos el silencio y la introversión tan propia de pueblos subyugados. Ha sido muy fácil observar que el indio en la actualidad se muestra inaccesible y pasivo frente al hombre moderno, aunque es locuaz y cooperativo dentro de su grupo comunal». ¿Cómo coinciden las palabras del poeta José Santos Chocano con las observaciones de los investigadores antropológicos?

B **Un mensaje** Las obras de la mayoría de los intelectuales o de los escritores latinoamericanos tienen algún mensaje para el pueblo. En estos versos, ¿qué le está diciendo el poeta al indio? ¿Quiere Chocano que el indio acepte su situación con una resignación fatalista?

LITERATURA

cuatrocientos siete 🌣 **407**

CAPÍTULO 8
Literatura

TEACHING TIPS

These *Comprensión* can be assigned for homework and presented the next day in class.

ANSWERS
Comprensión

A 1. **El indio labra tierras.**
2. **Es posible que él no sepa que scn suyas las tierras, que audaz codicia se las quitó hace siglos y que él es el amo.**
3. **¡Quién sabe, señor!**
4. **No se sabe si el indio tiene las respuestas.**

B and **C** Answers will vary.

TEACHING TIPS

These *Actividades* give more able students ample opportunities to discuss the Indian question in more depth.

Actividades comunicativas

ANSWERS
A and **B** Answers will vary.

ABOUT THE SPANISH LANGUAGE

La «guagua» es el saco de tela en que se lleva al bebé. Por extensión, en Chile, el Perú y Bolivia al bebé o nene pequeño se le llama «guagua». En el Caribe y las islas Canarias, la «guagua» es el ómnibus.

Critical Thinking Activity

Thinking skills: identifying causes Los indígenas en las dos fotos no se parecen mucho. Los de la foto de abajo son yaguas, de la región amazónica. La señora de la foto de arriba es del altiplano. ¿A qué atribuyen estas diferencias? ¿Solamente al clima? ¿Hay otros factores? ¿Cuáles serán?

Did You Know?

Los yaguas varones llevaron faldas de colo- res brillantes hechas de un tipo de paja. Los primeros europeos que los vieron creyeron que eran mujeres. De allí, se dice, vino la leyenda de «las amazonas», tribus de feroces mujeres guerreras.

407

VISTAS DE VENEZUELA

OVERVIEW

The **Vistas de Venezuela** were prepared by National Geographic Society. Their purpose is to give students greater insight, through these visual images, into the culture and people of Venezuela. Have students look at the photographs on pages 408A-408B for enjoyment. If they would like to talk about them, let them say anything they can, using the vocabulary they have learned to this point.

National Standards

Cultures
The **Vistas de Venezuela** photos, and the accompanying captions, allow students to gain insights into the people of Venezuela.

Learning From Photos

1. **Selva tropical y salto de El Hacha** The Hacha Falls are in El Parque Nacional Canaima in the region of Guayana. The park covers some 3 million hectares and has a variety of rivers, tropical forests, waterfalls, and an exceptional array of flora and fauna.

2. **Caracas** Venezuela's capital and major city is near the Caribbean, but its port is La Guaira. At 950 meters (3,100 ft.) above sea level, the climate is springlike. Caracas is the economic and cultural hub of the nation.

3. **Mural de Bolívar, Ciudad Bolívar** Ciudad Bolívar is the capital of Bolívar state; Venezuela's largest in area, but not in population. It was founded in 1764 and was given the name *Santo Tomé de*

1. Selva tropical y cataratas de Hocha
2. Caracas
3. Pintando un mural de Simón Bolívar, Ciudad Bolívar
4. Guacamayo escarlata, Parque Nacional Canaima
5. Llanero con ganado, Río Orinoco
6. Hacienda cerca de Mérida
7. Monumento a los Próceres (héroes) de la Independencia, Caracas

408A

NATIONAL GEOGRAPHIC SOCIETY — TEACHER'S CORNER

INDEX TO NATIONAL GEOGRAPHIC MAGAZINE

The following articles may be used for research relating to this chapter:

- "Tracking the Anaconda," by Jesús Rivas, January 1999.
- "The Orinoco: Into the Heart of Venezuela," by Donovan Webster, April 1998.
- "Venezuela's Island in Time," by Uwe George, May 1989.
- "Simón Bolívar," by Bryan Hodgson, March 1994.

NATIONAL GEOGRAPHIC

VISTAS
DE VENEZUELA

(Continued from p. 408A) Guayana de Angostura del Orinoco, or simply *Angostura*.

4. **Papagayo, Parque Nacional Canaima** An example of the exquisite fauna to be found in the park. This is a scarlet macaw *(ara macao)*, one of the world's most beautiful birds and one of its most endangered.

5. **Ganado y llanero, el Llano** El Llano, is the area bordering on Colombia, including parts of the states of Bolívar, Apure, Guarico, Cojedes, Barinas, and Portuguesa. Herding is a major occupation of the region. The Llano has given its name to *llanero*, the cattle herder.

6. **Finca rural** An isolated valley farm. Although oil is Venezuela's major commodity today, agriculture is still important. Coffee is grown in the highlands and cacao on the lower slopes.

7. **Paseo los Próceres, Caracas** On each side of this walk are statues of the heroes of Venezuelan independence, *Los Próceres.* The *Paseo de los Próceres* is replete with paths, statuary, and fountains.

PRODUCTS AVAILABLE FROM GLENCOE/MCGRAW-HILL

To order the following products call Glencoe/McGraw-Hill at 1-800-334-7344.

CD-ROMs
· Picture Atlas of the World
· The Complete National Geographic: 109 Years of National Geographic Magazine

Software
· ZingoLingo: Spanish Diskettes

Transparency Set
· NGS PicturePack: Geography of South America

Videodisc
· STV: World Geography (Volume 3: "South America and Antarctica")

PRODUCTS AVAILABLE FROM NATIONAL GEOGRAPHIC SOCIETY

NATIONAL GEOGRAPHIC SOCIETY

To order the following products call National Geographic Society at 1-800-368-2728.

Books
· Exploring Your World: The Adventure of Geography
· National Geographic Satellite Atlas of the World

Video
· South America ("Nations of the World" Series)

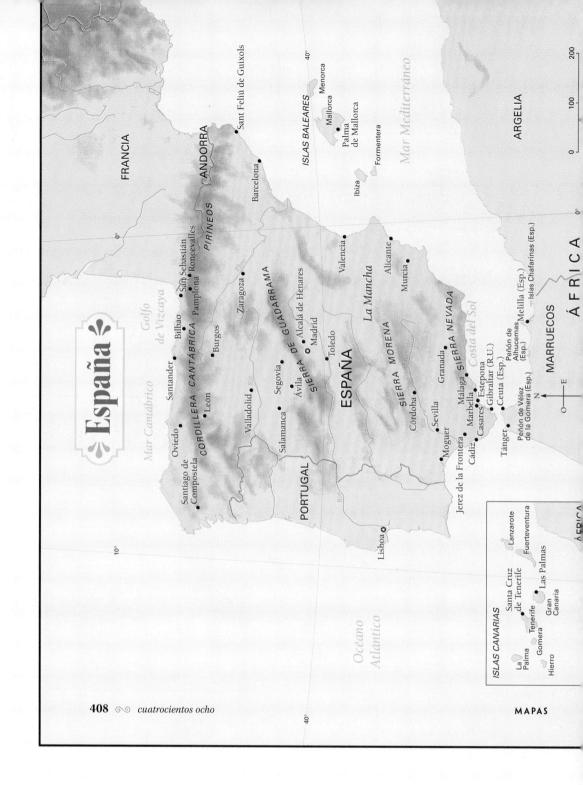

España

MAPAS

FRANCIA

ANDORRA

Sant Feliú de Guixols

Barcelona

Golfo de Vizcaya

Mar Cantábrico

San Sebastián
Pamplona Roncevalles
Bilbao
Santander
Oviedo
Burgos
Santiago de Compostela
León

PIRINEOS

CORDILLERA CANTÁBRICA

Zaragoza

Valladolid

Segovia
Salamanca
Ávila

SIERRA DE GUADARRAMA

Alcalá de Henares
Madrid
Toledo

ESPAÑA

La Mancha

Valencia

Alicante

Murcia

SIERRA MORENA

SIERRA NEVADA

Costa del Sol

Granada
Córdoba
Sevilla
Málaga
Marbella
Casares
Estepona
Cádiz
Jerez de la Frontera
Moguer
Tánger

Gibraltar (R.U.)
Ceuta (Esp.)
Peñón de Vélez
de la Gomera (Esp.)

Peñón de
Alhucemas
(Esp.)
Melilla (Esp.)
Islas Chafarinas (Esp.)

PORTUGAL

Lisboa

Océano Atlántico

Mar Mediterráneo

ISLAS BALEARES

Menorca
Mallorca
Palma
de Mallorca
Ibiza
Formentera

ARGELIA

MARRUECOS

ÁFRICA

N
O — E
S

40°

40°

10°

0°

0°

0 100 200

ISLAS CANARIAS

La Palma
Tenerife
Gomera
Hierro
Santa Cruz
de Tenerife
Gran
Canaria
Las Palmas
Lanzarote
Fuerteventura

ÁFRICA

408

La América del Sur

Mar Caribe

Cartagena
Maracaibo
Caracas
VENEZUELA
GUYANA
SURINAM
Georgetown
Paramaribo
Cayena

Medellín
Río Orinoco
Tolima
Santafé de Bogotá
GUAYANA FRANCESA
Cali
COLOMBIA

Océano Atlántico

Islas Galápagos (Ecuador)

Otavalo
Quito
Volcán Cotopaxi
ECUADOR
Guayaquil
Cuenca
Iquitos

Río Amazonas

PERÚ
Lima
MACHU PICCHU
Cuzco
Pisac
BOLIVIA
Miraflores
Lago Titicaca
Ica
La Paz
TIWANAKU
Sucre

BRASIL
Brasilia

ATACAMA DESERT

CORDILLERA DE LOS ANDES

PARAGUAY
Asunción
São Paulo
Río de Janeiro
Salta

Océano Pacífico

Vicuña
Córdoba
Viña del Mar
Mendoza
URUGUAY
Valparaíso
Rosario
Montevideo
Santiago
Buenos Aires
CHILE
ARGENTINA
Lago Villarrica
Mar del Plata
Pucón

Puerto Montt
Bariloche
Chiloé

PATAGONIA

0   500   1000
Kilómetros

Islas Malvinas (R.U.)

N
O   E
S

PARQUE NACIONAL TORRES DEL PAINE
Punta Arenas

MAPAS   cuatrocientos nueve ∿ 409

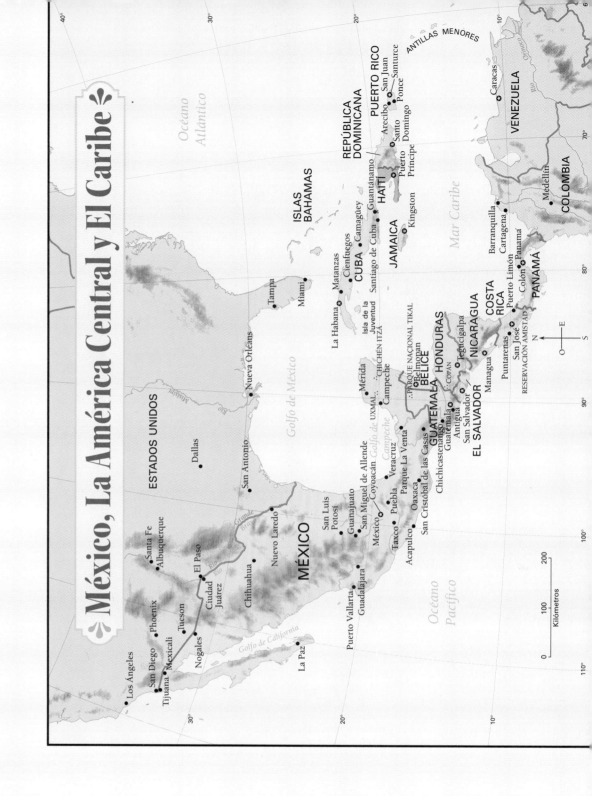

México, La América Central y El Caribe

ESTADOS UNIDOS

Los Angeles
San Diego
Tijuana • Mexicali
Phoenix
Nogales
Tucson
Santa Fe
Albuquerque
El Paso
Ciudad Juárez
Chihuahua
La Paz
Nuevo Laredo
Dallas
San Antonio
Nueva Orleans
Tampa
Miami

Golfo de California

MÉXICO

Puerto Vallarta
Guadalajara
San Luis Potosí
Guanajuato
San Miguel de Allende
México
Coyoacán
Taxco
Puebla
Veracruz
Parque La Venta
Oaxaca
Acapulco
San Cristóbal de las Casas
Mérida
Campeche
Golfo de UXMAL
Campeche
CHICHÉN ITZÁ

Océano Pacífico

Golfo de México

Río Grande
Río Bravo
Río Missouri

Océano Atlántico

ISLAS BAHAMAS

La Habana
Matanzas
Cienfuegos
CUBA
Camagüey
Isla de la Juventud
Santiago de Cuba
Guantánamo
HAITÍ
Puerto Príncipe
Santo Domingo
REPÚBLICA DOMINICANA
Arecibo • San Juan
Santurce
Ponce
PUERTO RICO

JAMAICA
Kingston

Mar Caribe

ANTILLAS MENORES

PARQUE NACIONAL TIKAL
Flores
Belmopan
BELICE
GUATEMALA
Guatemala
Antigua
COPÁN
Chichicastenango
HONDURAS
Tegucigalpa
San Salvador
EL SALVADOR
Managua
NICARAGUA
COSTA RICA
Puntarenas
San José
Puerto Limón
Colón • Panamá
RESERVACIÓN AMISTAD
PANAMÁ

Barranquilla
Cartagena
Medellín
COLOMBIA

Caracas
VENEZUELA
Río Orinoco

N
O — E
S

0   100   200
Kilómetros

40°   30°   20°   10°

110°   100°   90°   80°   70°

30°   20°   10°

410

Verbos

A. Verbos regulares

INFINITIVO	hablar *to speak*	
PARTICIPIO PRESENTE[1]	hablando	
PRESENTE	yo hablo tú hablas él, ella, Ud. habla	nosotros(as) hablamos *vosotros(as) habláis* ellos, ellas, Uds. hablan
PRETÉRITO	yo hablé tú hablaste él, ella, Ud. habló	nosotros(as) hablamos *vosotros(as) hablasteis* ellos, ellas, Uds. hablaron
IMPERFECTO	yo hablaba tú hablabas él, ella, Ud. hablaba	nosotros(as) hablábamos *vosotros(as) hablabais* ellos, ellas, Uds. hablaban
FUTURO	yo hablaré tú hablarás él, ella, Ud. hablará	nosotros(as) hablaremos *vosotros(as) hablaréis* ellos, ellas, Uds. hablarán
CONDICIONAL	yo hablaría tú hablarías él, ella, Ud. hablaría	nosotros(as) hablaríamos *vosotros(as) hablaríais* ellos, ellas, Uds. hablarían
PRESENTE PERFECTO[2]	yo he hablado tú has hablado él, ella, Ud. ha hablado	nosotros(as) hemos hablado *vosotros(as) habéis hablado* ellos, ellas, Uds. han hablado
PLUSCUAMPERFECTO	yo había hablado tú habías hablado él, ella, Ud. había hablado	nosotros(as) habíamos hablado *vosotros(as) habíais hablado* ellos, ellas, Uds. habían hablado
CONDICIONAL PERFECTO	yo habría hablado tú habrías hablado él, ella, Ud. habría hablado	nosotros(as) habríamos hablado *vosotros(as) habríais hablado* ellos, ellas, Uds. habrían hablado
FUTURO PERFECTO	yo habré hablado tú habrás hablado él, ella, Ud. habrá hablado	nosotros(as) habremos hablado *vosotros(as) habréis hablado* ellos, ellas, Uds. habrán hablado
SUBJUNTIVO PRESENTE	yo hable tú hables él, ella, Ud. hable	nosotros(as) hablemos *vosotros(as) habléis* ellos, ellas, Uds. hablen
SUBJUNTIVO IMPERFECTO	yo hablara tú hablaras él, ella, Ud. hablara	nosotros(as) habláramos *vosotros(as) hablarais* ellos, ellas, Uds. hablaran
PRESENTE PERFECTO DEL SUBJUNTIVO	yo haya hablado tú hayas hablado él, ella, Ud. haya hablado	nosotros(as) hayamos hablado *vosotros(as) hayáis hablado* ellos, ellas, Uds. hayan hablado
PLUSCUAMPERFECTO DEL SUBJUNTIVO	yo hubiera hablado tú hubieras hablado él, ella, Ud. hubiera hablado	nosotros(as) hubiéramos hablado *vosotros(as) hubierais hablado* ellos, ellas, Uds. hubieran hablado
IMPERATIVO FORMAL	hable Ud. hablen Uds.	
IMPERATIVO FAMILIAR	habla tú	

[1] Verbos con gerundio irregular: *caer: cayendo, construir: construyendo, contribuir: contribuyendo, distribuir: distribuyendo*

[2] Verbos con participio pasado irregular: *abrir: abierto, cubrir: cubierto, devolver: devuelto, escribir: escrito, freír: frito, morir: muerto, ver: visto*

Verbos regulares

INFINITIVO	comer *to eat*	
PARTICIPIO PRESENTE	comiendo	
PRESENTE	yo como tú comes él, ella, Ud. come	nosotros(as) comemos *vosotros(as) coméis* ellos, ellas, Uds. comen
PRETÉRITO	yo comí tú comiste él, ella, Ud. comió	nosotros(as) comimos *vosotros(as) comisteis* ellos, ellas, Uds. comieron
IMPERFECTO	yo comía tú comías él, ella, Ud. comía	nosotros(as) comíamos *vosotros(as) comíais* ellos, ellas, Uds. comían
FUTURO	yo comeré tú comerás él, ella, Ud. comerá	nosotros(as) comeremos *vosotros(as) comeréis* ellos, ellas, Uds. comerán
CONDICIONAL	yo comería tú comerías él, ella, Ud. comería	nosotros(as) comeríamos *vosotros(as) comeríais* ellos, ellas, Uds. comerían
PRESENTE PERFECTO	yo he comido tú has comido él, ella, Ud. ha comido	nosotros(as) hemos comido *vosotros(as) habéis comido* ellos, ellas, Uds. han comido
PLUSCUAMPERFECTO	yo había comido tú habías comido él, ella, Ud. había comido	nosotros(as) habíamos comido *vosotros(as) habíais comido* ellos, ellas, Uds. habían comido
CONDICIONAL PERFECTO	yo habría comido tú habrías comido él, ella, Ud. habría comido	nosotros(as) habríamos comido *vosotros(as) habríais comido* ellos, ellas, Uds. habrían comido
FUTURO PERFECTO	yo habré comido tú habrás comido él, ella, Ud. habrá comido	nosotros(as) habremos comido *vosotros(as) habréis comido* ellos, ellas, Uds. habrán comido
SUBJUNTIVO PRESENTE	yo coma tú comas él, ella, Ud. coma	nosotros(as) comamos *vosotros(as) comáis* ellos, ellas, Uds. coman
SUBJUNTIVO IMPERFECTO	yo comiera tú comieras él, ella, Ud. comiera	nosotros(as) comiéramos *vosotros(as) comierais* ellos, ellas, Uds. comieran
PRESENTE PERFECTO DEL SUBJUNTIVO	yo haya comido tú hayas comido él, ella, Ud. haya comido	nosotros(as) hayamos comido *vosotros(as) hayáis comido* ellos, ellas, Uds. hayan comido
PLUSCUAMPERFECTO DEL SUBJUNTIVO	yo hubiera comido tú hubieras comido él, ella, Ud. hubiera comido	nosotros(as) hubiéramos comido *vosotros(as) hubierais comido* ellos, ellas, Uds. hubieran comido
IMPERATIVO FORMAL	coma Ud. coman Uds.	
IMPERATIVO FAMILIAR	come tú	

Verbos regulares

INFINITIVO	**vivir** *to live*	
PARTICIPIO PRESENTE	viviendo	
PRESENTE	yo vivo tú vives él, ella, Ud. vive	nosotros(as) vivimos *vosotros(as) vivís* ellos, ellas, Uds. viven
PRETÉRITO	yo viví tú viviste él, ella, Ud. vivió	nosotros(as) vivimos *vosotros(as) vivisteis* ellos, ellas, Uds. vivieron
IMPERFECTO	yo vivía tú vivías él, ella, Ud. vivía	nosotros(as) vivíamos *vosotros(as) vivíais* ellos, ellas, Uds. vivían
FUTURO	yo viviré tú vivirás él, ella, Ud. vivirá	nosotros(as) viviremos *vosotros(as) viviréis* ellos, ellas, Uds. vivirán
CONDICIONAL	yo viviría tú vivirías él, ella, Ud. viviría	nosotros(as) viviríamos *vosotros(as) viviríais* ellos, ellas, Uds. vivirían
PRESENTE PERFECTO	yo he vivido tú has vivido él, ella, Ud. ha vivido	nosotros(as) hemos vivido *vosotros(as) habéis vivido* ellos, ellas, Uds. han vivido
PLUSCUAMPERFECTO	yo había vivido tú habías vivido él, ella, Ud. había vivido	nosotros(as) habíamos vivido *vosotros(as) habíais vivido* ellos, ellas, Uds. habían vivido
CONDICIONAL PERFECTO	yo habría vivido tú habrías vivido él, ella, Ud. habría vivido	nosotros(as) habríamos vivido *vosotros(as) habríais vivido* ellos, ellas, Uds. habrían vivido
FUTURO PERFECTO	yo habré vivido tú habrás vivido él, ella, Ud. habrá vivido	nosotros(as) habremos vivido *vosotros(as) habréis vivido* ellos, ellas, Uds. habrán vivido
SUBJUNTIVO PRESENTE	yo viva tú vivas él, ella, Ud. viva	nosotros(as) vivamos *vosotros(as) viváis* ellos, ellas, Uds. vivan
SUBJUNTIVO IMPERFECTO	yo viviera tú vivieras él, ella, Ud. viviera	nosotros(as) viviéramos *vosotros(as) vivierais* ellos, ellas, Uds. vivieran
PRESENTE PERFECTO DEL SUBJUNTIVO	yo haya vivido tú hayas vivido él, ella, Ud. haya vivido	nosotros(as) hayamos vivido *vosotros(as) hayáis vivido* ellos, ellas, Uds. hayan vivido
PLUSCUAMPERFECTO DEL SUBJUNTIVO	yo hubiera vivido tú hubieras vivido él, ella, Ud. hubiera vivido	nosotros(as) hubiéramos vivido *vosotros(as) hubierais vivido* ellos, ellas, Uds. hubieran vivido
IMPERATIVO FORMAL	viva Ud. vivan Uds.	
IMPERATIVO FAMILIAR	vive tú	

B. Verbos con cambio radical

INFINITIVO	pedir[3] (e>i) *to ask for*	
PARTICIPIO PRESENTE	pidiendo	
PRESENTE	yo pido tú pides él, ella, Ud. pide	nosotros(as) pedimos *vosotros(as) pedís* ellos, ellas, Uds. piden
PRETÉRITO	yo pedí tú pediste él, ella, Ud. pidió	nosotros(as) pedimos *vosotros(as) pedisteis* ellos, ellas, Uds. pidieron
IMPERFECTO	yo pedía tú pedías él, ella, Ud. pedía	nosotros(as) pedíamos *vosotros(as) pedíais* ellos, ellas, Uds. pedían
FUTURO	yo pediré tú pedirás él, ella, Ud. pedirá	nosotros(as) pediremos *vosotros(as) pediréis* ellos, ellas, Uds. pedirán
CONDICIONAL	yo pediría tú pedirías él, ella, Ud. pediría	nosotros(as) pediríamos *vosotros(as) pediríais* ellos, ellas, Uds. pedirían
PRESENTE PERFECTO	yo he pedido tú has pedido él, ella, Ud. ha pedido	nosotros(as) hemos pedido *vosotros(as) habéis pedido* ellos, ellas, Uds. han pedido
PLUSCUAMPERFECTO	yo había pedido tú habías pedido él, ella, Ud. había pedido	nosotros(as) habíamos pedido *vosotros(as) habíais pedido* ellos, ellas, Uds. habían pedido
CONDICIONAL PERFECTO	yo habría pedido tú habrías pedido él, ella, Ud. habría pedido	nosotros(as) habríamos pedido *vosotros(as) habríais pedido* ellos, ellas, Uds. habrían pedido
FUTURO PERFECTO	yo habré pedido tú habrás pedido él, ella, Ud. habrá pedido	nosotros(as) habremos pedido *vosotros(as) habréis pedido* ellos, ellas, Uds. habrán pedido
SUBJUNTIVO PRESENTE	yo pida tú pidas él, ella, Ud. pida	nosotros(as) pidamos *vosotros(as) pidáis* ellos, ellas, Uds. pidan
SUBJUNTIVO IMPERFECTO	yo pidiera tú pidieras él, ella, Ud. pidiera	nosotros(as) pidiéramos *vosotros(as) pidierais* ellos, ellas, Uds. pidieran
PRESENTE PERFECTO DEL SUBJUNTIVO	yo haya pedido tú hayas pedido él, ella, Ud. haya pedido	nosotros(as) hayamos pedido *vosotros(as) hayáis pedido* ellos, ellas, Uds. hayan pedido
PLUSCUAMPERFECTO DEL SUBJUNTIVO	yo hubiera pedido tú hubieras pedido él, ella, Ud. hubiera pedido	nosotros(as) hubiéramos pedido *vosotros(as) hubierais pedido* ellos, ellas, Uds. hubieran pedido
IMPERATIVO FORMAL	pida Ud. pidan Uds.	
IMPERATIVO FAMILIAR	pide tú	

[3]Verbos similares: *freír: friendo, repetir: repitiendo, seguir: siguiendo, sentir: sintiendo, medir: midiendo, sonreír: sonriendo*

Verbos con cambio radical

INFINITIVO	**preferir**[4] **(e>ie)** *to prefer*	
PARTICIPIO PRESENTE	prefiriendo	
PRESENTE	yo prefiero tú prefieres él, ella, Ud. prefiere	nosotros(as) preferimos *vosotros(as) preferís* ellos, ellas, Uds. prefieron
PRETÉRITO	yo preferí tú preferiste él, ella, Ud. prefirió	nosotros(as) preferimos *vosotros(as) preferisteis* ellos, ellas, Uds. prefirieron
IMPERFECTO	yo prefería tú preferías él, ella, Ud. prefería	nosotros(as) preferíamos *vosotros(as) preferíais* ellos, ellas, Uds. preferían
FUTURO	yo preferiré tú preferirás él, ella, Ud. preferirá	nosotros(as) preferiremos *vosotros(as) preferiréis* ellos, ellas, Uds. preferirán
CONDICIONAL	yo preferiría tú preferirías él, ella, Ud. preferiría	nosotros(as) preferiríamos *vosotros(as) preferiríais* ellos, ellas, Uds. preferirían
PRESENTE PERFECTO	yo he preferido tú has preferido él, ella, Ud. ha preferido	nosotros(as) hemos preferido *vosotros(as) habéis preferido* ellos, ellas, Uds. han preferido
PLUSCUAMPERFECTO	yo había preferido tú habías preferido él, ella, Ud. había preferido	nosotros(as) habíamos preferido *vosotros(as) habíais preferido* ellos, ellas, Uds. habían preferido
CONDICIONAL PERFECTO	yo habría preferido tú habrías preferido él, ella, Ud. habría preferido	nosotros(as) habríamos preferido *vosotros(as) habríais preferido* ellos, ellas, Uds. habrían preferido
FUTURO PERFECTO	yo habré preferido tú habrás preferido él, ella, Ud. habrá preferido	nosotros(as) habremos preferido *vosotros(as) habréis preferido* ellos, ellas, Uds. habrán preferido
SUBJUNTIVO PRESENTE	yo prefiera tú prefieras él, ella, Ud. prefiera	nosotros(as) prefiramos *vosotros(as) prefiráis* ellos, ellas, Uds. prefieran
SUBJUNTIVO IMPERFECTO	yo prefiriera tú prefirieras él, ella, Ud. prefiriera	nosotros(as) prefiriéramos *vosotros(as) prefirierais* ellos, ellas, Uds. prefirieran
PRESENTE PERFECTO DEL SUBJUNTIVO	yo haya preferido tú hayas preferido él, ella, Ud. haya preferido	nosotros(as) hayamos preferido *vosotros(as) hayáis preferido* ellos, ellas, Uds. hayan preferido
PLUSCUAMPERFECTO DEL SUBJUNTIVO	yo hubiera preferido tú hubieras preferido él, ella, Ud. hubiera preferido	nosotros(as) hubiéramos preferido *vosotros(as) hubierais preferido* ellos, ellas, Uds. hubieran preferido
IMPERATIVO FORMAL	prefiera Ud. prefieran Uds.	
IMPERATIVO FAMILIAR	prefiere tú	

[4]Verbos similares: *pensar: pensando, perder: perdiendo, sugerir: sugiriendo*

Verbos con cambio radical

INFINITIVO	**servir (e>i)** *to serve*	
PARTICIPIO PRESENTE	sirviendo	
PRESENTE	yo sirvo	nosotros(as) servimos
	tú sirves	*vosotros(as) servís*
	él, ella, Ud. sirve	ellos, ellas, Uds. sirvieron
PRETÉRITO	yo serví	nosotros(as) servimos
	tú serviste	*vosotros(as) servisteis*
	él, ella, Ud. sirvió	ellos, ellas, Uds. sirvieron
IMPERFECTO	yo servía	nosotros(as) servíamos
	tú servías	*vosotros(as) servíais*
	él, ella, Ud. servía	ellos, ellas, Uds. servían
FUTURO	yo serviré	nosotros(as) serviremos
	tú servirás	*vosotros(as) serviréis*
	él, ella, Ud. servirá	ellos, ellas, Uds. servirán
CONDICIONAL	yo serviría	nosotros(as) serviríamos
	tú servirías	*vosotros(as) serviríais*
	él, ella, Ud. serviría	ellos, ellas, Uds. servirían
PRESENTE PERFECTO	yo he servido	nosotros(as) hemos servido
	tú has servido	*vosotros(as) habéis servido*
	él, ella, Ud. ha servido	ellos, ellas, Uds. han servido
PLUSCUAMPERFECTO	yo había servido	nosotros(as) habíamos servido
	tú habías servido	*vosotros(as) habíais servido*
	él, ella, Ud. había servido	ellos, ellas, Uds. habían servido
CONDICIONAL PERFECTO	yo habría servido	nosotros(as) habríamos servido
	tú habrías servido	*vosotros(as) habríais servido*
	él, ella, Ud. habría servido	ellos, ellas, Uds. habrían servido
FUTURO PERFECTO	yo habré servido	nosotros(as) habremos servido
	tú habrás servido	*vosotros(as) habréis servido*
	él, ella, Ud. habrá servido	ellos, ellas, Uds. habrán servido
SUBJUNTIVO PRESENTE	yo sirva	nosotros(as) sirvamos
	tú sirvas	*vosotros(as) sirváis*
	él, ella, Ud. sirva	ellos, ellas, Uds. sirvan
SUBJUNTIVO IMPERFECTO	yo sirviera	nosotros(as) sirviéramos
	tú sirvieras	*vosotros(as) sirvierais*
	él, ella, Ud. sirviera	ellos, ellas, Uds. sirvieran
PRESENTE PERFECTO DEL SUBJUNTIVO	yo haya servido	nosotros(as) hayamos servido
	tú hayas servido	*vosotros(as) hayáis servido*
	él, ella, Ud. haya servido	ellos, ellas, Uds. hayan servido
PLUSCUAMPERFECTO DEL SUBJUNTIVO	yo hubiera servido	nosotros(as) hubiéramos servido
	tú hubieras servido	*vosotros(as) hubierais servido*
	él, ella, Ud. hubiera servido	ellos, ellas, Uds. hubieran servido
IMPERATIVO FORMAL	sirva Ud.	
	sirvan Uds.	
IMPERATIVO FAMILIAR	sirve tú	

Verbos con cambio radical

INFINITIVO	**volver[5] (o>ue)** *to return*	
PARTICIPIO PRESENTE	volviendo	
PRESENTE	yo vuelvo tú vuelves él, ella, Ud. vuelve	nosotros(as) volvemos *vosotros(as) volvéis* ellos, ellas, Uds. vuelven
PRETÉRITO	yo volví tú volviste él, ella, Ud. volvió	nosotros(as) volvimos *vosotros(as) volvisteis* ellos, ellas, Uds. volvieron
IMPERFECTO	yo volvía tú volvías él, ella, Ud. volvía	nosotros(as) volvíamos *vosotros(as) volvíais* ellos, ellas, Uds. volvían
FUTURO	yo volveré tú volverás él, ella, Ud. volverá	nosotros(as) volveremos *vosotros(as) volveréis* ellos, ellas, Uds. volverán
CONDICIONAL	yo volvería tú volverías él, ella, Ud. volvería	nosotros(as) volveríamos *vosotros(as) volveríais* ellos, ellas, Uds. volverían
PRESENTE PERFECTO	yo he vuelto tú has vuelto él, ella, Ud. ha vuelto	nosotros(as) hemos vuelto *vosotros(as) habéis vuelto* ellos, ellas, Uds. han vuelto
PLUSCUAMPERFECTO	yo había vuelto tú habías vuelto él, ella, Ud. había vuelto	nosotros(as) habíamos vuelto *vosotros(as) habíais vuelto* ellos, ellas, Uds. habían vuelto
CONDICIONAL PERFECTO	yo habría vuelto tú habrías vuelto él, ella, Ud. habría vuelto	nosotros(as) habríamos vuelto *vosotros(as) habríais vuelto* ellos, ellas, Uds. habrían vuelto
FUTURO PERFECTO	yo habré vuelto tú habrás vuelto él, ella, Ud. habrá vuelto	nosotros(as) habremos vuelto *vosotros(as) habréis vuelto* ellos, ellas, Uds. habrán vuelto
SUBJUNTIVO PRESENTE	yo vuelva tú vuelvas él, ella, Ud. vuelva	nosotros(as) volvamos *vosotros(as) volváis* ellos, ellas, Uds. vuelvan
SUBJUNTIVO IMPERFECTO	yo volviera tú volvieras él, ella, Ud. volviera	nosotros(as) volviéramos *vosotros(as) volvierais* ellos, ellas, Uds. volvieran
PRESENTE PERFECTO DEL SUBJUNTIVO	yo haya vuelto tú hayas vuelto él, ella, Ud. haya vuelto	nosotros(as) hayamos vuelto *vosotros(as) hayáis vuelto* ellos, ellas, Uds. hayan vuelto
PLUSCUAMPERFECTO DEL SUBJUNTIVO	yo hubiera vuelto tú hubieras vuelto él, ella, Ud. hubiera vuelto	nosotros(as) hubiéramos vuelto *vosotros(as) hubierais vuelto* ellos, ellas, Uds. hubieran vuelto
IMPERATIVO FORMAL	vuelva Ud. vuelvan Uds.	
IMPERATIVO FAMILIAR	vuelve tú	

[5] Verbos similares: *envolver: envolviendo, devolver: devolviendo.*

Verbos irregulares

INFINITIVO	buscar *to look for*	
PARTICIPIO PRESENTE	buscando	
PRESENTE	yo busco tú buscas él, ella, Ud. busca	nosotros(as) buscamos *vosotros(as) buscáis* ellos, ellas, Uds. buscan
PRETÉRITO	yo busqué tú buscaste él, ella, Ud. buscó	nosotros(as) buscamos *vosotros(as) buscasteis* ellos, ellas, Uds. buscaron
IMPERFECTO	yo buscaba tú buscabas él, ella, Ud. buscaba	nosotros(as) buscábamos *vosotros(as) buscabais* ellos, ellas, Uds. buscaban
FUTURO	yo buscaré tú buscarás él, ella, Ud. buscará	nosotros(as) buscaremos *vosotros(as) buscaréis* ellos, ellas, Uds. buscarán
CONDICIONAL	yo buscaría tú buscarías él, ella, Ud. buscaría	nosotros(as) buscaríamos *vosotros(as) buscaríais* ellos, ellas, Uds. buscarían
PRESENTE PERFECTO	yo he buscado tú has buscado él, ella, Ud. ha buscado	nosotros(as) hemos buscado *vosotros(as) habéis buscado* ellos, ellas, Uds. han buscado
PLUSCUAMPERFECTO	yo había buscado tú habías buscado él, ella, Ud. había buscado	nosotros(as) habíamos buscado *vosotros(as) habíais buscado* ellos, ellas, Uds. habían buscado
CONDICIONAL PERFECTO	yo habría buscado tú habrías buscado él, ella, Ud. habría buscado	nosotros(as) habríamos buscado *vosotros(as) habríais buscado* ellos, ellas, Uds. habrían buscado
FUTURO PERFECTO	yo habré buscado tú habrás buscado él, ella, Ud. habrá buscado	nosotros(as) habremos buscado *vosotros(as) habréis buscado* ellos, ellas, Uds. habrán buscado
SUBJUNTIVO PRESENTE	yo busque tú busques él, ella, Ud. busque	nosotros(as) busquemos *vosotros(as) busquéis* ellos, ellas, Uds. busquen
SUBJUNTIVO IMPERFECTO	yo buscara tú buscaras él, ella, Ud. buscara	nosotros(as) buscáramos *vosotros(as) buscarais* ellos, ellas, Uds. buscaran
PRESENTE PERFECTO DEL SUBJUNTIVO	yo haya buscado tú hayas buscado él, ella, Ud. haya buscado	nosotros(as) hayamos buscado *vosotros(as) hayáis buscado* ellos, ellas, Uds. hayan buscado
PLUSCUAMPERFECTO DEL SUBJUNTIVO	yo hubiera buscado tú hubieras buscado él, ella, Ud. hubiera buscado	nosotros(as) hubiéramos buscado *vosotros(as) hubierais buscado* ellos, ellas, Uds. hubieran buscado
IMPERATIVO FORMAL	busque Ud. busquen Uds.	
IMPERATIVO FAMILIAR	busca tú	

Verbos irregulares

INFINITIVO	conducir *to drive*	
PARTICIPIO PRESENTE	conduciendo	
PRESENTE	yo conduzco tú conduces él, ella, Ud. conduce	nosotros(as) conducimos *vosotros(as) conducís* ellos, ellas, Uds. conducen
PRETÉRITO	yo conduje tú condujiste él, ella, Ud. condujo	nosotros(as) condujimos *vosotros(as) condujisteis* ellos, ellas, Uds. condujeron
IMPERFECTO	yo conducía tú conducías él, ella, Ud. conducía	nosotros(as) conducíamos *vosotros(as) conducíais* ellos, ellas, Uds. conducían
FUTURO	yo conduciré tú conducirás él, ella, Ud. conducirá	nosotros(as) conduciremos *vosotros(as) conduciréis* ellos, ellas, Uds. conducirán
CONDICIONAL	yo conduciría tú conducirías él, ella, Ud. conduciría	nosotros(as) conduciríamos *vosotros(as) conduciríais* ellos, ellas, Uds. conducirían
PRESENTE PERFECTO	yo he conducido tú has conducido él, ella, Ud. ha conducido	nosotros(as) hemos conducido *vosotros(as) habéis conducido* ellos, ellas, Uds. han conducido
PLUSCUAMPERFECTO	yo había conducido tú habías conducido él, ella, Ud. había conducido	nosotros(as) habíamos conducido *vosotros(as) habíais conducido* ellos, ellas, Uds. habían conducido
CONDICIONAL PERFECTO	yo habría conducido tú habrías conducido él, ella, Ud. habría conducido	nosotros(as) habríamos conducido *vosotros(as) habríais conducido* ellos, ellas, Uds. habrían conducido
FUTURO PERFECTO	yo habré conducido tú habrás conducido él, ella, Ud. habrá conducido	nosotros(as) habremos conducido *vosotros(as) habréis conducido* ellos, ellas, Uds. habrán conducido
SUBJUNTIVO PRESENTE	yo conduzca tú conduzcas él, ella, Ud. conduzca	nosotros(as) conduzcamos *vosotros(as) conduzcáis* ellos, ellas, Uds. conduzcan
SUBJUNTIVO IMPERFECTO	yo condujera tú condujeras él, ella, Ud. condujera	nosotros(as) condujéramos *vosotros(as) condujerais* ellos, ellas, Uds. condujeran
PRESENTE PERFECTO DEL SUBJUNTIVO	yo haya conducido tú hayas conducido él, ella, Ud. haya conducido	nosotros(as) hayamos conducido *vosotros(as) hayáis conducido* ellos, ellas, Uds. hayan conducido
PLUSCUAMPERFECTO DEL SUBJUNTIVO	yo hubiera conducido tú hubieras conducido él, ella, Ud. hubiera conducido	nosotros(as) hubiéramos conducido *vosotros(as) hubierais conducido* ellos, ellas, Uds. hubieran conducido
IMPERATIVO FORMAL	conduzca Ud. conduzcan Uds.	
IMPERATIVO FAMILIAR	conduce tú	

Verbos irregulares

INFINITIVO	conocer *to know*	
PARTICIPIO PRESENTE	conociendo	
PRESENTE	yo conozco tú conoces él, ella, Ud. conoce	nosotros(as) conocemos *vosotros(as) conocéis* ellos, ellas, Uds. conocen
PRETÉRITO	yo conocí tú conociste él, ella, Ud. conoció	nosotros(as) conocimos *vosotros(as) conocisteis* ellos, ellas, Uds. conocieron
IMPERFECTO	yo conocía tú conocías él, ella, Ud. conocía	nosotros(as) conocíamos *vosotros(as) conocíais* ellos, ellas, Uds. conocían
FUTURO	yo conoceré tú conocerás él, ella, Ud. conocerá	nosotros(as) conoceremos *vosotros(as) conoceréis* ellos, ellas, Uds. conocerán
CONDICIONAL	yo conocería tú conocerías él, ella, Ud. conocería	nosotros(as) conoceríamos *vosotros(as) conoceríais* ellos, ellas, Uds. conocerían
PRESENTE PERFECTO	yo he conocido tú has conocido él, ella, Ud. ha conocido	nosotros(as) hemos conocido *vosotros(as) habéis conocido* ellos, ellas, Uds. han conocido
PLUSCUAMPERFECTO	yo había conocido tú habías conocido él, ella, Ud. había conocido	nosotros(as) habíamos conocido *vosotros(as) habíais conocido* ellos, ellas, Uds. habían conocido
CONDICIONAL PERFECTO	yo habría conocido tú habrías conocido él, ella, Ud. habría conocido	nosotros(as) habríamos conocido *vosotros(as) habríais conocido* ellos, ellas, Uds. habrían conocido
FUTURO PERFECTO	yo habré conocido tú habrás conocido él, ella, Ud. habrá conocido	nosotros(as) habremos conocido *vosotros(as) habréis conocido* ellos, ellas, Uds. habrán conocido
SUBJUNTIVO PRESENTE	yo conozca tú conozcas él, ella, Ud. conozca	nosotros(as) conozcamos *vosotros(as) conozcáis* ellos, ellas, Uds. conozcan
SUBJUNTIVO IMPERFECTO	yo conociera tú conocieras él, ella, Ud. conociera	nosotros(as) conociéramos *vosotros(as) conocierais* ellos, ellas, Uds. conocieran
PRESENTE PERFECTO DEL SUBJUNTIVO	yo haya conocido tú hayas conocido él, ella, Ud. haya conocido	nosotros(as) hayamos conocido *vosotros(as) hayáis conocido* ellos, ellas, Uds. hayan conocido
PLUSCUAMPERFECTO DEL SUBJUNTIVO	yo hubiera conocido tú hubieras conocido él, ella, Ud. hubiera conocido	nosotros(as) hubiéramos conocido *vosotros(as) hubierais conocido* ellos, ellas, Uds. hubieran conocido
IMPERATIVO FORMAL	conozca Ud. conozcan Uds.	
IMPERATIVO FAMILIAR	conoce tú	

Verbos irregulares

INFINITIVO	construir[6] *to build*	
PARTICIPIO PRESENTE	construyendo	
PRESENTE	yo construyo tú construyes él, ella, Ud. construye	nosotros(as) construimos *vosotros(as) construís* ellos, ellas, Uds. construyen
PRETÉRITO	yo construí tú construiste él, ella, Ud. construyó	nosotros(as) construimos *vosotros(as) construisteis* ellos, ellas, Uds. construyeron
IMPERFECTO	yo construía tú construías él, ella, Ud. construía	nosotros(as) construíamos *vosotros(as) construíais* ellos, ellas, Uds. construían
FUTURO	yo construiré tú construirás él, ella, Ud. construirá	nosotros(as) construiremos *vosotros(as) construiréis* ellos, ellas, Uds. construirán
CONDICIONAL	yo construiría tú construirías él, ella, Ud. construiría	nosotros(as) construiríamos *vosotros(as) construiríais* ellos, ellas, Uds. construirían
PRESENTE PERFECTO	yo he construido tú has construido él, ella, Ud. ha construido	nosotros(as) hemos construido *vosotros(as) habéis construido* ellos, ellas, Uds. han construido
PLUSCUAMPERFECTO	yo había construido tú habías construido él, ella, Ud. había construido	nosotros(as) habíamos construido *vosotros(as) habíais construido* ellos, ellas, Uds. habían construido
CONDICIONAL PERFECTO	yo habría construido tú habrías construido él, ella, Ud. habría construido	nosotros(as) habríamos construido *vosotros(as) habríais construido* ellos, ellas, Uds. habrían construido
FUTURO PERFECTO	yo habré construido tú habrás construido él, ella, Ud. habrá construido	nosotros(as) habremos construido *vosotros(as) habréis construido* ellos, ellas, Uds. habrán construido
SUBJUNTIVO PRESENTE	yo construya tú construyas él, ella, Ud. construya	nosotros(as) construyamos *vosotros(as) construyáis* ellos, ellas, Uds. construyan
SUBJUNTIVO IMPERFECTO	yo construyera tú construyeras él, ella, Ud. construyera	nosotros(as) construyéramos *vosotros(as) construyerais* ellos, ellas, Uds. construyeran
PRESENTE PERFECTO DEL SUBJUNTIVO	yo haya construido tú hayas construido él, ella, Ud. haya construido	nosotros(as) hayamos construido *vosotros(as) hayáis construido* ellos, ellas, Uds. hayan construido
PLUSCUAMPERFECTO DEL SUBJUNTIVO	yo hubiera construido tú hubieras construido él, ella, Ud. hubiera construido	nosotros(as) hubiéramos construido *vosotros(as) hubierais construido* ellos, ellas, Uds. hubieran construido
IMPERATIVO FORMAL	construya Ud. construyan Uds.	
IMPERATIVO FAMILIAR	construye tú	

[6]Verbos similares: *destruir: destruyendo, disminuir: disminuyendo, distribuir: distribuyendo, huir: huyendo, incluir: incluyendo, sustituir: sustituyendo*

VERBOS

Verbos irregulares

INFINITIVO	**dar** *to give*	
PARTICIPIO PRESENTE	dando	
PRESENTE	yo doy tú das él, ella, Ud. da	nosotros(as) damos *vosotros(as) dais* ellos, ellas, Uds. dan
PRETÉRITO	yo di tú diste él, ella, Ud. dio	nosotros(as) dimos *vosotros(as) disteis* ellos, ellas, Uds. dieron
IMPERFECTO	yo daba tú dabas él, ella, Ud. daba	nosotros(as) dábamos *vosotros(as) dabais* ellos, ellas, Uds. daban
FUTURO	yo daré tú darás él, ella, Ud. dará	nosotros(as) daremos *vosotros(as) daréis* ellos, ellas, Uds. darán
CONDICIONAL	yo daría tú darías él, ella, Ud. daría	nosotros(as) daríamos *vosotros(as) daríais* ellos, ellas, Uds. darían
PRESENTE PERFECTO	yo he dado tú has dado él, ella, Ud. ha dado	nosotros(as) hemos dado *vosotros(as) habéis dado* ellos, ellas, Uds. han dado
PLUSCUAMPERFECTO	yo había dado tú habías dado él, ella, Ud. había dado	nosotros(as) habíamos dado *vosotros(as) habíais dado* ellos, ellas, Uds. habían dado
CONDICIONAL PERFECTO	yo habría dado tú habrías dado él, ella, Ud. habría dado	nosotros(as) habríamos dado *vosotros(as) habríais dado* ellos, ellas, Uds. habrían dado
FUTURO PERFECTO	yo habré dado tú habrás dado él, ella, Ud. habrá dado	nosotros(as) habremos dado *vosotros(as) habréis dado* ellos, ellas, Uds. habrán dado
SUBJUNTIVO PRESENTE	yo dé tú des él, ella, Ud. dé	nosotros(as) demos *vosotros(as) deis* ellos, ellas, Uds. den
SUBJUNTIVO IMPERFECTO	yo diera tú dieras él, ella, Ud. diera	nosotros(as) diéramos *vosotros(as) dierais* ellos, ellas, Uds. dieran
PRESENTE PERFECTO DEL SUBJUNTIVO	yo haya dado tú hayas dado él, ella, Ud. haya dado	nosotros(as) hayamos dado *vosotros(as) hayáis dado* ellos, ellas, Uds. hayan dado
PLUSCUAMPERFECTO DEL SUBJUNTIVO	yo hubiera dado tú hubieras dado él, ella, Ud. hubiera dado	nosotros(as) hubiéramos dado *vosotros(as) hubierais dado* ellos, ellas, Uds. hubieran dado
IMPERATIVO FORMAL	dé Ud. den Uds.	
IMPERATIVO FAMILIAR	da tú	

Verbos irregulares

INFINITIVO	**decir** *to tell*	
PARTICIPIO PRESENTE	diciendo	
PRESENTE	yo digo tú dices él, ella, Ud. dice	nosotros(as) decimos *vosotros(as) decís* ellos, ellas, Uds. dicen
PRETÉRITO	yo dije tú dijiste él, ella, Ud. dijo	nosotros(as) dijimos *vosotros(as) dijisteis* ellos, ellas, Uds. dijeron
IMPERFECTO	yo decía tú decías él, ella, Ud. decía	nosotros(as) decíamos *vosotros(as) decíais* ellos, ellas, Uds. decían
FUTURO	yo diré tú dirás él, ella, Ud. dirá	nosotros(as) diremos *vosotros(as) diréis* ellos, ellas, Uds. dirán
CONDICIONAL	yo diría tú dirías él, ella, Ud. diría	nosotros(as) diríamos *vosotros(as) diríais* ellos, ellas, Uds. dirían
PRESENTE PERFECTO	yo he dicho tú has dicho él, ella, Ud. ha dicho	nosotros(as) hemos dicho *vosotros(as) habéis dicho* ellos, ellas, Uds. han dicho
PLUSCUAMPERFECTO	yo había dicho tú habías dicho él, ella, Ud. había dicho	nosotros(as) habíamos dicho *vosotros(as) habíais dicho* ellos, ellas, Uds. habían dicho
CONDICIONAL PERFECTO	yo habría dicho tú habrías dicho él, ella, Ud. habría dicho	nosotros(as) habríamos dicho *vosotros(as) habríais dicho* ellos, ellas, Uds. habrían dicho
FUTURO PERFECTO	yo habré dicho tú habrás dicho él, ella, Ud. habrá dicho	nosotros(as) habremos dicho *vosotros(as) habréis dicho* ellos, ellas, Uds. habrán dicho
SUBJUNTIVO PRESENTE	yo diga tú digas él, ella, Ud. diga	nosotros(as) digamos *vosotros(as) digáis* ellos, ellas, Uds. digan
SUBJUNTIVO IMPERFECTO	yo dijera tú dijeras él, ella, Ud. dijera	nosotros(as) dijéramos *vosotros(as) dijerais* ellos, ellas, Uds. dijeran
PRESENTE PERFECTO DEL SUBJUNTIVO	yo haya dicho tú hayas dicho él, ella, Ud. haya dicho	nosotros(as) hayamos dicho *vosotros(as) hayáis dicho* ellos, ellas, Uds. hayan dicho
PLUSCUAMPERFECTO DEL SUBJUNTIVO	yo hubiera dicho tú hubieras dicho él, ella, Ud. hubiera dicho	nosotros(as) hubiéramos dicho *vosotros(as) hubierais dicho* ellos, ellas, Uds. hubieran dicho
IMPERATIVO FORMAL	diga Ud. digan Uds.	
IMPERATIVO FAMILIAR	di tú	

Verbos irregulares

INFINITIVO	estar *to be*	
PARTICIPIO PRESENTE	estando	
PRESENTE	yo estoy tú estás él, ella, Ud. está	nosotros(as) estamos *vosotros(as) estáis* ellos, ellas, Uds. están
PRETÉRITO	yo estuve tú estuviste él, ella, Ud. estuvo	nosotros(as) estuvimos *vosotros(as) estuvisteis* ellos, ellas, Uds. estuvieron
IMPERFECTO	yo estaba tú estabas él, ella, Ud. estaba	nosotros(as) estábamos *vosotros(as) estabais* ellos, ellas, Uds. estaban
FUTURO	yo estaré tú estarás él, ella, Ud. estará	nosotros(as) estaremos *vosotros(as) estaréis* ellos, ellas, Uds. estarán
CONDICIONAL	yo estaría tú estarías él, ella, Ud. estaría	nosotros(as) estaríamos *vosotros(as) estaríais* ellos, ellas, Uds. estarían
PRESENTE PERFECTO	yo he estado tú has estado él, ella, Ud. ha estado	nosotros(as) hemos estado *vosotros(as) habéis estado* ellos, ellas, Uds. han estado
PLUSCUAMPERFECTO	yo había estado tú habías estado él, ella, Ud. había estado	nosotros(as) habíamos estado *vosotros(as) habíais estado* ellos, ellas, Uds. habían estado
CONDICIONAL PERFECTO	yo habría estado tú habrías estado él, ella, Ud. habría estado	nosotros(as) habríamos estado *vosotros(as) habríais estado* ellos, ellas, Uds. habrían estado
FUTURO PERFECTO	yo habré estado tú habrás estado él, ella, Ud. habrá estado	nosotros(as) habremos estado *vosotros(as) habréis estado* ellos, ellas, Uds. habrán estado
SUBJUNTIVO PRESENTE	yo esté tú estés él, ella, Ud. esté	nosotros(as) estemos *vosotros(as) estéis* ellos, ellas, Uds. estén
SUBJUNTIVO IMPERFECTO	yo estuviera tú estuvieras él, ella, Ud. estuviera	nosotros(as) estuviéramos *vosotros(as) estuvierais* ellos, ellas, Uds. estuvieran
PRESENTE PERFECTO DEL SUBJUNTIVO	yo haya estado tú hayas estado él, ella, Ud. haya estado	nosotros(as) hayamos estado *vosotros(as) hayáis estado* ellos, ellas, Uds. hayan estado
PLUSCUAMPERFECTO DEL SUBJUNTIVO	yo hubiera estado tú hubieras estado él, ella, Ud. hubiera estado	nosotros(as) hubiéramos estado *vosotros(as) hubierais estado* ellos, ellas, Uds. hubieran estado
IMPERATIVO FORMAL	esté Ud. estén Uds.	
IMPERATIVO FAMILIAR	está tú	

Verbos irregulares

INFINITIVO	hacer *to do*	
PARTICIPIO PRESENTE	haciendo	
PRESENTE	yo hago tú haces él, ella, Ud. hace	nosotros(as) hacemos *vosotros(as) hacéis* ellos, ellas, Uds. hacen
PRETÉRITO	yo hice tú hiciste él, ella, Ud. hizo	nosotros(as) hicimos *vosotros(as) hicisteis* ellos, ellas, Uds. hicieron
IMPERFECTO	yo hacía tú hacías él, ella, Ud. hacía	nosotros(as) hacíamos *vosotros(as) hacíais* ellos, ellas, Uds. hacían
FUTURO	yo haré tú harás él, ella, Ud. hará	nosotros(as) haremos *vosotros(as) haréis* ellos, ellas, Uds. harán
CONDICIONAL	yo haría tú harías él, ella, Ud. haría	nosotros(as) haríamos *vosotros(as) haríais* ellos, ellas, Uds. harían
PRESENTE PERFECTO	yo he hecho tú has hecho él, ella, Ud. ha hecho	nosotros(as) hemos hecho *vosotros(as) habéis hecho* ellos, ellas, Uds. han hecho
PLUSCUAMPERFECTO	yo había hecho tú habías hecho él, ella, Ud. había hecho	nosotros(as) habíamos hecho *vosotros(as) habíais hecho* ellos, ellas, Uds. habían hecho
CONDICIONAL PERFECTO	yo habría hecho tú habrías hecho él, ella, Ud. habría hecho	nosotros(as) habríamos hecho *vosotros(as) habríais hecho* ellos, ellas, Uds. habrían hecho
FUTURO PERFECTO	yo habré hecho tú habrás hecho él, ella, Ud. habrá hecho	nosotros(as) habremos hecho *vosotros(as) habréis hecho* ellos, ellas, Uds. habrán hecho
SUBJUNTIVO PRESENTE	yo haga tú hagas él, ella, Ud. haga	nosotros(as) hagamos *vosotros(as) hagáis* ellos, ellas, Uds. hagan
SUBJUNTIVO IMPERFECTO	yo hiciera tú hicieras él, ella, Ud. hiciera	nosotros(as) hiciéramos *vosotros(as) hicierais* ellos, ellas, Uds. hicieran
PRESENTE PERFECTO DEL SUBJUNTIVO	yo haya hecho tú hayas hecho él, ella, Ud. haya hecho	nosotros(as) hayamos hecho *vosotros(as) hayáis hecho* ellos, ellas, Uds. hayan hecho
PLUSCUAMPERFECTO DEL SUBJUNTIVO	yo hubiera hecho tú hubieras hecho él, ella, Ud. hubiera hecho	nosotros(as) hubiéramos hecho *vosotros(as) hubierais hecho* ellos, ellas, Uds. hubieran hecho
IMPERATIVO FORMAL	haga Ud. hagan Uds.	
IMPERATIVO FAMILIAR	haz tú	

Verbos irregulares

INFINITIVO	**ir**	
	to go	
PARTICIPIO PRESENTE	yendo	
PRESENTE	yo voy	nosotros(as) vamos
	tú vas	*vosotros(as) vais*
	él, ella, Ud. va	ellos, ellas, Uds. van
PRETÉRITO	yo fui	nosotros(as) fuimos
	tú fuiste	*vosotros(as) fuisteis*
	él, ella, Ud. fue	ellos, ellas, Uds. fueron
IMPERFECTO	yo iba	nosotros(as) íbamos
	tú ibas	*vosotros(as) ibais*
	él, ella, Ud. iba	ellos, ellas, Uds. iban
FUTURO	yo iré	nosotros(as) iremos
	tú irás	*vosotros(as) iréis*
	él, ella, Ud. irá	ellos, ellas, Uds. irán
CONDICIONAL	yo iría	nosotros(as) iríamos
	tú irías	*vosotros(as) iríais*
	él, ella, Ud. iría	ellos, ellas, Uds. irían
PRESENTE PERFECTO	yo he ido	nosotros(as) hemos ido
	tú has ido	*vosotros(as) habéis ido*
	él, ella, Ud. ha ido	ellos, ellas, Uds. han ido
PLUSCUAMPERFECTO	yo había ido	nosotros(as) habíamos ido
	tú habías ido	*vosotros(as) habíais ido*
	él, ella, Ud. había ido	ellos, ellas, Uds. habían ido
CONDICIONAL PERFECTO	yo habría ido	nosotros(as) habríamos ido
	tú habrías ido	*vosotros(as) habríais ido*
	él, ella, Ud. habría ido	ellos, ellas, Uds. habrían ido
FUTURO PERFECTO	yo habré ido	nosotros(as) habremos ido
	tú habrás ido	*vosotros(as) habréis ido*
	él, ella, Ud. habrá ido	ellos, ellas, Uds. habrán ido
SUBJUNTIVO PRESENTE	yo vaya	nosotros(as) vayamos
	tú vayas	*vosotros(as) vayáis*
	él, ella, Ud. vaya	ellos, ellas, Uds. vayan
SUBJUNTIVO IMPERFECTO	yo fuera	nosotros(as) fuéramos
	tú fueras	*vosotros(as) fuerais*
	él, ella, Ud. fuera	ellos, ellas, Uds. fueran
PRESENTE PERFECTO DEL SUBJUNTIVO	yo haya ido	nosotros(as) hayamos ido
	tú hayas ido	*vosotros(as) hayáis ido*
	él, ella, Ud. haya ido	ellos, ellas, Uds. hayan ido
PLUSCUAMPERFECTO DEL SUBJUNTIVO	yo hubiera ido	nosotros(as) hubiéramos ido
	tú hubieras ido	*vosotros(as) hubierais ido*
	él, ella, Ud. hubiera ido	ellos, ellas, Uds. hubieran ido
IMPERATIVO FORMAL	vaya Ud.	
	vayan Uds.	
IMPERATIVO FAMILIAR	ve tú	

Verbos irregulares

INFINITIVO	**jugar** *to play*	
PARTICIPIO PRESENTE	jugando	
PRESENTE	yo juego tú juegas él, ella, Ud. juega	nosotros(as) jugamos *vosotros(as) jugáis* ellos, ellas, Uds. juegan
PRETÉRITO	yo jugué tú jugaste él, ella, Ud. jugó	nosotros(as) jugamos *vosotros(as) jugasteis* ellos, ellas, Uds. jugaron
IMPERFECTO	yo jugaba tú jugabas él, ella, Ud. jugaba	nosotros(as) jugábamos *vosotros(as) jugabais* ellos, ellas, Uds. jugaban
FUTURO	yo jugaré tú jugarás él, ella, Ud. jugará	nosotros(as) jugaremos *vosotros(as) jugaréis* ellos, ellas, Uds. jugarán
CONDICIONAL	yo jugaría tú jugarías él, ella, Ud. jugaría	nosotros(as) jugaríamos *vosotros(as) jugaríais* ellos, ellas, Uds. jugarían
PRESENTE PERFECTO	yo he jugado tú has jugado él, ella, Ud. ha jugado	nosotros(as) hemos jugado *vosotros(as) habéis jugado* ellos, ellas, Uds. han jugado
PLUSCUAMPERFECTO	yo había jugado tú habías jugado él, ella, Ud. había jugado	nosotros(as) habíamos jugado *vosotros(as) habíais jugado* ellos, ellas, Uds. habían jugado
CONDICIONAL PERFECTO	yo habría jugado tú habrías jugado él, ella, Ud. habría jugado	nosotros(as) habríamos jugado *vosotros(as) habríais jugado* ellos, ellas, Uds. habrían jugado
FUTURO PERFECTO	yo habré jugado tú habrás jugado él, ella, Ud. habrá jugado	nosotros(as) habremos jugado *vosotros(as) habréis jugado* ellos, ellas, Uds. habrán jugado
SUBJUNTIVO PRESENTE	yo juegue tú juegues él, ella, Ud. juegue	nosotros(as) juguemos *vosotros(as) juguéis* ellos, ellas, Uds. jueguen
SUBJUNTIVO IMPERFECTO	yo jugara tú jugaras él, ella, Ud. jugara	nosotros(as) jugáramos *vosotros(as) jugarais* ellos, ellas, Uds. jugaran
PRESENTE PERFECTO DEL SUBJUNTIVO	yo haya jugado tú hayas jugado él, ella, Ud. haya jugado	nosotros(as) hayamos jugado *vosotros(as) hayáis jugado* ellos, ellas, Uds. hayan jugado
PLUSCUAMPERFECTO DEL SUBJUNTIVO	yo hubiera jugado tú hubieras jugado él, ella, Ud. hubiera jugado	nosotros(as) hubiéramos jugado *vosotros(as) hubierais jugado* ellos, ellas, Uds. hubieran jugado
IMPERATIVO FORMAL	juegue Ud. jueguen Uds.	
IMPERATIVO FAMILIAR	juega tú	

Verbos irregulares

INFINITIVO	**leer** *to read*	
PARTICIPIO PRESENTE	leyendo	
PRESENTE	yo leo tú lees él, ella, Ud. lee	nosotros(as) leemos *vosotros(as) leéis* ellos, ellas, Uds. leen
PRETÉRITO	yo leí tú leíste él, ella, Ud. leyó	nosotros(as) leímos *vosotros(as) leísteis* ellos, ellas, Uds. leyeron
IMPERFECTO	yo leía tú leías él, ella, Ud. leía	nosotros(as) leíamos *vosotros(as) leíais* ellos, ellas, Uds. leían
FUTURO	yo leeré tú leerás él, ella, Ud. leerá	nosotros(as) leeremos *vosotros(as) leeréis* ellos, ellas, Uds. leerán
CONDICIONAL	yo leería tú leerías él, ella, Ud. leería	nosotros(as) leeríamos *vosotros(as) leeríais* ellos, ellas, Uds. leerían
PRESENTE PERFECTO	yo he leído tú has leído él, ella, Ud. ha leído	nosotros(as) hemos leído *vosotros(as) habéis leído* ellos, ellas, Uds. han leído
PLUSCUAMPERFECTO	yo había leído tú habías leído él, ella, Ud. había leído	nosotros(as) habíamos leído *vosotros(as) habíais leído* ellos, ellas, Uds. habían leído
CONDICIONAL PERFECTO	yo habría leído tú habrías leído él, ella, Ud. habría leído	nosotros(as) habríamos leído *vosotros(as) habríais leído* ellos, ellas, Uds. habrían leído
FUTURO PERFECTO	yo habré leído tú habrás leído él, ella, Ud. habrá leído	nosotros(as) habremos leído *vosotros(as) habréis leído* ellos, ellas, Uds. habrán leído
SUBJUNTIVO PRESENTE	yo lea tú leas él, ella, Ud. lea	nosotros(as) leamos *vosotros(as) leáis* ellos, ellas, Uds. lean
SUBJUNTIVO IMPERFECTO	yo leyera tú leyeras él, ella, Ud. leyera	nosotros(as) leyéramos *vosotros(as) leyerais* ellos, ellas, Uds. leyeran
PRESENTE PERFECTO DEL SUBJUNTIVO	yo haya leído tú hayas leído él, ella, Ud. haya leído	nosotros(as) hayamos leído *vosotros(as) hayáis leído* ellos, ellas, Uds. hayan leído
PLUSCUAMPERFECTO DEL SUBJUNTIVO	yo hubiera leído tú hubieras leído él, ella, Ud. hubiera leído	nosotros(as) hubiéramos leído *vosotros(as) hubierais leído* ellos, ellas, Uds. hubieran leído
IMPERATIVO FORMAL	lea Ud. lean Uds.	
IMPERATIVO FAMILIAR	lee tú	

Verbos irregulares

INFINITIVO	oír
	to hear

PARTICIPIO PRESENTE	oyendo	

PRESENTE	yo oigo	nosotros(as) oímos
	tú oyes	*vosotros(as) oís*
	él, ella, Ud. oye	ellos, ellas, Uds. oyen
PRETÉRITO	yo oí	nosotros(as) oímos
	tú oíste	*vosotros(as) oísteis*
	él, ella, Ud. oyó	ellos, ellas, Uds. oyeron
IMPERFECTO	yo oía	nosotros(as) oíamos
	tú oías	*vosotros(as) oíais*
	él, ella, Ud. oía	ellos, ellas, Uds. oían
FUTURO	yo oiré	nosotros(as) oiremos
	tú oirás	*vosotros(as) oiréis*
	él, ella, Ud. oirá	ellos, ellas, Uds. oirán
CONDICIONAL	yo oiría	nosotros(as) oiríamos
	tú oirías	*vosotros(as) oiríais*
	él, ella, Ud. oiría	ellos, ellas, Uds. oirían
PRESENTE PERFECTO	yo he oído	nosotros(as) hemos oído
	tú has oído	*vosotros(as) habéis oído*
	él, ella, Ud. ha oído	ellos, ellas, Uds. han oído
PLUSCUAMPERFECTO	yo había oído	nosotros(as) habíamos oído
	tú habías oído	*vosotros(as) habíais oído*
	él, ella, Ud. había oído	ellos, ellas, Uds. habían oído
CONDICIONAL PERFECTO	yo habría oído	nosotros(as) habríamos oído
	tú habrías oído	*vosotros(as) habríais oído*
	él, ella, Ud. habría oído	ellos, ellas, Uds. habrían oído
FUTURO PERFECTO	yo habré oído	nosotros(as) habremos oído
	tú habrás oído	*vosotros(as) habréis oído*
	él, ella, Ud. habrá oído	ellos, ellas, Uds. habrán oído
SUBJUNTIVO PRESENTE	yo oiga	nosotros(as) oigamos
	tú oigas	*vosotros(as) oigáis*
	él, ella, Ud. oiga	ellos, ellas, Uds. oigan
SUBJUNTIVO IMPERFECTO	yo oyera	nosotros(as) oyéramos
	tú oyeras	*vosotros(as) oyerais*
	él, ella, Ud. oyera	ellos, ellas, Uds. oyeran
PRESENTE PERFECTO DEL SUBJUNTIVO	yo haya oído	nosotros(as) hayamos oído
	tú hayas oído	*vosotros(as) hayáis oído*
	él, ella, Ud. haya oído	ellos, ellas, Uds. hayan oído
PLUSCUAMPERFECTO DEL SUBJUNTIVO	yo hubiera oído	nosotros(as) hubiéramos oído
	tú hubieras oído	*vosotros(as) hubierais oído*
	él, ella, Ud. hubiera oído	ellos, ellas, Uds. hubieran oído
IMPERATIVO FORMAL	oiga Ud.	
	oigan Uds	
IMPERATIVO FAMILIAR	oye tú	

Verbos irregulares

INFINITIVO	**poder** *to be able*	
PARTICIPIO PRESENTE	pudiendo	
PRESENTE	yo puedo tú puedes él, ella, Ud. puede	nosotros(as) podemos *vosotros(as) podéis* ellos, ellas, Uds. pueden
PRETÉRITO	yo pude tú pudiste él, ella, Ud. pudo	nosotros(as) pudimos *vosotros(as) pudisteis* ellos, ellas, Uds. pudieron
IMPERFECTO	yo podía tú podías él, ella, Ud. podía	nosotros(as) podíamos *vosotros(as) podíais* ellos, ellas, Uds. podían
FUTURO	yo podré tú podrás él, ella, Ud. podrá	nosotros(as) podremos *vosotros(as) podréis* ellos, ellas, Uds. podrán
CONDICIONAL	yo podría tú podrías él, ella, Ud. podría	nosotros(as) podríamos *vosotros(as) podríais* ellos, ellas, Uds. podrían
PRESENTE PERFECTO	yo he podido tú has podido él, ella, Ud. ha podido	nosotros(as) hemos podido *vosotros(as) habéis podido* ellos, ellas, Uds. han podido
PLUSCUAMPERFECTO	yo había podido tú habías podido él, ella, Ud. había podido	nosotros(as) habíamos podido *vosotros(as) habíais podido* ellos, ellas, Uds. habían podido
CONDICIONAL PERFECTO	yo habría podido tú habrías podido él, ella, Ud. habría podido	nosotros(as) habríamos podido *vosotros(as) habríais podido* ellos, ellas, Uds. habrían podido
FUTURO PERFECTO	yo habré podido tú habrás podido él, ella, Ud. habrá podido	nosotros(as) habremos podido *vosotros(as) habréis podido* ellos, ellas, Uds. habrán podido
SUBJUNTIVO PRESENTE	yo pueda tú puedas él, ella, Ud. pueda	nosotros(as) podamos *vosotros(as) podáis* ellos, ellas, Uds. puedan
SUBJUNTIVO IMPERFECTO	yo pudiera tú pudieras él, ella, Ud. pudiera	nosotros(as) pudiéramos *vosotros(as) pudierais* ellos, ellas, Uds. pudieran
PRESENTE PERFECTO DEL SUBJUNTIVO	yo haya podido tú hayas podido él, ella, Ud. haya podido	nosotros(as) hayamos podido *vosotros(as) hayáis podido* ellos, ellas, Uds. hayan podido
PLUSCUAMPERFECTO DEL SUBJUNTIVO	yo hubiera podido tú hubieras podido él, ella, Ud. hubiera podido	nosotros(as) hubiéramos podido *vosotros(as) hubierais podido* ellos, ellas, Uds. hubieran podido
IMPERATIVO FORMAL	(no usado)	
IMPERATIVO FAMILIAR	(no usado)	

Verbos irregulares

INFINITIVO	**poner**	
	to put	
PARTICIPIO PRESENTE	poniendo	
PRESENTE	yo pongo	nosotros(as) ponemos
	tú pones	*vosotros(as) ponéis*
	él, ella, Ud. pone	ellos, ellas, Uds. ponen
PRETÉRITO	yo puse	nosotros(as) pusimos
	tú pusiste	*vosotros(as) pusisteis*
	él, ella, Ud. puso	ellos, ellas, Uds. pusieron
IMPERFECTO	yo ponía	nosotros(as) poníamos
	tú ponías	*vosotros(as) poníais*
	él, ella, Ud. ponía	ellos, ellas, Uds. ponían
FUTURO	yo pondré	nosotros(as) pondremos
	tú pondrás	*vosotros(as) pondréis*
	él, ella, Ud. pondrá	ellos, ellas, Uds. pondrán
CONDICIONAL	yo pondría	nosotros(as) pondríamos
	tú pondrías	*vosotros(as) pondríais*
	él, ella, Ud. pondría	ellos, ellas, Uds. pondrían
PRESENTE PERFECTO	yo he puesto	nosotros(as) hemos puesto
	tú has puesto	*vosotros(as) habéis puesto*
	él, ella, Ud. ha puesto	ellos, ellas, Uds. han puesto
PLUSCUAMPERFECTO	yo había puesto	nosotros(as) habíamos puesto
	tú habías puesto	*vosotros(as) habíais puesto*
	él, ella, Ud. había puesto	ellos, ellas, Uds. habían puesto
CONDICIONAL PERFECTO	yo habría puesto	nosotros(as) habríamos puesto
	tú habrías puesto	*vosotros(as) habríais puesto*
	él, ella, Ud. habría puesto	ellos, ellas, Uds. habrían puesto
FUTURO PERFECTO	yo habré puesto	nosotros(as) habremos puesto
	tú habrás puesto	*vosotros(as) habréis puesto*
	él, ella, Ud. habrá puesto	ellos, ellas, Uds. habrán puesto
SUBJUNTIVO PRESENTE	yo ponga	nosotros(as) pongamos
	tú pongas	*vosotros(as) pongáis*
	él, ella, Ud. ponga	ellos, ellas, Uds. pongan
SUBJUNTIVO IMPERFECTO	yo pusiera	nosotros(as) pusiéramos
	tú pusieras	*vosotros(as) pusierais*
	él, ella, Ud. pusiera	ellos, ellas, Uds. pusieran
PRESENTE PERFECTO DEL SUBJUNTIVO	yo haya puesto	nosotros(as) hayamos puesto
	tú hayas puesto	*vosotros(as) hayáis puesto*
	él, ella, Ud. haya puesto	ellos, ellas, Uds. hayan puesto
PLUSCUAMPERFECTO DEL SUBJUNTIVO	yo hubiera puesto	nosotros(as) hubiéramos puesto
	tú hubieras puesto	*vosotros(as) hubierais puesto*
	él, ella, Ud. hubiera puesto	ellos, ellas, Uds. hubieran puesto
IMPERATIVO FORMAL	ponga Ud.	
	pongan Uds.	
IMPERATIVO FAMILIAR	pon tú	

Verbos irregulares

INFINITIVO	**querer**
	to want, to love

PARTICIPIO PRESENTE	queriendo	
PRESENTE	yo quiero	nosotros(as) queremos
	tú quieres	*vosotros(as) queréis*
	él, ella, Ud. quiere	ellos, ellas, Uds. quieren
PRETÉRITO	yo quise	nosotros(as) quisimos
	tú quisiste	*vosotros(as) quisisteis*
	él, ella, Ud. quiso	ellos, ellas, Uds. quisieron
IMPERFECTO	yo quería	nosotros(as) queríamos
	tú querías	*vosotros(as) queríais*
	él, ella, Ud. quería	ellos, ellas, Uds. querían
FUTURO	yo querré	nosotros(as) querremos
	tú querrás	*vosotros(as) querréis*
	él, ella, Ud. querrá	ellos, ellas, Uds. querrán
CONDICIONAL	yo querría	nosotros(as) querríamos
	tú querrías	*vosotros(as) querríais*
	él, ella, Ud. querría	ellos, ellas, Uds. querrían
PRESENTE PERFECTO	yo he querido	nosotros(as) hemos querido
	tú has querido	*vosotros(as) habéis querido*
	él, ella, Ud. ha querido	ellos, ellas, Uds. han querido
PLUSCUAMPERFECTO	yo había querido	nosotros(as) habíamos querido
	tú habías querido	*vosotros(as) habíais querido*
	él, ella, Ud. había querido	ellos, ellas, Uds. habían querido
CONDICIONAL PERFECTO	yo habría querido	nosotros(as) habríamos querido
	tú habrías querido	*vosotros(as) habríais querido*
	él, ella, Ud. habría querido	ellos, ellas, Uds. habrían querido
FUTURO PERFECTO	yo habré querido	nosotros(as) habremos querido
	tú habrás querido	*vosotros(as) habréis querido*
	él, ella, Ud. habrá querido	ellos, ellas, Uds. habrán querido
SUBJUNTIVO PRESENTE	yo quiera	nosotros(as) queramos
	tú quieras	*vosotros(as) queráis*
	él, ella, Ud. quiera	ellos, ellas, Uds. quieran
SUBJUNTIVO IMPERFECTO	yo quisiera	nosotros(as) quisiéramos
	tú quisieras	*vosotros(as) quisierais*
	él, ella, Ud. quisiera	ellos, ellas, Uds. quisieran
PRESENTE PERFECTO DEL SUBJUNTIVO	yo haya querido	nosotros(as) hayamos querido
	tú hayas querido	*vosotros(as) hayáis querido*
	él, ella, Ud. haya querido	ellos, ellas, Uds. hayan querido
PLUSCUAMPERFECTO DEL SUBJUNTIVO	yo hubiera querido	nosotros(as) hubiéramos querido
	tú hubieras querido	*vosotros(as) hubierais querido*
	él, ella, Ud. hubiera querido	ellos, ellas, Uds. hubieran querido
IMPERATIVO FORMAL	quiera Ud.	
	quieran Uds.	
IMPERATIVO FAMILIAR	quiere tú	

Verbos irregulares

INFINITIVO	**saber** *to know*	
PARTICIPIO PRESENTE	sabiendo	
PRESENTE	yo sé tú sabes él, ella, Ud. sabe	nosotros(as) sabemos *vosotros(as) sabéis* ellos, ellas, Uds. saben
PRETÉRITO	yo supe tú supiste él, ella, Ud. supo	nosotros(as) supimos *vosotros(as) supisteis* ellos, ellas, Uds. supieron
IMPERFECTO	yo sabía tú sabías él, ella, Ud. sabía	nosotros(as) sabíamos *vosotros(as) sabíais* ellos, ellas, Uds. sabían
FUTURO	yo sabré tú sabrás él, ella, Ud. sabrá	nosotros(as) sabremos *vosotros(as) sabréis* ellos, ellas, Uds. sabrán
CONDICIONAL	yo sabría tú sabrías él, ella, Ud. sabría	nosotros(as) sabríamos *vosotros(as) sabríais* ellos, ellas, Uds. sabrían
PRESENTE PERFECTO	yo he sabido tú has sabido él, ella, Ud. ha sabido	nosotros(as) hemos sabido *vosotros(as) habéis sabido* ellos, ellas, Uds. han sabido
PLUSCUAMPERFECTO	yo había sabido tú habías sabido él, ella, Ud. había sabido	nosotros(as) habíamos sabido *vosotros(as) habíais sabido* ellos, ellas, Uds. habían sabido
CONDICIONAL PERFECTO	yo habría sabido tú habrías sabido él, ella, Ud. habría sabido	nosotros(as) habríamos sabido *vosotros(as) habríais sabido* ellos, ellas, Uds. habrían sabido
FUTURO PERFECTO	yo habré sabido tú habrás sabido él, ella, Ud. habrá sabido	nosotros(as) habremos sabido *vosotros(as) habréis sabido* ellos, ellas, Uds. habrán sabido
SUBJUNTIVO PRESENTE	yo sepa tú sepas él, ella, Ud. sepa	nosotros(as) sepamos *vosotros(as) sepáis* ellos, ellas, Uds. sepan
SUBJUNTIVO IMPERFECTO	yo supiera tú supieras él, ella, Ud. supiera	nosotros(as) supiéramos *vosotros(as) supierais* ellos, ellas, Uds. supieran
PRESENTE PERFECTO DEL SUBJUNTIVO	yo haya sabido tú hayas sabido él, ella, Ud. haya sabido	nosotros(as) hayamos sabido *vosotros(as) hayáis sabido* ellos, ellas, Uds. hayan sabido
PLUSCUAMPERFECTO DEL SUBJUNTIVO	yo hubiera sabido tú hubieras sabido él, ella, Ud. hubiera sabido	nosotros(as) hubiéramos sabido *vosotros(as) hubierais sabido* ellos, ellas, Uds. hubieran sabido
IMPERATIVO FORMAL	sepa Ud. sepan Uds.	
IMPERATIVO FAMILIAR	sabe tú	

Verbos irregulares

INFINITIVO	**salir** *to leave*	
PARTICIPIO PRESENTE	saliendo	
PRESENTE	yo salgo tú sales él, ella, Ud. sale	nosotros(as) salimos *vosotros(as) salís* ellos, ellas, Uds. salen
PRETÉRITO	yo salí tú saliste él, ella, Ud. salió	nosotros(as) salimos *vosotros(as) salisteis* ellos, ellas, Uds. salieron
IMPERFECTO	yo salía tú salías él, ella, Ud. salía	nosotros(as) salíamos *vosotros(as) salíais* ellos, ellas, Uds. salían
FUTURO	yo saldré tú saldrás él, ella, Ud. saldrá	nosotros(as) saldremos *vosotros(as) saldréis* ellos, ellas, Uds. saldrán
CONDICIONAL	yo saldría tú saldrías él, ella, Ud. saldría	nosotros(as) saldríamos *vosotros(as) saldríais* ellos, ellas, Uds. saldrían
PRESENTE PERFECTO	yo he salido tú has salido él, ella, Ud. ha salido	nosotros(as) hemos salido *vosotros(as) habéis salido* ellos, ellas, Uds. han salido
PLUSCUAMPERFECTO	yo había salido tú habías salido él, ella, Ud. había salido	nosotros(as) habíamos salido *vosotros(as) habíais salido* ellos, ellas, Uds. habían salido
CONDICIONAL PERFECTO	yo habría salido tú habrías salido él, ella, Ud. habría salido	nosotros(as) habríamos salido *vosotros(as) habríais salido* ellos, ellas, Uds. habrían salido
FUTURO PERFECTO	yo habré salido tú habrás salido él, ella, Ud. habrá salido	nosotros(as) habremos salido *vosotros(as) habréis salido* ellos, ellas, Uds. habrán salido
SUBJUNTIVO PRESENTE	yo salga tú salgas él, ella, Ud. salga	nosotros(as) salgamos *vosotros(as) salgáis* ellos, ellas, Uds. salgan
SUBJUNTIVO IMPERFECTO	yo saliera tú salieras él, ella, Ud. saliera	nosotros(as) saliéramos *vosotros(as) salierais* ellos, ellas, Uds. salieran
PRESENTE PERFECTO DEL SUBJUNTIVO	yo haya salido tú hayas salido él, ella, Ud. haya salido	nosotros(as) hayamos salido *vosotros(as) hayáis salido* ellos, ellas, Uds. hayan salido
PLUSCUAMPERFECTO DEL SUBJUNTIVO	yo hubiera salido tú hubieras salido él, ella, Ud. hubiera salido	nosotros(as) hubiéramos salido *vosotros(as) hubierais salido* ellos, ellas, Uds. hubieran salido
IMPERATIVO FORMAL	salga Ud. salgan Uds.	
IMPERATIVO FAMILIAR	sal tú	

Verbos irregulares

INFINITIVO	ser *to be*	
PARTICIPIO PRESENTE	siendo	
PRESENTE	yo soy tú eres él, ella, Ud. es	nosotros(as) somos *vosotros(as) sois* ellos, ellas, Uds. son
PRETÉRITO	yo fui tú fuiste él, ella, Ud. fue	nosotros(as) fuimos *vosotros(as) fuisteis* ellos, ellas, Uds. fueron
IMPERFECTO	yo era tú eras él, ella, Ud. era	nosotros(as) éramos *vosotros(as) erais* ellos, ellas, Uds. eran
FUTURO	yo seré tú serás él, ella, Ud. será	nosotros(as) seremos *vosotros(as) seréis* ellos, ellas, Uds. serán
CONDICIONAL	yo sería tú serías él, ella, Ud. sería	nosotros(as) seríamos *vosotros(as) seríais* ellos, ellas, Uds. serían
PRESENTE PERFECTO	yo he sido tú has sido él, ella, Ud. ha sido	nosotros(as) hemos sido *vosotros(as) habéis sido* ellos, ellas, Uds. han sido
PLUSCUAMPERFECTO	yo había sido tú habías sido él, ella, Ud. había sido	nosotros(as) habíamos sido *vosotros(as) habíais sido* ellos, ellas, Uds. habían sido
CONDICIONAL PERFECTO	yo habría sido tú habrías sido él, ella, Ud. habría sido	nosotros(as) habríamos sido *vosotros(as) habríais sido* ellos, ellas, Uds. habrían sido
FUTURO PERFECTO	yo habré sido tú habrás sido él, ella, Ud. habrá sido	nosotros(as) habremos sido *vosotros(as) habréis sido* ellos, ellas, Uds. habrán sido
SUBJUNTIVO PRESENTE	yo sea tú seas él, ella, Ud. sea	nosotros(as) seamos *vosotros(as) seáis* ellos, ellas, Uds. sean
SUBJUNTIVO IMPERFECTO	yo fuera tú fueras él, ella, Ud. fuera	nosotros(as) fuéramos *vosotros(as) fuerais* ellos, ellas, Uds. fueran
PRESENTE PERFECTO DEL SUBJUNTIVO	yo haya sido tú hayas sido él, ella, Ud. haya sido	nosotros(as) hayamos sido *vosotros(as) hayáis sido* ellos, ellas, Uds. hayan sido
PLUSCUAMPERFECTO DEL SUBJUNTIVO	yo hubiera sido tú hubieras sido él, ella, Ud. hubiera sido	nosotros(as) hubiéramos sido *vosotros(as) hubierais sido* ellos, ellas, Uds. hubieran sido
IMPERATIVO FORMAL	sea Ud. sean Uds.	
IMPERATIVO FAMILIAR	sé tú	

Verbos irregulares

INFINITIVO	**tener**	
	to have	
PARTICIPIO PRESENTE	teniendo	
PRESENTE	yo tengo	nosotros(as) tenemos
	tú tienes	*vosotros(as) tenéis*
	él, ella, Ud. tiene	ellos, ellas, Uds. tienen
PRETÉRITO	yo tuve	nosotros(as) tuvimos
	tú tuviste	*vosotros(as) tuvisteis*
	él, ella, Ud. tuvo	ellos, ellas, Uds. tuvieron
IMPERFECTO	yo tenía	nosotros(as) teníamos
	tú tenías	*vosotros(as) teníais*
	él, ella, Ud. tenía	ellos, ellas, Uds. tenían
FUTURO	yo tendré	nosotros(as) tendremos
	tú tendrás	*vosotros(as) tendréis*
	él, ella, Ud. tendrá	ellos, ellas, Uds. tendrán
CONDICIONAL	yo tendría	nosotros(as) tendríamos
	tú tendrías	*vosotros(as) tendríais*
	él, ella, Ud. tendría	ellos, ellas, Uds. tendrían
PRESENTE PERFECTO	yo he tenido	nosotros(as) hemos tenido
	tú has tenido	*vosotros(as) habéis tenido*
	él, ella, Ud. ha tenido	ellos, ellas, Uds. han tenido
PLUSCUAMPERFECTO	yo había tenido	nosotros(as) habíamos tenido
	tú habías tenido	*vosotros(as) habíais tenido*
	él, ella, Ud. había tenido	ellos, ellas, Uds. habían tenido
CONDICIONAL PERFECTO	yo habría tenido	nosotros(as) habríamos tenido
	tú habrías tenido	*vosotros(as) habríais tenido*
	él, ella, Ud. habría tenido	ellos, ellas, Uds. habrían tenido
FUTURO PERFECTO	yo habré tenido	nosotros(as) habremos tenido
	tú habrás tenido	*vosotros(as) habréis tenido*
	él, ella, Ud. habrá tenido	ellos, ellas, Uds. habrán tenido
SUBJUNTIVO PRESENTE	yo tenga	nosotros(as) tengamos
	tú tengas	*vosotros(as) tengáis*
	él, ella, Ud. tenga	ellos, ellas, Uds. tengan
SUBJUNTIVO IMPERFECTO	yo tuviera	nosotros(as) tuviéramos
	tú tuvieras	*vosotros(as) tuvierais*
	él, ella, Ud. tuviera	ellos, ellas, Uds. tuvieran
PRESENTE PERFECTO DEL SUBJUNTIVO	yo haya tenido	nosotros(as) hayamos tenido
	tú hayas tenido	*vosotros(as) hayáis tenido*
	él, ella, Ud. haya tenido	ellos, ellas, Uds. hayan tenido
PLUSCUAMPERFECTO DEL SUBJUNTIVO	yo hubiera tenido	nosotros(as) hubiéramos tenido
	tú hubieras tenido	*vosotros(as) hubierais tenido*
	él, ella, Ud. hubiera tenido	ellos, ellas, Uds. hubieran tenido
IMPERATIVO FORMAL	tenga Ud.	
	tengan Uds.	
IMPERATIVO FAMILIAR	ten tú	

Verbos irregulares

INFINITIVO	**traer** *to bring*	
PARTICIPIO PRESENTE	trayendo	
PRESENTE	yo traigo tú traes él, ella, Ud. trae	nosotros(as) traemos *vosotros(as) traéis* ellos, ellas, Uds. traen
PRETÉRITO	yo traje tú trajiste él, ella, Ud. trajo	nosotros(as) trajimos *vosotros(as) trajisteis* ellos, ellas, Uds. trajeron
IMPERFECTO	yo traía tú traías él, ella, Ud. traía	nosotros(as) traíamos *vosotros(as) traíais* ellos, ellas, Uds. traían
FUTURO	yo traeré tú traerás él, ella, Ud. traerá	nosotros(as) traeremos *vosotros(as) traeréis* ellos, ellas, Uds. traerán
CONDICIONAL	yo traería tú traerías él, ella, Ud. traería	nosotros(as) traeríamos *vosotros(as) traeríais* ellos, ellas, Uds. traerían
PRESENTE PERFECTO	yo he traído tú has traído él, ella, Ud. ha traído	nosotros(as) hemos traído *vosotros(as) habéis traído* ellos, ellas, Uds. han traído
PLUSCUAMPERFECTO	yo había traído tú habías traído él, ella, Ud. había traído	nosotros(as) habíamos traído *vosotros(as) habíais traído* ellos, ellas, Uds. habían traído
CONDICIONAL PERFECTO	yo habría traído tú habrías traído él, ella, Ud. habría traído	nosotros(as) habríamos traído *vosotros(as) habríais traído* ellos, ellas, Uds. habrían traído
FUTURO PERFECTO	yo habré traído tú habrás traído él, ella, Ud. habrá traído	nosotros(as) habremos traído *vosotros(as) habréis traído* ellos, ellas, Uds. habrán traído
SUBJUNTIVO PRESENTE	yo traiga tú traigas él, ella, Ud. traiga	nosotros(as) traigamos *vosotros(as) traigáis* ellos, ellas, Uds. traigan
SUBJUNTIVO IMPERFECTO	yo trajera tú trajeras él, ella, Ud. trajera	nosotros(as) trajéramos *vosotros(as) trajerais* ellos, ellas, Uds. trajeran
PRESENTE PERFECTO DEL SUBJUNTIVO	yo haya traído tú hayas traído él, ella, Ud. haya traído	nosotros(as) hayamos traído *vosotros(as) hayáis traído* ellos, ellas, Uds. hayan traído
PLUSCUAMPERFECTO DEL SUBJUNTIVO	yo hubiera traído tú hubieras traído él, ella, Ud. hubiera traído	nosotros(as) hubiéramos traído *vosotros(as) hubierais traído* ellos, ellas, Uds. hubieran traído
IMPERATIVO FORMAL	traiga Ud. traigan Uds.	
IMPERATIVO FAMILIAR	trae tú	

Verbos irregulares

INFINITIVO	venir *to come*	
PARTICIPIO PRESENTE	viniendo	
PRESENTE	yo vengo tú vienes él, ella, Ud. viene	nosotros(as) venimos *vosotros(as) venís* ellos, ellas, Uds. vienen
PRETÉRITO	yo vine tú viniste él, ella, Ud. vino	nosotros(as) vinimos *vosotros(as) vinisteis* ellos, ellas, Uds. vinieron
IMPERFECTO	yo venía tú venías él, ella, Ud. venía	nosotros(as) veníamos *vosotros(as) veníais* ellos, ellas, Uds. venían
FUTURO	yo vendré tú vendrás él, ella, Ud. vendrá	nosotros(as) vendremos *vosotros(as) vendréis* ellos, ellas, Uds. vendrán
CONDICIONAL	yo vendría tú vendrías él, ella, Ud. vendría	nosotros(as) vendríamos *vosotros(as) vendríais* ellos, ellas, Uds. vendrían
PRESENTE PERFECTO	yo he venido tú has venido él, ella, Ud. ha venido	nosotros(as) hemos venido *vosotros(as) habéis venido* ellos, ellas, Uds. han venido
PLUSCUAMPERFECTO	yo había venido tú habías venido él, ella, Ud. había venido	nosotros(as) habíamos venido *vosotros(as) habíais venido* ellos, ellas, Uds. habían venido
CONDICIONAL PERFECTO	yo habría venido tú habrías venido él, ella, Ud. habría venido	nosotros(as) habríamos venido *vosotros(as) habríais venido* ellos, ellas, Uds. habrían venido
FUTURO PERFECTO	yo habré venido tú habrás venido él, ella, Ud. habrá venido	nosotros(as) habremos venido *vosotros(as) habréis venido* ellos, ellas, Uds. habrán venido
SUBJUNTIVO PRESENTE	yo venga tú vengas él, ella, Ud. venga	nosotros(as) vengamos *vosotros(as) vengáis* ellos, ellas, Uds. vengan
SUBJUNTIVO IMPERFECTO	yo viniera tú vinieras él, ella, Ud. viniera	nosotros(as) viniéramos *vosotros(as) vinierais* ellos, ellas, Uds. vinieran
PRESENTE PERFECTO DEL SUBJUNTIVO	yo haya venido tú hayas venido él, ella, Ud. haya venido	nosotros(as) hayamos venido *vosotros(as) hayáis venido* ellos, ellas, Uds. hayan venido
PLUSCUAMPERFECTO DEL SUBJUNTIVO	yo hubiera venido tú hubieras venido él, ella, Ud. hubiera venido	nosotros(as) hubiéramos venido *vosotros(as) hubierais venido* ellos, ellas, Uds. hubieran venido
IMPERATIVO FORMAL	venga Ud. vengan Uds.	
IMPERATIVO FAMILIAR	ven tú	

Vocabulario español–inglés

Words without chapter references indicate either receptive vocabulary (not taught in the vocabulary sections) in Level 3 or vocabulary presented in Levels 1 and 2. Words followed by boldface numbers indicate vocabulary introduced for the first time in Level 3. Many of the meanings given in this glossary are taken directly from the context in which they appear in the text.

The following abbreviations are used in this glossary.

adj.	adjective
adv.	adverb
conj.	conjunction
dem. adj.	demonstrative adjective
dem. pron.	demonstrative pronoun
dir. obj.	direct object
f.	feminine
fam.	familiar
form.	formal
ind. obj.	indirect object
inf.	infinitive
inform.	informal
interr.	interrogative
interr. adj.	interrogative adjective
interr. pron.	interrogative pronoun
inv.	invariable
irreg.	irregular
m.	masculine
n.	noun
past. part.	past participle
pl.	plural
poss. adj.	possessive adjective
prep.	preposition
pron.	pronoun
sing.	singular
subj.	subject
subjunc.	subjunctive

A

a bordo on board
a eso de about, around
a menudo often
abajo below, **1**; down
abalanzar to contribute
abandonar to leave
el **abandono** abandonment, neglect
abarcar to comprise
el **abdomen** abdomen, **3**
la **abeja** bee, **4**
abnegado(a) self-sacrificing, **4**
el/la **abogado(a)** lawyer
abominable hateful
el/la **abonado(a)** subscriber
abordar to get on, board; to approach
   el **pase de abordar** boarding pass
aborrecer to hate, detest
abotagado(a) puffy
abotonar to button
abrazar (c) to embrace, hug
el **abrazo** hug
la **abreviatura** abbreviation
el **abrigo** overcoat
abril April
abrir to open
abrocharse to fasten
el **absceso** abscess
absolutamente absolutely
absoluto(a) absolute
absorber to absorb
la **abstinencia** abstinence
la **abstracción** abstraction
abstracto(a) abstract
abstraer to abstract
el/la **abuelo(a)** grandfather (grandmother)
   los **abuelos** grandparents
la **abundancia** abundance
abundante abundant
abundar to abound
aburrido(a) boring
el **aburrimiento** boredom
aburrir to bore
el **abuso** abuse
acabar de to have just (done something); to finish, **3**
   No te los acabas. Incredible.
la **academia** academy
académico(a) academic
el/la **académico(a)** academician

acampanado(a) in great danger
acampar to camp
acariciar to caress, **4**
el **acceso** access
el **accidente** accident
las **acciones** stock
el **aceite** oil
la **aceituna** olive, **8**
aceleradamente quickly
acelerar to accelerate
aceptar accept
la **acera** sidewalk
acercarse to approach
aciago(a) unfortunate
el **acíbar** bitterness
el **acierto** success
acomodado(a) well-to-do
acomodar to accommodate
acompañado(a) accompanied, **1**
el **acompañamiento** escort, **4**; accompaniment
acompañar to accompany
acondicionado(a) conditioned
aconsejable advisable
aconsejar to advise
el **acontecimiento** event, **3**
acorchado(a) lined with cork
acordarse (ue) to remember
acostado(a) stretched out
acostarse (ue) to go to bed
acostumbrarse to get used to, **2**
acrecentar to increase
la **actividad** activity
activo(a) active
el **acto** act, **3**
el **actor** actor
la **actriz** actress
la **actualidad** present time
las **actualidades** news, current events
actualmente at the present time
la **acuarela** water color
acuático: el esquí acuático water skiing
acudir a to go to; to attend, **1, 2, 3**
el **acueducto** aqueduct
el **acuerdo** agreement, pact, **7**
   de acuerdo according to; in agreement; okay, all right

acuífero(a) aquiferous, water-bearing
acusar to accuse; to acknowledge (receipt of a letter)
adaptar to adapt
adecuado(a) adequate
adelantar to overtake
además (de) besides
adentrar to search deeper
adentro inside
el/la **adherente** adherent
la **adicción** addiction
adinerado(a) wealthy
adiós good-bye
la **adivinanza** riddle, puzzle
adivinar to guess; to foretell, **6**
la **administración** administration
la **admiración** admiration
el **admirador** admirer
la **adolescencia** adolescence
el/la **adolescente** adolescent
adonde where
¿adónde? (to) where?
adoptar to adopt
adorable adorable
adorar to adore
adornar to adorn
el **adorno** ornament
adquirir to acquire
la **adquisición** acquisition
la **aduana** customs
el **adulto** adult, **2**
el/la **adversario(a)** adversary
la **advertencia** warning
aéreo(a) air (adj.)
   la **línea aérea** airline
   por correo aéreo by air mail
aeróbico(a) aerobic
el **aerodeslizador** hydrofoil
aerodinámico(a) aerodynamic
el **aerograma** aerogram
el **aeropuerto** airport
afectar to affect
el **afecto** affection, fondness, **6**
afectuoso(a) affectionate
afeitarse to shave
   la **crema de afeitar** shaving cream
aferrar to grasp, seize
la **afición** liking, enthusiasm, **6**

aficionado(a) fond of
afirmar to affirm
afirmativo(a) affirmative
africano(a) African
afrocubano(a) Afro-Cuban
afuera out; outside
las afueras outskirts
agachar to lower, bend
agarrar to get; to seize
agasajar to entertain
    splendidly
la agencia de viajes travel
    agency
el/la agente agent
ágil agile
la aglomeración collection
agonizante dying
agosto August
agotado(a) exhausted; sold-
    out
agotador(a) exhausting
agraciado(a) graceful,
    charming
agradable pleasant
agradar to please, 6
agradecer to thank
agregar (gu) to add
el/la agricultor farmer
la agricultura agriculture
agridulce bittersweet, 2
agrio(a) sour
agropecuario(a) pertaining
    to farming
la agrupación group
el agua (f.) water
    el agua bendita holy water
    el agua corriente running
        water
    el agua de colonia
        cologne
    el agua mineral mineral
        water
    las aguas negras sewage
el aguacate avocado
el aguacero downpour, 1
el aguamanil washstand
aguantar to bear; to tolerate;
    to hold up
aguardar to wait for
agudo(a) keen, sharp, 7
el águila (f.) eagle
el aguinaldo Christmas present
ahí there (adv.)
el/la ahijado(a) godchild

ahora now
ahorrar to save
los ahorros savings
ahuyentar to drive away
el aire air
    al aire libre outdoors
    el aire acondicionado air
        conditioning
aislado(a) isolated
ajeno(a) foreign, 2
el ajo garlic
ajustado(a) fitted
ajustar to adjust
al (a + el) to the, at the
el ala (f.) wing
el alambre wire
alargar to stretch out
el/la albañil mason
la alberca swimming pool
el albergue juvenil youth hostel
alborotado(a) rumpled
el alcalde mayor
la alcaldía city hall
el alcance reach
alcanzar (c) to reach
el alcázar castle, 5
el alcohol alcohol
la alcoholemia blood alcohol
    level
el alcoholismo alcoholism
la aldea village
alegrarse de to be glad about
alegre happy
la alegría happiness
alejarse to go far away, 3; to
    move away, leave
alemán (alemana) German
alentar to encourage
la alergia allergy
la alfabetización literacy
alfabetizar to teach to read
    and write, 8
el alfabeto alphabet, 8
el alga (f.) seaweed
el álgebra algebra
algo something
    ¿Algo más? Something
        more?
el algodón cotton
alguien somebody
algún, alguno(a) some, any
la alhambra Alhambra
el aliento breathing, 6
la alimentación food
alimentar to feed

alimentario nourishing
alimenticio(a) nutritional, 7
el alimento food, 7
aliviar to alleviate
allá there
allegado(a) near, close;
    related, 4
allí there
el alma (f.) soul, 4
el almacén department store
almacenar to store; to
    accumulate
la almeja clam
el almidón starch
el almirante admiral
la almohada pillow
almorzar to lunch
el almuerzo lunch
alojar to lodge, stay
la alpaca alpaca
el alpargatero shoemaker
el alpinismo mountain
    climbing
alquilar to rent
el alquiler rent
alrededor (de) around
los alrededores outskirts
el altar altar
la alteración alteration
alterar to alter
alternar to alternate
alternativo(a) alternate
el altiplano high plateau
la altitud altitude
alto(a) tall; high
la altura height; altitude
el/la alumno(a) student
alzar to raise, lift, 1
el ama (f.) de casa housewife, 2
la amabilidad kindness
amable kind
el amago beginning
amanecer to dawn, 7
la amapola poppy
amar to love, 1
amargo(a) bitter
la amargura bitterness
amarillo(a) yellow
Amazonas: el río Amazonas
    Amazon River
amazónico(a) Amazon,
    Amazonian
la ambición ambition
ambicioso(a) ambitious
ambiental environmental

el **ambiente** environment
ambos(as) both
la **ambulancia** ambulance
la **ameba** amoeba
amenazar to threaten
la **América del Sur** South
America
americano(a) American
el/la **amigo(a)** friend
el **aminoácido** amino acid
la **amistad** friendship
el/la **amo(a)** master; owner;
boss, **8**
las **amonestaciones** (marriage)
banns, **4**
el **amor** love
amoroso(a) amorous
amplio(a) large, roomy
amurallado(a) walled
el **análisis** analysis
analizar (c) to analyze
análogo(a) analogous
anaranjado(a) orange (color)
el/la **anarquista** anarchist
el/la **anatomista** anatomist
ancho(a) wide
la **anchura** width
el/la **anciano(a)** old person, **2**
el **ancla** (f.) anchor, **1**
andar (irreg.) to move; to
travel; to function; to walk
andar en monopatín to
skateboard
el **andén** railway platform
andino(a) Andean
andrajoso(a) ragged
la **anestesia** anesthesia
la anestesia local local
anesthesia
el/la **anestesista** anesthetist
el **ángel** angel
anglicanizado(a) anglicized
angosto(a) narrow, **1**
el **ángulo** angle
el **anillo** ring
el anillo de boda wedding
ring
el **animal** animal
animar to encourage
el **aniversario** anniversary
anoche last night
anónimo(a) anonymous
el **anorak** anorak
la **añoranza** nostalgia
anotar to write down, **8**

antaño long ago
antártico(a) antarctic
la **Antártida** Antarctic
anteayer day before
yesterday
el **antecedente** antecedent
antemano beforehand
antenupcial prenuptial
el **antepasado** ancestor, **8**
los **anteojos** eyeglasses, **2**
**los anteojos de (para el)
sol** sunglasses
anterior previous
antes de que before
los **antibióticos** antibiotics
anticipar to anticipate
la **antigüedad** antiquity, **8**
antiguo(a) ancient, old
antipático(a) unpleasant
(person)
el **antojo** craving
la **antropología** anthropology
el/la **antropólogo(a)**
anthropologist
anual annual
anualmente annually
anudar to tie, **7**
anular to cancel
anunciar to announce
el **anuncio** advertisement,
announcement
añadir to add
añejo(a) old
el **año** year
el año pasado last year
este año this year
hace muchos años many
years ago, it's been many
years
¡Próspero año nuevo!
Happy New Year!
apacible peaceful
apagar (gu) to turn off
el **aparato** apparatus,
appliance, **7**
aparcar (qu) to park
aparecer (zc) to appear
aparentar to feign
la **aparición** appearance, **4**
la **apariencia** appearance
el **apartado postal** post office
box
el **apartamento** apartment
apartar to separate
aparte separate

apasionadamente
passionately
el **apellido** last name
apenado(a) sad
apenas scarcely, barely
apesadumbrado(a)
saddened
apetecer to long for, **1**
el **apetito** appetite
el **apio** celery
aplaudir to applaud
el **aplauso** applause
aplicar to apply, employ
apocado(a) bashful, timid
el **apoderado** manager
apoderarse de to seize, take
possession of, **5**
el **apodo** nickname
el **apogeo** height (of power)
aportar to contribute,
bring, **6**
el **aporte** contribution
la **apostura** bearing
el **apotegma** maxim
apoyar to support
el **apoyo** support, help, **5**
apreciar to appreciate
aprender to learn
el/la **aprendiz(a)** apprentice,
beginner, **2**
el **aprendizaje** learning
apresurarse to hurry,
hasten, **7**
apretar (ie) to pinch
Me aprieta(n). It (They)
pinch(es) me. It's tight on
me.
aprobar to approve, **5**
apropiado(a) appropriate
aprovecharse to take
advantage
aproximadamente
approximately
apuesto(a) handsome,
elegant, **7**; tanned
los **apuntes** notes
tomar apuntes to take
notes
aquel, aquella that
aquél, aquélla that, that one
(dem. pron.)
aquesa that (Old Spanish)
aquí here
el/la **árabe** Arab
la **araña** spider

los **araucanos** Araucanians
el/la **árbitro(a)** referee
el **árbol** tree
  el **árbol genealógico** family
    tree
  el **árbol de Navidad**
    Christmas tree
ardiente burning, **1**
el **área** (f.) area
la **arena** sand; arena
arenisco(a) sandy
el **arete** earring, **1**
argentino(a) Argentinian
la **aristocracia** aristocracy
el/la **aristócrata** aristocrat
la **aritmética** arithmetic
el **arma** (f.) firearm, **2**
  armar una tienda to put up
    a tent
el **armario** closet
el **arnés** harness
el **aro** hoop
el **aroma** aroma
la **arqueología** archaeology
arqueológico(a)
  archaeological
el/la **arqueólogo(a)** archeologist
el **arquitecto** architect
la **arquitectura** architecture
arrancar to uproot
las **arras** dowry; thirteen
  coins the groom gives
  to the bride
arrasar to level
arrastrar to drag, **2**
arrebatado(a) impetuous
arreglar to fix
arreglarse to be settled
arrepentirse to be sorry
arriba above
arribar to arrive
arrimar to put or place near
arrojar to hurl
el **arroyo** stream; bed (of a
  stream), **8**
el **arroz** rice
arrugado(a) wrinkled
el **arte** art
  las bellas artes fine arts
el **artefacto** artifact
la **arteria** artery, main road
arterial arterial
artesanal craft (adj.)
la **artesanía** handicraft
el/la **artesano(a)** artisan

el **artículo** article
  el artículo de tocador
    toiletry
el **artilugio** gadget
el/la **artista** artist
  artístico: el patinaje artístico
    figure skating
el **asalto** assault
asar to broil
la **ascendencia** ancestry, **1, 8**
el **ascenso** promotion (in
  position), **6**
el **ascensor** elevator
asco: Me da asco. It disgusts
  me.
asegurar to insure;
  to assure, **2**
asemejarse to be similar, **6**
el **aseo** lavatory
asesinar to assassinate
el **asesinato** assassination
el **asfalto** asphalt
así thus
el **asiento** seat
  el número del asiento seat
    number
la **asignatura** subject
asimismo also
la **asistencia** assistance;
  attendance
el/la **asistente** attendant
  el asistente (la asistenta)
    de vuelo flight attendant
asistir to attend; to assist
asociar to associate
el **asombro** amazement
el **aspecto** aspect
el/la **aspirante** candidate
aspirar to breathe in
  aspirar a to aspire to
asqueroso(a) disgusting
la **astronomía** astronomy
asumir to assume
el **asunto** matter; subject
asustar to frighten, **6**
atacar (qu) to attack
el **ataque** attack
el **atardecer** late afternoon
el **ataúd** coffin, **2**
la **atención** attention, kindness
atender (ie) to attend to, take
  care of
atentar to attempt
atento(a) polite, courteous
el **aterrizaje** landing

aterrizar (c) to land
atesorar to treasure, store up
atestiguar to testify
Atlántico: Océano Atlántico
  Atlantic Ocean
el/la **atleta** athlete
la **atmósfera** atmosphere
atmosférico(a) atmospheric
el **atolondramiento** confusion
atómico(a) atomic
atontar to stun
atractivo(a) attractive
atraer to attract
atrapar to catch
atrás behind; back,
  backward, **8**
atravesar (ie) to cross, **2, 6;**
  to go through
atreverse to dare
el **atún** tuna
aturdido(a) dazed;
  bewildered, **6**
la **audacia** audacity
audaz bold
la **audición** hearing, **7**
los **audífonos** earphones
auditivo(a) auditive
el **auditorio** auditorium
el **auge** summit, apex, **8**
  en pleno auge at its peak
el **aula** (f.) classroom, **7**
aumentar to increase, **7**
el **aumento** increase
  en aumento on the
    increase
aun even
aún yet, still
aunque although
el **auricular** receiver (of
  telephone)
auscultar to listen with a
  stethoscope
la **ausencia** absence
ausente absent
austral southern
el **autobús** bus
  perder el autobús to miss
    the bus
autóctono(a) aboriginal,
  native, **8**
automáticamente
  automatically
automático(a) automatic
el **automóvil** car
la **autonomía** autonomy

la **autopista** super highway

el/la **autor(a)** author

las **autoridades** authorities

autorizado(a) authorized

autorizar to authorize, permit, **6**

el **autotransporte** transportation system

la **autovía** super highway

avanzado(a) advanced

avanzar to move forward

el **ave** (f.) bird

el ave picuda stork, **4**

la **avenida** avenue

la **aventura** adventure

el/la **aventurero(a)** adventurer

avergonzarse to be ashamed

la **aviación** aviation

el/la **aviador(a)** aviator

el **avión** airplane

el avión reactor jet

en avión by plane

la **avioneta** small airplane

avisar to notify, **1**

el **aviso** warning

el aviso luminoso neon sign, **2**

la **avispa** wasp

el **axioma** axiom

ayer yesterday

ayer por la mañana yesterday morning

ayer por la tarde yesterday afternoon

el **aymará** language of the Aymarás, **8**

los **aymarás** Indians of Bolivia and Peru, **2, 8**

la **ayuda** help

ayudar to help

el **ayuno** fast, **3**

el **ayuntamiento** city hall

el **azafrán** saffron

los **aztecas** Aztecs

el **azúcar** sugar

azucarar to add sugar, **2**

azul blue

azul marino navy blue

el **azulejo** tile, **7**

B

las **bacanales** orgies

el **bachillerato** bachelor's degree

la **bacteria** bacteria

el **bagaje** equipment, baggage

bailar to dance

el **baile** dance

bajar to go down

bajar del tren to get off the train

bajo below (prep.)

bajo cero below zero

bajo(a) short (person); low

el **balcón** balcony

la **baldosa** tile, **7**

la **ballena** whale

el **balneario** beach resort

el **balón** ball

el **baloncesto** basketball

la **banana** banana

bancario(a) banking

el **banco** bench; bank

el estado de banco (de cuenta) bank statement

la **banda** band, **3**

la **bandera** flag, **5**

el **bandido** bandit

el **bandoneón** concertina, **3**

el/la **banquero(a)** banker

el **banquete** banquet

el **bañador** bathing suit

bañarse to go for a swim; to take a bath

la **bañera** bathtub

el **baño** bathroom

el cuarto de baño bathroom

el traje de baño bathing suit

el **bar** bar

la **baraja** pack, deck (of cards), **6**

barato(a) cheap

la **barba** beard

bárbaro(a) barbarian; enormous

la **barbería** barber shop

el/la **barbero(a)** barber

el **barco** boat

el **barquito** small boat

la **barra** bar (of soap); (Argentina) group of friends, **3**

el **barril** barrel, **6**

el **barrio** neighborhood

basar to base

basarse to be based

la **báscula** scale

la **base** base

básico(a) basic

el **básquetbol** basketball

basta enough

bastante rather, quite

bastar to be enough

el **bastón** pole; club (golf)

basurear to throw away as trash

la **batalla** battle

el **bate** bat

el/la **bateador(a)** batter (baseball)

batear to hit (baseball)

la **batería** battery

batir to beat, **2**

la **batidora** beater

bautizar to baptize

el **bautizo** baptism, **5**

el **bazar** bazaar; marketplace, **1**

el/la **bebé** baby, **2**

beber to drink

la **bebida** drink

el/la **becario(a)** scholarship student

el **béisbol** baseball

belga Belgian

bélico(a) hostile, warlike

la **belleza** beauty

bello(a) beautiful

las bellas artes fine arts

bendecir to bless, **4**

bendito: ¡Ay, bendito! Dear Lord!

el **beneficio** benefit

benévolo(a) benevolent

besar to kiss

el **beso (besito)** kiss

bestial fabulous

la **biblioteca** library

la **bicicleta** bicycle

bien fine, well

bien cocido (hecho) well-done (meat)

los **bienes** goods

los bienes raíces real estate

el **bienestar** well-being

bienhechor(a) kind

la **bienvenida** welcome

el **biftec** steak

el **bigote** mustache

los **bigotes** whiskers, **2**

bilingüe bilingual

la **bilis** bile

el **billete** ticket; bill (money)

el billete sencillo one-way ticket

el billete de ida y vuelta round-trip ticket

biográfico(a) biographical

la **biología** biology

biológico(a) biological

el/la **biólogo(a)** biologist

el/la **bisabuelo(a)** great-grandparent, **8**

el/la **bisnieto(a)** great-grandchild, **4**

el **bizcocho** cookie

blanco(a) white

el **blanqueador** bleach

el **bloc** writing pad

bloquear to block

los **blue jeans** blue jeans

la **blusa** blouse

la blusa de cuello sin espalda halter, **13**

el **blusón** jacket

la **boca** mouth

la boca del metro entrance to subway, **2**

la **bocacalle** intersection

el **bocadillo** sandwich

el **boceto** sketch

la **bocina** receiver (of telephone); car horn

la **boda** wedding

el anillo de boda wedding ring

la **bofetada** slap, **6**

la **boina** beret, **3**

la **bola** (golf) ball

la **boletería** ticket window

el **boleto** ticket

el **bolígrafo** ballpoint pen

boliviano(a) Bolivian

la **bolsa** bag

la bolsa de plástico plastic bag

el **bolsillo** pocket, **5**

la **bomba**

la bomba de bencina gas pump, **2**

la **bondad** goodness, kindness, **6**

bondadoso(a) kind

bonito(a) pretty

bordado(a) embroidered, **1**

el **borde** edge; rim, **1, 7**

al borde de on the brink of

los **bordes de rush** hemline, **4**

bordo: a bordo de aboard, on board

el **bosque** forest

la **bota** boot

botado(a) en pinta better looking

la **botánica** botany; herbalist's shop

el **bote** can

la **botella** bottle

el **botiquín** medical kit, first-aid kit

el **botón** button

de (a) botones push button

el **botones** bellhop

el **boxeador** boxer

brasileño(a) Brazilian

el/la **bravucón(a)** braggart

la **bravura** bravery

el **brazo** arm; branch (of candelabra)

brillante bright, shining

brillar to shine

brincar to bounce

el **brinco** skip, hop, **3**

brindar to toast (to one's health), **4**

el **brindis** toast (to one's health), **4**

la **brisa** breeze

británico(a) British, **8**

la **broma** joke

bronceado(a) tanned

bronceadora: la crema bronceadora suntan lotion

broncearse to get a tan

bruñido(a) tanned

brusco(a) abrupt

bucear to skin-dive

el **buceo** skin diving

el **buche** mouthful

el **bucle** curl

la **buenaventura** fortune (as told by a fortune teller)

bueno(a) good

Buenas noches. Good evening. Good night.

Buenas tardes. Good afternoon.

Buenos días. Hello. Good morning.

la **buganvilla** bougainvillea

el **bulevar** boulevard

el **bullicio** noise

el **burro** donkey

el **bus** bus

la **busca** search

en busca de in search of, searching for

el/la **buscador(a)** searcher

buscar to look for

la **butaca** orchestra seat

la butaca de patio (orquesta) orchestra seat, **3**

el **buzo** jogging suit, diver

el **buzón** mailbox

C

el **caballero** knight; man, gentleman

el **caballo** horse

la **cabellera** hair

el **cabello** hair

caber: no cabe duda there is no doubt

el **cabestro** leading bull, **3**

la **cabeza** head

el dolor de cabeza headache

el **cabezal** small head pillow, **7**

la **cabina** booth

la cabina telefónica telephone booth

la cabina de mando (vuelo) cockpit

el **cable** cable

cabotaje: de cabotaje domestic

el **cacahuete** peanut

la **cacerola** saucepan, **7**

el **cacharro** useless thing, **2**

el **cacique** chief

cada each

el **cadáver** corpse, **2**

la **cadena** chain

la **caducidad** expiration

caerse (irreg.) to fall down

Se me cae el pelo. My hair is falling out.

el **café** coffee; café

la **cafetería** cafeteria, **7**

la **caída** downfall

la **caja** cash register; box, checkstand; cashier's desk

el/la **cajero(a)** cashier; teller

el **calabozo** jail, **8**

el **calamar** squid

los **calcetines** socks

el **calcio** calcium

el/la **calculador(a)** calculator

el **cálculo** calculus

el **caldo** stock, **2**

el **calendario** calendar

el **calentamiento** warming up, **3**

calentarse (ie) to warm, become warm

la **calidad** quality

caliente warm

la **calificación** grade

calificado(a) qualified

la **calistenia** calisthenics

callar(se) to be quiet, **3**

la **calle** street

callejero(a) pertaining to the street

la **callejuela** side street; alley

el **calmante** sedative

calmo(a) calm

el **calor** heat

Hace calor. It's hot.

la **caloría** calorie

la **calzada** highway, **1**

calzar to wear (shoes)

los **calzones** underpants, **3**

calzonudo(a) stupid

la **cama** bed

la **cámara: de cámara** court, royal

la **camarera** maid

el/la **camarero(a)** waiter (waitress)

el **camarón** shrimp, prawn

cambiar to change, exchange

cambiar de velocidad to shift gears

el **cambio** change; exchange rate

en cambio on the other hand

el **cambista** broker

el **camello** camel

el **camerino** dressing room, **3**

la **camilla** stretcher

caminar to walk

la **caminata** hike

dar una caminata to take a hike

caminero(a) (adj.) road

el **camino** road

el **camión** truck

la **camisa** shirt

la **camisa de deporte** sports shirt

la **camiseta** undershirt; T-shirt

el **campamento** camp

la **campana** bell, **1**

el **campanario** bell tower, **1**

la **campaña** campaign

la **tienda de campaña** tent

el/la **campeón(a)** champion

el **campeonato** championship

el/la **campesino(a)** peasant

el **camping** camping, campgrounds

ir de camping to go camping

el **campo** country; field

el **campo de fútbol** soccer field

el **camposanto** cemetery

la **caña de azúcar** sugar cane

canadiense(a) Canadian

el **canal** channel

el **canario** canary

la **canasta** basket

el **canasto** basket

el **cancel de tela** cloth screen

el **cáncer** cancer

la **cancha** court (sports)

la **cancha de tenis** tennis court

la **canción** song

la **candela** candle, **8**

el **candelabro** candelabra

el/la **candidato(a)** candidate

la **canica** marble, **4**

el **cañón** canyon, **1**

cansado(a) tired

cansarse to tire oneself

el/la **cantante** singer

el **cantar** song

cantar to sing

la **cantidad** quantity

la **cantimplora** canteen

la **cantina** lunchroom, **7**

el **canto** song

el/la **cantor(a)** singer, **3**

el **caos** chaos

la **capa** layer

en capas layered

el **capacho** basket

la **capacidad** capacity

capear un temporal to weather a storm

la **capital** capital

el/la **capitalino(a)** inhabitant of the capital

el **capitán** captain

capitanear to captain

el **capó** hood

el **capricho** whim, **2**

captar to capture

capturar to capture

la **cara** face

la **carabela** caravel, **5**

el **caracol** cochlea (internal ear)

el **carácter** character

la **característica** characteristic

característico(a) characteristic (adj.)

caracterizar to characterize

la **caravana** trailer; caravan

el **carbohidrato** carbohydrate

cardíaco(a) (adj.) cardiac, heart, **7**

la **careta** mask

los **cargadores** suspenders

el **cargo** care, control, **6**

a cargo de in charge of

el **Caribe** Caribbean

los **caribes** Caribs

la **caricatura** caricature, **1**

la **caridad** charity

la **caries** tooth cavity, **7**

el **cariño** affection

cariñosamente affectionately, **2**

cariñoso(a) affectionate

el **carmín** carmine, **2**

el **carnaval** carnival

la **carne** meat

la **carne de res** beef

la **carne molida** ground meat, **7**

el **carné** identification card, **6**

el **carnero** mutton

la **carnicería** butcher shop

el/la **carnicero(a)** butcher

carnívoro(a) carnivorous

caro(a) expensive

la **carpa** tent

el/la **carpintero(a)** carpenter

la **carrera** race, **7**; career

la **carretera** highway

el **carril** lane (of highway)

la **carrillada** jowl fat of a hog

el **carrito** shopping cart

el **carro** car

la **carta** letter

la **carta de memoria** memory chart

el **cartelón** poster, **6**

la **cartera** portfolio, **2**; wallet, **5**

el **carterista** pickpocket, **5**

el/la **cartero(a)** mail carrier
la **cartilla** reading primer, **8**
el **cartón** cardboard
la **casa** house
    la casa de huéspedes guest house
    la casa particular private house
    en casa at home
    ir a casa to go home
la **casa-remolque** trailer
el **casamiento** marriage, wedding
    casarse to get married
los **cascos azules** United Nations troops
el **caserío** country house, **6**
    casi almost
    casi crudo rare (cooked meat)
la **casilla** post office box
el **casillero** locker, **7**
el **casino** casino
el **caso** case
el **casquillo** cartridge
la **casta** caste; class (of society), **6**
    castaño(a) brown
el **castigo** punishment
el **castillo** castle
    castizo(a) real, legitimate, genuine
    catalán(a) Catalan
el **catálogo** catalogue
el **catarro** cold (medical)
    tener catarro to have a cold
la **catástrofe** catastrophe
el/la **cátcher** catcher
    cate failing (grade)
la **catedral** cathedral
la **categoría** category
el **catolicismo** Catholicism
    católico(a) Catholic
    caudaloso(a) abundant
la **causa** cause
    a causa de because of
    causar to cause
    cauteloso(a) cautious
el **cautiverio** captivity
    cautivo(a) captured
el/la **cautivo(a)** prisoner, captive, **5**
la **caza** (wild) game
    cazar (c) to hunt
la **cazuela** pot
la **cebolla** onion

la **celebración** celebration
    celebrar to celebrate
la **célula** cell
    celular cellular
el **cementerio** cemetery
el **cemento** cement
la **cena** dinner
    cenar to dine
la **censura** censorship
    censurar to criticize
el **centígrado** centigrade
el **centro** center
    el centro comercial shopping center
    Centroamérica Central America
    cepillarse to brush one's hair
el **cepillo** brush
el **cepillo de dientes** toothbrush, **7**
la **cera** wax
la **cerámica** ceramics, pottery
    cerca de near
la **cerca** fence, **4**
las **cercanías** outskirts
    cercano(a) near, close
el **cerdo** pork
el **cereal** cereal
la **ceremonia** ceremony
    ceremoniosamente ceremoniously
    ceremonioso(a) formal
la **cereza** cherry
la **cerilla** wax
    cero zero
    cerrar to close
el **cerro** hill, **1**
    cesar to cease
el **césped** grass, lawn, **7**
el **cesto** basket
la **chabola** shack
el **chaleco salvavidas** life vest
el **chaman** shaman
el **champú** shampoo
    chao good-bye
la **chaqueta** jacket
    charlar to chat
    chasquear to click
    checar to check
el **cheque** check
    el cheque de viajero traveler's check
la **chequera** checkbook

    chévere terrific
el/la **chico(a)** boy (girl)
    chico(a) young; little
    chileno(a) Chilean
el **chimpancé** chimpanzee
    chino(a) Chinese
el **chiste** joke
el **chocolate** chocolate
el **chofer** driver, **5**
la **chompa** jersey; sweater
el **chorizo** pork and garlic sausage
el **chorro** spurt
la **choza** shack
el **chubasco** squall, **1**
la **chuleta** chop
el **chuño** frozen dried potato
el **chupe** stew of fresh fish
el **churro** a type of doughnut
    churro(a) good-looking
la **chusma** crew, **1**
la **cicatriz** scar
el **ciclismo** cycling, **7**
el **ciclo** cycle
el **ciclomotor** motorbike
el/la **ciego(a)** blind person, **7**
el **cielo** sky
    el cielo raso ceiling
    cien(to) one hundred
la **ciencia** science
    la ciencia política political science
    las ciencias naturales natural sciences
    las ciencias sociales social sciences
    de ciencia ficción science fiction (adj.)
el/la **científico(a)** scientist
    científico(a) scientific (adj.)
    cierto(a) certain
el **cigarrillo** cigarette
el **cigarro** cigar
la **cigüeña** stork, **4**
    cinco five
    cincuenta fifty
el **cine** movie theater
    cinematográfico(a) cinematographic
    cínico(a) cynical
la **cinta** tape; ribbon
la **cintura** waist
el **cinturón** belt
    el cinturón de seguridad seat belt

el **circuito** circuit

la **circulación** circulation; traffic

circular circular (adj.); to circulate, travel

el **círculo** circle

la **circuncisión** circumcision

la **cirugía** surgery

el/la **cirujano(a)** surgeon

la **cita** date

citar to cite

la **ciudad** city

el/la **ciudadano(a)** citizen

la **ciudadela** citadel

civil civil; civilian, **2**

la **civilización** civilization

la **clara** egg white, **2**

el **clarinete** clarinet

claro (que sí) of course (adv.)

claro(a) clear (adj.)

la **clase** class

    la **clase alta** upper class

    la **clase media** middle class

    la **clase preferente** first class

clásico(a) classical

la **clasificación** classification

clasificar to classify

clavar to nail, stick

la **clave** key

    la **clave de área** area code

el **clavicordio** clavicord

el **claxon** car horn

el/la **cliente** client, customer

el **clima** climate

climático(a) climatic

la **clínica** clinic; private hospital

el/la **cobarde** coward, **6**

cobijar to cover

la **cobijita** baby blanket, **4**

la **coca** coca

la **cocción** cooking

el **coche** car; train car

    el **coche deportivo** sports car

    el **coche-cafetería** dining car

    el **coche-cama** sleeping car

el **coche-comedor** dining car

cocido(a) cooked

    bien cocido (hecho) well-done (meat)

la **cocina** cooking; kitchen

cocinar to cook

el/la **cocinero(a)** cook

el **coco** coconut

el **cóctel** cocktail

la **codicia** cupidity, greed

el **código de área** area code

el **código postal** zip code

el **codo** elbow

coeducacional coeducational

la **cofia** headwear

coger to seize

el **cohete** rocket, **3**

la **coincidencia** coincidence

coincidir to coincide

la **cola** line (of people); tail

    la **cola de caballo** pony tail

    hacer cola to line up

colaborar to collaborate

colar to strain, **2**

la **colección** collection

la **colecta** collection

el **colectivo** passenger vehicle, **5**

el **colegio** high school

el **colesterol** cholesterol

la **coleta** pigtail, queue

colgado(a) hanging on

el **colgador** clothes hanger

colgar (ue) to hang up

la **coliflor** cauliflower

la **colina** hill

el **collar** collar, necklace

colmar to lavish, heap

el **colmo** limit

    ¡Eso es el colmo! This is the last straw!

    para colmo to make matters worse

colocar to place, put

colombiano(a) Colombian

el **colón** colon

la **colonia** colony

colonial colonial

la **colonización** colonization

el/la **colonizador(a)** colonist

colonizar to colonize

el/la **colono** colonist

el **color** color

de color crema, vino, café, oliva, marrón, turquesa cream-, wine-, coffee-, olive-, brown-, turquoise-colored

la **comadrona** midwife

el/la **comandante** captain

el **combate** combat

la **combinación** combination

combinar to combine

la **comedia** comedy

comedido(a) discreet, **4**

el **comedor** dining room

el **comentario** commentary

comenzar (ie) (c) to begin, **7**

comer to eat

comercial of or pertaining to business

el/la **comerciante** businessman(woman); merchant

el **comercio** business

el **comestible** food

cometer to commit

la **comida** meal

    la **comida chatarra** junk food, **2**

    la **comida rápida** fast food

el **comienzo** beginning

la **comisaría** police station, **5**

como as, like

¿Cómo? What?; How?

    ¿Cómo estás? How are you?

    ¡Cómo no! Of course!

cómodamente comfortably

la **comodidad material** material comfort

las **comodidades** comforts

cómodo(a) comfortable

la **compañía** company

el/la **compañero(a)** friend, companion

comparable comparable

la **comparación** comparison

comparar to compare

la **comparsa** costumed group, **3**

el **compartimiento** compartment

compartir to share, **6**

compás: al compás de to the rhythm of, **3**

el/la **compatriota** compatriot

el **compendio** compendium

la **competencia** competition

competir to compete

completamente completely

completar to complete
completo(a) complete,
  perfect; full
  a tiempo completo full-
    time
la complicación complication
complicado(a) complicated
componer to compose
el comportamiento behavior
comportarse to behave
la composición composition
el/la compositor(a) composer
la compra y venta trade
el/la comprador(a) buyer
comprar to buy
compras: de compras
  shopping
comprender to understand
la comprensión comprehension
el comprimido pill
comprobar (ue) to prove
comprometer to pledge
comprometerse to get
  engaged
el/la comprometido(a) fiancé(e)
el compromiso engagement
  la sortija de compromiso
    engagement ring
el compuesto compound
compuesto(a) composed;
  made, produced, 8
el/la computador(a) computer
común common
la comunicación
  communication
el comunicado comuniqué, 4
comunicar to communicate;
  to inform, 8
comunicativo(a)
  communicative
la comunidad community
la comunión communion
con with
  con cuidado carefully
  con frecuencia frequently
  con lo bien que se pasa
    considering all the fun
    it is
  con retraso late
  con tal que provided that
  con una demora late
conceder to concede
concentrar to concentrate
el concepto concept
la concha shell

la conciencia conscience
el concierto concert
conciliar to reconcile
conciliar el sueño to induce
  sleep
conciliar la cuenta to
  balance the checkbook
el/la concurrente attendee, 4
el concurso contest
el conde count
condenar to condemn
condensar to condense
la condolencia condolence
el condominio condominium
la conducción driving
conducir (zc) to drive
la conducta conduct
el/la conductor(a) driver
conectar to connect
el conejo rabbit
la conexión connection
confeccionado(a) made
confeccionar to make,
  prepare, 1
la conferencia conference;
  lecture
la confianza confidence, trust
confiar to confide
la confirmación confirmation
la conflagración conflagration
el conflicto conflict
conforme con in agreement
  with
la confrontación confrontation
confrontar to confront
confundirse to be confused
confuso(a) confused
congelado(a) frozen
el congelador freezer
congregar to congregate,
  assemble
conmemorar to
  commemorate
conmigo with me (pron.)
conocer (zc) to know (a
  person)
el/la conocido(a) acquaintance
el conocimiento knowledge;
  understanding, 8
la conquista conquest
el/la conquistador(a) conqueror
conquistar to conquer
consciente conscious
la consecuencia consequence
consecutivo(a) consecutive

conseguir to obtain
el/la consejero(a) advisor
  el/la consejero(a) de
    orientación counselor
el consejo advice
conservador(a)
  conservative
conservar to conserve,
  preserve
considerar to consider
consiguiente: por
  consiguiente consequently
consistir to consist
el consomé consommé
constante constant
constantemente constantly
constar de to consist of, 4
constituir to constitute
la construcción construction
construir (y) to build,
  construct
la consulta del médico doctor's
  office
el consultorio del médico
  doctor's office
consumado(a) consummate
el/la consumidor(a) consumer
consumir to use up, 7; to
  consume
el consumo consumption
la contabilidad accounting
el/la contable accountant
la contaminación
  contamination
el contaminante contaminant
contaminar to contaminate
contemplar to contemplate
contemporáneo(a)
  contemporary
contener (irreg.) to contain
el contenido content
contento(a) happy
la contestación answer
el contestador answering
  machine
contestar to answer
la contienda fight
contigo with you (pron.)
el continente continent
el contingente contingent (of
  troops)
continuación: a
  continuación following,
  next
continuar to continue

contra against
en contra de against
contraer (irreg.) to contract
el **contralor** comptroller
la **contraloría** comptrollership
el **contrapeso** counterbalance
contrario(a) opposite
lo contrario the opposite
por el contrario on the contrary, vice versa, **2**
el **contraste** contrast
la **contribución** contribution
contribuir to contribute
el **control** inspection; control
el control de seguridad security inspection
el control de pasaportes passport inspection
controlado(a) controlled
el/la **controlador(a)** controller
controlar to control
controversial controversial
convencer to convince
convencido(a) convinced
la **convención** convention; agreement
conveniente convenient
convenir to agree
el **convento** convent
la **conversación** conversation
convertir (ie) to convert
convidar to invite
la **convivencia** reunion
el/la **cónyuge** spouse, **4**
la **coordinación** coordination
la **copa** cup
la Copa mundial World Cup
el/la **copiloto(a)** copilot
el **copo** flake, **1**
el copo de maíz cornflake
el **Corán** Koran
el **corazón** heart
el latido del corazón heartbeat
la **corbata** necktie
el **cordal inferior** bottom wisdom tooth
el **cordero** lamb
la **cordillera** mountain range
el **cordón** cord, **7**
coreano(a) Korean
la **corona** crown, **5, 8**
el **coronel** colonel
correcto(a) correct

corregir (j) to correct
el **correo** mail; post office
por correo aéreo by air mail
por correo certificado certified mail
por correo ordinario regular mail
por correo recomendado certified mail
correr to run
la **correspondencia** correspondence
corresponder to correspond
correspondiente corresponding
la **corrida de toros** bullfight
el **corrido** Mexican ballad
corriente common, usual
cortar to cut
la **corte** court
el **corte de pelo** haircut
cortés courteous
la **cortesía** courtesy
corto(a) short
el pantalón corto shorts
la **cosa** thing
la **cosecha** crop; harvest
la cosecha de maíz corn harvest, **8**
cosechar to harvest, reap, **2, 4**
los **cosméticos** cosmetics
cosmopolito(a) cosmopolitan
el **coso** bullring
la **costa** coast
costal coastal
costar (ue) to cost
costarricense Costa Rican
la **costilla** rib
la **costumbre** custom
costumbrista folkloric
cotidiano(a) (adj.) daily, **7**
el **cráneo** skull
el **cráter** crater
la **creación** creation
crear to create, establish
crecer to grow
crecido(a) big, large
creer (y) to believe
la **crema: la crema bronceadora** suntan cream
la crema de afeitar shaving cream

la crema protectora sunblock
la **cremallera** zipper
crespo(a) curly
la **criada** maid, **1**
el **criadero** breeding place
criar to raise
la **criatura** creature
el **crimen** crime, **5**
cristalino(a) crystalline, transparent
cristiano(a) Christian
criticar to criticize
el **croto** hedge plant
el **cruce** intersection
crucial crucial
la **crudeza** crudeness
crudo(a) raw
casi crudo rare (meat)
cruel cruel
el **crujido** crackle, creak
crujir to creak, **1**
la **cruz** cross, **2, 6**
cruzar (c) to cross
el **cuaderno** notebook
la **cuadra** (city) block
cuadrado(a) square
el **cuadrante** quadrant
el **cuadro** painting, picture
cuadros: a cuadros plaid
cual which
¿Cuál? What?; Which?
¿Cuál es la fecha de hoy? What is today's date?
la **cualidad** quality
la **cualificación** qualification
cualquier any
cualquiera lo sabe who knows
cuando when
de cuando en cuando from time to time
¿Cuándo? When?
cuanto as
en cuanto a as to
en cuanto as soon as
unos cuantos a few
¿Cuánto(a)? How much?
¿A cuánto está(n)? How much is it (are they)?
¿Cuánto cuesta? How much does it cost?
¿Cuánto es? How much is it?
¿Cuánto le debo? How much do I owe you?

cuarenta forty
la cuaresma Lent
cuarto fourth
y (menos) cuarto a
quarter after (to) (the
hour)
el cuarto room; quart
el cuarto sencillo single
room
el cuarto de dormir
bedroom
el cuarto de baño
bathroom
el cuarto doble double
room
el/la cuate (Mex.) friend
cuatro four
cubano(a) Cuban
cubierto(a) covered
cubrir to cover
la cuchara spoon
la cucharada spoonful, 2
la cucharita teaspoon
los cuchicheos whisperings
la cuchilla blade
el cuchillo knife
el cuello neck
la cuenta bill; account
la cuenta corriente
checking account
la cuenta de ahorros
savings account
el cuentagotas dropper
el/la cuentista storyteller
el cuento story
el cuerpo body
el Cuerpo de Paz Peace
Corps
el cuerpo diplomático
diplomatic corps
la cuesta slope
en cuesta baja going
downhill
la cuestión question
el cuidado care
con cuidado carefully
¡Cuidado! Be careful!
cuidar to take care of
culpable guilty, culpable, 8
el/la cultivador(a) cultivator
cultivar to develop; to
cultivate; to grow
el cultivo farming, 8
la cultura culture
cultural cultural

el cumpleaños birthday
¡Feliz cumpleaños! Happy
birthday!
el cumplimiento fulfillment
cumplir to be (so many
years) old; to fulfill
cumplir años to have one's
birthday
el/la cuñado(a) brother-in-law
(sister-in-law)
el cupé coupe
la cúpula dome
el cura priest
la cura cure, treatment
el curandero witch doctor
curar to cure
curiosamente curiously
la curiosidad curiosity
curioso(a) curious
el currículo profesional
curriculum vitae
el curso course
la curvatura curvature
curvo(a) curved
el cutis skin
cuyo(a) whose; of which

D

la dama lady
la dama de honor
bridesmaid
el/la damnificado(a) victim of a
disaster, 5
dañado(a) damaged, 7
dañar to damage
el daño damage
la danza dance, 3
el/la danzarín(a) dancer, 3
dar (irreg.) to give
dar a luz to deliver, give
birth, 4
dar la bienvenida to
welcome
dar la vuelta to turn
around
dar palmaditas to slap
gently
dar un dedazo to stick a
finger in
dar un paseo to take a
walk, 3
dar un paso to take a
step, 8
dar una caminata to
take a hike

dar una patada to
stamp, 1
dar una representación
to put on a
performance
dar vergüenza to feel
ashamed; to be
embarrassed, 6
dar vuelta to go around
darle cuerda a una
victrola to wind up a
victrola, 2
darse cuenta de to
realize
darse la mano to offer
one's hand; to shake
hands
darse prisa to rush,
hurry
darse una vuelta to go
for a walk
el dátil date (fruit)
el dato fact
de of, from, for
de equipo (adj.) team
de jazz (adj.) jazz
De nada. You're welcome.
de nuevo again
de rock (adj.) rock
de vez en cuando now
and then
debajo de under
deber to owe; (+ infinitive)
should, ought
debido a due to
debido(a) due, proper
débil weak
debilitarse to become
weak
la debutante debutant
debutar to make one's
debut
la década decade
la decadencia decadence
decapitar to decapitate
la decena ten (group of ten)
el decibel decibel
decidido(a) determined
decidir to decide
decimal decimal
décimo tenth
decir (irreg.) to tell, to say
la decisión decision
decisivamente decisively
declarar to declare

decrépito(a) decrepit
decretar to decree
la **dedicación** dedication
dedicado(a) dedicated
dedicar(se) to dedicate (oneself)
el **dedo** finger
  el dedo pequeño little
    finger
deducir to deduct, 1
el **defecto** defect
defender to defend
el/la **defensor(a)** defender
el **déficit** deficit
la **definición** definition
definitivo(a) final
  en definitiva finally
degustar to taste, sample, 4
dejar to leave (something
    behind); to allow
  dejar claro to make
    obvious, 2
  dejar por limosna to give
    as charity
  dejar una propina to leave
    a tip
del (de + el) from the,
    of the
delante de in front of
delantero(a) front
delicado(a) delicate
delicioso(a) delicious
el/la **delincuente** criminal
la **demanda** demand
  demandar to file a suit
    against, 5
los **demás** others, 3
  demasiado too, too much
democrático(s) democratic
la **demografía** demography
la **demora** delay
  con una demora late
demostrar to demonstrate
la **denominación** denomination
la **densidad** density
  denso(a) thick
la **dentadura postiza** set of false
    teeth
el **dentífrico** toothpaste, 7
el/la **dentista** dentist, 7
dentro de in; inside (adv.);
    within
  dentro de poco soon
denunciar to report (a crime)
el **departamento** province,
    district; department

el **departamento
    (servicio) de personal**
    personnel (human
    resources) department
el **departamento de
    recursos humanos**
    personnel (human
    resources) department
depender (ie) to depend
los **deportes** sports
deportivo(a) related to
    sports
depositar to deposit
el **depósito** deposit
depredador(a) plunderer
deprimido(a) depressed
la **derecha** right
  a la derecha to the right
el **derecho** law; right
  derecho(a) straight; right,
    right-hand
deriva: a la deriva adrift
derivar to come from
derretir to melt
derrocar to overthrow
la **derrota** defeat
derrotar to defeat
derruido(a) pulled down
derrumbado(a) fallen
derrumbar to fail; to knock
    down
el **derrumbe** collapse
desabotonar to unbutton
el **desacuerdo** disagreement
desafiar to dare
desaparecer (zc) to
    disappear
desaprobado(a) failing
desarmado(a) disarmed
desarmar to disarm
desarrollar to develop; to
    promote, 8
el **desarrollo** development
el **desasosiego** uneasiness
el **desastre** disaster
desayunarse to eat breakfast
el **desayuno** breakfast
el **desbarajuste** disorder, mess
descalzo(a) barefoot
el **descampado** open country
descansado(a) rested
descansar to rest
el **descanso** intermission, 3
el **descapotable** convertible
descargar to unload

descender (ie) to descend; to
    go down, to get off (bus,
    etc.) 1
el/la **descendiente** descendent
descifrar to decipher
descolgar (ue) to pick up
    (the telephone)
descollar to excel
descomponer to decompose
descomponerse to break
    down
el/la **desconocido(a)** stranger, 6
descortés discourteous
describir to describe
la **descripción** description
descriptivo(a) descriptive
descubierto(a) discovered
el/la **descubridor(a)** discoverer
el **descubrimiento** discovery
descubrir to discover
el **descuido** carelessness
desde from; since
deseable desirable
desear to wish, want
desechable disposable
desembarcar to disembark
la **desembocadura** mouth,
    outlet (of river), 5
desembocar to empty
desempeñar to fulfill, carry
    out
desempleado(a) unemployed
    (adj.)
el/la **desempleado(a)** unemployed
    person
el **desempleo** unemployment
desentrañar to get to the
    bottom of
el **deseo** wish, desire
el **desequilibrio** lack of
    equilibrium
la **desesperación** desperation
desesperar to despair
desfilar to parade
el **desfile** parade, 3
desfondado(a) broken
el **desgano** reluctance
desgastado(a) weakened
desgraciadamente
    unfortunately
desgraciado(a) unfortunate, 4
la **deshidratación** dehydration
deshidratado(a) dehydrated
la **deshonra** dishonor, 6
deshonrado(a) dishonered

deshonroso(a) dishonorable
el **desierto** desert
la **desintegración** decay
desmedido(a) excessive
desnudo(a) naked
desocupado(a) unemployed
la **desocupación**
unemployment
el **desodorante** deodorant
despachar to sell, dispense
el **despacho** study
despacio slowly
despedirse (i, i) to say good-
bye
despegar (gu) to take off
(airplane)
el **despegue** taking off
despejado(a) cloudless, **1**
desperdiciar to waste, **8**
desperezarse to stretch
despertarse (ie) to wake up
desplazar to displace; to
move, shift
el/la **desposado(a)** newlywed
desposar to wed, marry
después de (que) after
desque since (Old Spanish)
destacarse to stand out
destemplado(a) loud; noisy
desterrar to exile, banish
el/la **destinatario(a)** receiver
el **destino** destination; destiny,
fate
con destino a to
destrozar to destroy; to ruin, **2, 7**
la **destrucción** destruction
destruir to destroy, **5**
el **desvelo** sleeplessness; anxiety
la **desventura** misfortune
desvestirse to undress
desviar to divert
desviarse to get lost, go
astray
la **detalle** detail
detectar to detect
detener (irreg.) to stop
el **detergente** detergent
determinado(a) specific
determinar to determine
detestable detestable
detestar to detest
detrás de behind
la **deuda** debt
develar to reveal
el **devenir** future

devolver (ue) to return
el **día** day
el **Día de los Reyes** Day of
the Three Kings
el **Día de los Difuntos** Day
of the Dead
el **día feriado** holiday
la **diagnosis** diagnosis
el **diálogo** dialogue
el **diamante** diamond
diariamente daily
diario(a) daily, **7**; diary
el/la **dibujante** sketcher, **1**
dibujar to draw, sketch, **1**
el **dibujo** sketch, drawing, **1**
el **diccionario** dictionary
la **dicha** happiness; good luck
diciembre December
la **dictadura** dictatorship
dictar to give a lecture
el **diente** tooth; clove
la **dieta** diet
diez ten
la **diferencia** difference
diferente different
difícil difficult
la **dificultad** difficulty
el/la **difunto(a)** dead person
el **Día de los Difuntos** Day
of the Dead
dignarse to deign
la **dignidad** dignity
dignificar to dignify
digno(a) deserving
diligente diligent
el **diluvio** flood
dinámico(a) dynamic
el **dineral** fortune, great sum of
money, **2**
el **dinero** money
el **dinero en efectivo** cash
el/la **dios(a)** god (goddess)
el/la **diplomado(a)** graduate
diplomático(a) diplomatic
la **dirección** address; direction,
management
la **direccional** turn signal
directamente directly
el **directivo** board of directors,
management
directo(a) direct
el/la **director(a)** conductor;
director; principal
dirigir to direct
discar to dial

el **discernimento** discernment, **2**
la **disciplina** subject
el **disco** record; dial (of
telephone)
la **discoteca** discotheque
el **discurso** speech
la **discusión** discussion;
argument
discutir to discuss; to argue
la **disección** dissection
el/la **diseñador(a)** designer
diseñar to design
el **diseño** design
disfrutar (de) to enjoy, **1, 3**
dislocar to dislocate
disminuir to diminish
el **disparo** discharge, **3**; shot, **7**
el **dispensario** dispensary
displicente indifferent
disponer to have at one's
disposal
disponible available
la **disposición** disposal
dispuesto(a) ready
la **disputa** argument
la **distancia** distance
distinguido(a) distinguished
distinguir to distinguish; to
identify
distinto(a) distinct
distraer to distract
la **distribución** distribution
distribuir (y) to distribute
el **distrito** district
la **diversidad** diversity
la **diversión** amusement
diverso(a) different
divertido(a) fun
divertirse (ie, i) to enjoy
oneself
dividir to divide
divino(a) divine
la **divisa** currency
divorciarse to get divorced
el **divorcio** divorce
la **dobla** old Spanish coin
doblado(a) dubbed
doblar to turn
doble double
la **docena** dozen
el/la **docente** teacher, **7**
la **documentación**
documentation
el **documento** document
el **dólar** dollar

doler (ue) to hurt, ache
  Me duele____. My____
    (part of body) hurts,
    aches.
  doliente sorrowful
el **dolor** ache, pain; sorrow, 1
  el dolor de cabeza
    headache
  el dolor de estómago
    stomachache
  el dolor de garganta
    sore throat
  dolorido(a) sore
la **dominación** domination
  dominante dominant
  dominar to dominate
el **domingo** Sunday
  dominicano(a)
    Dominican
el **dominio** power
el **dominó** domino
  ¿dónde? where?
  doquier wherever
  dorar to gild
  dormir (ue, u) to sleep
    dormirse (ue, u) to fall
      asleep
el **dormitorio** bedroom
  dos two
la **dosis** dose
el **dote** dowry
  dramáticamente
    dramatically
  dramático(a) dramatic
el **dramaturgo** dramatist
  driblar con to dribble
    (sports)
la **droga** drug
la **drogadicción** drug addiction
la **droguería** drug store
la **ducha** shower
  tomar una ducha to
    take a shower
la **duda** doubt
  no hay duda there is no
    doubt
  sin duda without a
    doubt
  dudar to doubt
el **duelo** sorrow, grief
  duele: Me duele____.
    My____(part of body)
    hurts.
la **dueña** chaperone
el/la **dueño(a)** owner

  dulce sweet
la **duna** dune
  durante during
  durar to last
  duro(a) hard; five pesetas, 1

E
  e and (used instead of **y** before
    words beginning with **i** or
    hi)
la **ebullición** boiling
  a la ebullición to a boil
  echar to throw
    **echar a correr escalera
      abajo** to run quickly
      downstairs, 1
    echar canas to have some
      fun
    echar los dados to throw
      the dice
    echar una siesta to take a
      nap
    echarse to apply oneself
    echarse unas asoleadas to
      get tanned
la **ecología** ecology
  ecológico(a) ecologic
la **economía** economy;
    economics
    la economía doméstica
      home economics
  económico(a) economical
el **ecosistema** ecosystem
el **ecuador** equator
  ecuatorial equatorial
  ecuatoriano(a) Ecuadorean
  ecuestre equestrian
la **edad** age
    la Edad Media Middle Ages
el **edén** Eden
  edificar to build, 1
el **edificio** building
la **educación** education
    la educación cívica social
      studies
    la educación física
      physical education
  educacional educational
  educado(a) well-mannered,
    polite
  educar to educate
  efectivamente indeed
el **efecto** effect
  en efecto in effect
  efectuar to take place, carry

    out, 4
la **eficiencia** efficiency
el **eje** axis; main point, 6
el **ejemplo** example
  por ejemplo for example
  ejercer (z) (una profesión) to
    practice (a profession)
el **ejercicio** exercise
    el ejercicio aeróbico
      aerobic exercise
    el ejercicio físico physical
      exercise
  ejercitar to exercise; to
    practice, 3
  el the (m. sing.)
  él he; (to, for) him
  elaborado(a) elaborate
la **elasticidad** elasticity
  elástico(a) elastic
el/la **electricista** electrician
  eléctrico(a) electric
el **electrodoméstico** domestic
    appliance
el **elefante** elephant
  el elefante marino walrus
la **elegancia** elegance
  elegante elegant
  elegir to choose, **6**; to elect
el **elemento** element
la **elevación** elevation
  elevar to elevate
  eliminar to eliminate
  ella she, (to, for) her
  ellos(as) they, (to, for) them
el/la **embajador(a)** ambassador
el **embarazo** pregnancy
  embarcar to embark
el **emblema** emblem
el **embotamiento** dullness,
    drowsiness
el **embotellamiento** traffic jam,
    bottleneck, 1
el **embutido** sausage, 7
la **emergencia** emergency
el/la **emigrante** emigrant
  emigrar to emigrate
la **emisión** emission
    la emisión deportiva
      sports broadcast
  emitir to emit
la **emoción** emotion;
    excitement
  emocionarse to be moved,
    touched
la **empalizada** stockade, palisade

empanizar to hold together, **2**
empatado(a) tied
empavonado(a) greased, slick
empedrado(a) paved with
  stones
el **empellón** shove
empeñar to pawn
el **empeño** undertaking
empezar (ie) (c) to begin
el/la **empleado(a)** employee,
  attendant
  el/la empleado(a) de
    correo postal employee
  el/la empleado(a) del
    banco bank clerk
emplear to employ; to use
el **empleo** job
  la solicitud de empleo job
    application
el **empobrecimiento**
  impoverishment
empollar to hatch
emprender to undertake
la **empresa** business; company
el/la **empresario(a)** manager
empujar to push
el **empujón** push, shove, **6**
en in
  en autobús by bus
  en avión by plane
  en carro (coche) by car
  en cuanto as soon as
  en cuanto a as to
  en el pucho right away
  en este momento right now
  en seguida right away
  en todas partes everywhere
el/la **enamorado(a)** sweetheart
enamorarse to fall in love
el **encabezamiento** heading
encalado(a) whitewashed
encantador(a) charming, **2**
encantar to love
encarcelar to imprison
encargarse to take charge of
encarnizado(a) bloody;
  cruel
encender (ie) to light
encerrar to lock in
encestar to make a basket
la **encía** gum (of mouth), **7**
el **encierro** penning (of bulls), **3**
encima above; overhead
  por encima de above, over
encoger(se) to shrink

encontrar (ue) to find
  encontrarse (ue) to meet
la **endogamia** inbreeding
endosar to endorse
el/la **enemigo(a)** enemy
energético(a) energetic
la **energía** energy
  la energía nuclear nuclear
    energy
enero January
enfadar to annoy, anger
enfatizar to emphasize, **8**
la **enfermedad** sickness
el/la **enfermero(a)** nurse
enfermizo(a) sickly, weak
enfermo(a) sick
el/la **enfermo(a)** sick person
enfrente de in front of;
  opposite
enfriarse to become cold
engañar to deceive, **8**
engreído(a) spoiled
¡Enhorabuena!
  Congratulations!
el **enigma** enigma
enigmático(a) puzzling
enjuto(a) lean
el **enlace** union
  el enlace nupcial wedding
enlatado(a) canned
enlazar to join, connect
enlodado(a) muddied
enojar to annoy, anger
enorme enormous
enrarecido(a) thin (air)
el **enrarecimiento** thinning (of
  the air)
enredarse to get entangled
enriquecerse to get rich, **8**
enrojecer to blush
la **ensalada** salad
ensayar to rehearse
la **enseñanza** teaching
enseñar to teach
enterarse de to find out about
enternecido(a) moved,
  touched
entero(a) whole
enterrar (ie) to bury
la **entidad** entity
el **entierro** burial, **4**
entonces: en aquel entonces
  at that time
la **entrada** entrance; inning;
  admission ticket

entrañable close, intimate, **4**
entrante next, coming
entrar to enter
  entrar en escena to come
    on stage
entre between, among
la **entrega** delivery
entregar to deliver; to hand
  over
el **entremés** appetizer
el/la **entrenador(a)** trainer, coach, **2**
el **entrenamiento** training, **8**
entretanto meanwhile
la **entrevista** interview
el **envase** container; packing, **7**
el **envejecimiento** aging, **2**
enviar to send
envidiable enviable
envidiar to envy, **6**
el/la **enviudado(a)** widow(er), **1**
enyesar to put in a plaster cast
épico(a) epic
la **epidemia** epidemic
el **episodio** episode
la **época** epoch; season
el **equilibrio** equilibrium,
  balance
el **equipaje** baggage, luggage
  el equipaje de mano hand
    (carry-on) luggage
  el reclamo de equipaje
    baggage claim
el **equipo** team; equipment
equivalente equivalent
equivocado(a) wrong
eres you (sing. fam.) are
la **ermita** hermitage
erosionar to erode
errar to rove, wander
el **error** mistake
eructar to belch, burp, **2**
es he/she/it is
esbozar to outline
la **escala** scale
la **escalera** stairway
el **escalofrío** shiver, chill, **6**
el **escalón** stair
el **escándalo** commotion
escandinavo(a) Scandinavian
escaparse to escape
el **escaparate** shop window
escaso(a) scarce
la **escena** scene; stage
  entrar en escena to come
    on stage

el **escenario** stage, scenery
el/la **esclavo(a)** slave, **8**
escoger (j) to choose
escolar school (adj.)
esconder to hide
escondido(a) hidden
el/la **escribidor(a)** writer
escribir to write
escrito(a) written
escuchar to listen
el **escudo** coat of arms
la **escuela** school
la escuela intermedia middle, junior high school
la escuela primaria elementary school
la escuela secundaria high school
la escuela superior high school
la escuela vocacional vocational school
el/la **escultor(a)** sculptor
la **escultura** sculpture
la **escupidera** spittoon, **7**
el **esfuerzo** effort; endeavor, **8**
eso: a eso de about
espacial space (adj.)
el **espacio** space
espacioso(a) spacious
el **espagueti** spaghetti
la **espalda** back
espantoso(a) frightful, dreadful
España Spain
español(a) Spanish
el **español** Spanish (language)
españolizar to hispanicize
la **especia** spice
la **especialidad** specialty
especialista specialist (adj.)
el/la **especialista** specialist
la **especialización** specialization
especializado(a) specialized
especializar to specialize
especialmente especially
la **especie** type, species
específicamente specifically
específico(a) specific
espectacular spectacular
el **espectáculo** show, performance
el/la **espectador(a)** spectator

el **espejo** mirror
la **espera** expectation
la **esperanza** hope
la esperanza de vida life expectancy
esperar to wait for; to hope
la **espinaca** spinach
el **espíritu** spirit
espléndidamente splendidly
espontáneo(a) spontaneous
las **esposas** handcuffs
el/la **esposo(a)** husband (wife)
la **esquela** obituary, **4**
el **esquí** ski, skiing
el esquí acuático water skiing
el esquí alpino downhill skiing
el esquí de descenso downhill skiing
el esquí de fondo, el esquí nórdico cross-country skiing
el/la **esquiador(a)** skier
esquiar to ski
esquiar en el agua to water ski
esquilar to shear (sheep)
el **esquileo** shearing
la **esquina** corner
estable stable
establecer (zc) to establish
el **establecimiento** establishment
la **estación** ski resort; station; season
la estación de ferrocarril train station
la estación de servicio service station
estacionar to park
la **estadía** stay, sojourn, **1**
el **estadio** stadium
el **estadista** statesman
la **estadística** statistic
el **estado** state
el estado de banco (de cuenta) bank statement
el estado libre asociado commonwealth
los **Estados Unidos** United States
estadounidense from the United States
estallar to break out, to explode, **3**

la **estampa** engraving; stamp
la **estampilla** stamp
están they/you (pl. form.) are
la **estancia** room
el **estanco** tobacco store
estar (irreg.) to be
estar a gusto to be satisfied, **2**
estar al acecho to be on the alert
estar de acuerdo to agree
estar dispuesto to be ready, be prepared, **6**
estar en (de) buena salud to be in good health, **7**
estar en onda to be in vogue
estar enfermo(a) to be sick
estar hasta la punta del pelo to be fed up
estás you (sing. fam.) are
estatal of or pertaining to the state, **7**
la **estatua** statue
el **este** east
este(a) this
éste, ésta this one (dem. pron.)
la **estela** inscribed stone slab
estereofónico(a) stereophonic
esterlino(a) sterling
la **estiba de arroz** mountain of rice sacks
el **estilo** style
estimular to stimulate
el **estiramiento** stretching, **3**
estirar to stretch, **4**
el **estómago** stomach
el dolor de estómago stomachache
estornudar to sneeze
éstos(as) these (dem. pron.)
estoy I am
estrechar la mano to shake hands
estrecho(a) tight; narrow, **1**
la **estrella** star, **1**
estrellar to smash
estremecido(a) shaken
el **estrés** stress
la **estrofa** stanza
la **estructura** structure
el/la **estudiante** student
estudiantil student (adj.)

estudiar to study
el estudio study
la estufa stove
estupendo(a) terrific
la etapa stage (of time), epoch, 2
eterno(a) eternal
la etnia ethnic background
la etnicidad ethnicity
étnico(a) ethnic, 8
etnocultural ethnocultural
la etnología ethnology
el/la etnólogo(a) ethnologist
el eucalipto eucalyptus tree
la Europa Europe
europeo(a) European
la evaluación evaluation
evaluar to evaluate
evangelista Evangelistic
el evento event
evidenciar to prove
evitar to avoid
evocar to evoke
exactamente exactly
la exactitud accuracy
exacto(a) exact
exagerar to exaggerate
el examen examination
examinar to examine
la excavación excavation
excelente excellent
la excepción exception
excepcional exceptional
excesivo(a) excessive
el exceso excess
exclusivamente exclusively
la excursión excursion
la excusa excuse
exigente demanding
el exilio exile
la existencia existence
existente existing
existir to exist
el éxito success, 3
el éxodo exodus
exótico(a) exotic
expandir to expand
la expansión expansion
el expansionismo expansionism
expansionista expansionist
la expectación expectation
la expectativa expectation
la expedición expedition; dispatch
expedir to issue

el expendio sale, distribution
la experiencia experience
experimentado(a) experienced
experimentar to experience
el experimento experiment
experto(a) expert
la explicación explanation
explicar (qu) to explain
la exploración exploration
el/la explorador(a) explorer
la explotación exploitation
el exponente exponent
exponer (irreg.) to explain, expound
exponerse to expose oneself
exportar to export
la exposición exhibition
expresar to express
la expresión expression
expuesto(a) exposed
expulsar to expel, drive out
extender (ie) to extend
extendido(a) extended, widespread
la extensión extension
extenso(a) extensive
el/la exterminador(a) exterminator
externo(a) external
el/la extinto(a) dead person, 4
la extracción extraction
extraer to extract; to remove, 4
extramuros (adv.) outside the city
extrañar to surprise, 6
extranjero(a) foreign
el extranjero abroad
extraño(a) strange
el/la extraño(a) stranger
extraordinario(a) extraordinary
extremadamente extremely
extremo(a) extreme

F
la fábrica factory
fabricar to make
fabuloso(a) fabulous
la facción faction; (pl.) features
fácil easy
la facilidad ease
fácilmente easily
el factor factor
la factura bill

facturar to check (luggage)
facultativo(a) optional
la faena job; work, 2
la faja sash, 3
la falda skirt
fallecer to die, 5
el fallecimiento death
fallido(a) frustrated; unsuccessful, 4
falso(a) false
la falta lack
faltar to lack
la fama fame
la familia family
el familiar member of the family
familiar of the family (adj.)
famoso(a) famous
el/la fanático(a) fanatic
fanfarrón(a) boastful
la fanfarronería bragging
la fantasía fantasy
fantástico(a) fantastic
el/la farmacéutico(a) pharmacist
la farmacia pharmacy
el faro headlight
la farra revelry, spree
fascinante fascinating
fascinar to fascinate
fastidiar to annoy, 3
fastidiarse to get annoyed
las fatigas sickness
la fauna fauna
el favor favor
el fax fax
la faz face, 4
la fe faith
febrero February
la fecha date
¿Cuál es la fecha de hoy? What is today's date?
la felicidad happiness
¡Felicitaciones! Congratulations!
felicitar to congratulate
feliz happy
¡Feliz cumpleaños! Happy birthday!
¡Feliz Navidad! Merry Christmas!
femenino(a) feminine
fenicio(a) Phoenician
fenomenal phenomenal
el fenómeno phenomenon
feo(a) ugly
el féretro coffin

la **feria** fair
la **fermentación** fermentation
el **ferrocarril** railway, railroad
el **fertilizante** fertilizer
fervoroso(a) fervent
festejar to celebrate
el **festejo** entertainment, banquet, **4**
la **festividad** festivity
festivo(a) festive
la **fibra** fiber
la **ficha** token; registration card
la **fiebre** fever
fiel faithful
la **fiesta** party
la fiesta de las luces celebration of lights
la **figura: la figura clave** key figure
fijar to fix
fijarse en to pay attention to; to take note of
la **fila** row; line
el **filete** fillet
la **filial** branch office
el **film(e)** film
filmar to film
el **filo** cutting edge (of knife)
el **filósofo** philosopher
el **fin** end
el fin de semana weekend
en fin finally
el **final** end
finalmente finally
financiero(a) financial
la **finanza** finance
fino(a) fine
el **fiordo** fiord
firmar to sign
firme firm, stable
la **física** physics
físicamente physically
el/la **físico(a)** physicist
físico(a) physical
la **fisiología** physiology
flaco(a) thin, **7**
flamenco(a) flamenco; Flemish
el **flequillo** bangs
la **flexibilidad** flexibility
flexible flexible
flojo(a) loose, **2**
el/la **flojonazo(a)** lazybones
la **flor** flower
la **flora** flora

floreciente flourishing
florido(a) full of flowers; ornate, flowery
flote: a flote afloat
la **flotilla** fleet of small vessels, **5**
fluctuar to fluctuate
fluir to flow, **6**
folklórico(a) folkloric
el **folleto** pamphlet
el **fondo** background; bottom; fund
a fondo thoroughly
el/la **fontanero(a)** plumber
la **forma** form; shape
la **formación** formation
formal formal
la **formalidad** formality
formalizar to formalize
formar to form, make
formativo(a) formative
formidable terrific
la **fórmula** method, pattern
la **formulación** formulation
formular la pregunta to pose the question
el **formulario** form
el formulario de retiro withdrawal slip
el **foro** forum
forrado(a) lined
la **fortaleza** fortress
la **fortificación** fortification
forzado(a) hard (labor); forced, **8**
el **fósforo** match
el **fósil** fossil
el **foso** pit
la **foto** photo
la **fotografía** photograph
fracasar to fail, be unsuccessful, **5**
el **fracaso** failure
la **fractura** fracture
fragante fragrant
la **fragata** frigate
frágil fragile
el **fragmento** fragment
francamente frankly
francés (francesa) French
el **franco** franc (monetary unit)
el **franqueo** postage
la **franqueza** frankness
el **frasco** jar
la **frase** sentence; phrase
la **fraternidad** fraternity

fratricida fratricidal
la **frecuencia** frequency
con frecuencia frequently
frecuentar to frequent
frecuente frequent
frecuentemente frequently
freír (i, i) to fry
frenado(a) held back, restrained
frenar to brake
el **freno** brake
la **frente** forehead
frente a facing, opposite
la **fresa** strawberry; drill, **7**
fresco(a) fresh, cool
Hace fresco. It's cool.
el **frijol** bean
el **frío** cold (weather)
Hace frío. It's cold.
frito(a) fried
la **frontera** frontier, border
fronterizo(a) from the border
la **fruición** pleasure
la **frustración** frustration
la **fruta** fruit
el **fuego** fire
la **fuente** fountain
fuerte strong
la **fuerza** strength, **1**
a fuerza de by means of
la fuerza aérea air force
la fuerza ascensional lifting force
las **fuerzas militares** forces (military)
fulgor: sin fulgor without spark or brightness
el/la **fumador(a)** smoker
fumar to smoke
la **función** function
el **funcionamiento** functioning
funcionar to function
el/la **funcionario(a)** city hall employee
la **funda** wrapper
la **fundación** founding
el/la **fundador(a)** founder
fundamental fundamental
fundamentar to lay the foundations of
fundar to found (establish)
fundir to found (unite)

furioso(a) furious
el **furor** furor, rage
la **fusión** fusion
el **fútbol** soccer
  el campo de fútbol
    soccer field
el **futuro** future

G

la **gabardina** raincoat
el **gabinete** laboratory, **7**
las **gafas** glasses, goggles
el **galápago** giant turtle, **1**
el **galeno** doctor, **7**
  Gales Wales, **1**
  galés (galesa) Welsh (adj.)
  gallego(a) Galician
la **galleta** biscuit, cracker, **8**
la **gallina** hen, **6**
el **gallinazo** buzzard
el **gallo** rooster
el **galón** gallon
la **gama** range
la **gamba** shrimp
la **gana** desire, wish
el **ganado** cattle; herd
el/la **ganador(a)** winner
  ganar to win; to earn
el **gancho** clothes hanger
la **ganga** bargain
el **garaje** garage
  garantizar to guarantee
  garboso(a) graceful
la **garganta** throat
  el dolor de garganta
    sore throat
la **garita de peaje** toll
    booth
  gas: con gas carbonated
la **gaseosa** soft drink, soda
la **gasolina** gas
la **gasolinera** gas station
  gastado(a) spent, barren
  gastar bromas to joke
    habitually
el **gasto** expense; charge
  gastronómico(a)
    gastronomic
el **gatillo** forceps
el **gato** cat; jack
la **gaveta** drawer, **7**
la **gelatina** gelatin
la **generación** generation
el **general** general

  el general a caballo
    general on
    horseback, **1**
  por lo general in
    general
  generalizar to
    generalize
  generalmente generally
el **género** genre, kind, sort,
    type
la **generosidad** generosity
  generoso(a) generous
  genial pleasant
el **genio** character;
    temperament, **8**
  genovés(a) Genoese
la **gente** people
la **geografía** geography
  geográfico(a)
    geographic
la **geometría** geometry
el **geranio** geranium
la **gesta** exploit; epic poem
el **gesto** gesture
  gigantesco(a) gigantic,
    huge
el **gimnasio** gymnasium
la **gira** tour
  girar to revolve, **6**
el **giro** turn
  el giro postal money
    order
el/la **gitano(a)** Gypsy
  glacial icy
el **glaciar** glacier
el **globo** globe, **5**
la **gloria** glory
el/la **gobernador(a)**
    governor
el **gobierno** government
el **gol** goal (soccer)
  meter un gol to score
    a goal
el **golf** golf
  el campo de golf golf
    course
  el juego de golf golf
    game
  la bolsa de golf golf
    bag
el **golfo** gulf
la **golosina** delicacy, tidbit,
    1
el **golpe** blow, hit, **5**
  de golpe suddenly, **2**

  golpear to hit
la **goma** eraser; tire
la **góndola** gondola
el **gorro** cap
la **gota** drop, **2, 6**
  gozar to enjoy
  gozar de buena salud
    to be in good health, **7**
  grabar to engrave
  gracias thank you
  gracioso(a) charming;
    attractive
el **grado** grade; degree
la **graduación** graduation
el **graduado** graduate
  graduarse to graduate
el **gramo** gram
  gran, grande big
    las Grandes Ligas
      Major Leagues
la **grandeza** greatness
  grandilocuente
    grandiloquent
el **granizo** hail, **1**
la **grasa** grease
  gratis free
la **gratitud** gratitude
  grato(a) agreeable,
    pleasant, **8**
  gratuitamente free
    (adv.)
  grave serious, grave
el **green** green (golf)
  griego(a) Greek
el/la **gringo(a)** yankee
la **gripe** influenza, cold, flu
  gris grey
  gritar to shout, **5**
el **grito** shout, cry
  grosero(a) rude, vulgar
  gruesamente grossly
la **grupa** rump (of horse)
el **grupo** group
la **guanábana** soursop (tree)
el **guante** glove
el **guapo** braggart
los **guaraníes** Guarani
los **guardabarros** fenders
  guardar to guard; to keep
  guardar cama to stay in
    bed
la **Guardia Civil** Spanish
    police force, **8**
  guatemalteco(a)
    Guatemalan

la **guayaba** guava
gubernamental governmental
la **guerra** war
la **guerrera** military jacket
guerrero(a) warlike
el **guerrillero** guerrilla
el/la **guía** guide, **6**
la **guía telefónica** telephone
book
el **guión** screen play, script
el **guisante** pea
el **guiso** stew
la **guitarra** guitar
gustar to like, enjoy
el **gusto** taste; pleasure
estar a gusto to be
satisfied, **2**

H

haber to have (auxiliary verb)
la **habichuela** bean
la habichuela negra black
bean
la **habilidad** ability
la **habitación** room
el/la **habitante** inhabitant
habitar to reside, **6**; to inhabit
el **hábitat** habitat
habla: de habla española
Spanish-speaking
hablar to speak
hacer (irreg.) to do; to make
hace mucho tiempo a long
time ago
hace muchos años many
years ago
hace poco a short time ago
hacer calor to be hot
(weather)
hacer cargo de to take
charge of
hacer cola to line up
hacer ejercicio to exercise
hacer el desaparecido to
play a disappearing act
hacer un viaje to take a
trip
hacer frío to be cold (weather)
hacer juego con to go with
hacer la cama to make the
bed
hacer la maleta to pack
one's suitcase
hacer los negocios to get
down to business

hacer obras to do repair
work
hacer sus veces to take
one's place
hacer una llamada to
make a call
hacerse cargo de to take
charge of, **4, 6**
hacerse daño to hurt oneself
hacia toward
el **hado** fate, destiny, **1**
halagar to delight
hallar to find
el **hallazgo** discovery; finding
la **hamaca** hammock
el **hambre** (f.) hunger
pasar hambre to go hungry
tener hambre to be hungry
la **hamburguesa** hamburger
Hanuka Hanukkah
la **harina** flour
hartarse to get one's fill of
harto(a) fed up
hasta even; also (adv.)
hasta (que) until; up to
Hasta la vista. See you
later.
Hasta luego. See you later.
Hasta mañana. See you
tomorrow.
Hasta pronto. See you soon.
hay there is, there are
hay que one must
Hay sol. It's sunny.
la **hazaña** deed, heroic feat, **6**
la **hebra** thread
hebreo(a) Hebrew
el **hecho** fact
la **helada** frost
la **heladería** ice cream parlor
el **helado** ice cream
helado(a) frozen, **1**; icy
las **hélices** propellers
el **helicóptero** helicopter
el **hemisferio** hemisphere
la **hemorragia** hemorrhage
herbívoro(a) herbivorous
el/la **herbolario(a)** herbalist
heredar to inherit, **6**
el/la **heredero(a)** heir, **4**
la **herencia** inheritance
la **herida** wound
herir to hurt, **8**
el/la **hermanastro(a)** stepbrother
(stepsister)

el/la **hermano(a)** brother (sister)
el **héroe** hero
heroico(a) heroic
hervir (ie) to boil
hervores boiling; figuratively,
heartaches
la **hibridación** hybridization
el **hidalgo** nobleman
el **hidrato de carbono**
carbohydrate
el **hidrofoil** hydrofoil
la **hiel** bitterness; adversity, **4**
el **hielo: el patinaje sobre hielo**
ice skating
la **hierba** herb; grass
el **hierro** iron
el **hígado** liver
higiénico(a) sanitary
el papel higiénico toilet
paper
el/la **hijastro(a)** stepson
(stepdaughter)
el/la **hijo(a)** son (daughter)
los hijos children (sons and
daughters)
hinchado(a) swollen
la **hiperinflación** hyperinflation
el **hipermercado** supermarket
el **hipopótamo** hippopotamus
la **hipótesis** hypothesis
hispánico(a) Hispanic (adj.)
hispano(a) Hispanic (person)
hispanohablante Spanish-
speaking
la **historia** history; story
el/la **historiador(a)** historian
el **historial profesional**
curriculum vitae
histórico(a) historic
el **hit** hit (baseball)
el **hogar** home, **8**
la **hoja** sheet; blade
la hoja de afeitar razor
blade, **2**
la hoja de papel sheet of
paper
la **hojalata** tin
hojear to leaf through, **2**
hola hello
holandés (holandesa) Dutch
el **holgazán (la holgazana)**
idler, loafer, **3**
el **hombre** man
el **hombro** shoulder
homogéneo(a) homogeneous

hondo(a) deep
honesto(a) honest
el **honor** honor
la **hora** hour; time
el **horario** schedule, **2**
la **horca** gallows
la **horda** horde
el **horizonte** horizon
hornear to bake
el **hornillo** portable stove
   el/la hornillo(a) (stove)
      burner
el **horno** oven
   el horno de microondas
      microwave oven
el **horóscopo** horoscope
la **horquilla** bobby pin
el **horror** horror
hospedar to lodge, stay
el **hospital** hospital
hostil hostile
el **hotel** hotel
hotelero(a) hotel (adj.)
el/la **hotelero(a)** hotelkeeper
hoy today
   hoy día nowadays; today
   hoy en día nowadays
   ¿Cuál es la fecha de hoy?
      What is today's date?
el **hoyo** hole
el **hueco** hole
la **huelga** strike
la **huella** impression
la **huerta** garden, orchard, **5**
el **huerto** fruit or vegetable
      garden, **1**
el **hueso** bone
el/la **huésped** guest
el **huevo** egg
   los huevos duros hard-
      boiled eggs
   los huevos pasados por
      agua soft-boiled eggs
   los huevos revueltos
      scrambled eggs
huir to flee
las **humanidades** humanities
el/la **humanista** humanist
humano(a) human
la **humedad** dampness
humilde humble, **8**
el **humor: de buen humor** in a
      good mood; **de mal humor**
      in a bad mood
el **hundimiento** sinking

hundir to plunge; to sink
   hundir la panza to pull in
      the belly
el **huracán** hurricane, **1**
huronear to pry, snoop
hurtadillas: a hurtadillas
      furtively, stealthily, **6**
el **huso horario** time zone

I

ibérico(a) Iberian
ida y vuelta round-trip (adj.)
la **idea** idea
   No tengo idea. I don't have
      any idea.
el **ideal** ideal
idéntico(a) identical
la **identidad** identity
identificar to identify
el **idioma** language
idolatrar to idolize, **3**
el **ídolo** idol
la **iglesia** church
ignorar to be ignorant of, not
      to know, **8**
igual equal
la **igualdad** equality
la **ilusión** illusion
ilusionado(a) hopeful, **2**
ilustre distinguished
la **imagen** image; picture
la **imaginación** imagination
imaginar to imagine
imitar to imitate
impar odd
la **impedimenta** equipment,
      supplies
el **impedimento** impediment,
      obstacle, **4**
impedir to impede, hinder
impeler to impel, push
imperdonable unforgivable
el **imperio** empire
el **impermeable** raincoat, **3**
la **impertinencia** impertinence
imponer (irreg.) to impose
la **importación** importation
importado(a) imported
la **importancia** importance
importante important
importar to be important; to
      import
   Le importa un pimiento.
      It doesn't mean a thing.

imposible impossible
imprescindible essential, **5**
impresionado(a) impressed
impresionante amazing,
      impressive
impresionar to impress
el **imprevisto** unforeseen event
improbable improbable
improvisar to improvise
el **impuesto** tax
el **impulso** impulse, **8**
inaccesible inaccessible
inalámbrico(a) cordless
inapropiado(a) inappropriate
la **inauguración** inauguration
inaugurado(a) inaugurated
incaico(a) Incan
incalculable incalculable
incapaz incapable
el **incendio** fire, **5**
la **incisión** incision
inclinado(a) slanted
incluir (y) to include
incluso including
incógnito(a) unknown
la **incomodidad** discomfort
incomparable incomparable
la **inconsciencia**
      unconsciousness
el **inconveniente** difficulty
inconveniente inconvenient
      (adj.)
incorporarse to incorporate
incorruptible incorruptible
increíble incredible
independiente independent
indeseable undesirable
indicar (qu) to indicate
el **índice** ratio, index
el/la **indígena** native (adj.), **8**
indigno(a) unworthy
el/la **indio(a)** Indian (adj.), **8**
indispensable indispensable
individual individual
el **individualismo** individualism
el/la **individuo** individual
indudablemente
      undoubtedly
la **industria** industry
industrializado(a)
      industrialized
industrialmente industrially
inexorable relentless
infalible infallible
la **infancia** infancy

la **Infanta** daughter of the King of Spain, **4**

el/la **infante(a)** infant

el **infarto** heart attack, **5**

infeliz unhappy

inferior inferior; lower

el **infierno** hell

la **inflación** inflation

inflexible inflexible, **6**

la **influencia** influence

influir to influence, **8**

la **información** information

informal informal

informar to inform

la **informática** computer science

informativo(a) informative

el **informe** report

el/la **ingeniero(a)** engineer, **2**

el **inglés (la inglesa)** English (person)

el **inglés** English (language)

inglés (inglesa) English (adj.)

el **ingrediente** ingredient

ingresar to deposit; to enter, become a member (of), **2**

el **ingreso** deposit; income

inhóspito(a) inhospitable

inicialmente initially

injusto(a) unfair

inmediatamente immediately

inmediato(a) immediate

de inmediato immediately

inmenso(a) immense

inmerecido(a) undeserved, **4**

el/la **inmigrante** immigrant

inmoral immoral

la **inocencia** innocence

el **inodoro** toilet

inolvidable unforgettable

inoportuno(a) inopportune

inoxidable rustproof

el **inquietud** uneasiness

el/la **inquilino(a)** tenant

la **Inquisición** Inquisition

inscribir to register; to enroll, **7**

la **inscripción** enrollment

inscrito(a) engraved

inseparable inseparable

insignificante insignificant

insistir to insist

inspeccionar to inspect

inspirar to inspire

la **instalación** installation

instalarse to establish oneself

la **institución** institution

el **instituto** institute

la **instrucción** instruction

el **instrumento** instrument

insular insular, island

el **insulto** insult

integrar to form, make up, **2**

íntegro(a) integral

inteligente intelligent

la **intemperie** inclemency (weather)

la **intención** intention

la **intensidad** intensity

intensivo(a) intensive

intentar to attempt; to intend

interactuar to interact

intercambiar to exchange

el **intercambio** exchange

el **interés** interest

interesante interesting

interesar to interest

el **interior** interior

el/la **interlocutor(a)** speaker

interminable interminable

intermitente intermittent (adj.)

el **intermitente** turn signal

internacional international

internar to lock up, **7**

interno(a) internal

la **interpretación** interpretation

interpretar to interpret

el/la **intérprete** interpreter

interrogativo(a) interrogative

interrumpir to interrupt

la **interrupción** interruption

interurbano(a) interurban

el **intervalo** interval

intervenir (irreg.) to intervene

la **intimidad** intimacy

íntimo(a) close, intimate

la **intriga** intrigue

la **introducción** introduction

introducir (zc) to insert; to introduce

invadir to invade

la **invención** invention

la **inversión** investment

la **investigación** investigation

el **invierno** winter

la **invitación** invitation

el/la **invitado(a)** guest

invitar to invite

la **inyección** injection, shot

ir (irreg.) to go

ir a to be going to

ir de camping to go camping

ir de compras to go shopping

ir de paseo to go for a walk

irlandés (irlandesa) Irish (adj.)

irrepetible not repeatable

irse to leave, depart, **1**

la **isla** island

islamita Muslim

el **istmo** isthmus

el **italiano** Italian (language)

izar to hoist

la **izquierda** left

a la izquierda to the left

izquierdo(a) left (adj.)

J

el **jabón** soap

el jabón en polvo soap powder

el **jade** jade

jadeante panting

jadear to pant

jamás never

el **jamón** ham

japonés (japonesa) Japanese (adj.)

el **jardín** garden

el/la **jardinero** outfielder (baseball)

el **jebe** elastic, rubber

el/la **jefe(a)** leader, chief

la **jerarquía** hierarchy

la **jeringa** syringe, **7**

el **jeroglífico** hieroglyphic

el **jersey** sweater

jesuíta Jesuit (adj.)

el **jet** jet

el **jíbaro encastado** Puerto Rican peasant

el **jonrón** home run

la **jornada** day

joven young (adj.)

el/la **joven** young person, **2**

las **joyas** jewelry

el/la **jubilado(a)** retired person, **2**

jubilarse to retire

la **judía verde** string bean

el/la **judío(a)** Jewish person

el **juego** game

hacer juego con to go with, match

el **jueves** Thursday

el/la **juez** judge

el/la **jugador(a)** player

jugar (ue) to play
el juglar minstrel
juglaresco(a) pertaining to
minstrels
el jugo juice
el jugo de china orange juice
jugoso(a) juicy
el juguete toy, 1, 4
el juicio opinion
juicioso(a) mature
julio July
la jungla jungle
junio June
junto(a) together
el juramento oath
justamente exactly
justificarse to justify oneself
justo(a) fair, reasonable
la juventud youth

K

el kilo(gramo) kilogram
el kilómetro kilometer

L

la the (f. sing.)
el laberinto labyrinth
el labio lip
la labor work, labor, 2
el laboratorio laboratory
laboristo(a) labor (adj.)
el/la labrador(a) farm worker
labrar (la tierra) to farm
(the land)
la laca hair spray
lacio(a) straight (hair)
la lactancia nursing period
el/la ladino(a) person of mixed
race
lado: al lado de to the side of
ladrar to bark, 7
el ladrido bark, barking, 7
el/la ladrón(a) thief, 6
la lagartija push-up
el lago lake
la lágrima tear, 7
la laguna lagoon, 5
lamentablemente
unfortunately
lamentar to mourn
la lámpara lamp
la lana wool
la langosta lobster
la lanza spear
el/la lanzador(a) pitcher

el lanzamiento throw, pitch
lanzar to throw
el lápiz pencil
largo(a) long
a lo largo de along
las the (f. pl.)
la lástima pity
ser una lástima to be a
pity
lastimar to hurt, wound, 3
lastimarse to get hurt
lastrado(a) weighted
la lata can
el latido beat
el latido del corazón
heartbeat
el latín Latin
Latinoamérica Latin
America
latinoamericano(a) Latin
American
la latitud latitude
el lavabo lavatory, sink
el lavado wash; laundry
el lavamanos washbasin, 1
la lavandería laundromat
lavar to wash
lavarse to wash oneself
le him, her, you (form.)
(pron.)
la lealtad loyalty
la lección lesson
la leche milk
el lechón roast suckling pig
la lechuga lettuce
el/la lector(a) reader
la lectura reading
leer (irreg.) to read
legendario(a) legendary
legítimo(a) legitimate
la legumbre vegetable, 1
lejano(a) distant, 1
lejos far
la lengua language
la lengua materna mother
tongue, native language
la lenteja lentil, 7
lento(a) slow
les them, you (form.) (pron.)
el letargo lethargy
la letra letter (of the alphabet),
8; lyrics
las letras literature
levantar to lift, 7; to raise
levantarse to get up

leve light, 1
la ley law
la leyenda legend
libanés (libanesa) Lebanese
(adj.)
el/la liberal liberal
la libertad freedom
el/la libertador(a) liberator
la libra pound
librarse to escape, 4
libre free
la libreta notebook; passbook
el libro book
la licencia driver's license
licenciarse to receive a
master's degree
el liceo primary school (in
Mexico), high school (in
most places)
la licuadora blender
el líder leader
el lienzo cloth
ligarse to become bound (by
an obligation)
ligeramente lightly
ligero(a) light, 1
el/la ligero(a) lightweight, 3
la lima lime
limeño(a) from Lima
limitar to limit
el límite limit; boundary
el limón lemon
la limonada lemonade
la limosna alms, charity
el limpiaparabrisas windshield
wiper
limpiar to clean
limpiar en seco to dry clean
la limpieza cleanliness; purity
la limpieza en seco dry
cleaning
limpio(a) clean
la línea line
la línea aérea airline
La línea está ocupada.
The line is busy.
la linfa lymph
la linterna flashlight
la liquidación sale
el líquido liquid
líquido(a) liquid (adj.)
lírico(a) lyric
liso(a) straight (hair);
smooth; even
la lista list

la **litera** berth
literario(a) literary
el/la **literato(a)** writer
la **literatura** literature
el **litoral** coast
el **litro** liter
la **llama** llama, 2; flame, 5
la **llamada** call
llamar por teléfono to phone
llamarse to be called, named
la **llanta** tire
la **llanura** plain
la **llave** key
la **llegada** arrival
el tablero de llegadas y salidas arrival and departure board
llegar to arrive
llenar to fill (out)
llevar to carry; to wear
llevar a cabo to carry out, perform, 4
llevar la casa to manage the house
llevar puesto(a) to be wearing
llover to rain
Llueve. It's raining.
la **lluvia** rain, 1
el **lobo de mar** sea lion
el/la **lobo(a)** wolf
local local
la **localidad** seat (in theater)
localizar to locate
loco(a) crazy
la **locura** craziness
lógico(a) logical
lograr to achieve; to obtain, 8
la **loma(da)** hill, slope, 1
la **longitud** longitude
longitudinal longitudinal
la **lonja** slice
los the (m. pl.)
la **loseta** tile
la **lozanía** vigor, exuberance, 4
el **lucero** bright star
la **lucha** fight, battle
luchar to fight
lucir (zc) to display; to stand out, shine, 4
luego then
Hasta luego. See you later.
el **lugar** place, 1
tener lugar to take place
el **lujo** luxury, 2

de (gran) lujo deluxe
la **luna** moon
la luna de miel honeymoon
el **lunes** Monday
la **luz** light

M

la **macarela** mackerel, 6
el **machete** machete
el **macho** male
la **madera** wood, 1
la **madre** mother
la **madreperla** mother-of-pearl
el/la **madrileño(a)** native of Madrid
la **madrina** godmother; maid of honor
el **madroño** madrone tree
la **madrugada** dawn, 4, 5
el/la **madrugador(a)** early riser
la **madurez** maturity
el/la **maestro(a)** master, teacher
magallánico(a) Magellanic
mágico(a) magic, magical
el **Magisterio Fiscal** public school teachers, 4
la **magnificencia** splendor
magnífico(a) magnificent
magullado(a) bruised
el/la **mahometano(a)** Muslim
el **maíz** corn
majestuoso(a) majestic
el **mal** illness
el/la **malcriado(a)** ill-mannered person, 2
la **maldad** evil
el/la **maleante** hoodlum, 5
el **malentendido** misunderstanding
el **malestar** malaise; unease
la **maleta** suitcase
hacer la maleta to pack one's suitcase
el/la **maletero(a)** trunk (of car); porter
malo(a) bad
el **maltrato** ill treatment, abuse, 8
maltrecho(a) battered
la **mamá** mom
el **mamífero** mammal
la **mañana** morning
esta mañana this morning
mañana tomorrow (adv.)

la **mancha** stain
manchado(a) stained
mandar to send; to order
la **mandíbula** jaw
el **mando** command
manejar to drive; to manage
el **manejo** management
manera way, manner
de manera que so that
de ninguna manera by no means
la **manga** sleeve
el **mango** handle
el **maní** peanut, 7
la **manía** mania, 1
el **manicomio** insane asylum
manipular to manage
el **manjar** food
la **mano** hand
dar la mano to offer one's hand
el equipaje de mano hand (carry-on) luggage
estrechar la mano to shake hands
la mano de obra manual labor
la **mansión** mansion
manso(a) gentle; tame, 1
la **manta** blanket
la **manteca** lard
el **mantel** tablecloth
el **mantenimiento** maintenance
la **mantequilla** butter
la **manzana** apple; (city) block
el **mapa** map
la **máquina de lavar** washing machine
la **maquinilla** electric hair clipper
el/la **maquinista** mechanic
el **mar** sea
el mar Caribe Caribbean Sea
la **maravilla** wonder, marvel
maravilloso(a) wonderful
marcado(a) marked
marcar to score (sports); to dial; to designate; to mark
la **marcha** departure, 4
en marcha in motion
marcharse to go, leave, 3, 6
marchito(a) faded
el **marco** frame, 4
la **marea** tide
mareado(a) dizzy

la **marejada** swell, wave
el **mareo** dizziness
el **margen** margin
la **marginalización** marginalization
el **maricón** sissy
el **marido** husband
el **marino** sailor, **5**
el **marisco** shellfish
marrón brown
el **martes** Tuesday
marzo March
mas but
más more
la **masa** mass
   la **masa harina** flour
mascar to chew
la **máscara** mask
   la **máscara de oxígeno** oxygen mask
masculino(a) masculine
la **mata de cardo** thistle bush
matar to kill, **6**
las **matemáticas** mathematics
la **materia** subject matter
   la **materia prima** raw material
materno(a) maternal
   la **lengua materna** native language
los **matorrales** underbrush, thickets
la **matrícula** registration
matricular to enroll
el **matrimonio** wedding; marriage; married couple, bride and groom
matutino(a) pertaining to the morning
máximo(a) maximum
el/la **maya** Maya, Mayan
el **maya-quiché** language of the Guatemalan Mayas, **8**
mayo May
la **mayonesa** mayonnaise
mayor great, greater, greatest; older
el **mayordomo** steward
la **mayoría** majority
mayoritario(a) pertaining to the majority
mayormente principally, mainly
la **mazorca** ear of corn, corncob
me (to, for) me

mecánico(a) mechanical (adj.)
el/la **mecánico(a)** mechanic
la **mecha** lock (of hair)
mechado(a) shredded
la **medianoche** midnight
mediante by means of (adv.)
las **medias** pantihose, stockings
el **medicamento** medication
la **medicina** medicine
médico(a) medical, (adj.) **7**
el/la **médico(a)** doctor
la **medida** measurement; method
medieval medieval
el **medio** mean, way
medio(a) middle (adj.)
   la **clase media** middle class
   a **término medio** medium (meat)
   y **media** half past (the hour)
el **Medio Oriente** Middle East
el **mediodía** midday, noon
medir (i, i) to measure
la **mejilla** cheek
el **mejillón** mussel
mejor better; best
   a **lo mejor** maybe, perhaps
mejorar to improve
melancólico(a) melancholy, sad, **8**
la **melena** mane (of lion), **2**
el **melocotón** peach
la **membrana** membrane
la **memoria** memory
   la **carta de memoria** memory chart
mencionar to mention
el/la **mendigo(a)** beggar, **6**
menor younger; less, least
la **menora** menorah
menos less
   a **menos que** unless
   menos cuarto a quarter to (the hour)
   menos de less than
menospreciar to underrate
el **mensaje** message
mensualmente monthly
mental mental
la **mente** mind
la **mentira** lie, **5**
el **mentón** chin, **6**

el **menú** menu
   menudo: a menudo often
el/la **mercader** merchant
el **mercado** market
la **mercancía** merchandise
merendar to snack
el **meridiano** meridian
la **merienda** snack
el **mérito** merit
la **mermelada** marmalade
el **mes** month
la **mesa** table
   la **mesa de operaciones** operating table
el/la **mesero(a)** waiter (waitress)
la **meseta** plateau
la **mesita** tray table
el/la **mestizo(a)** of mixed race
la **meta** goal, objective, **6, 8**
la **metáfora** metaphor
el **metal** metal
la **meteorología** meteorology
meteorológico(a) meteorological
meter to put in
   meter en el cesto to make a basket
   meter un gol to score a goal
el **método** method
la **metodología** methodology
métrico(a) metric
el **metro** meter; subway
la **metrópoli** metropolis
metropolitano(a) metropolitan
mexicano(a) Mexican
la **mezcla** mixture, compound, **8**
mezclar to mix
la **mezcolanza** mixture
mezquino(a) stingy
la **mezquita** mosque, **5**
mi my
mí me
el **microbio** microbe
el **micrófono** microphone
microscópico(a) microscopic
el **microscopio** microscope
el **miedo** fear
la **miel** honey, **2, 4**
   la **miel de abeja** honey
el/la **miembro** member
mientras while
miércoles Wednesday
   el **miércoles de ceniza** Ash Wednesday

la **migración** migration
migrar to migrate
mil (one) thousand
la **milicia** militia
el **milímetro** milimeter
militar military (adj.)
el **militar** soldier
militarizar to militarize
la **milla** mile
el **millar** a thousand
el **millón (de)** million
el/la **millonario(a)** millionaire
la **milpa** field, 8
la **mina** mine
mineral mineral
la **miniatura** miniature, 1
el/la **miniaturista** miniaturist
el **minibús** minibus, 1
mínimo(a) minimum
el **ministerio** ministry
minoritario(a) minority (adj.)
el **minuto** minute
la **mirada** look, 8
mirar to look at
mirarse to look at oneself
la **misa** mass
la misa del gallo midnight mass
el/la **miserable** wretch
la **miseria** misery
la **misericordia** compassion
la **misión** mission
mismo(a) same; myself,
yourself, him / her / itself,
ourselves, yourselves,
themselves
lo mismo the same
el **misterio** mystery
misterioso(a) mysterious
la **mitad** half
mitigar to soften
la **mitología** mythology
mixto(a) mixed
la **mochila** bookbag, knapsack
la **moda** style
de moda in style
los **modales** manners
modelar to model
el **modelo** model
moderado(a) moderate
moderno(a) modern
modesto(a) modest
modificar to modify
el/la **modisto(a)** designer (clothes)
modo: de modo que so that
mojando wetting

el **molde** mold
la **molécula** molecule
molestar to bother
molesto(a) annoying
molido(a) exhausted
momentánea momentary
el **momento** moment
en este momento right now
de momento for the time
being
Un momento, por favor. One
moment, please.
la **monarquía** monarchy
la **moneda** coin
el **monje** monk
el **moño** bun, chignon
el **monocultivo** monoculture
el **monopatín** skateboard
andar en monopatín to
skateboard
el **monopolio** monopoly
el/la **monoteísta** monotheist
monótono(a) monotonous
el **monstruo** monster
la **montaña** mountain
montañoso(a) mountainous
montar to assemble
el **monte** mountain, 5
el **monto** total; sum, 1
el **monumento** monument, 1
la **mora** wild berry
el **moral** ethics
la **moraleja** moral
mordaz corrosive, sarcastic
moreno(a) dark
la **morería** Moorish quarter
morir (ue, u) to die
el **morisco** Moorish
el/la **moro(a)** Arab, 5
morrocotudo(a) big; strong
el **morrón** large, red, sweet
pepper
el **mostrador** counter
mostrar (ue) to show
el **motel** motel
motivar to motivate
el **motivo** motive, reason
la **moto** motorcycle
la **motoconformadora** road
grader
la **motonave** motorboat
el **motor** motor, engine
la **motricidad** motor function
mover (ue) to move
el **movimiento** movement

el/la **mozo(a)** young man (woman),
3; porter; bellhop
la **muchachada** group of young
people
el/la **muchacho(a)** boy (girl)
mucho(a) a lot; many
Mucho gusto. Nice to meet
you.
el **mueble** piece of furniture
la **muela** molar, 7
la **muerte** death, 5
el **muerto** corpse
el/la **muerto(a)** dead person
la **muestra** sample, 7
la **mujer** wife; woman
el/la **mulato(a)** mulatto
la **muleta** crutch
la **multa** fine
multinacional multinational
múltiple multiple
multiplicar to multiply
mundial worldwide
la Copa mundial World
Cup
la Serie mundial World
Series
el **mundo** world
el Nuevo Mundo New
World
la **muñeca** wrist; doll
el **municipio** municipality
el **muñón** stump (of amputated
limb)
el **mural** mural
la **muralla** city wall, 6
el **murmullo** murmur
muscular muscular
el **músculo** muscle, 3
el **museo** museum
la **música** music
musical musical
el/la **músico** musician
musulmán (musulmana)
Moslem, Muslim,
Mohammedan, 8
muy very

N
nacer (zc) to be born
el **nacimiento** birth
la **nación** nation
nacional national
la **nacionalidad** nationality
el **nacionalismo** nationalism

nada nothing
nadar to swim
nadie no one, nobody
la **naranja** orange
los **narcóticos** narcotics
la **nariz aguileña** aquiline nose, **7**
narrar to narrate
la **natación** swimming
natal native
natural natural
la **naturaleza** nature
el/la **naturalista** naturalist
el **naufragio** shipwreck, **5**
la **navaja** razor
la **nave** ship, **5**
navegable navegable
el **navegante** navigator, **5**
navegar to navigate, sail
la **Navidad** Christmas
  el **regalo de Navidad** Christmas present
  ¡Feliz Navidad! Merry Christmas!
  la **víspera de Navidad, la Nochebuena** Christmas Eve
el **navío** ship, **5**
la **neblina** fog, mist, **1**
necesariamente necessarily
necesario(a) necessary
la **necesidad** necessity
necesitar to need
negar to deny
negativo(a) negative
la **negociación** negotiation
negociarse to trade
el **negocio** business
negro(a) black
el **nervio** nerve
nervioso(a) nervous
nervudo(a) sinewy
el **neumático** tire
la **nevada** snowfall
nevado(a) snowy
nevar (ie) to snow
la **nevera** refrigerator
ni... ni neither... nor
  ni siquiera not even
  Ni yo tampoco. Me neither.
nicaragüense Nicaraguan
la **nicotina** nicotine
el/la **nieto(a)** grandchild
los **nietos** grandchildren
la **nieve** snow

la **niñez** childhood
ninguna: de ninguna manera by no means
el **niño(a)** boy (girl), **2**
el **nivel** level
  el nivel del mar sea level
nivelar to make even or level
no no
  No hay de qué. You're welcome.
  No hay más vuelta de hoja. No ifs, ands, or buts.
el/la **no conformista** nonconformist
el **noble** noble
la **nobleza** nobility
la **noche** night
  esta noche tonight
la **Nochebuena** Christmas Eve
nocturno(a) night (adj.)
nombrar to name
el **nombre** name
  el nombre de pila Christian name, first name
el **nordeste** northeast
la **norma** norm, standard, **8**
normal regular (gas)
el **noroeste** northwest
el **norte** north
  norteamericano(a) North American
la **Noruega** Norway
nos us (pron.)
nosotros(as) we
nostálgico(a) nostalgic
la **nota** grade; bill; note
notable outstanding; notable
notar to note; to notice
las **noticias** news
notorio(a) well-known
el/la **novato(a)** beginner, **3**
la **novela** novel
el/la **novelista** novelist
el **novenario** nine days of mourning
noveno(a) ninth
noventa ninety
noviembre November
la **novillada sin picadores** novice bullfight
el **novillero** novice bullfighter
el/la **novio(a)** fiancé(e), boyfriend (girlfriend), **4**

la **nube** cloud
nublado(a) cloudy
  Está nublado. It's cloudy.
la **nuca** nape (of neck)
nuclear nuclear
  la energía nuclear nuclear energy
el **núcleo** nucleus
el **nudo** knot, **1, 4**
  el nudo en la garganta lump in the throat, **4**
nuestro(a) our
nueve nine
nuevo(a) new
el **número** number
  el número de teléfono telephone number
  el número del asiento seat number
  el número del vuelo flight number
numeroso(a) numerous
nunca never
las **nupcias** nuptials
la **nutrición** nutrition
el **nutrimento** nutriment

O

o or
el **oasis** oasis
obediente obedient
el **objetivo** objective
el **objeto** object
oblicuo(a) angled, oblique
la **obligación** obligation
obligar to force
obligatorio(a) obligatory
la **obra** work; opus, **3**
obrar to work
el/la **obrero(a)** worker
obsequiar to give, present with, **4**
la **observación** observation
observar to observe
la **obsidiana** obsidian
obstante: no obstante nevertheless
la **obstetricia** obstetrics
la **obstinación** obstinacy
obtener (irreg.) to obtain
obviamente obviously
obvio(a) obvious
la **ocasión** occasion
  de ocasión secondhand
ocasionar to cause, **5**

el **ocaso** sunset; decline, end, **4**
occidental western
el **occidente** West, **8**
el **océano** ocean
    el océano Atlántico Atlantic Ocean
    el océano Pacífico Pacific Ocean
ochenta eighty
ocho eight
octavo eighth
octubre October
ocultar to hide
oculto(a) hidden
ocupado(a) occupied; busy
    el tono de ocupado busy signal
    La línea está ocupada. The line is busy.
    Suena ocupado. It is busy.
ocupar to occupy
    ocupar de to worry about
la **ocurrencia** incident
ocurrir to occur, happen, **1**
odiar to hate
el **odio** hate, hatred, **6**
el **oeste** west
    del oeste Western (movie)
ofender to offend
el/la **oferente** offerer
la **oferta** offer
oficialmente officially
oficiar to officiate, celebrate
la **oficina** office
    la oficina de cambio exchange office
    la oficina de correos post office
    la oficina de recepción (hospital) admitting office
el **oficio** trade; job, occupation, **3**
ofrecer (zc) to offer
el **oído** ear; hearing, **1, 7**
    oír (y) (irreg.) to hear
    Ojalá (que) I hope (that)
la **ojeada** quick glance
el **ojo cuadrado** amazed
la **ola** wave
el **oleaje** surf
el **óleo** oil painting
olímpico(a) Olympic
la **oliva** olive
la **olla** pot
el **olmo** elm
el **olor** odor

olvidar to forget
    ¡No te olvides! Don't forget!
omitir to omit
el **ómnibus** omnibus
omnívoro(a) omnivorous
la **onda** wave
    las ondas sonoras sound waves
el **ónix** onyx
la **onza** ounce
opaco(a) opaque; gloomy
la **opción** option
la **ópera** opera
el/la **operado(a)** post-operative patient
el/la **operador(a)** operator
    operar to operate
la **opereta** operetta
opinar to think; to express an opinion
la **opinión** opinion
oponer (irreg.) to oppose
la **oportunidad** opportunity
la **oposición** opposition
el/la **opresor(a)** oppressor, tyrant, **8**
el/la **oprimido(a)** oppressed person
oprimir to push
la **oración** sentence; prayer
    oral oral
el **orangután** orangutan
la **órbita** orbit
el **orden** order
el/la **ordenador(a)** computer
    ordenar to arrange
la **oreja** ear, **7**
    orgánico(a) organic
el **organillo** hand organ, **3**
el **organismo** organism
la **organización** organization
    organizar to organize
la **organza** organza
    orgulloso(a) proud, **2**
el/la **orientador(a)** counselor
    oriental eastern
el **oriente** East, **8**
el **origen** origin
    original original
    originar to originate
    originario(a) originating; native, descendant
la **orilla** bank (of a river)
el/la **oriundo(a)** native
el **ornamento** ornament

el **oro** gold, **8**
la **orquesta** orchestra
    ortopédico(a) orthopedic
el/la **ortopedista** orthopedist
la **osadía** daring
la **osamenta** skeleton, bones
la **oscuridad** darkness, gloom
    oscuro(a) gloomy
el **oso** bear
el **otoño** autumn
    otro(a) other
    el uno del otro each other
el **out** out (baseball)
la **ovación** ovation
    ovalado(a) oval
la **oveja** sheep, **2**
el **oxígeno** oxygen

P

la **paciencia** patience
    pacífico(a) peaceful, **8**; Pacific
    padecer to suffer
el **padrastro** stepfather
    padre (Mex.) really great
el **padre** father
    los padres parents
el **padrino** godfather; best man
    los padrinos godparents
la **paella** Valencian rice dish with meat, chicken, or fish and vegetables
la **paellera** paella pan
el **pagano de la fiesta** the person who pays
    pagar to pay
el **pago** pay; payment
el **país** country
el **paisaje** countryside; landscape, **1**
la **paja** straw
el **pajarillo volador** flying bird, **2**
el **pájaro** bird, **1**
el **paje de honor** usher
la **palabra** word
    tomar la palabra to take the floor
el **palacio** palace
    palidecer to turn pale
el **palillo** toothpick, **7**
la **palmadita** slap
    dar palmaditas to slap gently, tap
    palmear to clap, **7**
la **palmera** palm tree
el **palo** (golf) club; drink

la **paloma** dove

   la paloma torcaz wood pigeon

palpar to feel, touch

el **pan** bread

   el pan tostado toast

la **panadería** bakery

el/la **panadero(a)** baker

   panameño(a) Panamanian

el **panqueque** pancake

la **pantalla** screen

los **pantalones** pants

   el pantalón corto shorts

   el pantalón vaquero blue jeans

   el traje pantalón pantsuit

   pantanoso(a) swampy, marshy

el **pañuelo** handkerchief

la **papa** potato

   las papas fritas French fries

el **papá** dad

la **papaya** papaya

el **papel** paper

   el papel higiénico toilet paper

   la hoja de papel sheet of paper

el **papel** role (theater)

la **papilla** papilla

el **paquete** package

   par equal (adj.)

el **par** pair

   para for; to

   para que in order that, so that

el **parabrisas** windshield

el **paracaídas** parachute, **2**

el/la **paracaidista** paratrooper, parachutist, **2**

el **parachoques** bumper

la **parada** stop

   la parada de taxis taxi stand, **1**

el **parador** inn

el **paraíso** paradise, **3**

el **paramecio** paramecium

   parar to stop

el **parasol** parasol

la **parcela** parcel

   parcial partial

   a tiempo parcial part-time

   parcialmente partially

   parear to pair, match

parecer (zc) to seem; to resemble

   parecido(a) similar

la **pared** wall, **6**

la **pareja** couple

el **parentesco** relationship; bond, **6**

el/la **pariente** relative

   los parientes lejanos distant relatives

   parir to give birth, **4**

el **paro** stop, stoppage of work, **5**

el **parque** park

el **parquímetro** parking meter

el **párrafo** paragraph

la **parrilla** grill

la **parroquia** parish

la **parte** part

   a ninguna parte nowhere

   ¿De parte de quién? Who is calling?

la **partera** midwife

el/la **participante** participant

   participar to communicate; to inform, **4**

   particular private; particular, **2**

   particularmente particularly

el **partido** game

   partir to depart, leave, **1**; to divide

   a partir de as of, from

el **parto** birth, **4**

   pasado(a) past, gone by

el **pasado** past

   el año pasado last year

el **pasador** pin

el **pasaje** passage, journey

el/la **pasajero(a)** passenger

el **pasaporte** passport

   el control de pasaportes passport inspection

   pasar to pass; to spend; to happen

   pasar hambre to go hungry

el **pasatiempo** pastime, hobby

la **Pascua** Easter

el **pase de abordar** boarding pass

el **paseíllo** parade of bullfighters

el **paseo** stroll, walk

el **pasillo** corridor; aisle

el **paso** passing, passage

   el paso de peatones pedestrian crosswalk

la **pasta dentífrica** toothpaste

el **pastel** pie; pastry

la **pastelería** pastry shop

la **pastilla** pill; bar (of soap)

el/la **pastor(a)** shepherd

   el pastor vasco Basque shepherd

los **patagones** Patagonians

la **patata** potato

   paterno(a) paternal

el **patíbulo** scaffold

la **patilla** sideburn

el **patín** skate

el **patinadero** skating rink

el/la **patinador(a)** skater

el **patinaje** skating

   el patinaje artístico figure skating

   el patinaje sobre hielo ice-skating

   el patinaje sobre ruedas roller skating

   la pista de patinaje skating rink

   patinar to skate

el **patio** patio, courtyard

el **pato** duck, **6**

la **patología** pathology

la **patria** homeland, native land

el **patriota** patriot

   patrocinado(a) sponsored

el **patrón** pattern

el **patrón (la patrona)** patron, boss

   patronal patronal

la **pausa** pause

el **pavo** turkey

la **paz** peace

el **peaje** toll

el **peatón** pedestrian

el **pecho** chest

el **pedacito** (little) piece

la **pedagogía** education

   pedalear to pedal

   pedir (i, i) to ask for

   pedir prestado to borrow

   pedradas: a pedradas throwing stones

el **pedrusco** rough, uncut stone

   pegar to stick; to fasten; to hit

   pegar un tiro to shoot

el **peinado** hairdo

   el peinado afro Afro hairstyle

   peinarse to comb one's hair

el **peine** comb

el **pejerrey** variety of mackerel, **2**
el/la **pelado(a)** penniless person, **6**
    pelar to peel
la **película** movie, film
    dar una película to show a
      movie, film
el **peligro** danger
    peligroso(a) dangerous
el **pellejo** skin, hide, **7**
el **pelo** hair
    tomar el pelo a alguien to
      pull someone's leg
la **pelota** ball
la **peluca** wig
la **peluquera** beautician
la **peluquería** hair salon
el/la **peluquero(a)** hair stylist
la **pena** sorrow; suffering
    a duras penas with great
      difficulty
    pendiente aware
    penetrante penetrating
la **península** peninsula
el/la **pensador(a)** thinker
el **pensamiento** thought
    pensar to think
    pensativo(a) pensive
la **pensión** boarding house;
    small hotel; room and board
el/la **pensionista** pensioner, retired
    person, **2**
    pentecostal Pentecostal
    peor worse; worst
el **pepino** cucumber
    pequeño(a) small
la **pera** pear
la **percepción** perception
la **percha** clothes hanger
    percibir perceive
    perder (ie) to lose
    perder el autobús to miss
      the bus
la **pérdida** loss
la **perdiz** partridge
    perdón excuse me
    perdonar to pardon
el **peregrinaje** pilgrimage
    perenne perennial
    perfectamente perfectly
la **perforadora de pavimento**
    jackhammer
el **perfume** perfume
la **perfumería** perfume shop
el **periódico** newspaper
el **periodismo** journalism

el/la **periodista** journalist
el **período** period, space of time
    perjudicial harmful
la **perla** pearl
    permanente permanent
el **permiso de conducir** driver's
    license
    permitido(a) permitted
    permitir to permit
    pero but
    perplejo(a) confused, **6**
el **perro** dog
la **persecución** persecution
    perseguir to pursue, chase, **8**
la **persona** person
el **personaje** character
    personal personal
    personalmente personally
    pertenecer (zc) to belong
las **pertenencias** belongings
    peruano(a) Peruvian
la **pesa** weight, **7**
    pesado(a) dull, tiresome (adj.)
el/la **pesado(a)** heavyweight, **3**
el **pésame** condolences
    pesar to weigh
    pesar: a pesar de in spite of
    pesca: de pesca fishing
la **pescadería** fish market
el **pescado** fish (when caught)
el/la **pescador(a)**
    fisherman/woman
    pescar to fish
el **peso** weight; monetary unit of
    several Latin American
    countries
    pesquero(a) (adj.) fishing, **7**
el **pez** fish (alive)
el/la **pianista** pianist
el **piano** piano
    picar to dice
el/la **pícher** pitcher (baseball)
el **pico** peak
el **pie** foot
    a pie on foot
    de pie standing
la **piedra** rock, stone, **6**
    la piedra caliza limestone
la **piel** skin
la **pierna** leg
la **pieza** piece
la **pila** (baptismal) font, **4**
el **pilar** pillar, **8**
la **píldora** pill
el/la **piloto(a)** pilot

la **pimienta** pepper
el **pimiento** bell pepper
el **pinar** pine grove
el **pingüino** penguin, **1**
el **pino** pine tree
la **pinta** pint
    pintar to paint
el/la **pintor(a)** painter
    pintoresco(a) picturesque
la **pintura** painting
la **pinza** clamp, **7**
    la pinza para el cabello
      hair clip
las **pinzas** tweezers, **7**
la **piña** pineapple
el/la **pionero(a)** pioneer
la **pirámide** pyramid, **1**
la **piscina** swimming pool
el **piso** floor, apartment, **2**
la **pista** ski trail; runway
    la pista de patinaje
      skating rink
la **pistola** pistol
la **pizarra** chalkboard
el **pizarrón** chalkboard
la **pizca** pinch
la **pizzería** pizza parlor
la **placa** license plate
    placentero(a) pleasant,
      agreeable, **1**
el **placer** pleasure
    plácido(a) calm, **1**
el **plan** plan; outline, **2**
la **plana** page
la **plancha** iron
    la plancha de vela wind
      surfboard
    planchar to iron
    planear to plan
el **planeta** planet
    planetario(a) planetary
la **planta** floor; plant
    la planta baja ground
      floor
la **plantación** plantation
    plantar to plant
    plantear to outline, set
      forth
    plástico(a) plastic
    de plástico plastic (adj.)
    la bolsa de plástico
      plastic bag
la **plata** silver; money, **8**
el **plátano** plantain; banana
el **platillo** home plate

(baseball); saucer
el **platino** platinum
el **plato** plate, dish
la **playa** beach
playero(a) beach (adj.)
la toalla playera beach
towel
la **plaza** job; employment;
place, space
la plaza de toros bull ring, **3**
plegable folding
plenamente fully, completely
el/la **plomero(a)** plumber
el **plomo** lead
con plomo leaded
sin plomo unleaded
la **pluma** feather
el **plumaje** plumage
la **población** population
el **poblado** town, village
poblado(a) populated
pobre poor
la **pobreza** poverty
la **poción** potion
poco(a) little, small (amount)
poco a poco little by little
podar to prune, **7**
poder (irreg.) to be able
puede ser maybe
el **poder** power, strength, **6**
el poder extranjero
foreign power
poderoso(a) powerful
el **poema** poem
la **poesía** poetry
el/la **poeta** poet
polar polar
polarización focus of
attention
el **polen** pollen, **4**
el/la **policía** police officer
policromo(a) multicolored
la **política** politics, **8**
político(a) political (adj.)
los **políticos (parientes)** in-laws
el **pollo** chicken
el **polo** pole
el **polvo** dust, **4**
en polvo powdered
polvoriento(a) dusty
el **pomo de loza** small
porcelain bottle
las **pompas** buttocks
el **poncho** poncho, cape
poner (irreg.) to put

poner al fuego to put on
the fire
poner la mesa to set the
table
ponerse to become, **2**; to
put on
popular popular
la **popularidad** popularity
poquito más a little more
por about, for, by
por consiguiente
consequently
por ejemplo for example
por encima over
por eso therefore
por favor please
por lo menos at least
por supuesto of course
¿por qué? why?
la **porcelana** porcelain
la **porción** portion
porque because
la **portada** cover
el **portal** city gate
portarse to behave
el **porte** bearing
la **portería** goal
el/la **portero(a)** goalkeeper, goalie
portugués(a) Portuguese
la **posibilidad** possibility
posible possible
la **posición** position
positivo(a) positive
posterior posterior
posteriormente afterwards
postizo(a) false
el **postre** dessert
el/la **postulante** applicant
el **potro** colt, **8**
el **pozo** well, **1, 2, 4**
el/la **practicante** hospital nurse
practicar to practice
práctico(a) practical
precario(a) precarious
el **precepto** precept
el **precio** price
la **preciosidad** beauty, charm
precioso(a) beautiful
la **precipitación** precipitation
precisado(a) forced
precisamente precisely
precisar to need, **2**; to
specify, determine
precolombino(a) pre-
Columbian

precoz precocious
predominante predominant
predominantemente
predominantly
el **predominio** predominance
la **preferencia** preference
preferir (ie, i) to prefer
el **prefijo** prefix
el prefijo telefónico area
code
el prefijo del país country
code
la **pregunta** question
preguntar to ask
la **prehistoria** prehistory
el **prejuicio** prejudice
el **premio** prize
el Premio Nóbel Nobel
Prize
la **prenda** garment, article of
clothing
el **prendedor** brooch, pin, **1**
prendidísimo: lo
prendidísimo what is
most interesting
prendido(a) interesting
el **prendimiento** capture, arrest
la **preocupación** preoccupation
preocuparse to worry
la **preparación** preparation
preparar to prepare
la **presencia** presence
presentar to present
presentar (dar) una
película to show a movie
el **presente** present
preservar to preserve
la **presidencia** presidency
el/la **presidente(a)** president
la **presión** pressure
la presión arterial blood
pressure
la presión sanguínea
blood pressure
prestar to lend
prestigioso(a) prestigious
presunto(a) presumed
el **presupuesto** budget, **6**
pretender (ie) to seek
el **pretendiente** suitor
prevalecer to prevail
la **prevención** prevention
la **previsión** forecast
primario(a) primary, elementary
la **primavera** spring

primer, primero(a) first
  el primer balcón first
    balcony, **3**
  primitivo(a) primitive
el/la **primo(a)** cousin
el/la **primogénito(a)** firstborn, **4**
  principal main
el **príncipe** prince
el/la **principiante** beginner
el **principio** beginning
  al principio in the
    beginning
la **prioridad** priority
la **prisa** hurry, haste, **1**
  dar prisa to rush, hurry
  de prisa fast, in a hurry
el/la **prisionero(a)** prisoner
  privado(a) private
la **privatización** privatization
  privatizar to privatize
el **privilegio** privilege
la **probabilidad** probability
  probable probable
  probar (ue) to try; to taste
el **problema** problem
  procedente coming
  proceder to proceed, come
  procesar to process
la **procesión** procession
el **proceso** process
  procurar to try, strive for
  producir (zc) to produce
  productivo(a) productive
el **producto** product
el/la **productor(a)** producer
  profano profane
la **profesión** profession; career
  profesional professional
    (adj.)
el/la **profesional** professional
    (person)
el/la **profesor(a)** teacher
el **profesorado** faculty
el **profeta** prophet
la **profundidad** depth
  profundo(a) profound
el **progenitor** direct ancestor
el **programa** program
el/la **programador(a)** programmer
el **progreso** progress
la **prohibición** prohibition
  prohibido(a) forbidden
  prohibir to prohibit
  prolongar to prolong
el **promedio** average

la **promesa** promise
  prometer to promise
el/la **prometido(a)** fiancé(e)
  promulgar to enact a law
  pronosticar to foretell, **1**
el **pronóstico** forecast
  pronto(a) quick, fast
la **propiedad** property
el/la **propietario(a)** owner
la **propina** tip
  propio(a) one's own, **2**
  proponer to propose, **6**
la **proporción** proportion
el **propósito** purpose
  a propósito by the way
  ¡Próspero año nuevo! Happy
    New Year!
el/la **protagonista** protagonist
  protagonizar to take a
    leading part in, **4**
la **protección** protection
  protector: la crema
    protectora sunblock
  proteger to protect
la **proteína** protein
la **protesta** protest
  protestante Protestant
el **provecho** benefit, advantage
  ¡Buen provecho! Enjoy
    your meal!
  proveer to provide
la **provincia** province
  provisionalmente
    temporarily
la **provocación** provocation
  provocar to provoke
la **proximidad** proximity,
    nearness
  próximo(a) next
  proyectar to plan, project
el **proyecto** project
la **prudencia** prudence
la **prueba** test
  a prueba on trial
  psicológico(a) psychological
  publicado(a) published
  publicar to publish
la **publicidad** advertising
  público(a) public (adj.)
el **público** public; audience
el **pueblo** town; people
  puede ser maybe
el **puente** bridge; dental bridge
el **puerco** pork
la **puerta** gate; door

  la puerta de salida
    departure gate; exit door
el **puerto** port, **5**
  puertorriqueño(a) Puerto
    Rican
  pues well
el **puesto** stall
la **pulgada** inch
  pulir to polish
el **pulmón** lung, **7**
  pulmonar pulmonary, **7**
la **pulsación** beat
la **pulsera** bracelet, **1**
el **pulso** pulse
el **puñado** handful
el **puñal** dagger
el **puñetazo** punch, blow, **6**
la **punta** point; tip
el **puntapié** kick
el **punto** stitch; dot
  el punto de vista point of
    view
  en punto on the dot
la **pupila** pupil (of the eye)
  puramente purely, strictly
el **puro** cigar, **4**

Q

  que that
¿Qué? What?; How?
  ¿Qué es? What is it?
  ¿Qué hora es? What time
    is it?
  ¿Qué tal? How are you?
  ¿Qué tiempo hace?
    What's the weather like?
el **quechua** Quechuan people
  and language, **8**
  quedar(se) to stay, remain
  Me queda bien. It fits me.
  quedar empatado(a) to be
    tied (sports)
  quemar to burn
  querer (irreg.) to want; to
    love
  querer decir to mean
el **queso** cheese
el **quicio de la puerta** door
  threshold, **4**
¿Quién? Who?
  ¿De parte de quién? Who
    is calling?
  ¿Quién es? Who is it?
  quieto(a) quiet
la **química** chemistry

químico(a) chemical (adj.)

el/la **químico(a)** chemist

la **quinceañera** young woman's fifteenth birthday

quinientos five hundred

quinto(a) fifth

el **quiosco** newsstand

el **quirófano** operating room

Quisiera... I would like...

quitar to remove, take away, **5**

　quitar del fuego to take off the fire

　quitarse to take off

quizá(s) perhaps

R

la **rabia** anger, fury

el **rabino** rabbi, **8**

racial racial

la **ración** portion; allowance, **7**

el **radiador** radiator

radical radical

el/la **radio** radio

radioactivo(a) radioactive

la **radiografía** X-ray

raído(a) frayed

la **raíz** root, **8**

rallar to grate

la **rama** branch

el **ramo de novia** bridal bouquet, **4**

el/la **ranchero(a)** rancher

el **rango** rank; class

la **ranura** slot (for money)

rápidamente quickly

la **rapidez** swiftness, speed

el **rápido** express train

rápido fast

la **raqueta** racket

raro(a) rare, **2**

ras: a ras de level with

el **rasgo** feature

el **rato** while, short time

　a cada rato at each moment

　mal rato nasty experience

el **ratón** mouse

la **raya** part (in hair)

　a rayas striped

el **rayo** ray

　los rayos equis X-rays

la **razón** reason

razonable reasonable

real real, actual

la **realidad** reality

el **realismo** realism

realista realistic

realizar to carry out, put into effect

realmente really; actually

la **rebaja** reduction

rebajar to reduce, **2**

la **rebanada** slice

rebanar to slice

la **rebelión** rebellion

el **recado** message, **3**

recambio: de recambio spare (tire)

la **recepción** reception

el/la **recepcionista** receptionist

el **receptor** catcher (baseball)

la **receta** prescription; recipe

recetar to prescribe

recibir to receive

el **recibo** receipt

recién recently

el/la **recién casado(a)** newlywed

　el/la recién nacido(a) newborn

reciente recent

recientemente recently

recitar to recite

reclamar to claim

el **reclamo de equipaje** baggage claim

recoger to pick up, collect; to shelter; to gather, **6**

la **recomendación** recommendation

recomendar (ie) to recommend

reconfortable comfortable

reconocer (zc) to recognize; to acknowledge, **8**

reconstruir (y) to reconstruct

recopilar to compile

recordar (ue) to remember

el **recordatorio** reminder

recorrer to travel, **1**

el **recorrido** distance traveled, trip

　de largo recorrido long-distance

recortar to trim

el **recorte** trim

la **rectitud** honesty

el **recuerdo** memory, **3**

el **recurso** resource

　los recursos resources, wealth, **6**

　los recursos naturales natural resources

el **servicio de recursos humanos** human resources department

la **red** net; network; screen

la **rededicación** rededication

redondo(a) round, **5, 8**

reducido(a) reduced

reducir (zc) to reduce; to diminish, **5**

　reducir la fractura to set the bone

reembolsar to reimburse, **1**

el **reembolso** refund

reemplazar to replace, substitute, **2**

referir (ie, i) to refer

refinar to refine

reflejar to reflect

el **reflejo** reflection

la **reforma** reform

el **refrán** refrain, proverb

refrescante refreshing

el **refresco** soft drink

el **refrigerador** refrigerator

refugiarse to take refuge

el **refugio** refuge

el **regalo** gift

　el regalo de Navidad Christmas present

regar to water, **2, 7**

regatear to bargain

el **regateo** bargaining

el **regidor** manager

el **régimen** regimen

regio(a) royal, regal

la **región** region

registrar to record; to take place

la **regla** rule

el **reglamento** rule

regodearse to take delight in

regresar to return

regulador(a) regulating (adj.)

regular regular; fair (grade) (adj.); to regulate (verb)

rehabilitado(a) restored

rehusar to refuse, **6**

reinar to reign

el **reino** kingdom

reír to laugh

la **relación** relationship

relacionar to relate

relativamente relatively

el **relato** story
la **religión** religion
religioso(a) religious
rellenar to fill
el **reloj** watch; clock, **5**
relucir to shine
remedio: sin remedio unavoidably
el/la **remitente** sender
remontar to go back (to some date in time)
remoto(a) remote
el **rencor** rancor
rendido(a) exhausted
rendir to render; to yield
renovar to renovate
renunciar to renounce
reparador(a) restorative
repartir to deliver; to share
el **reparto** delivery
repentino(a) sudden
repetir (i, i) to repeat
la **representación** performance
dar una representación to put on a performance
el/la **representante** representative
representar to represent
la **represión** repression
la **reprobación** reproof, censure
el **réprobo** criminal
la **reproducción** reproduction
el **reptil** reptile
la **república** republic
repuesto: de repuesto spare (tire)
la **repugnancia** repugnance
repugnante repugnant
la **reputación** reputation
requerir (ie, i) to require
el **réquiem** requiem (mass)
resbalarse to slip
rescatar to rescue; to save, **5**
resentido(a) resentful
la **reserva** reserve
la **reservación** reservation
reservado(a) reserved
reservar to reserve
el **resfriado** (head) cold
la **residencia** residence, home
residencial residential
residir to reside
resignarse to resign oneself
resistir to resist
resolver (ue) to resolve
el **resorte** spring (mechanical)

el **respaldo** seatback; backing, support
respectivo(a) respective
respecto a with respect to
respetarse to respect one another
el **respeto** respect
respetuoso(a) respectful
la **respiración** breathing
respirar to breathe
responder to respond, answer
la **responsabilidad** responsibility
responsabilizarse to take the responsibility
la **respuesta** answer
el **restaurante** restaurant
los **restos** remains
la **restricción** restriction
restringir to restrict
el **resultado** result
resultar to result
el **resumen** summary
el **resurgimiento** revival
la **resurrección** resurrection
la **retirada** withdrawal
retirar to withdraw; to remove
retirar del fuego to take off the fire
retirarse to retire
el **retiro** withdrawal
el formulario de retiro withdrawal slip
el **retraso** delay
con retraso late
el **retrato** portrait
el **retrete** toilet, **1**
la **reunión** meeting, gathering
reunirse to get together
revés: al revés backwards
revisionista revisionist
el/la **revisor(a)** (train) conductor; auditor
la **revista** magazine
revitalizar to revitalize
la **revolución** revolution
revolucionario(a) revolutionary
revolver (ue) to stir; to revolve
revueltos scrambled (eggs)
el **rey** king, **5, 8**
los **Reyes Magos** Three Wise Men
el día de Reyes Twelfth-night
rico(a) rich; tasty

ridiculizar to ridicule
el **riesgo** danger, **5**
rígido(a) rigid
rigor: de rigor essential
riguroso(a) rigorous
el **rincón** nook, cozy corner, **1**
los **riñones** kidneys
el **río** river
rioplatense Argentinian (from the River Plate region)
la **riqueza** riches; wealth
el **ritmo** rhythm
el **rito** rite
el **rizado** curling
rizado(a) curly
el **rizador** curling iron
rizar to curl
el **rizo** curl
robar to rob; to steal
el **robo** theft, robbery, **5**
rociar to sprinkle, **2**
rodar (ue) to shoot a movie
rodear to surround
la **rodilla** knee
rogar (ue) to beg; to request
rojo(a) red
el **rol** roll, part
rollizo(a) roly-poly
el **rollo** roll (of paper)
el **romance** romance, ballad
el **romancero** collection of romances, ballads
el/la **romano(a)** Roman
romántico(a) romantic
romperse to break; to tear
el **ron** rum
la **ropa** clothes
la ropa interior underwear
poner la ropa en la maleta to pack
la **rosa** rose
el **rosal** rosebush
el **rostro** face
la **rotación** rotation
el **rótulo** sign
rubio(a) blond(e)
rudo(a) hard, difficult, **4**
la **rueda** wheel; roller
el **ruedo** bullring
el **ruido** noise, **7**
ruidoso(a) noisy, **1**
la **ruina** ruin
el **rulo** hair roller
rumbo a toward, in the direction of

rural rural, 8
ruso(a) Russian
la **ruta** route
la **rutina** routine
rutinario(a) routine

S

sábado Saturday
la **sábana** sheet
sabatino(a) pertaining to Saturday
saber (irreg.) to know (how)
el/la **sabio(a)** wise person
el **sabor** flavor
sabroso(a) tasty
sacar (qu) to get, receive; to take out
  sacar notas buenas (malas) to get good (bad) grades
  sacar provecho de to benefit from
el **sacerdote** priest
el **saco** jacket; sack
  el saco de dormir sleeping bag
el **sacramento** sacrament
sacrificar to sacrifice
el **sacrificio** sacrifice
el **sacro** sacred
sagrado(a) sacred, 8
la **sal** salt
la **sala** living room
  la sala de clase classroom
  la sala de emergencia emergency room
  la sala de espera waiting room
  la sala de operaciones operating room
  la sala de recepción waiting room
  la sala de recuperación recovery room
  la sala de restablecimiento recovery room
  la sala de urgencias emergency room
salarial wage (adj.)
el **salario** salary
la **salchicha** sausage
el **salchichón** sausage
el **saldo** total; balance (bank)
la **salida** departure; exit

el tablero de llegadas y salidas arrival and departure board
la puerta de salida departure gate
la salida de emergencia emergency exit
salir (irreg.) to leave; to go out
el **salón** room, lounge
  el salón de clase classroom
  el salón del hotel hotel ballroom
la **salsa** sauce
saltar to jump, 7
el **salto** jump, leap, 3
la **salud** health
  estar de buena salud to be in good health
saludable healthy
saludar to greet
el **saludo** greeting; salute
salvaje wild
el **sanatorio** sanatorium
las **sandalias** sandals
la **sandía** watermelon
el **sándwich** sandwich
la **sangre** blood, 7, 8
la **sanidad** health
sano(a) healthy
santamente virtuously
el/la **santo(a)** saint
  el santo patrón patron saint, 3
el **santuario** sanctuary
el **sargento** sergeant, 5
sarnoso(a) mangy
el/la **sartén** frying pan
la **sátira** satire
satirizar to satirize
la **satisfacción** satisfaction
satisfacer (irreg.) to satisfy
satisfecho(a) satisfied
las **saturnales** Saturnalia
el **saxofón** saxophone
el **secador** hair dryer
la **secadora** clothes dryer
secar to dry
la **sección** section
  la sección de no fumar no smoking section
seco(a) dry
el/la **secretario(a)** secretary
el **secreto** secret

secreto(a) secret
el **sector** section
la **secuencia** sequence
secundario(a) secondary
  la escuela secundaria high school
la **secuoya** sequoia
la **sed** thirst
  tener sed to be thirsty
la **seda dental** dental floss, 7
el **sedán** sedan
la **sede** headquarters
el/la **sefardí** Sephardic Jew
el **segmento** segment
segregar to segregate
seguida: en seguida at once, immediately
seguido(a) successive
el **seguimento** following
seguir (i, i) to follow; to continue
según according to
segundo second
la **seguridad** security
  el cinturón de seguridad seat belt
  el control de seguridad security control
el **Seguro Social** Social Security
seguro(a) reliable, dependable; sure; safe
seis six
la **selección** selection
el **sello** stamp
la **selva** jungle, rainforest, 1
el **semáforo** traffic light
la **semana** week
  la Semana Santa Holy Week
  la semana pasada last week
sembrar to plant, 2, 8
el **semestre** semester
el/la **senador** senator
el **sencillez** simplicity
sencillo(a) one-way; single
la **senda** path
el **sendero** path
la **sensación** sensation
sensacional sensational
sensible sensitive, 4
las **sentadillas** sit-ups, 3
sentarse (ie) to sit down
  Me sienta bien. It fits me well.

sentenciar to pass judgment on
el **sentido** sense; way, direction
de sentido único one-way
el **sentimiento** feeling
sentirse (ie, i) to feel
Lo siento. I am sorry.
la **señal** dial tone; signal; sign
la señal de no fumar no smoking signal
señalar to point out; to indicate, **8**
señor(a) Mr., sir; (Mrs., ma'am)
la **señorita** Miss
la **separación** separation
separado(a) separated
separar to separate
septiembre September
séptimo(a) seventh
ser (irreg.) to be
ser una lástima to be a pity
el **ser** being
el ser viviente living being
sereno(a) serene
seriamente seriously
la **serie** series
la Serie mundial World Series
serio(a) serious
serpentear to wind; to meander
la **serpiente** snake
el **servicio** service
el servicio de primer socorro first-aid service
el servicio de primeros auxilios first-aid service
el servicio de recursos humanos human resources department
el servicio militar military service
la estación de servicio service station
el/la **servidor(a)** servant
su seguro(a) servidor(a) your humble servant
la **servidumbre** servants
la **servilleta** napkin
servir (i, i) to serve
sesenta sixty
la **sesión** show (movies)
setenta seventy

severo(a) severe
el **sexo** sex
sexto(a) sixth
si if
sí yes; used for emphasis
el **SIDA** AIDS
siempre always
la **sien** temple (of the face), **6**
la **sierra** mountain range, **2**
la **siesta** nap
echar (tomar) una siesta to take a nap
siete seven
la **sigla** abbreviation by initials
el **siglo** century
el **significado** meaning
significar to mean
significativo(a) significant
el **signo** sign
siguiente following
el **silencio** silence
la **silla** chair
la silla de ruedas wheelchair
la silla plegable folding chair
el **sillín** seat, saddle
el **sillón** large chair, **7**
el **silo** silo
silvestre wild
el **símbolo** symbol
el **símil** simile
similar similar
la **simpatía** sympathy
simpático(a) pleasant, likeable
simple simple
simplemente simply
sin without
sin embargo nevertheless
sin escala nonstop
sin que without
la **sinagoga** synagogue, **8**
sincero(a) sincere
siniestrado(a) unlucky
sino but
el **sinónimo** synonym
el **síntoma** symptom
la **sirena** siren
sirio(a) Syrian
el **sistema** system
el sistema nervioso nervous system
sitiar to besiege
el **sitio** siege; site; place

la **situación** situation
situar to situate
el **slálom** slalom
el/la **soberano(a)** sovereign, **8**
sobre above, over; about
sobre todo especially, above all
el **sobre** envelope
el/la **sobrecargo** flight attendant
sobrepasar to exceed, surpass, **5**
sobresaliente outstanding
sobresalir to stand out
sobrevolar to fly over
el/la **sobrino(a)** nephew (niece)
social social
la **sociedad** society
sociología sociology
el/la **sociólogo(a)** sociologist
el/la **socorrista** first-aid worker
el **socorro** help
el **sodio** sodium
sofisticado(a) sophisticated
la **soga** rope, cord, **7**
el **sol** sun
Hay (Hace) sol. It's sunny.
tomar el sol to sunbathe
solamente only
el/la **soldado** soldier
soleado(a) sunny, **1**
solemne solemn
la **solemnidad** solemnity
soler (ue) to be accustomed to, **8**
solicitar (trabajo) to apply for (work)
la **solicitud de empleo** job application
sólido(a) solid
solitario(a) solitary, lone
sólo only
solo(a) alone
soltar to let go
la **soltería** single life
el/la **soltero(a)** unmarried person, **6**
la **solución** solution
la **sombra** shade
el **sombrero** hat
el **sombrerillo** little hat
la **sombrilla** umbrella
sombrío(a) somber
someter to subject
somos we are
sonar (ue) to ring

Suena ocupado. It is busy.

el **soneto** sonnet

el **sonido** sound, 7

sonorífero(a) noisy

sonreír to smile

sonriente smiling, 3

la **sonrisa** smile

soñar (ue) to dream, 6

soñoliento(a) sleepy, 2

la **sopa** soup

soplar to blow, 1

soportar to bear, endure; to support

la **sordera** deafness, 7

el/la **sordo(a)** deaf person, 7

sordo(a) deaf, 7

el **soroche** mountain sickness

sorprender to surprise

sorprenderse to be surprised, 2

la **sortija** ring

la **sortija de compromiso** engagement ring

soso(a) dull, inane

el **sostén** support

sostener (irreg.) to sustain; to support

su his, her, your (form.), their

suave soft

la **subcultura** subculture

subir to go up; to take up

subir a to get on, to board

súbito(a) sudden

sublime sublime

subscribir to subscribe

subsistir to continue to exist

la **substancia** substance

el **subterráneo** subway, 5

subterráneo(a) underground

el **subtítulo** subtitle

los **suburbios** suburbs

sucesivo(a) successive

el **suceso** event, happening

sucio(a) dirty

la **sucursal** branch (office)

sudamericano(a) South American

el **sudor** sweat, 8

sudoroso(a) sweaty

el/la **suegro(a)** father-in-law (mother-in-law)

la **suela** sole (of shoe), 3

el **suelo** ground; soil, land, 1

tocar el suelo to touch the ground

suelto(a) loose, free, 2

el **sueño** dream

la **suerte** luck

tener suerte to be lucky

el **suéter** sweater

suficiente sufficient, enough

el **sufragio** aid

sufrir to suffer

sugerir (ie, i) to suggest

suicido(a) suicidal

suizo(a) Swiss

sujeto(a) held (adj.)

el **sujeto** individual, person

sumamente extremely

suministrar to supply, 2

suministrado(a), supplied

sumo(a) highest, greatest

suntuosamente sumptuously

súper super

superar to surpass

la **superficie** surface

superior superior; higher; top, upper

el **supermercado** supermarket

supervisar to supervise

el/la **superviviente** survivor

el **suplemento** supplement

el **supremo** Supreme Court

supuesto: por supuesto of course

el **sur** south

la **América del Sur** South America

el **surgimiento** springing up

surgir to appear

el **suroeste** southwest

suspenso(a) failing (grade)

el **suspensor** suspender

el **suspiro** sigh

la **sustancia** substance

sustancioso(a) substantial

sustituir (y) to substitute

la **sutura** stitch

suyo(a) his, hers, yours, theirs, its, one's

T

el **T shirt** T-shirt

el **tabaco** tobacco

la **tabla** board, 3

la **tabla hawaiiana** surfing

el **tablero** backboard (basketball)

el **tablero de llegadas y salidas** arrival and departure board

el **tablero indicador** scoreboard

la **tableta** tablet

el/la **tablista** surfer

el **tabú** taboo

taciturno(a) taciturn, reserved, 8

el **tacón** heel (shoe)

los **tainos** Tainos (natives of the Caribbean area)

la **tajada** slice

el **tajo** cut, slash

el **tajo de perrillo** knife cut

tal such

tal vez perhaps

la **tala** stalk

el **taladro** drill, 7

el **talco** talcum powder

el **talento** talent

talentoso(a) talented; gifted

la **talla** size

tallar to deal (cards), 6

el **taller** artisan's shop

el **tallo** stalk

el **talón** luggage claims ticket; heel (foot)

el **talonario** checkbook

el **tamaño** size

el **tamarindo** tamarind

también also, too

tampoco neither, either

Ni yo tampoco. Me neither.

tan so

tan pronto como as soon as

el/la **tanguista** interpreter of the tango

el **tanque** tank

el **tanto** score, point

tanto... como as much... as

tantos(as) so many

la **tapa** cover; cap, 7

tapar to cover; to clog

la **tapia** wall

el **tapón** plug, 7

la **taquilla** ticket office

tarde late (adj.)

la **tarde** afternoon

esta tarde this afternoon

la **tarea** homework; task, job, work, 8

la **tarifa** fare, rate

la **tarjeta** card; registration card

la tarjeta de crédito credit card

la tarjeta de embarque boarding, pass

la tarjeta postal postcard

la **tasa de cambio** exchange rate

taurino(a) of or about bullfighting, **6**

el **taxi** taxi

el **taxímetro** taximeter, **1**

la **taza** cup

te you (fam. pron.)

el **té** tea

teatral theatrical

el **teatro** theater

la **tecla** key

el **teclado** keyboard

la **técnica** technique

técnico(a) technical

el/la **técnico(a)** technician

el **tejado** roof, **6**

tejer to weave

el **tejido** fabric, cloth, **2**

la **telaraña** spider's web

la **tele** TV

la **telecomunicación** telecommunication

la **telecopiadora** fax machine

telefonear to telephone

telefónico(a) telephone (adj.)

el/la **telefonista** telephone operator

el **teléfono** telephone

por teléfono on the phone

el **telégrafo** telegraph

la **telenovela** soap opera

el **telesilla** chair lift

el **telesquí** ski lift

la **televisión** television

el **televisor** television set

el **telón** curtain

el **tema** theme, subject

temblar to tremble

temer to be afraid

temerario(a) reckless, bold

la **temeridad** boldness

el **temor** fear, **6**

la **temperatura** temperature

la **tempestad** storm, **1**

templado(a) temperate

templar to moderate

el **templo** temple

la **temporada** period, spell, **3**

el **temporal** storm, **1**

temprano early

la **tendencia** trend

tender (ie) to tend

tender la cama to make the bed

tendido(a) stretched out

el **tenedor** fork

tener (irreg.) to have

tener... años to be... years old

tener cuidado to be careful

tener hambre to be hungry

tener lugar to take place

tener miedo to be afraid

tener prisa to be in a hurry

tener que to have to

tener que ver con to have to do with

tener razón to be right, **2**

tener sed to be thirsty

tener sueño to be sleepy

el **teniente** lieutenant

el **tenis** tennis

la cancha de tenis tennis court

el juego de tenis tennis game

los **tenis** tennis shoes

la **tensión arterial** blood pressure

la **teoría** theory

tercer, tercero(a) third

la **tercera edad** third age, old age, **2**

la **terminal** terminal, **1**

terminantemente categorically; conclusively, **6**

terminar to end, finish

el **término** term, word

a término medio medium (meat)

la **ternera** veal chop

la **ternura** tenderness

la **terraza** terrace

el **terreno** land, terrain

terrero(a) mud, earthen

territorial territorial

el **territorio** territory

terrorista terrorist

el **tesoro** treasure

el/la **testigo** witness

la **tía** aunt

tibio(a) tepid, **7**

el **tiempo** half (soccer game); weather; time

a tiempo on time

a tiempo completo full-time

a tiempo parcial part-time

al mismo tiempo at the same time

hace mucho tiempo a long time ago

la **tienda** store; tent

armar una tienda to put up a tent

la tienda de abarrotes grocery store

la tienda de campaña tent

la tienda de departamentos department store

la tienda de ropa para caballeros (señores) men's clothing store

la tienda de ropa para damas (señoras) women's clothing store

la tienda de video video store, **2**

la tienda por departamentos department store

tientas: a tientas groping

la **tierra** earth, land, **8**

la Tierra Santa Holy Land

el **tigre** tiger

las **tijeras** scissors

el **timbre** tone

la **timidez** shyness

tímido(a) timid, shy

el **tímpano** eardrum

tinto(a) red

la **tintorería** dry cleaners

el **tío** uncle

los tíos aunt(s) and uncle(s)

típicamente typically

típico(a) typical

el **tipo** type; character

el tipo de cambio exchange rate

tirar to throw

tiritar to shiver

titulado(a) entitled

el **titular** headline

el **título** degree

el título universitario university degree

la **tiza** chalk
la **toalla** towel
  la toalla playera beach
    towel
el **tobillo** ankle
el/la **tocador(a)** player, performer, **8**
  tocar to play (an instrument);
    to touch
el **tocino** bacon
  todavía yet, still
  todavía no not yet
  todo everything (noun)
  sobre todo especially
  todo(a) every, all
  en todas partes
    everywhere
  todo el mundo everybody
la **tolerancia** tolerance
  tolerante tolerant
  tolerar to tolerate
  tomar to take; to drink
  tomar el pelo a alguien to
    pull someone's leg
  tomar el sol to sunbathe
  tomar en serio to take
    seriously, **2**
  tomar fotografías to take
    pictures, **1**
  tomar la palabra to take
    the floor
  tomar una ducha to take a
    shower
el **tomate** tomato
la **tonelada** ton
el **tono** dial tone; pitch
  el tono de ocupado busy
    signal
la **tonsura** tonsure
la **tontería** foolishness, **6**
  tonto(a) silly, **1**
  tope: al tope at the highest
    level
el **tórax** thorax, **3**
  torcer (ue) to twist
  tordillo(a) dapple-gray
  torear to fight bulls
el **toreo** bullfighting, **6**
  torera: la larga torera pass
    with a cape in a bullfight
el **torero** bullfighter, **6**
la **tormenta** storm, **1**
  torno: en torno a about,
    regarding
el **toro** bull, **3**
la **toronja** grapefruit

la **torpeza** slowness
la **torre** tower
  la torre de control control
    tower
  tórrido(a) torrid
la **torsión** twisting
la **torta** cake
la **tortilla** tortilla
la **tortura** torture
  torturar to torture
la **tos** cough
  tener tos to have a cough
  tostadito(a) tanned
el **tostón** fried plantain slice
el **total** total
  totalmente totally
  tóxico(a) toxic
el/la **trabajador(a)** worker
  trabajar to work
el **trabajo** work, job
  el trabajo a código work
    slowdown
  el trabajo a tiempo
    completo (parcial) full-
    time (part-time) job
la **tradición** tradition
  tradicional traditional
  tradicionalmente
    traditionally
la **traducción** translation
  traer (irreg.) to bring
el/la **traficante** dealer, trader, **8**
el **tráfico** traffic
  tragar to swallow, **6**
la **tragedia** tragedy
  trágico(a) tragic
  traído(a) brought
el **traje** suit
  el traje de baño bathing
    suit
  el traje de novia bridal
    gown, **4**
  el traje pantalón pantsuit
el **tramo** span, stretch (of
    distance), **1**
  tranquilamente peacefully
la **tranquilidad** tranquility
  tranquilo(a) calm, tranquil, **3**
  transbordar to transfer
  transcendental far-reaching
el **transcurso** passage (of time)
  transformarse to be
    transformed
el **tránsito** traffic
  transmitir to transmit

  transpirar to sweat, **8**
  transportarse to be
    transported
el **transporte** transportation
el **trapo** rag, **6, 7**
  tras after
  trascender to transcend
  trasero(a) back, rear
  trasladar to transfer
el **trasteo** bustle
el **trastorno** disorder
el **tratado** treaty
el **tratamiento** treatment
  tratar to deal with; to treat
  tratar de to be about; to try
  traumático(a) traumatic
  través: a través de through,
    across
el **trayecto** road; distance, **1, 6**
  treinta thirty
  tremendo(a) tremendous
el **tren** train
  el tren de vía estrecha
    narrow-gauge train
  subir al tren to get on the
    train
la **trenza** braid
  tres three
la **tribu** tribe
el **tribunal** court
el **tricornio** three-cornered hat,
  8
el **trigo** wheat
la **trigonometría** trigonometry
  trilingüe trilingual
los **trillizos** triplets
la **tripulación** crew
  triste sad
  tristemente sadly
la **tristeza** sadness
  triunfante triumphant
  triunfar to win, triumph
el **trocito** little piece
la **trompeta** trumpet
el **trompicón** blow, punch
la **tronada** thunderstorm
el **tronco** trunk
el **trono** throne, **4**
la **tropa** troop, **2**
  tropezarse to trip
  tropical tropical
el/la **trotamundos** globetrotter
el **trozo** piece, part
el **truco** trick, **5**; device
  tu your (sing. fam.)

tú you (sing. fam.)
el **tubo** tube
la **tumba** tomb
   la tumba familiar family
     tomb, **4**
  tumbar to knock down
  tumultuoso(a) tumultuous
  turbado(a) disturbed
la **turbulencia** turbulence
  turbulento(a) turbulent
  turgente swollen
el **turismo** tourism
el/la **turista** tourist
  turístico(a) tourist (adj.)
el **turno** turn
el **turrón** nougat, **2**
  tutear to be on familiar
    terms with

U

  u or (used instead of **o** before
    words beginning with **o** or
    ho)
  ubicado(a) located, **1**
  ubicar to locate, place
  Ud(s)., usted(es) you (sing.
    [pl.] form.)
  último(a) last; latest
el **ultraje** insult
el **umbral** doorway
  un(a) a, an
  únicamente only
  único(a) only
la **unidad** unit
  la unidad de cuidado
    intensivo intensive care
    unit
el **uniforme** uniform
  llevar uniforme to wear a
    uniform
la **unión** union
  unir to unite
  universal universal
la **universidad** university
  universitario(a) university
    el título universitario
     university degree
  uno one
    el uno del otro each other
    unos cuantos a few
  untar to spread (butter on
    bread), **2**
  urbano(a) urban
el **urbe** city
  uruguayo(a) Uruguayan

  usado(a) used
  usar to use
el **uso** use
  usted(es), Ud(s.) you (sing.
    [pl.] form)
  útil useful, **2**
  utilísimo(a) very useful
  utilizar to use
la **uva** grape

V

  va he/she/it goes, is going
la **vaca** cow
las **vacaciones** vacation
  vaciar to pour, **2**
el **vacío** vacuum
  vacío(a) empty
el **vacuno** cattle
el/la **vagabundo(a)** vagabond
el **vagón** train car
  vaina: la misma vaina the
    same thing
la **vainilla** vanilla
la **vajilla** dish, **7**
la **valentía** courage
  valer to be worth
    valer la pena to be worth
     it
la **valía** value
  valiente brave, valiant
  valioso(a) valuable
la **valla** fence, **4, 7**
el **valle** valley
el **valor** value; courage, **2**
  valorar to value
  vamos we go, are going
  van they/you (pl. form.) go,
    are going
la **vanidad** vanity
la **vara de mimbre** reed stick
la **variación** variation
  variado(a) varied; diverse
la **variante** variant
  variar to vary
la **variedad** variety
  vario(a) various, varied;
    several (pl.)
el **varón** male, **3**
  vas you (sing. fam.) go, are
    going
la **vasija** vessel
el **vaso** (drinking) glass
  vasto(a) vast
el **váter** toilet
  veces: a veces sometimes

el/la **vecino(a)** neighbor, **2**
la **vegetación** vegetation
el **vegetal** vegetable
el/la **vegetariano(a)** vegetarian
el **vehículo** vehicle
  veinte twenty
la **veintena** score, about twenty
la **vela** candle; sail, **1**
el **velo** veil, **1, 4**
la **velocidad** speed
  la velocidad máxima
    speed limit
el **velorio** wake, vigil, **4**
la **vena** vein, **6**
  vencer to overcome, conquer
la **venda** band-aid
el **vendaje** bandage
el/la **vendedor(a)** salesperson, **1**
  vender to sell
  venenoso(a) poisonous
  venezolano(a) Venezuelan
  vengar to avenge, **6**
  venir (irreg.) to come
    venir a menos to lose status
la **venta** sale
    en venta for sale
la **ventaja** advantage
la **ventanilla** ticket window;
    window
el **ventorrillo** roadhouse
  ver (irreg.) to see, to watch
el/la **veraneante** summer vacationer
  veraniego(a) summery
el **verano** summer
la **verbena** fair, festival
el **verbo** verb
la **verdad** truth
    ¿No es verdad? Isn't it
     true?
    ¿Verdad? Right?
  verdadero(a) real, true
  verde green
la **verdulería** greengrocer's shop
el/la **verdulero(a)** greengrocer
la **verdura** vegetable
  verificar to check; to verify
  versátil versatile
la **versión** version
el **verso** verse
el **vestido** dress
    el vestido de boda
     wedding dress
  vestirse (i, i) to get dressed
el **vestuario** clothing; dressing
    room

la **vez** time

    de vez en cuando now and then

    en vez de instead of

la **vía** track; way

    viajar to travel

el **viaje** trip

    ¡Buen viaje! Have a good trip!

    el viaje de novios honeymoon trip

    hacer un viaje to take a trip

el/la **viajero(a)** traveler, **1**

la **víbora** snake

la **vibración** vibration

    vibrar to vibrate

la **víctima del crimen** crime victim, **5**

la **victoria** victory

    victorioso(a) victorious

la **vida** life, **5**

    vida: en mi vida never

el **video** video

la **vidriera** shop window

    viejo(a) old (adj.)

el/la **viejo(a)** old person, **2**

el **viento** wind

    hace viento it's windy

el **vientre** stomach, **7**

    viernes Friday

    vigilar to guard

la **villa** town, **6**

la **villanía** despicable act

el **vino** wine

la **violencia** violence

    violentamente violently

el **violín** violin

    virar to turn

la **virgen: las Islas Vírgenes** Virgin Islands

la **virtud** virtue, **6**

las **viruelas** measles, smallpox

el **virus** virus

las **vísceras** innards

el **visillo** sheer window curtain, **7**

la **visión** vision

la **visita** visit

    visitar to visit

la **víspera de Navidad** Christmas Eve

la **vista** view

la **vitamina** vitamin

la **vitrina** shop window

el/la **viudo(a)** widower (widow), **6**

la **vivienda** housing, dwelling, **8**

    vivir to live

    vivo(a) living; bright, vivid

el **vocabulario** vocabulary

la **vocación** vocation

    volar (ue) to fly

el **volcán** volcano

el **vólibol** volleyball

    voltear to turn around; to capsize, **3**

el **volumen** volume

la **voluntad** will; desire, **8**

el/la **voluntario(a)** volunteer

    volver (ue) to go back, **1**

    vosotros(as) you (pl. fam.)

la **voz** voice, **8**

el **vuelo** flight

    el asistente (la asistenta) **de vuelo** flight attendant

    el número del vuelo flight number

la **vuelta** turn; rotation

    dar vuelta to turn around

    de vuelta on returning; back, **3**

    vuestro(a) your (pl. fam.)

Y

y and

ya already

    ya no no longer

el **yate** yacht

la **yema** egg yolk, **7**

el **yen** yen

el **yeso** cast; plaster

    yo I

Z

    zambullir to dive

la **zanahoria** carrot

la **zanja** ditch, trench

el **zanjón** large ditch

la **zapatilla de deporte** sports shoe

el **zapato** shoe

la **zarza** bramble

el **zíper** zipper

la **zona** district, zone

    la zona postal zip code

la **zoología** zoology

el **zoológico** zoo

el **zumbido** buzzing, ringing

el **zumo de naranja** orange juice (Spain)

Vocabulario inglés–español

The *Vocabulario inglés-español* contains all productive vocabulary from the **Glencoe Spanish** series, Levels 1, 2, and 3. Boldface numbers indicate vocabulary introduced in Level 3. Many of the meanings given in this glossary are taken directly from the context in which they appear in the text.

The following abbreviations are used in this glossary.

adj.	adjective
adv.	adverb
conj.	conjunction
dem. adj.	demonstrative adjective
dem. pron.	demonstrative pronoun
dir. obj.	direct object
f.	feminine
fam.	familiar
form.	formal
ind. obj.	indirect object
inf.	infinitive
inform.	informal
interr.	interrogative
interr. adj.	interrogative adjective
interr. pron.	interrogative pronoun
inv.	invariable
irreg.	irregular
m.	masculine
n.	noun
past. part.	past participle
pl.	plural
poss. adj.	possessive adjective
prep.	preposition
pron.	pronoun
sing.	singular
subj.	subject
subjunc.	subjunctive

A

a, an un(a)
abdomen el abdomen, 3
aboriginal autóctono(a), 8
about a eso de
above sobre; arriba
to **accelerate** acelerar
accident el accidente
accompanied acompañado(a), 1
account la cuenta
accountant el/la contable
to **ache** doler (ue)
　My ____ hurts, aches. Me duele ____.
to **achieve** lograr, 8
to **acknowledge** reconocer, 8
act el acto, 3
active activo(a)
actor el actor
actress la actriz
to **add** agregar (gue)
to **add sugar** azucarar, 2
address la dirección
admission ticket la entrada
admitting office (hospital) la oficina de recepción
to **adore** adorar; idolatrar, 3
adult el adulto, 2
adversity la hiel, 4
to **advise** aconsejar
aerobic aeróbico(a)
aerogram el aerograma
affection el afecto, 6
affectionately cariñosamente, 2
Afro hairstyle el peinado afro
after después de; después de que
afternoon la tarde
　Good afternoon. Buenas tardes.
　this afternoon esta tarde
to **age** envejecer, 2
agent el/la agente
to **agree** convenir
agreeable placentero(a), 1; grato(a), 8
agreement el acuerdo, 7
agriculture la agricultura
air el aire; aéreo(a)
　air conditioning el aire acondicionado
　air mail por correo aéreo

airline la línea aérea
airplane el avión
　by (air)plane en avión
airport el aeropuerto
aisle el pasillo
algebra el álgebra
allergy la alergia
allowance la ración, 7
alphabet el alfabeto, 8
already ya
also también
altar el altar
although aunque
altitude la altura, la altitud
always siempre
ambulance la ambulancia
American americano(a)
ancestor el antepasado, 8
ancestry la ascendencia, 1, 8
anchor el ancla (f.), 1
and y
anesthetist el/la anestesista
to **anger** enojar, enfadar
ankle el tobillo
to **announce** anunciar
announcement el anuncio
to **annoy** enojar, enfadar, fastidiar, 3
anorak el anorak
to **answer** contestar
answering machine el contestador automático
antiquity la antigüedad, 8
apartment el apartamento; el piso, 2
apex el auge, 8
apparatus el aparato, 7
appearance la aparición, 4
to **applaud** aplaudir
apple la manzana
appliance el aparato, 7
application la solicitud
　job application la solicitud de empleo
to **apply for (work)** solicitar (trabajo)
apprentice el/la aprendiz(a), 2
to **approach** acercarse (qu)
to **approve** aprobar, 5
April abril (m.)
aquiline nose la nariz aguileña, 7
Arab el/la moro(a), 5
architecture la arquitectura

area code la clave de área, el código de área, el prefijo telefónico
Argentinian argentino(a)
arithmetic la aritmética
arm el brazo
armament el arma (f.), 2
around alrededor de; a eso de (time)
arrival la llegada
　arrival and departure board el tablero de llegadas y salidas
to **arrive** llegar
art el arte
arterial arterial
artisan el/la artesano(a)
　artisan's shop el taller
artist el/la artista
as soon as en cuanto; tan pronto como
to **ask** rogar (ue), 3
to **assist** asistir
to **assure** asegurar, 2
at a
at once en seguida
at the (m. sing.) al
to **attend** asistir; acudir a, 1, 2, 3
attendant el/la empleado(a)
attendee el/la concurrente, 4
attractive atractivo(a)
audience el público
auditor el/la revisor(a)
August agosto (m.)
aunt la tía
　aunt(s) and uncle(s) los tíos
author el/la autor(a)
to **authorize** autorizar, 6
automatic automático(a)
autumn el otoño
to **avenge** vengar, 6
avenue la avenida
avocado el aguacate
Aymará language el aymará, 8
Aymará Indians los aymarás, 2, 8

B

baby el/la bebé, 2
baby blanket la cobijita, 4

bachelor's degree el bachillerato

back (n.) la espalda, (adv.) de vuelta, **3**; atrás, **8**

backboard (basketball) el tablero

backpack la mochila

backward atrás, **8**

bad malo(a)

bad-mannered malcriado(a)

bad-mannered person el/la malcriado(a), **2**

bag la bolsa

    plastic bag la bolsa de plástico

baggage el equipaje

    baggage claim el reclamo de equipaje

    hand baggage el equipaje de mano

bakery la panadería

balance (bank) el saldo

balcony el balcón

    first balcony el primer balcón, **3**

ball el balón; la pelota; la bola

ballpoint pen el bolígrafo

banana el plátano, la banana

band la banda, **3**

bandage el vendaje

band-aid la venda

bangs el flequillo

bank el banco

    bank clerk el/la empleado(a) del banco

    bank statement el estado de banco (de cuenta)

bank (of a river) la orilla

banns (marriage) las amonestaciones, **4**

banquet el banquete; el festejo, **4**

baptism el bautizo, **5**

to **baptize** bautizar

bar (of soap) la barra; la pastilla

barber el/la barbero(a)

bark(ing) (of dog) el ladrido, **7**

to **bark** ladrar, **7**

barrel el barril, **6**

base la base, el platillo

baseball el béisbol

basket el cesto, el canasto; la canasta

basketball el baloncesto, el básquetbol

bat el bate

bathing suit el traje de baño, el bañador

bathroom el cuarto de baño; el baño

bathtub la bañera

batter (baseball) el/la bateador(a)

battery la batería

bazaar el bazar, **1**

to **be** ser (irreg.); estar (irreg.)

    to be a pity ser una lástima

    to be able poder (irreg.)

    to be accustomed to soler (ue), **8**

    to be afraid temer, tener miedo

    to be born nacer (zc)

    to be called llamarse

    to be embarrassed dar vergüenza, **6**

    to be glad about alegrarse de

    to be hungry tener hambre

    to be ignorant of ignorar, **8**

    to be in good health estar en (de) buena salud, gozar de buena salud, **7**

    to be named llamarse

    to be prepared estar dispuesto, **6**

    to be quiet callar(se), **3**

    to be ready estar dispuesto, **6**

    to be right tener razón, **2**

    to be satisfied estar a gusto, **2**

    to be similar asemejarse, **6**

    to be surprised sorprenderse, **2**

    to be thirsty tener sed

    to be tied (sports) quedar empatado(a)

    to be unsuccessful fracasar, **5**

    to be... years old tener... años

beach la playa

    beach la playa; playero(a) (adj.)

    beach resort el balneario

    beach towel la toalla playera

bean la habichuela, el frijol

to **beat** batir, **2**

beautiful precioso(a)

to **become** llegar a ser, ponerse, **2**

to **become a member (of)** ingresar, **2**

bed (of a stream) el arroyo, **8**

bed la cama

bedroom el cuarto de dormir, el dormitorio

bee la abeja, **4**

beef la carne de res

before antes de que

to **beg** rogar (ue)

beggar el/la mendigo(a), **6**

to **begin** empezar (ie) (c), comenzar (ie) (c)

    beginner el/la principiante; el/la aprendiz(a), **2**; el/la novato(a), **3**

to **behave** comportarse

behavior el comportamiento

behind atrás; detrás de

to **belch** eructar, **2**

to **believe** creer (y)

bell la campana, **1**

    bell tower el campanario, **1**

bellhop el botones, el mozo

to **belong to** pertenecer a, **4, 6**

below bajo; abajo, **1**

below zero bajo cero

belt el cinturón

    seat belt el cinturón de seguridad

bench el banco

beret la boina, **3**

berth la litera

best man el padrino

better mejor

bewildered aturdido(a), **6**

bicycle la bicicleta

big gran, grande

bill la cuenta; la nota; **(money)** el billete

biologist el/la biólogo(a)

biology la biología
bird el pájaro, **1**
birth el nacimiento; el parto, **4**
birthday el cumpleaños
  Happy birthday! ¡Feliz cumpleaños!
biscuit la galleta, **8**
bitterness la hiel, **4**
black negro(a)
  black bean la habichuela negra, el frijol negro
blade la cuchilla, la hoja
bleach el blanqueador
to **bless** bendecir, **4**
blind person el/la ciego(a), **7**
to **block** bloquear parar
block (city) la manzana, la cuadra
blond(e) rubio(a)
blood la sangre, **7, 8**
  blood pressure la tensión arterial, la presión arterial
blouse la blusa
blow el golpe, **5**; el puñetazo, **6**
to **blow** soplar, **1**
blue azul
  blue jeans los blue jeans
board el tablero; la tabla, **3**
  arrival and departure board el tablero de llegadas y salidas
to **board** abordar, subir a
boarding house la pensión
boarding pass la tarjeta de embarque, el pase de abordar
boastful fanfarrón(a)
boat el barco; el buque, **1**
  small boat el barquito
bobby pin la horquilla
to **boil** hervir (ie)
bomb explosion el bombazo, **8**
bond el parentesco, **6**
bone el hueso
  to set the bone reducir la fractura
book el libro
bookbag la mochila
boot la bota
to **bore** aburrir
boring aburrido(a)
boss el/la amo(a), **8**

to **bother** molestar
bottle la botella
box office la taquilla, **3**
boy el muchacho; el niño, **2**
boyfriend el novio, **4**
bracelet la pulsera, **1**
braid la trenza
brake el freno
to **brake** frenar
branch (of candelabra) el brazo
bread el pan
to **break** romperse
breakfast el desayuno
  to eat breakfast desayunarse
breathing el aliento, **6**
bridal bouquet el ramo de novia, **4**
bridal gown el traje de novia, **4**
bridesmaid la dama de honor
to **bring** traer (irreg.); aportar, **6**
British británico(a), **8**
to **broil** asar
broker el cambista
brooch el prendedor, **1**
brother el hermano
brown castaño(a), marrón
  brown-colored de color marrón
brush el cepillo
to **brush one's hair** cepillarse
budget el presupuesto, **6**
to **build** edificar, **1**
building el edificio
bull el toro, **3**
bullfighter el torero, **6**
bullfighting el toreo, **6**; taurino(a) (adj.), **6**
bull ring la plaza de toros, **3**
bumper el parachoques
bun (hair) el moño
burial el entierro, **4**
burner (stove) el/la hornillo(a)
burning ardiente (adj.), **1**
to **burp** eructar, **2**
to **bury** enterrar (ie)
bus el autobús, el bus

  to miss the bus perder el autobus
busy ocupado(a)
  busy signal el tono de ocupado
  It is busy. Suena ocupado.
  The line is busy. La línea está ocupada.
butcher shop la carnicería
butter la mantequilla
button el botón
to **buy** comprar
by (plane, car, etc.) en

C
cafeteria la cafetería, **7**
cake la torta
calculator el/la calculador(a)
call la llamada
to **call by telephone** llamar por teléfono
  Who is calling? ¿De parte de quién?
caller el/la interlocutor(a)
calm plácido(a), **1**; tranquilo(a), **3**
calorie la caloría
camel el camello
camp el campamento
to **camp** acampar
camping el camping
  to go camping ir de camping
can la lata, el bote
candelabra el candelabro
candidate el/la candidato(a), el/la aspirante
candle la vela; la candela, **8**
canteen la cantimplora
canyon el cañón, **1**
cap (of bottle) la tapa, **7**
cap el gorro
to **capsize** voltear, **3**
captain el/la comandante
captive el/la cautivo(a), **5**
car el coche, el carro; **(train)** el vagón; el coche
  sports car el coche deportivo
caravel la carabela, **5**
carbohydrate el carbohidrato
card la tarjeta
  credit card la tarjeta de crédito

cardiac cardíaco (adj.), **7**
care el cargo, **6**
career la profesión
careful: Be careful!
  ¡Cuidado!
carefully con cuidado
to **caress** acariciar, **4**
caricature la caricatura, **1**
carmine el carmín, **2**
carpenter el/la carpintero(a)
carrot la zanahoria
to **carry** llevar
  carry-on luggage el
    equipaje de mano
  to carry out llevar a cabo,
    4
cart el carrito
cash el dinero en efectivo
  cash register la caja
to **cash** cobrar
cashier el/la cajero(a)
  cashier's desk la caja
cast el yeso
caste la casta, **6**
castle el alcázar, **5**
cat el gato
to **catch** atrapar
catcher el/la cátcher, el/la
  receptor(a)
categorically
  terminantemente, **6**
cauliflower la coliflor
to **cause** suscitar, **4**; ocasionar, **5**
to **celebrate** celebrar
  celebration of lights la fiesta
    de las luces
celery el apio
cellular celular
cemetery el cementerio, el
  camposanto
centigrade el centígrado
ceremony la ceremonia
certified mail por correo
  certificado, por correo
  recomendado
chair la silla
  chair lift el telesilla
  folding chair la silla
    plegable
  large chair el sillón, **7**
chalk la tiza
chalkboard la pizarra; el
  pizarrón
to **change** cambiar
channel el canal

chaperone la dueña
character el genio, **8**
to **charge** cobrar, **6**
charge el gasto
charming encantador(a), **2**
to **chase** perseguir, **8**
cheap barato(a)
check el cheque
  to check (luggage) facturar
checkbook el talonario, la
  chequera
checking account la cuenta
  corriente
checkstand la caja
cheek la mejilla
cheese el queso
chemistry la química
cherry la cereza
chest el pecho
chicken el pollo
chignon el moño
children los hijos
chills los escalofríos
chin el mentón, **6**
to **choose** elegir, **6**
chop la chuleta
Christmas la Navidad
  Christmas Eve la víspera de
    Navidad, la Nochebuena
  Christmas present el
    regalo de Navidad, el
    aguinaldo
  Christmas tree el árbol de
    Navidad
  Merry Christmas! ¡Feliz
    Navidad!
church la iglesia
cigar el puro, **4**
city la ciudad
  city hall la alcaldía, el
    ayuntamiento
  city hall employee el/la
    funcionario(a)
civilian civil (adj.), **2**
to **claim** reclamar
clam la almeja
clamp la pinza, **7**
to **clap** palmear, **7**
class la clase; **(of society)** la
  casta, **6**
classic clásico(a)
classroom la sala de clase; el
  salón de clase; el aula (f.), **7**
to **clean** limpiar
clerk el/la dependiente(a)

client el/la cliente
clinic la clínica
clock el reloj, **5**
close entrañable; íntimo(a);
  allegado(a), **4**
closet el armario
cloth el lienzo; el tejido, **2**
clothes la ropa
  clothes dryer la secadora
  clothes hanger la percha,
    el colgador, el gancho
  clothing store la tienda de
    ropa
cloud la nube
cloudless despejado(a), **1**
cloudy nublado(a)
  It's cloudy. Está nublado.
club (golf) el palo, el bastón
coach el/la entrenador(a), **2**
cockpit la cabina de vuelo
  (mando)
cocktail el cóctel
coconut el coco
code el prefijo
  country code el prefijo del
    país
coffee el café
  coffee-colored de color
    café
coffin el ataúd, **2**
coin la moneda
cold (medical) el catarro, la
  gripe; **(weather)** el frío
  It's cold. Hace frío.
Colombian colombiano(a)
color el color
colt el potro, **8**
comb el peine
to **comb one's hair** peinarse
to **come** venir (irreg.)
  to come on stage entrar
    en escena
to **communicate** participar, **4**;
  comunicar, **8**
communiqué, el
  comunicado, **4**
compartment el
  compartimiento
complicated complicado(a)
compound la mezcla, **8**
computer la computadora, el
  ordenador
  computer science la
    informática
concert el concierto

concertina el bandoneón, 3
conclusively terminantemente, 6
conductor el/la director(a), (train) el/la revisor(a)
to confide confiar
confused perplejo(a), 6
Congratulations! (n.); ¡Enhorabuena! ¡Felicitaciones!
to consist of constar de, 4
container el envase
to continue seguir (i, i)
contrary: on the contrary por el contrario, 2
to contribute aportar, 6
control el cargo, 6
control tower la torre de control
controller el/la controlador(a)
conversation la conversación
convertible el descapotable
cook el/la cocinero(a)
to cook cocinar
cookie el bizcocho
copilot el/la copiloto(a)
cord el cordón, la soga, 7
cordless inalámbrico(a)
corn el maíz
corn harvest la cosecha del maíz, 8
corner la esquina
corpse el cadáver, 2
to correspond corresponder
correspondence la correspondencia
corridor el pasillo
to cost costar (ue)
costumed group la comparsa, 3
cough la tos
to have a cough tener tos
counselor el/la consejero(a) de orientación, el/la orientador(a)
counter el mostrador
country el campo
coupe el cupé
couple la pareja, 4
courage el valor, 2
course el curso
court la corte, el tribunal; (sports) la cancha
tennis court la cancha de tenis

courteous cortés
courtesy la cortesía
cousin el/la primo(a)
cover la tapa
to cover tapar
covered cubierto(a)
coward el/la cobarde, 6
cozy corner el rincón, 1
cracker la galleta, 8
cream la crema
cream-colored de color crema
credit card la tarjeta de crédito
crew la tripulación
crime el crimen, 5
crime victim la víctima del crimen, 5
cross la cruz, 2, 6
to cross cruzar (c); atravesar, 2, 6
crosswalk el paso de peatones
crown la corona, 5, 8
crutch la muleta
cucumber el pepino
culpable culpable, 8
to cultivate labrar, 5, 8
cup la taza
curl el rizo, el bucle
to curl rizar
curling el rizado
curling iron el rizador
curly rizado(a), crespo(a)
curriculum vitae el historial profesional, el currículo profesional
curtain el telón
sheer window curtain el visillo, 7
custom la costumbre
customer el/la cliente
customs la aduana
to cut cortar
cycling el ciclismo, 7

D
dad el papá
daily cotidiano(a), diario(a) (adj.), 7
damaged dañado(a), 7
dance la danza, 3
to dance bailar
dancer el danzarín (la danzarina) 3
danger el riesgo, 5

dark moreno(a)
date (calendar) la fecha; (appointment) la cita
daughter la hija
daughter of the King of Spain la Infanta, 4
to dawn amanecer, 7
dawn la madrugada, 4, 5
day el día
day before yesterday anteayer
dazed aturdido(a), 6
dead person el/la muerto(a), el/la difunto(a); el/la extinto(a), 4
deafness la sordera, 7
to deal (cards) tallar, 6
dealer el/la traficante, 8
death la muerte, 5
to deceive engañar, 8
December diciembre (m.)
deck (of cards) la baraja, 6
decline el ocaso, 4
decrepit old house el caserío, 6
to dedicate (oneself) dedicar(se)
to deduct deducir, 1
deed la hazaña, 6
degree el grado
delay el retraso, la demora
delicacy la golosina, 1
delicious delicioso(a)
to delight encantar
to deliver repartir, entregar
delivery la entrega, el reparto
to demand exigir
dental floss la seda dental, 7
dentist el/la dentista, 7
deodorant el desodorante
to depart irse, partir, 1
department store la tienda por departamentos
departure la salida; la marcha, 4
arrival and departure board el tablero de llegadas y salidas
departure gate la puerta de salida
deposit el depósito, el ingreso
to deposit depositar, ingresar
desire la voluntad, 8
dessert el postre

destination el destino
destiny el hado, 1
to destroy destruir, 2, 5; destrozar, 7
detergent el detergente
to develop desarrollar, 8
diagnosis la diagnosis
dial (of telephone) el disco
dial tone la señal, el tono
to dial discar; marcar
to dice picar
to die morir (ue, u); fallecer, 5
diet la dieta
difficult difícil; rudo(a), 4
to diminish reducir, 5
dining car el coche-comedor
dining room el comedor
dinner la cena
direction la dirección; el sentido
dirty sucio(a)
discernment el discernimiento, 2
discharge el disparo, 3
discourteous descortés
discreet comedido(a), 4
to disembark desembarcar
dish la vajilla, 7
dishonor la deshonra, 6
distance el trayecto, 1, 6
distant lejano(a), 1
to distribute distribuir
to do hacer (irreg.)
to do again volver (ue) a
doctor el/la médico(a); el/la galeno(a), 7
doctor's office la consulta del médico, el consultorio del médico
dog el perro
door la puerta
door threshold el quicio de la puerta, 4
dose la dosis
double doble
to doubt dudar
There's no doubt. No hay duda.
dowry las arras
to drag arrastrar, 2
to draw dibujar, 1
drawer la gaveta, 7
drawing el dibujo, 1
to dream soñar (ue), 6
dress el vestido

dressing room el camerino, 3
to dribble driblar con
drill el taladro; (dentist's drill) la fresa, 7
drink la bebida
to drink tomar; beber
to drive conducir (zc); manejar
driver el/la conductor(a); el chófer, 5
driver's license la licencia, el permiso de conducir
to drive out expulsar, 8
drop la gota, 2, 6
drug la droga
to dry clean limpiar en seco
dry cleaners la tintorería
dry cleaning la limpieza en seco
duck el pato, 6
during durante
dust el polvo, 4
dwelling la vivienda, 8

E

each cada
each other el uno del otro
ear el oído, 1, 7; la oreja, 7
early temprano
earphones los audífonos
earring el arete, 1
earth la tierra, 8
east el este; el oriente, 8
easy fácil
to eat comer
to eat breakfast desayunarse
economics la economía
edge el borde, 1, 7
education la pedagogía
effort el esfuerzo, 8
egg el huevo
egg white la clara, 7
egg yolk la yema, 7
eight ocho
eighth octavo(a)
eighty ochenta
elastic elástico(a)
elbow el codo
electric hair clipper la maquinilla
electrician el/la electricista
elegant apuesto(a), 7
elevator el ascensor

to embrace abrazar (c)
embroidered bordado(a), 1
emergency la emergencia
emergency exit la salida de emergencia
emergency room la sala de urgencias, la sala de emergencia
to emphasize enfatizar, 8
employee el/la empleado(a)
end el ocaso, 4
endeavor el esfuerzo, 8
to endorse endosar
energy la energía
nuclear energy la energía nuclear
engagement el compromiso
engagement ring la sortija de compromiso
engine el motor
engineer el/la ingeniero(a), 2
English el inglés; inglés (inglesa) (adj.)
engravings las estampas, 1
to enjoy disfrutar (de), 1, 3
to enjoy oneself divertirse (ie, i)
enough bastante; suficiente
to enroll inscribir, 7
to enter entrar; ingresar, 2
entertainment el festejo, 4
enthusiasm la afición, 6
entrance la entrada
entrance to subway la boca del metro, 2
envelope el sobre
to envy envidiar, 6
epoch la etapa, 2
eraser la goma
to escape librarse, 4
escort el acompañamiento, 4
essential imprescindible, 5
ethnic étnico(a), 8
Europe la Europa
eve: Christmas Eve la víspera de Navidad, la Nochebuena
evening la noche
Good evening. Buenas noches.
event el acontecimiento, 3
everyone todos
examination el examen
to examine examinar; revisar, 2
to exceed sobrepasar, 5
exchange el cambio

exchange office la oficina de cambio

exchange rate el tipo de cambio, la tasa de cambio

What is the exchange rate? ¿Cuál es el tipo de cambio?

to **exchange** cambiar; intercambiar

to **exercise** ejercitar, **3**

exercise el ejercicio

  aerobic exercise el ejercicio aeróbico

  physical exercise el ejercicio físico

exhibition la exposición

exit la salida

  exit door la puerta de salida

to **expel** expulsar, **8**

expensive caro(a)

expert experto(a)

to **extract** extraer, **4**

exuberance la lozanía, **4**

eyeglasses los anteojos, **2**

F

fabric el tejido, **2**

face la cara; la faz, **4**

factory la fábrica

to **fail** fracasar, **5**

to **fall** caerse (irreg.)

  to fall asleep dormirse (ue, u)

  to fall in love enamorarse

family la familia

fantastic fantástico(a)

to **farm (the land)** labrar (la tierra)

farm worker el/la labrador(a)

farming el cultivo, **8**

fast el ayuno, **3**

fast rápido

to **fasten** abrocharse

fate el hado, **1**

father el padre

fear el temor, **6**

February febrero

to **feel** sentir (ie, i)

  to feel ashamed avergonzarse, **6**

fence la cerca, **4**; la valla, **4, 7**

fever la fiebre

fiancé(e) el/la novio(a), el/la comprometido(a)

fiber la fibra

field el campo; la milpa, **8**

  soccer field el campo de fútbol

fifteenth: young woman's fifteenth birthday la quinceañera

fifth quinto(a)

fifty cincuenta

figure skating el patinaje artístico

to **file a suit against** demandar, **5**

to **fill (out)** llenar

film la película, el film(e)

fine bien

finger el dedo

to **finish** acabar, **3**

fire el fuego; el incendio, **5**

first primer, primero(a)

  first-aid kit el botiquín

  first-aid service el servicio de primeros auxilios, el servicio de primer socorro

  first-aid worker el/la socorrista

firstborn el/la primogénito(a), **4**

fish (when caught) el pescado

  fish market la pescadería

fishing pesquero(a) (adj.); de pesca, **7**

to **fit** sentar (ie) bien a

  It fits me. Me sienta bien.

five cinco

five pesetas duro, **1**

five hundred quinientos

flag la bandera, **5**

flake el copo, **1**

flame la llama, **5**

flashlight la linterna

fleet of small vessels la flotilla, **5**

flight el vuelo

  flight attendant el asistente/la asistenta de vuelo; el/la sobrecargo

  flight number el número del vuelo

floor el piso

to **flow** fluir, **6**

flower la flor

flu la gripe

to **fluctuate** fluctuar

to **fly over** sobrevolar (ue)

flying bird el pajarillo volador, **2**

fog la neblina, **1**

folding plegable

  folding chair la silla plegable

to **follow** seguir (i, i)

fondness el afecto, **6**

font (baptismal) la pila, **4**

food el comestible; el alimento, **7**

foolishness la tontería, **6**

foot el pie

  on foot a pie

football el fútbol americano

forbidden prohibido(a)

forced forzado(a), **8**

forehead la frente

foreign ajeno(a), **2**

forest el bosque

to **foretell** pronosticar, **1**; adivinar, **6**

fork el tenedor

form el formulario

to **form** integrar, **2**

fortune el dineral, **2**

forty cuarenta

four cuatro

fourth cuarto(a)

fracture la fractura

frame el marco, **4**

free libre, suelto(a), **2**

freezer el congelador

French francés (francesa)

French fries las papas fritas

frequently con frecuencia

Friday viernes (m.)

friend el/la amigo(a)

to **frighten** asustar, **6**

from de

  from the (m. sing.) del

front: in front of enfrente; delante de

frozen congelado(a); helado(a), **1**

fruit la fruta

  fruit garden el huerto, **1**

frustrated fallido(a), **4**

to **fry** freír (i, i)

  frying pan el/la sartén

  full-time a tiempo completo

fun divertido(a)
furtively a hurtadillas, 6

G

game el partido; el juego
   tennis game el juego de
   tenis
gang la barra, 3
garage el garaje
garden el jardín; la huerta, 5
   botanical garden el jardín
   botánico, 2
garlic el ajo
gas la gasolina
   gas pump la bomba de
   bencina, 2
   gas station la gasolinera
gate la puerta
   departure gate la puerta
   de salida
to gather recoger, 6
general: in general por lo
   general
general on horseback el
   general a caballo, 1
geography la geografía
geometry la geometría
to get sacar (qu)
   to get dressed vestirse (i, i)
   to get engaged
   comprometerse
   to get good (bad) grades
   sacar notas buenas
   (malas)
   to get hurt lastimarse
   to get married casarse
   to get off the train
   bajar(se) del tren
   to get on subir a
   to get on the train subir al
   tren
   to get rich enriquecerse, 8
   to get together reunirse
   to get up levantarse
   to get used to
   acostumbrarse, 2
gift el regalo
girl la muchacha; la niña
girlfriend la novia, 4
to give birth dar a luz, parir, 4
glass (drinking) el vaso
glasses (eye) las gafas; los
   anteojos, 2
globe el globo, 5
glove el guante

to go ir (irreg.); marcharse, 3, 6
   to go back volver (ue), 1
   to go camping ir de
   camping
   to go down bajar;
   descender, 1
   to go far away alejarse, 3
   to go for a swim bañarse
   to go home ir a casa
   to go out salir (irreg.)
   to go to acudir a, 1, 2, 3, 4;
   ir a
   to go to bed acostarse (ue)
   to go up subir
   to go with hacer juego con
goal el gol, la portería; la
   meta, 6, 8
goalkeeper el/la portero(a)
godfather el padrino
godmother la madrina
gold el oro, 8
golf el golf
   golf bag la bolsa de golf
   golf club el palo, el bastón
   golf course el campo de
   golf
   golf game el juego de golf
good bueno(a)
   Good afternoon. Buenas
   tardes.
   Good evening. Good night.
   Buenas noches.
   Good morning. Buenos
   días.
good-bye adiós, chao
goodness la bondad, 6
grade la nota, la calificación
grandchild el/la nieto(a)
grandfather el abuelo
grandmother la abuela
grandparents los abuelos
grape la uva
grapefruit la toronja
grass el césped, 7
to grate rallar
great-grandchild el/la
   bisnieto(a), 4
great-grandparent el/la
   bisabuelo(a), 8
green verde; el green (golf)
greengrocer's shop la
   verdulería
to greet saludar
grey gris
grill la parrilla

grocery store la tienda de
   abarrotes
ground el suelo
   ground floor la planta
   baja
   ground meat la carne
   molida, 7
group of friends la barra, 3
Guatemalan Mayan
   language el maya-quiché,
   8
to guess adivinar, 6
   guest el/la huésped; el/la
   invitado(a)
   guide el/la guía, 6
   guilty culpable, 8
   guitar la guitarra
   gum (of mouth) la encía, 7

H

hail el granizo, 1
hair el pelo; el cabello
   hair clip la pinza para el
   cabello
   hair dryer el secador
   hair roller el rulo
   hair salon la peluquería
   hair spray la laca
   hair stylist el/la
   peluquero(a)
haircut el corte de pelo
half (soccer game) el tiempo
ham el jamón
hammock la hamaca
hand la mano
   hand organ el organillo, 3
handle el mango
handsome apuesto(a), 7
to hang up colgar (ue)
to happen ocurrir, 1
Hanukkah Hanuka
happiness la felicidad
happy contento(a); alegre;
   feliz
   Happy birthday! ¡Feliz
   cumpleaños!
   Happy New Year!
   ¡Próspero año nuevo!
hard rudo(a), 4; (labor)
   forzado(a), 8
to harvest cosechar, 2, 4
to hasten apresurarse, 7
hat el sombrero
hate, hatred el odio, 6

to **have** tener (irreg.)
    to have just (done something) acabar de
    to have one's birthday cumplir años
    to have to tener que
he él
head la cabeza
headache el dolor de cabeza
headlight el faro
health la salud
to **hear** oír (y)
    hearing el oído, **1, 7;** la audición, **7**
heart cardíaco(a) (adj.), **7**
    heart attack el infarto, **5**
heat el calor
heavyweight el/la pesado(a), **3**
Hebrew hebreo(a)
heel (shoe) el tacón
heir el/la heredero(a), **4**
helicopter el helicóptero
hello hola, Buenos días
help el apoyo, **5**
hen la gallina, **6**
heroic feat la hazaña, **6**
hide (of animal) el pellejo, **7**
high alto(a)
    high plateau el altiplano
    high school el colegio, la escuela secundaria
highway la carretera, la autopista, la calzada, **1**
hike la caminata
    to take a hike dar una caminata
hill la colina; la loma(da), el cerro, **1**
history la historia
hit el golpe, **5; (baseball)** el hit
to **hit** golpear; **(baseball)** batear
to **hold together** empanizar, **2**
hole el hoyo
home la casa; el hogar, **8**
    at home en casa
    home economics la economía doméstica
home plate el platillo
home run el jonrón
honest honesto(a)
honey la miel, **2, 4**
honeymoon la luna de miel
    honeymoon trip el viaje de novios

hood el capó
hoodlum el/la maleante, **5**
hoop el aro
hop el brinco, **3**
hope: I hope (that) Ojalá (que)
hopeful ilusionado(a), **2**
horn la bocina, el claxon
hospital el hospital
hot: It's hot. Hace calor.
hotel el hotel
    hotel ballroom el salón del hotel
house la casa
housewife el ama (f.) de casa, **2**
How? ¿Qué?; ¿Cómo?
    How are you? ¿Qué tal?
    How much? ¿Cuánto(a)?
    How much do I owe you? ¿Cuánto le debo?
    How much does it cost? ¿Cuánto cuesta?; ¿A cuánto está(n)?; ¿Cuánto es?
    How much is it? ¿Cuánto es?
hug el abrazo
to **hug** abrazar (c)
human humano(a)
    human resources department el departamento (el servicio) de recursos humanos
humble humilde, **8**
hunger el hambre (f.)
    to be hungry tener hambre
    to go hungry pasar hambre
hurricane el huracán, **1**
to **hurry** apresurarse, **7**
    hurry la prisa, **1**
to **hurt** doler (ue); lastimar, **3;** herir, **8**
    My____(part of body) hurts, aches. Me duele ____.
to **hurt oneself** hacerse daño
husband el marido, el esposo

I

I yo
ice el hielo
    ice cream el helado
    ice skating el patinaje sobre hielo

identification card el carné, **6**
idler el holgazán (la holgazana), **3**
ill treatment el maltrato, **8**
immediately en seguida
impediment el impedimento, **4**
important importante
impossible imposible
improbable improbable
impulse el impulso, **8**
in en
to **increase** aumentar, **7**
    Indian el/la indio(a), **8**
to **indicate** señalar, **8**
    individual el individual, **7**
    inflexible inflexible, **6**
to **influence** influir, **8**
to **inform** participar, **4;** comunicar, **8**
to **inherit** heredar, **6**
    inning la entrada
to **insert** introducir (zc)
    inside dentro de
to **insist** insistir
to **inspect** revisar; inspeccionar
    inspection el control
        passport inspection el control de pasaportes
        security inspection el control de seguridad
    instructions las instrucciones
to **insure** asegurar, **2**
    intelligent inteligente
    intensive intensivo(a)
        intensive care unit la unidad de cuidado intensivo
to **interest** interesar
    interesting interesante
    intersection el cruce; la bocacalle
    intimate íntimo(a); entrañable, **4**
    invitation la invitación
to **invite** invitar (a)
    iron la plancha
to **iron** planchar
to **irritate** dar la lata, **2**
    is es; está
    Italian italiano(a) (adj.); el italiano (language)

J

jack el gato
jacket la chaqueta, el saco, el blusón

jail el calabozo, **8**
January enero (m.)
jar el frasco
jazz de jazz (adj.)
jet el avión reactor, el jet
Jewish person el/la judío(a)
job el trabajo, el empleo; la faena, **2**; el oficio, **3**; la tarea, **8**
   job application la solicitud de empleo
judge el/la juez
July julio (m.)
jump el salto, **3**
to **jump** saltar, **7**
June junio (m.)
jungle la selva, **1**
junk food la comida chatarra, **2**

K

keen agudo(a), **7**
key la llave
keyboard la tecla, **1**; el teclado
to **kill** matar, **6**
kilogram el kilo(gramo)
kind amable
kindness la bondad, **6**
king el rey, **5, 8**
kiss el beso
kitchen la cocina
knapsack la mochila
knee la rodilla
knife el cuchillo
to **knot** anudar, **7**
knot el nudo, **1, 4**
to **know (a person)** conocer (zc)
to **know how** saber (irreg.)
   knowledge el conocimiento, **8**

L

labor la labor, **2**
laboratory el laboratorio; el gabinete, **7**
lagoon la laguna, **5**
lake el lago
lamb el cordero
land el suelo, **1**; la tierra
to **land** aterrizar (c)
landing el aterrizaje
landscape el paisaje, **1**

lane (of highway) el carril
language la lengua
   native language la lengua materna
last: last night anoche
   last week la semana pasada
   last year el año pasado
to **last** durar
late tarde; con retraso, con una demora
Latin el latín
laundromat la lavandería
laundry el lavado
lavatory el aseo, el lavabo
lawyer el/la abogado(a)
leaded con plomo
to **leaf through** hojear, **2**
leap el salto, **3**
to **learn** aprender
to **leave** salir; abandonar; irse, partir, **1**; marcharse, **3, 6**
   to leave (something behind) dejar
left la izquierda
   to the left a la izquierda
leg la pierna
lemon el limón
lemonade la limonada
lentil la lenteja, **7**
lesson la lección
letter la carta
   letter (of the alphabet) la letra, **8**
lettuce la lechuga
level el nivel
   sea level el nivel del mar
library la biblioteca
lie la mentira, **5**
life la vida, **5**
   life vest el chaleco salvavidas
to **lift** alzar, **1**; levantar, **7**
light ligero(a), leve, **1**
light la luz
to **light** encender (ie)
lightweight el/la ligero(a), **3**
to **like** gustar
liking la afición, **6**
lime la lima
line la línea; la cola (of people)
   The line is busy. La línea está ocupada.
to **line up** hacer cola
lip el labio

liquid líquido(a)
to **listen** escuchar
   to listen with a stethoscope auscultar
little poco(a)
to **live** vivir
   living room la sala
llama la llama, **2**
loafer el holgazán (la holgazana), **3**
lobster la langosta
located ubicado(a), **1**
lock (of hair) la mecha
to **lock up** internar, **2**
locker el casillero, **7**
long largo(a)
to **long for** apetecer, **1**
look la mirada, **8**
to **look at** mirar
   to look at oneself mirarse
to **look for** buscar (qu)
loose suelto(a), flojo(a), **2**
to **lose** perder (ie)
to **love** querer (irreg.); amar, **1**
low bajo(a)
luck la suerte
luggage el equipaje
   carry-on luggage el equipaje de mano
lump in the throat el nudo en la garganta, **4**
lunch el almuerzo
lunchroom la cantina, **7**
lung el pulmón, **7**
luxury el lujo, **2**

M

mackerel la macarela, **6**; (a variety of) el pejerrey, **2**
madam señora
made confeccionado(a), **4**; compuesto(a), hecho(a), **8**
magazine la revista
maid la camarera; la criada, **1**
   maid of honor la madrina
mail el correo
   air mail por correo aéreo
   certified mail por correo certificado, por correo recomendado
   mail carrier el/la cartero(a)
   regular mail por correo ordinario
mailbox el buzón
main point el eje, **6**

to **make** hacer (irreg.); confeccionar, **1**
  to make a basket (basketball) encestar
  to make a call hacer una llamada
  to make obvious dejar claro, **2**
  to make the bed hacer (tender) la cama
  to make up integrar, **2**
male el varón, **3**
man el caballero; el hombre
mane la melena, **2**
mania la manía, **1**
manner la manera
manners los modales
many muchos(as)
marble la canica, **4**
March marzo
market el mercado
marketplace el bazar, **1**
married couple el matrimonio
to **marry** casarse, **3, 5**
mass la misa
  midnight mass la misa del gallo
master el/la amo(a), **8**
material la materia
mathematics las matemáticas
maximum máximo(a)
May mayo (m.)
maybe puede ser
mayonnaise la mayonesa
Me neither. (Ni) yo tampoco.
meal la comida
means: by no means de ninguna manera
meat la carne
mechanic el/la mecánico(a)
medical médico(a), **7**
  medical kit el botiquín
medication el medicamento
medicine la medicina
medium (meat) a término medio
melancholy melancólico(a), **8**
memory el recuerdo, **3**
menorah la menora

menu el menú
merchant el/la comerciante, el/la mercader
Merry Christmas! ¡Feliz Navidad!
message el recado, **3**
Mexican mexicano(a)
microwave oven el horno de microondas
midday el mediodía
midnight la medianoche
milk la leche
mineral mineral
miniature la miniatura, **1**
minibus el minibús, **1**
mirror el espejo
Miss señorita
to **miss the bus** perder el autobús
mist la neblina, **1**
mixture la mezcla, **8**
molar la muela, **7**
mom la mamá
moment momento
  at this moment en este momento
  One moment, please. Un momento, por favor.
Monday lunes (m.)
money el dinero; la plata, **8**
  great sum of money el dineral, **2**
monument el monumento, **1**
mood el humor
  in a bad mood de mal humor
  in a good mood de buen humor
more más
morning la mañana
  Good morning. Buenos días.
  this morning esta mañana
Moslem musulmán (musulmana), **8**
mosque la mezquita, **5**
mother la madre
motorbike el ciclomotor
mountain la montaña; el monte, **5**
  mountain range la cordillera; la sierra, **2**
mouth la boca
  mouth (of river) la desembocadura, **5**

movie la película; el film(e)
  movie theater el cine
  to show a movie dar una película
Mr. señor
Mrs. señora
mural el mural
muscle el músculo, **3**
museum el museo
music la música
musical musical
musician el/la músico
mussel el mejillón
mustache el bigote

N
name el nombre
nap la siesta
  to take a nap echar (tomar) una siesta
napkin la servilleta
narrow estrecho(a); angosto(a), **1**
national nacional
nationality la nacionalidad
native autóctono(a); el/la indígena, **8**
  native language la lengua materna
  natives of Bolivia and Peru los aymarás, **2, 8**
navigator el navegante, **5**
near allegado(a), **4**
necessary necesario(a)
neck el cuello
necktie la corbata
to **need** necesitar; precisar, **2**
neighbor el/la vecino(a), **2**
neighborhood el barrio, **2**
neither: Me neither. (Ni) yo tampoco.
neon sign el aviso luminoso, **2**
nephew el sobrino
nervous nervioso(a)
net la red
never nunca; jamás
new nuevo(a)
newlywed el/la recién casado(a)
news las noticias
newspaper el periódico
newsstand el quiosco
next próximo(a)
Nice to meet you. Mucho gusto.

niece la sobrina
  niece(s) and nephew(s) los sobrinos
night la noche
  Good night. Buenas noches.
  last night anoche
nine nueve
ninety noventa
ninth noveno(a)
no no
  by no means de ninguna manera
  no one, nobody nadie
  no smoking section la sección de no fumar
  no smoking signal la señal de no fumar
noise el ruido, 7
noisy ruidoso(a), 1
noncarbonated soft drink el refresco
nook el rincón, 1
noon el mediodía
norm la norma, 8
north el norte
not yet todavía no
notebook el cuaderno; la libreta
notes los apuntes
nothing nada
to notify avisar, 1
nougat el turrón, 2
novel la novela
November noviembre (m.)
now ahora
  now and then de vez en cuando
nuclear nuclear
  nuclear energy la energía nuclear
number el número
  flight number el número del vuelo
  seat number el número del asiento
  telephone number el número de teléfono
nurse el/la enfermero(a)
nutritional alimenticio(a), 7

O

obituary la esquela, 4
objective la meta, 6, 8
obstacle el impedimento, 4

to obtain lograr, 8
occupation el oficio, 3
occupied ocupado(a)
to occur ocurrir, 1
October octubre (m.)
of de
of the (m. sing.) del
to offer one's hand dar la mano
office la oficina
often a menudo
oil el aceite
old viejo(a) (adj.)
old person el/la anciano(a), el/la viejo(a) 2
older mayor
olive la aceituna, 8
  olive-colored de color oliva
on board a bordo
one uno
  one hundred cien(to)
  One moment, please. Un momento, por favor.
  one's own propio(a), 2
  one-way (adj.) sencillo
onion la cebolla
only solamente
to open abrir
operating room la sala de operaciones, el quirófano
operating table la mesa de operaciones
operator el/la operador(a)
operetta (Spanish) la zarzuela, 2
opposite contrario(a); enfrente de
oppressor el/la opresor(a), 8
opus la obra, 3
orange la naranja (fruit); anaranjado(a) (color)
orchard la huerta, 5
orchestra la orquesta
  orchestra seat la butaca; la butaca de patio (orquesta), 3
orthopedic ortopédico(a)
orthopedist el/la ortopedista
other otro(a)
others los demás, 3
out (baseball) el out
outdoors al aire libre
outfielder (baseball) el/la jardinero(a)

outlet (of river) la desembocadura, 5
outline el plan, 2
outskirts las afueras
oven el horno
over por encima
overcoat el abrigo
to overtake adelantar
owner el/la amo(a), 8
oxygen el oxígeno
  oxygen mask la máscara de oxígeno

P

to pack one's suitcase hacer la maleta
package el paquete
packing el envase, 7
pact el acuerdo, 7
painter el/la pintor(a)
painting el cuadro
pair (couple) la pareja, 4
pantihose las medias
pants los pantalones
papaya la papaya
paper el papel
  sheet of paper la hoja de papel
  toilet paper el papel higiénico
parachute el paracaídas, 2
parade el desfile, 3
paradise el paraíso, 3
parasol el parasol
paratrooper el/la paracaidista, 2
parents los padres
park el parque
to park aparcar, estacionar
parking meter el parquímetro
part (in hair) la raya
part-time a tiempo parcial
party la fiesta
to pass pasar
passbook la libreta
passenger el/la pasajero(a)
  passenger vehicle smaller than a bus el colectivo, 5
passport el pasaporte
  passport inspection el control de pasaportes
pastry el pastel
  pastry shop la pastelería

path la senda, el sendero
patient el/la enfermo(a)
patron saint el santo patrón, **3**
to **pawn** empeñar, **1**
to **pay** pagar
pea el guisante
peaceful pacífico(a), **8**
peach el melocotón
peak el pico
peanut el maní, **7**
pear la pera
pedestrian el peatón
to **peel** pelar
pencil el lápiz
penguin el pingüino, **1**
penniless person el/la pelado(a), **6**
penning (of bulls) el encierro, **3**
pensioner el/la pensionista, **8**
people la gente
pepper la pimienta
pepper (bell) el pimiento
to **perform** llevar a cabo, **4**
performance la representación, el espectáculo
  to put on a performance dar una representación
performer el/la tocador(a), **8**
perhaps tal vez, quizá(s)
period (of time) la temporada, **3**
to **permit** autorizar, **6**
person la persona
  person of mixed race el/la ladino(a), **8**
  personnel department el departamento (servicio) de personal, el departamento de recursos humanos
pharmacist el/la farmacéutico(a)
pharmacy la farmacia
physical físico(a)
  physical education la educación física
physics la física
piano el piano
to **pick up** recoger; descolgar (ue)
pickpocket el carterista, **5**
picture el cuadro

pie el pastel
piece (little) el pedacito, el trocito
pill la pastilla, la píldora, el comprimido
pillar el pilar, **8**
pillow la almohada
  head pillow el cabezal, **7**
pilot el/la piloto(a)
to **pinch** apretar (ie)
  It (They) pinch(es) me. Me aprieta(n).
pineapple la piña
pitcher (sports) el/la pícher, el/la lanzador(a)
pity la lástima
  to be a pity ser una lástima
place el lugar
  to take place tener lugar
plaid a cuadros
plain la llanura
plan el plan, **2**
plane el avión
  by plane en avión
plant la planta
to **plant** sembrar, **2, 8**
plastic de plástico
  plastic bag la bolsa de plástico
plate el plato
  home plate el platillo
plateau (high) el altiplano, **2**
to **play** jugar (ue) (a sport); tocar (an instrument)
player el/la jugador(a); el/la tocador(a), **8**
playing cards la baraja, **6**
pleasant placentero(a), **1**; grato(a), **8**
to **please** agradar, **6**
please por favor
plug el tapón, **7**
plumber el/la plomero(a), el/la fontanero(a)
pocket el bolsillo, **5**
point (score) el tanto
to **point out** señalar, **8**
pole el bastón
police officer el/la policía
police station la comisaría, **5**
police: Spanish police force la Guardia Civil, **8**
polite educado(a)
politics la política, **8**

pollen el polen, **4**
pony tail la cola de caballo
pool la alberca, la piscina
popular popular
population la población
pork el cerdo
port el puerto, **5**
portable stove el hornillo
porter el/la maletero(a), el/la mozo(a)
portfolio la cartera, **2**
portion la ración, **7**
possible posible
post office la oficina de correos
  post office box el apartado postal, la casilla
postage el franqueo
postal employee el/la empleado(a) de correo
postcard la tarjeta postal
poster el cartelón, **6**
pot la olla, la cazuela
to **pour** vaciar, **2**
potato la papa; la patata
powdered en polvo
  powdered soap el jabón en polvo
power el poder, **6**
to **practice** ejercitar, **3**
  to practice (a profession) ejercer (una profesión)
prawn el camarón
to **prefer** preferir (ie, i)
to **prepare** preparar; confeccionar, **1**
to **prescribe** recetar
prescription la receta
to **present** presentar
  to present with obsequiar, **4**
present el regalo
  Christmas present el regalo de Navidad, el aguinaldo
  president of a university el/la rector(a), **2**
pressure la presión
pretty bonito(a)
price el precio
priest el cura
principal el/la director(a)
prisoner el/la cautivo(a), **5**
private particular, privado(a), **2**
probable probable
profession la profesión

programmer el/la programador(a)

to **promote** desarrollar, **8**

promotion (in position) el ascenso, **6**

propellers las hélices

to **propose** proponer, **6**

protein la proteína

proud orgulloso(a), **2**

provided that con tal que

to **prune** podar, **7**

public público(a)

public school teachers el Magisterio Fiscal, **4**

Puerto Rican puertorriqueño(a)

pulmonary pulmonar, **7**

pulse el pulso

punch el puñetazo, **6**

purse la bolsa, **5**

to **pursue** perseguir, **8**

push el empujón, **6**

push button de (a) botones

to **push** empujar

to **put** poner (irreg.)

to put in meter

to put in a plaster cast enyesar

to put on (clothes) ponerse

to put on the fire poner al fuego

to put on a performance dar una representación

to put up a tent armar una tienda

pyramid la pirámide, **1**

Q

quarter: a quarter to (past) (the hour) menos (y) cuarto

Quechuan people and language el quechua, **8**

quite bastante

R

rabbi el rabino, **8**

race la carrera, **7**

racket la raqueta

radiator el radiador

rag el trapo, **6, 7**

railway platform el andén

railway track la vía

rain la lluvia, **1**

to **rain** llover (ue)

It's raining. Llueve.

raincoat la gabardina; el impermeable, **3**

to **raise** levantar; alzar, **1**

rare (meat) casi crudo; raro, **2**

rather bastante

raw crudo(a)

ray el rayo

razor la navaja

razor blade la hoja de afeitar, **2**

to **read** leer (y)

reading primer la cartilla, **8**

to **reap** cosechar, **2, 4**

to **receive** sacar (qu); recibir

receiver el/la destinatario(a)

receiver (of telephone) el auricular, la bocina

reception la recepción

receptionist el/la recepcionista

to **recognize** reconocer, **8**

to **recommend** recomendar (ie)

to **reconcile** conciliar

record el disco

recovery room la sala de recuperación, la sala de restablecimiento

red rojo(a)

to **reduce** reducir (zc), **2**

referee el/la árbitro(a)

refrigerator el refrigerador, la nevera

to **refuse** rehusar, **6**

to **register** inscribir, **7**

registration card la tarjeta, la ficha

regular (gas) normal

regular mail por correo ordinario

to **reimburse** reembolsar, **1**

related allegado(a), **4**

relationship el parentesco, **6**

to **remain** quedarse

to **remove** extraer, **4**; quitar, **5**

renowned renombrado(a), **1**

to **rent** alquilar

to **repeat** repetir (i, i)

to **replace** reemplazar, **2**

to **request** rogar (ue)

to **require** requerir (ie, i); exigir, **1, 7**

to **rescue** rescatar, **5**

reservation la reservación

to **reserve** reservar

reserved reservado(a); taciturno(a), **8**

to **reside** habitar, **6**

resources los recursos, **6**

rest el descanso, **3**

restaurant el restaurante

retired person el/la jubilado(a), **2**

to **return (something)** devolver (ue)

returning de vuelta, **3**

to **revolve** girar, **6**

rhythm: to the rhythm of al compás de, **3**

rib la costilla

rice el arroz

Right? ¿Verdad?

right la derecha

to the right a la derecha

right away en seguida

right now en este momento

rim el borde, **1, 7**

ring el anillo, la sortija

engagement ring la sortija de compromiso

wedding ring el anillo de boda

to **ring** sonar (ue)

rink: ice skating rink la pista de patinaje, el patinadero

river el río

road el trayecto, **1, 6**

roast suckling pig el lechón

robbery el robo, **5**

rock la piedra, **6**

rock (adj.) de rock

rocket el cohete, **3**

roll (of paper) el rollo

roller la rueda

roller skating el patinaje sobre ruedas

roof el tejado, **6**

room el cuarto, la habitación

classroom la sala (el salón) de clase

double room el cuarto doble

single room el cuarto sencillo; la habitación simple

waiting room la sala de espera

root la raíz, **8**

rope la soga, **7**

round redondo(a), **5, 8**
round-trip de ida y vuelta
row la fila
to ruin destrozar, **2, 7**
to run correr
to run quickly downstairs
echar a correr escalera
abajo, **1**
runway la pista
rural rural, **8**

S

sacred sagrado(a), **8**
sad triste; melancólico(a),
8
safe seguro(a)
sail la vela, **1**
sailor el marino, **5**
salad la ensalada
salesperson el/la
dependiente; el/la
vendedor(a), **1**
salt la sal
to sample degustar, **4**
sample la muestra, **7**
sand la arena
sandals las sandalias
sandwich el sándwich, el
bocadillo
sanitary higiénico(a)
sash la faja, **3**
Saturday sábado
saucepan la cacerola, **7**
saucer el platillo
sausage la salchicha; el
embutido, **7**
to save rescatar, **5**; ahorrar
savings account la cuenta
de ahorros
to say decir (irreg.)
to say good-bye
despedirse (i, i)
scale la báscula
scar la cicatriz
scene la escena, **3**
schedule el horario, **2**
school el colegio, la escuela;
escolar, (adj.)
high school la
escuela secundaria
science la ciencia
science fiction de
ciencia ficción (adj.)
scissors las tijeras
to score (sports) marcar

scoreboard el tablero
indicador
screen la pantalla
sculptor el/la escultor(a)
sea el mar
sea level el nivel del mar
search: in search of en busca de
season la estación
seat el asiento
seat belt el cinturón de
seguridad
seat number el número
del asiento
seat (in a theater) la
localidad; la butaca
second segundo(a)
secondary secundario(a)
secret el secreto
secretary el/la secretario(a)
security la seguridad
security inspection el
control de seguridad
sedan el sedán
to see ver
See you later. Hasta la
vista. Hasta luego.
See you soon. Hasta
pronto.
See you tomorrow. Hasta
mañana.
to seize apoderarse de, **5**
self-sacrificing abnegado(a), **4**
to sell vende; despachar
to send enviar; mandar
sender el/la remitente
sensitive sensible, **4**
September septiembre (m.)
sergeant el sargento, **5**
serious serio(a)
to serve servir (i, i)
service station la estación de
servicio
to set the bone reducir la
fractura
seven siete
seventh séptimo(a)
seventy setenta
several varios(as), **1**
to shake hands estrechar la
mano
shampoo el champú
to share compartir, **6**
to shave afeitarse
shaving cream la crema de
afeitar

she ella
sheep la oveja, **2**
sheet la hoja; la sábana (bed)
sheet of paper la hoja de
papel
shellfish el marisco
to shelter recoger, **6**
to shift gears cambiar de
velocidad
to shine brillar; lucir, **4**
ship el buque, **1**
shipwreck el naufragio, **5**
shirt la camisa
loose-fitting man's shirt
worn in some tropical
Hispanic countries la
guayabera, **1**
shiver el escalofrío, **6**
shoe el zapato
shop window el escaparate,
la vitrina
shopping de compras
shopping center el centro
comercial
short (person) bajo(a);
(length) corto(a)
shot el disparo, **7**
shoulder el hombro
to shout gritar, **5**
shove el empujón, **6**
show el espectáculo; la sesión
to show a movie dar una
película
shower la ducha; el aguacero
(of rain), **1**
to take a shower tomar
una ducha
shrimp la gamba; el camarón
to shrink encoger
shy tímido(a)
sick enfermo(a)
sick person el/la enfermo(a)
side: to the side of al lado de
sideburn la patilla
sidewalk la acera
sign el rótulo
to sign firmar
silly tonto(a), **1**
simple sencillo(a)
sincere sincero(a)
to sing cantar
singer el/la cantor(a), el/la
cantante, **3**
single sencillo(a); simple
sir señor

sister la hermana
to **sit down** sentarse (ie)
sit-ups las sentadillas, 3
six seis
sixth sexto(a)
sixty sesenta
size el tamaño, la talla
skate el patín
to **skate** patinar
skater el/la patinador(a)
skateboard el monopatín
skating el patinaje
   figure skating el patinaje
     artístico
   ice skating el patinaje
     sobre hielo
   roller skating el patinaje
     sobre ruedas
   skating rink el patinadero,
     la pista de patinaje
sketch el dibujo, 1
to **sketch** dibujar, 1
sketcher el/la dibujante, 1
ski el esquí
   ski lift el telesquí
   ski pole el bastón
   ski resort la estación de esquí
   ski slope la pista de esquí
to **ski** esquiar
skier el/la esquiador(a)
skiing el esquí
   cross-country skiing el esquí
     de fondo; el esquí nórdico
   downhill skiing el esquí
     alpino, el esquí de descenso
skin el pellejo, 7
to **skin-dive** bucear
skindiving el buceo
skip el brinco, 3
skirt la falda
sky el cielo
slalom el slálom
slap la palmadita; la bofetada, 6
to **slap gently** dar palmaditas
slave el/la esclavo(a), 8
to **sleep** dormir (ue, u)
sleeping bag el saco de (para)
   dormir
sleeping car el coche-cama
sleepy soñoliento(a), 2
sleeve la manga
   long-(short-) sleeved de
     manga larga (corta)
slice la tajada; la lonja; la
   rebanada

to **slice** rebanar
to **slip** resbalarse
slope la cuesta; la loma(da), 1
slot (for money) la ranura
small pequeño(a); **(amount)**
   poco(a)
smiling sonriente, 3
smoking (no smoking)
   section la sección de (no)
   fumar
snack la merienda
to **sneeze** estornudar
snow la nieve
to **snow** nevar (ie)
   It's snowing. Nieva.
snowfall la nevada
so that para que, de manera
   que, de modo que
soap el jabón
   powdered soap el jabón en
     polvo
soap opera la telenovela
soccer el futból
   soccer field el campo de
     futból
social sciences las ciencias
   sociales
social studies la educación
   cívica
sociology la sociología
socks los calcetines
soda la gaseosa
soft drink la gaseosa
soil el suelo, 1
sojourn la estadía, 1
sole (of shoe) la suela, 3
some algún, alguno(a)
somebody alguien
something algo
   Something more? ¿Algo más?
sometimes a veces
son el hijo
soon: as soon as tan pronto
   como
sore throat el dolor de
   garganta
sorrow el dolor, 1
soul el alma (f.), 4
sound el sonido, 7
soup la sopa
south el sur
   South America la América
     del Sur
sovereign el/la soberano(a), 8
span el tramo, 1

Spanish español(a), el
   español (language)
Spanish-speaking de
   habla española
spare de repuesto, de
   recambio (tire)
to **speak** hablar
specialist especialista
spectator el/la espectador(a)
speed la velocidad
   speed limit la velocidad
     máxima
spell la temporada, 3
to **spend (time)** pasar
spittoon la escupidera, 7
spoon la cuchara
spoonful la cucharada, 2
sport los deportes
   sports broadcast la
     emisión deportiva
   sports car el coche
     deportivo
spouse el/la cónyuge, 4
to **spread (butter on bread)**
   untar, 2
spring la primavera
sprinkle rociar, 2
squall el chubasco, 1
squid el calamar
stadium el estadio
stage la escena (theatre); la
   etapa (time), 2
   to come on stage entrar en
     escena
stain la mancha
stained manchado(a)
stairway la escalera
stall el puesto
stamp el sello, la estampilla
to **stamp** dar una patada, 1
to **stand out** lucir, 4
standard la norma, 8
star la estrella, 1
starch el almidón
state estatal (adj.), 7
station la estación
   service station la estación
     de servicio
   train station la estación
     de ferrocarril
statue la estatua
stay la estadía, 1
to **stay** quedarse
   to stay in bed guardar cama
to **steal** robar

stealthily a hurtadillas, **6**
stereophonic estereofónico(a)
to **stir** revolver (ue)
stitch el punto, la sutura
stock el caldo, **2**
stockings las medias
stomach el estómago; el vientre, **7**
stomachache el dolor de estómago
stop la parada
to **stop** parar
stoppage of work el paro, **5**
store la tienda
  department store la tienda de departamento (por departamentos)
  grocery store la tienda de abarrotes
  men's clothing store la tienda de ropa para caballeros (señores)
  women's clothing store la tienda de ropa para damas (señoras)
stork la cigüeña, el ave picuda, **4**
storm la tempestad, el temporal, la tormenta, **1**
stove la estufa
straight liso(a), lacio(a), (hair); derecho (direction)
to **strain** colar, **2**
stranger el/la desconocido(a), **6**
straw la paja
strawberry la fresa
stream el arroyo, **8**
street la calle
strength la fuerza, **1**; el poder, **6**
stretch (of distance) el tramo, **1**
to **stretch** estirar, **4**
stretcher la camilla
stretching el estiramiento, **3**
string bean la judía verde
striped a rayas
student el/la alumno(a); el/la estudiante
to **study** estudiar
subject la asignatura, la disciplina, la materia
to **substitute** reemplazar, **2**
suburbs los suburbios
subway el metro; el subterráneo, **5**
success el éxito, **3**

suddenly de golpe, **2**
sufficient suficiente
sugar el azúcar
to **suggest** sugerir (ie, i)
suit el traje
suitcase la maleta
  to pack one's suitcase hacer la maleta
sum el monto, **1**
summer el verano
summit el auge, **8**
sun el sol
  sunblock la crema protectora
to **sunbathe** tomar el sol
Sunday domingo
sunglasses los anteojos de (para el) sol
sunny soleado(a), **1**
  It's sunny. Hay (Hace) sol.
sunset (of life) el ocaso, **4**
suntan lotion la crema bronceadora
super súper
  super highway la autopista, la autovía
supermarket el supermercado, el hipermercado
supplied suministrado(a), **2**
to **supply** suministrar, **2**
support el apoyo, **5**
sure seguro(a)
surgeon el/la cirujano(a)
to **surpass** sobrepasar, **5**
to **surprise** sorprender; extrañar, **6**
to **swallow** tragar, **6**
sweater el suéter, el jersey
sweetheart el/la enamorado(a)
to **swim** nadar
swimsuit el traje de baño, el bañador
swimming pool la piscina, la alberca
swollen hinchado(a)
symptom el síntoma
synagogue la sinagoga, **8**

T
T-shirt el T shirt
table la mesa
tablecloth el mantel

tableland la meseta
tablet la pastilla
taciturn taciturno(a), **8**
to **take** tomar
  to take a bath bañarse
  to take a hike dar una caminata
  to take a leading part in protagonizar, **4**
  to take a nap echar (tomar) una siesta
  to take a shower tomar una ducha
  to take a step dar un paso, **8**
  to take a walk dar una caminata, **1**; dar un paseo, **3**
  to take away quitar, **5**
  to take charge of hacerse cargo de, **4, 6**
  to take off (airplane) despegar
  to take off the fire quitar del fuego, retirar del fuego
  to take out sacar
  to take pictures tomar fotografías, **1**
  to take place tener lugar; efectuar, **4**
  to take possession of apoderarse de, **5**
  to take seriously tomar en serio, **2**
  to take up subir
take-off el despegue
tall alto(a)
tame manso(a), **1**
tank el tanque
tape la cinta
task la tarea, **8**
to **taste** degustar, **4**
tasty rico(a)
taxi el taxi
  taxi stand la parada de taxis, **1**
taximeter el taxímetro, **1**
to **teach** enseñar
  to teach to read and write alfabetizar, **8**
teacher el/la profesor(a); el/la docente, **7**; el/la maestro(a)
team el equipo; de equipo (adj.)
tear la lágrima, **7**

teaspoon la cucharita
technician el/la técnico(a)
telephone (adj.) telefónico(a)
telephone (n.) el teléfono
 on the telephone por teléfono
 telephone book la guía telefónica
 telephone booth la cabina telefónica
to telephone telefonear
television la televisión
 television set el televisor
to tell decir
teller el/la cajero(a)
temperament el genio, 8
temperature la temperatura
temple (anat.) la sien, 6
ten diez
tennis el tenis
 tennis court la cancha de tenis
 tennis game el juego de tenis
 tennis shoes los tenis
tent la tienda de campaña, la carpa
 to put up a tent armar una tienda
tenth décimo(a)
tepid tibio(a), 7
terminal la terminal, 1
test el examen
thank you gracias
that eso; aquel, aquella
the el, la
theater el teatro
theatrical teatral
theft el robo, 5
then luego
there is/are hay
thief el/la ladrón(a), 6
thin flaco(a), 7
third tercer
third age la tercera edad, 2
thirst la sed
 to be thirsty tener sed
thirty treinta
this este (esta)
thorax el tórax, 3
thousand mil
three tres
Three Wise Men los Reyes Magos
throat la garganta

sore throat el dolor de garganta
 to have a sore throat tener dolor de garganta
throne el trono, 4, 8
to throw tirar, lanzar; echar
Thursday jueves (m.)
ticket el boleto, el billete; la entrada, 3
 one-way ticket el billete sencillo
 round-trip ticket el billete de ida y vuelta
 ticket window la boletería, la ventanilla; la taquilla
tidbit la golosina, 1
tied empatado(a)
to tie together anudar, 7
tight estrecho(a)
time tiempo
 At what time? ¿A qué hora?
 full-time a tiempo completo
 on time a tiempo
 part-time a tiempo parcial
timid tímido(a)
tip la propina
tire el neumático, la goma, la llanta
 spare tire la llanta de repuesto (de recambio)
tired cansado(a)
to a; con destino a
 to the (m. sing) al
toast (to one's health) el brindis
to toast (one's health) brindar, 4
today hoy
together junto(a)
toilet el inodoro, el váter; el retrete, 1
 toilet paper el papel higiénico
toll el peaje
 toll booth la garita de peaje
tomb la tumba
 family tomb la tumba familiar, 4
tomorrow mañana
tone el tono
tonight esta noche
too también
too (much) demasiado
tooth el diente

tooth cavity la caries, 7
toothbrush el cepillo de dientes, 7
toothpaste la pasta dentífrica; el dentífrico, 7
toothpick el palillo, 7
tortilla la tortilla
total el total, el monto
to touch tocar
tourist el/la turista
towel la toalla
 beach towel la toalla playera
town el pueblo; la villa, 6
toy el juguete, 1, 4
trade el oficio, la compra y venta
trader el/la traficante, 8
traffic la circulación, el tráfico, el tránsito
 traffic jam el embotellamiento, 1
 traffic light el semáforo
trail la pista
trailer la caravana, la casa-remolque
train el tren
 train station la estación de ferrocarril
trainer el entrenador, 2
training el entrenamiento, 8
tranquil tranquilo(a), 3
to transfer transbordar
transportation el transporte
to travel recorrer, 1
 traveler el/la viajero(a), 1
 traveler's check el cheque de viajero
tray table la mesita
tree el árbol
 Christmas tree el árbol de Navidad
trick el truco, 5
tricorn el tricornio, 8
trigonometry la trigonometría
trim el recorte
to trim recortar
trip el viaje
 to take a trip hacer un viaje
troop la tropa, 2
true verdadero(a)
 Isn't it true? ¿No es verdad?
trumpet la trompeta

trunk (of a car) el/la maletero(a)

truth la verdad

tube el tubo

Tuesday martes (m.)

tuna el atún

to turn doblar

to turn around dar la vuelta, voltear, **3**

to turn off apagar

turn signal el intermitente, la direccional

turquoise-colored de color turquesa

turtle (giant) el galápago, **1**

tweezers las pinzas, **7**

twenty veinte

to twist torcer (ue)

two dos

tyrant el/la opresor(a), **8**

U

umbrella la sombrilla

uncle el tío

uncles and aunts los tíos

under debajo de

underground subterráneo(a)

underpants los calzones, **3**

undershirt la camiseta

to understand comprender

understanding el conocimiento, **8**

undeserved inmerecido(a), **4**

unemployed desocupado(a), desempleado(a)

unemployed person el/la desempleado(a)

unemployment el desempleo

unfortunate desgraciado(a), **4**

university la universidad; universitario(a) (adj.)

university diploma el título universitario

unleaded sin plomo

unless a menos que

unmarried person el/la soltero(a), **6**

unpleasant antipático(a)

unsuccessful fallido(a), **4**

until hasta; hasta que

to use usar

to use up consumir, **7**

useful útil, **2**

useless thing el cacharro, **2**

usher el paje de honor

V

valley el valle

veal la ternera

vegetable la legumbre, la verdura, el vegetal

vegetable garden el huerto, **1**

veil el velo, **1, 4**

vein la vena, **6**

to verify verificar

verse, improvised with music la bomba, **8**

very muy

vice versa por el contrario, **2**

victim of a disaster el/la damnificado(a), **5**

crime victim la víctima del crimen, **5**

video store la tienda de videos, **2**

view la vista

vigil el velorio, **4**

vigor la lozanía, **4**

violin el violín

virtue la virtud, **6**

vitamin la vitamina

voice la voz, **8**

volleyball el vólibol

W

to wait for esperar

waiter el mesero

waiting room la sala de recepción

waitress la mesera

wake el velorio, **4**

to wake up despertarse (ie)

Wales Gales, **1**

to walk caminar; andar (irreg.)

wall la pared, **6**

city wall la muralla, **6**

wallet la cartera, **5**

to want querer (irreg.); desear

warm-up el calentamiento, **3**

wash (n.) el lavado

to wash (oneself) lavar(se)

washbasin el lavamanos, **1**

washing machine la máquina de lavar

to waste desperdiciar, **8**

to watch ver

watch el reloj, **5**

water el agua (f.)

to **water** regar, **2, 7**

watermelon la sandía

water skiing (n.) el esquí acuático

to go water skiing esquiar en el agua

wave la ola; la onda

way la manera; el sentido

we nosotros(as)

wealth los recursos, **6**

wedding la boda, el enlace nupcial

Wednesday miércoles (m.)

week la semana

last week la semana pasada

this week esta semana

to weigh pesar

weight la pesa, **7**

welcome (n.) la bienvenida

to welcome dar la bienvenida

well bien

well-done (meat) bien cocido (hecho)

well-mannered educado(a)

well el pozo, **1, 2, 4**

west el oeste, el occidente, **8**

What? ¿Cuál?, ¿Qué?; ¿Cómo?

What is it? ¿Qué es?

What is today's date? ¿Cuál es la fecha de hoy?

What time is it? ¿Qué hora es?

What's the weather like? ¿Qué tiempo hace?

wheel la rueda

wheelchair la silla de ruedas

when cuando

When? ¿Cuándo?

Where? ¿Dónde?, ¿Adónde?

Which? ¿Cuál?

while mientras

whim el capricho, **2**

whiskers los bigotes, **2**

white blanco(a)

egg white la clara, **2, 7**

Who? ¿Quién?

Who is calling? ¿De parte de quién?

Who is it (he, she)? ¿Quién es?

wide ancho(a)

widow la viuda, **4, 5, 6**

widowed, enviudado(a), **1**
widower el viudo, **6**
wife la esposa, la mujer
will la voluntad, **8**
to **win** ganar
wind el viento
to **wind up a victrola** darle
cuerda a una victrola, **2**
window la ventanilla
windshield el parabrisas
windshield wiper el
limpiaparabrisas
windsurfboard la plancha
de vela
windy: It's windy. Hace viento.
wine-colored de color vino
wing el ala (f.)
winter el invierno
to **wish** desear
to **withdraw** retirar
withdrawal el retiro
withdrawal slip el
formulario de retiro
without sin (que)
woman la mujer

wool la lana
work la obra; el trabajo;
la faena, la labor, **2;**
la tarea, **8**
to **work** trabajar
worker el/la obrero(a), el/la
trabajador(a)
to **wound** lastimar, **3**
wrinkled arrugado(a)
wrist la muñeca
to **write** escribir
to write down anotar, **8**
writing pad el bloc
wrong equivocado(a)

X
X-ray la radiografía
X-rays los rayos equis

Y
year el año
Happy New Year!
¡Próspero año nuevo!
last year el año pasado
this year este año

yellow amarillo(a)
yesterday ayer
the day before yesterday
anteayer
yesterday afternoon ayer
por la tarde
yesterday morning ayer
por la mañana
you tú, Ud., usted, Uds.,
ustedes (pl. form.), vosotros
You're welcome. De nada., No
hay de qué.
young joven
young man el mozo, **3**
young person el/la joven, **2**
younger menor
youth el mozo, **3**
youth hostel el albergue
juvenil

Z
zero cero
zip code la zona postal, el
código postal
zipper la cremallera, el zíper

Índice gramatical

504

506